Contemporary Authors
Autobiography Series

ISSN 0748-0636

Contemporary Authors

Autobiography Series

Mark Zadrozny

Editor

volume 10

Gale Research Inc. • Detroit, New York, Fort Lauderdale, London

EDITORIAL STAFF

Mark Zadrozny, *Editor*
Laurie Collier and Carleton Copeland, *Associate Editors*
Shelly Andrews and Motoko Fujishiro Huthwaite, *Assistant Editors*
Marilyn O'Connell, *Editorial Associate*

Mary Rose Bonk, *Research Supervisor, Biography Division*
Jane Cousins-Clegg, Alysa I. Hunton, Andrew Guy Malonis,
and Norma Sawaya, *Editorial Associates*
Pamela Atsoff, Reginald A. Carlton, Christine Ferran, Shirley Gates,
Elizabeth Parker Henry, and Sharon McGilvray, *Editorial Assistants*

Deborah Gillan Straub, *Senior Editor*

Mary Beth Trimper, *Production Manager*
Marilyn Jackman, *External Production Assistant*

Art Chartow, *Art Director*
C. J. Jonik, *Keyliner*

Laura Bryant, *Internal Production Supervisor*
Louise Gagné, *Internal Production Associate*
Sharana Wier, *Internal Production Assistant*

Donald G. Dillaman, *Index Program Designer*

Copyright © 1989
Gale Research Inc.
835 Penobscot Bldg.
Detroit, MI 48226-4094

Library of Congress Catalog Card Number 84-647879
ISBN 0-8103-4509-9
ISSN-0748-0636

Contents

Preface

Each volume in the *Contemporary Authors Autobiography Series (CAAS)* presents an original collection of autobiographical essays written especially for the series by noted writers. *CAAS* has grown out of the aggregate of Gale's long-standing interest in author biography, bibliography, and criticism, as well as its successful publications in those areas, like the *Dictionary of Literary Biography, Contemporary Literary Criticism, Something about the Author, Author Biographies Master Index,* and particularly the bio-bibliographical series *Contemporary Authors (CA),* to which this *Autobiography Series* is a companion.

As a result of their ongoing communication with authors in compiling *CA* and other books, Gale editors recognized that these wordsmiths frequently had more to say—willingly, even eagerly—than the format of existing Gale publications could accommodate. Personal comments from authors in the "Sidelights" section of *CA* entries, for example, often indicated the intriguing tip of an iceberg. Inviting authors to write about themselves at essay-length was the almost-inexorable next step. Added to that was the fact that the collected autobiographies of current writers were virtually nonexistent. Like metal to magnet, Gale customarily responds to an information gap—and met this one with *CAAS.*

Purpose

This series is designed to be a congenial meeting place for writers and readers—a place where writers can present themselves, on their own terms, to their audience; and a place where general readers, students of contemporary literature, teachers and librarians, even aspiring writers can become better acquainted with familiar authors and make the first acquaintance of others. Here is an opportunity for writers who may never write a full-length autobiography (and some shudder at the thought) to let their readers know how they see themselves and their work, what carefully laid plans or turns of luck brought them to this time and place, what objects of their passion and pity arouse them enough to tell us. Even for those authors who have already published full-length autobiographies there is the opportunity in *CAAS* to bring their readers "up to date" or perhaps to take a different approach in the essay format. At the very least, these essays can help quench a reader's inevitable curiosity about the people who speak to their imagination and seem themselves to inhabit a plane somewhere between reality and fiction. But the essays in this series have a further potential: singly, they can illuminate the reader's understanding of a writer's work; collectively, they are lessons in the creative process and in the discovery of its roots.

CAAS makes no attempt to give an observer's-eye view of authors and their works. That outlook is already well represented in biographies, reviews, and critiques published in a wide variety of sources, including *Contemporary Authors, Contemporary Literary Criticism,* and the *Dictionary of Literary Biography.* Instead, *CAAS* complements that perspective and presents what no other source does: the view of contemporary writers that is reflected in their own mirrors, shaped by their own choice of materials and their own manner of storytelling.

CAAS is still in its youth, but its major accomplishments may already be projected. The series fills a significant information gap—in itself a sufficient test of a worthy reference work. And thanks to the exceptional talents of its contributors, each volume in this series is a unique anthology of some of the best and most varied contemporary writing.

Scope

Like its parent series, *Contemporary Authors*, the *CA Autobiography Series* aims to be broad-based. It sets out to meet the needs and interests of the full spectrum of readers by providing in each volume twenty to thirty essays by writers in all genres whose work is being read today. We deem it a minor publishing event that more than twenty busy authors from throughout the world are able to interrupt their existing writing, teaching, speaking, traveling, and other schedules to converge on a given deadline for any one volume. So it is not always possible that all genres can be equally and uniformly represented from volume to volume. Of the eighteen authors from five countries in Volume 10, about half are poets, with the other half made up of novelists. Like most categories, these oversimplify. Only a few writers specialize in a single area. The range of writings by authors in this volume also includes drama, translation, and criticism as well as work for movies, television, radio, newspapers, and journals.

Format

Authors who contribute to *CAAS* are invited to write a "mini-autobiography" of approximately 10,000 words. In order to give the writer's imagination free rein, we suggest no guidelines or pattern for the essay. The only injunction is that each writer tell his or her own story in the manner and to the extent that each finds most natural and appropriate. In addition, writers are asked to supply a selection of personal photographs, showing themselves at various ages, as well as important people and special moments in their lives. Barring unfortunate circumstances like the loss or destruction of early photographs, our contributors have responded graciously and generously, sharing with us some of their most treasured mementoes, as this volume readily attests. This special wedding of text and photographs makes *CAAS* the kind of reference book that even browsers will find seductive.

A bibliography appears at the end of each essay, listing the author's book-length works in chronological order of publication. If more than one book has been published in a given year, the titles are listed in alphabetic order. Each entry in the bibliography includes the publication information for the book's first printing in the United States and Great Britain. Generally, the bibliography does not include later reprintings, new editions, or foreign translations. Also omitted from this bibliography are articles, reviews, and other contributions to magazines and journals. The bibliographies in this volume were compiled by members of the *CAAS* editorial staff from their research and the lists of writings provided by many of the authors. Each of the bibliographies has been submitted to the author for review. When the list of primary works is extensive, the author may prefer to present a "Selected Bibliography." Readers may consult the author's entry in *CA* for a more complete list of writings in these cases.

Each volume of *CAAS* includes a cumulative index that cites all the essayists in the series as well as the subjects presented in the essays: personal names, titles of works, geographical names, schools of writing, etc. The index format is designed to make these cumulating references as helpful and easy to use as possible. For every reference that appears *in more than one essay,* the name of the essayist is given before the volume and page number(s). For example, W.H. Auden is mentioned by several essayists in the series. The index format allows the user to identify the essay writers by name:

For references that appear *in only one essay,* the volume and page number(s) are given but the name of the essayist is omitted. For example:

Stieglitz, Alfred **1**:98, 99, 104, 109, 110

CAAS is something more than the sum of its individual essays. At many points the essays touch common ground, and from these intersections emerge new mosaics of information and impressions. *CAAS* therefore becomes an expanding chronicle of the last half-century—an already useful research tool that can only increase in usefulness as the series grows. And the index, despite its pedestrian appearance, is an increasingly important guide to the interconnections of this chronicle.

Looking Ahead

All of the writers in this volume begin with a common goal—telling the tale of their lives. Yet each of these essays has a special character and point of view that set it apart from its companions. Perhaps a small sampler of anecdotes and musings from the essays ahead can hint at the unique flavor of these life stories.

Rosellen Brown, wondering why an elusive time remains so powerful in memory: "Although reason tells me that every year of those four that I lived in Mount Vernon consisted of the requisite four seasons, and even though I can recall any number of winter and summer scenes if I try, still, for whatever entirely subterranean reason, when I remember what I think of as the central years of my childhood—the others trickled away a year or two at a time in places that left no particular emotional residue—it is always fall and I am kicking up noisy leathery leaves in a particular stretch of woods within sight of the solid stone castlelike bridges that cross the old winding highways of Westchester County. I don't know why this is the abiding image I have taken from the full years of my childhood—nothing special happened there, either ecstatic or traumatic, I have no whole picture that tells me whether I played there once or twice or a hundred times, and I don't remember who I played with. I must have felt some heart-centered, solitary, sensual delight, some essence of childhood freedom otherwise denied me, in that place. I remember that certain oblique sunlight that precedes winter-in-earnest, and the kind of temperature in which you keep your jacket open because it's not quite cold, but yet your ears hurt with the hinted beginning of serious weather."

Robert Creeley, mulling over our sense of importance and place in the large, old world: "I recall one night in Placitas, New Mexico. Restless, I had stepped just outside the door of our living room into a small courtyard. It must have been fall because there was a sharp odor of burning piñon in the air, and it was one of those magnificent sharp, dry, immensely clear and star-filled nights. Just back of me in the room there was a bleak argument going on, the rehearsal of a very painful and blocked sense of relation, a classic human debate which can never end except in exhaustion. But outside, less than ten feet away, was such a vast and inhuman place, so indifferent to those almost insectlike flailings I'd left. About a mile distant, up into the canyon, there was a cave which dated human habitation here some thirty thousand years into the past. All around us were the fossils from a sea which had been here long before that, fish, shells, timeless. The Hopi say, 'First came the Navajo, and then the white man.' We are a curious fact."

Arthur Gregor, reflecting on what might and might not be learned from remembered lives: "I always held—and continue to hold—that while the artist's life is inseparable from his work, much of it, of the life, can be discounted, those details which are of strictly personal character and of little value beyond their occurrences, and that those which were significant have been embedded—though transformed, molded to its requirements—in the work itself. In my view, the artist's life is his material but only those aspects of it are worth using which are more generally applicable and relevant to the human condition as such. I continue to maintain that what can mingle with musings and what memory finds worth retaining has been woven into the poems, and it is the poems themselves that remain as the best source and evidence of my true engagement. Still, I know from my own pleasure in reading that curiosity about a work's history and about the author's life increases the more the work itself has seized me and made me its adherent. But the pleasure with which one has become the work's captive surely exceeds the interest with which one learns later of its genesis. Nevertheless, it is intriguing to discover—or at least to be made aware of—the secrets of the creative process by being able to see the author's life as the soil of the work."

These brief examples can only suggest what lies ahead in this volume. The essays will speak differently to different readers; but they are certain to speak best, and most eloquently, for themselves.

Acknowledgments

A special word of thanks to all the writers whose essays appear in this volume. They have given as generously of their enthusiasm and good humor as of their talent. We are indebted.

Authors Forthcoming in *CAAS*

Ai
American poet

Mulk Raj Anand
Indian novelist, nonfiction writer,
and critic

Hal Bennett
American novelist

James Broughton
American poet and filmmaker

Algis Budrys
American science-fiction writer
and editor

Ed Bullins
American playwright

Cyprian Ekwensi
Nigerian novelist and short-story
writer

Philip José Farmer
American science-fiction writer

Charles Gordone
American playwright, actor, and
director

Kay Green
English novelist

Daniel Halpern
American poet and editor

Ihab Habib Hassan
American critic and editor

Marianne Hauser
American novelist

John Hollander
American poet

Danilo Kiš
Yugoslavian novelist and short-story
writer

Etheridge Knight
American poet

Samuel Menashe
American poet

Jessica Mitford
English essayist and journalist

Bharati Mukherjee
Canadian novelist and short-story
writer

Larry Niven
American science-fiction writer

Fernand Ouellette
Canadian novelist

Harry Mark Petrakis
American novelist and screenwriter

Tom Raworth
English poet

Alastair Reid
Scottish poet, essayist, and
translator

Martin Rosenblum
American poet

John Ryan
Irish poet and editor

Nawal el-Saadawi
Egyptian novelist

Sonia Sanchez
American poet

James Schevill
American poet

Vladimir Voinovich
Russian novelist

Paul Weiss
American philosopher

Acknowledgments

Grateful acknowledgment is made to those publishers and photographers whose works appear with these authors' essays.

Carol Bergé: p. 1, Bernard Mindich; p. 3, Berekian, Nice, France; p. 5, David Ready; p. 11, Bill Yoscary.

Marion Zimmer Bradley: p. 19, Rachel E. Holmen; p. 23, Dean A. Grennell; p. 24, Frank J. Johns/*Staten Island Advance.*

Rosellen Brown: p. 29, Marvin Hoffman.

Camilo José Cela: p. 45, César Lucas; p. 56, © Barratts, London.

Robert Creeley: pp. 68, 69, Special Collections, Washington University, St. Louis, Missouri; p. 73, Bruce Jackson; p. 75, Elsa Dorfman.

Roy Fisher: p. 97, Dennis J. Bussey.

Penelope Fitzgerald: p. 102, Valentine, Hampstead, England.

Roy Fuller: p. 114, Edward Hutton; p. 117, P. Fewell; p. 119, © Martin Breese; p. 120, John Vickers; p. 121, © Barrsit's Photo Press, Ltd.; p. 125, © Stanley Graham; p. 126, Studio Edmark; p. 127, © Michael Ward/*The Sunday Times.*

Brewster Ghiselin: p. 129, Busath Photography; Poetry by Brewster Ghiselin from *Windrose: Poems 1929–1979.* Copyright © 1980 by Brewster Ghiselin. Reprinted by permission of the University of Utah Press.

Lee Hoffman: p. 174, Aaron M. Rennert.

Damon Knight: p. 219, Katherine MacLean; p. 227, Cine-Foto Real, Brazil.

Sławomir Mrożek: p. 265, © Simone Oppliger, Switzerland; p. 275, H. Schabenbeck.

Contemporary Authors

Autobiography Series

Carol Bergé

1928-

Carol Bergé, 1984

It is fashioned like a novel of ideas, and of our time, in which the characters' own natures and motives form the otherwise unpredictable turns . . . The 60 years are divided in half. Whatever more there may be after that is a gift from the gods, and each day an amazement and a discovery.

I. *The Novelist/Editor Approaches Her Youth in Third Person.*

She was born in Manhattan. The first 30 years were lived to the design of parents and society. Years of learning and of frustration. The Natural History Museum, Swan Lake Ballet, Verdi, Puccini. By age 11, she had read Mark Twain, Dickens, Peter Freuchen; later, Poe, the Brontes, Conan Doyle, Saki, the DuMauriers, Jules Verne, Elizabeth Goudge, H. G. Wells, Richard Halliburton, Oliver LaFarge, Doc Savage, the Satevepost Short-Shorts . . . WWII, and A. B. Davis High School, in Westchester: a proper sorority, clothes from Lord & Taylor, Peck & Peck, boyfriends, proms, and not one friend or relative who spoke her language. A feeling of unexplainable isolation. The father went to Manhattan to work at 1 p.m. when the kids were at school, returned after midnight; he saw the kids on weekends. He handled all the physical discipline and there was plenty of it: he had a temper. When the daughter "waited up" to see him, he was tired and withdrawn, needing to be alone. The mother: capable, brisk,

1

cold, efficient, *Für Elise* on the baby grand, mah jongg and filets mignon and servants. Light through the picture window on snow bowing the blue spruce branches. A beloved baby brother grown from a friend into a stranger. A dog named Tip to run through Hunts Woods with on autumn afternoons.

Always a memory of Fieldston School (Ethical Culture), where dreams could become goals for a bright child. They'd chosen to use tuition money instead to move to Westchester. The children went into public schools: a shocking move downward into a mediocrity of standards and vision. She had begun to write. A story in a camp newspaper at 8, a poem in a local newspaper at 14. No diaries or journals. Then, as now, if it was worth saying, it was worth hewing, honing, shaping into a form, putting it out there for the world to share.

A red-star-leafed Japanese maple, hydrangeas, peonies, forsythia. An unforgettable kiss from Charlie on the screened-in porch glider. Riding a bike through Bronxville, staring at the homes which seemed new stone towers, not like King Arthur's castle. The Gramatan Hotel: sliding in to be a voyeuse at the parties, weddings, enriching the interior life. The parents shipped the lonely, miserable girl off to summer-camps while they toured Europe, Asia. She had no names for wanting to escape. Everything seemed perfect. She met all the rules. A first marriage, because one was supposed to marry, so she married her good friend, Bill. Before that, a sweet man had asked and been refused; by the time she turned to him, he'd married a lesser woman. Carol's marriage was convenient, uncomfortable but useful, brief. She left him when they got an apartment in Manhattan and she could be on her own. She loved that earlier love but not Bill. The sex was simply unbearable. One day, she just quit.

Before and after the first marriage, there were 8½ years of college—3½ at NYU, where she met Martin Tucker, Alfred Chester, Si Perchik, Richard Barker, Herb Hauser, important in her life over the years. Barker, in the same Philosophy class, was the brightest, the one who asked questions, gave challenges. He had a tiny walk-up apartment, cold-water, on Cornelia St., and a wife from Appalachia whom he'd brought home to shock his parents. She was pregnant and older than he, and did not understand his books, which filled the entire flat, or the crowd of literary students of whom he was the energy center. Carol would go there for parties and conversation, fine stories about how he'd smuggled in copies of Frank Harris and Henry Miller (whom he'd gone to meet, at Big Sur) when he'd stowed away on a ship to

"Carol Peppis, surburban bobby-soxer,"
about 1944

Paris . . . Her parents feared and hated "Reb" Barker—he was The Enemy. They were Le Petit Bourgeois, he was La Vie Bohème. And they knew their proper daughter was mortally attracted to him and to his lifestyle. But Carol was never more alive than at Reb's apartment, with Jesse Gordon, Cliff Hall, Nick Karolides, Marv Schiller—all part of *Lines & Letters,* the literary mag which had offices in the Ed Building of NYU at Washington Square.

Everyone was writing. Si Perchik was a vet, the elder of the crowd. Carol had poems published and admired in *L&L.* After 3½ years, she quit the Degree track and began to educate herself, taking night classes at NYU, Columbia, The New School. She took what she hungered for: Shakespeare (the Historical Plays, the Comedies, the Tragedies, the Poetry), Book Editing, Magazine Editing, Printing Inks & Paper, Book Production, Writing Advertising Copy, Typing & Shorthand. She studied with Margaret Mead, Clyde Kluckhohn, Louise Bogan, S. Stephenson Smith, more. She remained close to Warren Bower of NYU, who would tell her years later, at her reading at the 92nd St. YMHA, that of all his students of writing, she had been the best and the brightest . . .

She lived at 265 Riverside Drive in the apartment she'd shared with Bill. Riding the Riverside bus to and from work, she read Shirley Jackson's early novel, *Hangsaman,* and then her collection *The Lottery;* John Updike's early stories in *The New Yorker; New Directions* and *discovery* until they loosened from their paperback bindings. The jobs she held, sequentially: Syndicate Publications (early health-food industry mags, based on Adelle Davis and Gayelord Hauser); Hart Publishing (children's lit); Simon & Schuster/Pocket Books (where she was friend to Dennis Wepman, who later got famous in a hurry for the champagne/cyanide murder of his parents—he worked in the stock room, and everyone left with books under their coats); Green-Brodie Advertising (Rudy Globus, Anatole Broyard, Alan Green, Julian Brodie); Forbes Magazine, where she was Assistant to the Book Editor, Chester Heck; and, enfin, Pendray & Co. (Industrial PR), where she was Assistant to G. Edward Pendray, had her own office, and worked with him and Bob McDevitt on Canadian Westinghouse, Allied Chemical & Dye and other accounts. Pendray was a marvelous, giving teacher of just what she wanted to learn next. Directly in the Pendragon line of descent (his children named Guinever, Lynet, Elain), he was a futurist who headed The American Rocket Society and hired his assistant because she knew who Ted Sturgeon, Hugo Gernsback and von Braun were, and had read the books.

At *Forbes,* she knew Robert S. Gordon, one of the stable of bright young editors. When she asked, about his Upper East Side highrise flat, filled with Swedish Modern, Orrefors, and hand-woven fabrics, "I've never seen anything like this, how is it accomplished?" he gave her an answer to live by: "Good taste *knows.* " At 24, Bob played the Market knowledgably enough to earn at it, and never turned away her questions with "Don't bother your pretty head about it," as had most men. Bob had taupe hair, green eyes, was bisexual, and looked like Nureyev, in "L'Après-midi."

By 1954, she lived in a studio apartment walkup on 76th St. just off Central Park. A fireplace of ombré Dutch tiles, brown to gold; a bathtub down the hall; a newlywed couple making love on the other side of a thin wall. Her name was still Bill's: Farand, and Noel Farrand (an heir of Farrand Optical) lived on the ground floor; they talked classical music and were friends. One evening, on the subway from work, a very romantic man offered her his seat: Jack Bergé,

tall, slender, a green-eyed Scorpio, handsome, an Argentine with a British accent. They left at the same stop (his bachelor flat was on 77th, facing the Museum). He offered her a cigaret; they sat on a bench at the edge of the Park and talked about the music they both loved: Bach, Vivaldi, Franck, Dvořák, opera . . . he was engaged to Beatriz, a fellow Argentine whom his parents favored. Carol said, "When you get free, give me a call," and a few months later, as she was working at her desk, he called from the phone in the lobby: would she come down for coffee? A year later, after a delicious mutual courtship, they married, and ten months later, Peter Iago Bergé was born to them, in 1956.

It was a perfect marriage, the source of all the clichés. They had the same sense of humor, danced divinely together, were always making love and being in love. It was joy being with this sweet sophisticate who was competent in 8 languages and knew how to cook artichokes. They learned together how to make, have, love and care for a baby. Their son, almost 8 pounds at birth, looked like her and had Jack's

Parents, Molly and Albert Peppis,
Nice, France, 1954

graceful, long fingers. Jack had a neat job with Commerce & Industry Association, in Manhattan, so he commuted from Westchester where they had an apartment.

She had begun again to write: stories and poems. The marriage was directed and supervised by their parents, and it began to feel constricting, confining; she had nothing in common with the other young mothers of suburbia who seemed content. She took long walks alone with the baby, stopping to make notes for story ideas. She had to look backward to the birth of the child to feel in touch with reality. She remembered what Margaret Mead said: "Love is the invention of a few high cultures, independent of marriage—society can make it a prerequisite for marriage, but . . . it's a cultural artifact. A lifelong marriage is exceedingly difficult and only a few people can achieve it . . ."

In winter 1957–8, after they'd moved to Bedford St. in The Village to see if locus would save the marriage, she sat with one line, from *Hamlet,* in her head: "This above all; to thine own self be true, and it must follow, as the night the day . . ." She left Jack and the marriage, asking only to keep the baby, her rings and watch—he could keep the rest. She cashed in the rings and Rolex watch, booked a tiny inside stateroom on the *Liberté* to Paris, stashed her baby, pro tem, with her unwilling yet cooperative parents (who thought she'd lost her mind), and left to be in Europe as a writer. Her luggage was one small satchel containing 2 changes of clothing, 2 books (one on Van Gogh, one on Art History), a notebook, 2 pairs of shoes, and a return ticket. Paris was her dream, made reality the night the boat train pulled into Gâre du Nord and the air of the sweet city was familiar . . . She managed to be in Europe almost 3 months, working illicitly for a perfume manufacturer (translating copy for tourist brochures), doing radio copy, modelling. A tiny room on rue Jacob. Travelling: hitchhiking and by train, through France (Provence and the caves at Lascaux), Italy (the hill towns near Siena, Florence, Rome, Naples, whence the boat back). Always writing: poems and notes for stories.

On her return, her parents relayed a telegram from Jack, who'd relocated to Mexico City: he sought a reconciliation; would she and the baby come there? Yes, with one stipulation: she and the baby must live separately from him, until she reached her decision. When she arrived, she found he'd taken her parents' advice and rented an apartment for himself, his wife and son. It lasted only 4 months. During that time, she painted, produced over 20 works, had a near-sell-out show and sale at Galleria Angel—but the pull was toward writing.

She met a writer: the Japanese novelist and journalist, Makoto Oda, who was travelling on a Guggenheim. He fit into her lifelong attraction to "The Other." Jack wanted a divorce—he'd met a blonde Mexican woman who would stay home and be a wife. They'd take care of the baby, who "needed two parents," if Carol wanted to travel. She gave Jack the divorce and travelled with Makoto: to Guanajuato, San Miguel, Tepoztlán, and then a second journey to Paris.

II. *"She" Begins to Be "I": Owning the Life.*

Makoto and I lived for 6 weeks at Hôtel de Cluny on rue de la Petite-Boucherie in Saint-Germaine-des-Prés. We walked everywhere. I was absorbed with the way he saw Paris; we both felt the centuries of history under our feet. A side trip to Rouen, another to Barbizon. I wrote, bought great objects at the Flea Market and at the bookstalls on the Rive Gauche. He invited me to come to Japan and live with him—I wanted to return to New York, open a Gallery and earn enough to support myself and my young son.

While in Europe, I got a letter from my parents, saying Jack had placed Peter (then not yet 2) in a boarding-school, so Jack might be with his now-pregnant new wife. He was also suing for full custody of Peter, and my parents were in alliance with him—they saw me as living in a way that made me an unfit mother. The group of artists I was identifying with were threatening to them. I had confided to Jack that I had experimentally smoked grass, and that cinched it. With my parents backing him, Jack won custody of Peter.

Now, it's not unusual for young people to take time to travel and learn the world, enriching their education with the perspective of history and other cultures; in the late 1950s, the moves that felt right to me were almost unheard of. I had the support of Elizabeth Lyon, one of the earliest therapists to work with women who sought to break creatively out of the conventional social structures. Libby was the only intimate who approved and encouraged my first and second trips to Mexico and Europe. She was outraged that I'd lost custody of Peter and that my parents sided with Jack. It was she who suggested that I find a way of earning a living which was compatible with my natural proclivities, such as opening a Gallery of the

Arts—this would enable me to gather strength and focus my creative energies.

All this pre-dated the Women's Liberation Movement by over 12 years. Back then, there were no co-op child-care facilities. Libby made the difference. She encouraged me to fight Jack on his own turf and win Peter back, and to construct a life made of my own choices, and she confirmed those choices as right and healthy. Just as she had supported my need to go alone to Europe a year earlier, when I was in Europe the 2nd time she encouraged me to start The Five Cities Gallery. She sent me $200 to buy beautiful things to stock the Gallery with.

I went back to Mexico, found (through my dear friend, Jorge Portilla) a great lawyer (Rául Medina Mora) who was willing to take my case for very little, and, armed with Libby's letter of support, won my child back. Jack and I were finally free to live our differing lives. I was overjoyed to have my baby back with me. At first, Peter (who spoke only Spanish then) would only call me "Carol," and I told him that was okay—as long as he let me be his friend. After

several months, he began to call me "Mommy," one of the most beautiful words in the language. Turned out he blamed me for the brutal year he'd spent in the Dickensian boarding-school that Jack had put him into. It took healing on both sides. There was a lot of love, and my child and I were to grow up together over the next 15 years, designing the life while living it as process.

In 1959, while Peter was still in Mexico, I found and rented an old, dirty space used till then as storage by a mechanic whose own door faced on 4th Ave.; the L-shaped area, with its own door and shop-front window, could be separate, and it had an upstairs room where I could live. This would become The Five Cities Gallery. Rent was $65 a month, no shower, no stove. After 3 weeks of intensive cleanup and paint, revealing the pressed-tin ceilings and wood wainscoting, it was great. The 10th St. area was the hub of the active Abstract Expressionists. Next to my Gallery was the Tenth Street Coffeehouse, owned by Ed Kaplan and Mickey Ruskin. I'd met Ed at the Hotel Albert, where I briefly had a rooftop room next to the writer Aileen Pippett, who was companionable and very encouraging to my writing.

On a month-long sojourn to San Francisco, I began a stormy affair with Reb, who'd meanwhile taken his Master's at Cornell. He was now a jazz musician, writing poetry, living in Monterey near Fisherman's Wharf in a communal cottage he shared with his friends. Reb wrote a well-received article for *Contact* on the Monterey Jazz Festival. I stayed there while Peter was in Mexico, and Reb went with me when I fought for Peter and regained custody. We all had an apartment in 1960 (?) on 6th St. between Aves. B & C, in a Molly Cohen building which also housed Allen Ginsberg and Peter Orlovsky, Eileen and Bob Kaufman and their son Parker, and other writers. We read our poems at the cafes on Bleecker and MacDougal, as we had on North Beach, in Mexico City and in Paris . . .

Poetry readings began at the Tenth St. Coffeehouse, next door to my Gallery. I met Serge and Anne-Marie Gavronsky, Kathleen Fraser (Marshall) and Jack Marshall; then Jackson Mac Low, Howard Ant, Diane Wakoski, Chester Anderson (whom I had met in San Francisco hawking his magazine *Beatitude* on Grant Ave., alongside Gordon Lish with his mag *Genesis/West*, and Barney Childs, co-editor of *G/W*). In NY, Chester published *Beatitude East*, with 10 of my poems in the centerfold . . . Jerry Rothenberg, David Antin, Paul Blackburn, George Economou, Rochelle Owens, Armand Schwerner, Denise Levertov, Diane di Prima—we all read at Tenth St. I was

Carol Bergé with her son, New York City, 1962: "Peter is six, his mom is thirty-four."

amazed and fascinated. The poems I heard were opening doors to new ideas about craft and the possibilities, such as chance-method work (which made me angry at first but which later served as a wedge to new information-systems and attitudes about what art was and could become).

All of us moved with Mickey and Ed when Tenth St. Coffeehouse became Les Deux Mégots, on 7th St. between B & C, in 1961. The next 6 seminal, exciting, remarkably productive and active years, involving some 125 vital poets, will be the subject of a book I'm putting together now. A dozen magazines flourished, like the friendships—we became each other's new family, *chosen* family, cronies. We were in and out of each other's lives, thoughts, conversations, magazines, beds, poems, gossip, energy, and parties . . . My book will chronicle what became of everyone: the books, the academic jobs, the fame, the deaths, the marriages, over the next 28 years.

III. *Friends, Lovers and Catalysts.*

Of my friends in the 1960s, Paul Blackburn was most influential. We'd met in 1958, at a Paul Carroll party for *Big Table*—Makoto introduced me to both Pauls, and also to Galway Kinnell. Paul B. introduced me to Cid Corman, editor of *Origin*. I met Paul again at the Tenth Street Coffeehouse. By 1962, both he and Denise had published me in *The Nation*, and Cid had published me in *Origin*; LeRoi Jones (now Amiri Baraka) included me in the Totem/Corinth collection *Four Young Lady Poets* (alongside Diane Wakoski, Barbara Moraff and Rochelle Owens); I had good press from Hayden Carruth, among others, for my work.

Paul had me invited into the anthology *Erotic Poetry*, Random House, 1963. Then came *Of Poetry & Power: Poems Occasioned by the Presidency & Death of JFK*, Basic Books. David Ignatow organized a WNYC reading from that anthology; I read my long threnody written from the perspective of the grieving widow, which had had special mention in John Barkham's review in the *World Telegram & Sun*. Ignatow said how much he admired my writing and stated surprise that I had no book out yet. He asked me to prepare a book-length manuscript of my poems, which he would then take to his publishers.

A month later, it was done, and after I sent it to David Ignatow, he disclaimed ever having asked for it. I was angry and crushed and ran crying to Paul. He spun the situation around in a way that was fully creative and compassionate. Instead of concentrating on the betrayal of that uncaring lizard, Ignatow, Paul

made something productive out of it: he asked if he could keep my ms. for a week and get back to me. In just a week, what he did was a masterful job of turning the large ms. into 3 discrete small-press-size chapbooks, ready to go. They came out just as he'd done them: *Poems Made of Skin,* from Weed/Flower Press in Canada (Nelson Ball, Editor); *The Chambers,* from Aylesford Review Press in England (Brocard Sewell, Editor); and *Circles, as in the Eye,* from Desert Review Press in Santa Fe (Terry Abbott, Editor), with an introduction by Paul Blackburn.

One never forgets one's first major editor, especially if he was teacher, friend, companion and lover as well. Paul taught me how many ways there were to publish, how to nurture one's reputation, and how to order and keep one's drafts of published work for archival collections. When Paul was by-passed in favor of Joel Oppenheimer to head up the St. Marks Poetry Project, Frank Murphy and I led the picket line—I think it was 1967. The Deux Mégots group had moved briefly to Le Métro Cafe and then disbanded; it had nurtured a prodigious number of active poets, novelists, playwrights and editors, many of whom became award-winners and teachers. The group rivalled Black Mountain College in quality and exceeded it in quantity, over a much briefer existence—the intensity of our productivity was incredible—"We were all the same age," to paraphrase a Taylor Mead one-liner of that glorious era: we were all burgeoning and becoming.

"At Les Deux Mégots coffee shop on Seventh Street with Diane Wakoski," about 1963

Life on the Lower East seethed and hummed. Ted and Sandy Berrigan were the first writers on 9th St. (though there were already a few painters there as well—Toby Urbont comes to mind). I found flats for Al Katzman, Susan Sherman and Jack Rader. Ed Sanders' Peace Eye Bookstore was around the corner on 10th St. between B & C. Peter and I rode our bikes in Tompkins Square Park, and ate pirogi at "The Uke," with the Russian immigrants. My mother's parents had been like them (from Kiev and Odessa), and had lived there. She was furious when I and my child moved to 9th St.—"We spent all our lives struggling to get out of that neighborhood, and now you move there on purpose!" We loved it. We had a floor-through 4-room apartment accessed by an iron staircase, on the middle floor of a 3-story building in back of a tall tenement. There was a courtyard. It reminded me of Paris. The floors were wide wood boards; the ceilings were patterned tin. It was sweet and cozy. We had our first cat, Alice Louise, and her son, dumb Woody. Peter asked that instead of a 7th Birthday Party, I make a dinner for his friends from City & Country School—he asked for a turkey with stuffing. After it was done and cleared, he opened the fridge, to find the kitten, Woody, in the dark interior of the turkey-frame, happily munching away . . .

The day I was first published in *Poetry: Chicago* (1964?), a goal since my teens, I floated a foot off the ground when I went to meet Peter at the crosstown bus-stop. "What's up?" he asked. "Oh, I was just published in the best poetry magazine in the country!" "That's great," he said, "Now quit bragging and get back to the typewriter and do something new." Peter has always had tremendous insights. I turned strongly toward fiction. I'd written my first "adult" short story, *The Farm Woman,* in Toronto earlier that year, when P. and I were returning from the Poetry Conference at UBC/Vancouver; I'd gone to *be there* as part of history, to meet and learn from Charles Olson, and to write it up for Ed Sanders' mimeo press (it was published as *The Vancouver Report*). Thus began 2 threads, fiction alongside reportage, which have taken precedence in my life, over poetry, to this day.

We moved over to 37½ St. Marks Place. Peter continued under his scholarship at the wonderful brownstone school, City & Country, on W. 12th St. near 6th Ave. Two poets whose kids were already there gained us access: Bob Nichols and Denise Levertov. Our lives were rich in friendships. Diane Wakoski and Shep Sherbell lived down the block in a brownstone. Early rock-&-roll at The Dom on the next block, alongside great, tiny boutiques and The

Bridge Theater. Bob Blossom, Aldo Tambellini's Gate Theater, Harry Smith, Jonas Mekas, Judith Malina's and Julian Beck's Living Theatre, the Katzman Twins and their *East Village Other,* Allen and Doris Planz, Hannah Wiener, Sue Sherman, Szabo, Tuli Kupferberg, Ed Sanders, La Mama Experimental Theater and Cafe, Bread & Puppets Theater, so much the life in motion intensely, Charlie Mingus at The Five Spot, Lennie Tristano/The Blue Note, music the fabric of our lives . . .

IV. *The Next Dimension.*

One winter, I asked Jackson Mac Low to include me in the new multi-media activities he was working with. I sensed it was my next area of learning. It involved performance pieces and was scored like music. He invited me to a rehearsal at Judson Church's basement. There I met Nam June Paik, Dick Higgins, Philip Corner, Yoko Ono, La-Monte Young, Marian Zazeela, Kenneth King, Al Hansen, Ray Johnson, Yvonne Rainer, Phoebe Neville, Meredith Monk—it was intended to change my ideas, and it worked. From then on, I was part of the new angle into art: I saw all of the arts expanding into each other and overlapping, in a most exciting way. I would never again be able to be solely passive audience. I would be a participant, as the art became synonymous with and not differentiated from the everyday life. Language would change for me, move into another dimension, when chance-method was applied to produce a different view of sound and meaning.

Cage's class at The New School spawned these concepts. I was a second-waver (I'd missed that class, in the late 50s, where Richard Maxfield, Al Hansen, Allen Kaprow, Jackson Mac Low, Dick Higgins and George Brecht had been with Cage to evolve the new arts). As I understood Cage's concepts, the music I'd always loved subtly shifted, expanding to include sounds of my everyday surround. The idea widened into the activities of my life after "The Family," at The Bridge Theater on St. Marks, in which ordinary familial activities take place on-stage over a week, showcasing them startlingly as "art," following through on the way Cage's "music" highlights ordinary sounds and Nam June Paik's amalgams transform musical instruments and TV sets into new art forms . . . The name of it was "DON'T TAKE ANYTHING FOR GRANTED" and "YOU ARE THE LENS."

I was active in many events of the Fluxus group, with Al Hansen, Nam June Paik, Dick Higgins, Alison

Knowles, Ray Johnson, Philip Corner, Dieter Roth; I was published in the Fluxus newspaper *CC V Tre.* I was there with Meredith Monk, Phoebe Neville, Simone Forti, Carolee Schneemann, Kenneth King, Bengt af Klintberg, Daniel Spoerri, Benjamin Patterson, Shigeko Kubota, Kosugi, Claude Pelieu, moving at the edges where poetry, music, dance, sculpture and painting overlapped and melded and caused our ordinary lives to be suffused into art. These were mind-expanders, like the events at Fillmore East with Timothy Leary and Richard Alpert. Nothing would ever be as before, for those of us who lived in the 60s.

My writing would change. Kenneth King's, Phoebe Neville's, Yvonne Rainer's, Simone Forti's "new dance" would cause me to see ordinary walking as dance. Yvonne's "The Mind is a Muscle," Carolee's "The Queen's Dog," a funny piece by Phoebe Neville parodying The Hippie Walk on a tightrope, all at Judson. At Café a Go-Go, Al Hansen made me think about news and newspapers when he ground them in blenders. Opera would never be the same to me after being in Dick Higgins' "Opera," and Central Park looked different after having seen it on stilts with Ray Johnson. "Poetry in motion" changed from a phrase to a meaningful infusion after being in Jackson Mac Low's theater pieces ("Walt Whitman's Birthday" comes to mind: planets, flashlights, music). The revelation: it is all music, all a poem being lived, all dance. A gift, back to the givers, full circle. We who had distilled facets of life to present them as art were given back the realization that *the life itself is the art,* that we are the art and the music, that the life itself is the poem. Andy Warhol, Jonas Mekas, Kenneth Anger, Stan Brakhage, Ron Rice, Harry Smith showed us on film that film was about being alive now. The changes were in perspective and concept. Ourselves as agar-cultures of the interior landscapes.

I knew there were 2 groups nearby into which I didn't fit: those who weren't participating in this change, but continued to divide life in the old way: I saw it as the way the masses live: holding down a job they hate, taking weekends/vacations/retirement to do what they love best. These other "artists" were being specialists, "writing" or "painting" or "dancing." I felt different from them, as I incorporated the other arts into my life and writing. And I was different from the Political Activists, many of whom were in our group. I was never able to identify with them, especially the anarchists. I could feel their passion but I saw it as a residual anger left from childhood, that wasn't being converted into positive creativity. I opted instead for a specific and personal

politics; I felt, then and now, I could be useful in any direct interpersonal dialogue toward changing the way the world is. I see the world as cyclical (physics) and irrational (philosophy)—and politics as useless nattering. The only political piece I've ever done was at Mickey Ruskin's "Longview Acres," when P. and I did resonance-echoes on the names "Daniel" and "Sinyavsky" to protest the arrest of those Russian writers. We chanted their names, Dan-*yell*, Sin-yavsky, until (briefer and quieter) they became one word: Dan-cin', in a mantra . . .

One evening, when I went to pick up P. from an after-school visit with Duncan, Bob Nichols' son, I saw Bob Nichols in the snowy winter twilight at the tiny triangle near Carmine St. and Waverly Place. Bob had a carton on a stick held over his head; on all sides was painted "PEACE"; I felt distanced from this beautiful, idealistic one-man march, as I did when I went on marches to Washington to "Exorcise the Pentagon" and such. I came to feel that my chances to improve things were as a writer, as a teacher, and as a friend, if anyone cared to listen to me. One of my major character flaws is that I do want to change the world, which is probably okay the way it is and moving toward change without my help—I take it upon myself to point out ways people could do their trip with less pain or in a more salubrious way, and this is not always well-received . . . Among my other flaws is over-reacting when I see my flaws reflected in others, bounced back in the mirror of you. Some of my other faults are envy, jealousy, self-absorption, the desire for immortality, impatience, a lack of confrontiveness, the inability to get past griefs and wounds, a certain elitism, and a need always to "be right." My friends help with these.

V. *Leaving New York City: Major Moves Outward.*

Frank Murphy introduced me to Carl Ginsburg in 1968 and then to Alan Dye. Alan and I fell into love, spent the summer in Utica at and near Carl/Phyllis' house, and then moved into an apartment at Hotel Chelsea with Peter. We had #211, @ $250 a month. Down the hall, in Dylan Thomas' old studio, was the novelist Joyce Elbert. We became friends; she asked to see my novel and other mss. In 1964, during one of many trips to New Mexico, I was at Wurlitzer Foundation in Taos, and began my first novel, *In Motion,* the story of a woman painter's life from 1930–1995. Anne Freedgood of Doubleday saw and liked it in winter 1969, and asked for major changes I didn't know how to make then (magnifying the role of one of the characters most interesting to her). This book foretells the development of SoHo and TriBeCa in great detail, and describes a computerized world-wide reference network resource for the arts, called "Total Center," or "Total See." This early novel is in rewrite now: call if interested.

Joyce liked this novel and my other writings. She writes conventional, commercial novels; she said, "My editors wouldn't go for these, but I know someone who would!" She had me meet Bob Amussen, of Bobbs-Merrill. Some weeks later, Bob called, saying he accepted all 3 of the mss. I'd submitted: a collected poetry (called, to honor Alan, who was a photographer for TIME, *From a Soft Angle: Poems About Women,* Bobbs-Merrill, NY, 1971); a collection of stories and novellas, *A Couple Called Moebius,* out in 1972; and a novel-in-progress, which would be called *Acts of Love: An American Novel,* out in boards in 1973 and (thanks to Chuck Neighbors, my agent) brought out by Pocket Books in 1974. I knew that moving to The Chelsea would be good for all of us! P. met Arthur C. Clarke there, and did a class project with him about Clarke's writings. I stayed friends with Joyce, and met Peggy Biderman, Stella Waitzkin, Virgil Thomson, Erje Ayden, Janis Joplin, and many other high creative energies there. Peter has said, "It's funny, how we always seemed to be living where it was happening," and that's surely true of The Chelsea—it's like an intensely packed small town, rife with Gossip of the Tribe, compressed within tight walls like a medieval hill-town. One can meet anyone at the bar of the Quijote Restaurant, with its perky margaritas and great paella and famous lobster with green sauce. I shared many such meals with Isabella Gardner, Stella, visiting firemen, Alan and Peter. There are more civilised artists' hotels in NYC, but none more lively or challenging. One even meets interesting people on the elevator and on the roof. There's nothing like it anywhere . . .

In winter 1968, Alan and I took over the lease on a Woodstock house from The Mothers of Invention (Bunk Gardner was a friend from the St. Marks days, and we ran into him at The Chelsea again). How we loved that beautiful, energetic, New England–looking small town! We ran to it every chance we had. I painted a mailbox to say BERGÉ/DYE (echoes of Ray Johnson, "Carol Bergé will die some day," at a Fluxus dinner I went to with Dieter Roth in the early 60s . . .). That mailbox stood on the country road long after we'd all moved elsewhere. When Alan and I split up the following year, we divided the turfs: Alan continued on at The Chelsea, Peter and I moved full-time to Woodstock, renting.

Carol Bergé with Alan Dye at the publication party for An American Romance, *Gotham Book Mart, New York City, 1969*

There we were to remain, for a total of 6 years. When Peter got his first dog, a beautiful Welsh Terrier, he named him "Arthur C. Clarke," an honor not acknowledged or appreciated by that writer. Arthur was our dog and friend for over 12 years; he brought us his buddy, "Corky," a Welsh Corgi, *naturalement,* and together with our two cats, Alice and NutZen, we were a family.

A family needs a homestead. I found a 110-year-old, run-down nine-room farmhouse, bordered by the Sawkill and the Beaverkill, surrounded with 21 acres of meadow, with a beautiful old barn and lean-to and 2 small out-buildings. I borrowed a down payment (price: $35,000!) and we moved in. It was 5 miles outside of town, in Lake Hill. 1971: Peter was in high school, and capable of both good work and of standing up to me, useful habits which continue to this day.

We had 4 wonderful years in that house. The 2 dogs bounding across the meadow at twilight. The cats bringing back tiny prizes of the kidneys of even smaller animals and leaving them for us to step on with bare feet on the doormat . . . smell of lilacs in spring; "silence in the snowy fields" (bless Bob Bly for that title!) in winter. Friendships, music, a small-town life with big-city resonances. The challenge of remodelling the big house and out-buildings, to make them livable, then for possible resale when we moved to another phase.

I learned on that house, the way parents learn on their firstborn child. I got my first writing grant, a CAPS/NY State Council on the Arts Fellowship in Fiction, and poured it into food and supplies. My novel, *Acts of Love,* was published and then sold to Pocket Books by Chuck Neighbors, and that money, too, went into the house. Carl Ginsburg came down from Utica to help build the shelves in the kitchen— we used old boards from the barn's lean-to to line the room and for shelves—what a beautiful kitchen— when the electricity failed one winter in a storm, I snuggled with the 4 animals in front of the stone fireplace; in the morning, when the electric system went on while I slept, the pipes in the kitchen had frozen; as they thawed, they burst, and the kitchen was all steam . . .

Ed and Miriam Sanders were among our renters; they stayed in our farmhouse while we were else-where, and then in our remodelled chicken-brooder. They and Dee-dee were lovely people, once you got past Ed's eccentricities. Ed used the tiny shed for a writing study and ignored me when I pointed out the corner that leaked; he kept his Olson letters there. Later, we had a falling-out over whether George Butterick should have paid me (or at least asked for permission) before lifting a paragraph of mine verba-tim from my *Vancouver Report* and using it as epi-graph for a chapter called "History" in his *Charles Olson Journal,* from U/Conn. I have always believed that writers should be paid for their work. Ed said I should thank Butterick for publishing my words. I guess I'm more of a capitalist than an anarchist.

The book of my love affair with Alan, *An American Romance,* came in winter 1969 from Black Sparrow, and was the source of the literary argument which preceded the one with Ed. John Martin and I had a terrible fight because he summarily cut, without asking and without notice, 12 pages from the page-proofs. I was beyond furious. A Woodstock friend, David Ballantine, brother of Ian of Ballantine books, gave me a piece of cogent advice that has staying power: "Don't you realize that writers are nothing special to publishers? All they are is mattress manufacturers, just selling a product, and you're providing the stuffing to fill their mattresses!" How

true, and so much for Ego, or Art. Thus was I enlightened . . . but I continued writing: the 3 "big books" from Bobbs-Merrill came after that, and many others.

The Woodstock years and furnishing that big house were a renewal of active antiquing. I bought at countless auctions, yard sales, flea markets. If only I still owned some of the Mission Oak furniture (Arts-and-Crafts Period) which I bought on instinct back then, and sold later for a song!

VI. *The Teaching Begins, and the Editing.*

My first teaching was with The Guidance Center in Woodstock: writing as therapy. There I learned that dyslexia can be perceived instantly in the material rather than in the handwriting; dyslexics give insight into a world simultaneous to our reality and otherwise inaccessible. They produce extraordinary, fascinating writings of great luminosity.

In Woodstock, in 1970, I began editing and publishing *CENTER Magazine,* which continued for some 13 years under generous grants from CCLM/NEA. This thread, encouraging writers of innovative fiction and prose, is about to begin again. Over the course of its years, *CENTER* and I published some 250 experimenting writers, many of whom then published books, extending their careers. *CENTER* is another manifestation of my love for "The Other," this time in the field of writing. I'm interested in the edges, the overlaps, the changes which point into the future of the medium. I can enjoy reading conventional writing, but it rarely excites me. We're talking here about sand-papered fingertips. All the creative editors and many great writers reach into the future, rather than simply following precedents. Ed Sanders was an early role model, on many levels: the audacity of his *Fuck You: A Magazine of the Arts* was at the cutting edge of the "Mimeo Revolution" of the early 60s.

By 1976, I had my first invitation to teach at college level, at Thomas Jefferson College, the innovative division of Grand Valley State Colleges, in Michigan. I learned to teach and I learned my own strengths and weaknesses. I wanted more of a personal exchange with students than the formal "I/They" school afforded, and we had this at TJC: enjoyable dialogues and personal friendships were formed. The assumption was that we were all on earth to learn from each other. I loved affording access to writing; I loved teaching "Multi-media: the Convergence of Contemporary Arts," which included all the high-spirited melding and explorations I'd experienced in

Saying something to Gary Snyder at a Gotham Book Mart party, about 1979

the 60s in NYC. I learned there was a price to pay on having even *some* rules/definitions at such a school. I was called "rigid" because I needed students to be on time and to attend classes and to fulfill assignments. It was an "all or nothing" school. Students' excuses for being late or absent or ignoring assignments got to me, and I found this defiance occurring no less at UNM in 1987 than it had at TJC in 1976; at the latter, one student told me she'd missed classes for a week because "she had to go see the Maharishi," and at UNM last year, same-same because "she had to see this Indian Chief," a wise man just passing through. Students made no correlation between a college format/education and the life they would later lead, and the need to be in a room in order to learn from the teacher hired to do that job.

I also learned, over the next 10 years of teaching at universities in CA, MS, OH, IN, NY, and NM, that education in this country now has little or nothing to do with preparing a student for the sort of life which includes resiliency, inventiveness and other survival skills. I experienced that the majority of teachers are not in it for love of teaching or with the aim of sharing their expertise, abilities or accrued wisdom, but for security, predictability, panache and paid vacations. They are bored, and so they are bores and bad teachers. I've concentrated on doing private workshops of the sort which make room for creativity and a real sharing and growth. And as an *éminence grise,* I also do editorial consultations, co-authoring and private tutorials.

VII. *The Writing: Sources, Processes, Commentaries.*

My desire, when I left the traditional life, was to experience as many emotions and aspects of life as possible, and write about them with veracity. I've always had absolute self-confidence—in the writing, and in a few other areas—not to the extent of smugness but more of willingness to extend and risk. I know that no one else writes what I write and I feel satisfied to have carved out a well-defined terrain which I love. Writing is now incorporate in the life, so that no division exists between the various constants. As I'd hoped, the writing has provided a circle of sweet friendships, interesting lovers, wise teachers and a width of *lebensraum,* and acknowledgment of achievement by way of feedback from readers and grants and awards. After the CAPS, there was a National Endowment for the Arts Fellowship in Fiction (1979), and there were invitations to serve on Grants Committees for CCLM/NEA and many other panels. *CENTER Magazine* had 12 grants to publish and to pay my authors. By the time the last "Full Set" of 13 issues of *CENTER* sold to The New York Public Library, at Fifth Avenue & 42nd St., across the street from where I'd had my last full-time office job at Pendray & Co., I felt the continuum of history; it was 1985, just 30 years after I'd met Jack for coffee and romance. I felt a crown of confirmation from the city where I was born.

Back then, I knew I wanted a life of challenge, filled with growth-provoking surprises, anything but suburbia. I've had plenty of time and room to check out the possibilities. I've studied the archetypes I myself fit into: in the Chinese Zodiac, I am an Earth Dragon; from Diane Wakoski, I learned, back in 1962, that I am Libra, with Cancer Ascendant and Moon in Gemini and with Mercury and Venus in Scorpio. I learned that I'm a female, and a Jew, and what these signify in our society, as advantages and detriments. I understood that I had my options because I was born in USA, and developed a career more likely to thrive here than anywhere else except perhaps in France in this time . . . When I went through the EST Training, in 1978, I acquired some practical applications of Zen (which I've been studying or being in since the late 1950s). I spotted what Iago Galdston, my first shrink, meant back in 1948 when he said I had "a most interesting *chiaroscuro* personality"—the roots and sources of the stuck positions I get into, and I copped to how I get lost in passions and how I resist taking responsibility for resolving problems.

In Woodstock, in 1970, in one of the first Women's Consciousness Raising Groups, I gained understanding of set-piece attitudes toward other women. In Berkeley, in an Anger Workshop, I got clear that anger means a need for motion to effect change, and how to work with dialogue and a view of the options. I never achieved compassion for the fashionable excuses women use to evade their lives: in the 1970s, it was hypoglycemia; in the 80s, it became PMS and Seasonal Affective Disorder, all variations on telling God, "I have a headache tonight, dear." In New York, I went to classes on Finances and How to Read the Stock Market. Always, I knew how to travel alone, finding the marvelous and remarkable in the most ordinary of landscapes—the pleasure in the pedestrian, when held at an angle to the light. I've realized that as long as I'm free to explore, I'm not limited or trapped.

The writing continues, apace. There are 20 books now, in fiction, poetry and non-fiction. My fiction is made of real people, often archetypes or composites, drawn from life but with exaggerated traits and habits, in fictional situations designed to limn intriguing crosscurrents. My characters are living out extrapolations of their basic natures, in interaction with each other. I never know at the beginning of a story how it will end or even how it will develop—that's the way the life itself is, so I trust myself and them and go ahead, using the initial idea as impetus. Once the characters stand and live on their own, they carry the story in its own direction—all I have to do is perceive and record. A story needs classical bases and interesting people. Some of mine are fabliaux not much different from those passing among the minnesingers or as folk-legends. To me, what is required is a sense of archetype, compression, and universality, and a point of shift or change within the tale. If a story has an energetic beginning (well-made, to draw the attention of the reader), a "middle" (not necessarily at the conventional ⅝ point) where *something changes,* and a dénouement or resolution which fits the characters' own natures, the story will work. I pay attention to titles, as mini-art-forms; I like reading other writers' T.O.C.s, which show if they, too, enjoy making titles.

Small, quirky traits point up the characters' lives. I know that everyone alive is divided into those who arrive at the airport an hour early and those who catch the plane by the skin of their teeth. The person who "doesn't like letters" or "doesn't like telephones" shows a certain attitude about communication. The person who doesn't drive a car—the person who collects Royal Doulton china, or guns, or dolls, or contemporary art, or pre-Columbian pottery—the person who smiles with only half his face, the person who keeps every scrap from her great-grandmother on down and doesn't own her own house, the person who lives in fear of displeasing the gods, each is evidential of our time, and we are all on earth together in a simultaneity of struggle to communicate and understand. And, given a situation which brings out a basic tension or commonality of conflict between any of them, and an interesting locus, we may have a successful story. My theory is that all writers

Peter and Jack Bergé, Mexico City, 1984: "Jack turned up in our lives after an absence of some twenty-one years. Imagine our surprise when Peter turns out to look more like his father than like me."

start out with nobody to listen to them, and if a universality is achieved, whereby lives are observed *in situ* and in motion and with story-telling skill, somebody will listen and be delighted.

One review of my stories, by Vivian Gornick, in *Village Voice,* touches what I'm about in the writing:

> Bergé invests her stories with an insinuating pliancy of tone, deftly emulating styles of conversation, writing monologue in a way that makes it seem she's imitating her characters rather than creating them. She invites suspicion, encourages vertigo; her male-female fables, sentimental, dry, acerbic, overwhelm with quotidian detail which gradually turns surreal. All are filled with pungent imagery and a solemn sense of ritual—part industrial sculpture, part Oriental sheen—with just a touch of John Fowles to keep things nasty.

Ishmael Reed did the other review which I feel most closely grasps my work, this time about my novels. Whereas the *Kirkus* and *PW* people seemed confused about *Acts of Love* ("The people in this novel have so many dimensions that the author has to use a kaleidoscope to show them all, but she does it brilliantly—compellingly interesting"), Ishmael Reed, an old friend and himself one hell of a novelist and observer of human behavior, had the wisdom to recognize that *Acts* is in the tradition of Thornton Wilder, Sherwood Anderson, Erskine Caldwell and William Inge, in portraying life in a small town—in the 1960s. After all, the part of the title that says "An American Novel" should be the give-away. Ish's review of *Acts,* in *The Washington Post,* gives good insights:

> The American small-town novel . . . what the characters eat and the objects with which they surround themselves take on a story line by themselves . . . The detail is reminiscent of that found in classical American realist paintings . . . the small-town hangouts have a Hopper-like eeriness . . .

People ask how long it takes to write a novel; my answer seems to correlate with what I've heard from other novelists: about 2 years withal. A book I'm working on underlies everything else I'm doing during that time. It pervades and is an immersion process. I do notes in longhand and shorthand and directly on the typewriter. I'm my own word-processor.

I had great models and grand goals in thinking about writing novels. As my heritage is half-Russian, I've always wanted the scope and grandeur of Tolstoi & Dostoievski, but since I'm of this time, I admire DHL's *The Rainbow* for generation-structure, and Rolvaag's *Giants in the Earth;* the intellectual acuity of Nabokov, and the energy of Edna Ferber's works. Henry James was no slouch, and one must not omit Lady Murasaki's *Genji Monogatari,* earliest and lastingly finest. When I read *The Naked Lunch,* in Paris, and Nancy Mitford's *Love in a Cold Climate,* I knew I wanted to include angularity, a sense of humor and irony, social criticism and commentary, and experimentation with the form. I admire Lucy Lippard's *I See/You Mean* and Leonard Cohen's *Beautiful Losers* for form and innovation. In non-fiction, it would be Burton Roueché, Eve Auchincloss, Paul Theroux. The magazine I like best is *FESSENDEN REVIEW;* next would be *Maine Antique Digest* and *Connoisseur.*

Mack Thomas' 1964 remark about writing fiction stays with me and is repeated to every class and workshop: "When building a character, consider the earth from which he or she is sprung." The story must be an integral evidence of the time in which it is set; then it has weight, tensile strength, and a motion forward into history by virtue of its classicism.

I admire writers whose works are universal, rounded, strong in time; the characters and situations are memorable, and one can identify the author without needing to see the signature, which is the main criterion for excellence of style in any art. I stand by my novels and short fiction as meeting these demands. People recognize my work.

Of the shorter fiction, my One-Page Novels touch a chord in many people. The stories in *Fierce Metronome* (1981) evolved from about 1964 on, with a history in the old Satevepost Short-Shorts and those of Saki and Poe. I had a note from Howard McCord in early 1972, asking if I'd done anything in that distillate area halfway between poetry and prose, and giving them that label. I wrote back that I'd done perhaps 20, and enclosing 3, and he printed them in his Tribal Press Series, which were some 70 in all. For me, the medium was a natural evolution, incorporating compression/intensity/tonalities—the One-Page Novel is the microchip of fiction. It's the sample cross-slice that goes under the high-power microscope. It lacks the ramifications and subtleties of the story; instead, it has the edge of observations and commentary, clearly in prose rather than in poetic diction. Making one is fast payoff, instant gratification, but the medium shouldn't be tackled by amateurs as if it could be brought off without experience in conventional forms of poetry and fiction. Not surprisingly, the medium turns out to attract amateurs like iron filings to a magnet; after Howard's original series, the form became popular. It's not a populist medium, though it has become *au courant*.

From *Fierce Metronome: The One-Page Novels*, Window Press, NY, 1981, "Forms: The Challenge, An Introduction":

> We record this era in current idiom . . . intense storage and report of information, fast takes and quick studies, bubble memories, recombinant DNA, encoded masks, fast speed forward and playback, electronic speech synthesis, charm and beauty to mean atomic particles . . . modular input, interfaces, lithium drift detectors, the brain as original databank. Forms follow time: if each cell contains humanity's history, lives can essence into a page: each punctuation-mark a gesture, a breath; a relationship in a paragraph, a family's anatomy in a sentence . . . A haiku of fiction forms, a terse garden of bonsai. Bloom of souls as lasers crystals filaments chips shining . . . Motion into the future from now.

Of my short stories, my choice of those which have enough substance to continue in memory would be *Contour Lines*, . . . *And Now, Alexandra, Fat Chance, In Trouble, Winter*; of the novellas, *Invitation to the Dance* (as yet unpublished) and *Hanging Tough*, published in *Aspect*. *Invitation* deals with a peculiar reaction to rape, and *Hanging* may be the first to deal with dyslexia in a social context . . . Of the innovative pieces, *Food & Love* (The Minnesota Review, 1978) and *Watch Out for Children* (New Departures in Fiction, 1975) were milestones for their time.

I knew what kind of writer I was by who published me. Like every beginning writer, I sent to *The New Yorker* and collected rejection slips. One day, my bourgeois brother, Phil Peppis, a Madison Ave. Creative Director with N. W. Ayer Advertising, gave me the clue in. I was bemoaning the lack of reading public for my writings, so he handed me the Theory of Multiplicity: I was creating a product which was valued or useful to only a tiny percentage of the population; if I wanted to make real money, I'd have to move to a product useful to the masses, like safety-pins or paper-clips. Or Romance Novels. He seemed

to be saying, "When you hear hoofbeats, think horses, not zebras," but I've always been the sort who thinks zebras. Or camelopards. I got the point. As long as I wrote in an elitist mode, the payoffs would be in intangibles, like becoming part of history (such as this Series), honors and honoraria, admiration and respect, invitations to teach, and low dollars. I made the adjustment in my expectations. I knew that my capabilities, though wide in vision, were within a narrow parameter, but that within them I could find both great and subtle ranges of terrain. I do what I love to do and the pleasure is my payoff; as long as there's no separation between the life and the art, I'm following one of the laws of nature.

VIII. *"The Portable Self"* Strikes Again.

In the 60s, 70s and early 80s, I wrote about other artists' works: Joseph DeNoto's sculpture, Carolee Schneemann's performances, Harry Smith's films; reviews of the writings of Isabella Gardner, Michael McClure, Howard Moss, others. Poems about paintings and about the photography of Dorothea Lange. Now, it's the late 80s, and time to move on. An article in *Art & Antiques* on the pottery of Maria Martinez; a book review in *Artspace* on the Art Deco designer, Eileen Gray; catalogue copy for the Osaka show of the sculptor, Tom Waldron. My perspective has to do with becoming "The Older Generation"—there are now 2 half-generations coming up fast behind me. Concepts of life on earth, causes, contexts, change at about 50, with the accessing of what I call "The Mantle." It means one can look back and look around, seeing it as from a mile up into the ionosphere, as history, as all of us in motion in history; it's a perspective which comes only from many decades of experience . . .

In June, 1988, my 6th investment/renovation/roll-over house finally sold. I took a loss and got out fast—even before the closing, I'd leased 309 Johnson St., a 10-room beauty in Santa Fe. I was ready for a comprehensive change: I'd had 4 Mall antique shops and was ready for autonomy, for the first time since The Five Cities Gallery on 10th St. In June, 1988, I opened The Gallery of Antiques/Blue Gate Art Gallery. Since then, I've acquired and utilized more practical skills than ever before (all in play simultaneously) and more simple life-skills (like getting along with strangers) than in the 8½ years I studied at schools or the 11 years I taught at schools. This venture has coalesced and focused information gathered apparently randomly over all my years. It's the big move to self-actualization, meaning that I earn while learning. I keep a ledger of inventory, draw up a P&L statement, apply for and get a business loan, do my own taxes down to the last summaries; I hire and supervise sales help, put together a productive advertising campaign and write copy for others' programs locally. I can do the demographics which show, over the first year's course, which investments pay off and which don't. (I'm still struggling with "expectations" and "disappointments.")

I'm studying the market, real estate, seasonal swings. I listen to fellow dealers, and I have advice and support from my son, my father, my friends and my brother, all of whom are heeded and valued, yet withal I try to look only to myself to make the project work, as old friend Howard McCord advised years ago about the writing . . . The hardest part has been becoming a Sales Person: one who must relate to the public constantly. Meeting people is arduous for me; I realize what an Ivory Tower my life has been till now. For 6 months, I protected my morning hours for being alone and reading and writing; then I realized that I have to have the shop open all day.

The Gallery of Antiques/Blue Gate Art Gallery, Sante Fe, New Mexico, Carol Bergé, proprietor

Richard Church compassionately gave me a guide-book, *How to Master the Art of Selling*. Santa Fe is a unique market, requiring constant resiliency (Peter, years ago: "You know, Ma, you're really pretty flexible, for a majorly rigid personality . . ."). This place requires a public mode quite different from that of my presentation as a university teacher or as a well-known writer. I am now a 60-year-old gallery-owner and antiques dealer.

Santa Fe: complex, strange beyond description, an anomaly: back in the 70s, small towns didn't seem to have this complexity of layering (I'm talking about unusual, arty towns, like Mendocino or Woodstock, not about Mapleton, Iowa, of course). One would suppose that a person who'd survived life at The Hotel Chelsea, Berkeley, Taos, Panna Grady's parties at The Dakota and Lita and Morton Hornick's parties on Park Avenue, and who was raised in Manhattan and Westchester, would have no trouble in Santa Fe. But it's like no other, a city which is also a small town in constant flux. The layers are staggering in contrast. Thousands of artists, successful or struggling. Thousands of wealthy retirees doing volunteer work for the Symphony and the Opera. A layer of Old Radicals left over from 1965 Berkeley, some of whom meld into the layer of New Agers, who, with no solid education or comparison bases, come up instead through *The Sword and the Stone*, Hesse, Vonnegut, Dianetics, Meher Baba, Shirley MacLaine and George Ohsawa; they invest in fantasy and mysticism (Did you know that Santa Fe is here because it sits on a giant bed of potent crystals? Did you know that the mesas were laid out as landing-pads for extraterrestrials? "I apologized to my crystal yesterday."). Another of Taylor Mead's great one-liners is on my wall here: "I WANT YOU SHOULD WORSHIP MY LITTLE STATUE!" In Santa Fe, I've found more in-place belief systems existing cheek-by-jowl than ever before, anywhere. Everyone is a card-carrying Something and wants you to agree and belong. This is the only place I've ever lived where I feel I'm Dull Normal or a conservative.

Can I disguise what I'm thinking, when confronted with aggressive defiance of my personal ethos? Can I be mannerly and social toward haughty women who know nothing of books and treat me like "the help"? Don't doubt it. If they don't see me, I see them. Can I, a New Yorker with a strong accent (and with a passable proficiency in 6 languages, including body-language) relate to a Texas woman in cobra boots and a rhinestoned shirt, who wants a painting to match her couch? Yes. After all, she cannot read, and she cannot read my mind.

*Carol Bergé, while teaching at the
University of New Mexico, Albuquerque, 1980*

All the lines of continuum are focused and in motion. I'm remembering that I finished high-school with a 99.6 on the English Regent Exam, bringing tears of frustration to the erstwhile star of that department, Robert Cipes (who later went on to become a well-known Washington attorney)—and that my Math Regent Exam mark had to be illicitly raised from 63 to 65 in order that I could graduate with my class . . . Being in my own business means that I am fast at math now, and enjoy it. I'm still in transition. Mack Thomas handed me another pearl recently: "I look for the process in their moment." I have a manuscript of short fiction circulating, and the outline for the book about the days of the Deux Mégots Poets. *CENTER Magazine* will start up again, with an added line of books of innovative fiction, under a not-for-profit status. I can do all of these alongside running my Gallery of Antiques. I don't claim to know the answers or endings any more than I can tell how a story will end when I begin it. It's taken a while to correlate everything and integrate the physical reality of being The Big Six-oh. I like challenges. The Chinese written symbol (ideogram) for the idea of CRISIS combines the symbols for *Danger* and for *Opportunity.*

I am finding it tough enough just to survive in this conflictive microcosm, much less write about it. Before I polish a chair or open the door of the Galleries, I may dash off a One-Pager: there are some 15 new ones from my first year here. Most of my writing has been articles about art or antiques. In a Republican regime, articles pay the utility bills, if not the rent. Of the stories written with Santa Fe as locus, all were created while elsewhere (*A City Story,* written about the Puye cliff-dwellings when back in NYC; *Fat Chance* and *On Sight,* written in Albuquerque).

I think of myself less and less as a "writer." The first section of my archival materia went to the Humanities Center at the University of Texas/Austin (covering the years 1959–1969). The years since are at Washington University in St. Louis. I've had Fellowships in Residence to work at The MacDowell Colony, and each of the 4 stays was productive and important. I realize however that I don't need to get away from anything in order to write. The writing is going to occur in the midst of and as part of and not divided from the life.

BIBLIOGRAPHY

Poetry:

Four Young Lady Poets, with Barbara Moraff, Rochelle Owens, and Diane Wakoski. Edited by LeRoi Jones. New York: Totem/Corinth Press, 1962.

The Vulnerable Island. Cleveland: Renegade Press, 1964.

Lumina. Cleveland: 7 Flowers Press, 1965.

Poems Made of Skin. Toronto: Weed/Flower Press, 1968.

An American Romance: The Alan Poems, a Journal. Los Angeles: Black Sparrow Press, 1969.

The Chambers. Abergavenny, England: Aylesford Review Press, 1969.

Circles, as in the Eye. Santa Fe, N.M.: Desert Review Press, 1969.

From a Soft Angle: Poems about Women. New York: Bobbs-Merrill, 1971.

Rituals and Gargoyles. Bowling Green, Ohio: Newedi Press, 1976.

The Unexpected: Poems Based in the Elements. Milwaukee: Membrane Press, 1976.

Alba Genesis: New Poems, 1978. Woodstock, N.Y.: Aesopus Press, 1978.

A Song, a Chant. Albuquerque, N.M.: Amalgamated Sensitivity Publications, 1978.

Alba Nemesis: The China Poems, 1969–1978. Albuquerque, N.M.: Amalgamated Sensitivity Publications, 1979.

Fiction:

The Unfolding (Part I). New York: Theo Press, 1969.

A Couple Called Moebius: Eleven Sensual Stories. New York: Bobbs-Merrill, 1972.

Acts of Love: An American Novel. New York: Bobbs-Merrill, 1973; New York: Pocket Books, 1974.

Timepieces. Union City, Calif.: Fault Publications, 1977.

The Doppler Effect. Emeryville, Calif.: Effie's Books, 1979.

Remembrance of Things to Come. New York: Theo Press, 1979.

Fierce Metronome: The One-Page Novel and Other Short Fiction. New York: Window Press, 1981.

Secrets, Gossip, and Slander. Berkeley, Calif: Reed & Cannon, 1984.

Nonfiction:

The Vancouver Report: A Report and Discussion of the Poetry Seminar at the University of British Columbia. New York: Fuck You Press, 1964.

Editorships:

CENTER Magazine, Editor/Publisher, 1970–1985, et seq.

Southwest Profile, Contributing Editor, 1983.

Ahsahta Press, Boise State University, Editor, 1983.

Woodstock Review, Contributing Editor, 1977–1981.

Shearsman, Contributing Editor, 1980–1982.

Mississippi Review, Editor-in-Chief, 1977–1978.

Student publications: *Wing Bones, Paper Branches, Subterranean,* University of New Mexico and Thomas Jefferson College.

Marion Zimmer Bradley

1930-

Marion Zimmer Bradley, 1981

They say that the first thing you remember is of vital importance in the life of the psyche. If that is true then my life must have been overpoweringly, shatteringly dull; for I have examined my earliest memory again and again for any significance whatever, and I can't find any. It is a simple flash out of darkness; a summer day—I can't have been much more than fifteen months old. I am walking along a hall in our old farmhouse with my mother and my grandfather; they are pushing a screened crib. I know how old I must have been because my younger brother, the occupant of the crib, outgrew it when he was about four months old, and I was no more than thirteen months his senior. Maybe the very presence of my brother is significant;

we were the bitterest of rivals all through my childhood, but I don't remember him in the memory at all, just Mother and Grandpa. And as Alice said, if anyone can discover an atom of meaning in that, I'd give him sixpence—if I could find a sixpence.

That one flash, and memory disappears again. Two or three other memories are clear before I can have been two years old; the night the old barn blew down, at which I do not remember being frightened, though it must have been terrifying, and a Christmas Eve when I cannot have been more than eighteen months old, in my aunt May's apartment, at which my mother taught me to sing all the words to *Good King Wenceslas*—quite a feat, I learned at teacher's college, for someone not yet two. My mother approved; and I spent my childhood looking for her approval—I knew that as the firstborn I *should* have been a boy, and spent my whole life trying to make up for the solecism of being a despised girl. I was always trying to do things that would please my mother. I seldom succeeded; I was an independent creature who was always wriggling off her lap and insisting I'd rather do whatever it was for myself. I'm told my first sentence was "Me do it all myself"; and my younger brother, a plump, pliant creature who would rather stay on her lap, was her favorite; he had the advantage anyway, because he was a *boy*. I never understood what was so good about being a boy, but the lack of it was something I could never, it seemed, overcome.

The next flood of memories concerns learning to read and sew; I do not remember learning to embroider, though I remember my mother teaching me to make French knots; but I do remember learning to read, from a book called *The Toy Town Primer*. Very clearly I remember a book called *What Happened to Tommy*, about a poor little kitten who had a can tied to his tail by some rude boys; I also remember a book called *Dorothy's Dolls*, and another called *The Magic Doll*, with incredibly beautiful illustrations which I can still see if I close my eyes—a sort of Aladdin's Cave, filled with jewels, a golden light, and the golden doll. The book itself, alas, vanished before I was seven.

I remember too the first real book—i.e., not a kiddie book, and without pictures, which I read all alone; it was by Dorothy Canfield Fisher and was called *Understood Betsy.* I still go back and read it every year or three.

Above and beyond that I remember learning to play on the piano; it must have been before I learned to read properly, because it was from a storybook called *Nan and Nanynka,* one of those fairy tales about a good girl who helped everyone and a bad girl who didn't; I can remember playing the piano pieces and then going to my mother to have the story read to me. One of the few punishments I remember for mild misbehavior was ingenious: having to sit and read the "Goop Book"—a huge scrapbook of cutout Goop poetry by Gelett Burgess—not much of a punishment, for even at that age I would rather read than anything else; but a way of making me, a hyperimaginative child, sit and ponder or meditate on my misbehavior.

My brother, Leslie, who was called Sonny by the whole family, my father being Leslie, Senior, does not play a very large part in these early memories, except that once I hit him; he ran crying to my father and Daddy said, "Well, hit her back." That had evidently never occurred to Leslie; so he came back and knocked me down. Daddy said it served me right; and my memory is that Leslie, spurred on by this permission, hit me every time he thought of it for at least the next ten years, unpunished; Mother seemed to be always saying, "Don't fight with your brother," or, "Why don't you give in? After all, he's the boy." Somehow I got the feeling that my having been born a girl was a great injury to my mother for which I could never really atone. (And then she wondered, when I was in my teens, why I had an inferiority complex!)

I don't want to give the impression, though, that I was an unhappy child: quite the reverse; I can't remember ever being unhappy over anything very often, though there were times when I would suffer inarticulate storms of unhappiness. My own daughter, Moira, suffered just such inexplicable fits of desperate unhappiness, where her father would say, "She's crying because she's a baby," and I suppose that was true of me; some feeling of utter misery at my own smallness and comparative weakness. I suppose I was crying because I was a baby—or because I was a girl. Even though I knew I *should* have been a boy, and made my mother very unhappy by being a girl. Until I was about seven or eight I frequently felt unhappy at *being* a girl, though I did know there was nothing I could do about it, and in general I liked being a girl just fine. I even played with dolls a good deal. I still do.

I was very small, and not particularly strong; and I thought I was ugly; I remember once or twice, at least—my mother insists she never said it except maybe once, but it seemed to me it was what I heard most often in my childhood—"Isn't it a shame Eleanor is a girl; Leslie is so pretty and boys don't need good looks. And she's so smart and girls don't need brains." But I thought most of the time that having brains was just fine, and I built my life on it, since I was stuck with it anyhow.

My father was an exceptionally brilliant but uneducated man; he held a good position with Western Union when I was small, and since he said the telegrams came over the wires—which he pointed out to me—I spent hours watching the wires, hoping to see one of the familiar yellow forms fly by, "over the wires."

Needless to say, I never saw one. Not till I was about thirteen did it occur to me that the familiar yellow forms did not actually fly by over the wires. Even now I have a picture in my mind of a yellow telegraph form flying over the wires; my first idea of magic.

Marion Eleanor Zimmer at age seven

*Parents, Leslie Raymond and Evelyn Conklin Zimmer,
about 1960*

He had, however, one bee in his bonnet, and that was to work for himself; what he said most often in my hearing was, "A man's got a right to be his own boss." Working as an employee seared his soul for some reason which I could never imagine. When I was about eight he began drinking intermittently; and it seemed that my beloved Daddy had become another man whom I did not even like; which was difficult, because I loved him unbelievably. This was the great conflict of my childhood; I often felt guilty because he had become, it seemed, sullen and morose, and when he was drinking it seemed he was another man—cruel and abusive to my mother, surly and unfriendly to my brother—but I, who could often interpose myself and tease him into being nicer, sometimes liked him better when he had been drinking a *little*. But he never stopped there, and I felt guilty because I felt I had set him off. Of course now I know that drinking and abuse are two sides of the same coin; the alcoholic does not abuse wife and kids because he is drunk, he gets drunk in order to abuse them without feeling intolerably guilty. But I did not understand that then, and thought if I was a better daughter he would have to be a better father.

There's no end to that kind of thing, and as a result I suffered, I suppose, thinking all my family's troubles were my fault. Most kids, I now know, feel

something like this; if I were a better daughter, my parents would have to be better parents. I did my best—although to my mother being a good daughter often meant not reading so much and doing more housework. I hated housework and refused to miss school even when my mother was not very well—and she felt I should stay home and help with the housework. I never wanted to miss school; I loved it, and never would miss a day if I could help it; unlike Leslie, who would leap at any excuse to get out of school. I now realize I wasn't lazy; just half-blind and allergic—literally—to dust. I know now that much of my hatred of housework was because of an undiagnosed dust allergy which made me hate sweeping; nor could I see properly to do much housework. But who knew about allergies then, and who can blame my mother? To her a daughter was a helpful household gadget; and I tried so hard to avoid housework, because it made me literally sick, that I got the reputation for being lazy. I wasn't; from childhood I did heavy farm work; my father felt that was what kids were for. There must have been precious little love in his life; it was surprising that in spite of everything I remember him as a kind and loving father—when he was sober, which after I was eight or ten was pretty seldom.

When I was sixteen I graduated from high school, having won a National Merit Scholarship; I went to college and, almost at the same time, discovered pulp science fiction. I think I can honestly say this was the turning point of my whole life.

Fred Pohl said once, in his autobiography—and he was speaking of himself—that if you introduce a hundred kids to science fiction, half of them will yawn and never read any more; half the rest will keep up a low level of involvement, and maybe half a dozen will go on to make it a way of life. It certainly became a way of life for me, and still is.

Soon after that, at least partly because my parents thought I should go to work, I left college and married Robert A. Bradley, whom I had met through science fiction fandom. Brad, as I always called him, was fifty; I was only nineteen and I can sympathize now with his moroseness; I must have been a very difficult wife. I wasn't old enough to be anyone's wife, but I managed. Brad said once to our son, when David asked how he had come to marry me when we were obviously so incompatible, that, "I could trust her with the last cent of my money, and she laughed at my jokes." I guess there are worse foundations for marriage.

I don't know what they could have been, though.

Brad was a very strange man; now that I am something of an expert on psychology—every novelist becomes an expert psychologist, or her characters won't be realistic enough to convince anyone—I realize that it wasn't me; it would have taken three saints working eight-hour shifts to live with him. He was gloomy and morose, and eccentric enough that I sometimes think he was dropped down out of a spaceship from Mars or something. Thus I was very unhappy. Just to start with, I wanted children; Brad, who had three children from his first marriage, had already had all the children he wanted. I did have one son, because (thank goodness) abortion was still illegal and he could not bully me into breaking the law.

With that background I should be firmly anti-abortion; but I think the only thing sadder than an abortion is an unwanted child. I love David as much as any mother could ever have loved a son; but he knows his father did not want him. Brad later managed to bully me into two abortions; after which I put my foot down. "Never again," I said, and as a result what one might call our love life came to a screeching halt. He never touched me again. My major regret is that I was faithful to him for the ten years more I lived with him.

The next few years were largely taken up with writing. Brad suggested at one point that I should get a job; but there was no way, he said, that he was going to baby-sit, and I made it clear that if I held down a job, no way was I going to work eight hours and then come home and do all the washing, ironing, cooking, etc., while he worked eight hours and came home, put his feet up, and read the newspaper. Nor did I want our son raised by an illiterate girl from the cotton fields; so he agreed that if I did not mind living on his rather small salary, that was all right with him.

I made him promise, before we were married, three things: that he would never drink himself insensible, that he would never gamble money we didn't have—I made it clear I didn't mean not taking a chance on a turkey or something like that—and that he would never hit me. He looked at me rather strangely and asked what kind of a family I had come from; but he promised, and only once broke that promise. In the middle of a fight, I slapped him hard, and he slapped me back hard enough to rattle my teeth; but I didn't count that; after all, I had started it. That was a fair fight, not legitimated abuse, and I thought it was fair enough, all round.

One thing I deeply appreciate; Brad taught me to drive. That in itself was hard enough because I was rather timid about it; but to give credit where credit

was due, Brad taught me well and patiently and I became a very good driver. Since my second stroke I don't drive—my eyes are going—but that does not diminish my fondness for driving. My daughter is an excellent driver and once said that I had been the best driver she knew. I think of driving as freedom; now that I have had to give up driving, I feel very deprived.

Eventually Brad came around to saying that as a young woman with a young child to support, as I would be in the normal course of events, I should return to college and get a teaching certificate. There were three colleges in Abilene, Texas, about seventy miles away, and I had the choice of the Methodist McMurry College, the Baptist Hardin-Simmons University, and Abilene Christian College.

I investigated all three. To enter ACC—the "holy hump"—would have involved signing a statement that my purpose in getting a college education was "To become a better Christian." No way I was going to sign a statement like that! I had no objection to becoming a better Christian, but it was far from being my major purpose in getting an education; so I at once eliminated ACC—Abilene Christian—from my considerations. I never seriously considered McMurry; it had about five hundred students. I had been living in a small town of six hundred people, and I didn't think I would get a very good education there. That left Hardin-Simmons; I enrolled there and proceeded to learn all about Christianity.

I had never been much of a churchgoer; but I had nothing against churches—and I was a Christian by default, meaning that I was neither a Jew nor an atheist. I went into HSU a fairly good Christian, meaning I tried to follow the principles of God as I understood them; I came out the next thing to an atheist. I had somehow got the idea that God liked good people better than bad ones; my religious education, such as it was, was limited to attending church and Sunday school at the local Lutheran church. I related "bad" and "good" to the Golden Rule: "Do as you would be done by." I thought the Sermon on the Mount—which I read, as I read everything that came under my eyes, because it was *there*—was a pretty good guide to life. To that extent, I was a Christian. I had been baptized—because my favorite aunt and uncle were Episcopalians, and my beloved uncle Fred later became an Episcopal priest (he was then an organist)—but I knew as much theology as the cat. I soon discovered that, in this small Texas town, being a Christian meant only one thing. Not being good or trying to live a good life— or even accepting the Thirty-nine Articles, which had

David Bradley, Marion Zimmer Bradley, and Walter Breen at Worldcon, 1962

kept me from being confirmed—but going to church and Bible class, and *nothing* else.

Segregation was a big thing—a big issue—just then; I couldn't see how they could square it with their consciences to enforce segregation, but they did. They even quoted the Bible to give authority for segregation; a piece of doublethink I found repulsive. (I still do.) One reason I am proud of being a graduate of Hardin-Simmons—the only reason, for I didn't care about their rodeo or football team (heresy in Texas)—was that Dr. Reiss, the college president, opened it as the first private college below the Mason-Dixon line to integrate. He said that no one could call himself a Christian who was unwilling to relate to any other Christian whatever his color; and anyone who was, was free to seek his education elsewhere.

My reaction? "Huzzah! This is Christianity!" Most people's reactions were that I was an infidel; they assured me there was biblical authority for segregation. My reaction was—and is—so much the worse for the church. I still feel that if Jesus could associate with lepers and such, then a few orderly, well-behaved Negroes could not harm me that much; after all, being black was not contagious. Another way

I was always in a minority. However, I remember the Rosalind Russell movie *A Majority of One.* The idea is that if a thousand think they are right and you are supposed to be wrong, but are right, you form a majority—of one. I still do.

About that time I formed a kind of love affair with another woman. When I was sixteen I had briefly had a love affair with another woman, but after my marriage I let a relatively unimportant piece of information—that I did not at all dislike sex, and suffered greatly from Brad's intransigence in this matter—blind me to that affair, and believed—in congruence with the best psychological theories of that day—that I had just been going through a phase; as many girls did. I never thought to ask myself why I did not find another man—one of my husband's apprentices, or the proverbial iceman, or the garbage-man, or a fan—with whom to deceive him. The fact is I never did. I thought of it sometimes, but as I later put it, Brad was content—we once discussed a divorce and he said he was perfectly happy, so I abandoned the thought of divorce, and took up with a young woman I will call Dorothy. (It happened to be

The author with her children Patrick Russell Donald and Moira Evelyn Dorothy Breen,
1970

her name; the woman of my first affair was a Dorothy too; and I later gave that name to my daughter.) However—Brad liked her, at that time, and seemed to like having her around. I now know that many men of low sexuality respond well to their wives having affairs of this sort; it's part of not taking anything seriously that women do if there is not another man involved. It doesn't offend their masculinity.

Anyhow, I at that time became a professional writer writing what were then thought of as sex books. I thought it was rather fun because I was attending a Baptist college which would have expelled me for having one of those books in my possession, far less writing them. What were then thought of as sex books are by today's standards very tame—I once explained it as "Lots of heaving bosoms"—no real sex at all. I later let my pre-teenage niece read them as another mother might have allowed a child to read Barbara Cartland. I had grown up on the mild romances of a turn-of-the-century writer called Myrtle Reed, and of Grace Livingston Hill; my own were just about that tame. I was really shocked by the best-sellers of Jacqueline Susann; I've been known to say

that it was not till my second marriage that I understood some of the "spicy" passages of Jacqueline Susann or Norman Mailer. I am fairly naive still; I have never read the works of Erica Jong—I think they would embarrass me; and I was really shocked when my friend Lisa told me that she had read *Lady Chatterley's Lover* in school. I read it, the most celebrated "dirty book" of a generation. *Lolita*— without a single four-letter word—was *the* shocker of the fifties. I loved it.

I had a friend—he wanted to marry me—who chided me for the relative tameness of my "sex novels" because I didn't use four-letter words; he said I must be censoring myself, and how could I avoid using this "freedom"? All I could say was that after listening to my drunken father, "freedom" for me lay in never having to hear those words again. I occasionally, when absolutely furious, rip out, "Shit!" but I don't think I have ever used what some people think of as the great "freedom" of what somebody called "the f-word." I know enough Middle English to know *exactly* what it means and do not use it as a catchall obscenity for anything I happen to dislike. My uncle

Fred once said to me something I have always remembered; I ripped out a casual "damn," and he observed mildly that it was silly to consign something to eternal theological punishment when what I really meant was, "How very tiresome." Never again did I say "damn," over the equivalent of a run in my stocking.

Verbal overkill does not excite me and I can well do without the "freedom" of such words; they usually indicate nothing more than a lack of imagination.

I remember a Talbot Mundy novel where the hero says, "Never talk fight unless you mean fight; then don't talk, fight." I once said that about "fuck." I don't mind it in its place; I'm not squeamish—but using it as a catchall substitute for every known objurgation or grossness seems to me overkill.

Be that as it may, I went on a cross-country trip, and there met a fan with whom I immediately "fell in love," if that phrase has any meaning. This was my second husband, Walter Breen; he regarded himself as gay, and was very turned on, I suppose, by my acceptance of him. We soon began an affair and as a result I quarreled with Dorothy, telling her truthfully that I preferred Walter—even sex with Walter—to anything she had ever done with me.

I managed my escape from Texas by telling Brad I wanted to do graduate research work at University of California, where Walter had been accepted. I moved to California, asking David to come with me. Brad had cut off talk of divorce long ago by saying he would cut himself off completely from David; I felt David, a shy and sickly child, needed a father. I should have known Brad was bluffing; when David chose to come with me, Brad readily agreed to try and keep up a relationship with David.

Well, to make a long story short, Dorothy immediately went to Brad and "confessed," and I found myself in a custody fight. He wanted David; I felt that an honorable homosexual—and Walter was nothing if not honorable—was a better father than an aging (seventy-seven) eccentric, so I fought for him by getting pregnant by Walter, then telling Brad I was willing, if he refused me a divorce, to swear it was his child, and let him support it.

This quickly brought him round and I married Walter.

They say there are two things that are very sad; never getting what you want, and getting it.

They also say, be careful what you pray for; you'll probably get it.

Well, I got Walter.

I still love him; he has many admirable qualities: absolute integrity, the only intelligence I have ever willingly conceded as superior to mine, and he was—and is—a good and loving father to our children. He is also *hopeless* as a husband. He is nevertheless the only male I have ever loved, but loving is a different thing from being in love. Walter now swears he did not ever love me, but for more than a year I could not move away from his side without his fear that I would abandon him, which once meant he pursued me across an airline terminal yelling "Beloved!" at the very top of his voice. What can I say? I loved him; he fell out of love with me, saying that his experiment in heterosexuality had failed. I still loved him, and by then I was bearing the burden of supporting us at least part of the time; I was still writing potboilers. We lost our big beautiful Berkeley house—the only thing, of many, I have not forgiven him—and moved to New York, where he had a total nervous breakdown, and I had to hold together the whole household—now including two kids under three years old: my beloved daughter, Moira, had been conceived almost the last time we slept together; my adored Patrick was our love child, and Walter adores him too.

Then I really began to take off as a writer; the Darkover series grew and grew, including what I now think of as my best books: *The Heritage of Hastur, Forbidden Tower,* and *Stormqueen.* I wrote about homosexuality in *Heritage of Hastur,* and in my first big book, which I called "The Flyers," and my editor called *The Catch Trap.* (It was probably the first full-

Patrick and Moira, 1973

length nonscandalous gay novel, which I had written in Texas during the affair with Dorothy and held back because I DIDN'T want to sell it as a cheap sex novel.) I was a full-time writer and, with the Darkover novels, finally started to make something more than a bare living, and Walter, now recovered from his breakdown, went out and got a good job in his field of expertise—numismatics—so I could stop writing potboilers. That is how I came to write my most famous novel, *The Mists of Avalon.* My original title was "Mistress of Magic," and it was the life story of Morgaine le Fay.

With this book, I hit the *zeitgeist,* I suppose. It was a lot more successful than anything else I had ever written; and may even have been better than anything else I have ever written; and I suppose if my name is to be remembered at all, it will be for this book, which will probably be remembered longer than I will.

About the time I started *Mists* my cousin Lisa Waters came to live with me, first as a sort of governess for my daughter, Moira, who was floundering in public school, and hated it. Like me,

and like her father, Moira found the public schools unendurable; if I could have afforded it I would have put her into a private school where she might have learned something. As it was, Moira was about as fit for public school as she was to keep elephants. Maybe less; she would have had some intellectual interest in the elephants. Sending her to private school, however, was against my principles and beyond the reach of my pocketbook; I could as easily have afforded to send her to Harvard. My "wealth" came too late for Moira.

Well, soon after, I wrote a book I thought as good as *Mists,* namely, *The Inheritor,* and then a major book, which my agent sold to a major publisher for more money than I ever thought there was in the world. First I tried to set Patrick up with some small property which will eventually support him, and Moira, discovering that she had a voice, decided to study for the opera. She turned out to have a voice I think is lovely; and I have now one major ambition: to see her established on the stage of a major opera house. I think—I hope—she'll make it. She has the talent and works very hard; but all too often talent

With Walter Breen during a lifeboat drill on a trip to Greece to conduct research for the novel The Firebrand, *1984*

On a library visit with daughter, Moira Breen, 1987

have a fine support system of friends and adopted daughters and such, and there is, according to my doctor, no reason I shouldn't live till ninety. Don Wollheim is nearly eighty; and he's still going strong. (May he do so for many, many years to come; everybody needs a father, and because of the deficiencies of my own father, I've adopted Don; he says he doesn't mind.)

If I live till ninety I firmly expect him to live to a hundred and seven; my grandfather lived to a hundred and three. I fully intend to. I suspect I will; because I'm still interested in what the next day's mail will hold. And that's really all; if you want any more, as the folk song says, you can write it yourself. Although I have been told that's a dangerous thing to say; because someone might take me at my word.

goes unrewarded, as mine did for many years and as Walter's did until very recently.

During the printing of *Firebrand*—which I think as good as *Mists*, so I can't imagine why it hasn't caught on, though it has done very well indeed in England, and in Europe, where they take a classical education for granted—I suffered the second major stroke, which put me into the hospital. I am still recovering from that one; but I hope to write another major book; in fact I have signed a contract to do a three-way collaboration with Andre Norton and Julian May.

We are still in the middle of it; I am recovering my strength after another slight stroke, and I have two more major books to write: a feminist version of Robin Hood, and a book about Roman Britain. And this is where I am now. God knows where I will go from here; but writing is a profession from which there is no retiring. The only way to kill off a writer is to shoot her; the very popular Agatha Christie finished her last book at eighty-six; Rex Stout, at eighty-nine. Toscanini was still conducting at eighty-nine. I fully intend to outlast all of them. I come from a long-lived family with no history of Alzheimer's. The way to live forever, they say, is to get a mild chronic disease and take great care of it. That's what I am doing. I am a diabetic; not a very serious one, and they may soon discover the way to conquer it; hopefully in my lifetime.

My cousin Lisa works as my secretary and takes very good care of me; Andre Norton, who is nearly twenty years older than I am, is still going strong. I

BIBLIOGRAPHY

Fiction:

The Door through Space (bound with *Rendezvous on a Lost World,* by Bertram Chandler). New York: Ace Books, 1961; London: Arrow, 1979.

Seven from the Stars (bound with *Worlds of the Imperium,* by Keith Laumer). New York: Ace Books, 1962.

The Colors of Space (juvenile). Derby, Conn.: Monarch, 1963; Edited by Hank Stine (illustrated by Barbi Johnson). Norfolk, Va.: Donning, 1983.

The Dark Intruder and Other Stories. New York: Ace Books, 1964.

Castle Terror. New York: Lancer, 1965.

Souvenir of Monique. New York: Ace Books, 1967.

Bluebeard's Daughter. New York: Lancer, 1968.

The Brass Dragon (bound with *Ipomoea,* by John Rackham). New York: Ace Books, 1969; London: Methuen, 1978.

Dark Satanic. New York: Berkley, 1972.

Falcons of Narabedla [and] *The Dark Intruder.* New York: Ace Books, 1972.

Hunters of the Red Moon. New York: DAW Books, 1973; London: Arrow, 1979.

In the Steps of the Master. New York: Tempo, 1973.

Can Ellen Be Saved? New York: Tempo, 1975.

The Endless Voyage. New York: Ace Books, 1975; expanded edition published as *Endless Universe.* New York: Ace Books, 1979.

The Parting of Arwen. Baltimore: TK Graphics, 1975.

Drums of Darkness: An Astrological Gothic Novel, Leo. New York: Ballantine, 1976.

The Ruins of Isis. Edited and illustrated by Polly and Kelly Freas. Norfolk, Va.: Donning, 1978; London: Arrow, 1980.

The Catch Trap. New York: Ballantine, 1979.

The Survivors, with Paul Edwin Zimmer. New York: DAW Books, 1979; London: Arrow, 1985.

The House between the Worlds. Garden City, N.Y.: Doubleday, 1980.

Survey Ship (illustrated by Steve Fabian). New York: Ace Books, 1980.

The Mists of Avalon. New York: Knopf, 1982; London: Michael Joseph, 1983.

The Web of Darkness (illustrated by V. M. Wyman and C. Lee Healy). Virginia Beach, Va.: Donning, 1983; Sevenoaks, England: New English Library, 1985.

The Web of Light (illustrated by C. Lee Healy). Edited by Hank Stine. Norfolk, Va.: Donning, 1983.

Falcons of Narabedla. London: Arrow, 1984.

Night's Daughter. New York: Ballantine, 1985; London: Sphere, 1985.

Lythande. New York: DAW Books, 1986.

The Firebrand. New York: Simon & Schuster, 1987; London: Michael Joseph, 1988.

The Best of Marion Zimmer Bradley. Edited by H. Greenberg. New York: DAW Books, 1988.

Warrior Woman. New York: DAW Books, 1988; London: Arrow, 1988.

"Darkover" series:

The Planet Savers. New York: Ace Books, 1962; London: Arrow, 1979.

The Sword of Aldones. New York: Ace Books, 1962; London: Arrow, 1979.

The Bloody Sun. New York: Ace Books, 1964; London: Arrow, 1978.

Star of Danger. New York: Ace Books, 1965; London: Arrow, 1978.

The Winds of Darkover. New York: Ace Books, 1970; London: Arrow, 1978.

The World Wreckers. New York: Ace Books, 1971; London: Arrow, 1979.

Darkover Landfall. New York: DAW Books, 1972; London: Arrow, 1976.

The Spell Sword. New York: DAW Books, 1974; London: Arrow, 1978.

The Heritage of Hastur. New York: DAW Books, 1975; London: Arrow, 1979.

The Shattered Chain. New York: DAW Books, 1976; London: Arrow, 1978.

The Forbidden Tower. New York: DAW Books, 1977; London: Arrow, 1980.

Stormqueen! New York: DAW Books, 1978; London: Arrow, 1980.

The Bloody Sun [and] *To Keep the Oath.* Boston: Gregg, 1979.

The Keeper's Price and Other Stories. New York: DAW Books, 1980.

The Planet Savers [and] *The Sword of Aldones.* New York: Ace Books, 1980.

Two to Conquer. New York: DAW Books, 1980; London: Arrow, 1982.

Sharra's Exile. New York: DAW Books, 1981; London: Arrow, 1983.

Children of Hastur (contains *Heritage of Hastur, Sharra's Exile*). Garden City, N.Y.: Doubleday, 1982.

Hawkmistress! New York: DAW Books, 1982; London: Arrow, 1985.

Sword of Chaos and Other Stories. New York: DAW Books, 1982.

Oath of the Renunciates (contains *The Shattered Chain, Thendara House*). Garden City, N.Y.: Doubleday, 1983.

Thendara House. New York: DAW Books, 1983; London: Arrow, 1985.

City of Sorcery. New York: DAW Books, 1983; London: Arrow, 1986.

Free Amazons of Darkover: An Anthology. New York: DAW Books, 1985.

Other Side of the Mirror. New York: DAW Books, 1987.

Red Sun of Darkover. New York: DAW Books, 1987.

Four Moons of Darkover. New York: DAW Books, 1988.

Nonfiction:

Checklist: A Complete, Cumulative Checklist of Lesbian, Variant, and Homosexual Fiction in English, with Gene Damon. Rochester, Tex.: Privately printed, 1960.

Men, Halflings, and Hero Worship (criticism). Baltimore: TK Graphics, 1973.

The Jewel of Arwen. Baltimore: TK Graphics, 1974.

The Necessity for Beauty: Robert W. Chambers and the Romantic Tradition. Baltimore: TK Graphics, 1974.

Experiment Perilous: Three Essays on Science Fiction, with Norman Spinrad and Alfred Bester. New York: Algol Press, 1976.

Editor of:

Greyhaven: An Anthology of Fantasy. New York: DAW Books, 1983.

Sword and Sorceress: An Anthology of Heroic Fantasy (5 vols.). Vols. 1–5. New York: DAW Books, 1984–88; Vol. 1. London: Headline, 1988.

Rosellen Brown

1939-

A FRAGMENT OF AUTOBIOGRAPHY

Rosellen Brown, 1984

Only because I acknowledge my own voyeuristic interest in other writers' lives do I even consider writing this mini-memoir. My life has been almost uniquely uneventful, nor have I even been one of those "demons of sensibility" who can thresh fascinating details out of, say, mastery of the yo-yo (Frank Conroy), or out of a love affair with a dog (J. R. Ackerley)—out of, that is, a profoundly conventional life. I have threatened, on occasion, that the next "live" interview I consent to will contain pure fiction—my birth in Baku, my girlhood in Fiji or Formosa. (But confronted with an equally "live" interviewer, I forever renege on my threat; it could

be damaging to someone's sense of competence to have so much wool pulled over such trusting eyes.)

In my case I tend to think the only question worth pursuing is: In such an ordinary life, how did the writing come about? And I, who don't dare much, how do I dare stake so much on so chancy an enterprise? Where do I get the nerve, or is it the need?

First memory of writing, which can still flood over me when it's a certain color outside and the lamps are making their warm dry spots in a damp day: Somewhere between three and four years old, I walk down the stairs on a rainy morning wearing a navy blue corduroy jumper. It is (what I remember as) the dingy, small, gray city of Reading, Pennsylvania, in wartime; my memory includes little sun but this is probably illusion. But it was a time of air raids and ration books, so a certain bleakness, occasionally tense, understandably pervades everything. My first experience of terrifying thunder overwhelmed me in Reading—though I never imagined we were being bombed, which should not have surprised me in view of the black window shades and the piercing sirens and my mother's frantic cry, frequently repeated, frequently justified, "Where is your brother?", I was sure the mountain behind the town was falling in on us.

But on this misty morning I am feeling extremely grown up. I must have been planning this for a while—I go to the desk and on a piece of paper, sitting very straight, write, exactly as I know my brothers are doing just then at school, long rows of *eeeeeeeee*'s and waves and, best of all, a loose succession of *mmmmm*'s that must seem to me like the emanation of something that tastes delicious. A few years later, at the beach, still young enough for a topless bathing suit, I will fake-swim one day with my elbows pointed precisely but my hands on the bottom. A woman will point to me and say, "Look how well that little girl swims!" Unfortunately that fraudulent crawl seemed to satisfy my meagre interest in swimming; fortunately my initial foray into writing did not exhaust my curiosity about the genuine alphabet.

My father, divinely compulsive—"German, after all," my mother always says as if this is an explanation—saved the piece of school-lined paper on which a few years later I really learned to write my name. (It was one of a lot of things he saved, and we moved around so much I can't imagine where he stashed them. Approaching his ninetieth birthday, he stubbornly retains a set of marbled "journals" in which he recorded, beginning at the age of nineteen, every game of tennis he played for years: weather, court conditions, outcome, even the personality of his opponent.) The exploratory sampler of curls and surf is gone though I have on my walls half a dozen second-grade extravaganzas documenting in crayoned technicolor how Little Jack Horner put in his thumb and pulled out a plum and how Jack-be-nimble made his leap over a candlestick that looks like a piece of penny candy. But by then the real words have begun, however shakily spelled, and anything seems possible.

I have no other memories of my early writing but reading excited me so much I recall, as wordlessly as a smell or a color, the exquisite physical thrill of reading a book of fairy tales, a musty book reclaimed by accident from some pile perhaps on its way to the rubbish. In black and white, nothing extravagant or fashionably beautiful, the twelve dancing princesses, with pictures, that long ward of a room and their worn slippers lined up neatly under their beds! A very small, very fat square of a book whose shape intrigued me, folktales from some Scandinavian country. Phyllis McGinley's *Plain Princess,* which my mother bought for my birthday at a book fair at my school—I could, this minute, identify the exact pink and the exact rough lineny texture of its cover without hesitation. One day I wrote a letter in answer to some question I've forgotten, which won from a predinner children's radio program called "Treasure Island" a book about a dog who lost his tail. Every one a stepping-stone, each one irreplaceable in my memory, without which I might not have kept on walking into words.

Our school librarian had us "sell" books to each other, make them sound irresistible—*Nicodemus and the Little Black Pig, Dr. Dolittle,* a set of orange-covered biographies, Clara Barton, Helen Keller, Jane Addams. (Interesting: no men? I don't remember any. A friend, male, recently told me about his addiction at the same age to a matching set called "The Boy Allies." Our turfs were certainly clearly marked early on.) My anticipation of library days was

almost unbearable. In recent years I've begun to think of myself as phototropic, obsessed with light in the room where I work, unable to function happily in shady spaces, and I wonder if I've influenced my memories to fit my adult temperament: Just as I remember the war years in Reading as sooty gray, I see that library as a bath in pure sunlight, the books we "advertised" standing propped open on low blonde shelves in an endless spring without shadows.

Equally unbearable, less pleasantly, were "club afternoons" when we were compelled to do crafts, work of such dazzling complexity as the unravelling of the thready edges of a cotton square into a fringe to make a "bridge cloth" to be presented on Mother's Day. My mother, I remember pleading, did not play bridge. Did I really have to do this thing? (What was so difficult about it? I can't imagine.) I have a perfect recollection of the stubborn square of brown-sprigged cotton whose edges held fast under my desperate fingers; I had yet to learn that the only things that unravel are the ones you don't want to.

Mother, Blossom Lieberman Brown, aged twenty-six, Philadelphia, 1930: "She was 8½ months pregnant with my oldest brother and the photographer blotted him out!"

Later I was crucified on the task of knotting yarn around a milk-bottle top with a hole gouged in its middle—a shade pull. Why was I being tortured? "We don't have shades. Do I have to?" Ditto the irises we tortured with wire and green florist's paper into mock orchids. My mother hated orchids and would have exempted me if only she could have.

But the same teacher had a glassed-in bookcase in the back of the room and we were sometimes "rewarded" with a chance to extract a book and read it (after class? during?). This is where I first met *Alice in Wonderland*, that giraffe neck strange enough to give me a nightmare in which Alice was played by a goose. One spring my father (having been given it by some benefactor) brought home two at a time for many weeks a British set of what we called the Book of Knowledge but which was in fact a compendium, real title by now mislaid, of every sort of sedate childhood pleasure from puzzles and word games to history and stories to rudimentary scientific explanations. (I remember an explanation of color—this was a predominantly black-and-white set—the spectrum broken down into squares of components, *roygbiv*.)

Father, David H. Brown, aged thirty-one, Philadelphia, 1930

To me these were the ultimate exotic gifts beyond price, a wonder, an astonishment—the British take fun and games in a spirit of high seriousness and the tone of the whole was perplexing, foreign, yet, in English, quite comprehensible. The children in these books spoke respectfully of the Queen—she was somehow truly theirs, not merely a character in a tale! I was dazzled. I was also impressed by their manners, the serene look of the little girls, their coats standing out rather starchily above their neat little shoes. The British, at least in these books, were and weren't different from us. (My understanding of this phenomenon was intact at age nine.)

My experiences with these books and others, which I remember with a slight speeding-up of breath, were stronger, I would venture, than any other experiences I had. (I do believe serious readers have a physiological response to the very idea of a book, as, perhaps, alcoholics have to their vision of a drink. Twenty years later, pregnant, I could feel my baby leap and kick every time I crossed the threshold of the library. Another twenty-one years later, an hour ago, in fact, she phoned me to tell me she'd just finished the first draft of her first novel. Blood tells.)

(Another parenthesis. I also can't help but think that my continuing physical relation to the page is exceptionally strong because of the primal pleasure of these books as objects, and of paper and pens and the feel of my moving hand. I have never been able to write on the typewriter, which, for me, imposes a deadening distance that makes me irresponsible, puts me (literally) out of touch with my words and their rhythms. These days people tend to look at me as a direct descendent of a pterodactyl when I say that I change notebooks—size of paper, lined or blank— and adapt with different pens and colors of ink depending on what I'm writing and what it seems, intuitively, to demand. Once when I had trouble finding a refill of the right size notebook paper for *Civil Wars* and had to settle for a pack of unlined sheets, the only way I could compensate for the absence of familiar blue lines correctly spaced was to put away my felt-tip and find a fountain pen with a nib that seemed to bite into the page, as if that compensated for the absence of a grid. Writing is still exactly as it was when I first came to it, a sensual experience, alive on my skin and in my hands, and without that I've often wondered if I'd lose interest in it.)

Our house had a good many books in it, read before my time or perhaps not read at all. I don't know how the books figured in their lives but their symbolic presence made me proud and pleased with my parents, neither of whom had gone to high school, let alone college, but who did not believe in the *Reader's Digest* or liverwurst or cats and dogs (I came to regret that later) or catechism or Easter hats or anything Christian for that matter, though my friends' parents seemed to believe in all of them. We had candles and a clean tablecloth on Friday nights and that meant we were Jewish, even if sometimes we were rather alone in that. Somehow, rightly or wrongly, because children don't understand much about hierarchies of importance, and can't tell the difference between taste and ineluctable identity, I threw the books in with my religious inheritance and thought they all belonged together.

My mother had come from a little town in the Ukraine to Baltimore and then New York City, at eight; she grew up smart and poor. Her parents had a candy store—her father was, in an international tradition, charming, a talker but not a worker, and he had time to be affectionate; her mother was tense, overworked, and abrupt. My mother, who learned English within a few months and learned it so well she assisted in tutoring other immigrants, was a wonderful student—she was taken, once, to a Dodgers' game as a reward for her good grades!—and she turned into an extraordinary writer, though only of letters, community bulletins, and organizational notes. She has huge talent, she is what Robert Bly called a natural "leaping" poet (who's never written a poem), but has never had—is it the will or the confidence or the underlying need, a hunger for clarification or the assertion to pursue it? (There is my leading question in one of its many manifestations.) She too has always loved books, so much that, by her own explanation, they've daunted her. While I, early on, would think, "Oh, to replenish, just a little bit, the pool of words I'm drinking from, to give back a book or two!" (as if my appropriation of them had diminished the supply), and made that my hallowed goal, a kind of reciprocation, my mother was so respectful she could only tiptoe in their presence, couldn't come close enough even to dream of writing, herself, even to dare to want to. I'm afraid it may be one of the costs of having had so little formal education that this brilliant woman never, in a sense, got inside the door and was asked to sit down, or allowed herself to; never relaxed in the presence of books sufficiently to acknowledge that they were written by mortals, that she might approach and somehow do the same. Is it possible she nipped her *wanting* in the bud?

My father, similarly, went out to work at the end of the eighth grade, a clerk for the Erie-Lackawanna Railroad, his own typewriter under his arm the way

Rosellen Brown, three years old, with her brothers, Ralph (left), eight, and Phil, twelve, Allentown, Pennsylvania

ghetto sewing-machine operators often brought their own machines to work hoisted on their shoulders. He was the youngest of four brothers whose mother was born in New Jersey (which, among Jews of that era, made her practically a candidate for the DAR) and whose father, who went from a pack-on-his-back peddler to proprietor of a modest dry-goods store on Hudson Street in Manhattan, was German. At their first opportunity his dashing older brothers took off for foreign parts—a coffee plantation in Colombia, freewheeling travel and some kind of anonymous work in Alaska, Panama; all my father seems to have gotten, by his own admission, was their indifference to the idea of a formal education. Presumably they were acquiring theirs in the field.

He, who stayed home, got neither. He was even cheated of the First World War by a day. He enlisted, his friends gave him a hail-and-farewell party, and he was off!—only to be sent home abruptly the next day because the armistice had been signed. Of course, by the standards of his day there was nothing unusual about not going to college, or even, I suppose, to high school. What he did by reading and by attention to the way he presented himself was that, extremely intelligent (a man with the face of a white Bill Cosby), he made himself literate, more than presentable, intellectually speaking. An eighth-grade education in 1910 or so was, at least in certain respects, worth half a college education today, or more. It was made of different stuff, great patience expended on learning to write and to recite (which he can still do, reaching back to nineteenth-century poetry learned before the eighth grade). He sold poems to the New York newspapers, good ones of their kind, many of them truly delightful, and wrote articulate letters to their readers' columns, commenting in the classical style of the day on world affairs—compared to today's ventilating letters-to-the-editor writers, he was Jonathan Swift incarnate. He kept Reading Journals (in the same marbled-paper ledgers as the Tennis Archives!) of the classics he had read, so beautifully lettered, with ornate titles and flawless calligraphy, that he ought to have suspected his real talent then—he became, at retirement, a uniquely daring artist: a painter and assemblage sculptor, uninterested in Your Standard Parental Still Lifes, rather given to wonderfully bizarre constructions of, say, dozens of laminated ladies' high heels, or car insignias, renderer of visionary scenes that have the feel of Magrittes, direct emanations of an interesting subconscious— trees with birds floating out of them, impastoed semiabstract forests, wonderful golden horses and imaginary birds, in three dimensions, on black wooden plaques. He could have had a lifetime of it but didn't know, never even asked himself if he'd dare be an artist. It was, for most, an unselfconscious time; one did one's duty. The "interest and aptitude" tests that present our children with 1,001 choices are this generation's middle-class luxury, a result of information glut. My father kept his nose obediently to the grindstone of conventional work.

But of their children, two of the three of us looked straight at the challenge of our talent, and took it. My middle brother, Ralph, the sanest and most competent of us by far, though he had considerable musical talent, chose to find his excitement being useful in the "real world," but my oldest brother, Phil, nine years my senior, was for many years a jazz drummer—he played with Stan Getz, Buddy Rich, Red Rodney—he even recorded a jam session with Charlie Parker—living in the tormenting, satisfying, dramatic, demanding world of life-on-the-road, druggy and irregular, tense and exhilarating. (And his son, like my elder daughter, has that talent whole, like something contained, intact, on a cassette.) And in my

early years I had the peacock-tail spread of talents that often arise side by side and whose presence I can acknowledge without immodesty because I had nothing to do with bringing it about: I was a good pianist (wasted it for laziness), a good artist, a shy indoor sort of person who (I've been told) didn't seem particularly retiring, but was always in pursuit of a solitary art. And writing chose me in a moment of crisis.

Let me go back a bit. Someone introducing me recently at a reading told the audience that I grew up in Philadelphia, which was a fair enough assumption, based on the information on some book jacket or vita that I was born in Philadelphia, but he was entirely wrong: I lived in Philadelphia for ten weeks. At the end of ten years of not much belonging there, my parents, forever New Yorkers, were obviously waiting with their bags packed for me to be born so that we could take off to what turned out to be a series of other places in which they also never felt at home.

Our vagabondage was not particularly exhilarating. We weren't natural gypsies who chose the next town over the hill because it looked inviting; nor was my father a circuit-riding preacher or a military man. He was following a job or two in the textile business to this or that unlikely outpost and was, by necessity, indifferent to the charm or charmlessness of our living arrangements. These days, "quality of life," as it's being quaintly called, is being written up in studies that tell us we should try to live in Palo Alto, California, but not, at any cost, in Haverhill, Massachusetts. But along with profession, choice was not always an active concept. I assume that for them, dutiful and loving parents, once having ascertained that we lived, as the ads say, "near schools and shopping," a good job was a lot more potent an attraction than a graceful skyline or a dozen lakes scattered across the horizon. For so many in America, moving up (or at least making it) has been more of an ideal than staying home and making do. As for family, in that kind of vertical move, family is necessarily left behind, or if it does not disappear, it hangs on the way my grandmother did once her own household had dispersed, moving as we moved, barnacle-like, for want of anyone else to live with or anywhere else to go.

In any event, until I was a teenager the longest I lived in any one place was four years, which I spent in a town in Westchester County outside of New York City. We all know that "where you come from," where you grew up, is a matter for the imagination. The date on a questionnaire doesn't begin to approach the significant center of one's experience. That town I lived in from ages five through nine—right after a bit more than a year in that dismally remembered Reading, Pennsylvania—was called Mount Vernon; it was a short and to me wondrous commuter-train ride away from Manhattan that we made on many a Thursday night (when the department stores stayed open late) or Saturday afternoon, for shopping or a concert. But when people say to me, You grew up in New York then, I have to demur—there are so many fine distinctions: from time to time I borrowed its vigor and its cultural endowments, and it was familiar to me, but the city wasn't my daily playground. We called it, in fact, The City, with capital letters, as if one had to go a longer distance to get there, to achieve it, than its true distance in miles would explain. I was not that kind of natural New Yorker.

Although reason tells me that every year of those four that I lived in Mount Vernon consisted of the requisite four seasons, and even though I can recall any number of winter and summer scenes if I try, still, for whatever entirely subterranean reason, when I remember what I think of as the central years of my childhood—the others trickled away a year or two at a time in places that left no particular emotional residue—it is always fall and I am kicking up noisy leathery leaves in a particular stretch of woods within sight of the solid stone castlelike bridges that cross the old winding highways of Westchester County. I don't know why this is the abiding image I have taken from the full years of my childhood—nothing special happened there, either ecstatic or traumatic, I have no whole picture that tells me whether I played there once or twice or a hundred times, and I don't remember who I played with. I must have felt some heart-centered, solitary, sensual delight, some essence of childhood freedom otherwise denied me, in that place. I remember that certain oblique sunlight that precedes winter-in-earnest, and the kind of temperature in which you keep your jacket open because it's not quite cold, but yet your ears hurt with the hinted beginning of serious weather.

But this is very nearly all. The rest of my memories from childhood, though they are numerous, are not continuous. They yield less than they ought to of pattern and ritual, and of rich pictures of neighbors in their characteristic places, of townspeople locally famous for their behavior which in time became predictable to a concentrating child (whose family would laugh about this one or that, or shake its collective head in disapproval at the dinner table). Though my parents were wonderfully adequate to

the tasks of parenthood, and this is the only detail of nurturing they didn't manage to provide, I think they suffered considerable loneliness themselves for the lack of a single place to call home. (Even that character who came, according to Flannery O'Connor, "not even from a place, just from near a place," was luckier than we.) I did not have the repetition of year-in year-out expectation that comes of belonging in a community and I think I have written about exile again and again because of that, about the thing I didn't have.

The only advantage to this kind of random childhood, I ought to say, is that when I want to date something in my mind I can think, ah yes, I must have done such and such in 1948, say, because that was the year, the only year, we lived in Los Angeles. There is a backdrop for the memories and it is always recognizable because it changes so distinctly with each move. So while those who lived in a single place may see a blur of years, I have them all too neatly separated and captioned, like photographs, according to city and landscape. How else would I know that I "learned" to write at three or four in cheerless Reading? Only because we had just come there and were soon to move on—a dubious reason to celebrate.

We had moved. I was nine. The only thing to be said for departing for Los Angeles lock, stock, and barrel, grand piano and weighty shelves of books, was that I was under the illusion that we were really going somewhere exotic, that I would wake at the other end of the continent transformed into a cowgirl. I imagined a new life on a street called Buttercup Lane. I saw high grass and a habitat of distinctly western creatures and a life lived out-of-doors. *Mariposa, tumbleweed, buckboard:* it was a lexical holiday, I saw it and heard it in hazy movie color and a whole new set of words. And the drive to Los Angeles along old Route 66 confirmed our approach to something radically new—we drove through the Texas Panhandle and saw a cattle skull or two, saw oil wells on the capitol lawn in Oklahoma City, spent a night at a lodge on the rim of the Grand Canyon where Hopi Indians danced for us, and the gift shop was dominated by turquoise, silver, and earthy oatmeal-colored blankets. We stayed in little motel cottages in which the lives of others, strangers, were still palpable—mildewed, soft-mattressed, no two rooms alike but certain things recurrent: Gideon Bibles with pebbly black covers, not-quite-white chenille bedspreads, the splay of neon lights blinking outside the window. I could take out a map today and put my finger on every town we stopped in.

But the step off the edge into this new life was apparently deeply troubling to me. I was so terrified, in some way I could never explain, that I couldn't eat—my parents spent every evening trying to get me to swallow a decent dinner but my throat stayed resolutely locked. They begged and cajoled, they reassured me that they were there with me, but nothing helped, until one evening in Omaha, beguiled by a set of paper placemats that offered paper-and-pencil games for children, I forgot to be stubborn and depressed and mysteriously relented.

Clearly the trip was everything a real psychic journey ought to be, not a plane ride that delivered us instantaneously, unprepared, into a new world but a slow, not always comfortable immersion in distance and differentness. By the time we'd worried about what was the best time to cross Death Valley, day or night, fleeing through the competing dangers of heat or cold (take your pick, our advisers suggested, but

Summer 1947, aged eight

keep a water bag with you just in case), and forged the Prescott Mountains of Arizona on a narrow road between tractor trailers, we *were* in fact changed—we had had an Experience. I felt like a pioneer, strengthened and brave. You'd think we'd come in a prairie schooner.

But Los Angeles was no more a different world than any unfamiliar city might have been. Four Buttercup Lane turned out to be 3315 West Thirtieth Street, surrounded by small neat lawns, no waving hay in sight, and used-car lots hung with flapping banners. Of course there were oddities: we lived in a small Spanish stucco bungalow edged with hibiscus and pomegranate bushes, and witnessed with a bewildered puritanical eye the peculiarities of Los Angeles architecture and Hollywood flamboyance. (Chiefly, I remember seeing my first pastel-colored buildings, all the "crazy" pink and aqua courtyards that belonged to a Mexican tradition none of us could recognize.) I attended my first supermarket and discount drugstore, brand-new, announced, like the Academy Awards, with klieg lights. New houses with no foundations went up on my school route like mushrooms, over the weekend. I ate school lunch outside all year around, under a sort of porch roof called the Pergola, a perpetual picnic.

Mild as these changes were, I did not take well to them. My father was intent on buying into a business—all this was new to him as well, he had worked in the textile business in other people's offices—and this threw him into company with a kind of underside of California prosperity that we all found odd, and I think I felt to be somehow unseemly, even threatening. In the evenings, after dinner, he would take my mother to see the best of the day's prospects for his investment: there was a rickety-floored five-and-ten, a movie theatre that had keno night and gave away dishes, a liquid coffee process that bottled something that looked like molasses or motor oil. This was an encounter with what (I suspect now) I felt to be fly-by-night America. At nine I had, of course, no such sociological categories, but I could tell flimsy goods and shoddy get-rich promises when I heard my parents discussing them, and they felt like the kind of things other people's fathers got involved in. Whoever it was—Nathanael West?—who said that it was as if the continent had been tilted and everything that wasn't securely screwed down rolled out to Los Angeles—whoever that was and however he said it, he had the feeling precisely. And, though children may pretend they want exotic new lives, in fact they are the world's true conservatives. I was surely one of them. Or maybe it's simpler, maybe I just didn't like being left alone (I didn't count my brothers as protection) in a new place.

My response, an extension of my trap-tight throat on the cross-country trip, was a very uncharacteristic one because, though I've always been most comfortable in my own company, I've also tended to be fairly buoyant and even-tempered. But on the evenings when my parents went out to investigate those unsavory "opportunities," I would stay home with Ralph and Phil, and the smell of some night-blooming flower—jasmine, I thought, but it might have been orange blossoms—would overwhelm me, smother me in a deep blanket of depression. This is the only memory of the purely irrational that I have, and one of the very few of any purely distilled childhood emotion. I don't remember what I did about it, if I hid in my bed or simply withdrew, or read a book to extinguish my terror. I only know that I was oppressed, lonely, and frightened. Either I told my parents how I felt or my father found his "opportunity" (which, after all the searching, didn't work out: a shag-rug company, not particularly sleazy given what I was afraid he'd be sucked into, in which his partner, named something-or-other Arnold, was

rapidly renamed Benedict and I learned a little about the historic betrayal by his namesake). In any event they stopped leaving me at home, and I stopped half wanting to die, flower-drugged, of melancholy.

That state, debilitating, to say the least, probably underlay my daytime desperation. Over the course of the summer of our arrival I had made decent friends down the block and around the corner, about as exotic as I could stand: one owned a dog named Rex, another had a fig tree. But on the first day of school, disappointed, I discovered that the whole lot of them walked in one direction to their school while I, divided from them by a zoning line as final as a sword, was compelled to go in the opposite direction to another. Perhaps I had depleted my friend-making energy on the set now lost to me; I was alone again, and furious. In class, a well-meaning teacher alienated me further from potential friends (at least I saw it that way; someone with more confidence or grace might have shrugged off such conspicuousness) by sending me to the blackboard incessantly to solve arithmetic and spelling problems—she had found a good solid student and it must have been convenient to overuse me. (There was a red-headed boy, too, who many years later turned up in a photo of a competition in China as the table-tennis champion of the world—each of us obviously driven to compensate for early stardom!) I skulked around on my own and no one made friendly advances. The smell of the school cafeteria tomato soup sickened me at lunch; good friends ran and played softball and left me out, at least for a while. Long enough.

Which is when I began to write. Perhaps I'd done so before and have no record of it in memory or on paper; I tend to remember designing extravagant costumes for my paper dolls and playing with jacks and trading cards. I only know that I discovered, then, the lush reflexive comfort that drives artists of every kind, and little pre-artists as well, the bitter pleasure to be found in alienation, in making the pearl that surrounds the sandy mote in the oyster.

I began bringing a stenographer's notebook to school with me—I remember looking forward all morning to my time alone with it, and at recess and after lunch I'd sit against the trunk of a tree just inside the playground fence, writing in a voice that never failed me: my own. I had nothing original to say, I imagine few children do. I told the archetypal story of the girl who wanted a horse desperately (oh lost Buttercup Lane and myself, half tomboy in chaps, half little lady, junior Doris Day, in gingham!) who wakes on her birthday morning to find the perfect black-stallion-with-white-star looking casually in her

High-school graduation, 1956

window. I wrote—this was at home on the old sticky family Underwood—a mystery, half lifted from a Classic Comic of Sherlock Holmes, called "Murder Stalks at Midnight," and I was devastated when my musician brother demonstrated how hopelessly unoriginal I was by showing me a record (Ray McKinley? Lionel Hampton?) called "Celery Stalks at Midnight."

Needless to say, that didn't stop me. My father has saved, in that bottomless box of finite moments, a poem about "the wonderful land of Rin-tin-tin." (Close to it as I lived, I didn't mean Hollywood—I thought I'd invented a kingdom. Nobody told me Rin Tin Tin was a dog.) "The daffodils are yellow-gold /And basking in the sun./ Their petals daintily unfold and open one by one." And so on.

Thus we hold open the place we will eventually fill with our own real voices; we show our facility, our willingness to learn from real models, our capacity to be seized by words, even if they're neither interesting nor, strictly, our own. I have a very hard time recalling myself as a child, either guessing at how I might have appeared objectively, or remembering what I felt about most things. But I certainly can reconstruct myself as child-author, and that little girl is a touching creature, all the desperation and hunger for solace in place, already capable of being assuaged by finding the right syllables and punctuation and structure, like the miniature organs of an embryo already pulsing long before it was ready to function in the world. I look back at myself at nine and I'm aghast.

I began announcing, then, that I knew what I was going to do with my life: I would write. (My sixth-grade autograph book has a note from a teacher saying, "Good luck with your writing!" I cringe trying to imagine how obnoxious I must have been already!) And, with an arrogance (so wild and lucky a child should not be allowed such prescience), I went further: Writing is a perfect life for a woman, I said at nine—I was still playing house, putting dolls, real or imagined, to sleep in their carriages, or at least infinitesimal creatures in matchboxes that slid open at a push, perfectly furnished with leaves and buttons and other miniature props—because she can do her writing and at the same time be at home with her husband and children. I seemed to understand that I wanted both, and I seemed to have no reason to think I couldn't have both.

But here comes the question again: How did I know I could combine the two, or that I deserved to? Had times already changed that much? (This was

1948 or 1949; I don't think they had.) My mother didn't work; I knew few women who did, or if they did they had "jobs," not "careers" that demanded commitment, and none who did odd things like write. Was I a sport? I think I was simply doing my ideal thing, innocently, with no understanding (and just as well) that women were expected to have problems—see V. Woolf—being so many things at once. I still have to ask, as Woolf did, how many Judith Shakespeares have made the same naive pronouncement only to find themselves foiled when the time came, by their frailty or—and/or—the excessive demands of the others in their lives? (Sylvia Plath probably planned to do both, but she had complicating factors like the death of her father at a psychologically vulnerable time.)

I believe I was lucky. Though I was a girl in a family of boys I had never had a moment's longing to be like them, or to have their alleged powers. I believe I was insulated against such envy by my parents' constantly expressed delight at "finally achieving" a baby girl after two boys. My mother used to tell me a story strong enough to be a lodestar: how she bet her doctor a bottle of champagne that I'd be just another boy, then waking, hearing "Mrs. Brown loses!" and trying to sort out her vague, ether-confused comprehension that losing this time meant

The author with her daughter Adina, Tougaloo, Mississippi, 1967

winning . . . A story like that is a good one to grow up on.

Sometimes, of course, the luck of having the wish come true, as if my fairy godmother were listening, is a weight I paradoxically flag under; as if, having been granted both books and children, Adina and Elana (not to mention one of the most profoundly support-ive husbands anyone could dream up), I dare not put it down for even a while, let alone fail it . . . Nor has it always been as easy as that makes it sound. (I'll come back to this with an example.)

I had teachers who pushed me hard, a faculty adviser to a junior-high newspaper I edited; a breath-of-fresh-air high-school journalism mentor at Forest Hills High School (outside of New York City again) named James J. Kernan who wore shirtsleeves and his hat pushed far back on his head as if he might have a press pass in its brim (though nasty rumor had it he had once taught classics!). If I needed proof that he respected me I got it when he'd alibi to my teachers and sit me in the newspaper office all day until I finished the essay I had promised. The essays were speculative, pretentious, plummy, and soft with ver-biage—patronizingly mature—but again, the prod-uct wasn't the point so much as the process, and the sense I had that someone cared enough about my words that he would push me hard and hope for the best. (Writers as diverse as the biographer and critic Judith Thurman and the sportswriter Robert Lipsyte passed through Mr. Kernan's hands at some point: he was iconoclastic, genuinely dedicated, benignly per-fectionist, and he took girls seriously. I got to thank him—one of those things you usually hate yourself for not doing—before he died.)

I was planning to go to Queens College, like so many of my friends—it was free and it was nearly around the corner from my house. It would have served me well enough, too, but when I won a New York State Regents Scholarship I changed my plans and took myself uptown to Barnard, astonished that I was welcome amidst what I saw as the glamour of an old, fine, private college whose buildings looked aged and indestructible, where we were served, as if it were an annointment, from silver samovars in parlors lush with Oriental rugs. (First-generation college students can do with a little of that kind of intoxication, though it often doesn't last very long.) But more important, my freshman English teacher, Inez Nel-bach, asked me if I intended to teach in college. The suggestion was like a blow between the eyes. Could she be talking to me? College? I took a long look at myself—I'd assumed I was "going into" journalism, at best—and confessed that such a thing had never

seemed possible. How much could you skip over in a generation, I wondered, though in retrospect the question seems foolishly self-conscious. I was ready for influence, eager to be pulled along a way. This time the catalyst was a poet, Robert Pack, with the sweet assistance of one of the most gentle and sensitive (and undervalued) writers of his day, George P. Elliott. For Pack I wrote only poetry; for Elliott I wrote one story, a dreamy seduction that tried to be coolly knowing, a dozen times. And when I say I wrote for them, I mean it, I think, quite literally. A little transference surely enters into such relation-ships, a need to please the teacher that stiffens the more problematic resolve to please the self before the self is truly formed.

After my sophomore and junior years I accompa-nied Bob Pack—what a thrill, to call a professor by his first name, though this professor wasn't yet thirty—to a wonderland that could not have been better designed for the likes of me, a sort of junior MacDowell Colony, called the Cummington School of the Arts. (It still exists, on its archetypally beautiful Berkshire acres thirty years later, as a "community" of adult artists.) There, on a scholarship that felt as if it were administered by the gods, I wrote poetry all day, much of the time leaning against a nineteenth-century tombstone. "Cummington Cemetery," which became the title of one of my earliest published poems (which appeared in *Mademoiselle*), demystified New England graveyards for me. There were college-aged painters and musicians hard at work in the rehearsal rooms and the art barn as well; though I had always listened to music, I learned to love chamber music at Cummington. And at night, in a colonial house, under antique portraits, in a parlor furnished in my dreams—as a quasi-New Yorker I was more unsophisticated about such an ambiance than anyone might have imagined; Queens didn't abound in real colonial furnishings—we heard lec-tures, had our work criticized, joined a passionate company of artists and mentors.

On what must have been one of my first nights at Cummington, I went down to Bob Pack's cabin, where I sat in the mountain cool with half a dozen older students and a few of the faculty, a composer, a sculptor. A playful argument was raging—absurd, now that I reconstruct it—over who was the greater, Mozart or Beethoven. I had grown up playing both on the piano, and not badly, but had never given much thought to either: I had better "fingers," I suspect, than head or intellectual training. I was drinking red wine in a paper cup. After half an hour or so, in which I felt myself so far out of my depth I

With daughter Elana, aged ten, 1980

could hardly breathe, let alone utter, I went out onto the porch to indulge my desperation and weep bitter tears into my wine. It was a moment of such pure longing I can close my eyes now and—almost—feel it; there have been jaded moments when I've called up the memory as a kind of touchstone to remind me of a purer time. No child has ever stood outside a toyshop window lusting so vigorously to be let in.

I had just turned nineteen; I had read nothing; for ten years I had wanted to be, though of course I had never dared call myself, a writer. Every fragile egg I had was in that one basket, and it was very clear to me that I didn't even begin to deserve to be there. I remember that Bob Pack came out at one point and gently asked me if I was all right. I'm sure I blamed the wine, it was much less shameful to claim to be sick on Gallo than to admit I was drowning in disappointment, self-disgust, terminal inadequacy. He went back inside and I truly made one of those vows a child makes, one of those "if only I get this, then I'll give that" pacts with myself. I don't know what I offered in return for the right to sit at the hearth, in a manner of speaking, around which the genuine writers clustered, where they took (and gave) their warmth. I

suppose I pledged my blood and sweat; I'd already wept my first installment of tears, out there shivering on the porch. I don't know if that fairy godmother was listening, but I was, of course, and I was the one who had to do the work. I was the one who spent that summer and the next, not to mention the time between, reading Emily Dickinson and Yeats, trying to read Ezra Pound, revising a single line till three in the morning, writing the poems I began to publish before I graduated. This was the late fifties; it was a time of formal, disciplined writing (unless you were daring enough—I wasn't, I was all too good a girl—to throw in your lot with Allen Ginsberg and Gregory Corso et al., the Beat Way toward liberation). My first published poem was a sestina that *Poetry*, that classic magazine, chose when I was a senior, I suspect because it was a tour de force. (A sestina is, by definition, always a tour de force.)

But just as surely as there are no finite happy endings, the moments on that little wooden porch are never over: the question of whether one belongs beside the fire with the genuine writers is never closed, and even if there were a way to put a seal on one's last work—the Guaranteed Real Thing—there

"Celebrating our parents' fiftieth wedding anniversary," New Hampshire, 1977: (from left) Ralph, Blossom, Rosellen, Philip, and David Brown

is always today's work waiting to be done. Here is an honest record of how that felt from the summer of 1968, a fragment of my first published prose (which was a sort of mixed-genre collage called "Finger-prints"). By coincidence I am sitting on another little porch in this paragraph, which I suppose only means that one habitually takes oneself out of the company of others to moon and mourn, to fall apart and put oneself back together:

An hour ago I was sitting on the side porch, nothing but a little peaked roof to keep the rain away, going through a ritual of the blues more regular and self-pitying than anything I ever give in to before my period. I will never be able to write anything again, good or bad; L. was speaking at dinner about her prolific friend who tosses off every form of brilliant work—I despise L. (who doesn't know how I happen to be feeling today); despise the friend; disparage, thus discredit, L.'s taste in writing; despise myself (which I should have begun with);

then all around again. I also despise the baby, who has spent the whole day hanging on me (reluctantly—she too can think of better fun but she is teething and very sad) so that I couldn't even read. Why didn't I wait to have a baby till I had *done* something, so that I wouldn't have to keep doing it when it got so treacherous to be many things on one hot sticky domestic day?

But I stop (sniffling and watching the undramatic drizzle roll off the roof and splatter at my feet). I have just argued convincingly with myself that having written means nothing in itself, that working must exist in the present tense to exist at all. And the baby has nothing to do with it. (Everything else I have in fact done besides writing I never count, thus starting with something of a handicap. I keep this spare part in the back of my mind.) I blow my nose with histrionic vigor, and feel my small self-conscious funk being ignored so loudly by my husband that he is telling me what he thinks of my indulgence without even having to look up from his book (for which he would never forgive me) or to have to stanch the tears that almost always make him angry. Defeated I stand up, let the screen door slam behind me like a backfire, and—never to write again—sit down in this chair and begin. . . .

I'm not really interested in rehearsing the facts of my adult life—a few years of unsatisfying graduate study (the last in a classful of would-be writers to drop out; I had contemplated going to the Iowa Writers' Workshop, one of the only programs of its kind at the time, but was appalled at the idea of living in the midst of the cornfields with a bunch of writers. But the alternative, my inattentive scholarly study of literature when I really wanted to be writing, was far worse); marriage, at twenty-three, which seems to me younger by the year, to a Harvard psychology student named Marv Hoffman, whom I didn't really know very well by today's standards but understood, in some totally inarticulate way, I wanted to and should marry. I was right, but I attribute this to extraordinary luck; if there was any conscious wisdom in the choice it was buried too far down for me to be able to recreate its specifics, let alone take credit for it. (I also, though, attribute much of the unstrained pleasure of these years to Marv's love of writing and, consequently, I've always thought, of this writer, whose opportunities to do what he sees as my "main work" he has passionately devoted himself to protecting from the multiplying distractions that menace it. My friends who have had to renegotiate their marriage contracts, in a manner of speaking, having come late to writing, or any other commitment, have had a much harder time.)

We began a replication of my parents' rootless life together the day after our marriage by getting on an airplane (my first, and I nearly had to be forced up the stairs onto it) and flying seventeen hours—there were still propeller flights in 1963—to San Francisco, where Marv was serving a year's internship at the University of California psychiatric hospital. We have subsequently lived in Boston, Mississippi, Brooklyn, New Hampshire, and, since 1982, in Houston (where we came to live so that I could teach in the University of Houston's Creative Writing Program, and where Marv teaches English to kids and teaches teachers how to help them to write)—we tend to choose to live in places that demand explanation, where kindred spirits are not common and are visible at twenty paces. Responding to an assortment of attractions in these disparate places, I'm afraid (though it's only half, perhaps, by my parents' example; Marv lived at one address until he went away to graduate school) we've visited the blight of our homelessness on our children. I regret that.

The best I can say for the habit of endless relocation is that it's yielded for my writing a kind of perpetual theme, sometimes an undercurrent but more often an outright preoccupation. And since I had a childhood uneventful enough to give me no deep emotional scores to settle, no psychological axes to grind (John Irving put it that way once), I make the most of having started nowhere, having no sense of my own place, the bedrock reality. My subject has turned out, time and again, to be exile; turned out to be *place,* which, unpossessed or forfeited—the obverse of home—can be just as deep an obsession as devotion to (or aversion to) home. I have immersed myself in a rather unwieldly number of borrowed terrains: in Mississippi, where we lived in the mid-sixties at the latter edge of the civil rights movement, an experience that redirected the energies of our lives, too large for me even to attempt to discuss here except to say that I wrote much of *Some Deaths in the Delta,* my first book of poems, in a little house just outside the gates of the campus of a black college, Tougaloo, to which we had come to teach at the beginning of 1965. I had my first child, Adina, there in 1967, and many years later, in 1984, still fascinated by the experiences I had and dreamed (mostly the latter), published *Civil Wars,* a novel which concerns two ex–civil rights activists, the husband a Mississippi native, his wife a New Yorker far from home, and an orphaned niece and nephew who come to live with them, ultimate exiles whose way of life has disappeared with their parents in a sudden accident. A block in Brooklyn inhabited by blacks, whites, Puerto Ricans, the poor, and the middle class, where we lived for three years at the end of the sixties (and where my second daughter, Elana, was born in 1970), became my book of stories, *Street Games* (1974). In New Hampshire (where we lived for eleven years), I've set one novel, *Tender Mercies* (1978), about a woman accidentally crippled by her husband, and not incidentally the story of a native small-town boy and a sophisticated Boston professor's daughter; and *Cora Fry* (1977), which is a kind of novel in the form of eighty-four short poems, a presumptuous ventriloqual act in which I dare to speak as a New Hampshire countrywoman persevering right down the road from where she was born. (That's the only book in which anyone *belongs,* and I think I enjoyed writing it more than any of my other books partly because I liked

Rosellen Brown with her husband, Marvin Hoffman, and daughters, Elana and Adina Hoffman, Houston, 1984: "We were taking pictures for a brochure advertising a book party for Civil Wars.*"*

trying on the feel of "home" for a change. Even Cora goes away—flees to Boston briefly but comes gratefully home again, quite clear, if conflicted, about the virtues and drawbacks of intimacy and anonymity.)

I am trying to finish, right now, a novel about exiles of a different kind, a group of Russian Jews who come to America to become farmers near the end of the nineteenth century, who try to build a sort of Yiddish-speaking Brook Farm in New Hampshire—that we, my husband and children and I, found ourselves Jews with an eighteenth-century farmhouse and one hell of a garden, if not exactly a farm, in benignly alien territory in the 1970s just might have something to do with the psychic genesis of this (still-untitled) book. (I think my growing interest in writing about the experiences of Jews in the world may be a kind of indirect attempt to find and take pleasure in the sort of "travelling home" that Jewish cultural and historical experiences provide, a shared identity even in the absence of a permanent address.)

And finally, though not in chronological order, my first novel, *The Autobiography of My Mother* (1976), took as its overt theme exile, the loss of home, the gains and losses that attend the life of the perpetual outsider. My (anti-) heroine, Gerda Stein, born in Alsace-Lorraine and catapulted into the world by violent historical events, says something I suppose I, her creator, might say myself, however undramatic my own displacement has been. A civil-liberties lawyer, aged seventy-two, she says impatiently of her law partner,

I can better comprehend the life of a hoarse-throated, one-legged, blind, garlic-scented, God-fearing Malaysian who has lived in any twelve cities of the world than, say, that of my partner, Jack Tenney, who was born in Washington Heights and has merely rolled downhill a few miles to the nearest viable neighborhood, barring Harlem, to live in a building which must be nearly identical to the first; and so, except for a short lifeless sojourn to the barracks of Fort Dix twenty years ago, he has moved gently through his life yet to be truly surprised, I would wager, or truly inconvenienced. Snug Jack.

Flannery O'Connor closed her essay on the regional writer this way: "The writer operates at a peculiar crossroads where time and place and eternity somehow meet. His problem is to find that location." It has surely been my problem, not easily solved but the one I've constantly, shiftingly, hungrily pursued. The fact that I began the search as a child sitting, lonely, under a tree three thousand miles from what I called home delights me, really—everything ties together like a poem we don't realize our lives are writing. When I write I always feel that the thing, the *it,* the essence is in there, in the silence somewhere, trapped like Michelangelo's slaves who are caught forever trying to thrust themselves out of shapeless marble into being. It is only for me to uncover the words, the structure, find the story and tell it, whether I think anyone wants to hear it or not. That's my sentence and my freedom and, I know by now, it's not negotiable.

BIBLIOGRAPHY

Fiction:

Street Games (short stories). Garden City, N.Y.: Doubleday, 1974.

The Autobiography of My Mother. Garden City, N.Y.: Doubleday, 1976; London: Sphere, 1981.

Banquet: Five Short Stories, with others. Edited by Jean Norris. Lincoln, Mass.: Penmaen Press, 1978.

Tender Mercies. New York: Knopf, 1978; London: Hutchinson, 1979.

Civil Wars. New York: Knopf, 1984; London: Michael Joseph, 1984.

Poetry:

Some Deaths in the Delta, and Other Poems. Amherst: University of Massachusetts Press, 1970.

Cora Fry. New York: Norton, 1977; Greensboro, N.C.: Unicorn Press, 1989.

Editor of:

The Whole Word Catalog: Creative Writing Ideas for Elementary and Secondary Schools, with others. New York: Teachers and Writers Collaborative, 1972.

Camilo José Cela

1916-

(Translated from the Spanish by Elaine Kerrigan)

Contemplating The Rose *a Good Many Years Later*

As time goes by and the lees settle, a man realizes that it is quite tedious to explain what has already been explained. Things happen because they happen—health and affliction, life and death, time and forgetfulness—they flow by, because there is nothing else they can do—like the water in the crystalline water bed or in the majestic and grandiose river—and one, in the end, during the course of events, is faced with history ready-made, for good or for bad, and with no chance of appeal, alteration, or indulgent rough drafts.

A man moves a finger and another is hanged; a man wrinkles his brow and another, looking at him, shits his pants; a man whistles in the night and a woman, behind a wall, is startled into action, with love or terror. This, the wise men call a conditioned reflex; the worst part of it is that in this state, we sometimes lose our lives or our liberty. History is the sequel of my conditioned reflexes, among which disorder prevails or, at least, chance.

In the tragicomedy of history, we all are, at once, actors, extras, and spectators: for men the attitude—not even the pretense—of being a mere decoration does not hold. History, to a greater or lesser degree, is made by all of us, whether we want it or not. History, Carlyle said, is the quintessence of innumerable biographies, and the biography of every human being happens without it being asked permission to happen (willpower rules, remember, but does not decide).

Yes: things happen because they happen—the woman who loves and the woman who hates, the opportune moment or the hostile one, the book that is saved by a narrow escape and the one that is lost irremediably—and one, at the end of all the swagger and other trifles, is faced with history ready-made, written badly and full of erasures, but ready-made, and if it is one's own, the only thing to do is to face up to it before growing old and wearisome.

When a man in his seventies begins to bore those around him to tears by telling of his incredible

Camilo José Cela

youthful exploits, he is already lost forever and beyond reprieve: he can no longer be saved either by peace or indulgence, even if they appeared together, hand in hand. No: at seventy a man has no reason to become a chronicler, rather he should continue to be a minstrel. And an actor in the great big theater of the world, that stage on which, behind the scenes, the tomb is already present. Many men, in order to forget this, die young or at the wrong time or out of turn, which is not a desirable conclusion for anyone, that is, to die of the boredom of being alive, which—at least until now—is not the case of some seventy-year-olds: your servant, to go no further.

The Rose

My Father and the Family of My Father

My father has the same name as I, and I have the same name as my son. My grandfather had the same name as my father, and my grandson, when I have one, will probably have the same name as all the rest of us.

Camilo is not a pretty name, it's a strange name that sounds French or Russian, but it would have seemed foolish if my parents, guided by an aesthetic standard or some long drawn-out tale, had named me Gustav Adolph, or Julius Caesar, or Victor Emanuel, or Mark Antony at my baptism; these are what blacks from the Antilles are called.

I believe one should not go against family tradition, because, among other things, no one can guarantee our making a change for the better and not the worse.

Camilo José seems nicer than Camilo on its own; but of these things—and of more—I'll talk when the time comes.

My father is a strange man to study; perhaps this idea is more prevalent among children who try to contemplate their parents impartially, with a certain serenity. The two attitudes usually adopted by children about their parents—that of veneration or that of scorn—both strike me as equally one-sided and prejudiced. No one, after the age of twenty, with a grain of common sense, can remain ignorant of the virtues or defects of a parent. I think it of little worth to evade the obvious topics, and the timid man who lets off steam seems as stupid as the rebel who grimaces as a matter of course.

My father is a reserved man, almost hermetic, serious and mysterious. Sometimes, however, he becomes loquacious, garrulous, and then he talks a blue streak, tells jokes and stories from the old days, and laughs uproariously. He seems another person, but to me he is always his same mysterious self. With a mystery of profound sorrow, inexplicable and wary. With a mystery that occurs a great deal among his countrymen and which seems to imply an underlying fatalism, like the eyes of horses and cats that shine in the night.

It took many years to get to know my father; it took him another few in getting to know me. We both thought the other was a fool, but later we realized that neither of us was. My father never placed too much trust in me, and that, no doubt, was why we took so long in getting to know each other deeply.

With father, Camilo Cela

My father's greatest virtue, what I admire most, is his absolute contempt for death; for him death is totally meaningless. I don't think he's pretending; my father is a violent and passionate man, nothing mellifluous or compliant about him, and this type of person usually has no knack for putting things on.

The most serious defect I find in him is his willfulness. My father is a man of great will, an iron and inflexible will, and if he gets something into his head, everyone around him should get ready to quake in his boots. It is totally futile to argue with him if he thinks he ought to go here and not there. I don't think his pigheadedness is mere rigidity; it is perhaps shyness: the shyness of not appearing malleable. When my father overcomes this shyness, and makes use of reasons that come to hand, he changes from night to day.

In those years my father was living in Foz, a village lost on the Cantabrian coast, where there must have been a scant thousand inhabitants, and where he had a fairly up-to-date library: Baroja, Blasco Ibáñez, Valle-Inclán, and Azorín were his favorite authors. I have the first edition of Valle-Inclán's *Sonatas* at home, two books of Azorín, from the time when he was still signing J. Martínez Ruiz: *The Confessions of a Little Philosopher* and *The Force of Love* (a tragicomedy of the seventeenth century). The rest have been lost. The books of Blasco Ibáñez and Baroja were lent to José Luis Hermida, brother-in-law of my aunt Teresa, my father's sister, who took them to my aunt's estate at Bouzabalada, in Túy, and never returned them. When she died I asked my cousins for the books, but they answered vaguely and did not give them to me.

The foreign authors my father preferred were Nietzsche and Schopenhauer. Later he read some of Lord Macaulay. He also liked the Russian novelists. The French, no. Poetry, except for the odd Galician poem, did not please him much either. He had all the issues of the magazine *Mercurio* in his library.

My father married on Saint Joseph's day in 1915, in Villagarcía de Arosa, where he had been appointed to the customs department. When he married he had already left Villagarcía and was serving in Almería. If I had not been a little careful I would have been born in Almería. This business of births is very mysterious. If I had happened to be born in Almería at this time, more than likely I'd have been a painter like Jesús de Perceval, and would speak passionately about the Iberian cultures.

My father, from the time he left home till he was assigned to Madrid for the second time, did nothing but move from place to place and, from his marriage on, he took his household, his wife, and children along. This, actually, is something fairly common among bureaucrats.

When we arrived in Madrid in 1925, to stay now, my father had a preparatory academy for customs officials, which was first on Vergara Street, by Plaza Isabel II, and then on Fernanflor Street. On the balconies of Fernanflor, I witnessed, as all my schoolmates did, the birth of the republic in 1931. Two houses further on, where the police station is now, were the premises of a republican circle, and the people flocked into the little plaza behind the congress and in front of Azorín's house, to listen to the speakers. They let out mild enough shouts and predicted harmony and work. In view of this, my father's pupils agreed not to attend class and pushed and shoved through the halls of the academy proclaiming and not proclaiming the republic. The people in the street were sporadically singing the *Marseillaise,* but since the words are in French and they did not know them very well, some only hummed and others sang at the tops of their lungs, chanting, "Lalara, lalara, lalara . . ."

My father as a professor was something awful. He taught classes in political and economic geography and his pupils were afraid of him. He wore a derby then and arrived every afternoon smoking a tremendous cigar, an almost offensive cigar, a cigar worthy of a big shot.

In class, I, besides being a pupil, was his son, and I was nowhere, with no possible recourse. Later, during the course of my life, I've at times been confronted with a very black panorama, but never as then, when I found myself cornered and helpless. In reality, I was not much of a student, not very bright or very conscientious, and the truth is that of the whole vast program of geography I only managed to learn the ports of Japan and Algeria, the states of Mexico, and the rivers of Spain more than forty kilometers in length. Yes, I learnt them so well that I still remember them and can reel them off by heart and without a mistake. I do so occasionally, but never get carried away.

I did not think much of the preparation for customs, and to study like a demon, in order, after endless effort, to be stationed on the Portuguese border, or in some out-of-the-way village in Cáceres or Salamanca, enchanted me even less. At that time I was already attending, half on the sly, as if I were committing a sin, Pedro Salinas's class in the department of philosophy and letters, and I shall never weary of thanking Salinas for his valuable encouragement. The business of customs I took as something inevitable, but which one day would come to an end.

The only one of my schoolmates of that time who achieved fame was Perico Regueiro, who was a star forward in the Madrid Football Club, and who went international.

In his academy my father was taciturn, his expression surly, and we pupils respected him and did not dare have any showdowns with him. When some strike or other was being hatched, it was always in his absence; with him on the scene, the most vehement strikers came down to earth. I generally played a passive role in the strikes; I did not denounce them, but neither did I join forces with them. The role of strikebreaker was repugnant to me, but what happened at home one day when I had felt inspired and managed to empty my father's academy, I prefer not to remember.

My father is not a man of artistic tastes; art and poetry are for him entertainments more suited to idlers. He has a bit more tolerance for the essay and the novel; not much, however.

I think my father would have been a good doctor or scientist. My father does not find any justification for things that are done "just because" or simply to pass the time. In this, and in many other things, my father is very English, more English than my mother, who has the English blood.

Despite what I say, my father is not a practical man. The English, if one delves a bit deeply, are not either; they seem to be, but they are not. My father is a theoretician; he thinks things out in theory, and if, later, they do not work out in practice as he had thought, he shrugs his shoulders and thinks that they are no longer any of his concern. My mother, when she wants to get at him, tells him he is the King of Theory. My mother is not wrong.

My father is a man—also like the English—who loves luxury and protocol. If he had had money, he would have been one of the men who lived high on the hog in Spain. As he did not have it, he resigned himself to knowing he was a gentleman—which is no small thing—and rejected, with an Olympian gesture, ersatz crème caramel, malt for coffee, and saccharine for sugar. If he is not given crème caramel made of real eggs, authentic coffee or sugar, he prefers nothing at all. I applaud his taste and envy it. But my time has not been his. He married with forty pairs of shoes; I with some slippers that lasted me until a short time ago. Physically, my father bears—at least in the portrait by Luis Mosquera—a certain resemblance to Wenceslao Fernández Flórez. This is not odd: they are both Galicians and both are the same age.

My father is not a tall man—his seven living children are taller than he—and his hair is white, his forehead wide, his expression profound and rarely tender.

My father is a man who thinks a man should never go nude.

My father is a man with conservative ideas, even though he does not deny evolution. Long underpants, which went out of style years ago, are a good example.

My father is correct in his behaviour, coldly pleasant.

My father is a man of deep feelings, shyly amorous.

My father has humor in his wit, a cautious, veiled, muted humor.

My father—I don't know if I'm mistaken—is an important man. I could go on talking about him all my life.

My Mother and the Family of My Mother

My mother has the same name as her husband, as her grandfather, as her son, and as her grandson. Her father-in-law, one of her sisters-in-law, and a nephew have the same name as well. Camilo is a name that seems to have been agreed upon by everyone in my family, above all on the paternal side of my father and the maternal side, the Italian side, of my mother.

My mother's maiden name was lovely: Camila Enmanuela Trulock y Bertorini, a name for a Byron heroine or the result of English spleen wintering in the sun of Capri.

My mother was born in Santiago de Compostela on the twenty-third of June, 1895. She is, therefore, fifty-five years old, fifteen years less than her husband. It's wonderful, without a doubt, to be the son of a young woman: I, at least, think so. I remember my mother when she was twenty-three and twenty-four, when she was the age of women that now seem too young.

My mother, Galician by birth, was English until she married. This nationality change is something quite usual in her family. When voyages and mixtures of blood abound, passports change escutcheon with frequency. My mother, who was born English, became Spanish; my grandmother Nina Bertorini, the Spanish daughter of an Italian and an Englishwoman, did the opposite; my great-grandmother María Margarita Jones, English when single, became Italian when she married and Spanish when her husband did the same. This great-grandmother of mine is the María Bertorini, a native of Wales, to whom the poet Rosalía de Castro dedicated verses written in memory of Sir John Moore, the English general who died on January 16, 1809, in the battle of Elviña, fighting against the French.

> How far, I sing, of dark mists,
> of green pines, of fervent waves
> that saw him born!

María Margarita Jones, or María Bertorini when she married, was born in Willock, Cheshire. Her husband, my great-grandfather, was named nothing less than Camilo Marco Decio (and he had a brother named Timoleón Teobaldo Juan and a sister who was baptized with the name of Margarita María Virginia) and was born in Barcelona, where his father had gone in flight from Italy.

My great-great-grandfather Pietro was married to a Cicogniani—or Cicognani, which is the same name spelled differently—to Virginia Cicognani, a woman who was distinguished by her beauty and personal bravery. These Cicognani were fairly outstanding in Italian history and have provided princes of the Church with some frequency; Bruno Cicognani, the abundantly bearded author of *Villa Beatrice*, belongs to this family, too.

This great-great-grandfather of mine, Pietro Bertorini, was governor of Parma, and it seems that one fine day things went badly for him and he had to take flight; if he hadn't, he would have been hanged. Pietro Bertorini departed with what he had on and, from Marseilles, sent a black servant to tell his wife that he was waiting for her in Barcelona. The whole tale is charming and very Italian and very much in keeping with the epoch. The black servant returned to Italy, and, as it did not seem prudent for him to enter his lady's house, he disguised himself and sang her a serenade, some of it in code, in which he told her what he had to tell her. Virginia Cicognani, a

woman who did not let anything get in her way, went off to Genoa, where the black man was waiting and ready to accompany her in her flight, chartered a boat, and appeared in Barcelona, where she was reunited with her husband. With the jewels Virginia Cicognani had been able to take from her house in Parma, the couple lived comfortably for many years, a comfort which allowed them, among other things, to educate their children in England, and thus the wedding of Camilo to María Margarita.

When Pietro Bertorini arrived in Barcelona, the first Carlist war was ablaze in Spain. My great-great-grandfather asked who was losing, and, when they told him the Carlists, he joined up with the forces of the Pretender, in whose ranks he reached the grade of lieutenant-colonel. The white beret and cutlass of Pietro Bertorini were still around my grandmother's house not so many years ago. My uncles and their friends resuscitated these "historical memories" unexpectedly at Carnival time and afterwards they must have let them drop. The expression "historical memories" was that of an insufferable and very well-read servant they had who also had been a seminarian and had studied a bit to be a doctor's aid.

My great-great-grandfather's black servant died in the war at the side of his master, and my great-great-grandfather ordered a hundred masses in his honor and a very luxurious funeral. I do not think any black has ever been so well buried.

My great-grandfather Camilo Bertorini was married, as I already mentioned, in England, to María Margarita Jones, and afterwards came to Spain as the director of the West Railway Galicia, the railroad he built. This train went from Carril to Santiago de Compostela—and is still running, today incorporated into the national network of Spanish railways, because it is a train of normal width—along an itinerary drawn up according to a criterion more aesthetic than economical, traversing a landscape that is truly beautiful. My great-grandfather, was, without a doubt, a man of excellent taste.

I have already spoken about this railway on other occasions. It was a family railway, on which the fishermen and milkmaids asked for a discount at the ticket counter, with pleasant trains, haltingly pulled by old engines that seemed to have been taken from the movies of the Far West. The locomotives—more human, much more so, than those that came later—had their own names engraved on them, on shining plaques fitted onto their bellies: *Princesa de Asturias, Príncipe de Gales, María Cristina, Ría de Arosa, Minero Primero, Vásquez Mella*. Each train had its engineer and its own fireman, always the same, and the people,

With mother, Camila Trulock de Cela, about 1917

instead of talking about mail trains or mixed cargo-passenger cars, called the trains by the surnames of their conductors: "There goes Pereira," "Lourido's on time," "Fernández is a little late," etc.

Certain writers picked quarrels with the train because it stopped in front of a house to let some of us off, or in a tunnel so the fireman could fill his jug with cold water. So much for them!

My great-grandfather built his house on the line, at the railway crossing of Iria-Flavia, like the good railway man he was, and in this house my grandmother Nina and I were born.

The house in Iria is a square house, with two floors and two galleries, one facing north and the other south, and with its main facade—which now, with the rerouting of the highway, is at the back—covered over totally with sweet peas, wild roses, and honeysuckle. Around the house there is a garden where in times past—times I remember, ay!, perfectly and sorrowfully—graceful palms grew, and an immense and strange orange tree, as well as a fragrant lemon tree and, at its side, the royal pine and the holly tree, the tree of English Christmases and the most classical Christmas cards, with its thorny leaves of shiny green and its miniscule fruit of shiny red.

Today, and it hasn't been many years now, the garden is dry and withered, overgrown with nettles and bramble bushes, its paths obscured, the myrtle not cut back and the grass growing any old place. The house, if God does not save it, will fall in, any day now. In short . . .

Nina Bertorini, my grandmother, married John Trulock, who came from England at the age of twenty to become director of the "West," the *Té Bés*, as the locals called it.

The Trulocks—surnames that will die away like certain company rosters—are natives of Truro in Cornwall, and make up a family toughened by piracy and sailing, but, when taken out of those surroundings, are brought low. Walter Starkie, who was the director of the British Institute in Madrid, told me a lot about this family and their wanderings over the high seas, chasing after Spanish and Portuguese galleons.

The last John Trulock pirate was my great-great-grandfather, who died at sea of yellow fever, as was his duty. An aunt of mine, given to extravagances and to family history, for a while collected family documents, but when she found out that a relative was hanged in Swansea for stealing a sheep, she became quite disillusioned.

My great-grandfather John Trulock was born in London, as was his wife, Henriette Glascott, and it was there he acquired a certain prestige and not a slight predicament. In London, even if somewhat far from the center of town—beyond the Tottenham playing field, the richest football club in England—there is a not too important street called Trulock Road, named thus in his honor. It was with great difficulty that I found it.

This John Trulock was economically powerful and came to own the most important wax-candle factory in the British Empire, a candle factory that supplied the entire world and which had its own ship at the London docks, such was its prosperity. My great-grandfather was ruined overnight by Edison, when it occurred to him to invent the electric light bulb. I realize that competition was not possible.

The John Trulock who followed him, my grandfather, was the exact opposite of what one would imagine a pirate to be. With his white beard, his light, gentle eyes, and his venerable aspect, my grandfather John Trulock had the air of an honest, good bourgeois Briton, lover of his home, his whisky, and his traditions.

My grandfather lived the greater part of his life in Spain, in Santiago de Compostela, in Villagarcía de Arosa, and in Iria-Flavia, but when he died, after spending forty-three years there, he still spoke a quaint and childish Spanish, using his verbs in the infinitive and his adjectives any old way.

In his marriage, he represented goodness, flexibility, tolerance, and my grandmother Nina Catalina Aida Bertorini, character, decision, wiseness, and a gift of command.

My grandfather, still a bachelor, lived in Santiago with his sister, my great-aunt Katherine, who now lives in Sussex and is the friend of Charles David Ley, the English poet of *Holy Week in Seville* and translator, in his country, of *Antonio Pérez* by Marañón. When Katherine Trulock lived in London, Charles Ley, on his trips there, would generally go to her house to visit on my behalf; my aunt Kate would invite him for biscuits and black beer, and then give him a pound sterling to deliver to me.

In Santiago, my grandfather and his sister Kate lived with an old and determined housekeeper who watched over them and was full of good advice. My grandfather, on one occasion, finding his sister more untidy than usual, called the housekeeper. The housekeeper, raising her hands to her head, as if to confess a grave and painful sin, exclaimed:

"Ay, señor, it shouldn't have to be mentioned! What's wrong with this young lady is that her bustle is listing off to one side." When my Aunt Kate centered the bustle and put it in its place she proved to be like all the other young ladies of Santiago.

My aunt, at that time, pulled some divine stunts, and if she was forgiven, it was because Grandfather was well liked and she was given the forgive-and-forget treatment which Galicia applies to all the English. If this had not been the case, perhaps there would have been a real uproar when she showed up on a bicycle with a white mantilla, spectacles, and an unequivocal "off to the continent" air, in the Corpus Christi procession.

Another relative who was somewhat strange was Aunt Ana, Mrs. Tomlinson her married name, a woman of very special ideas, who, when she died, left all her capital, which consisted of a good many thousands of pounds sterling, to the town pharmacist, for him to poison cats painlessly. I imagine the pharmacist heir of my Aunt Ana as a character out of Dickens, with beady eyes and a smug look, rubbing his hands with glee while he prepared the sausage the cats were to eat. Truly, the source of his fortune was as convenient as it was sinister.

On the lap of his grandfather, John Trulock,
at Iria-Flavia, 1916

These three bloodlines—the Spanish, the Italian, and the English—are those that produced me, and this is what is meant by the slogan "Blood of three nations Don Camilo carries in his veins," which bordered the self-portrait that illustrated my article *Camila and Camilo,* which Juan Aparicio published in *El Español.* To be sure, this self-portrait did not appear with Aparicio's article except in part of the magazine's edition; later, something must have happened or someone must have protested, because it was replaced by another drawing, a vignette which bore little relation to the text and which could have equally well been used to accompany some news item on the exploitation of pine resin to illustrate a newspaper serial on Germano-Russian relations during the nineteenth century.

Digging a little deeper into my mother's family history, some French surname or other emerges, euphonious and of good vintage. Lafayette and Château-Laffitte are on the list, but already somewhat distant.

To be tied to several geographies does not seem to me, at least for a writer, at all inconvenient. Some bloods or lineages file down the harshness of others, and the mixture of all of them allows things to be seen with a certain serenity, with the necessary coolness and sufficient perspective.

I, who feel very truly and deeply Spanish, believe that I see and know and love Spain with more common sense than the majority of my Spanish friends. Perhaps this reality is supported by the fact that the mixture of blood is simplicity itself compared to what is foreign, because what is foreign feels familiar and close, quotidian and common, usual and domestic. I do not know. In any case, I am satisfied not being pure-blooded. I do not think there are any purebreds left in the world except for the Bantus, the Zulus, and the pure Aryans, who, if they were not, would manage to believe they were.

I, on the other hand, am happy to think that my blood is a mixture of Galician and English, with a dash of Italian. It seems to me, in order of importance, the second mixture in the world; the first, to my way of thinking, is that of German and Jewish.

My mother came to enlarge the ranks of her complex family on June 23, 1895, at twenty to two in the morning, to be most precise. My mother was number four among her brothers and sisters, three before her and three after. And in course of time, seven would also be the number of her children altogether, all of whom are alive today. Being born into a crowd, in a house, marks the spirit with a trace of independence, a virtue which, if corrupted, ends up in selfishness. The firstborn son, or at least the oldest, is usually fastidious, capricious, authoritarian, lazy, and aesthetic. The second-born cannot help but harbor in his soul a veiled and unconfessable desire for his older brother to be carried off to the other world. The last-born sees things with a certain sadness, somewhat as though borrowed. Only those born in the middle are useful, which is not to say important—clever, which is not to say intelligent, or even less, brilliant—those who in life are never left behind, though neither are we saying they'll necessarily scale the highest peaks.

Importance, inspiration, triumph are the patrimony of fools, of men always in danger of going adrift, of people who walk with one foot in a vacuum, with a strange glow in their expression, a deep hollow in their emotional and embittered hearts. This is the general rule—a rule which, like almost all other rules, has its exceptions.

My mother, in my opinion, is the exception. My mother has an artistic and even literary temperament, with all its extraordinary advantages and all its immense inconveniences. My mother has an aesthetic understanding of life even if, at times, and for complicated reasons difficult to explain, this exactitude comes disguised in the most varied and unsuspected garb.

I think my mother's importance as a woman can be attributed to her strange education. My mother, when she married, did not know how to cook or sew, which I consider an important advantage. The Spanish woman is usually given a partial education, a maid's education. What is called the traditional education of the Spanish woman is one of the last vestiges of slavery. Mothers, at the marriage markets at the beaches, the spas, and summer resorts, when they want to plead the cause of their marriageable daughters to a likely young suitor, say that their daughters know how to cook, iron, wash, sew, dust, etc. Since the likely young suitor is usually a silly fellow with modest ideas, he falls for the bait and gets married. Afterwards, if a remote grain of talent is left to him, he realizes that his wife, so diligent, is sloppy, sly, mean, despotic, uncultured, egotistical, etc. Her parents, who wanted her to be so well educated, created a maid, but not a wife, out of her. Then the signs of disillusion set in, the letdown and the casino for the husband, and resignation, filth, and slippers for the wife.

My mother, who did not know how to cook or sew, raised all her children, ran the house with skill, looked after her husband, and made life comfortable and pleasant for all of us. And not by calculation,

Camilo José with his aunt Ana Trulock Bertorini at Iria-Flavia

certainly, since hers is a passionate and romantic temperament, but rather by intuition, which is the best way.

As is only logical, I do not mean to go to the ridiculous extreme of thinking that a married woman should have the soul of a useless and decorative coquette. This is something that can no doubt have its importance, but not in marriage. My idea is that a married woman should study to be a wife, just as her husband, when young, studied to be a doctor, an architect, or took a degree in chemistry. At the same distance from the starlet as from the maid, a woman, when she gets married, should feel like a wife, which is really the most difficult thing to do. In this, as in so many other things, balance indicates health.

This balance that I refer to is what I always seemed to see in my mother. If I am mistaken, then the gods should forgive my lack of repentance.

My mother had a tumultuous childhood and adolescence. Walking on rooftops, leaping over walls, scaling the cliffs along the coast, throwing stones at neighbors, going down wells, and swimming for hours at a time was the occupation of her first years. Afterwards, when she married, the change was sudden and automatic. In this attitude of my mother I found a clear explanation by observing my sister Maruxa, who, as a single woman, showed an evident mastery in crossing the facade of our house, from one balcony to another, and today, now married, gets vertigo if she looks down at the street from a window a little high up.

The courtship of my parents was a little like a sentimental novel. My father was a friend of my grandfather John Trulock and went often to his house for tea or to have a whisky with him. My mother, who was then a child, did not take part in the visits except for the greetings. It was pre-wartime and things went along with a healthy slowness, an elegant cadence. The first symptom of my father's inclination towards my mother—an inclination, probably, still unsuspected—was, according to my conjectures, to do with a difficult whim of hers, which he resolved with wise gallantry. My mother had taken it into her head to have a burro, and Grandfather, in whose vocabulary the word "no" did not exist, was troubled and wanted to convince his daughter how inappropriate it would be to put a burro in a house without a stable and without any tradition at all of raising burros. My mother persisted, and my father, when he saw his future father-in-law trapped, intervened and conciliated:

"Don't worry, Camila. In a few days you'll have your burro."

My grandfather put his hands to his head in despair, but said nothing. My mother went off happy, and my father ordered a tiny gold donkey from a silversmith in Santiago. It was the first gift my mother had ever had. In the novels of John Galsworthy similar things happen.

My mother led an active youth at a time when Spanish women had not yet even taken off their corsets. The Ría de Arosa was witness to her feats as a swimmer and rower. In the shadow of the Home Fleet, in constant visits to the river, my mother trained herself in the art of staying afloat for hours on end, without tiring, bravely and with good style. Her plan at the time—which she had thought out well and which probably would have been crowned with success—to dive into the sea at Cape Gris-Nez and cross the English Channel, was interrupted by the war and died, in the department of forgotten good intentions, with her marriage.

Harum-scarum times were still alive in her memory: mornings in school, where she was the schoolmate of William Powell—who was the devil himself—days, when for a seventy-*centime* bet she would lower herself to the water level in a ten-meter well; the hours of scaring off praying mantises, which took nine baths a day; the bad moments of pushing the guard on the docks into the water. With the memory of her childhood still fresh in her mind, my mother changed her name from Miss Camila Trulock to the more solemn and binding one of Señora de Cela.

I was the first concrete symptom of this transformation, and I did not arrive in the world at Baden-Baden for the same reason I did not do so in Almería: by a true miracle of God.

My parents honeymooned in Portugal, the only peaceful country there was at hand, and, on the way back to Galicia, they embarked in Vigo on the *Príncipe de Asturias* of the Compañía Pinillos—the ship that months later would sink tragically off the coast of Brazil—in order to sail as far as Almería, where my father was being posted.

The trip was going along placidly, when, at Leixões, opposite Oporto, alarm began to spread among the passengers and crew: around the boat, exactly as in war films, two German submarines were maneuvering. Looking back on it, the joke was not bad.

One of the submarines surfaced and—with a cannon-shot half a hundred meters from the prow—signalled the *Príncipe de Asturias* to halt. The ship stopped and the submarine sent its boarding party aboard.

The Germans inspected the boat from top to bottom and slowly examined everyone's papers. The German officer—cold, correct, and a martinet—conducted a rather unnerving conversation with my father.

"This woman," referring to my mother, "must come with us. She is English and must be taken prisoner."

I suppose my father had a real scare.

"I beg your pardon. This woman is Spanish. She's my wife, and I am Spanish: look at my passport."

The German officer did not bat an eye.

"We have orders to take prisoner all subjects of enemy countries that we encounter. Your wife is a Trulock; the surname is English and the English are our enemies."

"Yes, Trulock is an English surname, no doubt of it. But this woman is Spanish; in European law the wife always takes the nationality of her husband."

The German officer cut the conversation short.

"Pardon me. The lady can take a small overnight case with her. Let's not waste time."

The German officer turned his back on my father and continued reviewing papers. My father approached the captain of the *Príncipe de Asturias.*

"What can I do?"

The captain of the *Príncipe de Asturias* was not a very able talker.

"Well, I don't know. As that officer is set on taking her prisoner, I don't think it's going to turn out very well."

My father was in a quandary. Perhaps thoughts of a dry plain, with its ploughed fields, its mule-drawn carts and springs without water, passed through his head during those moments.

"Yes, you're right."

The captain of the *Príncipe de Asturias* adopted the voice that preaches conformity.

"The English women they take on the high seas go to Baden-Baden, the spa. They're all right there. See if they won't take you with her; at least you'll be together."

The Spanish captain was a practical philosopher, full of resignation and good sense.

"Yes . . . it could be a solution . . ."

The German officer, when he finished the inspection, came up to my father again. He was smoking a cigarette, and in his eyes glowed a remotely tender little light. The man had thought better of it. Germans have a strange and capricious child inside their heads, arbitrary and dreamy, poetic and cruel, rigid and sentimental, all at the same time.

"Is your wife on your passport?"

"No, no, she's not on it. My passport dates from before our wedding . . . We were married a short time ago . . . I didn't bother including her in my passport because we weren't thinking of leaving the peninsula . . . We Spaniards don't need passports for Portugal . . ."

"Good. Your passport, does it have any English or French visas in it?"

"No, none. See for yourself . . ."

"Good. Your wife can stay aboard. I want to believe that everything you're telling me is true."

"Yes, completely."

My father took a deep breath.

My mother, seated on a chaise lounge on the deck, had not gleaned very much. After a while she asked:

"What was that German officer saying?"

"Nothing. He wanted to know if we had passed any English boats."

In Almería, about 1918

My mother watched absent-mindedly as the submarine grew more distant, sailing off on the surface of the water.

"He seemed a correct enough young man, didn't he?"

"Yes, very much so."

There are two kinds of Englishwomen: true Englishwomen, who are rare, romantic, and spiritual, and those who are practical, and they are many, suffragettes and members of animal-protection societies. My mother is a true Englishwoman.

"What a terrible war! Politicians should busy themselves avoiding wars. Wars never bring anything good, isn't that so?"

"No, never . . ."

The trip returned to its monotonous and blessed normality, the passengers calmed down, and it was clear sailing as the *Príncipe de Asturias* continued on its Portuguese route, along the Gulf of Cádiz and the straits. My father went to the bar and ordered a whisky. Then he lit a cigarette. Later he realized his voice was quavering.

But the second fright of the trip awaited him at Gibraltar, at passport control. The English, not to be outdone by the Germans, made just as much trouble and were equally tiresome and distrustful.

My father had a conversation with the English officer very similar to the one he had had with the German officer, the difference being that the latter had a remote shred of reason, while the Englishman had none. The English officer deemed it his duty to consider my mother German and, with his interrogation, was also a considerable nuisance.

From these two incidents I have been able to draw two immediate conclusions: first, that my mother actually does not look either German or English, and by her looks she can confuse any petty naval officer, no matter from what country; and second, that the belligerents of the war of 1914—on both sides—made imaginary shadow guests and saw phantoms where there were not even shadows. In short,

As a boy, 1921

fear is free, and the manifestations of fear are countless, like the sand of the sea.

My mother, as I say, does not look English, although neither does she look German. My mother looks more Scandinavian, or perhaps Russian. In these complicated families, in these families where bloods cross as in a labyrinth, it is not uncommon for the children to come out with features and characters difficult to identify, diverse and even opposed. It is easy to observe what I am saying in my mother's family.

If my mother, superficially, because of her strange ash blond hair, and her delicately blue eyes, looks like a Russian from the best and most decadently refined families, within, with her very complex personality, she is not very different from a Tolstoy heroine. My mother, a woman of great tenderness, an almost pathological tenderness, is also a woman capable of letting herself get carried away by anger, as often as not for no good reason, by an anger bordering on the unhealthy, and the extent of her reactions cannot possibly be predicted.

I, particularly, think that this fluidity of her character, this imbalance, if one likes, is one of her greatest charms. I also feel in myself—with the incalculable force of the tides—this heritage that my mother bequeathed me, this understanding of life through raptures, intuitions, gusts.

My mother is a difficult woman to classify, and all her efforts to become ordinary have always been, luckily, crowned with failure.

My Arrival in the World and My First Few Steps

At nine twenty on the night of May 11, 1916, Thursday, I entered this vale of tears in the house at the railway crossing of Iria-Flavia, the municipal seat of Padrón, diocese of Santiago de Compostela, province of La Coruña, starboard side of the Ría de Arosa, where the Sar and Ulla rivers meet. I was the first child of the several my parents had.

My mother was attended by Don Manuel Carballido, an old country doctor who prescribed infusions of herbs so as not to take any chances, played cards, talked to his horse, and preached conformity.

Seven hundred and twenty-seven years before, the Emperor Barbarossa left the city of Regensburg, on the way to the third crusade.

I was born the descendant of railway men, as I said in previous pages, in my mother's bed as it rumbled with the passage of the train.

Torquato Tasso is three hundred and seventy-two years older than I am.

*Cela paying a visit to Trulock Road, named in honor of his great-grandfather,
London, 1953*

They held a big celebration in my house when I was born; my decision to be born a male and not a female was much feted and with it I scored my first and one of my few family successes. When it comes to cattle it's just the reverse, curiously enough.

A century and a year before, on the same day that Pope Pius VII founded his Noble Guards, Barbudo, the Salamancan bull, killed Pepe Hillo in the Madrid plaza. Goya did a drawing of it.

The beggars, the lovely lame fellows, the noble blind, the funny one-armed chaps, the pleasant cripples, the ostentatious idiots, the tender and silent paralytics, the charming lepers of the vicinity, dined that day on soup with slices of ham.

Sixty-seven years had gone by since Madame Récamier went off to the other world.

I weighed three kilos, six hundred grams.

The year my father, Juan Ramón Jiménez, and Pablo Picasso were born, and the same day and month I was born, Frédéric Amiel died, without putting the final period in his diary. He probably didn't have it in him.

Scarcely two days after being born, I began to die, and from then on, from time to time, I have still given my family a fright. This thing about my health is a little like the story of the wolf, and on the least likely day, I'm really going to die and no one is going to believe me.

Sometimes I leap through the corridors of my house and roar, and climb on the doorjambs, and everyone is used to this. One day, however, I was poisoned by an injection and began to shiver so I couldn't even speak, and my wife, laughing her head off, told me if I didn't keep still, God was going to punish me.

As a result of my first swoon at forty-eight hours of life, as I say, my grandmother, so that I should at least not go to purgatory but to paradise, gave me a dose of sugared, spiked water, and she must have done her job with such zeal that I caught an intestinal infection to match, or more, and without much more ado, I'd have been on my way to the cemetery, which to be sure is quite close to my house, though not as close as my father's in Túy.

Later I thought better of it and did not go to purgatory or to paradise and, for the moment, stayed in Iria. Viewing the event from a distance of forty years, I don't know if, in staying, I was right or wrong; whatever the case may be, it is something that can no longer be remedied. It must be quite nice to be in heaven, that's the truth, and I, at the time, the little angel, would have gone straight to heaven, but . . .

I was baptized when I had recovered a little, in the Colegiata de Santa María la Mayor de Adina, where in times past San Pedro de Mezonzo, the inventor of the *Salve,* was bishop. They gave me enough names: Camilo, for my father and mother and out of family tradition; José, for my godmother and maternal grandmother; Manuel, for my godfa-ther; Juan, for my maternal grandfather; Ramón, like all of my brothers, in honor of San Ramón Nonato, and Francisco de Jerónimo for being one—and the most discreet—of the saints of the day. If I had happened to be born in Palencia or Zamora at this time, I would be named Anastasio, or Evelio, or Antimo, or Basso, or Fabio, or Sisinio, or Dioclecio, or Gangulfo, or Mamerto, or Mayolo, or Iluminado, which are, among others, the saints of the day. I think that if I had come to be named Evelio Cela, I would not have found a publisher for my books. Evelio Cela is a name for a company bugler.

What they did not name me at the baptismal font was Zacarías, or Abraham, or David, all names I have assumed on occasion, as I said, to be a bother, when the Nazis were going about the woeful business of the pure-blooded Aryans. In other places, instead of David I put down Leví; there's pleasure in variety. Some people believed it, which pleased me, because I think that a little confusion is always salubrious. Others did not believe it very much. Now that the Nazis are defeated, the ones causing trouble with gobbledygook about the races are the Yankees and the South Africans. Tomorrow, God willing, will be another day.

I was baptized by Don Victoriano Catoira, an old card-playing priest, and my godparents were my maternal grandmother and my uncle Manolo, my father's brother. If I had wanted to marry either of them, I'd have had to ask for special dispensation. My godfather gave me a silver watch, with my name on the back; it lasted until the Civil War, when it was stolen from me. My godmother gave me a gold medal with the Virgen del Carmen on one side and Santiago Apostle on the other; it lasted until the cow Toxenta ate it, mistaking it perhaps for the wild spikelet of the yellow dyer's-woad herb.

I remember absolutely nothing of that year, neither a little nor a lot, and I think it's a lie when people tell you they're sure they remember their baptism perfectly. Except for prisoners and soldiers, some of whom are baptized at twenty-odd years to better take advantage of the gift—and also the wise advice—of the godfather, who's usually the civil governor, or the colonel, the rest, the run-of-the-mill chaps, who are baptized a few days after birth, we don't even remember the most striking details. Anyone who says he does is lying like a trooper and his words should not be believed.

BIBLIOGRAPHY

Fiction:

La familia de Pascual Duarte. Madrid: Aldecoa, 1942; New York: Appleton-Century-Crofts, 1961; translation by John Marks published as *Pascual Duarte's Family.* London: Eyre & Spottiswoode, 1946; translation by Anthony Kerrigan published as *The Family of Pascual Duarte.* Boston: Little, Brown, 1964; London: Weidenfeld & Nicolson, 1965; translation by Herma Briffault published as *Pascual Duarte and His Family* (bilingual edition). New York: Las Américas, 1965.

Pabellón de reposo (illustrated by Suárez de Árbol). Madrid: Afrodisio Aguado, 1943; translation by Herma Briffault published as *Rest Home* (bilingual edition). New York: Cypress/Las Américas, 1961.

Nuevas andanzas y desventuras de Lazarillo de Tormes. Madrid: La Nave: 1944.

Esas nubes que pasan. Madrid: Afrodisio Aguado, 1945.

El bonito crimen del carabinero, y otras invenciones. Barcelona: José Janes, 1947.

Caminos inciertos: La colmena. Buenos Aires: Emecé, 1951; also published as *La colmena.* Barcelona: Noguer, 1955; translation by J. M. Cohen in consultation with Arturo Barea published as *The Hive.* New York: Farrar, Straus, 1953; London; Gollancz, 1953.

Nuevas andanzas y desventuras de Lazarillo de Tormes, y siete apuntes carpetovetónicos. Madrid, 1952.

Santa Balbina, 37: Gas en cada piso. Melilla, Spain: Mirto y Laurel, 1952.

Timoteo, el incomprendido. Madrid: Rollán, 1952.

Baraja de invenciones. Valencia, Spain: Castalia, 1953.

Café de artistas. Madrid: Tecnos, 1953.

Mrs. Caldwell habla con su hijo. Barcelona: Destino, 1953; translation by Jerome S. Bernstein published as *Mrs. Caldwell Speaks to Her Son.* Ithaca, N.Y.: Cornell University Press, 1968.

Historias de Venezuela: La catira (illustrated by Ricardo Arenys). Barcelona: Noguer, 1955; also published as *La catira.* Barcelona: Noguer, 1966.

El molino de viento, y otras novelas cortas (illustrated by Lorenzo Goñi; includes *El molino de viento; Timoteo, el incomprendido; Café de artistas;* and *Santa Balbina, 37: Gas en cada piso*). Barcelona: Noguer, 1956.

Mis páginas preferidas (selections). Madrid: Gredos, 1956.

Historias de España: Los ciegos, los tontos (illustrated by Manuel Mampaso). Madrid: Arión, 1957; expanded edition published as *A la pata de palo.* Vol. 1: *Historias de España* (illustrated by Lorenzo Goñi). Madrid: Alfaguara, 1965.

Nuevo retablo de don Cristobita: Invenciones, figuraciones y alucinaciones (includes *Esas nubes que pasan, El bonito crimen del carabinero,* and part of *Baraja de invenciones*). Barcelona: Destino, 1957.

Los viejos amigos (illustrated by José María Prim). 2 vols. Barcelona: Noguer, 1960–61.

Gavilla de fábulas sin amor (illustrated by Pablo Picasso). Palma de Mallorca: Papeles de Son Armadans, 1962.

Obra completa. 14 vols. Barcelona: Destino, 1962–83.

Tobogán de hambrientos (illustrated by Lorenzo Goñi). Barcelona: Noguer, 1962.

Las compañías convenientes y otros fingimientos y cegueras. Barcelona: Destino, 1963.

Once cuentos de fútbol (illustrated with eleven paintings of Pepe). Madrid: Nacional, 1963.

Toreo de salón: Farsa con acompañamiento de clamor y murga (photographs by Oriol Maspons and Julio Ubiña). Barcelona: Lumen, 1963.

Izas, rabizas y colipoterras: Drama con acompañamiento de cachondeo y dolor de corazón (photographs by Juan Colom). Barcelona: Lumen, 1964.

A la pata de palo: Florilegio de carpetovetonismos y otras lindezas de C.J.C. y su amigo Lorenzo Goñi, el Sordico. (illustrated by Lorenzo Goñi). Vol. 1: *Historias de España.* Madrid: Alfaguara, 1965; vol. 2: *La familia del héroe; o, Discurso histórico de los últimos restos; ejercicios para una sola mano.* Madrid: Alfaguara, 1965; vol. 3: *El ciudadano Iscariote Reclús.* Madrid: Alfaguara, 1965; vol. 4: *Viaje a U.S.A.: o, El que la signe la mata.* Madrid: Alfaguara, 1967; published in one volume as *El tacatá oxidado: Florilegio de carpetovetonismos y otras lindezas.* Barcelona: Noguer, 1973.

Nuevas escenas matritenses (photographs by Enrique Palazuela). 7 vols. Madrid: Alfaguara, 1965–66; published in one volume as *Fotografías al minuto.* Madrid: Organización Sala, 1972.

Antología. Madrid: Coculsa, 1968.

La bandada de palomas (for children; illustrated by José Correas Flores). Barcelona: Labor, 1969.

Café de artistas y otros cuentos. Zaragoza, Spain: Salvat/Alianza, 1969.

Vísperas, festividad y octava de San Camilo del año 1936 en Madrid. Madrid: Alfaguara, 1969.

Timoteo el incomprendido y otros papeles ibericos. Madrid: Magisterio Español, 1970.

Obras selectas (includes *La familia de Pascual Duarte; Viaje a la Alcarria; La colmena; Mrs. Caldwell habla con su hijo; Izas, rabizas y colipoterras;* and *El carro de heno; o, El inventor de la guillotina*). Madrid: Alfaguara, 1971.

Oficio de tinieblas 5; o, Novela de tesis escrita para ser cantada por un coro de enfermos. Barcelona: Noguer, 1973.

Cuentos para leer después del baño. Barcelona: La Gaya Ciencia, 1974.

Prosa (selections), edited by Jacinto-Luis Guereña. Madrid: Narcea, 1974.

Rol de cornudos. Barcelona: Noguer, 1976.

Café de artistas y otros papeles volanderos. Madrid: Alce, 1978.

El espejo y otros cuentos. Madrid: Espasa-Calpe, 1981.

Mazurca para dos muertos. Barcelona: Seix Barral, 1983; Hanover, N.H.: Ediciones del Norte, 1983.

Cristo versus Arizona. Barcelona: Seix Barral, 1988.

Nonfiction:

Mesa revuelta (essays). Madrid: Ediciones de los Estudiantes Españoles, 1945; expanded edition (includes text of *Ensueños y figuraciones*). Madrid: Taurus, 1957.

San Juan de la Cruz, under pseudonym Matilde Verdu. Madrid, 1948.

El gallego y su cuadrilla y otros apuntes carpetovetónicos. Madrid: Ricardo Aguilera, 1949.

Ensueños y figuraciones. Barcelona: Ediciones G.P., 1954; also published as part of *Mesa revuelta*. Madrid: Taurus, 1957.

La rueda de los ocios. Barcelona: Mateu, 1957.

La obra literaria del pintor Solana: Discurso leído ante la Real Academia Española el día 26 de mayo de 1957 en su recepción pública por el Excmo. Sr. D. Camilo José Cela y contestación del Excmo. Sr. D. Gregorio Marañón. Madrid: Papeles de Son Armadans, 1957.

Cajón de sastre (articles). Madrid: Cid, 1957.

Recuerdo de don Pío Baroja (illustrated by Eduardo Vicente). Mexico City: De Andrea, 1958.

La cucaña: Memorias. Barcelona: Destino, 1959; portion reprinted as *La Rosa*. Barcelona: Destino, 1979.

Cuatro figuras del 98: Unamuno, Valle Inclán, Baroja, Azorín, y otros retratos y ensayos españoles. Barcelona: Aedos, 1961.

El solitario: Los sueños de Quesada (illustrated commentary on the art of Rafael Zabaleta). Palma de Mallorca: Papeles de Son Armadans, 1963.

Garito de hospicianos; o, Guirigay de imposturas y bambollas (articles). Barcelona: Noguer, 1963.

Xam (illustrated commentary on the art of Pedro Quetglas Ferrer), with Cesáreo Rodríguez Aguilera. Palma de Mallorca: Daedalus, 1966.

Diccionario secreto. Vol. 1: Madrid: Alfaguara, 1968; vol. 2: Madrid: Alfaguara, 1972.

Al servicio de algo. Madrid: Alfaguara, 1969.

La bola del mundo: Escenas cotidianas. Madrid: Organización Sala, 1972.

A vueltas con España. Madrid: Seminarios y Ediciones, 1973.

Cristina Mallo (monograph). Madrid: Theo, 1973.

Crónica del cipote de Archidona, with Alfonso Canales (illustrated by Lorenzo Goñi). Madrid: Gisa, D.L., 1977; first published as *La insólita y gloriosa hazaña del cipote de Archidona*.

Enciclopedia de erotismo. Madrid: D. L. Sedmay, 1977.

Los sueños vanos, los ángeles curiosos. Barcelona: Argos Vergara, 1979.

Los vasos comunicantes. Barcelona: Bruguera, 1981.

Vuelta de hoja. Barcelona: Destino, 1981.

Album de taller (illustrated commentary on the art of José María Subirachs). Barcelona: Ambit, 1981.

El juego de los tres madroños. Barcelona: Destino, 1983.

El asno de Buridán (articles). Madrid: El País, 1986.

Travel:

Las botas de siete leguas: Viaje a la Alcarria, con los versos de su cancionero, cada uno en su debido lugar. Madrid: Revista de Occidente, 1948; also published as *Viaje a la Alcarria*. Palma de Mallorca: Papeles de Son Armadans, 1958; London: Harrap, 1961; translation by Frances M. López-Morillas published as *Journey to the Alcarria*. Madison: University of Wisconsin Press, 1964.

Avila. Barcelona: Noguer, 1952; translation by John Forrester published under the same title (photographs by Eugene Haas). Barcelona: Noguer, 1956.

Del Miño al Bidasoa: Notas de un vagabundaje. Barcelona: Noguer, 1952.

Vagabundo por Castilla (illustrated by Marcos Aleu). Barcelona: Seix Barral, 1955.

Judíos, moros y cristianos: Notas de un vagabundaje por Avila, Segovia y sus tierras. Barcelona: Destino, 1956.

Cuaderno del Guadarrama (illustrated by Eduardo Vicente). Madrid: Arión, 1959.

Primer viaje andaluz: Notas de un vagabundaje por Jaén, Córdoba, Sevilla, Huelva y sus tierras (illustrated by José Hurtuna). Barcelona: Noguer, 1959.

Páginas de geografía errabunda. Madrid: Alfaguara, 1965.

Viaje al Pirineo de Lérida: Notas de un paseo a pie por el Pallars Sobirà, el Valle de Arán y el Condado de Ribagorza. Madrid: Alfaguara, 1965.

Calidoscopio callejero, marítimo y campestre de C.J.C. para el reino y ultramar. Madrid: Alfaguara, 1966.

Madrid (illustrated by Juan Esplandíu). Madrid: Alfaguara, 1966.

Barcelona (illustrated by Federico Lloveras). Madrid: Alfaguara, 1970.

La Mancha en el corazón y en los ojos. Barcelona: EDISVEN, 1971.

Balada del vagabundo sin suerte y otros papeles volanderos. Madrid: Espasa-Calpe, 1973.

Madrid, color y silueta (illustrated with watercolors by Estrada Vilarrasa). Sabadell, Spain: AUSA, 1985.

Nuevo viaje a la Alcarria. 3 vols. Madrid: Información y Revistas, 1986.

Poetry:

Pisando la dudosa luz del día: Poemas de una adolescencia cruel. Barcelona: Zodíaco, 1945; Barcelona: Seix Barral, 1960.

Dos romances de ciego. Málaga, Spain: Libraría Anticuaria El Guadalhorce, 1966.

María Sabina. Madrid: Papeles de Son Armadans, 1967; second edition published bound with *El carro de heno; o, El inventor de la guillotina.* Madrid: Alfaguara, 1970.

Poesia y cancioneros. Madrid, 1968.

Plays:

Homenaje al Bosco, I: El carro de heno; o, El inventor de la guillotina. Palma de Mallorca: Papeles de Son Armadans, 1969; published bound with *María Sabina* as *María Sabina* [and] *El carro de heno; o, El inventor de la guillotina.* Madrid: Alfaguara, 1970.

Editor of:

Homenaje y recuerdo a Gregorio Marañón (1887–1960). Madrid: Papeles de Son Armadans, 1961.

La Celestina, puesta respetuosamente en castellano moderno por Camilo José Cela quien añadio muy poco y quitó aún menos (original by Fernando de Rojas). Barcelona: Destino, 1979.

El Quijote, by Miguel de Cervantes Saavedra. Alicante, Spain: Ediciones Rembrandt, 1981.

Robert Creeley

1926-

I've spent all my life with a nagging sense I had somehow the responsibility of that curious fact, that is, a substantial *life*, like a dog, but hardly as pleasant, to be dealt with no matter one could or couldn't, wanted to or not. This must be what's thought of as Puritanism, a curious split between the physical fact of a person and that thing they otherwise think with, or about, the so-called mind. I kept thinking of possible qualifications therefore, like Duchamp's "Besides, it's always the others who die . . . ," or Wittgenstein's "Tell them it's been wonderful . . ." Even Beethoven's "More light!" seemed a fit echo of what was, presumably, a decent wish to stay with it.

Anyhow I have no reifying memories that tell me this is where I was then and there. They are far more echoes, that came or come to me, a sense of shadow, or the comforting poignancy of old affections. "A cigarette that bears a lipstick's traces . . . ," like they say. Charles Olson had told me years ago that the first imagined sign for *self* in such language as had record was a boat, and that made an adamant if harsh sense—much as Noah's Ark did. The great flood of seeming chaos had only one apparent agency for its signifying order, and that was oneself, that verifying agency without equal, because it was the one and only one for each of us. "Mine eyes have seen the glory, etc." Who could argue with that?

Now it is attractive to suspend a life as an afterthought, a well-earned pleasure of discretion and justifiable revision, just that one has lived long enough to see the time precedent as a cause of the present, a reward, as it were, for having lived long enough to know the value of such fact. One of the songs I can remember my family having, on a player-piano roll as I recall, was "Ah, sweet mystery of life, at last I've found you . . ." But it would be truly a fool who presumed any life to be simple consequence, or earned, or understood. It is the pleasure and authority of writing that it invents a life to live in the first place—as Walt Whitman so made one, or Daniel Defoe, or Samuel Beckett.

My father, a doctor working in the Boston area, having moved us all out to West Acton, Massachu-

Robert Creeley with his father, Oscar Slade Creeley, Watertown, Massachusetts, 1928

setts, died in the early spring of 1930, when I was four. I have very faint memories of him—certain smells of tobacco, whiskey highballs, a curious scale I can never quite identify nor relate as a specific measure. Many years later the son of a close friend of his, who'd been named Creeley Buchanan and was a few years older than my sister and I, told us my father's voice and intonation were very like the actor Pat O'Brien's. The emphasis was on a dry wit, a male, reflective confidence, a quick humor. My mother had told me he could keep attention for hours on end and gave as one instance the night he'd not come home till morning, having talked all through it to his patient. Because I didn't know him, I wondered if he might have been fooling her.

But there were nonetheless echoes no other fact of the family had. For example, there was a little street, "Creeley Road," in Belmont, and in the Mount Auburn Cemetery in Watertown there was the Creeley family lot with its predominant Lauries close to the Bowditch lot, a patent of some sort, however specious. My mother's family were, in contrast, poor relations and had come to Massachusetts from Stonington, Deer Isle, Maine, when their luck there was exhausted and the young still dependent. My mother told a story of working as an all-service maid, when still a teenager, in the household of an invalid woman, and of how she had been impressed that the nurse would eat with the family, whereas she was served in the kitchen. It was that fact, so she said, which determined her to become a nurse, which she did and which was her primary identity for me in every way as her son.

My father's death must have been bitterly hard for her. Not only did she lose his literal company and the income he managed as a successful doctor, but she was left with property she had little sense of how to deal with. He had invested heavily in a clinic, and all its equipment was sold for the proverbial song within a year. Our house in Acton was very attractive but huge and impractical to heat. We had an old coal furnace the women, now entirely the resource, struggled over all winter. I remember their trying to mow the vast lawns as well, with an archetypal power mower that, once started, simply shot forward till shut off again. Turning corners with it was an act of great skill and strength. It was cause of my grandfather's death from a heart attack in one real way. Watching the women trying to work with it, he became so exasperated that he finally took it away from them one day, and so was hauled along himself, in his mid-eighties, the one-time-cabin-boy-to-second-mate of the last Yankee clipper out of Maine to the Far East, laid low by a lawn mower. I remember his swearing behind the closed door of the bedroom after the doctor had come out with my grandmother.

Both my mother's parents lived with us until they died, another responsibility, as was Teresa Turner, a maid of my father's time whom he had befriended when he found her shocked in a home for the mentally retarded, to which she'd been sent by the immigration authorities. She became our housekeeper, and my mother used to say that the salary she'd been given on Friday was all borrowed back again by Monday. Teresa was particularly dear to me and indulged me, the boy, with awkward and

consistent devotion even past my adolescence. Sometime in my early teens I suddenly realized I could utterly baffle her with verbal constructs or numbers, and had that sick, sad recognition of power. It wasn't a fair world that made such people so brutally vulnerable.

In any case, my sister's memories of our father are very different because she could actually remember him whereas I could not, and she had known that time of our family's affluence, with maids and a chauffeur, big houses and cars, and a sense of significant authority. No doubt my curious "poor boy" insistences have been fostered far more by this echo than they have been by any factual want. Once, visiting in Hull a graduate seminar of Geoffrey Moore's, I was displaced to hear him tell the company I had a typical middle-class education and was, in some respects, an instance thereof. He was quite right. I went to a boarding school and then to Harvard, both certainly exceptional provisions for the time and place, and all the more so for someone coming from a small country town in the New England of the thirties. Still I seem to have grown up with an immense sense of my family's particular limits, and it is my luck that has gained me the possibilities I've had, far more than either my company's provision or my own inherent abilities.

Two instances can make the point clear. When two, seated on the lap of a nurse on the front seat of the car beside my father as he drove through the city of Boston on some errand or other, I was showered with broken glass full in the face when a stray lump of coal shattered the side window. Again I recall nothing of it, and perversely the year that followed must have been a very happy one because I was not allowed to cry for fear of causing the affected left eye further damage. For some time, then, the eye was left in place although it seems to have had little function. It began to grow larger, however, and so, when I was five, just a year after my father's death, the eye was taken out. That I do remember because my mother had told me we were to go to the hospital on some routine business of her own, and once there, she suggested I wait inside, which was common enough. But from there I was taken to the doctor, and so on and so forth, till I came to with a great bandage covering my head and the eye gone. I so wish she had told me, although I rationally understand why she did not, and why also she had not made clear to us our father wasn't coming back after we saw him taken away in the ambulance across our front lawn in the snow. We knew nothing of the funeral, or let me speak for myself. Those tracks fading in the spring thaws mark for me the end of that previous time entirely.

But it is luck, which was the point, and the paradoxical fact that this death and injury had a curious consequence. The company employing the person responsible for the careless shovelful of coal paid damages of some nine thousand dollars, enough to see me through college, toward which I'd been determinedly propelled by my mother's sense of duty to the memory of my father. Neither of my elder half-brothers had gone but neither seemingly wanted to. Our side of the family, which had no such advanced education as immediate habit, valued it far more.

So, as luck would have it, I did get to college, although I fled it in the last half of my senior year, some meager credits short of a degree. Luck had got me to prep school by way of my sister's having a friend at Northfield, to which she went in her senior year, whose brother was at Holderness. The girls thought it would be charming if both brothers were to be at the same school, as they were. My sister secured applications, prodded my mother to arrange for scholarship tests, and shortly thereafter I was admitted with substantial financial provision and was allowed to bring my pigeons with me. A sports coat, as they were called, bought at Grover Cronin's in Waltham, shed its simulated-leather buttons on first cleaning, and my glass eye took getting used to in the new environment. But it was during those years I learned more expansively and intensively than ever before or since, and I have only luck, and my immensely dear sister's imagination, to thank for any of it.

Whatever is presumed of a life that designs it as a fixture of social intent, or form of family, or the effect of an overwhelming event, has little bearing here, even if one might in comfortable hindsight say that it all followed. What else was, in any case, possible? As living, each moment seemed to me utterly impossible to anticipate. Physical love was such—so immensely sweet a human pleasure, who could claim it as determined? Was I simply to follow it forever? That first effortless, ancient depth of feeling, so wisely knowing in such confused participants—it was luck again that got me through all the hostile misunderstanding and distortion of that time,

With maternal grandfather, Ira Jules, West Acton, Massachusetts, 1930

Mother, Genevieve Jules Creeley, with Robert and his sister Helen, West Acton, 1934

even to the man in the black suit appearing out of nowhere to demand that I "take that girl home," on Belmont Hill as it happened.

I have far more a sense of comfortable wandering, as momently bearings were lost or discarded, and the world occurred with intense particularity. It seems sad that so often the recognition of such presence has to be fact of some overwhelming crisis or despair. I don't know that I had the least intent to be so at sea. My sense of apparent order is irritatingly, almost obsessively neat, so that my very young children often followed me about picking bits of lint off the carpet, "just like Daddy." Both my sister Helen and I had been given, somewhere back there, a habit of cleaning surfaces, tabletops, counters, floors, anyplace that accumulates expectable bits and pieces of whatever. Each of us tidies incessantly, and I have been known to dump an ashtray just after someone had flicked an ash into it. Yet I could eat off the floor, or finish someone's plate, or wear soiled clothes without concern. But I must have the feel of clean hands, or hair, and recall a long bus trip of years ago whereon I began, it seemed to me, almost to mutate into the filth and odor of myself.

Possibly because of those sudden losses spoken of, my childhood is more a fact of places now than a sense of changing progression. My own favorite was

Four Winds Farm, which is where our father had left us and where too I knew my grandfather, who saved me at least from some confusions of maleness. Best were the woods well back of the barn that we'd go off into, with the sense one could go for miles and miles—"all the way to Canada!"—without being bothered by adamant, boxed-in people. There we kids played endless patterns of Robin Hood (my friend Harry Scribner would be Robin—I was Will Scarlet), and occasionally Tarzan. One time my cousin Laurie, two years older and living then in Stow with my younger cousin Barbara, Uncle Hap, and Aunt Vera (who had come exotically from near Marlborough and was Scandinavian), took my stocking cap right off my head with a spear we commonly fashioned from sumac, alders, or willows. We figured it as consummate marksmanship rather than imminent disaster.

School was two grades to a room, and my mother was the school nurse by the time I got there. Miss Dickenson was a sharp, specific teacher of the third and fourth grades, was it? Miss Allard, bosomy and young, taught the primary ones. Then Miss Suhusky prepared us for the shift to junior high and the further world. Just across from the school was a great, steep hill for sliding. I went into a tree at the bottom once without too much damage and walked home. There was much in that way one got up from, like Luxy Davis sticking a pitchfork tine through his palm while playing in our barn. Soak it in hot water and Lysol, and bandage it up. Infections were insistent, I remember, and sulfa drugs finally helped with them, thank god. Things were always draining, or about to. We fished a lot, got hooks caught in fingers, cut ourselves with jackknives, hatchets, sticks more generally. Splinters were a persistent curse and I think it was Harry again who managed to slide one up under much of the palm of his hand, so that it had to be cut out. I was fascinated by the hands of elder men, with those scarred knuckles, broken nails, sometimes a finger or more missing altogether. These were farmers and there were so many ways to get caught in that occupation, despite care and competence.

For some time it was my intent to become a veterinarian when I finished school. Probably it was the echo of that initial place though even with my own childhood it seemed to be changing. Still then it was a much more ingenuous and rooted place than it seems to have become. One could skate from West Acton to South Acton on Teel's Brook, having to hop occasionally over branches and whatnot that crossed its small width in places but nonetheless getting there, to end in broad millpond by the railroad bridge. We swam in Teel's Brook in the summer, a comfortable collection of boys and the men who came down after work to rinse off the sweat and hayseed. We contrived mud slides so as to end in a great splash, raced and wrestled, picked off abundant bloodsuckers and watched for the reported water moccasins, whose bite, we believed, would kill us in seconds. We rehearsed, though not literally, the procedure of making a slash by the bite and sucking out the poison. It sounds awful even now—like sliding down a razor blade on your heels, another childhood proposal we used to scare ourselves. A friend's father showed us how to make willow whistles and a more enduring kind from short lengths of copper or lead pipe we'd cut into with a hacksaw, to make the notch, then plug partially with wood at one end. I recall there being endless things to learn and do of that kind, slingshots, huts (as we called them) in the woods, traps, and a great proliferating lore of rituals and locations, paths through the woods, secret signs, provisions for all manner of imagined possibility including at one point the attempt to make a glider out of bed sheets and poles tied together.

So it's probable that what I most wanted was a world, if not of that kind, at least of that place. And while I could not emulate my dead father by becoming a doctor—the thought of being thus responsible for people's lives was terrifying to me—I could be a doctor of sorts for far more tractable and patient beasts.

The year I graduated from school it all got sidetracked by a creeping sophistication, to be sure, gained from the diversity of other boys at Holderness and also the elders' sense of a far more various occupation of people's intelligence than had been the case in Acton. It wasn't better or worse. It was simply different, as such things are forever. Years later I had friends in North Lisbon, New Hampshire, who, some of them, had been no more than twenty-five miles from where they were born. One neighbor went away to war, the South Pacific, and on return simply settled in again as though he had never been gone. One time I asked his brother to come with me to Cambridge, where my mother then lived, a drive of some three or four hours. But he chose not to, saying, "I don't know anybody there." It seemed to him absurd to go where one had no relationships.

Whatever prompted me, I think I must have begun moving about the age of fourteen, first to that school, which changed all my sense of things, and

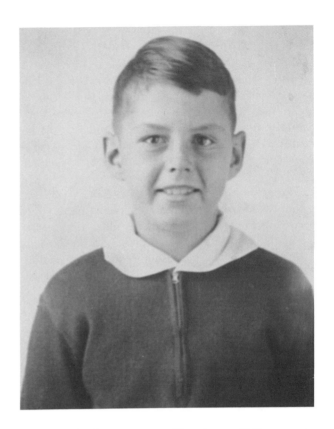

Creeley at age ten, West Acton, 1936

then increasingly as I discovered there was, as Thomas Wolfe had said, no returning. A few years ago I counted over forty houses on just one side of the road between the house we then lived in till I was ten and the neighboring farmer's, the Lockes', down the way. Across the road, over the field, to the swimming hole—my mother would say, "If there's no one there, come home!"—there is now a large middle school, as they are called, and no trace of the farming is much left at all. Two summers ago, driving through the town with my friend Warren Tallman and slowing to point out this or that place, I soon realized from blasts of horns and cars gunning past me that my world, if that's what it ever was, was altogether gone. The railroad station and the trains, so specific a place then, even Mac's Garage a block back of it, aren't there anymore and haven't been for years. I went into the Acton Center Library, where our mother would take us Saturdays to get books, and, on impulse, checked out the card catalog to see if by any chance a book of mine might be there. All I managed was to spill the cards all over the floor. "Horseman, pass by!"

When finally I got to college, I came by way of Northeast Harbor, Maine, where my mother had taken the job of Red Cross nurse to be closer to my sister Helen, whose first husband, Arthur Reynolds, came from there, person of a classic old-time Maine family. His aunt had lost the fingers of both hands in a mangle but raised a substantial family no matter. They were tough people and had obvious questions about the outlander married to their significant son, who was an extremely sweet man. He had already wandered far afield, by studying philosophy at the University of Maine but even more so by becoming a middleweight boxer, billed as the Mad Greek. He made it all the way to the Boston Gardens with his classic but increasingly vulnerable profile. The young couple had been married in the West Acton Baptist Church, which was our place of worship, as they say, and for a time lived with us in the Willow Street house. There was a great moment when I had first experimented with drinking by going with three friends to a remote river bank whose location now escapes me. Was it the Concord River in some imagination of our significant endeavor? In any case, we drank quickly several quarts of Ballantine's Ale, all we could hold, and several of us vomited then and there. Now it was time to go home but the alcohol was just beginning to work. When I came staggering into our house, thankfully I was spotted by my brother-in-law who deftly got me out of there, into the car, and off to some back road where he had me trot as best I could after the car until I was back together. It was a delight, even drunk, to be object of his amused and resourceful affection.

Clearly what I needed, and probably still do, was a sense of what constitutes manhood. I have three sons who can speak for themselves, finally, as to how capable as a father I proved for them. It was certainly a broken trip very often, even with years of separation in two relationships. But I feel confident nonetheless. Being a man myself, as one says, has proven something quite otherwise.

The years of college, broken by the war and the endless shifting of our company, were still an immensely valuable time. And why shouldn't they be, I suppose. Yet with very few exceptions I can think of little taught me in the fact of courses. F. O. Matthiessen, Harry Levin, Kenneth Murdoch, and Werner Jaeger—with a care indeed for Douglas Bush though he never persuaded me of Milton—and that about does it, though one, Fred McCreary, a writer turned teacher whose daughter Phoebe was a brilliant, beautiful young woman I must have had

chance to talk to only a very few times, was the one most crucial. He taught an English A course for students unable to bypass it by scoring well on the qualifying test, and one day well into the term he asked that I see him after class. I was expectably scared, confused that I might dumbly have done something wrong not knowing it. When all the others had left, he spoke to me quite sternly, asking if I had thought of what I might like to do after college. It seemed an ironic emphasis upon my uselessness in all respects, but I answered that I hoped to be a writer. He answered that if I kept at it long enough, I just might make it—or words to that effect. It was the only literal encouragement of that kind I ever got at Harvard, but it was enough.

Reading some time ago of the various character of Harvard, Yale, and Stanford, I was struck by the point that it was the peer group that made Harvard effective educationally, the literal company one kept. For me that was very much the case, and the relationships, in no clubby sense, often continued for life. It was there I first met Alison Lurie, John Hawkes, Kenneth Koch, and Willy Gaddis—and Seymour Lawrence and Bubsy Zimmerman, as Barbara Epstein was then known. Musicians were crucial and very close friends—Buddy Berlin, Race Newton, and Joe Leach. It was Buddy and Race who first played me Charlie Parker, and Joe had come from Detroit and Wayne State, a transfer student, and actually knew Milt Jackson, Howie McGhee, and many more. There was a note in *Downbeat* to announce his arrival in Boston.

Academically I floundered at Harvard, or so I felt. My eager thirst for knowledge, almost Jude-the-Obscurian in its innocence, was all but shut down by the sardonic stance of my elders. It was Andrew Wanning, for example, who began a second lecture on Wallace Stevens's poetry with a remark I *think* I will never forget: "The only thing I can find to say about the later poetry of Wallace Stevens is that it is very obscure." He then played us a record of Stevens reading. Even Matthiessen was a disappointment, finding the work of Pound too ugly politically and beyond his comprehension in its structure. He let me give a paper on Hart Crane but it was a lost cause instantly I opened my mouth. In depressing contrast, Richard Wilbur was a graduate student in that same class and gave a brilliant exegesis, as they say, of Marianne Moore's nifty poem "See in the Midst of Fair Leaves and Much Fruit the Swan . . ." I must have seen him again at least twenty years later and instantly asked him if she'd ever seen his terrific analysis. He told me he had sent her a copy, shyly, in respect. Next question was obvious: *what* did she answer? To which he replied, she said she didn't understand it. Wow!

The American sense of education as the filling of a vessel otherwise empty is probably the confusion I, as many others, was facing, both with my teachers and in myself. I expected to be taught but whether manners, taste, sophistication, or simply how specifically to do something was never clear to me. I didn't, as one says, know what I wanted to do, despite the hope to be a writer, because I didn't have the faintest sense of who or what a writer was. A classmate, Craig Gilbert, took the classic pose of Hemingway, or tried to, trench coat, hat, the bottle of bourbon. It was a very impressive attempt. Then there was the character in one of Huxley's novels who did act in every respect the writer so therefore felt no need to *write* anything. Later Olson quoted the remark of someone apropos the aggressively sexual conduct of some man on the beach with his patient girl. "Getting experience for his nuvvel?" I know I read a lot of writers writing about writing, not really those who were suggesting procedures as those who were bearing witness to their own significant states of mind. Andre Gide's *Journals* were heroic instance, and I think I read all three volumes as they appeared.

But the writer who most delighted and saved me was Stendhal, the pronunciation of whose name I still can't manage comfortably. His extraordinary self-perception—at least the *person* he so presents—is very attractive. His characters are seen with such intimate clarity and yet they are as objective as statistics or phone numbers. Just so, there is a shot in a Fellini film taken from a helicopter flying over a city. The people, sunning on the roofs, look up, waving, and one sees them from the perspective of the pilot, specific, yet passing and painfully small.

As a parallel instance of sorts, I recall one night in Placitas, New Mexico. Restless, I had stepped just outside the door of our living room into a small courtyard. It must have been fall because there was a sharp odor of burning piñon in the air, and it was one of those magnificent sharp, dry, immensely clear and star-filled nights. Just back of me in the room there was a bleak argument going on, the rehearsal of a very painful and blocked sense of relation, a classic human debate which can never end except in exhaustion. But outside, less than ten feet away, was such a vast and inhuman place, so indifferent to those almost insectlike flailings I'd left. About a mile distant, up into the canyon, there was a cave which dated human habitation here some thirty thousand years into the past. All around us were the fossils

from a sea which had been here long before that, fish, shells, timeless. The Hopi say, "First came the Navajo, and then the white man." We are a curious fact.

But it's not a diminution of humanness I wish to make, rather a scale for its diverse presence. In all of Stendhal's work there is a lovely measure in such sense, of the significance of actions and of persons, neither sneering nor enlarging. All that would matter to me, finally, as a writer, is that the scale and the place of our common living be recognized, that the mundane in that simple emphasis be acknowledged. Wendell Berry one time said there were two premises people almost always used in their thinking that really terrified him. One was that they knew what was good for themselves, and the other, that what was good for people was good for all other worlds pertaining. At times our life seems much as if we lived in a terrarium, which we somehow ourselves have got to take care of.

Another friend, John Chamberlain, had a wry qualification apropos babies, i.e., the most complicated artifact possible made by the least-skilled labor. One hardly knows what one's doing, like they say. My own first experience was a terror that I'd drop it, and I felt no capability at all to be a father. I hardly managed as a husband, if I did. When David, my first child, was being born in the hospital in Hyannis, Massachusetts, I kept pestering the nurse at reception for news of my wife's progress. Her humiliating answer was, "Wife? Wife? You're too young to have a wife, much less a baby!" I was twenty-one and our being on the Cape was consequence of our friendship with (William) Slater Brown, whom I'd met in Cambridge at (the now-gone) McBride's, a tavern right in the square used mostly by the noncollege people. I'd gone in to get away from the usual company, and also to drink, and found myself at the far end of the crowded bar with just one older man at the wall beyond me. It was Slater. As we talked, he asked me my interests as a student, and then, as I made clear my reading and hopes to write, he told me in a way I can't now recall, but it must have been decisively self-effacing, that he was the character "B" in Cummings's *The Enormous Room*.

Amazing that one might meet, that casually, a person so curiously present in two such decisive places—as if he'd stepped from the literal book itself. When he also said he knew Hart Crane, I felt very much like running because it all seemed such a fragile and vulnerable possession, that I should so simply meet someone so significant to my own life's need. I guess I love Thomas Hardy because he had such a dogged determination of the world's scale, its presences, an architecture as real as any other he gave attention. Heroes, as they say, are not simply grandiose pretentions of person nor echoes of some lost measure only. They are the imagined possibility of whatever makes the potential of a life seem just that—what Kitaj recalls cannily in his echo of Pound in the series of three prints *A Site*: "working on the life vouchsafed." How one discovers that "material" is what so-called "heroes" can provide means to know, else reflect as sun on water.

So Slater led me, in a specific way, not only to the Cape but to an increasingly distinct life from that determined by the academic. I recall our going in to see Matthiessen, whom he knew, and my recognizing from that secular vantage of my company the professor's curious absence from the terms of world I most valued, but had least means then to know. It's ironic that so much of my own life has been spent teaching, uneasily, I suppose, but certainly with commitment. I had no intention, nor training, to be a teacher at all. After the brief time at Black Mountain College in the early fifties, I'd assumed those days were over.

In any case, my life felt a shambles. The marriage, after a year on the Cape, then three in New Hampshire, then France and Spain, had collapsed as I myself did, following the revelation, I want to say, which Black Mountain meant for me, and the parallel recognition of that previous world I had otherwise thought to hide in. It neither would nor could work any longer and my wife fled for her own survival, angered to this day I had seemingly proved so little competent or faithful. In the last days, or hours, I remember asking her what it was she did so want, and her answer, *to be right*. In that, of course, I could have no part at all. So I headed west from North Carolina, on a Trailways bus, to Albuquerque where friends from college had settled. I remember getting into the bus station and being met by Race Newton, driven up to Imported Motors, our friends Buddy and Mary Ann's business selling Volkswagens on Central, and then out, in a old, white, boatlike Jaguar with open top, across the river to the west mesa, and off on a side road, then a dirt one, into a box canyon, where, with immense blue sky overhead and no end to all that arching space, we stopped. I

At Rock Pool Farm with wife Ann and son David, Lisbon, New Hampshire, 1949

said some classic American thing like, where are we. His answer, far more memorable, was, *here.*

What one might now say is that years and years went by, almost overnight. Ed Dorn, first met in Black Mountain and continuingly a measure for all I'd value as poetry or person, thought for some years that I'd one day write a narrative of that place, the Southwest. It's inextricably part of my head, like they say, and was a rite of passage even more significant than Black Mountain. It was in Albuquerque that I finally faced unequivocally first terms of my own life, its need for love, dignity, consequence, and responsibility, all equally.

I fell in love again. We thought to marry, and had got a marriage license, but when it came the literal time, neither of us believed in it enough to go through it again. So we made a commitment to stay together for as long as it felt specific, some fact of love. It was probably a far more secular agreement than a society can finally accommodate because it so depends on singular choice. It can be brutal to those related certainly, thoughtful as it may feel itself to be. Children can hardly know why people start hating one another, and the old have no further

choices. We stayed together for twenty years, and whatever it came to mean, beyond our vulnerable and extraordinary children, the poignance of its clarity often and the risks it could survive seem as much as a life can think to depend upon, despite it isn't enough.

I also managed a common qualification to teach by going to the University of New Mexico, while also working days at a newly constituted school for boys, now known as Albuquerque Academy. The school was three days from opening without a French teacher, I was living in some despair in Ranchos de Taos, the novelist Ramon Sender had somehow heard of both dilemmas, told a mutual friend, Mercedes Garoffalo (first met in Mallorca by direction of Ken Lash, then editor of the *New Mexico Quarterly*), who put me in touch with the school's headmaster. So it was I began teaching again, this time seventh to twelfth graders, French, English, Latin, and other "subjects" I now completely forget. On the books I was a janitor.

No pedagogic presumptions seem to me worth much without an experience at least of common circumstance or world relating. For example, the

Robert Duncan and John Altoon, Bonanova, Mallorca, 1955

latter could be helping a child gain control of bowel movements, as my mother would call them, or learning to drive or do an altogether usual human thing. Mark Hopkins's sense of it, of student on one end of log and teacher on the other, always seemed right to me—or Olson's proposal: suggestion/teacher—recognition/student. There seems no static "place" which can permit a containing procedure, no matter the needs or the things literally to be done are as old as time itself. The initiation, so to speak, is intensely critical for all. I remember, for instance, the doctor who refused my hand, just after telling me our daughter Sarah had been born. I remember dear Ira Grant, an older friend and breeder of Barred Plymouth Rock chickens in Hanover, New Hampshire, telling me, really as instruction, a lovely story of a crew of painters he was foreman of, sent to some edge of northern Massachusetts for a job. After work they would go to a local tavern and one, always a bit surly and standoffish, would never take his turn buying a round for the rest. Of course, he'd always drink what they provided but would never share otherwise. Naturally it got to the others, and Ira sensed a lot of irritation was backing up.

It happened that they crossed over a bridge to get to the bar, and it was late winter. So one early evening, still on the bridge, Ira proposed that he could drop a beer bottle, remnant from the day, down to the ice some twenty or thirty feet below, and have it land upright, unbroken, and stay there. It seemed, if not impossible, highly unlikely, but Ira persisted, challenging all to either agree or contest by betting a round on the loser as the forfeit. He cannily knew who could not let him go unchallenged, and so it was that he and the loner were faced off.

As you'll know, he said, which I didn't, a warm day melts the snow on the ice of the river just enough to make it yielding, and that chilling again at evening firms it up. If you take both your index fingers, putting them on either side of the bottle's neck, and then simultaneously withdraw them, if there is no breeze to disturb the fall, which there wasn't, it seems, the bottle will fall plumb a distance, landing flush on its bottom with sufficient weight to bed in the slush, yet hold there upright and unbroken as that impact dissipates. Whatever he said, that's what happened, and the man bought drinks, was brought to the common table, and that was the end of that.

It was Ira also who could get down on his knees and pray to a radio to catch out of the blotch of conflicting stations the faint signal of the one in St. Johnsbury, Vermont, whereon I spoke weekly for a

hysterical half-hour of my literary respects, Joyce, Pound, Williams, Crane. God knows who could have heard me, other than him. I was diligent and ambitious. It was a fifty-mile drive one way from where we lived in North Lisbon, New Hampshire. But it was my own way of being serious—as I read Porter Sargent's extraordinary qualification of secondary private schools in America, sent me by Ezra Pound, who thought he'd be an active addition to the magazine I was trying to get started. His prefaces were bedrock judgements I still believe, and I wonder now if anyone remembers them, or Pound's interest. Certainly we recall John Kasper, and the rest.

I am thinking now of Red Pigmy Pouters, of all things, and Charles Schultz, of Lincolnwood, Illinois, who in 1948 won Grand Champion on a young cock bird exhibited in the major show of that year. There was a picture of the bird in the *Pigeon News,* and it was a haunting one. All the genetic patterns that qualify this pigeon's required look are recessive, the upright stance, the peculiarly inflated crop, the white crescents on the wings and breast, the feathered feet, even the color red itself. Rightly or wrongly, the fancier holds this bird's very existence as his determination. I wrote Mr. Schultz in respect, and asked him the breeding involved. He answered in an old-fashioned handwriting that, in 1912, he had acquired a pair of a particular strain to line breed with his own, thus to stabilize color and posture, and slowly, in subsequent years, worked on size and markings, ridding the red of smut, gaining adequate scale, and so slowly came to that moment thirty-six years later, when the bird (a male, which is not the dominant in the process) finally was there.

It was Ira's son Lincoln, who called me years after his father's death, when I thought I'd lost track of him forever, to tell me he had finally stabilized the Barred Plymouth Rock bantam, an ambition of his father's, and that his stock was now breeding true. It's curious how this is really as much my life as any books might be. I bought breeding stock, a trio, from Harold Tompkins of Concord, Massachusetts, whose Rhode Island Reds set the standard for that breed with their intense brownish red. The barnyard chicken of that kind was the New Hampshire Red, far more orange and gangly, whereas Tompkins's birds had proportions like a brick, the body well over the legs and rectangular. Tompkins was a solid, rather quiet man with a son I much liked, though clearly he drank too much, but that is a professional hazard with poultrymen for whatever reason. I raised chickens myself for a time, Barred Rocks, Dark Brahmas, Rhode Island Reds—and pigeons, ducks, geese, and

The author with his wife Bobbie and daughters "Kirsten eldest, Leslie (blonde) next, Sarah about three, and Kate the baby," San Jerónimo, Patulul, Suchitepéquez, Guatemala, 1959

goats. A regular ranch, as they used to say in New Hampshire. The last time I had any was when we were last living in Placitas, and I got some Rollers and a few Fantails, just for the company. Then again in Albuquerque, when Willy was not yet three, we got some white Leghorns, and our friends had left pigeons in the cote attached to the front porch. We used to walk out to the hen coop in the evening, Willy and I, to make sure all was secure for the night, and that sound of chickens going to roost, the clucking sporadic, inevitably comforts and delights me. Chickens are so obviously vulnerable that they present a curious trust, and one feels large, competent, and benign, seeing that they are all right once again.

I should have stayed put much more than I ever managed to, and I am once again, with patient family, weighing the choices of here and there. It is really the going that must be the point, and now, increasingly, that movement gets simply hard and distracting. One time in conversation with students at Cortland back in the sixties, Olson emphasized for them how long it took to accomplish "a habit and a haunt," a place so habituated by one's being there that it isn't even thought of as apart. In contrast, I've been such a tourist in the world despite I find a company much as a gypsy might—or so I'd like to think. Just having been made State Poet of New York for the years 1989–91, I look at what the governor, Mario Cuomo, says of me. "With courage and cunning, he has made the discreet loneliness of the solitary individual into a universal experience." People must love me for that. Last night talking to the poet Claes Andersson, who is also a member of the Finnish parliament and a psychologist, he tells us he had encouraged a young woman, a patient, to look to books for a relieving sense that many feel as threatened as she in the world. The book she randomly finds is Kafka's *The Trial*.

When did all this displacement first start might be a question, but a far too late one at this point. Still, if one's ever actually witnessed another human altogether at home, entirely present, it's unforgettable. Years ago now, in San Cristóbal de las Casas, the self-determined anthropologist Franz Blum asked if we would like to meet a Lacandone Indian from the

Yucatan peninsula. It was the late fifties as I recall. I was fascinated, particularly because of all Olson had told me, and momently an inexplicably contained person came into the room. But I mean by "contained" that he was *all* there, all of him was present, as an intensive animal might be, a tiger, but not the least threatening. All the seeming capacity of his senses was alert to the fact of his existence, not to its projection or recall. I can't now make clear how impressive and how tender that human capacity was. So far beyond thought, or belief, or any eventual abstraction at all, requiring no exercise or intent, no commitment or reason. Paradise must be a faint echo indeed.

But how long could such bittersweet innocence last in this world, as they say. William Burroughs points out the response of the European newcomers to these ultimately indigenous people is to cut off the hands held out to them. Would you then trust such people, he says simply enough.

A meager emphasis finally, but the world has hardly been a nice place to live in. But that too is indulgent if one has been given as much as I have. What I no doubt want is a clearer conscience, so that I can enjoy the privileges without concern that so few others share them. So I attempt, as many in my place, to acknowledge my blessings, my curious success. I wonder that we can look at our lives, any one of us, as if that reflective judgement constituted the point and thereby permitted our uselessness. Now one is so bitterly weary of the self-excuse, the elsewheres of proposed solution. Many times I've found people from my own country in absent corners of the world, in some metaphysical crouch, babbling that they have escaped the horror of their origins, and can think, it would seem, of very little else. They've come to nowhere, only gone, and I find their sense of security contemptible. No one gets away anymore.

Most awful is the memory of the death of my daughter Leslie, beyond ability to recall in detail. But as we dug to try to find her body in the vagueness of the sand's dimension at the top of the arroyo—into which they had made a tunnel which had collapsed— a crew of television people, a news team, suddenly were there too, trying to get close in for a shot of our finding her. I threatened one with the shovel, saying if he didn't get back, I'd smash him to bits. Moments later we found her, but it was too late. She was eight years old, a quirky, brilliant kid with a wry and singular wit. One time I remember she'd set her older sister Kirsten to a contest of counting telephone poles, and when, miles later, Kirsten said, I've got three thousand four hundred and eighty-six, how

Charles Olson, Berkeley Poetry Conference, 1965

many have you got?—Leslie's answer was, oh, I wasn't counting. She had a way with words, like they say.

A year later I had got something or other at the supermarket nearby, and was in the car again, just starting it up, when there was a knock on the car roof, someone trying to get my attention obviously, despite the rolled-up windows. I opened the window and looked out to see a man beside the car staring down at me with an angry face. He said, do you remember what you said to me a year ago, when you were trying to find your daughter? I couldn't at first quite believe he was saying this. I was the man you threatened, he continued, and I would like an apology. I don't now remember just what I answered, but something to the effect that if he didn't go away immediately, I'd give him far worse. He left, disgruntled.

Never mind, then, because it seems useless to. Allen Ginsberg had an accurate, early qualification, something like, "So what's the use escaping the cops and dentist's drills? Somebody will invent a Buchenwald next door . . ." At moments, stopped in traffic, I look out to either side to see such packed-in, determinedly depressed faces, I fear for what inept, soft delights might otherwise be. My memory is so flooded with instance, such "fragile, passing pleasure," which was air, sunlight, water, earth—very basic, one wants to say. As a kid I was so pleased one *could* make fire by rubbing two sticks together, despite it took a long time and often didn't work. Buddy Berlin once spoke of that fact in childhood, of waking up with such a vivid sense of a whole *day* as prospect, such a space of forward *time* in which so much could happen. As Simone de Beauvoir well reminds us, that sense fades with youth itself.

Olson—the way I so use him for measure here must emphasize how he was so much a brother to my own ways of thinking—would say that art is the only true twin life has. As I understood him, the point is there isn't any point, more than what being human itself can make. "No further than in itself." I would love to think that living became a progress, a fact of something's having been gained. But Louis Zukofsky

serves here to note the problem, just that the singular is (he quotes Wittgenstein) that point in space which is place for an argument. Whatever "it" can ever be known to be, the fact is, "the more so all have it . . ." In that respect, no one goes anywhere alone, and no one survives to get there even. The door is endlessly being opened and closed.

My sister tells a story of me when we still lived in the house on Elm Street in West Acton next to the Lockes' farm. I had one of those flags you get on Memorial Day, and had put a march possibly on our old wind-up phonograph, and was going around and around the dining room table, chanting, "The town's all out for Creeley!" I can't have been too young since I knew the idiom of such approval. For someone who has so often sent people up the wall with frustrated, impotent anger, I've a nearly perverse wish to please, or, more truly, to be told I do. A character I thought repellent and sinister was Dickens's Uriah Heap, because he is so patently a liar of utter, obvious convenience. There is an awful, self-consciously recognized limit to what may be called my sincerity. In some curious way, I cannot finally believe anything I think. Only feeling can survive there, and if, as with

Wife Penelope with daughter Hannah and son Willy, Waldoboro, Maine, 1984

those obscenely rubbed hands of that malevolent person, it's all a calculated intent, then reason itself is only another artifice, artfully employed. I suppose that is as it should be, but it frightens me nonetheless.

Just so I distrusted fiction, feeling the term "something made-up" argued an intentional distortion of the "truth," whatever that proved. I wanted to call such work "prose" simply. No doubt this feeling echoes again the Puritan aura of where I grew up, but also the fact that being told the truth, as I felt it, was the only location possible for me. Those crucial lies of my childhood, the one covering my father's death and the other the necessary removal of my eye, left truth a peculiar authority.

But, more to the point, some confusion as to just what the proposals of writing might be underlay all of these terms. Williams notes emphatically, "To tell what subsequently I saw and what heard . . ." But how answer Olson's equal point in *In Cold Hell*— "What has he to say?" Then again there was the fact of the words themselves, so that Duncan made playful and exact sense: "To tell the truth the way the words lie." When young, I'd written Olson with almost pious exclamation: "Form is never more than an extension of content." Now I might say equally, "Content is never more than an extension of form." It depends, as they say in New England. Back of it all I hear Williams again, saying all those years ago, "Why don't we tell them that it's *fun* . . ." Such *fun*, such *delight*, when all possibilities of such act come together in words moving in mind's recognition with body's weight and measure.

Getting the children ready for school this morning, in this still very strange country, Finland, I wonder what will become of them. It's a comfortable thought as I consider it, just that the moment is empty of anything but the two of them, as Hannah attempts to have her older brother accept her saying "goodbye" to him, and he, expectably, wants to be ponderously preoccupied. Fair enough. I've watched both move out from the limits of our own household the past months into physical edges of city here, into social places we can't really follow them, into increasing confidence. On the street as Willy walks to his school tram, there's an early morning collection of men, drinking usually, roughly dressed for this secure neighborhood (though all neighborhoods in Finland seem secure), waiting for whatever. They disperse quite soon after he's left. The Finns tell you Chernobyl had no effect on their country, because it wasn't raining that day, so the radioactive matter didn't fall with the rain to the earth and water. Duncan told me

that during the last painful months before Jaime d'Angulo died, he got paradoxically cheerful letters from Jane Harrison, in which she said things like, "Soon you'll be with them all, Homer, Hesiod, possibly even the gods themselves!" We believe a world or have none.

I can watch, from this window, an insistent height of sky that has been all this past fall and winter a companion to my being here, and a subtle, unaggressive information of where, in fact, it is. It's as if I can't really see ground but, rather, the tops of birches, planted in the back common ground of this large apartment block, which are on eye level. One could reach out, with sufficiently long arms, and pick off twigs from their crowns. Elsewise I look across at the other apartment windows, which are of regular dimensions, set and abstracting, in the flat yellowish-brown stucco. Above there are details of brickwork, the point where an edge of roof meets another. There are galvanized tin roofs, one painted a barn red, another black, both common colors of industrial cover paints. And the sky is another thing entirely, persistently, though it is within a set frame, the window, a place, simply up there. It isn't only its being far, or indeterminant, or just this shifting, massive place of light and weather. It is that it proposes no human convenience, that it isn't simple, that it won't go away. Thus I love Ginsberg's line in *Kaddish*, "And the sky above, an old blue place."

Zukofsky was shy of such writing as this, because it fouls up the gauges, makes them stick. There is a broken-record tone of necessity in it that keeps coming back to the beginning of the proposition, that there was someone to begin with, and that something therefore followed. Wittgenstein proposes that it is the "I" that is "deeply mysterious," not "you" or "them." What cannot be objectified is oneself. Yet the fiction, finally for real, is attractive—that the Walt Whitman of *Song of Myself* is, as Borges says, one of the consummate literary fictions of all time.

When Olson was dying in the New York hospital of cancer, and Duncan had come to see him—hoping, I think, in an old-fashioned sense for advice concerning that prospect—their sense of it all was that it had been a great adventure. That would seem the point, echoing Ted Berrigan's "I'd like to take the whole trip." Can I now recall how impressive first sounded "Who dare not share with us the breath released . . . "

Anchises' navel, dripping of the sea,—
The hands Erasmus dipped in gleaming tides,
Gathered the voltage of blown blood and vine;

Robert Creeley, Cambridge, Massachusetts, 1985

Delve upward for the new and scattered wine,
Oh brother-thief of time, that we recall.
Laugh out the meager penance of their days
Who dare not share with us the breath released,
The substance drilled and spent beyond repair
For golden, or the shadow of gold hair.
Distinctly praise the years, whose volatile
Blamed bleeding hands extend and thresh the
  height
The imagination spans beyond despair,
Outpacing bargain, vocable and prayer.

  One had the company.

                    Helsinki, Finland
                    March 23, 1989

BIBLIOGRAPHY

Poetry:

Le Fou. Columbus, Ohio: Golden Goose Press, 1952.

Ferrini and Others, with others. Gloucester, Mass.: Ferrini, 1953; Berlin: Gerhardt, 1955.

The Immoral Proposition (illustrated by René Laubiès). Karlsruhe-Durlach, Germany: J. Williams, 1953.

The Kind of Act Of. Palma de Mallorca: Divers Press, 1953.

A Snarling Garland of Xmas Verses. Palma de Mallorca: Divers Press, 1954.

All That Is Lovely in Men (illustrated by Dan Rice). Asheville, N.C.: J. Williams, 1955.

If You (illustrated by Fielding Dawson). San Francisco: Porpoise Bookshop, 1956; London: Lion and Unicorn Press, 1968.

The Whip. Worcester, England: Migrant, 1957; Highlands, N.C.: J. Williams, 1957.

A Form of Women. New York: Jargon/Corinth, 1959.

For Love: Poems, 1950–1960. New York: Scribner, 1962.

Distance (illustrated by Bobbie Creeley). Lawrence, Kan.: T. Williams, 1964.

Two Poems. San Francisco: Oyez, 1964.

Hi There! Urbana, Ill.: Finial Press, 1965.

Words. Rochester, Mich.: Perishable Press, 1965.

About Women (illustrated by John Altoon). Los Angeles: Gemini, 1966.

For Joel. Madison, Wis.: Perishable Press, 1966.

Poems, 1950–1965. London: Calder & Boyars, 1966.

Robert Creeley Reads (booklet with 7-inch gramophone record). London: Turret/Calder & Boyars, 1967.

A Sight. London: Cape Goliard Press, 1967.

Words. New York: Scribner, 1967.

The Boy. Buffalo: Gallery Upstairs Press, 1968.

The Charm: Early and Uncollected Poems. Mount Horeb, Wis.: Perishable Press, 1968; London: Calder & Boyars, 1971.

Divisions and Other Early Poems. Mount Horeb, Wis.: Perishable Press, 1968.

The Finger (illustrated by Bobbie Creeley). Los Angeles: Black Sparrow Press, 1968.

5 Numbers. New York: Poets Press, 1968.

Numbers (illustrated by Robert Indiana). Edited by Dieter Honisch. Translated into German by Klaus Reichert. Stuttgart: Domberger, 1968; Düsseldorf: Galerie Schmela, 1968.

Pieces (illustrated by Bobbie Creeley). Los Angeles: Black Sparrow Press, 1968.

Hero. New York: Indianakatz, 1969.

Mazatlan: Sea. San Francisco: Poets Press, 1969.

Pieces. New York: Scribner, 1969.

A Wall. New York: Bouwerie, 1969; Stuttgart: Domberger, 1969.

America. Miami: Press of the Black Flag, 1970.

As Now It Would Be Snow. Los Angeles: Black Sparrow Press, 1970.

Christmas: May 10, 1970. Buffalo: Lockwood Memorial Library, 1970.

The Finger: Poems, 1966–1969. London: Calder & Boyars, 1970.

For Benny and Sabina. New York: Samuel Charters, 1970.

For Betsy and Tom. Detroit: Alternative Press, 1970.

In London. Bolinas, Calif.: Angel Hair, 1970.

Mary's Fancy. New York: Bouwerie, 1970.

For the Graduation. San Francisco: Cranium Press, 1971.

1°2°3°4°5°6°7°8°9°0 (illustrated by Arthur Okamura). Berkeley: Shambala, 1971; San Francisco: Mudra, 1971.

St. Martin's (illustrated by Bobbie Creeley). Los Angeles: Black Sparrow Press, 1971.

Sea. San Francisco: Cranium Press, 1971.

Change. San Francisco: Hermes Free Press, 1972.

One Day after Another. Detroit: Alternative Press, 1972.

For My Mother. Rushden, England: Sceptre Press, 1973.

His Idea (with photographs by Elsa Dorfman). Toronto: Coach House Press, 1973.

Kitchen. Chicago: Wine Press, 1973.

Sitting Here. Storrs: University of Connecticut Library, 1974.

Thirty Things (illustrated by Bobbie Creeley). Los Angeles: Black Sparrow Press, 1974.

Backwards. Knotting, England: Sceptre Press, 1975.

Away (illustrated by Bobbie Creeley). Santa Barbara, Calif.: Black Sparrow Press, 1976; Solihull, England: Aquila, 1976.

Hello. Christchurch, New Zealand: Hawk Press, 1976.

Selected Poems. New York: Scribner, 1976.

Myself. Knotting, England: Sceptre Press, 1977.

Thanks. Deerfield, Mass.: Deerfield Press, 1977.

The Children. St. Paul: Truck Press, 1978.

Desultory Days. Knotting, England: Sceptre Press, 1978.

Hello: A Journal, February 29–May 3, 1976. New York: New Directions, 1978; London: Boyars, 1978.

Later. West Branch, Iowa: Toothpaste Press, 1978.

Later. New York: New Directions, 1979; London: Boyars, 1980.

Corn Close. Knotting, England: Sceptre Press, 1980.

Mother's Voice (illustrated by Tom Clark). Santa Barbara, Calif.: Am Here Books/Immediate Editions, 1981.

The Collected Poems of Robert Creeley, 1945–1975. Berkeley: University of California Press, 1982; London: Boyars, 1983.

Echoes. West Branch, Iowa: Toothpaste Press, 1982.

A Calendar, 1984. West Branch, Iowa: Toothpaste Press, 1983.

Mirrors. New York: New Directions, 1983; London: Boyars, 1984.

Memories. Durham, England: Pig Press, 1984.

Memory Gardens. New York: New Directions, 1986; London: Boyars, 1987.

The Company. Providence, R.I.: Burning Deck Press, 1988.

Window. Buffalo: State University of New York at Buffalo, 1988.

Dreams. New York: Periphery & the Salient Seedling Press, 1989.

It (illustrated by Francesco Clemente). Zurich: Edition Bischofberger, 1989.

Prose:

The Gold Diggers (short stories). Palma de Mallorca: Divers Press, 1954; London: Calder, 1965.

The Island. New York: Scribner, 1963; London: Calder, 1964.

An American Sense (essay). London: Sigma, 1965.

The Gold Diggers and Other Stories. London: Calder, 1965; New York: Scribner, 1965.

A Quick Graph: Collected Notes and Essays. Edited by Donald Allen. San Francisco: Four Seasons Foundation, 1970.

A Day Book (illustrated by R. B. Kitaj). Berlin: Graphis, 1972; New York: Scribner, 1972.

Notebook. New York: Bouwerie, 1972.

A Sense of Measure (notes, essays, and interviews). London: Calder & Boyars, 1972.

The Creative (lecture). Los Angeles: Black Sparrow Press, 1973.

Contexts of Poetry: Interviews, 1961–1971. Edited by D. Allen. Bolinas, Calif.: Four Seasons Foundation, 1973.

Inside Out: Notes on the Autobiographical Mode (lecture). Los Angeles: Black Sparrow Press, 1973.

Mabel: A Story and Other Prose. London: Boyars, 1976.

Presences: A Text for Marisol (with 61 photographs of Marisol's sculptures). New York: Scribner, 1976.

Was That a Real Poem or Did You Just Make It Up Yourself (essay). Santa Barbara, Calif.: Black Sparrow Press, 1976.

Mabel: A Story (illustrated by Jim Dine). Paris: Atelier Crommelynck, 1977.

Was That a Real Poem and Other Essays. Edited by D. Allen. Bolinas, Calif.: Four Seasons Foundation, 1979.

Charles Olson and Robert Creeley: The Complete Correspondence. Edited by George F. Butterick. 9 vols. continuing. Santa Barbara, Calif.: Black Sparrow Press, 1980–89.

The Collected Prose of Robert Creeley. London and New York: Boyars, 1984; Berkeley: University of California Press, 1987.

Collected Essays. Berkeley: University of California Press, 1989.

Sound recordings:

Today's Poets 3, with others. New York: Scholastic Magazines, Inc., 1968.

Robert Creeley Reads (7-inch gramophone record with booklet). London: Turret/Calder & Boyars, 1967.

For Love (phonotape). New York: Scribner, 1972.

The Door: Selected Poems (audiocassette). Düsseldorf and Munich: S Press, 1975.

Radio play:

Listen, first produced in London, 1972. (Illustrated by Bobbie Creeley) Los Angeles: Black Sparrow Press, 1972.

Editor of:

Mayan Letters, by Charles Olson. Palma de Mallorca: Divers Press, 1953; London: J. Cape, 1968; New York: Grossman, 1968.

New American Story, with Donald Allen. New York: Grove Press, 1965; Harmondsworth, England: Penguin, 1971.

Selected Writings of Charles Olson. New York: New Directions, 1966.

The New Writing in the U.S.A., with D. Allen. Harmondsworth, England: Penguin, 1967.

Black Mountain Review, 1954–1957. New York: AMS Press, 1969.

Whitman: Selected Poems. Harmondsworth, England: Penguin, 1973.

The Essential Burns. New York: Ecco Press, 1989.

Roy Fisher

1930-

I must have been conceived during those days in late 1929 when Wall Street was falling in ruins; I was a latecomer in a poor but prudent family which thought itself complete, and although nobody ever hinted as much to me, I can see now that my birth, in June 1930, will have been accompanied by a revival of economic fear and some privation. These were to last until the arrival of the prosperity which the war of 1939 brought to working people. My father was a craftsman, working for the same small, paternalist jewellery firm ("Walter, you're a good workman, and if you ever leave here I'll see to it that you never get another job anywhere in this trade") to which he'd been apprenticed at fourteen, in 1903. It was a luxury trade which withered with the Depression and took a long while to recover; my father was to earn far better wages when the war came, but for assembling aircraft, not setting diamonds. The fact that he then felt it demeaning to become for a while just another factory worker, even for three times the pay, tells something about the family ethos.

Not that he actually enjoyed making jewellery, even though he did take a certain pride in his minute skill: he was in it only because he had been put to it as a boy. Jewellery of some sort had been the family trade for at least three generations; they'd lived in a succession of homes never more than walking distance from the same nest of small workshops just outside the city centre. This was the Jewellery Quarter, a congested patch maybe three-quarters of a mile square on the crest of Hockley Hill. It was the archetype, almost a concentrate, of the Birmingham system of proliferating small manufactures which developed through the eighteenth and nineteenth centuries. The "masters" would start by having their workshops attached to their houses, all over the district; the workshops would extend piecemeal to cram the backyards, then the gardens. At that stage the master would move his family a mile or two out to a new suburb, and every room of the original house would be filled with workbenches or clerks' desks. There were hundreds of these establishments in Hockley, dark and chaotic, their work spaces linked by rickety stairways and catwalks. It was an area I saw for the first time only in my teens, working as a

Roy Fisher, 1981

telegram delivery boy one school holiday; certainly my father never saw any reason to take me there, and although I once called at W. H. Small's front office with a message when he was in hospital, I never set eyes on the room where, apart from the two wars, he spent every working day for over fifty years. It's quite possible that my mother never learned exactly where the place was.

I think my father would probably have been better suited by temperament to some sort of clerical, white-collar job; he was certainly literate enough. But that would have meant, under the crazy but insidiously effective English system, changing social classes; and for the large family of my grandfather (also Walter Fisher) the game was one of consolidation rather than movement upward. Nobody was put to an education involving expense which future fortune might or might not repay; that would be the plan for my own generation, once the consolidation had taken effect. That family—Lizzie, Ern, Wal, Doris, Jessie, Rose, Albert, Florrie—earned their livings early. My uncle Ern was the only one ever to become his own boss, and that was in a very small way, as half of a two-man japanning business he ran in partnership with his sister Florrie's husband, Will, but which neither of them owned.

I write of that household as being my grandfather's partly as a fact of memory, for my grandmother was dead three years before I was born; but by every account the setup had always been patriarchal, right from the elder Walter's marriage in 1885, at nineteen (twenty-one on the marriage lines), to Mary Jane Kite. She was two years older, living a few doors away in James Street, Lozells, and on the point of giving birth to my aunt Lizzie. When I came to know him—or rather to witness him, for he didn't have much interest in children—he was an impressive old man, bald, lean, and hard, with a down-turned moustache and an outfit that included polished leather leggings and made him look more like a shepherd or a stockman dressed up for market day than a man who had spent all his life within a couple of miles of the centre of Birmingham. He was a little bowed, but loping and agile. He stank of tobacco smoke, and his speech was a direct, articulate Old Brummagem, a strong, railing accent, very different from the sodden and nondescript English usually thought of nowadays as the local language. Just by his presence he dominated any room he was in, though I don't remember him as interacting with other people much; for his last ten years or so he was accompanied everywhere by his golden retriever, which both served as an intimate and did all his socialising for him. You could make contact with him via the dog; and he'd usually give the children a few of the dog's chocolate drops, when the dog had had enough. I was brought up to think of him as something of a household tyrant and a miser, and there was probably some truth in both. He certainly had an unusually large amount of savings for a retired working man who had raised a big family: when he died in 1945 he

The Fisher family at Anglesey Street, about 1914: (back row) Ern, Lizzie, Walter, Jessie, Doris; (middle row) Walter, Sr., Rose, Mary Jane; (front row) Albert, Florrie

left over a thousand pounds, enough to buy outright a couple of houses of the sort we were then living in for a rent of ten shillings a week.

He never moved from the house, 77 Anglesey Street, Lozells, in which he'd spent most of his adult life. It was a plain brick street of terrace houses, without bay windows or front gardens, and it ran down from the Lozells Road, which was something of a shopping street, into the factory-filled valley east of Hockley; beyond that, the hill rose by way of Great King Street, where he'd been born, to the Jewellery Quarter, where he worked. In the other direction, away from the city centre, he would in his earlier years have come quickly into open country; and that was the clue to the other side of his life. At the time of his birth, Great King Street will have been almost at the edge of the built-up area, and the other places he lived in—all within a square half-mile or so of one another—were in the zone to which the edge of town had pushed itself by the time he married; James Street looked out into farmland. Once he was settled in Anglesey Street, the suburbs went on spreading beyond him, a good ten miles or more, till they almost met, as they now do meet, Walsall, the next town. He didn't, however, do what many small householders did, his own father among them: cultivate his backyard and an allotment garden as well. Although a complete product of the city and its economy, he didn't at all, so far as I know, *use* the city, and feed off its atmospheres and opportunities in the way really urbanised people do. Whenever he could, he got out.

He was exactly of the generation of workingmen who were liberated by the safety bicycle back into the countryside from which their parents or grandparents had probably come. He took his holidays and weekend excursions in male company or alone, by bicycle, covering considerable distances. And the machines he rode were the only extravagance he had. He would have them built to his specifications: not racers, but well-engineered, rugged road cycles. The last of them came to my father as a premature legacy, and quickly to me; it was so heavily constructed that the old man could hardly move it. I found it hard work, too: a smooth, black brute with a broad, sprung saddle, oil-bath chain guard and so much equipment of one sort and another slung low on its bodywork that it would almost stand up by itself.

As he grew older he restricted himself more and more to an old haunt nearer town, the wide stretch of protected wild heath and woodland called Sutton Park, in Sutton Coldfield. He would get away through the suburbs into that. He had been a noted swimmer in the pools there, particularly in the depths

of winter, belonging to a group of ice-breaking swimmers; their successors probably still swim for the Walter Fisher Cup, a winter trophy. And it was in that park that he met his death, early in 1945. Since the deaths of my aunt Lizzie and her family in an air raid (this was the incident I described in my poem "The Entertainment of War") he'd become more and more remote and confused; there were perpetual ringing noises in his head. His trouble was probably tinnitus, but the general opinion—which he may have shared—was that he was losing his wits as he approached eighty. He didn't come visiting any more, communicated with people very little, and finally didn't stir from the house, as if in a terminal feebleness. One January day, he disappeared, and the dog with him. Late the next day, and a dozen miles away in Sutton Park, the dog led a passerby to where he lay dying of exposure after a freezing night. I think everybody considered it a good death for him. Uncle Ern and my father cycled out to the park with his ashes, no doubt strapped to the carrier of his own massive bicycle, and scattered them near Blackroot Pool.

The style of all the Fishers was one of alert, short-range attention; humour was brisk and dismissive, even abrupt. Their voices could be sharp or declamatory, and their movements and facial expressions tended to the vigorous and, on occasion, manic. They coped with life as they went along, and on the level they found themselves on. Constitutionally, they kept their noses clean and a little money in the bank. Of my grandfather's children, none, so far as I know, ever faced insolvency, traumatic unemployment, or breakdown; none engaged in crime; none met with a great increase in fortune, or went looking for such a thing. When they came to have taller, better-educated children, electric light, and indoor lavatories, it was only at the pace at which those things came to many other people. They didn't direct themselves much to the future, and spent little time reminiscing—mostly, I think, because the past had been so harsh they didn't enjoy thinking about it. Of my grandfather's numerous brothers and sisters, for instance, I only ever heard one talked about, and that in long retrospect. This was Great-Uncle John, who was uncharacteristic. Born in 1859, he made the move away from manual work two generations early, becoming the first qualified "high-speed typewriter" in Birmingham. He then married into a Catholic family; his wife was judged to have been a woman of some pretensions; and on her he begot, it was said, three headmistresses. Dominated by his womenfolk, he became eccentrically speculative, and would happily give his money away; I suppose he was a steady hypomanic. At any rate, his family consigned him to institutions from time to time. I should like to have known him. But for the rest, virtually everything I know about them from the time before I was born comes not from anecdote but from searching the public records. Those searches haven't yet reached back beyond Great King Street. In 1861, my great-grandfather William Fisher, an electroplater (probably working in the bulkier end of the jewellery trade), was recorded as living there with his wife, Georgina Mason, and their six children (and there were more to come, including my grandfather) in a household headed by her mother, a widow born in Hornton in Oxfordshire and working as a mangler. The Kites and the other tributary family, the Mousleys, were almost certainly already in the same parish somewhere.

I never heard of any of the Fishers having any political allegiance; nor any trace of felt religion. My father would describe his father as having been a

Father, Walter Fisher, as a chorister,
about 1902

Freethinker, but I think that just meant he was a sceptic. There exist photographs of my father and his brother Ern as young men, in a Methodist cricket team; there are also photographs of them, from the same period, in a Church of England football eleven. My father also passed the most exalted period of his life as a boy chorister at that same church. The religion seemed to have no effect on him, but socially the church choir affected him a good deal. For one thing, it came close to removing him from his family, from his class, and from Birmingham. That was when, as head chorister and principal soloist, he was talent-spotted for the choir of Canterbury Cathedral with, I suppose, the offer of a free scholarship to the Cathedral Choir School and all the opportunities for social mobility that would carry with it. For some reason, my grandfather didn't give his consent; the refusal wasn't thought to be out of character. At any rate, my father stayed on at Saint Mary's, Handsworth, for as long as his voice lasted, and beyond: far from being eager to drop his register and come out as a man, he wanted to preserve his position, and the excitement of singing the high line, long past the natural time. He forced his voice to stay up till it was a falsetto, probably ruining any prospect of having a reasonable adult singing voice. He certainly never acquired anything more than a rather strained tenor, and as a man didn't sing much. In a rare moment of reminiscence he once gave me the best possible summary of his relationship with my grandfather. "I only ever heard my father sing once," he said; "I came home early, and as I came up the entry I heard a man singing in a most beautiful tenor voice. And that was my dad. And when he heard me he stopped, and then pretended he hadn't been doing it. I never heard him do it again."

Saint Mary's choir was an interesting choice. Handsworth was then an altogether leafier and more affluent place than Lozells, and Saint Mary's was several churches away from my father's home territory. He must have been drawn there by an ambition to sing in the strongest team. The church was the handsome mediaeval parish church of an independent Staffordshire borough, not annexed by Birmingham till 1911, and at that time one of the districts where the manufacturers had their mansions and the clerical and business classes their villas. It was a place of parlour maids and tennis courts, and the quality came to church in carriages. The church itself had numerous clergy, a huge choir, and was a centre of social power; at the same time it had—as it still has—something of the atmosphere of a village church, sandstone-built and set in a spacious graveyard under a canopy of tall trees. It embodied the English tradition which the industrial nineteenth century was reaching for, inventing where necessary and taking to itself as a talisman; and I'm sure its sub-Gothic dignities had a strong and romantic effect on my father's imagination. It didn't prompt him to social climbing, but was more of an escapism, allied to the old man's cycle rides, which he often shared.

One of the local girls who sat in the front pew and made eyes at the choirboys was a jobbing gardener's daughter called Emma—or Pem, the only person I've ever heard of with that name—Jones. Their courtship turned out to be long: they were married in Saint Mary's in the autumn of 1918, by which time she was twenty-seven and my father twenty-nine, a signals lance-corporal in the London Fusiliers on leave from France. But my father's careful pencil drawing of the church was already in her autograph album by the time he was a sixteen-year-old jeweller's apprentice and boy soprano and she was just starting work in a small sweetshop in the area everybody called "the village," the group of shops round the old toll bar in Villa Road, about midway between her family territory and his.

Whereas the Fishers seem to have been established on their small patch for generations, the Joneses were new arrivals in Handsworth. They'd lived for a time near Harborne, further round the semirural western edge of the city, and my grandfather Edward Jones had at some time worked for the Chamberlain family: possibly Joseph, the creator of the modern Birmingham; certainly Austen, who became Foreign Secretary. My grandmother Emma Lane had had some family connection with a laundry business, and had done housekeeping work in one of the smaller outlying hospitals; I have the impression that she'd also been in domestic service. Something of that sort was certainly the family style, which was in marked contrast to that of the Fishers; the contrast was worked out year after year in the household I grew up in, and it made an uncomfortable inheritance. The Joneses had the air of servants who'd been paid off, given their freedom, and who weren't too happy with the bargain; life was an ache, a trial to be faced with cheerfulness and charm amid slowly declining fortunes. I don't know whether this air of decline was based in anything substantial. The Joneses didn't reminisce any more than did the Fishers; and although their thoughts seemed to be turned towards the past, they were thoughts that lay too deep for tears, or words. Usually, at any rate; I can remember seeing my mother and my aunts weeping for times gone by. And there was always something wistful

about the charm and the cheerfulness. There was certainly nothing of the bluff pugnacity of the Fishers.

This was, of course, the mood I learned to know in the thirties, and it may be that the one focus of reminiscence and overt regret which they had was the real cause of the pervading wistfulness. This was the loss of Ivy Cottage, something which happened quite a few years before I was born. Somehow, on arriving in Handsworth around the turn of the century, the family had gained the tenancy of an idyllic old yeoman cottage, left marooned in woodland and among fields as the prosperous suburb developed all round it; and there they seem to have lived an almost rural life for a quarter of a century. In speech and manner they gave the impression of being country people, and by preserving that style for so long within a couple of miles of the city centre, they seemed also to be preserving a pre-industrial past. It was only when they lost Ivy Cottage—the story went that they were in some way tricked out of the lease—that they had to become urbanized. Even so, Howard Road, to which they had moved by the time I was born, was far from being a harsh city street. It was a quiet little cut-through, with varied housing, mostly quite old, and a small farmhouse and yard still tucked away behind the houses. But Ivy Cottage had been a complete survival, with climbing roses, old brickwork, and a pump in the yard. It sat among its birch trees half a mile or so up beyond Saint Mary's, and I suppose that for my father it was a powerful additional magic to be added to whatever the church gave him.

The other contrast to the life he was used to lay in the fact that the Jones family was emphatically matriarchal. My soulful-eyed grandmother ran things, persuasively and without resistance. She did it mostly from her bed in later years. My grandfather Edward Jones I knew as a slow, sweet-natured old man, white-bearded, straw-hatted, and with distant blue eyes: the type-figure of a retired gardener. I was told he'd been perhaps a little less uncomplicated in earlier years, before a fall through a hothouse roof and a crack on the head; there was no knowing. He outlived my grandmother by ten years, but didn't liberate himself from his chimney-corner existence.

The family wasn't a matriarchy of the strong sort, where daughters breed daughters and men are peripheral; it was a home base near the end of a line, and it exerted a steady, soft, sweet magnetism. When my mother used the word "home" we knew that she meant—although she'd never lived in it—her parents' house in Howard Road. My grandparents had five children, four of whom lived to adulthood, and

Maternal grandfather, Edward Jones

of those four only my mother married and had children. Her elder sister Elsie worked from home as a dressmaker to the local well-to-do, and became, when past child-bearing, the third wife of an elderly *rentier* who lived opposite, enjoying, while she lasted, the slight elevation of position which had come to her by way of a little patience. My mother herself was to marry quite late. Uncle Ted, a bighearted, affectionate bachelor, who worked as a builder's labourer, died in his middle forties, a few months after his mother. The youngest, Ethel, born in 1900, was by general agreement pampered and brought up to idleness, after which she spent thirty years or so keeping house for her parents till they died. She went out to work, cleaning and then doing light factory work, only when she was near retiring age; she never married.

I've said that the contrast between the styles of the Fishers and the Joneses made for an uncomfortable inheritance. On the credit side, the Joneses' quasi-rural nostalgia combined with my father's inherited commitment to country excursions to provide, through my childhood, blissful, almost visionary experiences on outings and walks, supported by an unshakable moral faith in something called Nature. That basic guidance, and many of those experiences, have stayed with me all my life. There are people who

know me for my writings about urban landscapes and city life and who find it impossible to square that knowledge with the fact that I now live, not as a lifelong denizen of those streets, but in a quite remote and wild place in the Derbyshire hills. But it's the paradox I was given as a child—the sensation of having been born in a state of exile from some unknown countryside—which forced me to stare so hard at all the particulars of my city surroundings.

The real discomfort was social, a matter of loyalties and emotional allegiances. My father was probably the least matter-of-fact, the most reflective of the Fishers; he would need to be, to marry into the Jones family, into which he fitted quite well, though as the years went by, he grew impatient and dismissive about what he considered their passivity, and the uselessness of their little bits of gentility. By the time I was born he probably saw much more of my mother's family than he did of his own. We children certainly did. Visits to Grandpa Fisher's house in Anglesey Street came once or twice a year, so that it felt physically like a foreign territory, whereas the Jones house in Howard Road was a home from home, visited on many weekends and filled with familiar objects and sensations. Being brought up close to my mother—and she was by nature possessive of her two sons—I absorbed, without explicit teaching, the very strong sense that the Jones way was the true way, and that the Fisher way was the way of a heartless world with no leaves on the trees, no flowers in the vases, and sharp edges everywhere. There was no enmity between the families—simply the assumption, from my mother's side, of an inherent incompatibility. And when my parents were at odds, usually about money, the incompatibility of the clans became personal: my father was characterised as a hot-tempered miser, my mother as a devious and indulgent spendthrift. These were just the positions they repeatedly took up; the money there was to argue over was pathetically little. But the slogans of those occasional wars made their impression on me.

My mother was thirty-nine and my father forty-one when I was born, and for our sort of people those were advanced ages for childbearing. My sister was ten years, and my brother eight years, my senior; and my parents seemed much older in relation to me than did those of other children. My mother, for instance, was prematurely gray: I never knew her with dark hair. And my father had received from his father the gene for early baldness which he passed on to me and thus to my sons. Moreover, there was nothing boyish about his demeanour. And I came to realise—though not really until I reached that time of life myself—

that they were both by then in quite poor shape, and had their troubles. They did well to be as animated as they were. I don't think, for instance, that giving me birth had done my mother any good at all. She didn't always walk well, couldn't go up or down stairs except one step at a time, and already had the beginnings of a tremor which plagued her later years.

As for my father, I think now that he was an uncompensated war casualty. After volunteering, being rejected as unfit because of a cartilage injury, and undergoing surgery to make himself eligible for service, he spent three years in the trenches, an experience about which he had little to say. He didn't set any value on it, or on his campaign medals, or on the results of the Allies' victory. Physically, he was a fairly small man, and I imagine he must always have been nervous, tensed like a spring; on the football field he'd been a fast wing forward, and at cricket a ferociously fast bowler. The stress of his war service, and the problems and frustrations which followed it, will have damaged him. By the time I knew him, there was not an atom of relaxation in him, most of the time. He'd continued with his sports past the age

when it would have been sensible to stop, and had pushed himself too far. He was in frequent pain from rheumatism and stomach ulcers, and he slept badly. His thyroid had become seriously overactive, and he repeatedly refused the surgery which was the only available treatment. He was hard for a child to get to know; much of what I thought of as his personality, the signs I read him by, must have been the phenomenology of his illness: the losses of temper, the overloud laughter, the friendliness that seemed far more forced and uneasy than it was. It alarmed me, I suppose, and distanced me from him, and it never occurred to me to model my behaviour on his in any way. When I took to doing things I'd learned from him, like roaming the countryside, on foot or bicycle, I arrogantly assumed I was doing it my way; and it was with real astonishment that I discovered, in adulthood, that it was his face I'd inherited more than my mother's. I'd ruled out any such possibility.

It's easy for me to see my whole character, and the course of my life, as determined by an early disposition to be, quietly and without fuss, as unlike him as possible in the way I did things. Where he was

The Jones family at Ivy Cottage, about 1920: (back row) Ted, Ethel, Elsie, Emma, Walter Fisher;
(front row) Emma, Sr., Edward, Great-Aunt Ann

keen, quick, and hyperactive, I grew up to be laid back, noncommittal, sceptical about the value of any action at all. This scepticism was strengthened by the spectacle of the fascinating but turbulent adolescent years of my sister and brother.

And I grew secretive. This wasn't purely temperamental. Either parent would sound me out about what the other might be thinking or doing. I didn't like that; but it taught me that the discovery of others' plans, motives, and feelings was a powerful currency. In consequence, I became disinclined fully to confide anything in anybody, a habit which was to stay with me long after it was of any possible tactical use. A few years ago I made a note: "My life is the history of my secrets." Which meant, not that my secrets ever amounted to anything, but that my whole sense of myself was as a carrier of secrets. Early on, I'd decided that if secrets spelled safety, the best course for me was to *be* a secret incarnate. Good for the contemplative life, if in a warped way; bad for the active.

And when the active life hit me, when I went at five to Wattville Road School, I was unprepared for it. I'd had the upbringing many youngest children receive, being capably but unconcernedly looked after by an experienced mother who was busy with the still-unfamiliar challenges generated by the older children. I was just kept close to my mother; the other people I met for five years were mostly relatives, and mostly adults. I had very little contact with other children. So my first day at school, when I suddenly encountered what felt like the whole of the rest of the human race, was a shock. I still haven't got over it. Something had got at all those children and brutalized them. They were loud and aggressive—even their friendliness was intrusive—and they were even more taboo-ridden than I was. Even when they didn't seem intelligent, they behaved as if far more worldly-wise than me. Since I was never worldly-wise, and not rebellious in an active way, I was always to be puzzled by the way the world seemed to run on taboos and bans, a life defined by its negatives. My parents, without any theology beyond a sentimental attachment to the church where they'd met, often seemed to have devised a secular Calvinism, overhung with calamity to come, a calamity in and of the world.

I hated school, apart from one or two encouraging relationships with teachers when I was ten or eleven, and I learned to survive in a paradoxical way. I soon found out that I was better than most, if not all, of the others at the lessons; and I could sing and draw, though I'm left-handed and writing was an agony, particularly with steel pens and filthy ink. I

had no talent for naughtiness, and so had all the qualifications of a teacher's pet. Insofar as I wanted to, I could always have a secure place close to the seat of authority, crazy as that authority might seem. At the same time, I had no standing in the playground, a place which always seemed to me a chaos of violence and spite. Out there, I was for years "the Daft Kid," the slow-on-the-uptake, the dim-witted. And since that was my name, that was who I believed I was. The knowledge that I always beat them all at schoolwork was a palliative, but no more. They were reality, after all. I was never without friends, but they were drawn from the quieter end of the mob. The rougher end was something to worry about: it had some wild and violent characters from down beyond the railway tracks, and I came to rely on my acquired *persona* as a talisman for physical safety—"Let him alone, he's only the Daft Kid!"

The railway line was a real, as well as a notional, boundary in the patch of ground where I grew up—a landscape which was, in fact, made by its shape and the uses it had in those days, into a moralized

A street party in Kentish Road, 1938. Roy is the eighth child from the front on the right side of the table.

landscape. That edge of Handsworth is an easy slope running down from the ridge carrying the Birmingham-Holyhead road and into Winson Green and Smethwick, at whose conjunction Matthew Boulton's Soho Foundry stood. Wattville Road (there never was a place called Wattville, though it may once have been projected) is a straight track from top to bottom of that slope, with the main railway line which leads northwest out of the city centre three miles away crossing it halfway down; the school is the last thing before the railway bridge as you go down. The zone above the railway was mainly given over to streets of fairly tidy terraced houses; these included Kentish Road, where I was born and lived till I was twenty-three. And up beyond those streets were newer houses, a park, sports grounds, a huge semirural municipal cemetery, and a patch of farmland. But below the railway, the hill seemed to steepen, dropping among slum houses to a valley bottom filled with all the gigantic signs of heavy industry: chimney stacks, black and rusting factory buildings, huge gasholders, a pandemonium of metallic noise, a network of oily green canals. The whole place was threatening, harsh, and mysterious. Also it was a zone to which we had no entrée, since my father worked a good way nearer town, in the Jewellery Quarter.

We were out there on the western edge of Handsworth by way of a temporary expedient which turned permanent. When my father came out of the army in 1919, he and my mother, then pregnant, lodged in the house, 74 Kentish Road, rented by his sister Lizzie and her husband. It was well away from either Jones or Fisher territory. Before long, Lizzie's family moved, first to a house in the same street, then eventually to the house down on the edge of Smethwick, where they were all to be killed twenty years later. My parents took on the tenancy of 74; their three children were born there and they themselves stayed there till they died, my father in 1959 and my mother in 1965.

Kentish Road was in a small edge-of-town development of four uniform terraced streets, built sometime between 1900 and 1910. Originally they had backed onto pastureland, but that had been taken over by the sports field and timber yard of the Birmingham Carriage and Wagon Company, whose main gate was at the bottom of our street and whose territory occupied the whole of the southern outlook from our backyard. It made a decent, docile, politically conservative working-class district which at that time showed hardly anything of the raw impulse towards affluence which was to drive almost all the inhabitants to flee from it in the fifties. When I was a

child, many of the adults around me had been born in vile slums; it was as if they were resting for a generation before moving on. It was a quiet, tired, fatalistic place, where the people made great efforts to establish and guard their privacy. There was very little of the proverbial working-class habit of being always in and out of one another's houses.

Our house was small, though I've lived in bigger ones that felt smaller. It had a tiny garden at the front, with a domed bush of yellow privet and a border of bluebells. There was a narrow hall, and a front parlour with a piano and an archaic three-piece suite. The living room had a deal table with a green chenille cloth, a blackleaded range, again with a chenille valance round its high mantelpiece, on which stood a polished brass shellcase and other ornaments. There was an old blue basket chair, and the remains of a suite upholstered in green and red. Down one step was the narrow little kitchen containing a stone sink with the house's one tap, a built-in copper boiler, a small range fireplace, a black gas cooker, a mangle that folded to make a table, and, in wet weather, my father's and my brother's bicycles. There was a canary in a cage, my father's pet; and outside in the blue-brick-paved yard he had others—fish in an aquarium on a stand, and a large wall-mounted cage for a song thrush. Along the yard were a coal house and a toilet with a scrubbed plank seat. The house was a set of closed compartments, in which it was possible for the five of us to have some seclusion from one another when we wanted it, if not from the neighbours, whose noise came through the walls on either side regardless. The staircase was hidden behind a door opening off the living room and led to three bedrooms, one very small. The house was lit, rather dimly, by gas, except for the bedrooms, where, since the gas was unreliable, we burned oil; I had a homemade lamp made from a coffee bottle filled with paraffin, with a bootlace for a wick. The whole place was floored with cold linoleum, and there were a couple of homemade rag hearth rugs. There were few books, and we took a newspaper and comics; there were some intensely memorable monochrome framed prints, and four gilt-framed original oil paintings by a local artist; I still have three of them. Nothing much changed in the house till the end of the thirties, when an upturn in the jewellery trade and, probably more significantly, the fact that my sister and brother had left school and were earning, brought electric light and some more modern furniture.

The gardens were the width of the houses, ten or twelve feet, and no more than thirty feet long: they were strips for hanging out washing. My father took ours over and populated it densely with plants and animals. Against the solid sports-field fence he improvised a shed for hens and rabbits; the other fences he raised to head-height with scrap wood from fruit crates and covered them with rambler roses; all the rest of the space was crammed with cottage garden flowers and whatever vegetables there was room for. Beyond the garden, the chief amenity was open sky. The sports field, much of it rough grass, stretched away for half-a-mile, with the next factory buildings miniaturised beyond it; and to the left, the works timber yard was spacious and remote, with a small locomotive and a couple of steam cranes puffing about in it. I always had one of the bedrooms facing out westwards over this area; there was nothing claustrophobic about being there.

That open view was important. Even more so was the access to the area of countryside which opened up ten minutes' walk away, across the Holyhead road. Although it lay at the city boundary it wasn't open country; that was a couple of hours' bus ride away. The few square miles of land we had, a single shallow valley under a crest of upland, was just a patch that hadn't yet been turned to city uses, lying across the widening stretch between that Holyhead road and the next one to the east, that went on to Stafford and Manchester. The Birmingham suburbs petered out just about where we lived, and gave way to this rather run-down bit of country, which, strangely, didn't go on reaching to the northwest as the roads diverged, but was hemmed in after a few miles by a string of industrial townships which gradually joined up to isolate it. But it was an enclosure whose edges you didn't have to think about, unless you wanted to react to the mysterious sight of sunlit cooling towers rising above a misty horizon ten miles away. It was a vista of fields and copses and rags of hedgerow, stands of tall trees, and the long sandstone wall of what had been the Earl of Dartmouth's estate. Its heart was made up of five or six farms, dominated by a pair of collieries; a railway branch line ran through the fields; and pushing quietly in from the edges were the spacious, landgrabbing outreaches of city life; two lonely golf courses with birch woods and scrub; a public park; the vast cemetery, still mostly unused, and, wherever the houses stopped, allotment gardens packed with weird shanties with their flue-pipes, rain-barrels, and bits of pub window.

So there was no clear distinction between the town and the country. The cemetery and the golf course had wild edges to them, and the desolate reed-bordered pool that was the destination for special excursions lay, with a complete scenic rightness, under the arid, black and red-brown spoil heap of Jubilee Colliery, with its baleful flat top and the deep scars of rain channels running down to the thickets of alder and willow around its base. Nobody ever suggested in my hearing that the collieries or the cemetery or the allotments were "spoiling" the landscape. They were part of it; it was a particular type of countryside that had those things in it.

When I was old enough I would spend, with friends or alone, walking or cycling, a great deal of time there. When I was younger it was a regular Sunday-morning excursion with my father, part of a routine set of activities. We'd walk the lanes while my mother cooked. In the afternoon she'd join us for a strange family party on one of the upper slopes of the cemetery, with sweeping views. A selection of my father's brothers and sisters, their spouses and children—up to a dozen people—would gather at the grave of my grandmother and my uncle Albert, who'd died young. My grandfather never came. They'd change the flowers in the marble urn, talk for an hour, and disperse. I grew to be quite at home there. When my mother's mother and uncle Ted were buried a couple of hundred yards down the slope, some of us would tend that too. It had a patch of turf, which my father would clip with a pair of kitchen scissors he carried in his pocket.

Sometimes we'd take our walks in the other direction, down into Hell, quiet and sunlit on a Sunday morning. Whereas I took the countryside to be righteous, there was a whiff of addiction about my appetite for the beauty of the great rusting sheds, the tarry stinks, and the slimy canals of Smethwick. It was a lonely and gigantic landscape, with hardly anybody in it.

Until I was in my teens we travelled very little indeed. Each year there'd be a trip or two to the city centre, little more than three miles away, and a day's outing by bus or tram to one of the traditional spots just outside the city—the Lickey Hills, or Kinver Edge. Before I was born, there had been family holidays by the sea, but I was never to go on holiday with my parents. I was thirteen before I slept a night outside Birmingham; and there had probably been only two or three nights away from home in all that time. There were a few day trips to more distant places, so rare and so unreal that they had for me the impact of transcendental spiritual visitations. At six I was taken to the Malverns, and in a neighbour's car to the Vale of Llangollen and the mountains and seacoast of North Wales. The same neighbours later

At Kentish Road, 1989

took us to the Vale of Evesham and Dovedale. These places—I didn't know where they were, or why they were as they were—excited me enormously.

I was already reading obsessively, the books coming not from school, where the provision was thin, but from the public library, which I joined shortly after starting school. And I was drawing. I started with a blackboard and coloured chalks, then went on to cover every paper surface that could be provided for me, usually with pencil and crayon drawings, sometimes with watercolour. I was fairly slapdash, but I don't think I conformed for long to what is expected of child artists. I was inspired by the illustrators of adventure stories, historical romances, and by the appearances of things as I saw them at the cinema. All these I set myself to copy, repeating and developing favourite scenes over and over again. The siege of Omdurman in *The Four Feathers*, episodes from the Errol Flynn *Robin Hood*, Trafalgar, from *Lady Hamilton*. I drew in a sort of panoramic realism, with scores of characters accurately costumed and equipped, and mostly stuck full of spears or arrows.

For years this activity was the most positive thing in my life. It led to the only real lift I got from my school days, something which should, I suppose, have set me on a career as a painter had I been able to seize the advantage. In September 1939, the school had been closed down and most of the children evacuated to the country. My parents elected not to send me, reasoning on my behalf that, were they to be killed, the double bereavement would be more than I could bear, and that hence I would no doubt prefer to be blown to bits along with them. I was told all this at the time, and was persuaded. Early in 1940, the school reopened for the few who remained, and I quickly passed the examination qualifying me to go on to the grammar school when I was old enough, in a year and a half's time. In doing so, I'd virtually exhausted the Wattville Road curriculum and had time to spare. Pop Lewis, my teacher, a shrewd and spirited Welshman, played a hunch and set me up in a corner with a full-sized blackboard and easel, a set of powder colours and brushes, the biggest sheet of paper I'd ever seen, and a commission to paint *The Knights of the Round Table Asleep under the Hill until Britain's Hour of Need*. It took days, and people came to watch. I rose to the challenge. When the picture was hung high on the classroom wall I had a little fame, and the status of court painter. I was excused lessons for long periods to paint subjects of my choice. My range was wide: *The Last Fight of the "Revenge," Marco Polo Setting Out from Venice for Asia, Everyday Life in Ancient Rome, Abraham Leading Isaac Away from the Family Tent to Be Sacrificed, Marco Polo Returning to Venice from Asia*. There was even a street scene, painted from the life. These all hung above the desks, a deep, lengthening frieze. I suppose I had talent. I certainly enjoyed my role, and took it seriously.

Outside the painting, however, there were things starting to go wrong for me. At seven I'd become myopic and had to wear glasses. I took this blow very badly, for it removed me overnight from any hope of normality. We were a family accustomed to dark good looks in youth, and I was now not going to make

it. As well as being the Daft Kid I had to join the very small number of children who were patronised, or worse, for having some physical disability. Adults were kind; children, boys and girls alike, were merciless, until the novelty wore off. My outer and inner lives started to drift away from each other. Anxiously overfed by my mother, I grew fat, and stayed so. My life started to move in a series of lurches, between mild hope and mild despair. The war itself had a mixed effect. The air raids of 1940, when I spent many of my nights in the Anderson shelter in the garden, with bombs and equally lethal British shrapnel whistling down, were exciting but appalling, not so much from the fear of a notional death as from the actual presence afterwards of acres of destruction and disorder, the still, featureless mountains of bricks which had been neighbouring streets. After that, my brother and my brother-in-law spent years in danger; I would engage in elaborate daily muttered rituals, which grew longer and longer, in order to ensure their safety, which I believed depended only on me. At the same time, there was, with the prolongation of stoicism, a deadening of areas of feeling.

Moving to Handsworth Grammar School cheered me up at first. Life was socially more comfortable, and the air of tradition—most of it fairly new in fact—was supportive and seductive for a while. But merely being selected to go there, a mile away from home, isolated me to an exaggerated extent from the place I'd grown up in. From my Wattville Road class of forty, only three of us went to the Boys' Grammar School and two or three to the Girls'. Nobody from Kentish Road had ever gone before, except my own sister and brother, years before. This fact, the expectation that all the Fisher children were on the conveyor belt and in the process of being educated out of the street, set the family apart, in an odd way. We weren't brash or go-getting, but there was a slight air of our having received a higher call.

Handsworth Grammar School was a nineteenth-century foundation. Like nearly all such places it had developed the function of educating the sons of local lower-middle-class families—technical, clerical, shopkeeping, the sort of people who didn't send their children away to boarding schools—to perpetuate that class, and in addition to draw promising working-class boys "up" into it. The handful of us from Wattville Road were of the latter sort; certain other schools in better-off neighbourhoods sent their boys to the grammar school *en masse*. The staff was fairly typical, except for its Head, a product of public school and Cambridge, a haughty, cold-mannered zealot, an

Anglican cleric and a Buchmanite, whose declared aim was to reproduce, as far as was possible in such a place, the ethos of a public school like Arnold's Rugby. Its application was to be local: to feed industry with technically and scientifically trained personnel, in the process declassing any whose class origins were likely to hamper their social mobility. We were encouraged, for instance, to lose the local characteristics in our speech; with the blood of servants running in my veins, and some talent for mimicry, I turned out to be quite good at this game. The family accent wasn't a strongly marked Brummagem, but tended to take on different characteristics according to the occupations its speakers followed. I easily acquired a neutral, go-anywhere accent—so easily that I later felt angry at the way it had smoothed out of my memory the speech I first had. I can't hear my own unaltered voice.

I soon learned that painting played no part in the school's plans for my advancement. The top stream into which I was put had no art in its curriculum, no examinable music, no geography or history. I let my painting and drawing go without a fight; I couldn't see what the fight could have been. I kept them going as private activities for a while, but the talent didn't survive puberty. By this time, though, I was singing, untrained, in the school choir, having taken to it too late to make the sort of mark my father and brother—who had followed him as head chorister at Saint Mary's, as did my son Joe—had made. Technically I did join that choir, conquering my distaste for the liturgy and the fancy dress, but so late that during a bout of pneumonia that came between my audition and my debut my voice had broken. But it was to be music that first replaced painting for me.

That illness, a couple of months away from the world after passing through mortal danger, was a rite of passage, a *Magic Mountain* in miniature. I spent most of it in my room, looking out at the sky over the factory yard and the field, watching the spring arrive, reading, drawing, and thinking. My feelings sharpened and clarified. After the confusion and pain of the illness had passed, I was happy in my isolation. I experienced, in fact, many of the sensations of Mann's hero. I was twelve. When I emerged, I was less of a child. I hadn't become a conventional, active adolescent; I lurked behind a vaguely juvenile manner for years. But it was as if I'd been somewhere unknown, and had come back altered. Wherever it was, it's the location of my imagination; it's still the place I have to find in order to write, and its essential qualities never alter. It combines a sense of lyrical remoteness with an apprehension of something tur-

bulent, bulky, and dark. There, I don't have to bother to grow older.

I didn't move towards writing at that time, though I was reading everything I could find—and also listening to the radio. We'd acquired a radio only a little while before the war began, and I spent, like almost everybody else, a great part of the next five years listening to BBC broadcasts indiscriminately. The BBC was still very much as Reith had left it; it was also wartime, and the British, disoriented, had inadvertently dropped some of their defences against experiencing the arts. It was from reading the *Radio Times,* in those days an earnest and responsible journal, that I first realised there was an adult world of music, painting, and writing all around me, out of immediate reach but capable of being sought after. Very gradually I found my way around. It was late in 1943, when I had the musical tastes of an unassisted thirteen-year-old—I knew all the popular tunes of the day, along with a little Handel, a little Rossini, Tchaikovsky, Holst, Grieg—that I was knocked permanently into a different trajectory by a single record heard on a request programme. This was Meade Lux Lewis's 1936 piano solo, "Honky Tonk Train Blues." In the three minutes it took to hear it, it seemed as if every cell I had was mobilized to go in search of those unimagined sounds, which seemed to have nothing to do with any music I'd ever heard—even jazz, which had simply sounded rackety, overurgent stuff.

In those same minutes, I realised that my new passion was to be yet another of my secrets: nobody would approve of it. I began listening to any programmes where the music might appear, dissembling my intense interest, even joining in the insults it provoked when it showed up. I started scraping away at our semiderelict piano in an attempt to reproduce what I was hearing, and kept on doing so until I had some success, believing all the while that my ambition was secret. I don't know how I persuaded myself that this could be. The noise, in a small house, was loud, brutal, and insistent; neighbouring shift-workers complained. My parents suggested I should take lessons, probably in the hope that my practice would become more euphonious, but I declined, believing that the lessons would come between me and what I wanted to play—and, by declining, storing up years of technical troubles; I was to reach fifty before I took any lessons.

It wasn't long before my pursuit of piano boogie opened up the whole of jazz. I listened to whatever was broadcast—we had no gramophone—and, almost more important, read whatever there was to read. Two books, Wilder Hobson's *American Jazz*

Music and Hugues Panassié's *Le Jazz hot,* modelled as they were on orthodox musical criticism and intent on assimilating the new art to the traditional ones, were the first developed writings about any of the arts I ever encountered. I read them over and over again, and can still call whole sentences up from memory. They had an enormous influence on the way I thought in general, and in particular, directed my taste to a congenial quarter, the white Chicago musicians who came up in the twenties and continued to work in association with Eddie Condon—Bud Freeman, Dave Tough, Joe Sullivan, Pee Wee Russell, Jess Stacy. Of all the men who had ever made jazz, these constituted the only group whose circumstances were at all like my own.

The passion for jazz and for the piano was one of the positive lurches. It kept me going through a dreary period of school examinations, and the last stages of the war and its aftermath. By the end of 1943 I'd grown out of feeding off the war in any way, and it had turned to an endless dull horror. I was not cheered by the atomic bomb, or by the manifest state of things as the Cold War set in. My father's brief prosperity ended, and he went back, none too happily, to his jewellery firm. The young men of the family came back, much older and without illusions. At school, I moved up into the vestigial Arts Sixth, without objectives and feeling much further out of my depth than I need have done. There was an undertow of what I can only describe as unfelt sadness, somehow drawing my spirits down, not dramatically but gently and steadily.

Sometime early in 1946 I left the world, and stayed away from it for three years. Afterwards, I found it hard to get back, and I still sometimes experience the recurring shadow of that time. What happened was that I radically revalued the currency of my dealings with my life: I renegotiated my contract. In the quiet madness that took hold of me I became convinced, without any evidence, that I had an unknown, virtually undetectable form of tuberculosis, and was already too far gone for treatment to be of any use. I had two or three years left at the most. I would certainly never see twenty. More to the point, I would never have to.

The disease was then still a common-enough killer of young people, and I'd seen it at work; and I imagine my particular form of hysteria is common enough in the literature—though the only person I've ever known who entertained it, and in an almost identical form, is another poet, Patricia Beer. At all events, I now held the biggest of all my secrets. I was

dead. No one must know. The shock would kill my parents, naturally; so delay their learning about it as long as possible. As the possessor of a deadly disease, I also had the power of life and death over everybody I met. I had no inclination to be other than merciful, so for three years I didn't, apart from the odd unavoidable handshake and an arm's-length dandling of my newborn nieces, touch another human being. This was easy. Nobody observed any change in my behaviour, and there probably was none.

I was extremely healthy. In order to guard my secret I didn't go near a doctor for the whole of the period, nor did I need to. I stayed fat, cycled everywhere—while I could, until the unmistakable signs should appear. I kept on reading, coasted through schoolwork, developed my piano playing to the point where I could start appearing in public, sitting in with a band and playing solo spots at local jazz clubs.

Everything, though, was temporary. I put down nothing for the future, prepared nothing, confided in nobody. The renegotiated contract meant that I needed to do nothing beyond dabbling, diverting myself from my awful fate. As for motivation and structure, they were taken care of by the daily business of preserving my cover—for I wanted to remain at large as long as I could get away with it, secure in the knowledge that it wouldn't be for an inconveniently long time. I'd had almost enough of life: I didn't want in, but I didn't want out strongly enough to commit suicide. Indeed, I didn't have the strength of feeling of a suicide.

I structured my life as a spy must—days of low-key activities, offbeat, bitchy humour, casual-seeming appearances here and there, all within the main concern of preserving cover. I did enough work, for instance, to get myself a university place (whatever that might be—*I* didn't know) simply because attending a university would delay the army medical which would expose me and consign me precipitately to the sanatorium where I would spend my last months in the composition of a few important poems, probably in the style of Matthew Arnold. When I learned that Birmingham University, where my place was, administered a medical to all freshmen, I stayed at school for a further year to try for a scholarship at Cambridge, which, so far as I knew, didn't do anything so intrusive. That step meant that I was made Head Prefect, a position of greater power than any I've held since. I was a quite efficient disciplinary bureaucrat, operating with the arrogance the job traditionally demanded and with an added quiet menace generated by my understandably distant attitude to the whole thing. It was splendid cover. On one occasion I even evaded a compulsory mass chest X ray call by marshalling the entire school, boys and masters, onto the buses that took them to the radiography centre, then omitting to join the trip myself.

I didn't get the Cambridge scholarship. My motivation was too oblique, and my preparation hopelessly inadequate; the school wasn't equipped for such work. I had to fall back on Birmingham and its medical, and make the most of the months that remained. When I left school my remote and disaffected manner earned me a beta-plus for Personality in place of the customary straight A awarded to Head Prefects. It was an unprecedented snub. I thought it no bad score, for a corpse.

Going to the university changed my spectral life hardly at all. I cycled a couple of miles beyond the school each day, to the old Arts Faculty building in the city centre. I didn't know at first what course my school had enrolled me for. It didn't matter. I didn't buy books; I made notes in the backs of old school exercise books. I got caught up in a student jazz band, and decided to stay alive until its November Carnival gig; my medical would probably not fall due till February or March.

But the call came early. I cycled halfway to the medical centre, hallucinated chest pains, and phoned in my excuses. I was told to see my own doctor. He told me I had flu, completely failing to observe the wrecked condition of my lungs. Nobody at the postponed medical spotted anything either. The chest X ray I had would show it all, though. Waiting for the recall, I heard of other students being called in for repeats. But no message came for me. My game was up and I had to recognise it. I was alive, and must immediately adjust to the fact. Instantly and completely, I forgot the delusion which had dominated my life for three years; I mentioned it to nobody, and didn't remember it for a further two years. It was only then that I understood how mad I'd been, and it was the forgetting I found more frightening than the delusion itself.

After that moment in my nineteenth year, I had to begin my life, at the point to which my long absence had let it drift. I had to learn—and quickly— to study, smoke, drink, dance, compete, talk to girls, get around generally. At first I worked frantically to catch up lost ground, with the simple aim of not getting thrown out of the university. I overshot and did rather well, made friends, got around. The local jazz scene of which I'd been a part for a year or two

was in a trough, and there was less in it for me. While I was still at death's door I'd played solo at a big concert (insisting, in the interests of secrecy, that my name be excluded from all publicity) and had been invited to make a record for review in the leading jazz magazine—which I did. But the game was turning sour; maybe I realised that in my years away I'd equipped myself, technically, only very poorly and wasn't going to be able to sustain the chances that were coming my way. I broke engagements abruptly, and gave up playing in public for quite a few years.

I came to feel, as I turned nineteen, that I ought to want to write. I seemed to be becoming the sort of young man who had that wish. Thomas Mann's *Doktor Faustus*, which I first read about this time, had a good deal to do with it; my recent experience qualified me to be sceptical about its thesis, but the account of Leverkühn's artistic education made deliberate creative work seem possible. The insights linked up with something that had happened three years before, at the very onset of my imaginary malady, but which had had to remain isolated and dormant. The school sent a party of us to a belated piece of wartime

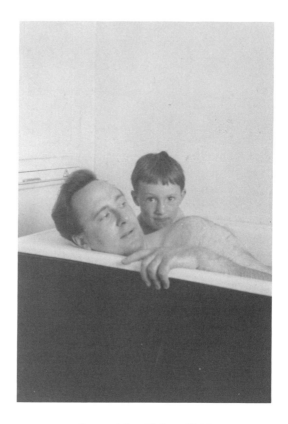

Roy and Joe Fisher, 1961

Basil Bunting, Roy Fisher, Michael Butler, and Gael Turnbull, about 1970

cultural education. For the time, it was something unheard of: a three-day course in film education. Fine gentlemen—Charles Frend, Michael Balcon, Roger Manvell—lectured us about their close experience of this art, and had us sitting goggling at films the like of which we'd never seen before: *Metropolis, Alexander Nevsky, The Plow That Broke the Plains, Night Mail, Steel, Drifters.* There was nothing academic about it all. It just hit hard. Again, there was a disruptive sense of what was possible. I don't think it strange that *Doktor Faustus* didn't make me want to be a composer, just as the film course didn't make me want to direct films; I've grown used to having poetic ideas opened up by arts other than poetry.

Gradually, I got the idea of writing into focus, chiefly by reading, wave on wave of whatever contemporary or recent work I could get hold of, altering taste and orientation by the week. In Septem-

ber 1949, I began keeping an intense, precious journal of my sensibility, and within a month had arrived at a poem. It was meant as a pledge of allegiance to early Dylan Thomas, and every word of it was false; but to be able to write it at all gave me a sense of exultant power. Naturally, I kept the whole thing to myself. I wrote more: pastiches of Auden, Empson, Henry Reed, in rapid succession. Writing was very difficult. I had a certain ability at phrase-making, but no facility of thought or form at all. I was working against resistances quite as formidable as the manual and theoretical problems posed by the piano keyboard.

After nearly a year, my reading had taken me to a stage where I could understand poetry as going beyond verbal sensations to a way of analysing cultures, and I wrote, in some excitement and with much more assurance, a short dramatic monologue in

94

pentameters. The speaker was a King Lear analogue, and he spoke severally through the mouths of Yeats, Rilke, Eliot, and Rafael Alberti—and probably more. There were a few poets around the university: R. F. Willetts was teaching Greek, D. J. Enright was an extramural tutor, and Paul West, not yet a novelist, was a final-year undergraduate. They often attended a staff-student writers' group. I read my piece there, and got plenty of encouragement. The university magazine published it; a door of sorts was opening.

I graduated, well enough to be given a research scholarship, and proceeded to go quietly to pieces again. I'd been good at quick, impressionistic criticism, but didn't know how to work systematically. I was setting out to solve some of the conundrums of metrical analysis, but was too full of a sort of libertarian dogmatism to get anywhere with it. I'd been running with a pack of Jungians and reading Robert Graves; my mind was animated but hardly open. I was obsessed with patterns and hierarchies. My poems became flat, dogmatic arrangements of symbols; my imagination was a panhistoric costume drama.

In an act which seems to me far more bizarre than my imaginary illness, but of which I'm more ashamed, since it was real, I joined a Christian church, on an intellectual whim. I decided that the cult of the Great Mother was magically perpetuated in the sacraments of the Christian church, and that I needed to receive those sacraments in order to share that magical linkage. The ultimate aim would be to subvert the Christian churches back into the Old Religion. I positioned myself at the highest, most ritualistic point of Anglo-Catholicism I could find, took the sacraments, and acquired a pious religiosity, while keeping my real intentions from my instructors. All this was most perverse, for I've always had a deep repugnance for Christianity, in its essence, and for its role in history—an attitude similar to that of Edward Gibbon, and held for similar reasons. But unaccustomed to action or commitment, I was forcing myself against my own nature—was, in fact, forcing my nature to abdicate and submit to something alien and uncongenial.

This went on for a year or two, fading slowly. It wasn't a good period. My scholarship wasn't renewed, for my intellect was being seriously disabled by its own efforts, and by my naïve flailing around for something—preferably something stuffy—to believe in. I'd edited the university magazine, but had run out of steam early and relinquished the editorship. I was still living with my parents, but was withdrawn into my own preoccupations, and oppressed by their many troubles; I was drawn to try to help them, but felt powerless. They were now in their sixties and seeming older. My father's health was breaking down by way of a series of strokes; he was often very anxious, and the damage to his brain brought his thinking and talk down into a more and more limited compass.

In my last year at the university I tried to continue my research while training as a teacher. It wasn't a career I wanted to follow, but I had no other plans, and it was the only job I'd ever watched anyone else doing extensively. Occasionally I wrote doctrinaire fantasy poems, but published only a few of them. I socialized a good deal; my friend Barbara Venables and I spent most of our time at the theatre or in pubs, dressing up and laying the law down. We got married while we were still both students. We were married for many years, and had two sons, Joe and Ben; we stayed friends through that, and remain so now.

My working life started in a characteristically ghostly fashion. When my student exemption from military service ran out, a couple of minor disabilities caused me to be declared unfit, but only on a temporary basis; I could be called in again at any time. The medical exemption was acceptable, for it saved me the trouble of going through the charade of disguising my political objections to military service as reservations of a more tender sort, and still paying a social penalty; but its temporary nature left me in a limbo of an all-too-familiar kind. I could only take a job under false pretences. Which I proceeded to do. I became a teacher at a grammar school in Newton Abbot, in Devon, expecting to be called away at any time, and for that reason living from day to day and putting down no roots. There was no way I could resolve my situation, and instead I treated it as unreal, even to the extent of concealing my address from the authorities and ignoring official summonses when they reached me. Again it was a life of temporary experiences, temporary sensations. It was over a year before an inescapable call caught up with me. This time I failed the medical conclusively. Once again I had to accept my situation as real, and catch up with it.

We lived in Torquay at first, in a squalid, rickety flat, and later in more comfort in Newton Abbot, and I found the area fascinating—for its towns more than its countryside: I'd never lived away from Birmingham before. I'd had no wish to become a schoolteacher; and it was perhaps this lack of seriousness and method which made me turn out to be, from my point of view, disconcertingly good at it. I hated schools as institutions as much as I had done as a pupil, so I treated it all as a compulsory game, and took risks I wouldn't have taken as a serious professional. I read Homer Lane and A. S. Neill, and taught accordingly. The results, of course, were pretty good. Although I didn't enjoy being a teacher, this experience, over the four years I spent there, taught me more about living in the real world than did all my explorations of the West Country. Those gave me enormous pleasure, but they contributed only to my increasingly tortuous fantasy life, which started, in about 1954, to break out into poems again. It was about that time that I came across the work of John Cowper Powys; different from me in almost every imaginable way, he was nevertheless able to show me how to accept an obsessional, quite unpresentable inner existence, a private madness, as a life force to be harnessed rather than locked in and ignored. For a while I worked more in the hope of producing massive novels like his than of making poems. Such poems as I did write were bulky and suffused, or

Bud Freeman, Henry Livings, Ron Parry, and Brian Wiltshire, with Roy Fisher at the keyboard, during a TV broadcast in 1980

manic, completely dedicated to psychic self-exploration. I'd grown out of the cold ritualism of a few years before, but there was nothing in my poems that might interest anybody else, except a certain energy and a perverse rhetorical force.

It was that odd energy which got me into publication and into touch with what has turned out to be my work. In 1954 a couple of my shorter fantasy poems were broadcast in a local radio programme run by Charles Causley, and some time later John Sankey took one for his nonconformist little magazine, *The Window.* I thought nothing of this. I'd been paid seven-and-sixpence, on condition that I let Sankey alter one line, and had grown out of the poem anyway; but I was surprised to receive a letter from one of the other contributors, Gael Turnbull, whose (as it seemed to me then) perilously slight, purist lyrics I'd noticed. He'd been commissioned to furnish a selection of new British poetry for an issue of Cid Corman's *Origin,* then still in its first series, and, importantly, close to the most vital initiatives in the poetry of Black Mountain College. The mandate was to find British poets who were outside the orthodoxy of the time. I was no Black Mountain poet; I was just another muffled English provincial eccentric. But I was certainly well outside the neat, socially oriented orthodox poetic, which had neither appeal nor meaning for me; I couldn't even mimic it.

Gael Turnbull, part Scot, part Swede, educated in England and the United States, and just returned from a spell in Canada to work in a London hospital before settling in Worcester, was another inevitable outsider; we had that much in common. Apart from the entrée to *Origin*—Corman approved of what I was doing and used three of my more lightly constructed fantasy pieces—he was able to show me a great deal. On a two-day visit to Worcester late in 1956, I saw for the first time the work of the later Williams, Basil Bunting, Robert Duncan, Allen Ginsberg, Louis Zukofsky, Irving Layton, Robert Creeley, Lawrence Ferlinghetti, Denise Levertov, Charles Tomlinson, Larry Eigner, and Charles Olson. I'd never seen poetry used as these people were, in their various ways, using it; nor had I seen it treated as so vital an activity. These people were behaving with all the freedom and artistic optimism of painters. Decidedly un-English.

I went home and tackled my writing from a new direction. I had already on occasion used chance operations to begin poems I didn't think important; now I used such methods extensively—usually short phrases picked at random, often by my wife, Barbara, who would sometimes arrive at them by automatic writing. The main effect of the method was to get me out of my own way. This was very necessary. I'd grown up with no trace of the compact self which most other people seemed to have; instead I had a diffused zone in which *ad hoc* selves would be generated for temporary purposes, and then dissolve again. Establishing a usable, consistent self was later to prove a lengthy business, like growing a windbreak. The self I'd tried in those days to fix as a writing *persona* was just a kind of self-important bruise, a posture. It got in the way, and didn't ring true. Once rid of it, though, I could get at observations, memories, earlier selves, lost feelings, casual things—reality, in short—and my clotted language cleared like a cloudy liquid left to settle. Almost immediately a poem called "Midlanders" turned up; it didn't quite succeed, but it showed me for the first time that I had material close to hand, from my own experience, and access to an unforced way of handling it. Although by my earlier standards my new poems were oblique, casual, and obscure, people started reading them and publishing them. Before long I was in receipt of postal tutorials from Cid Corman, and correspondence from Denise Levertov, Larry Eigner, and the British poets and editors Robert Cooper and Bill Price Turner. I was out when Louis and Celia Zukofsky called at our flat in Newton Abbot; but they called, nevertheless.

Gael Turnbull was, in the years that followed, single-handedly responsible for whatever currency I had as a poet. I'd send bundles of work off to him as I wrote it. He was in touch with many editors, and would quietly place my work in magazines I'd not even heard of. I seldom tried pushing my work even then, having a gift for choosing the wrong places. Soon I gave up, and left nature to take its course; for twenty or thirty years I've been able to rely on invitations—partly since I write relatively little.

I was in a liberated mood, too, because I had, or thought I had, the prospect of giving up full-time teaching. I was being given advancement at the school, and that made me uncomfortable, for I was thereby losing my position as a licensed young experimenter and being brought into the hierarchy. In a year or two I'd be in charge of a department, then in line for a headship, which would involve my identifying myself, to a greater extent than I was willing to do, with the generally Christian and conservative ethos of schools of that sort—indeed, most schools. We decided to go back to Birmingham. Barbara would teach—in Devon I'd had the only job, for which we were both qualified—while I'd work part-time in a primary school, and, for the rest, build

up a connection as a piano player. As it turned out, her teaching job turned into our son Joe, and I had to hang on to a full-time post in a school so hellishly unruly that I resigned before my year was out, with no job to go to.

Luck, and my teaching testimonials, landed me comfortably on my feet in a college of education, in one of the Black Country towns on the western edge of Birmingham. The place was run on breathtakingly hypocritical and paternalist lines, and my political education was considerably advanced; what I learned, I endeavoured to pass on to my students. But the duties were pleasant, and I was more effective as a teacher of teachers than of children directly. The pay was poor, though, and the penury I'd experienced ever since I went onto a payroll was deepening with a family to keep, so I needed all the piano-playing work I could get. We lived for the next thirteen years back in Handsworth, in a house we couldn't at first afford, a few hundred yards from my mother's old home, Ivy Cottage, by then embedded in a housing estate. For the first five

Joyce Holliday, 1987

Fisher's home in the Derbyshire hills (surrounded by a wall, at center)

of those years I was constantly out at nights, playing in Dixieland bands, bebop quartets, and Black Country dance bands; for a while I was the token white in the Andy Hamilton Caribbean Combo. I played in jazz clubs, town halls, village halls, strip clubs, dance halls, drinking clubs, and hotels. There was still plenty wrong with my playing, but I got by, and enjoyed it. It was a belated version of my surrendered adolescence.

Living in constant, and apparently inescapable, debt darkened my spirits to some extent, and I wrote poetry less freely. But I found that returning to Birmingham after an absence had given me an artist's distance from it; I wanted to write about it, and became immersed in its associative power. My journeys through it in connection with my educational work and my piano playing were in all directions at all hours of the day and night. I saw it from the oddest of angles. Without any particular aim I started on the voluminous series of prose pieces and poems which I was to help Michael Shayer to edit down to the Migrant pamphlet *City,* which appeared, as my first collection, in 1961.

With that publication, my inner and outer lives at last had no choice but to confront each other. I didn't at all enjoy being displayed as the author of the pamphlet, in spite of the favourable attention it got, and I retired, bewildered, into a writer's block and a nervous breakdown. I did find other things to write in the next few years, the most enjoyable for me being the prose work *The Ship's Orchestra,* which I started in 1962, after prolonged staring at Picasso's *Three Musicians.* With that, and the sequence of poems *Ten Interiors with Various Figures,* I knew I'd found a tone and a way of relating to material I could feel at home with. I'd also saddled myself with my troublesome inability to repeat formulae, which puts me to the bother of inventing a new form every time I start writing again. I'm happy, though, to continue to avoid people's attempts to put final labels on what I do.

I set myself so many challenges that I experienced a virtually complete block from 1966 to 1970; inconvenient because during that period *The Ship's Orchestra* and *Collected Poems, 1968* (so titled because I believed it was my last, although only my second, book) were being handsomely published by Stuart and Deirdre Montgomery's Fulcrum Press, and I was being invited to contribute to magazines and give readings. I evaded the block finally by taking a year's sabbatical from Bordesley College, Birmingham (to which I'd moved as Head of Department in 1963, the year my son Ben was born), to read, shake myself out of a fugitive period when I'd spent most of my time hiding away and making a garden, and look over my earlier writings. It worked. In the first six months of 1970 I wrote two books, *The Cut Pages* and *Matrix,* and a master's thesis. Since then, I've written when I've wanted to, and have kept busy with readings and broadcasts; sometimes I've been paid to give thoroughly egocentric talks on what it's like to be born without a self.

In 1971 I joined the Department of American Studies at Keele University, fifty miles north of Birmingham, and the following year moved house there. After forty years spent almost continuously in Birmingham, this small removal was more momentous than it sounds. I'd been using Birmingham less and less through the sixties, as it and I changed. I'd come to another trough in the local music scene, and had virtually given up performing. I was reacting to the place only retrospectively, and I had few strong ties there. When I go there again now, as I quite often do, I regard it much as I regard other cities I visit.

Keele treated me well, and I taught there till 1982, when I was able to quit teaching and live by my wits as a free-lance writer and musician, a life which suits me very well. Falling in quickly with the jazz musicians of the area, I'd spent more and more time playing, working in local bands, or as an accompanist to visiting American musicians—even my boyhood heroes, Bud Freeman and Wild Bill Davison, and their heirs, Kenny Davern and Bob Wilber. More recently I've been working also as a soloist at jazz festivals.

Living in North Staffordshire gave me more access to hills than I'd ever had before. Keele's western skyline has the Shropshire hills, from the Wrekin to Caer Caradoc, with the hills of the Welsh border beyond; eastwards I could look across the Potteries towns to the jagged edge of the Staffordshire moorlands, giving onto the southern Pennines and Derbyshire. By my late forties, having become a somewhat tougher and less phobic character than I'd been when younger, I took to living alone, as a sort of gregarious hermit, and did so for seven years or more, first on the campus at Keele, then, when I left the university, in an isolated house thirteen hundred feet up among those crags. It was virtually in the centre of what has become my adoptive landscape, an

area I've described as being about the same size as Birmingham, and, in its way, equally complex; its topography is beautiful, and so intricate that it's almost impossible to hold its shapes in the mind. In the long poem I wrote while living in that house, *A Furnace,* I call it a "land-maze." I'd found my way into the maze during years of exploring it with the playwright Joyce Holliday, who already knew her way round it. In 1986 she came to join me in it, and we moved to a house big enough for us both to work in. In 1987 we were married.

We live on an acre of rocky ground—a larger plot than my father's, but not yet so productive—above a crossroads and looking over the little quarrying and farming village of Earl Sterndale. We're in that strange, miniaturized mountain landscape at the edge of the Derbyshire limestone, where green conical hills shoot up fantastically hundreds of feet from the banks of the upper Dove. It feels remote, with, on the hilltops all around us, the low, grassy bumps of the emptied tombs of Bronze Age chieftains, and with their descendants quite possibly still working the farms; but half the population of England are living somewhere within sixty or seventy miles of us, in a ring of cities. It's a good place.

BIBLIOGRAPHY

Poetry:

City. Worcester, England, and Ventura, Calif.: Migrant Press, 1961.

Then Hallucinations: City II. Worcester, England, and Ventura, Calif.: Migrant Press, 1962.

The Ceremonial Poems. Cradley, England: Gael Turnbull, 1966.

Ten Interiors with Various Figures. Nottingham, England: Tarasque Press, 1966.

The Memorial Fountain. Newcastle upon Tyne, England: Northern House, 1967.

Collected Poems, 1968. London: Fulcrum Press, 1969.

Titles. Nottingham, England: Tarasque Press, 1969.

Matrix. London: Fulcrum Press, 1971.

Nineteen Poems and an Interview (interview conducted by Jed Rasula and Mike Erwin). Pensnett, England: Grosseteste Press, 1975.

Four Poems. Newcastle upon Tyne, England: Pig Press, 1976.

Barnardine's Reply. Knotting, England: Sceptre Press, 1977.

The Thing about Joe Sullivan: Poems, 1971–1977. Manchester: Carcanet New Press, 1978.

Comedies. Newcastle upon Tyne, England: Pig Press, 1979.

Wonders of Obligation. Bretenoux, France: Braad Editions, 1980.

Poems, 1955–1980. Oxford and New York: Oxford University Press, 1980.

Consolidated Comedies. Newcastle upon Tyne, England: Pig Press, 1981.

The Half-Year Letters: An Alphabet Book (designed by Ronald King). Guildford, England: Circle Press, 1983.

A Furnace. Oxford and New York: Oxford University Press, 1986.

Poems, 1955–1987. Oxford and New York: Oxford University Press, 1988.

Prose Poetry:

The Ship's Orchestra. London: Fulcrum Press, 1967.

Correspondence, with Tom Phillips. London: Tetrad Press, 1970.

Metamorphoses (illustrated by Tom Phillips). London: Tetrad Press, 1970.

The Cut Pages. London: Fulcrum Press, 1971.

Three Early Pieces. London: Transgravity Press, 1971.

Also There, with Derrick Greaves. London: Tetrad Press, 1972.

Bluebeard's Castle (designed by Ronald King). Guildford, England: Circle Press, 1973.

Cultures, with Ian Tyson. London: Tetrad Press, 1975.

Scenes from the Alphabet (illustrated by Ronald King). Guildford, England: Circle Press, 1978.

Nonfiction:

Talks for Words. Cardiff: Blackweir Press, 1980.

A Birmingham Dialogue, with Paul Lester. Birmingham: Protean, 1986.

Turning the Prism: An Interview with Roy Fisher, conducted by Robert Sheppard. London: Toads Damp, 1986.

The Left-handed Punch (designed by Ronald King). Guildford, England: Circle Press, 1987.

Sound recordings:

City. Monmouth, England: Amber Records AMBER 7102, 1977.

Roy Fisher: Readings at Coracle Press, No. 4. London: Audio Arts, 1982.

Roy Fisher: City Poems. Keele, England: University English Department, 1988.

Penelope Fitzgerald

1916-

The presentation of the Booker Award for fiction, 1979: (from left)
award committee chairman, Lord Asa Briggs; award winner, Penelope Fitzgerald;
chairman of Booker, Sir Michael Caine; shortlist author Fay Weldon;
shortlist author Julian Rathbone

1

I consider myself lucky, because when I was four years old I lived in a house with a garden, and in the garden was a double rose hedge, two hedges, that is, planted close to each other, but with enough space between them, even now they'd grown thick, for a person of my size to sit there without difficulty. Into this space the briar roses shed pale pink petals and heavy drops of rainwater or dew, so that it never quite dried out. I collected the petals into small heaps, each heap representing one of the dozen or so other regular inhabitants of the rose-hedge space. I knew their names then, but now can remember only a few. (One of them was Fatty Arbuckle, which gives you the date, but not the circumstances. I am sure nobody in the village knew anything then about the misfortunes of Arbuckle. It was simply a name for anyone fat, whether male or female.)

Every day, of course, one or more of the piles of rose leaves perished, withered at the top, mouldering underneath. They had no fragrance while they were alive, but a curious smell when they were dead. I buried them where the ground was soft, at the foot of the hedge. Prayers and a hymn had to be said over

101

them, but that was no problem to me, we were churchgoers and I knew plenty of both. After they were decently laid to rest, however, a new anxiety began. No empty spaces must be left by the time I was called back into the house. More fallen petals to collect, more piling up. And so Fatty and his companions rose again from the earth.

All this talk about hedges may suggest that we lived in a big place, but that we certainly didn't. When my father came back from the First World War, wounded through the shoulder, houses to rent were so scarce in London that he began to think he would have to live, with his family, in a furniture van. His job was on the staff of *Punch* (of which he eventually became the editor). Making your living by being funny is always hard work, and, in the 1920s, not well paid. So my mother, a quietly spoken woman whom nothing defeated, found a house in the village of Balcombe in Sussex, an hour by train from London, and a walk from the station.

I had a brother, much loved and admired, but three-and-a-half years older, at that time an unbridgeable gap. He was not a rose-heap builder, but, to his credit, not a destroyer of rose heaps either. While I was conducting my funerals he would have been down at the village carpenter's, where I wasn't wanted, or at the blacksmith's (which by then was a

Penelope with her brother, Rawle Knox,
Hampstead, England, about 1924

garage, hiring out two Citroëns), or competing with his friends to see who could pee farthest out of the window, disturbing the hens as they pecked about the grass. He was Rawle, a family name on my mother's side. It seemed to me that in the conversation which went on, quite literally, above my head, in church and at home, his name was mentioned frequently. "We thank Thee, Lord, for Rawle Thy mercies . . . ," "after Rawle . . . ," "they're Rawle as bad as each other. . . ." And this struck me as quite natural, for he was very important to me.

Twenty years or so later Rawle came out of a Japanese prisoner-of-war camp to become a journalist and a distinguished Far Eastern correspondent, so that in the end both of us finished up as writers.

2

The truth was that we came of a writing family, and I suppose some people might think an eccentric one. When I was young I took my father and my three uncles for granted, and it never occurred to me that everyone else wasn't like them. Later on I found that this was a mistake, but after all these years I've never quite managed to adapt myself to it. I suppose they were unusual, but I still think that they were right, and in so far as the world disagrees with them, I disagree with the world.

They were a vicarage family, and vicarages were the intellectual powerhouses of nineteenth-century England. Their father, Edward Knox, left his country parish for industrial Birmingham, crowded and thick with soot, because he thought there was more important work to do there, and the Knoxes grew up in an immensely hard-working Evangelical household where comfort and beauty counted for very little and money for almost nothing—there was always a good reason to give it away. They remained faithful to their upbringing—I say this because I count a violent reaction against an upbringing as a kind of faithfulness. My Uncle Dillwyn, for example, who came next after my father, was an extreme agnostic, referring to Jesus Christ as "that deluded individual, J.C." He was a brilliant scholar of ancient Greek texts, and using, I suppose, the same part of his mind, a great cryptographer; in the First World War he broke the German flag code, and his work on the "spy" variation of the Enigma cipher shortened the Second World War by roughly six months. One would expect from him clarity and coldness, but in point of fact nobody could understand his working methods, and although he could be ruthless if you made a foolish remark he was tenderhearted to a fault when anybody was in real trouble. The same was true of my second and third uncles, Wilfred and Ronnie, but they, on the other hand, were two of the most convincing Christians it would be possible to meet, and both became priests. All of them, including of course my father, were distinguished by courage and a frightening honesty. (My uncle Wilfred never told a lie in his entire life—he never saw the necessity.) But I won't write more about this, because, as they would have said themselves, what's the use of courage and honesty if you can't take them for granted? I should like, however, to mention their wit. Some of it lay in their fondness for quiet understatement. "One gets so little practice at this," said my father gently when, in 1971, he lay dying. Indeed all of them (although Ronnie published so many books that he lost all count of the titles) had a horror of talking too much. Wilfred said that no congregation ought to have to listen to a sermon for more than ten minutes, and any priest or minister who went on longer than that ought to have his income cut down proportionately every thirty seconds. I, too, feel drawn to whatever is spare, subtle, and economical.

3

My mother's family were called Hicks. She too came from a vicarage, and from a "long family," so musical that they could give an entire parish concert between them. Both my grandfathers became bishops, and both of them started out with next to nothing. Edward Hicks, in fact, had even less than that—his father was a small tradesman in Oxford who went bankrupt, and Edward had to set himself, in the old way, to free his family from debt. This may have been the reason why, during his ministry, he never refused to see anyone who came to the door for help. He was a great enemy of poverty and injustice, having come, while he was at Oxford, under the influence of John Ruskin. Ruskin he admired, not only for his teaching but for his delight in even the smallest details of life. Ruskin, he said, would describe "with the keenest relish" the joy of shelling peas—"the pop which assures one of a successful start, the fresh colour and scent of the juicy row within, and the pleasure of skilfully scooping the bouncing peas with one's thumb into the vessel by

"My father, Edmund V. Knox, the editor of Punch *from 1932 to 1940, in Hampstead, about 1930"*

one's side." I can honestly say that I never shell peas in summer without thinking of Ruskin and of my grandfather.

Well, those were my ancestors, and I can only say once again that I should like to have lived up to them. I should like to have been musical, I should like to be mathematical, and above all I should like never to have told a lie.

4

We left Sussex, the village, the hens, and the rose hedges, in 1922. Commuting had become impossible, since my father had been asked to act as theatre critic for *Punch,* as well as deputy-assistant editor. We went to number 34 Well Walk, a small eighteenth-century house in Hampstead, to the northwest of London. The rent at that time was forty pounds a year. If I may be allowed to quote from what I wrote about it some years ago, Hampstead at that time was a place of "high thinking, plain living and small economies. The steep, charming old streets were full of ham-and-beef shops, old bookstalls, and an amazing number of clothes-repairers, all helpful to shabby refugees and literary men. There was even a jeweller's where one bead could be bought at a time, for all the Hampstead ladies wore long necklaces." Poets, conspicuous in their wide-brimmed black hats, roamed the streets, as indeed they always had done. At one end of Well Walk, under the lime trees, was the wooden seat where John Keats was supposed to have sat down to rest. Certainly he had lived just round the corner. At dusk the lamplighters came round and, one by one, the gas lamps flickered into brightness. Muffinmen appeared on the streets in winter, and in summer the lavender sellers. To go down into London was an expedition. I was taken, for example, to the Poetry Bookshop, where you could buy, for sixpence, coloured rhyme sheets illustrated by fine artists—new ones every month or so. We travelled by underground railway, because Hampstead's hill was too steep for a bus to get up it.

I hadn't expected to be happy in Hampstead, but I was. Then, partly because of my mother's illness, I had to be sent away to boarding schools. I got a very good education, leading to an Oxford scholarship, but I learned only too quickly that homesickness is a real illness and that reason has no power against it. I still believe this is true, even though while I'm writing it down I realise what a small thing my wretchedness must sound, in view of the partings that were to come and the haunting faces that television now shows us day by day of the displaced, the rejected, the bewil-

dered, and the totally lost. "Even before they set out on life's journey they seem weary already of the way." There are children now who are homesick without ever having had a home to remember.

5

I've never been able to write short stories. In my whole life I've only written three, and then only because I was asked to. It took me almost as long to finish one as to write a novel. Biographies and novels are the forms which I feel I can just about manage. They are the outcome of intense curiosity about other people and about oneself. I think that the best way to continue with these notes about my life would be to look back through the novels I have written.

I left Oxford with an honours degree and might perhaps have stayed there, but it was 1938 and it hardly seemed to be the right thing to do at the time. In 1939 I took a job at Broadcasting House, the London headquarters of the wartime BBC. Broadcasting House was designed to look, and does look, like a great ship headed south, and in 1939, "with the best engineers in the world, and a crew varying between the intensely respectable and the barely sane, it looked ready to scorn any disaster of less than Titanic scale. At night, with all its blazing portholes blacked out, it towered over a flotilla of taxis, each dropping off a spectator or two." Reading that I can see that I was impressed, almost in spite of myself, by the seven-decked building, the sole source of news and wartime instructions for the British public over the next six years. But I myself was only a recorded-programme assistant—almost, I think, the lowest of the low. We were not even junior programme engineers, who were allowed to turn knobs which we were forbidden to touch and had the right to join a union. We were busy all day, and (since the BBC was on twenty-four-hour shifts) often all the night, and yet I have to think hard now to remember exactly what it was we did. To a large extent we were beasts of burden—very young ones. We had to make sure that things were in the right place at the right time by actually carrying them there. There were some tapes in existence, but the enormous everyday traffic in recorded sound was all carried on aluminium 78 discs coated with acetate. The acetate smelled very strong, particularly as the whole building was now sealed off, its entrance packed with sandbags, its windows (so we believed) not to be opened until peace was declared. Quantities of these discs seemed to be needed for every transmission—speeches, interviews, messages, broadcasts from enemy countries patiently transcribed by refugee scholars who toiled quietly in a department of their own. Some of them were standbys—there had to be an alternative recording ready, for instance, when King George VI was speaking to the nation, because his stammer was unpredictable, and for the chimes of Big Ben, because in very cold weather there was a chance that the mechanism might slow down.

I dream, sometimes, of those many thousands of discs. All of them were perishable. They melted easily—a cup of tea put down on top of them would do that—and in winter the teams on the mobile recording vans found that they also froze. They had a tendency, also, to disappear. There is, I think, a strong human instinct which prompts anyone who sees a neat stack of anything to move it somewhere else, and this (not only at the BBC) defeats all that filing systems and catalogues can do. But even when the discs were in their expected place they were distinguished from each other only by handwritten labels, and these labels were not always filled in correctly, or filled in at all. Or they were illegible— was it "Church bells" (which were to be rung only in case of invasion) or "Churchill"? In the basement transmission studios the announcers, whose familiar voices, during the wartime years, brought reassurance to millions, were waiting. As part of a system of finders, fetchers, and carriers in a building where the lifts had been halted, for security reasons, at the third floor, leaving four more flights of stairs to be struggled up and down, I can't claim to have been the strongest link in the chain, but I can say that I was willing.

The novel that I wrote about my years at Broadcasting House was called *Human Voices* (1980). The reviewers called it "light," and I suppose it is, although novelists never like to be called light. All I can say is that I never went far away from the truth. Broadcasting House in wartime was a life within a life. We so often had to sleep, when we were on night shift, in the concert hall, rigged up as a dormitory with a line of grey blankets supposed to separate male from female. It was a fitful sleep, disturbed by the anxious torchlights and muffled alarm clocks of those going on and off duty. Twice in the concert hall I had to help out when someone had an epileptic fit. In my novel I changed this to the birth of a baby, but that wouldn't have surprised me either. Broadcasting House had become the capacious, all-providing shelter for us all.

I remember, too, that I learned to listen there. From room after room, if the patent self-sealing rooms were open for the moment, bursts of music

*The author with her husband,
Desmond Fitzgerald, 1972*

from replays and editing sessions beguiled the passersby. I had never heard anything by Satie before, or by Fauré, or by Kurt Weill, except for the *Dreigroschenoper*. The programme editors considered me a little savage, but they kindly let me stay and listen. I have said that my mother's family was born, as birds are born, musical. I wasn't, so I am all the more grateful for the education in hearing which the BBC gave me. I also fell in love, with someone very much older and more important, without the least glimmer of a hope of any return. This was quite common in those days, but I suggested in *Human Voices* that we were the last generation to behave like this and that after the Second World War the human species no longer found it biologically useful. Certainly, towards the end of the war or just after it we all of us married, had children, and forgot why and even how we'd managed to love without return. In 1953 I married an Irish soldier and my three children are now respectively a professor of economics, a teacher of Spanish, and a research physiologist enquiring into the nature of pain. With my youngest grandchildren I

"In Cornwall with two of my eight grandchildren and my daughter, Dr. Maria Lake," 1986

can gain a little credit by telling them that I can remember a time when there was no television, and I carried recordings about, like Jill and her pail of water.

6

In the late 1950s we were living in Southwold, which is on the east coast of England, a flat, sandy, Holland-like coast with wide skies and bright clouds, beloved of painters, and a temptation to those who think they can paint, but can't. Southwold at that time was largely cut off from public transport. The branch railway had been closed for thirty years, the river had silted up in the nineteenth century, and the car ferry had collapsed during the great floods of 1953. We had no car, and hardly any money; we lived down by the harbour which was no longer a harbour since the seawall caved in sometime in 1910. The house we got had once been an oyster warehouse, and had been plastered with sea salt, which meant that it was never quite dry. Underneath the living room there was a flood cellar, where the water slopped about at very

high tides. The children lived like aquatic animals, taking no harm.

While they were at the local primary school, just across the marshes, I took a job in what was then the only bookshop in Southwold, and the novel I wrote about those years was called *The Bookshop* (1978). I still miss, and shall always miss, the wide shining horizons of East Suffolk, and the sight of the rooks and the seabirds balancing themselves on boundless currents of air. The human community of Southwold, however, was divided into friends and enemies. In my story I called the town Hardborough. (In the matter of "calling names" writers have an advantage.) The novel is really the report of a battle, a very minor engagement, of course, but important to the wounded.

My employer, however, Mrs. Neame, was kindness itself, and it seemed unjust that the shop (admittedly the building was three hundred years old) should be haunted—haunted, too, by that most mindless form of the supernatural, a poltergeist. It manifested itself, on what you might call its days on, by first tapping, then knocking, then drumming furiously. At first I thought the noise must have come from next door, which was a shoe store, part of a large chain. I didn't reflect that the assistants in shoe stores don't, nowadays, spend their time hammering, like goblins in fairy tales, at the cobbler's last. "They're a noisy lot," I said to Mrs. Neame, who turned pale, and told me not to talk about it to the customers, or we'd soon lose them all. It was a rapper—that was what they were called in East Suffolk. They were known, too, to "bring a chill with them," and unquestionably the temperature dropped during the uproar and the shop (although it was summer) became almost cold. But it would have seemed odd to light the paraffin heater in June. As we shut up shop there was a silence, then came a tremendous battering, more like a series of small explosions, not on the wall this time, but on the locked back door—the rapper triumphant. I recognised that afternoon something I had never met with before—malignancy.

This was my first novel—before that I had only published a biography and a mystery story—and not long after it came out the publisher rang up to tell me that it was on the shortlist for the Booker Award, which is the best known of Britain's fiction prizes. That raised the problem of evening dress, because the Booker dinner is a formal occasion. Still, it isn't difficult to make a long skirt, and I was advised to wear earrings and not to take off my shoes under the table, because at some point each writer would have to go up separately and shake hands with the chairman. For the same reason, I ought to make sure that I looked all right from behind. This advice has taken me through three Booker dinners.

7

At the beginning of the sixties we had to go back to London, and not being able to find a house that we could afford, we settled for a boat. It was moored on Chelsea Reach, between Battersea Bridge and Albert Bridge, so that we were in one of the very grandest parts of London. On the other hand, we were living on an old wooden barge which for many years had carried cargoes up and down the east coast under sail, but was now a battered, patched, caulked, tar-blackened hulk, heaving up with difficulty on every rising tide. Her name was *Grace,* and she had never been fitted with an engine, so that there was plenty of room for us in the huge belly of the hold. There was a very old stove, in which we burned driftwood. Driftwood will only light when it has paint or tar on it, and we knew its bitter fragrance well from the foreshore at Southwold, just as we were

used to a more or less permanent state of damp and to the voices, at first light, of the seagulls. Now we had to get used to the movement of *Grace,* rocking on the high tide, and the echoing wail of the hooters from the passing colliers on their way to the Port of London.

Grace was anchored next to the wharf, so that she was the first of a long line of lived-in craft—barges, landing craft, and even one minesweeper. They were connected by a series of gangplanks which were anything but safe, so that the postman and the milkman had, very sensibly, refused to go on delivering. There were other drawbacks, too—the boat owners were only allowed to let out wastewater, and to use the lavatories, on a falling tide. Our great consolation was that a Thames barge, because of the camber of the deck, never sinks completely. On this point I could give evidence, because we went down twice, and on both occasions the deck stayed just above water. We were taken off the first time by a kindly Swede in a dinghy, and the second time by the river police in their patrol launch. Among our drenched and floating possessions I saw a bottle of champagne which had been intended for a party. I was glad to be able to retrieve the champagne so as to have something to give, in gratitude, to the police, who reminded me that they were not allowed to drink on duty, but agreed to put it aside for later. Poor *Grace,* much loved, was towed away to the Essex marshes to be broken up. I dedicated my novel *Offshore* (1979) to "*Grace* and all who sailed in her."

It was a pity that the title was translated into various European languages with words meaning "far away" or "far from the shore," which meant the exact opposite of what I intended. By "offshore" I meant to suggest the boats at anchor, still in touch with the land, and also the emotional restlessness of my characters, halfway between the need for security and the doubtful attraction of danger. Their indecision is a kind of reflection of the rising and falling tide, which the craft at anchor must, of course, follow. This novel *did* win the Booker prize, and I knew then that some of the people who read it must have understood it.

8

Why don't you teach? people used to ask me, for women are supposed to be born able to do this. I did teach while we were on *Grace,* and one of the places where I taught was a theatrical school, Italia Conti's. It has moved premises since, but at that time it was in the depths of south London. The large front

"In Battersea, where we lived for a time after Grace sank"

room was used on Sundays by a Christian community who practised adult baptism, so that there was a large bath on the raised stage. The Conti children (who seemed to be much wilder than ordinary children, as though they were giving a performance of wildness) knew how to unlock the cold tap, and, if they didn't care for their classes, flooded the hall.

Freddie, the school's owner in *At Freddie's* (1982), was not at all like Italia Conti. I transferred her, or rather she appeared to transfer herself, from another school where I worked later. She was a freakish tyrant, kindhearted by fits and starts, a natural grande dame of a species which, allowed to flourish unchecked, becomes in time uncontrollable.

Penelope Fitzgerald, looking across the Moscow River toward the Kremlin: "My last novel, The Beginning of Spring, *is about Russia in 1913, and was partly the result of several winter visits."*

paid to teach them to spell. They might, in the future, need a tedious everyday job, such as I had. And under their bravado, they knew this, and even knew that I knew it.

I have tried, in describing these books of mine, to say something about my life. In my last two novels I have taken a journey outside of myself. *Innocence* takes place in Italy in the late 1950s, *The Beginning of Spring* in Moscow in 1913. Most writers, including the greatest, feel the need to do something like this sooner or later. The temptation comes to take what seems almost like a vacation in another country and above all in another time. V. S. Pritchett, however, has pointed out that "a professional writer who spends his time becoming other people and places, real or imaginary, finds he has written his life away and become almost nothing." This is a warning which has to be taken seriously. I can only say that however close I've come, by this time, to nothingness, I have remained true to my deepest convictions—I mean to the courage of those who are born to be defeated, the weaknesses of the strong, and the tragedy of misunderstandings and missed opportunities which I have done my best to treat as a comedy, for otherwise how can we manage to bear it?

My job at Conti's, on the other hand, I have described pretty nearly exactly as it was. I had to help give the pupils what was called their "education," and they did not disguise their lack of interest in it. I don't mean that they were bored—it was much more positive than that, a fierce electric thrill of rejection which ran from one end of the class to the other. They wanted not education, but "work." Work was largely in TV commercials and small movie roles, but there were those, especially around Christmastime, who actually got a stage part, and this gave them a certain dignity, the almost-vanished magic of belonging to a venerable profession. The authorities allowed them to stay in one show for six months at a time, and to make up for their lost schooling I had to go round backstage and attempt, as they came back to their dressing room in a state of pitiable excitement, to calm them down and give them their lessons. A little arithmetic (we still taught arithmetic then), a little spelling. They were brilliant with confidence. "How was I, Miss? Why don't you go and see it from the front?" But after a certain age—say ten or eleven—these children, particularly the dancers, were never likely to get another part. That was why I was being

BIBLIOGRAPHY

Fiction:

The Golden Child. London: Duckworth, 1977; New York: Scribner, 1977.

The Bookshop. London: Duckworth, 1978.

Offshore. London: Collins, 1979; New York: Holt, 1987.

Human Voices. London: Collins, 1980.

At Freddie's. London: Collins, 1982; New York: David Godine, 1985.

Innocence. London: Collins, 1986; New York: Holt, 1987.

The Beginning of Spring. London: Collins, 1988; New York: Holt, 1989.

Nonfiction:

Edward Burne-Jones. London: Michael Joseph, 1975.

The Knox Brothers. London: Macmillan, 1977; also published as *The Knox Brothers: Edmund, 1881–1971, Dillwyn, 1883–1943, Wilfred, 1886–1950, Ronald, 1888–1957.* New York: Coward McCann, 1978.

Charlotte Mew and Her Friends. London: Collins, 1984; New York: Addison-Wesley, 1988.

Roy Fuller

1912-

RECOLLECTIONS OF THE BLACKHEATH POETS

Roy Fuller in his study

1

The Woolwich Equitable Building Society (what Americans know as a Savings and Loan Association), though when I joined its staff in 1938 it was already well on the way to becoming a national institution, still had its headquarters in Woolwich (where it was founded in 1847), a mainly industrial and commercial area of southeast London. Two or three miles to the east is Blackheath, a residential suburb, looking green on the map, which is why, in my then ignorance of London suburbia, I chose it to find accommodation for myself, my wife, and my infant son on taking up my new post. The war soon interrupted our early married life, but in 1945 we all returned to Blackheath, and early in 1946 I resumed my prewar occupation with the Woolwich (or the Equitable, as the locals called it).

Before the war I had started to publish poems in little magazines, though my job as a lawyer and utter lack of fame prevented me from leading any sort of literary life, even had I wanted to. I had formed an enduring friendship with Julian Symons, then a poet and little-magazine editor, later a notable critic and author of crime novels, and through him had become acquainted with a few fairly minor thirties poets, like Gavin Ewart, H. B. Mallalieu, and Ruthven Todd. But in no sense did I move in "literary circles." I may well have known—in fact, I believe I did know—that Blackheath was the home of Charles Madge (in those prewar days a poet whose relative eminence I would not have attempted to approach) and Kathleen Raine (a poet of scarcely less *réclame*). But they, and any other poetic residents, remained unknown, unseen.

Postwar, all was changed. For one thing, Julian Symons and his wife (through my knowing of the vacancy in a time of housing shortage) took the top-floor flat in a large Victorian house where we occupied the ground-floor flat. Also, I had brought out two wartime books of verse with modest success, and after the war began to publish prose fiction. So that when a number of *littérateurs,* each celebrated in his own way, came to live in Blackheath, it was perhaps not surprising that I eventually came across them.

Blackheath was a rather unfashionable suburb before the war. In 1938 the estate agents had offered us a selection of flats at rentals around £1 5s. ($5.00) a week. Its architecture, mainly Victorian but with a substratum of Georgian, had by and large decayed. After the war, steeply rising prices in desirable north-of-the-river districts caused many discriminating accommodation-seekers to look southwards, and Blackheath began to go up in the world, particularly as its war-damaged buildings were repaired and brought back into use. Among the discriminating were some intellectuals.

After the rarely edifying journey from central London along the New and Old Kent Roads, the way rises steeply from the squalour of Deptford to the heath of Blackheath, an open area of grassland bordered by, on the whole, interesting domestic architecture, some distinguished. The openness is augmented by the contiguous Greenwich Park, descending from the heath almost to the Thames. A poet who lived at Blackheath in the 1890s has given a good idea, in a poem called "A Nocturne at Greenwich," of the atmosphere and topography of this ambience. The poet was Victor Plarr, now remem-

bered, if at all, as the original of "Monsieur Verog" in Ezra Pound's *Hugh Selwyn Mauberley*—the "Plarr talking of mathematics" of *The Pisan Cantos.*

Far out, beyond my window, in the gloom
  Nightly I see thee loom,
Thou vast black city. Oh, but night is kind
  Here where Thames' waters wind,
To the grim formless features of thy face.
  They do assume such grace
In the deep darkness, starred through leagues
    of night,
  With long streets, fringed with light,
Or with the lanthorns of the ships that aye
  Ascend the water-way . . .
Up from the darkness echoes sleepily
  The shipman's wandering cry,
Or, like a wild beast's call heard in a dream,
  The siren's undulant scream
Whistles the darkling midnight through and
    through,
  While with her labouring screw
Some dim leviathan of ships drops down
  Past storied Greenwich town . . .
Past the great hospital she drops, and past
  The marshes, still and vast,
Below the lines of Woolwich and the lines
  Of Bostal's shadowy pines,
On to that world of Saxon brine and fen,
  Old races, vanished men,
Where Thames, from heron-haunted shores set
    free,
  Merges in northern sea.
Here, in my chamber, 'mong my books, at
    peace,
  I watch thee without cease,
Thou ancient stream, mysterious as the sky
  Which starless glooms on high.
About me, on the volume-peopled wall,
  The famed old authors all
Sleep their just sleep, and in the hearth's clear
    beams
  Dante's medallion gleams,
And Brutus and great Tully o'er the shelves
  Commune among themselves.
This silent music of what once hath been
  Suits well with that night scene:
Nay, its essential sweetness sweeter grows,
  Because that river flows
Through northern midnight, big with life and
    doom,
  Out yonder in the gloom.

That is the Greenwich side, my side, of Black-heath: on the opposite or south side lies Blackheath Village, so called from ancient times, with its shops and railway station—a stop on the Southern Railway, as it was known before nationalization, nineteen minutes from Charing Cross, much less from London Bridge.

Bonamy Dobrée came to live near the Village when he retired in the early fifties from his professorship in English literature at Leeds University. A mutual friend, finding that Bonamy and I were separated only by the heath, said to me I ought to get to know him. I feel sure I made no move to obey this behest. I can't be said to have been at any time of my life keen to extend my acquaintances, and in Bonamy's case I would have been diffident about imposing myself on him. He was not only a distinguished academic and anthologist whose work was well known even outside the scholarly world; he had also in 1935 been joint author of a book which at the time made a great impression on me—*The Floating Republic,* an account of the mutinies in the Royal Navy in 1797. In

With son, John, and wife, Kate, in the Strand, London, about 1950

the early thirties I had been deeply committed to left-wing politics, the ideas of Marxism, suddenly come upon, seeming utterly revelatory. Lenin's *State and Revolution,* for instance, I saw as incontrovertible, the apparatus of army, police, and the courts the means of keeping a bourgeois regime imposed on the more numerous and less privileged proletariat. But how could the power of this apparatus, particularly the armed forces, be broken so as to allow the takeover of the state by the working class? It seemed a quite impossible event, in Britain at any rate, where the repressive machine was so well disciplined. *The Floating Republic* gave an inkling of how it might come about. It had to recount the final defeat of the mutineers, but its sympathy with their ideas and personalities made vivid an early example of working-class enterprise and solidarity, and gave hope to the left in the grim days of the thirties economic crisis.

But however it happened, my wife and I came to know Bonamy and his wife. Valentine Dobrée was a dark, Mediterranean type, three years younger than Bonamy, who was born in 1891. Accomplished paintings by her hung on the walls of their house, though by the time of our meeting her she had abandoned oils for collages. Eventually it came out (or perhaps I read somewhere) that in earlier days she had published several prose works, and in due course I discovered in the London Library a novel of hers called, strikingly enough, *Your Cuckoo Sings by Kind.* She had a further literary surprise in store: in 1965 Faber and Faber, England's premier poetry publishers, brought out a collection of her verse, *This Green Tide.* Though the book was far from negligible, no doubt her appearance in a list with such fashionable figures as Auden, Larkin, and Ted Hughes was due to Bonamy's long friendship with T. S. Eliot, the Faber director with the poetry say-so. Perhaps I may quote an entire poem to give some notion of the collection's quality:

The Enchantment of Raquel Meller

The fragrance of violets was more potent than
   violets,
Dark-mantled flowers, full of false modesty,
Their pungency distilled, bottled and
   advertised
To create bewilderment in men, adding
   mystery
And illusive charm to the ladies,
Suggesting limits of discreet seduction.
A birthday gift for Mamma
Disdainful of patchouli:
More homely than lilies.

The Dobrée family, about 1972: "Georgina, Valentine, and Bonamy, outside their Pond Road house"

When in Paris, City of Discovery far in the
    'twenties,
That rare singer, Raquel, peddled violets.
The freshness of her voice and presence,
A song of violets, shocked the long-corrupted
    air;
The hot excitement of the late night
    performance
—Back to lost childhood and its own
    innocence—
Awoke confusion in the heart of youth
    deprived,
Gave benison to a shell-shocked generation,
Ousting stale odours, shaming the lechers,
Knitting those who had been taken apart.
Strange props for the halls,
The cordials and simples of an old healing art
Borne in a plain reeded basket
By a bewitching deceiver.
Her knacks, small bunches of button-hole
    flowers;
With her distilling, the aroma of violets
Became more poignant than violets.

It was even more of a surprise when a few years after Valentine's death I read in Virginia Woolf's *Diary* of Valentine's part in the Partridge/Carrington/Brenan amatory mix-up in the period of the poem I have quoted, for in the years when we knew them Bonamy and Valentine were a singularly devoted couple. During the latter part of that time Valentine was more or less an invalid, Bonamy head cook and bottle-washer. To this day my wife will refer to Bonamy's virtuous morning habit of taking the newspapers to Valentine's bed and getting in it to read and discuss the news with her.

Valentine had an easy and amiable conversational style, yet one frequently lost the thread of her argument on any subject save the simplest. Some of her poems betray the same difficulty, but of course that is what one has become used to encountering on the printed poetic page. Orally, it was best to assent to her recondite propositions, try to bring the exchanges nearer earth.

Valentine's darkness formed a contrast to Bonamy's silver hair and moustache. His slim, erect figure added to the military impression conveyed—indeed, not misleadingly, for he had once been in the regular army, and served with distinction in both the German wars. In the Second World War, Virginia Woolf noted him as "Spick and span, clipped, grey, with a rainbow of medal ribbons across his breast" (*Diary*, 6 April 1940). He took up his post at Leeds University in the mid-thirties, and returned there after the war. One of his early pupils was Richard Hoggart, later to become famous as (*inter alia*) the author of *The Uses of Literacy*. In the early sixties, for a *Festschrift* in Bonamy's honour, Hoggart wrote a remarkable account of his relations with his master, illuminating both men (a somewhat different version appears in volume one of Hoggart's autobiography). To begin to quote from it would be fatal, for every word is telling. But one thing particularly emerges, pointed by Hoggart's origins in an utterly different society—Bonamy was quintessentially Cambridge and upper middle class, tempered by the generally leftish intellectualism of the Bloomsbury epoch. All this was allied with a sort of inspecting army officer's sharp regard for neatness, cleanliness, good behaviour, and tradition. No doubt it was his deep-dyed leftism that prompted his support, often of a practical nature (and by no means discouraged by Valentine), of poets and painters. He bought and read books of new verse, and when I first knew him had paid a young painter to contribute unskilled help in the garden. Valentine's patronage once brought notoriety in the local newspaper: at a show by the Blackheath Art Society she purchased a sculpture, essentially a small, upright, wooden member, with an aperture near the top à la Henry Moore, mounted on a modest base. It subsequently emerged that the "sculpture" had been a piece of firewood, the aperture a knothole; that anyone should pay a guinea or two for this was derided in the newspaper. But Valentine spiritedly defended her purchase, said she liked it, firewood though it may have been.

In the early days of our knowing them we were invited to a large Christmas party, a good proportion of the guests being their daughter Georgina's young friends, though some of the proceedings seeming to hark back to the twenties, if not earlier. Gambling games went on, but the stakes—a large amount of copper coin distributed equally among the guests—were provided by (and eventually lost or, I think, returned to) the "house," so that the pleasure and pain of winning and losing was divorced from financial advantage or anxiety. The climax of the party involved Bonamy's sudden appearance in evening dress, with top hat and cane, to make (I forget what) some announcement or speech, an event unde-

niably effective, though not without faint embarrassment for an uncommitted onlooker.

The house the Dobrées bought in Blackheath where this took place was rather misleadingly called Wemyss Cottage, since it was a commodious villa with extensive outbuildings and a garden that ran downhill a long way to an adjoining road, Pond Road. In those days Georgina was still at home, so that the house was not too commodious. When we first knew them she was just making her way as a professional clarinetist (doubling enterprisingly on the basset-horn), and she later became professor at the Royal Academy of Music. I think it was after the Dobrées' purchase that the Borough Council filled in the pond and marshy land in Pond Road opposite the rear of the Dobrées' garden, and created a housing estate in neo-Georgian style among the otherwise agreeable architecture. But Bonamy and Valentine, unlike most house-owners in the area, would not have seen this as anything other than to be accepted—even welcomed—*pro bono publico*.

To the *Festschrift* referred to, I contributed a set of couplets that bring in some of the foregoing themes:

Wemyss Cottage, 1956

A street of battered laisser faire
Leads to the house: past its parterre
Blushes the bogus-Georgian of
The Borough Council's awful love.
Thus the twin shadows of the State
Fall upon stucco, lawn and slate
And on the Afric god who smiles
Across the little Flemish tiles
To where a painter keeps alive
By helping with the spade. Birds strive
Against a clarinet's long curl
Swayed by the breathing of a girl.
From the professor peeps a slim
Volume of poetry—for him
Neither the best nor past's enough:
He really buys the newest stuff,
Indulgent with the private dream
Though longing for a public theme.
So often since that former song
Corporate decisions have been wrong.
Committees set to make a choice
Have mostly raised a stupid voice.
Now it's a marvel that there still
Remain good things for groups to kill.
Before such ambiguities
The poet only murmurs his,
Revulsed by almost every faction

And quite incapable of action.
Moved by the emblems here, his pen
Writes of the obvious again.
Magnolias offer on dead wood
Their tiny lip-sticked cups; the good
Inherent in briar starts to show
And what the tag says soon will blow.
The mistress of the house imparts
Nurture to soil in which the arts
Extend: the tendrils of a tune
Creep up the windows: in the noon
Hues leap from beds; and, ordered by
A critical hand, the shrubbery
Of verse (that flowers on gloomy caves)
Reminds the sense of all that raves.
The guest must take his leave at last
By the unequal way that's past
Or through the future's juster hell.
Precarious happiness, farewell!

These lines were originally written in heroic couplets, abandoned as utterly NBG. When a request to contribute to the *Festschrift* arrived, I shortened the lines and so made them just about publishable, given the geniality of the occasion; a lesson about poetic form. They are accurate in detail and therefore possibly worth exhuming. What is depicted comes back to me vividly as spring or summer evenings returning with Bonamy from some (more or less stupid) committee meeting in town either by train or, in early days, when parking was easier, in his motor car. At that epoch he and Valentine had a car each, neither of any distinction. As Richard Hoggart says, Bonamy "would always buy only the cheapest serviceable car; it was simply a means of getting quickly from here to there." He was a driver some of whose eccentricities I used when describing the driving of the aged poet Daniel House in *The Carnal Island,* absentmindedness about the choke being a notable feature.

Yes, happy days—the house and garden full of interest, Valentine still physically active, a glass or two of sherry and always some titbits provided to go with them, often the clarinet roulades in the background. Then time began to take its toll, as I fear will often be recounted in these pages.

The last body Bonamy and I sat on together was the board of the Poetry Book Society. Bonamy had joined at the suggestion of its secretary, Eric Walter White (the expert on Stravinsky and Benjamin Britten), who I believe may well have been the person who brought us together in the first place. I remember thinking that Bonamy, for all his enthusiasm for

new poetry, was rather elderly to be asked to serve, and, sure enough, since the meetings were held after lunch, he now and then dropped off to sleep during the course of them. But it may well have been that Eric's motive was to give Bonamy an outside interest in his domesticated old age.

We would return by rail from the Arts Council's premises in St. James's Square, where the board meetings were held, and repair for a drink not to Wemyss Cottage but to a house with Pond Road frontage which Bonamy and Valentine had built at the end of the Wemyss Cottage garden. Valentine's health had broken down, never to be recovered. The Pond Road house, modest though it was, constituted a remarkable embodiment of their idiosyncratic personalities and way of life. They had designed it as essentially three large rooms: one for Valentine, one for Bonamy, plus a large kitchen in which to eat as well as cook. They had sold Wemyss Cottage and were saddened at certain unaesthetic developments of it and its garden by subsequent owners. The kind of unostentatious, cultivated life the Dobrées expected the middle class to live had sunk further into decline.

Two expeditions made with Bonamy at this period remain in mind. Regular poetry readings used to be held in an upper room of a public house in Dulwich called the Greyhound, an awkward journey by public transport from Blackheath. For some reason—could I myself have been performing?—Bonamy and I attended, driving there in my car. We were in good time (or perhaps the start of proceedings was tardy, not unusual at such events), and there was sufficient margin for a number of drinks, most, if not all, bought by me, which rather suggests a reader taking the edge off his nerves. After the show there was a return to the bar. I was astonished, brought up to eschew mixing one's drinks, that on the occasion of each round Bonamy ordered a different beverage, eventually arriving at such comparative rarities as rum. It occurred to me that it was a regression to a former mode of behaviour, or possibly cementing the novelty of a "night out." At the end of the evening he was not in the least the worse for drink.

On the other occasion Bonamy had come by, perhaps bought, two tickets for a poetry reading in one of the South Bank halls by Edith Sitwell, and invited me to accompany him. Had I had less regard for Bonamy I would have declined, for at that time my opinion of the Dame was at its nadir. She was not, in any case, a good reader of verse. The memory that endures is of a rendering of the sleepwalking scene from *Macbeth,* in which she also read the names of the characters before each speech, an eminently prosaic

"In my Woolwich Equitable Building Society office,"
1966

procedure. Bonamy accepted all that happened as he had accepted the range of alcohol on offer at the Greyhound. The vision comes to me of sitting in the interval outdoors by the Thames surrounded by the South Bank concrete, in the summer air, our exchanges not altogether fluent. I have never been a great conversationalist, certainly not unless my *vis-à-vis* shared some everyday life, quite far removed from literature and ideas.

Undoubtedly Valentine's ill-health limited the intercourse between Kate and myself and the Dobrées, and my sharing committee duties with Bonamy came to an end in the course of time. It must have been during my five years as Oxford's Professor of Poetry that I met Bonamy by chance in Blackheath Village. Was it a prior intimation by some third party or simply through observing the signs of age (slight shabbiness, uncut hair, imperfect shaving, abstracted locomotion) that I immediately knew his intellectual grasp had deteriorated? Moreover, after I had greeted him he said: "How's the Poet Laureate?" At once I realised that though he almost certainly knew who I was, he had read of my being voted to the Oxford Chair (which at the time had gained media publicity through there being a number of *outré* candidates, including the Soviet poet Yevtushenko) and momentarily imagined I had succeeded to the Laureateship, the question being rhetorical. The mistake was less venal than may be imagined, for Bonamy and I both knew the Poet Laureate, who in fact lived in adjacent Greenwich. I played along with his error, saying that

as far as I knew the Laureate was all right. The enquiry had further plausibility, for at that time C. Day Lewis's final period of illnesses had already begun.

It must have been two years or so after this encounter that Georgina spoke to me on the telephone. The year was 1974; Valentine was dead. Georgina lived in north London, could not see her father as much as she would have liked, and he, now more or less housebound, lacked people he could talk to. I said I would visit him, and so I did, I suppose about half a dozen times. I used to walk across the heath mid-morning to the house in Pond Road, where Bonamy would be lying, fully dressed, on a bed downstairs. On an early visit I encountered one of his neighbours on a similar mission: she told me that sometimes Bonamy had called on them in the middle of the night, oblivious to the unsuitability of the hour, difficult to get rid of. But I found him by no means completely gaga; rather, in the state of Act V *Lear*—though the book by his bedside was the Everyman volume of Shakespeare's *Comedies,* a choice that greatly impressed me, bringing to mind Yeats's "Hamlet and Lear are gay; Gaiety transfiguring all that dread." He was being looked after by a lady evidently used to such a task, competent and well-meaning, though conversing with him as though he were a child or simpleton, in the usual manner of nurses or para-nurses, and therefore getting far less response than if she had behaved to him normally. As in the old days, he offered me sherry: I was somewhat appalled when she diluted his glass with water, remarking only fairly *sotto voce* on her action. Whether or not he knew what was going on, he made no comment, pursuing what seemed to be his strategy of treating the nurse-housekeeper as though she did not exist, or at any rate had no real role to play in his affairs.

No doubt in our conversational exchanges I made a greater effort to amuse him than on the South Bank terrace years before. More than once on these visits he asked: "How old am I?" I told him he was eighty-three: it so happened that I'd looked up his date of birth in *Who's Who.* He was still a handsome—even beautiful—man, the hair remaining shining silver, matching the military moustache. He sometimes mentioned Valentine. He knew she was dead, yet referred to her rather as though she had gone unaccountably into some permanent exile, yet was physically not utterly remote. His current life was without interest to him, so I tried to open up his memory by asking about his literary past, which stretched back to the years just after the First World

War, when he contributed to the *London Mercury* and *New Statesman* and brought out his book on Restoration comedy. He talked about "Tom" (T. S. Eliot) and "Herbert" (Read), but his recollection of interesting detail was absent. The occasion reminded me of two radio interviews I had once conducted with Arthur Waley, when getting out of him early—any!—memories of Pound and Eliot was like the proverbial blood from a stone.

At the time of these visits I was writing the poems in triplets that now appear in part eight of *New and Collected Poems, 1934–84:* included is the memorial poem for Bonamy, "Last Dreams," which takes up some of the foregoing themes and shows how deep was his last impression on me:

Sagacious Ella Freeman Sharpe says dreams
Are typical of the human mind and adds:
"The only dreamless state is death." I note

The place. Again some pages later: "Our
Essential life knows no mortality."
The obvious poignard strikes home to the
    heart.

When I release the walnuts' brainy shells
The husks' insides are as vein-netted as
Our human embryos. And gardening late

(The robin's song like snapping twigs or garden
Chairs being shut, the low sky jaundiced
    through
The trees), I see such things' nobility.

Each species has its general character—
The dunnock's patient pecking, say, at nothing;
Or human dreams—that conquers special
    marks.

The father, in the manner of all fathers
Once brushed the daughter's hair. Time has
    reversed
The roles. To mark my visit, silver silk

Above the mortal face. I wish I'd said:
"How beautiful you look!" Now it's too late.
In any case, would you have deigned to care?

In those last weeks we used to talk of Tom
And Herbert, best remembered of your friends:
Demotic names, high poets. Gone before you.

"How old am I?" you questioned more than
    once.
"You're eighty-three," I said. "I looked you
    up."

You liked it not those months without your
    wife.

Your life at last seemed almost wholly dreams.
I chose for your committal lines those friends
Would have been sad though scarcely shocked
    to find

Apt for the grim but not ignoble rite:
"From an island of calm a limpid source of
    love."
And "Old men ought to be explorers." It's

The final folding of the summer chair
The robin mimics. Now you can never know
The meaning of the strange recurring dream

In each man's life—one's reason to believe
It's always about some move into a great
And ruined house. Or have you fathomed it?

One day Georgina telephoned me to say that Bonamy had died; it was not long after my last visit. I do not know what the death certificate named as the cause of death: to me, as I put it in the poem, it seemed a case of the famous epitaph by Sir Henry Wotton. I thought the *Times* ought to be told of his death, not sure whether Georgina was going to announce it in the "Births, Marriages, and Deaths" columns. When I telephoned the obituaries department they seemed unacquainted with the name; in any case wanted to check with a relative. It was an insight into the risk of dying in old age, unnoticed by a world that had passed on, easily envisaged for oneself.

I travelled to the crematorium with Georgina and Valerie Eliot. Georgina had rigorously carried out what undoubtedly was Bonamy's wish—no religious ceremony—and had asked me to read something suitable. I thought the undertakers coped well with the unusual absence of a clergyman (a suitable firm for one's own obsequies), and they (or perhaps the verger) showed me two buttons by the lectern which I was to use in the right order when I had finished my reading: they were labelled MUSIC and INTERMENT. I had chosen two quite short passages from poems by Herbert and Tom. It was easy to find appropriate lines in Eliot—the last paragraph of *East Coker,* which turned out in the context to be extremely affecting, to the reader at least. Read proved a tougher nut to crack. I possessed his *Collected Poems,* knew them fairly well, but looking through the book for something that would strike home, however obliquely, I realised what a withdrawn and tenuous poet he was, matching his personality which, long before, I had awkwardly encountered once or twice at parties. When in due course I came to know his son, the novelist Piers Paul Read, though I was slightly taken aback at his saying unfilially that he did not care for his father's verse, on reflection I very well understood such a view. This is what I read, perhaps in the end not inappositely:

> Vision itself is desperate: the act
> Is born of the ideal: the hand
> Must seize the hovering grail.
> The sense of glory stirs the heart
> Out of its stillness: a white light
> Is in the hills and the thin cry
> Of a hunter's horn. We shall act
> We shall build
> A crystal city in the age of peace
> Setting out from an island of calm
> A limpid source of love.

Whether the mourners in the crematorium chapel (mainly Bonamy and Valentine's local friends) made anything of the words at first hearing, *quaere.*

and their family. Indeed, the Hamiltons stood for a whole literary ancestry, albeit a minor and quite out-of-fashion branch. For example, in their drawing room I met Francis Meynell, son of the poet, founder of the Nonesuch Press, and Lady Noyes, widow of Sir Alfred. Alfred Noyes was the author of a poem, most of which I can still recite, in an anthology I "did" for the Oxford Junior Local examination as a boy of fourteen:

> The moon is up: the stars are bright:
>   The wind is fresh and free!
> We're out to seek for gold to-night
>   Across the silver sea! . . .
>
> We're sick of all the cringing knees,
>   The courtly smiles and lies!
> God, let Thy singing Channel breeze
>   Lighten our hearts and eyes!

Thus it goes on. George Rostrevor Hamilton's poetry is in a less antiquated mode, but the Eliot-Pound revolution had passed him by. Or, rather, he had taken no account of it: his criticism proves him to

2

Like Bonamy, Sir George Rostrevor Hamilton had moved to Blackheath on his retirement. His knighthood had come through his distinction as a civil servant. Though he had a First in Greats from Oxford, he started humbly in the Inland Revenue at Somerset House, ending eventually (after being plucked from the ranks for a series of special posts) as Presiding Special Commissioner of Income Tax. But, as he said in the prefatory note to his *Collected Poems and Epigrams,* he "never regarded poetry as a second string to that honourable profession [of civil servant], or as a hobby." That volume of 1958 contains 356 pages but even so omits a large part of his previous work. A further collection, *Landscape of the Mind,* appeared in 1963.

The Hamiltons knew the Dobrées, but they are not associated in my mind as being together in physical space or in anything else. George and Marion were the children of clergymen and remained Christians, with conservative views and a high regard for decent and proper conduct. I am sure Bloomsbury seemed to them on the whole a raffish lot, and the leftwards swing of intellectual society in the thirties was without effect on them. George's literary forebears could be said to be the Georgian poets—Walter de la Mare had been a valued friend. Other friends had been J. C. Squire, and Alice and Wilfrid Meynell

The author with his cat, Domino

Julian Symons

have read widely, and a once, justly, famous essay called *The Tell-Tale Article* had some acute words about modernist poetic diction. He was fortunate in his publisher. When George was a young man William Heinemann took a great fancy to his verse, and the firm, through all its changes of personnel, stayed loyal to him, so that he was spared the lowering searches for a publisher forced on many of us aged and unfashionable poets.

I must surely have first known George through a curious institution called "The English Festival of Spoken Poetry." It was held every year, mainly to confer awards for verse-speaking, but with a few ancillary events that concerned poetry in general. The organizers were on the alert to recruit younger poets as judges (not long after I started so serving I was joined by a girlish Elizabeth Jennings). Older hands included L. A. G. Strong and Richard Church, names to conjure with in their day, now perhaps forgotten. I daresay I was flattered to be asked to figure in such a galaxy (also, I have been afflicted all my life with the kind of conscientiousness apt to lead to boring or uncongenial activities, then to be made

the best of), but the thing was really not my cup of tea. After a few years, however, the competitive verse-speaking was dropped, and the occasion became simply a "Festival of Poetry," later "Poetry International," when native bards were joined by such as Allen Ginsberg, Ungaretti, and Hans Magnus Enzensberger—though I doubt if the proceedings engaged me much more. The first time I ever saw in the flesh my idol of the thirties, W. H. Auden, was when at a Poetry International recital on the South Bank (very likely in the same auditorium where Dame Edith sleepwalked) he came on the platform in a shabby brown suit. It must have been a very early (perhaps the first) public appearance of his in this country since his prewar exile, and the audience, as moved as I was, accorded him remarkably prolonged applause.

Eventually we saw more of the Hamiltons than of the Dobrées. This may have been because of Valentine's illness, though on the whole George and Marion offered much the easier social intercourse. They lived at first in a flat on the ground floor of Paragon House, a Georgian house at the corner of the heath and Pond Road forming the end of a fine Georgian crescent known as the Paragon. Later they moved to a rather more spacious flat in the Paragon itself. Over the years they had accumulated some choice furniture, paintings, and books: nothing extravagantly valuable, merely what could have been afforded out of a discriminating civil servant's salary. There especially spring to mind a fine collection of Nonesuch Press books, and a painting bought from Victor Pasmore when they were neighbours of his in their previous house in Chiswick Mall. It may have been pure coincidence that in Blackheath they were still neighbours, for Victor and his wife had for some time owned a house on the east side of the heath. The painting in question was in Victor's attractive impressionist style: the intervening years had diverted him wholly to abstractionism.

The Pasmores were only two of a good few we first met, or renewed acquaintance with, round the Hamiltons' dining table. The process continued after George's death: Marion liked me to do the drinks, and open and serve the wine, though neither she nor I attempted to concoct the cocktail that George had invariably mixed and offered his guests, a brew I always avoided and whose ingredients I never discovered. Except for puddings, Marion was not a *cordon bleu*, but she took a great deal of trouble, and the guests, even after she was left a widow, were usually of interest—for instance, Burke Trend, when he was Secretary to the Cabinet and ever at the risk of being called to Downing Street, even after the dinner party was over. She was a strong woman, in mind and body (despite a chronic internal affliction), indefatigible in theatre- and concertgoing, especially devoted to opera. George, I should say, was practically tone-deaf, but nobly tagged along on these musical occasions. Each was the great love of the other's life.

When we became friends with the Hamiltons I knew his name as a poet, but had scarcely read his work. In earlier days I was a stern—even rude—reviewer of verse. I expect I should have been stern, though probably not rude, about George's. At one time I would have condemned out of hand those poets who had not accepted the challenge of Eliot/Pound, and the American poets of the interwar years, and the Auden generation. I did not lose this over-devotion to the *zeitgeist* until quite late in life, and thus for a long time was partially blind to the virtues of a poet like Ruth Pitter. Fortunately I had never had to review George, for I doubt I should have found much in his favour—though I liked the poem of his I knew best, the four-line epigram in, of all places, Auden and Garrett's anthology, *The Poet's Tongue:*

Don's Holiday

Professor Robinson each summer beats
The fishing record of the world—such feats
As one would hardly credit from a lesser
Person than a history professor.

But when *Landscape of the Mind* came out I thought it marked a fresh turn to his verse, and agreed to review it for the *London Magazine.* The editor then, Alan Ross, probably had a soft spot for George on account of his elegaic "Ode to a Cricketer: W. G. Quaife," otherwise I doubt if a notice would have appeared in such an *avant garde* place. A couple of years later George published a book I admired still more (indeed, in its way a forgotten minor classic)—the autobiographical *Rapids of Time.* It reveals a transparently good and innocent man, which he was. I remember him saying he did not know the meaning of the word "condom" (now bandied about by babes and sucklings), which I had used in a poem, but fortunately some diversion spared my giving a definition. This is a trivial, even ambiguous, indication of character, yet it has stuck with me as touchingly typical.

One of the earliest indications of George's failing powers occurred when he and Marion were greeting us on a visit to their Paragon flat. Men and women had exchanged kisses—probably the women, too—and then as the final act of the sequence George

implanted a kiss on *my* cheek. He was at once embarrassed, far more than I—though in Victorian times the osculation would have gone unremarked: Alfred Lyttelton records Ruskin giving a tender kiss of greeting to Carlyle (received "kindly enough"). Two subsequent instances come vividly to mind. Ensconced in the corner of a settee in our sitting room, George stretched out a leg (he was a tall man) into the settee's vacant space. It was a gesture to be thought nothing of, but Marion was horrified, and ordered the offending limb down. On a later occasion, at our dining table, George utterly uncharacteristically used his fingers to convey to himself some morsel of food. If Marion saw this, she refrained from comment: it may be by then such lapses were more common. I remember thinking that the action was a regression to childhood days.

Apropos of George's decline, Marion said that in her experience it was the keenest brains that were most liable to decay. George's amiability, good manners even, tended to make one forget he had written a book on Bergson and philosophy (subtitled "An Essay on the Scope of Intelligence"), and indeed that

Sir George Rostrevor Hamilton

in his final year at Oxford he had been as good as offered (and had rejected) a fellowship at his college. His chapter on Bergson, brief though it is, has abiding interest. On one of his visits to Bergson in Paris, he one day found with him "a studious-looking bearded figure" who proved to be none other than Lorenz, whom Einstein had called the greatest man, the most powerful thinker he had known.

It was not long before George deteriorated physically, as well as mentally, but we did not see him at that time. One day, during our stay at Torquay for a Building Societies Association conference, I opened the *Times* and with sadness saw his obituary. It was ample and, I think, judicious. It surprised Marion, she told us later, by its amplitude. It did not surprise me, since I was the author: writing it had been a rather grisly duty of a few years before, alleviated by the sense that I was doing justice to a man who had never written (and probably never uttered) an unworthy word. I wonder if Marion guessed the authorship: I have the feeling she did, but she never let on.

Marion lived a courageous widowhood, by no means slowing up on entertaining, holidays abroad, listening to music. She seemed indestructible (even

her hair never lost its brown), but of course in the end she had to rejoin George—and I am sure she believed it would be in a mode superior to common mortality. One evening when we had dined with her she asked me if I would like to have George's *OED*. It was the thirteen volumes of the original edition, each volume (except possibly the last supplementary and miscellaneous one) requiring a feat of strength to consult (in fact, when Logan Pearsall Smith needed to consult them in old age he used to call in the young Robert Gathorne Hardy to lug them about). Somehow the volumes seemed even heavier through having had to endure a flooding by the Thames when they reposed in the Hamiltons' house in Chiswick Mall that had formerly belonged to J. C. Squire. It was a gift of unlimited potential. Some time after Marion's death, in a secondhand bookshop in Blackheath Village, I saw the slender india-paper edition of Robert Bridges's *Spirit of Man,* a book I quite wished to possess. When I opened it, I found Marion's bold signature on the inside cover, with the date, 1920. She had then been a bride of two years. I bought the anthology and, with conscious sentiment, added my own name, and the date—28 November 1979.

C. Day Lewis presenting the Duff Cooper Memorial Prize to Roy Fuller (left)

3

I had no clear critical sheet in respect of two other poets who came to live in Blackheath after the war. *Twentieth Century Verse* was a little magazine of the thirties: through my contributing to it had come my friendship with its editor, Julian Symons. In its December 1938 issue I had reviewed C. Day Lewis's new book of poems, *Overtures to Death.* After a first paragraph of rather schoolmasterish analysis of its contents, I went on to write the following. (It should be explained that at that time Day Lewis was a convinced and active Marxist, a stance I wholeheartedly approved of: my words demonstrate how much I must have disliked the actual poems.)

Most of the virtue belonging to conviction and activity is cancelled out by the extraordinary way in which these poems are written. Sleep has night-scented borders, the night a grave manifold of stars, smoke rolls forth, the week is russet and rejoicing, elms toss their heads and are spring-garlanded, three cloud-maidens rise wind-flushed . . . Mr. D. L. has now lost the knack, which even a minor poet with sufficient ambition and application may acquire, of writing verse one might care to re-read. There are too many poems here which could have been improved by ten minutes' work, too many which are merely lazy literary responses to questions which (to Mr. D. L.'s credit) are posed to all of us. His talent is not so lovely that it can afford to go about ungroomed, even on party business.

Did Cecil ever see this? If so, it would have stuck in his memory, for he was affected by bad notices. After the war I came across him a few times on various literary chores, but there was nothing untoward in those meetings. By then he was a distinguished literary figure, and his authorship of the successful "Nicholas Blake" crime novels was widely known. He was an extremely good-looking man, always well dressed in a faintly horsy style (raglan overcoats, small-checked suits). At first an austere manner was conveyed, appropriate to encountering a whippersnapper who had once impudently reviewed him; but eventually the features would break into a smile, and he would prove himself to be someone who liked a joke, not averse to telling one at his own expense.

At the end of 1957 he came to live, with his second wife (Jill Balcon, the actress) and two children by her, in a Georgian house at the bottom of Croom's Hill, a road that runs from Blackheath heath down to Greenwich containing a conspectus of British domestic architecture from the middle of the seventeenth century onwards. It was a few years before we began to exchange visits, I think first getting to know one another better round the Hamiltons' dining table. Jill proved to have a great talent for entertaining and being entertained, and her personality prompted Cecil the more easily to let his hair down. No doubt there lurked always in his manner his sense of being a great man—not that he was in any way affected or pretentious; more that a feeling of his being on the *qui vive* was conveyed, against what precisely rather difficult to define. It is somewhat extraordinary that when one comes to give an account of him, personality and anecdotal memories are thin on the ground. Somewhere in his autobiography he says how much he hated large parties, and it may well have been that despite his success with women and in public appearances as verse reader, he was basically shy, a quality easily mistaken for other qualities, not always endearing.

When I read his son's posthumous biography (a fascinating though sometimes startlingly unfilial book) I was surprised to find that in 1960 Cecil (who was on the relevant committee) had advanced my claim (though in vain) to a Queen's Gold Medal for Poetry. If he had ever known of my review of *Overtures to Death* he had magnanimously put it out of mind, nor was it as though by 1960 I knew him really well. When we started to go to Croom's Hill, his children by Jill, Tamasin and Daniel, were out of infancy, both showing the striking looks that contributed to their following their mother into the world of the theatre. Sometimes a, to me, legendary figure would be a fellow dinner guest: I would instance John Garrett, the joint editor, with Auden, of *The Poet's Tongue,* already mentioned—influential anthology of 1935 (which followed Bridges's *Spirit of Man* in withholding the poets' name beside the poems) whose introduction was a sacred text of my youth; and Alec Brown, who to the Spring 1936 number of *New Writing* contributed an English version of Pasternak's "1905." I should emphasise again that though I followed closely the thirties movement in literature, it was mainly from afar. And when I say "closely," I wonder if I really read through, and with any critical insight, Alec Brown's Pasternak translation—which, having taken down from the shelf the dusty and foxed relevant issue of *New Writing*, I now find skilful and effective:

> Think; in our time; and turned to a lecturer's
>   catchword;
> and the fettering years since then have made
>   such a clatter
> the whole damn thing is forgotten, and all that
>   occurred
> is no legend inspiring, but a frigid "historical"
>   matter . . .

I expect, if I read the version at all attentively in the spring of 1936, I would have been interested in its "revolutionary" content and how to bring such matters into verse, rather than its "poetic" qualities and its usage of the characteristic tone of native English verse. And as to thirties political beliefs, Cecil once expressed surprise (and, I think, a touch of sympathetic fellow feeling) that I had been then, like him, for a short time a member of the Communist party.

The last years of Cecil's life were marked by a number of illnesses, all of which he treated with stoicism, even levity. After a gallstones operation he kept the offending minerals on the mantelpiece of his study, part of the relics on show there, which included a framed holograph poem by Wilfred Owen. This room, at the front of the ground floor, with stripped panelling and many bookshelves, was as elegant as its inhabitant. On my first entering it I had observed twin, floor-standing loudspeakers of discriminating make, so when I called after one of his hospitalizations (perhaps the gallstones removal) I brought as a gift the duplicate of a disc, cheap, but which had given me great pleasure. It was a realization of Bach's *Musical Offering* by a Czech ensemble, which made of that somewhat enigmatic piece a work of inexhaustible interest. I liked to think it helped Cecil to get shot of a poem or two—a process which involved also the smoking of many cigarettes, as Jill once told me.

By consulting a pocket diary of engagements I find I last saw Cecil on 20 January 1972. The occasion was a sort of business lunch at L'Escargot restaurant in Soho to which he and I had been invited by Jack Clark, old friend of mine who had become the brother-in-law of Julian Symons. Jack, and his partner in a firm of advertising agents, had conceived and carried into effect an enterprise called "Poem of the Month Club." The notion was that subscribers would receive every month a new poem, specially printed, and signed by the author. To confer prestige on what

was designed to be a profit-making venture, the selectors were the Poet Laureate and the Oxford Professor of Poetry, offices held by Cecil and me respectively. At L'Escargot it seemed plain that Cecil had cancer: he had lost weight, said he couldn't keep warm. But he attributed his illness to diabetes, which symptomwise may have been correct, for he had an inoperable tumour on the pancreas. He was forbidden wine, opened capsules and sprinkled the powder on his food, implied it might not go down at all well. His hands seemed to be taking on a transparency. But he was not in the least sorry for himself, and indeed had to leave for some other engagement while Jack and I were still at table. I saw him being helped on with his overcoat by a waiter, an office he seemed really to require, by no means a mere restaurant courtesy. I often thought of him with compassion thereafter, thinking of the suffering of both my parents from his disease.

Cecil died on 22 May. At quite short notice I was asked by Alan Haydock, a BBC radio producer I had worked with before, to compile and read a memorial programme of Cecil's poems. It was broadcast on 24 May. Looking through Cecil's poetry for this occasion, I saw clearly that his talent had survived Auden's overpowering influence, the crude political demands of the thirties, and his own tendency to lapse into the received "poetic" (it must be remembered he was born in 1904, passed his adolescence in a time when the Georgian poets—and worse—were still influential). Rehearsing and recording the poems I had chosen, I realised how well they were laid out for the voice (he was an excellent reader of verse), even the complex stanza forms, and how observing the metrics made plainer the sense. The experience touched me: I felt things had moved on for the better since that rude review nearly thirty-four years before.

4

Virtually at the top of Croom's Hill, within the curtilage of Greenwich Park, a fine old house, Macartney House, had long been converted into flats. One of them had once been occupied by the Woolwich executive Sandy Meikle; into another, or possibly the same one, had come John Pudney and his second wife, Monica. He was a poet I had known about ever since his first book had been scathingly reviewed in the February 1934 number of *New Verse* by Geoffrey Grigson, that little magazine's editor. Pudney had been in the Royal Air Force during the war, and, though starting out as a minority poet, his wartime verse had caught the imagination of a wider

John Pudney

public, one short poem actually being quoted in a famous film of the period, *The Way to the Stars.* It was called "Airman" and began:

> Fetch out no shroud
> For Johnny-in-the-cloud;
> And keep your tears
> For him in after years.

I, too, had written poetry while in the forces during the war; no doubt had a pang or two of envy at John Pudney's popularity (the sales of his wartime work were said by his publishers in 1948 to have exceeded 100,000 copies).

In 1948 I reviewed a new collection of his for the left-wing weekly, *Tribune.* I was very severe with it and, what was quite unfair, mocked his popularity, asserting he was now not so much a poet as a phenomenon, having "taken a place in the glass-fronted bookcase beside Omar Khayyam and Rupert Brooke." In next week's *Tribune* a letter to the editor from the poet appeared, which began:

The rather silly views of Mr. Roy Fuller upon Recent Poetry [the heading of the notice] are of no particular consequence in themselves. He is evidently a person who must first express a measure of bile before facing his own problems in literature.

What surprises me, sir, is that your journal, which at one time seemed to be concerned with the propagation of thought and culture among the rank-and-file of the country, should encourage this person to sneer at the fact that my former volumes reached a wide public . . .

The editor appended a note about the freedom of opinion of his contributors, but it must be admitted John Pudney had made an effective point. This exchange was very much in my mind when I was due to meet the poet and his wife at the Hamiltons', perhaps twenty years after. But the encounter passed off unremarkably: neither of us disinterred the past. I expect I silently confirmed on that occasion that John abstained from any alcoholic drink. He had made no secret of his former addiction; indeed, it formed the subject of some of his occasional journalism. Drink had perhaps contributed to the break-up of his first marriage, to the daughter of the once-celebrated author and M.P., A. P. Herbert. His second wife, Monica—intelligent and agreeable—seemed devoted to him, and one guessed she had played no small part in his conquest of the Demon Drink. John had gone on writing verse, but since he lived by his pen was also the author of many miscellaneous books and much journalism.

I went to a party the Pudneys gave at Macartney House; perhaps came across them on other occasions, but I never got to know John at all closely. He was only three years older than me; we could have had a good deal in common, but in person he has left little more impression than a middle-aged individual of medium height and average looks. What stays in my mind is his enviable courage. I don't know how I heard he had contracted cancer of the throat: it may well have been that he turned the disaster to journalistic account, as he had his alcoholism. The malady was possibly a legacy of his drinking past, but that would not have made it any easier to come to terms with. It was after he had undergone surgery that he, Monica, and I attended a tree-planting ceremony in Greenwich Park. Could it have been in 1977 to mark the Silver Jubilee of the Queen's accession? The reason for two poets being invited also eludes me. The episode is one of many become mysterious in the recollection of old age. But I remember feeling, that bright, sharp morning, as we met, like conferring monarchs, from our opposite sides of the park, a greater intimacy with him than before. Probably the faintly lunatic proceedings, and certainly one's concerned enquiries about his health, brought us closer; and Monica's presence was always a catalyst. George Rostrevor Hamilton had loved to walk on the heath, Cecil Day Lewis in the park—both had written poems about their peregrinations—but John and I seemed the last of the Blackheath poets. (In the eighties a young poet, Blake Morrison, came to live in the Pudney's old flat, but that is another story, as must remain the recent Blackheath presence of yet another poet, Herbert Lomas.) John was optimistic about his health, and in fact his looks and demeanor seemed to justify optimism. But eventually I read a newspaper article by him, characteristically forthcoming and gay, in which he recounted his inability to swallow, and his being fed direct into (I think) the oesophagus. His words were intended to reassure—perhaps did reassure—fellow sufferers, but they upset me, evidence of one further step into the inevitable pit.

John Fuller, about 1958

After his death Monica asked me to join with several other poets (including Bertie Lomas) in a memorial reading for her husband, held in the Ranger's House, another fine old house, near Macartney House, on the edge of the park. We could choose the poems we wished to read, Monica even supplying typescripts of uncollected, perhaps unpublished, poems. The choice was more difficult than had been the case with Cecil's commemorative programme. Quite strange, the itch to associate oneself only with what one is capable of defending—a sort of snobbery. But as I looked through John's work, I saw that he was best as a writer of light, even comic, verse—subsequently proved by the reactions of a live audience. I was obtuse not to have seen that in 1948, and thus been able to express sympathy in my review instead of contumely.

5

So, while others declined and passed away, I was spared to become (so I hope) by and large a better poet, certainly to write a good deal of poetry.

Roy Fuller in his Blackheath garden

Julian Symons was spared with me (we were both born in 1912), but he eventually deserted Blackheath and, to a great degree, the writing of verse. Jill Day Lewis and Monica Pudney also moved elsewhere. But I will not end on a note of change and decay. A book of poems I published in 1954, *Counterparts,* includes a poem with the dedication "J.L.F., his poem." It had been written during, or soon after, a family holiday in 1952 on the Côte des Maures, and the dedication acknowledges the contribution by my son to some of the imagery at the start of the poem:

> The azure marbled with white and palest grey:
> The cactuses with buds like hand grenades:
> The roman candle palms: a lonely house
> Against a hill, a wrong piece of a jig-saw.
> The terraces descend in armour plating,
> The grapes a violet shadow in their vines.

John was then only fifteen, but I suppose I must have guessed he was going to join the number of the Blackheath poets.

BIBLIOGRAPHY

Poetry:

Poems. London: Fortune Press, 1940.

The Middle of a War. London: Hogarth Press, 1942.

A Lost Season. London: Hogarth Press, 1944.

Epitaphs and Occasions. London: Lehmann, 1949.

Counterparts. London: Verschoyle, 1954.

Brutus's Orchard. London: Deutsch, 1962.

Collected Poems, 1936–1961. London: Deutsch, 1962; Philadelphia: Dufour, 1962.

Buff. London: Deutsch, 1965; Chester Springs, Pa.: Dufour, 1965.

New Poems. London: Deutsch, 1968; Chester Springs, Pa.: Dufour, 1968.

Pergamon Poets 1, with R. S. Thomas. Edited by Evan Owen. Oxford, England, and New York: Pergamon Press, 1968.

Off Course. London: Turret, 1969.

Penguin Modern Poets 18, with Alfred Alvarez and Anthony Thwaite. London: Penguin, 1970.

To an Unknown Reader. London: Poem-of-the-Month Club, 1970.

Song Cycle from a Record Sleeve. Oxford, England: Sycamore Press, 1972.

Tiny Tears. London: Deutsch, 1973.

An Old War. Edinburgh: Tragara Press, 1974.

Waiting for the Barbarians: A Poem. Richmond, England: Keepsake Press, 1974.

From the Joke Shop. London: Deutsch, 1975.

The Joke Shop Annexe. Edinburgh: Tragara Press, 1975.

An Ill-Governed Coast. Sunderland, England: Ceolfrith Press, 1976.

Re-treads. Edinburgh: Tragara Press, 1979.

The Reign of Sparrows. London: London Magazine Editions, 1980.

The Individual and His Times: A Selection of the Poetry of Roy Fuller. Edited by V. J. Lee. London: Athlone Press, 1982.

House and Shop. Edinburgh: Tragara Press, 1982.

As from the Thirties. Edinburgh: Tragara Press, 1983.

Mianserin Sonnets. Edinburgh: Tragara Press, 1984.

New and Collected Poems, 1934–1984. London: Secker and Warburg, 1985.

Subsequent to Summer. London: Salamander Press, 1985.

Outside the Canon. Edinburgh: Tragara Press, 1986.

Consolations. London: Secker and Warburg, 1987.

Available for Dreams. London: Collins Harvill, 1989.

Fiction:

With My Little Eye. London: Lehmann, 1948; New York: Macmillan, 1957.

The Second Curtain. London: Verschoyle, 1953; New York: Macmillan, 1956.

Fantasy and Fugue. London: Verschoyle, 1954; New York: Macmillan, 1956; also published as *Murder in Mind.* Chicago: Academy Chicago, 1986.

Image of a Society. London: Deutsch, 1956; New York: Macmillan, 1957.

The Ruined Boys. London: Deutsch, 1959; also published as *That Distant Afternoon.* New York: Macmillan, 1957.

The Father's Comedy. London: Deutsch, 1961.

The Perfect Fool. London: Deutsch, 1963.

My Child, My Sister. London: Deutsch, 1965.

The Carnal Island. London: Deutsch, 1970.

Omnibus (contains *With My Little Eye, The Second Curtain, Fantasy and Fugue*). Manchester, England: Carcanet, 1988.

Nonfiction:

Owls and Artificers: Oxford Lectures on Poetry. London: Deutsch, 1971; New York: Library Press, 1971.

Professors and Gods: Last Oxford Lectures on Poetry. London: Deutsch, 1973; New York: St. Martin's Press, 1974.

Souvenirs (memoirs). London: London Magazine Editions, 1980.

Vamp till Ready: Further Memoirs. London: London Magazine Editions, 1982.

Home and Dry: Memoirs 3. London: London Magazine Editions, 1984.

Twelfth Night: A Personal View. Edinburgh: Tragara Press, 1985.

The Strange and the Good: Collected Memoirs. London: Collins Harvill, 1989.

For Children:

Savage Gold: A Story of Adventure. (Illustrated by Robert Medley) London: Lehmann, 1946; Baltimore: Penguin, 1957; (illustrated by Douglas Hall) London: Hutchinson Educational, 1960.

Catspaw (illustrated by David Gollins). London: Alan Ross, 1966.

See Grandpa Lately? (illustrated by Joan Hickson). London: Deutsch, 1972.

Poor Roy (illustrated by Nicolas Bentley). London: Deutsch, 1977.

The Other Planet and Three Other Fables (illustrated by Peter Paul Piech). Richmond, England: Keepsake Press, 1979.

More about Tompkins and Other Light Verse. Edinburgh: Tragara Press, 1981.

Upright Downfall, with Barbara Giles and Adrian Rumble. Oxford, England, and New York: Oxford University Press, 1983.

The World through the Window: Collected Poems for Children. London: Blackie, 1989.

Editor of:

Byron for Today. London: Porcupine Press, 1948.

New Poems 1952, with Clifford Dyment and Montagu Slater. London: Joseph, 1952.

The Building Societies Acts, 1874–1960: Great Britain and Northern Ireland. Third edition. London: Franey, 1957; Fifth edition. London: Franey, 1961; Sixth edition. London: Franey, 1962.

Supplement of New Poetry. London: Poetry Book Society, 1964.

Fellow Mortals: An Anthology of Animal Verse (illustrated by David Koster). Plymouth, England: Macdonald & Evans, 1981.

The Penguin New Writing 1940–1950: An Anthology, with John Lehmann. London: Penguin, 1985.

Brewster Ghiselin

1903-

Brewster Ghiselin, at home in the garden, Salt Lake City, 1981. Photograph for display with those of other recipients of the first "Honors in the Arts" awards of the Salt Lake Area Chamber of Commerce

Very early in life, invited to express my love for "the little birdy," I rejected such paltry sentiment by proclaiming my love for the "big blue jye," that raucous jabber at fruit and robber of nests, sharp-beaked and crested, flashing his brilliance, exuberant, unstinted. Rebuked but not wholly repressed by human disapproval, I learned to modify my behavior, to heed the eye of appraisal and the cautions of parents and nurse and teachers, and a good many others of less intimate acquaintance.

Yet my life has been shaped by delight in transcendence, in overpassing established limits of custom and habit, in opposing finality of closure—arrest of the spirit, that turns the key in the lock and rusts it there.

For years I had no clear notion of that moving force. I sensed it in action, in impulse—as in climbing the difficult height of a woodland oak to look into a big bundle of twigs, the nest of crows absent a while from the cluster of darkly speckled pale green eggs, or invading thorny tangle of wild plum in flower to look into the nest of a cardinal that a cowbird had defiled with her freckled gift of death to the nestlings of the owner.

I thought of becoming an ornithologist. I collected and properly labeled a clutch of eggs, white, nearly round, from the hollow in a sycamore tree that a screech owl had deserted. I learned to call the owls to their chorus of dusk on the hill where I lived for a while in Marin County. And from the high school that I attended, some miles by electric train toward San Francisco, I used to walk home up the steep south slope of Mount Tamalpais, across the peak from which I could see the far Farallones in the glitter of westward ocean, before I turned to run down the rollrock slither of the firebreak toward home.

I had little understanding of the course I followed, yet knew it was an escape from constrictions. A love of poetry, that my mother had fostered by reading Shakespeare and Tennyson and others to her children from their earliest years, led me to register as a major in English when I began attending the University of California in August 1922. My instructor in Freshman English stuttered. I attended only for one term.

Though talented in drawing and painting, I thought to become a writer. Somewhat naively, I looked for work on a newspaper, found a position as reporter, then, soon, as assistant editor of a small newspaper in San Anselmo, soliciting advertising, writing news stories and editorials, and acting as Marin County correspondent for the San Francisco *Bulletin,* that later I worked for, as a cub reporter.

Enticed by relatives who offered support for a term at the Southern Branch of the University of California, I returned to college. Already dissatisfied with the limited life of a reporter, I remained to continue studies that might lead to employment as a teacher. I took courses in art—and was told by the head of the Department of Art that I was one of the two most talented students in the program. But to my inquiry as to the reason for my low grades in those courses, only "C," the response was that I probably had produced too little finished work. My disgust at that measure of value in terms of sheer quantity weakened my respect for institutional procedures. It contributed a little to my growing conviction that the established ways of mankind are intolerably limited.

Working my way through the next two years of college, I was not always well fed, yet I was nourished sufficiently in mind, and sometimes in spirit. My aunt owned a house on a cliff overlooking the ocean, in Laguna Beach, where a high rise now stands above crowded shores and polluted water. In those days the beaches were unlighted—except on some evenings by campfires. I swam by day and by night. I learned the ways of the waves in all weathers.

Though I had come long before to distrust the pleasures of discursive thought, that I pursued with

Brewster with elder sister, Mary, and younger sister, Eleanor, at home in Kirkwood, Missouri, about 1910

discriminate interest in many areas and with emulous intensity in some, I was saved from commitment to a life of intellectual specialization by the savor of original salt in the thoughtless ocean. Much later, at the University of Utah, while teaching courses in the writing of fiction and poetry, I discovered that even the most talented students needed to cultivate, with precise understanding, the oceanic liberties of the spirit and the focal disciplines of the mind. I devised a course that, in 1941, was announced in the catalogue as "The Creative Process." Shortly, it was drawing registrants from many areas of study besides English. After some years, a selection of materials that I had found most effectual, thirty-eight statements of workers in a great diversity of disciplines intellectual and esthetic, preceded by a long introduction condensing substance essential to the course I was teaching, became the book *The Creative Process.* Written and put into final shape in the summer of 1946, it was offered to half a dozen publishers—and refused, sometimes with explicit regrets and always on the assumption that it could not have the appeal which would assure sale of the ten thousand copies required for recovery of the costs of publication. Since its publication in 1952 by the University of California Press, it has never been out of print, and it has sold more than half a million copies. Its subject—sometimes confused with what is called "problem solving"—has become popular without attaining very wide or precise understanding. Watching development of interest in "creativity" has been monitory.

Prescriptive disciplines continue to be cherished, and routine remains in favor, as in my helpless childhood in suburbs of St. Louis, where I lived from my birth in Webster Groves—June 13, 1903—till removal to California at the age of seventeen. Learning by rote was the mode of preparation for a life of conformity. In grade school, mathematics was inculcated through assiduous practice, in obedience to pedagogical regulations exacted without inquiry. Though when I read Tennyson aloud in the fifth grade the whole class listened, the teacher with them, I was backward in arithmetic. I was demoted to the care of a pedantic scold. She merely exacted practice of the usual sort, through which I gained a little facility. But her sharp corrective interruptions of her pupils' recitations impaired the confidence of their tongues.

I endured that profitless punishment as if there were no remedy for it, but it was in fact only the first of many abuses that I learned—slowly and tardily— to oppose, by rejective efforts and, at best, through expansive adventures such as those I have cited.

When after taking an M.A. in English at the University of California in Berkeley I went to England in hope of finding at Oxford University a more liberal discipline in graduate studies—and was disappointed, I neglected some of the courses prescribed for an advanced degree, in order to attend others more rewarding in themselves, such as a series of seminars in study of classical Greek vases, taught among the treasures of the Ashmolean Museum by the preeminent authority J. D. Beazley. During vacations between terms, I traveled through Belgium, France, Germany, and Austria, into Italy, meeting a few of the most eminent artists of our century, among them Llewelyn Powys and D. H. Lawrence. I have written elsewhere of my ten days with Lawrence in Bandol.

I had looked forward to Oxford in vague hope of meeting D. H. Lawrence in Europe, yet made neither plans nor inquiries till in the Christmas vacation in Paris, at the bookshop Shakespeare and Company, Sylvia Beach informed me that Lawrence was "dying in Bandol." Finding him there, alone on the plage one afternoon, I talked with him of his work that I thought unrivaled in our time and for myself indispensable. At his suggestion a few days later, I moved to the Hôtel Beau Rivage to share in the daily life of Lawrence and Frieda, noonday through evening, as if I were a visitor in their household. Frieda's daughter Barbara Weekley was visiting them. Often after dinner while we sat in Frieda's small bedroom, Lawrence read aloud what he had written during the day. We made some excursions, to Toulon, and once in a motorboat far out toward the small islands on the sea. One afternoon I walked with Lawrence to wild uplands where, looking to the coast, the brightly painted houses below us, and inland to the snowy Maritime Alps, he said, "It's not far enough south."

He outlined a course of travel for my next vacation, across the Continent, north and south, up the valley of the Isar, over the Brenner Pass, to choice regions and cities of Italy. In Capri, his friend the painter and Buddhist scholar Earl Henry Brewster took me into his home, introduced me to friends, showed me such secrets of the island as a tract of sea-washed masonry of a palace of Tiberius, and a cave, down the steeps of a hill toward the sea, which was believed to have been sacred to Mithras, and from the heights of Monte Solaro the Mediterranean stretching beneath us into the past. He sent me to visit his friend Llewelyn Powys.

These men, mature in intellect and sensibility, proved in the flesh the value of the way I had trusted and years earlier had figured ideally in saying that "the precincts of the mind should also be the courts of the sun."

On that afternoon when I walked with Powys among greening vineyards, there had been little conversation. In a poem published years later, when I had read more of his work, I praised the wealth of abstention that enriched it, as it had enhanced that afternoon: "silence, a perfect courtesy of breath." With Brewster I talked briefly of Buddhism, of which I already knew a little. In 1923 I had bought and read Richard Maurice Bucke's *Cosmic Consciousness,* just then republished, and at about the same time I first heard in its full trisyllabic—and poetic—substance the long-drawn, deeply intoned AUM that breathes music and meaning as one and concludes with ultimate eloquence in silence. In Europe I began to see in what way the arts are one art, why "the Tao that is the subject of discussion is not the true Tao," why a poet must be free of words. That insight is central in my poem "The Vision of Adam," written in England but unpublished till eight years after.

Still hoping a scholarly career might not preclude the life of discovery, I went, that fall, to teach at the University of Utah. On returning from England, I had married Olive Franks, four years younger than I, yet my contemporary in college. From the train, as we entered the valley at the edge of the Great Basin, we saw the dun hills of October, alien to our eyes.

There, except for a summer in Laguna Beach, we stayed two years, till I obtained a half-time position at the University of California as assistant in English, teaching two classes, taking all the courses required for the Ph.D., and some others, during the two-year appointment. In 1933, with no prospect of employment in the midst of the Depression, we went to Laguna Beach for a year of deliverance from commitments too exclusively intellectual. I had written no poetry, but had read *La Chanson de Roland* in Old French and, with passionate comprehension, the *Beowulf* that I had known only superficially in earlier years. My impulse was toward the concrete experience I had been deprived of: the wild hills inland and the ocean.

We were housed without cost, with my elder sister, Mary, and younger sister, Eleanor, a talented artist just beginning to be noticed. During weeks of futile looking for work, I went to the sea and the sands for food and fuel. A small old vessel stranded and rotting near that jut of high sandstone and foam-washed conglomerate known as Wood's Point supplied firewood. I fished from shore or wave-washed rock, or more rarely swimming with trident spear.

One gray day I salvaged from stormy breakers, that threatened the rocks I stood on, a lobster trap drowning and shattering as it came with its walloping rope through the foam, its catch still caged. When the lowest low tides of winter were farthest down, I sprawled under boulders into cold dusk scented with sea wrack and iodine, to pry abalone from the stone. I wallowed in foam and green eelgrass, where sometimes an octopus could be wrenched from its grip among tiderocks. When the rains came that winter, wild mustard on the hills provided savory greens.

Yet before I found any work, I had to apply for government relief: eight dollars of credit, for groceries. At midyear I began work, half-time, as janitor at the local high school, though already I had begun earning nearly a dollar a day through teaching in the Emergency Education Program, that the poet Alfred Young Fisher and I organized in Laguna Beach. Fisher, in lack of an academic appointment for that year, and his wife M. F. K. Fisher, later the famous gastronomist, were living in her family's summer cottage after their return from France, where he had earned the degree of *docteur ès lettres.* Moving fast, he and I found appropriate work in the program for all the qualified teachers in the community who needed employment. The classes were various and popular.

The rarest experience of that year was far from the ocean: a two-week expedition into the Sonoran areas of southern Arizona to collect reptiles, with a dealer in specimens for museums. In an old Ford dragging a homemade trailer, we drove in wild country, to camp and to walk over desert and mountains. I was paid what I sacrificed through absence from my teaching. Olive was cook and camp-watcher.

During daylight hours the snakes lay hidden from the summer in darkest recesses under rock or roots. There we found them by tilting sunlight from a small mirror into the dusk where they coiled till evening, or till dawn brought them to the open before the sun became hot. In cool uplands they were abroad at any hour. Though careful, I came one afternoon, as I climbed across granite and pine needles, jaw to jaw with a black rattler laced with gold fretwork. My poem "The Catch," written thirty years after, records our capture, and celebrates the later escape, of a badger—actually a pair—that we found feeding underground on a broad rattler that had been raiding the burrows of rodents.

I was long in learning to heed my early intuitive insight—more instinct than understanding—that concrete experience teaches more surely and completely than intellect can conceive or report.

In October, under pressure of necessity—our first child would be born in May of the next year—I returned to the University of Utah to teach four classes of Freshman English, to read and correct, with comment and suggestions for improvement, the weekly themes of one hundred and twenty-two students during the autumn term. Thereafter the burden was less. As I continued publishing poetry and fiction, I began teaching courses in "creative" writing.

In 1936, my paintings and drawings were exhibited at the "Art Barn" gallery. The young director of the Federal Art Project in Utah, Judy Lund, engaged me to organize and direct the work of its subsidiary the Index of American Design, that employed some of the artists of the project in recording in color the work of pioneer craftsmen and talented laymen in the years before 1900. As supervisor of the index that summer, I traveled over most of the state, including remote communities, gathering information and some of the original artifacts. On my return I made sure that the paintings recording them were exact. One expert at headquarters in Washington reported

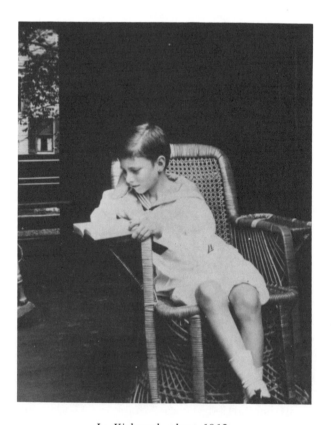

In Kirkwood, about 1912

*Brewster and Olive Ghiselin,
Altadena, California, 1930*

his impulsive temptation to pick up the image of a textile from the paper of the painting we had sent. The original, with other such objects that I collected, is preserved in the Museum of Fine Arts at the University of Utah. An experienced staff continued the work of the index under a new supervisor, Elzy Bird, when I returned to my teaching in September.

The following summer I was Fellow in Poetry at the three-week writers' conference directed by the poet Edward Davison at the University of Colorado in Boulder—a forerunner of the many to come. Most of the large staff of writers were at the height of their fame: Ford Madox Ford, Sherwood Anderson, John Crowe Ransom, John Peale Bishop, Whit Burnett, Evelyn Scott, Howard Mumford Jones, Thomas Hornsby Ferril. Halfway between students and staff, I gave no lectures, but with the latter I read my poetry, and participated as one of the speakers at a roundtable conference on poetry, during which my suggestion that the "sprung rhythm" of Gerard Manley Hopkins might strongly influence our sense of poetic form in the future was opposed by a student in the

audience—Robert Lowell—who declared that sprung rhythm resembled free verse "in lack of control." Lowell, then about twenty years old, had come to the writers' conference mainly to enjoy the influence there of his famous teacher John Crowe Ransom, an influence manifest in Lowell's remark.

John Peale Bishop, the most brilliant speaker of the conference leaders, was also the most discerning of those who read my poems and advised me. Whit Burnett, founder and editor of *Story,* then at the height of its prestige, taught me, one weekend, to fly-fish in upland lakes and streams. On another weekend, with Olive, I drove Ford Madox Ford and the artist Biala to Denver to hang and view an exhibit of her paintings, and to visit the Denver Museum of Art, where we admired in delight a magnificent bronze image of Shiva—Naṭarāja, lord of the dance, in bliss at the center of his circle of flames. Biala, appreciative of Olive's quick wit and grace, remarked that she was charming.

We went home round-about through New Mexico, Santa Fe and Taos, to the Lawrence ranch, where Frieda was living with Capitano Angelo Ravagli, about whom she had spoken to me briefly in 1929. Aldous Huxley and his family were guests. I admired Ravagli's current paintings, folk art of a sensitive eye and deft hand. At lunch he praised red wine well watered, drinkable therefore all day. Frieda had baked bread. She detailed some gossip thriving in Taos, mainly Mabel Luhan's report that Frieda sold hot dogs near the little chapel at the ranch, where Lawrence's ashes were enshrined.

In Laguna, in the summer of 1939, we heard the first news of war in Europe, and under that darkening we drove home to Utah for the year of teaching that preceded my first sabbatical. Our second child, Michael, four years younger than Jon, had been born in May. Conceived within sound of summer ocean, they wakened to light in spring, where uplands of the Great Basin tilt to the Wasatch range and the high Uintas. They were reared in a literate family addicted to delights of language and the open world. Both were to become biologists of wide interests, including deep concern for behaviors affecting the environment. Before illness and death in 1985, Jon supported his family by settling questions of environmental impact. Michael, after publication of a magisterial first book on the achievement of Charles Darwin, is exploring in a series of books the bases of a unitary discipline of intellect and its practical applications.

Michael was a quiet child. Jon at age five was delightfully ebullient, self-pleasing, headstrong, and original in vigorous language. In our rented house, above a noisy basement assigned to the use at all hours of the landlord's son, I escaped every morning for some hours of writing in the cold unheated but glassed-in isolation of the front porch. There I wrote slowly my novella *Death of the Past,* published in *Story* two years later, and, among other things, my poem "Bath of Aphrodite," written in the midst of the summer session of 1940. The poem, published in *Poetry,* and followed there by an analysis of the process of its composition, with remarks upon the relation of elements of its form with one another and with the elusively shifting grounds of subjective excitement from which they emerged, appears with my commentary in my book *The Creative Process.* It was an exploration of the meaning and power of our relation to the sea and of various possibilities of formal innovations, concretely developed in actual composition and tested by their service in satisfaction of intellect and sensibilities simultaneously and equally.

The next academic year, my sabbatical, in Laguna Beach, was financed by a diminished stipend, $1,400, a fraction of my salary provided by the University of Utah, and by my production of a large syllabus for guidance of students in a correspondence course I was to teach in following years for the Extension Division of the university. For that, I was paid thirty dollars. My outdoor study during the writing of the first draft was an open hilltop yellow with wild oats, where now the asphalt and its suburban adjuncts have been a long while.

That year, we learned to relish the white flesh of rattlesnakes, that when brought fresh from the morning hills commingles the flavor of frogs' legs and breast of chicken. I dived for abalone, with little equipment, only my swimming trunks and faceplate and sharp-tipped iron, end of a carriage spring honed to a bright edge to pry up the rim of the univalve shell sucked tight to rock. Damaged by phlebitis when a doctor who knew better failed to get me on my feet after removing my appendix, I wore no swim fins. Yet I swam deep enough, and in more intimate contact with the sea, deep enough that once, when tempted to take a second abalone from the rock that had yielded the one I had thrust into my trunks, I remembered the long way up through dim water swayed by waves, and pushed off to rise to the air.

Leaving the children for a week, we drove upcoast to Marin County, without expenses except for gasoline, since we camped on the beaches and slept in a borrowed sleeping bag. At Pismo Beach I grilled a big Pismo clam picked up at dawn on wide sand of the ebb. The nostalgia of shores and head-

lands and mountain in Marin County might have been foremost, except for the overwhelming revelation of fresh form and spirit in a landscape seen with changed eyes. I made many quick drawings, of rhythmic hills and shores, and wind-carved laurel in the open or trailing from the lee of huge boulders.

A highway up the slopes of Tamalpais had impaired the isolation of height. Inland, the valley below the mountain was beginning to suffer the influx that in a few years would crowd it with commerce and pack it along most of its length with housing, and reclaim the sloughs that had flooded the tides over tules and weeds up to the highway below the high school I attended. Seeing, I recalled my news stories and editorials favoring the project of the Golden Gate Bridge that would carry the influx of progress. We followed the coast back to Laguna.

Aside from that trip north our farthest ranging was into the nearer canyons, still lonely and wild in those days before the war—which changed all the coast by bringing in soldiers in training or guarding the coastline against invasion—many of whom re-

With Jon, Torrey Pines State Reserve,
La Jolla, California, 1937

turned to the region they had discovered when the war was over. One afternoon, upcanyon from San Juan Capistrano, I enticed a young black-headed grosbeak, innocent of fears learned in places settled by men, to come to my hand to perch and feed. Even in Laguna Beach wild animals often came from the hills, deer, coyote, fox, raccoon, skunk, opossum, weasel, and the most elusive of all—the nocturnal ringtail, the cacomistle, that I saw once racing the dawn down a strip of asphalt. And for several nights when we were living only a few blocks from the center of town, we heard from the unbuilt slopes above us harsh, hoarse cries, followed by a whistling mew, the unmistakable call of a cougar. When I went for several afternoons to paint a landscape from a vantage on the outskirts of the small settlement called the Top of the World, just above Laguna Beach, I heard at the approach of dusk along the inland canyon below me the music of bands of coyotes running their kill.

Inland again in October, we rented a small house. Two months later planes struck Pearl Harbor. Men in uniform attended regular classes and others of special purpose, some of which I taught. A colonel visiting the campus said, "Tell them to write short."

Most of the men who came back to study at the university were changed in more than age. The university changed, a little.

During years of war, there was shortage of gasoline. In the tideless Great Salt Lake, I could swim only briefly, eyes protected by a faceplate against splatter of stinging salt. One summer at Bear Lake, high and cold a hundred miles to the north, I taught our two children to fly-fish for trout in the streams that ran over gravel toward shores of sand bared by receding water. There along rippled shallows troupes of huge carp feeding in tandem, big brown backs rising and sinking in sequence resembling one wallowing body, made plausible the stories of sightings of the Bear Lake Monster. Disturbed when I sprinted to see them, they shattered into writhing fragments submerging in foam. Ospreys hung over water and dropped and rose with a fish to strip at once or to carry to nests on the farther shore.

No longer in exile, I was writing more and more of inland and upland country and the life there. At the same time, I was writing the long poem "Sea," overtly realistic, implicitly metaphoric of that ground of our nescience which, against the word of the greater mystics, organized religions have tended to delimit in doctrine and creed. One reviewer, Kathleen Raine, described the poem as wholly naturalistic, but I have not seen it so. Its central image, the ocean

in concrete presence, as it is for our senses, is not therefore the less what it is for mind and intuitive intelligence: not allegoric, emblematic, but immediate as light. Supplemented by "The Wheel" and "Aphrodite of the Return," "Sea" in its latest publication, in *Windrose: Poems 1929–1979*, stands first in the sequence entitled *Triptych*.

Writing and teaching, I tried to counter contractions of vision that harden the heart and block the circulation of thought. That was my foremost intention in the essays, reviews, and scholarly articles I published. "Paeonic Measures in English Verse," in *Modern Language Notes*, 1942, was designed, through enlarging the prevailing theory, to liberate practice. "Reading Sprung Rhythms," *Poetry*, 1947, an analysis of Gerard Manley Hopkins' poetic theory and consequent practice, was openly controversial and corrective.

Poetry and fiction, written in avidity wider and richer than forethought, can be subdued and contracted to no ulterior purpose—least of all to academic ambition. Through inmost impulsion I was writing more and more and publishing widely in preferred places and with critical recognition. My novella *Death of the Past* that appeared in *Story* in 1940 was given the highest rating—"three-starred"—by the anthologist Edward J. O'Brien, contemporary arbiter of fictional values, who had approved some of my earlier work. Years of such writing and publishing preceded the academic advancement that a doctoral degree would have provided promptly.

After advancements came, with assurance of continuing security in the Department of English at the University of Utah and of expanding opportunities for significant teaching there, I still thought of returning to California, especially during the years before the end of world war, when nostalgia for the unvisited ocean became recurrently painful. Perhaps deprivation increased the intensity of imaginative embrace in my writing that dealt with it, and with all that related to the enlargement of being and of insight which in recall of it even at great distance vibrated like the rote of its shore that I used to listen for when I climbed on the shorelong hills.

A strong inducement to remain year by year at the university came with my appointment as director of the Writers' Conference which I organized as a continuing project of the College of Letters and Science. The first conference, in the summer of 1947, drew more than a hundred registrants for one or both of the two weeks of workshops and lectures. It provided also a series of evening lectures by staff

Photograph by Brewster Ghiselin of Olive holding Michael, and Jon displaying his birdhouse, Laguna Beach, California, 1940

and director that were open to the public at large. That year, it was self-supporting—a notable enhancement of its value in the eyes of the administration. It rarely was so thereafter. Some of the local writers complained that the whole affair was too loftily conceived and conducted. The staff included one Utahn, Ray B. West, Jr., distinguished as writer and editor and as director of a writers' conference held the preceding year at the agricultural college in Logan but not designed to continue. There, as one of the staff for a single week, I had met Allen Tate; we had heard each other's discussions of writers and writing and had gone fishing for trout together. Tate and Caroline Gordon—Mrs. Allen Tate, a noted writer of fiction and a subtle critic and penetrating theorist of the art—were staff members in 1947. The others were Eric Bentley, Walter Van Tilburg Clark, Mark Schorer, and William Carlos Williams. I had long ago learned the value of first-rate minds. Year after year I labored—not always successfully—to bring them to Utah, despite the low honorariums that

were all we could offer, and sometimes against the opposition of administrative wisdom. In 1949, Vladimir Nabokov was a member of our conference staff, some years before the publication of *Lolita.*

Records of that venture in education—of self as of others—are in archives of the University of Utah Marriott Library: nine feet of files comprising financial reports, letters of invitation to the projected staff and responses of refusal or acceptance, my typed instructions to the staff, with brief admonitions, and their notes recording advice and criticism given in consultation over manuscripts, copies of their letters of appreciation and of reasoned opposition to threatened dissolution of the conference, and other matter more or less central and crucial. I gave up direction of the conference in 1966, primarily in disburdenment of administrative work that preceded and followed the two weeks of activity that justified such effort. The conference continued for a few years under a sequence of directors. It became simplified, less exacting and less rewarding for everyone concerned. When it was abandoned, the budget of several thousand dollars that I had won for it became a resource for payment and accommodation of writers engaged to visit the university to lecture and to consult with students.

Meanwhile I was freed for other things. My first book of poems, *Against the Circle,* attracted no great attention. As the title intimates, it was designed to transgress some ordinarily respected limits and to transcend expectations. The publisher, E. P. Dutton and Company, printed my second book also, in 1955, but I took leave of the firm when I was refused a guarantee of the commonly recommended ten-percent royalty for every copy of my next book that might be sold. I was working outside the circle.

Before Allen Tate and I met in Utah, he had accepted an early version of "Sea" for *A Southern Vanguard: The John Peale Bishop Memorial Volume,* which he was editing for publication in 1947. Later he published some of my new poems in the *Sewanee Review,* which he edited for two years. He included my poems in the anthology *Modern Verse in English: 1900–1950,* for which he edited the poetry written by Americans. After reading *Against the Circle* in the summer of 1946, he sent copies to several of his friends who were influential in the world of letters, among them Eliot and Auden, and in many other ways, early and late, he moved with similar intention, and on the whole with comparable effect.

Tate and our mutual friend Andrew Lytle returned several times to teach at the Writers' Conference. Rich in perception and technical skill and in ability to persuade understanding and to incite superlative effort, both men were invaluable. When Lytle published his novel *The Velvet Horn*, I reviewed it, at his suggestion, for the issue of the *Sewanee Review* that appeared concurrently with the book. At dusk, under trees beside water, we had been talking of fictional imagery in relation to the deeper perceptions that elude the ordinary reach of language. In pursuit of explicit understanding, with utmost care for the particulars of concrete substance in *The Velvet Horn*, I examined it, and found in it what had not emerged as topic for discussion in our evening's conversation, a dominant imagery of water and trees. In that context, I was able to tell myself, in exposition entailed by purposes of the review, but nowhere explicitly stated in the novel, "that to place anything first except life is to fell the tree of life." In immense complexity of action, the story exceeds any such summary insight. So did the triple experience of discussion, reading, and writing. It lighted like a flare the course I had held—the wake of difficult passage—and turned my face to the future. Exalting the gliding instant of our embodied life which is neither past nor future, delusive abstractions, the novel displayed its centrality as art. Its public success was moderate. What seems now, as then, more deplorable than the paucity of accolades and financial and other advantage that ought to have come to its author is the consequent deprivation of a society in need of what *The Velvet Horn* provides.

My ability to influence opinion was slight except in the growing area of interest and research that was coming to be called "creativity." My book *The Creative Process,* still a Mentor Book as it has been since 1955, and now also in the larger paperback edition issued by the University of California Press, with my "Foreword, 1985," has remained in wide and various use, often in classrooms but more commonly at large. I continue to encounter men and women of high accomplishment and reputation who tell me it was invaluable in guiding their youthful advance. Some of the half million copies sold in the third of a century since its first publication have been read to pieces. It quickly became known to people other than writers, especially in the graphic arts and in psychological research. It was the occasion of invitations to lecture in many places throughout the country, as at the Fifteenth Annual Meeting of the National Committee on Art Education, sponsored by the Museum of Modern Art, at the University of Michigan in 1957, or to act as consultant, as at the Institute of Personality Assessment and Research of the University of California in Berkeley in 1957 and

1958. Frequently during such assignments, I was engaged to read my poetry, for a smaller honorarium. So it was, for example, at the meeting in Michigan, and years later in Colorado when I gave the keynote address at the National Convention of the Society for Photographic Education. Reading on such occasions always to an audience far fewer than the assembled specialists, I saw how hard it is for people to put two and two together.

The character of my book *The Creative Process*, displaying the diversity of the one subject, and its rich complexity, and the rewards of insight into the nature of the complex procedure explored and explained, has involved me in lecturing and in consultation with a great variety of specialists, particularly at the national meetings of organizations devoted to the various sciences and arts. In highly focal examination of the specialties of those I was preparing to address,

With Michael, on the sands, the point north of Wood's Cove in the background, Laguna Beach, 1940

*Brewster as host at his birthday luncheon, a
black-headed grosbeak feeding from his hand,
Cleveland National Forest, upcanyon from
San Juan Capistrano, California, June 13, 1941*

cal research being conducted in universities throughout the country and in various offices of the national government.

In 1952 I applied for and was awarded a Faculty Fellowship of the Fund for the Advancement of Education, popularly referred to as a Ford Fellowship. It freed me to travel—with my wife, Olive, and our younger son, Michael—across the continent and into further contact with men and women of great capacity and dedication. Designated as "a post-doctoral visiting scholar," I went with the declared purpose of studying the education of creative writers in several universities, beginning with the University of Iowa, an obvious choice. Actually my purpose was much more inclusive. There I attended, for instance, some life classes taught by James Lechay, and besides observing and discussing aims and procedures with students and the instructor, I made some watercolor paintings of the posed subjects.

During that fellowship year I was abundantly confirmed in understanding that universities do not differ profoundly from one another in the temper of the faculty and their objectives. The poet and novelist Robert Penn Warren, teaching at Yale, was not a member of the Department of English. As a Rhodes scholar at Oxford, he had contented himself with the sufficient degree of B.Litt., rather than the still more advanced doctoral degree, the D.Phil. When I was at Oxford in 1929, the D.Phil. was widely reputed to be—perhaps not quite fairly—a concession to the needs of students from overseas.

Living for six months at Milford, Connecticut, in a beach house on Long Island Sound, I was privileged to see the wash of evidence of growing pollution that has for decades been defiling the shores of our civilization.

Conveniently situated between city and country and two great centers of academic life that I observed, Yale and Columbia, I continued my marginal investigations, and at the same time, for several weeks during the winter, I planned the next summer's Writers' Conference. A great deal of correspondence was necessary, both with the prospective staff—as always a prolonged process of inquiry and inducement—and with various offices and individuals at the University of Utah. Though I invited Lionel Trilling and Robert Penn Warren to be with us in Utah for the summer conference, I could not engage them. Always there was the question of adjusting the commitments of eminent writers to our own schedule, and the difficulty of inducing them to leave their more regular work for two weeks of heavy assign-

and in subsequent discussion, I learned in greater diversity than if I had concentrated only on the central matters of my own most cherished specializations. On the whole, that diversification was liberally educative. I was examining motivations and modes of advance which lead to discovery of the means of expanding and advancing human insight, of varied perspectives, and of refining perception and evaluation of ends proposed for examination, and of transcending the limits of expectation, which so easily foreclose in fatuous delusion of final attainment.

I engaged in some psychological research for the army and the air force. I participated in some conferences solely for specialists in creative performance of various sorts. In several of the biennial meetings of the University of Utah Research Conference on the Identification of Creative Scientific Talent, founded and directed by Calvin W. Taylor, supported by the National Science Foundation, I found myself among scientists—chiefly psychologists—addressing the questions of current psychologi-

ments in the west. The staff of the conference in 1953 were nevertheless a varied and distinguished group: Malcolm Cowley, M. F. K. Fisher, Vardis Fisher, Caroline Gordon, Virginia Sorensen, and Stephen Spender.

Despite my heavy commitments, we saw much of New England, and in New York particularly the greater museums of art. In Boston I was accosted by a museum guard as I was in the act of drawing a silver tablespoon made by the first of my family in America, the goldsmith Cesar Ghiselin, a Huguenot refugee who settled in Philadelphia in the seventeenth century. The first name was misspelled and the date of death was later than the fact, but the museum rules were preserved. I came away with a record only of the identifying mark of the maker that had been struck into the metal, an inverted heart with the initials in the curve of the lobes.

With our elder son, Jon, enrolled at the University of Wisconsin under provisions of the Ford Foundation for early advancement of qualified students, we drove to Virginia in the flowering time of azaleas and dogwood, through the tidewater country of my paternal grandparents. In part we went to see, and to show our children, where Richard Ghiselin had watched *Monitor* and *Merrimac* battle in Hampton Roads—where as a boy he had dived from high rigging of sailing ships. We saw marshes of azalea in flower above sunning turtles. We came to a steep shore of tan Atlantic sand where the open ocean fell in clean waves.

At home again in Utah, preparing for the session of the Writers' Conference in June, reflecting upon procedures in the universities, I was strengthened in conviction that despite all pressures to the contrary the conference must continue to foster the highest performance of staff and students and director. The universities must not be characterized by the societies they serve.

In November of that year the death of Dylan Thomas was announced. Thomas was the first of several prominent writers, among them Randall Jarrell, Marianne Moore, and Richard Wilbur, whom I drew to the University of Utah for appearances unrelated to the Writers' Conference, usually for readings and discussions of their own work. Supervision and entertainment of such visiting writers, my obligation, was by and large pleasurable.

On his first cross-country tour I had sat with Dylan Thomas for half an hour at the Salt Lake Airport, discussing the possibility of engaging him for such an occasion or even as one of the Writers' Conference staff. In April 1952, he came for a

reading and an afternoon session primarily for my students and members of the Department of English who might be interested. When he arrived, I drove him and his wife Caitlin from the airport to their quarters in the Temple Square Hotel, where the resources of the city would be available at their pleasure when Thomas was not fulfilling his obligations at the university. Later, I drove them eighteen miles to the west, for a satisfactory inspection of the Great Salt Lake.

Dire predictions of difficulties in prospect, based on reports from other university campuses, mainly fearful insults to academic self-esteem and to the chastity of wives, were not fulfilled in Utah. As Olive Ghiselin reported, in a witty and sympathetic account of his visit (published in the Utah *Alumnus* in 1967), "he behaved like an angel—much as he *looked* when Augustus John painted him, a curly-haired cherub with round credulous eyes and a pouting mouth." With his wife, he was our guest in the evening after his reading on the campus. And they were guests of others at dinner on his last evening in Utah. Early next morning, he telephoned to ask me to give his apologies to his hosts, because when he left—long after I had gone home—he was "not aware." They reported that he had seemed completely sober when he left them.

Marianne Moore was one of the most effectual, and delightful, of the visiting readers and speakers. We drove her to the grounds of the state capitol to see California quail that I knew would be plentiful there. In California, her well-meaning hosts, intent on everything of interest, had whisked her fast past the natural objects of her greatest concern. As she sat with us in the stopped car, she observed with pleasure that the backs of the quail nearby had exactly the same dark luster as the leaves of some bushes they wandered among. In California she had been the guest of academic people—as of course she was in Utah. The whole situation invited reflection upon responsibilities.

There was little novelty in it, however, in that autumn of 1957. In recent years I had been often at universities and elsewhere throughout the country in the company of specialists in various fields, participating in research or observing it, or lecturing and reading, remarking incidentally the characteristic ways of intellectuals in our time.

During that winter, I worked at the Institute of Personality Assessment and Research on the several weekends that gathered groups of eminent writers for psychological testing and inquiry, in exploration of such essentials as the sources and discipline of their

Photograph by Brewster Ghiselin of Opal and Vardis Fisher, Olive Ghiselin, and Michael Ghiselin with his catch of trout, above the lake on the Fisher estate, Hagerman, Idaho, 1950

power and the perspectives of their lives. They submitted to batteries of psychological tests. My duty was to elicit and record remarks on their ways of attaining the ends they prized. Their participation was nominally confidential. Some, like Kenneth Rexroth, exploited it in published report. Among those I interviewed was William Carlos Williams. We talked of such matters as "the variable foot" and sexuality in the life of the poet. At the summary meeting he startled and amused his examiners with his judgment, tinctured with reprimand, "You didn't ask the right questions." That protest, lighting a perennial problem in research as in life at large, was typical of Williams' simple phrasing of essentials, in poetry as in prose.

In Europe together for the first time, in 1962, Olive and I were guests of Leone Vivante and his wife at their villa not far from Siena, on a weekend that had gathered most of the members of that distinguished family of intellectuals and artists, among them the writer of short stories Arturo Vivante, now an American citizen. My acquaintance with Leone Vivante had begun in Salt Lake City, when as a visiting lecturer in the United States he had puzzled some philosophers, his hosts, to whom I attempted to explain some aspects of his thought that dealt with elements of literature and intuitive experience. In 1953 when his next book was published, *Elementi di*

una filosofia della potenzialità, he had sent me a copy and I had begun studying Italian under the most ideal conditions, avidity for light. As our correspondence continued, he had sent me *La poesia inglese,* which had not yet appeared in the United States, though as I learned later, it had been published in England in Vivante's own English translation, with a perceptive "Introduction" by T. S. Eliot. Ten years after Vivante's death, I wrote an interpretive "Foreword" for the book that he considered the ultimate expression of his insight, his *Essays on Art and Ontology,* translated by Arturo Vivante and published in 1980 by the University of Utah Press.

We had crossed the Atlantic on a vessel of the Italian Line, disembarked in Naples, and explored streets and museums and the waterfront before going to Capri, where we were to await delivery of a Mercedes. After two weeks there among the known pleasures of the island, we crossed by night on a small vessel to Palermo, rented a car, and drove round the whole coast and inland, concentrating on the splendors of antiquity, among them the Doric temple of Segesta. It is that "tempio aperto al vento" ("temple open to the wind") referred to in my poem "Austro" ("Southwind") that in 1968 I wrote directly in Italian and published in the periodical *Letteratura.* It appears, with a literal translation, in my book *Country of the Minotaur.*

Bringing the new language into intimate use enhanced understanding of how all our means of designation both order and intensify perception and simultaneously delimit and confine. Older than human memory, that realization is inculcated gradually in course of concrete experience. Traveling through Italy and France was a delight of discovery, then as in later years. So it has been in countries of the Spanish language, though in sojourns in Mexico, beginning in 1960, I have tended to glide awry into Italian idiom. Yet writing—years later—a few poems in Spanish, experimental but approved by trustworthy native speakers, has strengthened impressions of advantage. Here is ground for my recent observation "A poet should be free of words."

On arrival in Palermo, I began reading an anthology of contemporary Italian poets, with their commentaries and biographical data. Avoiding lexicographical trots, enunciating as truly as I could, listening, talking with people, I learned fast. When after further travels, in the car delivered to us in Naples, we arrived in Rome, I was ready to attempt interviews with some of the poets whose work seemed to me vital.

Our travels had included the inevitable greatly illuminating visit to Pompeii, and a long exploration of the Sorrentine peninsula, that in after years drew us to closer encounters with inexhaustible riches, during a time when I was searching for the whole course of D. H. Lawrence's movements there, between Amalfi by the sea and Ravello on the heights, and in dark Atrani, between those extremes of light.

In Rome I began the interviews illuminating ways of life and work of eminent writers, my professional commitment abroad. At lunch with Signor and Signora Luca Pinna (Margherita Guidacci), the first poet I interviewed, conversation was mainly in English, except in discussion of passages of her poetry, of which she gave me the latest volume, *La sabbia e l'angelo.* I managed to phrase in English and Italian a characterization of the writer's creative process in which we all concurred: "Attainment of a form satisfying the organic need of the writer—body-and-soul—*un incremento d'essere, di vita essenziale, dato in una configurazione nuova*" (an increment of being, of life essential, given in a new configuration). That abstraction, as it was brought to proof in scrutiny of the poetry, gained meaning. When I repeated it in the context of a long discussion with Vittorio Sereni in Milan, he said, "I would sign that!"

I interviewed Attilio Bertolucci, and the day after, Alberto Moravia and Giuseppe Ungaretti. Bertolucci, our guest at a leisurely lunch, approved

my reading of his "Amore," a lyric elusive beyond reach of mere explication. We discussed it and others at length. Next day, during our half hour at noon with Moravia, polite but on the alert for imminent arrival of journalists with cameras, he answered questions briefly and volunteered some opinions—most notably that creative writing is like love, and the two go poorly together.

Giuseppe Ungaretti had agreed to be our guest at lunch, on condition that we meet at his preferred restaurant, Il Buco, in the heart of the city. Arriving early, we were shown to "his" table: we were expected and, as the waiter explained, were to be his guests. White-haired, blue-eyed, and in chuckling good humor, he greeted us like preferred friends. Since he was reluctant to speak English, though fluent in reading it, I improved my inferior Italian. During a dinner of native delicacies such as scampi, and fine wines, we talked of his poetry and its production. With helpful comment, he heard my reading of one of his poems. In a low voice he read from my anthology his poem "Chiaroscuro" and inscribed his

Brewster and Olive Ghiselin,
Salt Lake City, 1980

name and the date and place of our meeting in the
margin—and an expression of thanks. After an
espresso and a sweet wine, we drove to the station
where he would board a train. There, thanking us
repeatedly, as we did him, he kissed Olive's hand, and
we said goodbye.

Many of those we encountered were friends of
my friends: of the Vivante family, Camillo Sbarbaro
and Eugenio Montale and his wife; or of Allen Tate,
among them Alfredo Rizzardi, translator of Tate's
poetry years later, and Mario Praz, Alessandro Bon-
santi, Mario Luzi. With Rizzardi we visited his friend
Ausonio Colorni, for whose exhibits of fiery paintings
of flowers many eminent Italian men of letters had
supplied critical introductions. So did I also, at his
request, soon after I had written him in appreciation,
when we reached Lago di Garda, the beloved lake of
D. H. Lawrence's first sojourn in Italy. The first
poem I wrote in Italian I read aloud—in a Florentine
restaurant—to Leone Traverso, translator of Rilke
and professor at the University in Urbino, who
moved at the center of intellectual life in Tuscany. He
questioned me severely, and after my responses,
relaxed in genial approval. Unaltered, entitled "Om-
aggio," it was published in *Letteratura* in 1965. In
Milan, late in March, conversations with Vittorio
Sereni and Salvatore Quasimodo went smoothly in
Italian. Some of these people remained our friends,
visited when we returned to Europe. Crossing thresh-
olds, in transgression of commonplace limits, widened
perspectives beyond those of cities and countryside
we enjoyed in travel.

It was different in Mexico, where over years
beginning in 1960, always driving, we saw the varied
land from Nogales in Arizona and across the border
toward the tropics, saw the people and the long coast
to Manzanillo and beyond, and inland over the winter
mountains, where in the heights the first peach trees
were in bloom, to Mexico City. Except for that
extended unlingering journey inland, we kept as
much as possible to wilder lands and the coast. Only
once we returned home over the jigzag highway up
rocky steeps to Durango and across the plains to El
Paso. Many times we were very fortunately lodged in
an apartment on a headland north of Guaymas,
overlooking the distances of the Gulf—Sea of Cortés.
There, incited and sustained more than anywhere
else abroad, I wrote many of the poems that for me
serve needs hardly to be satisfied otherwise. "Song at
San Carlos Bay" celebrates illuminations of day and
night that came from the shifting sea and the stone
heights, the cactus and ironwood and ocotillo and

tulipán, from the stars of summer in early spring over
the sea before dawn, and from the life there.

From dawn until blue twilight, sea birds were
over the water, near and far, pelicans falling in spouts
of foam, gannets—brown or white—circling high air
and dropping like diving rocks. Fish spattered
sunflash. Once at dawn I saw a charge of dolphins like
riderless horses rounding our headland in a hissing
froth of pursuit. I wrote of such things in the context
of the present instant and of the past, that I found
scattered on a lower headland, artifacts of gray stone
and black obsidian among chips in the dust.

During months of a sabbatical in Europe, autumn 1964 to late spring, the burden of directing the
Writers' Conference had been great, even with
efficient help in Utah. And it appeared no longer
necessary. It had changed the outlook of writers and
of the university administration. After the session of
1966 I resigned as director.

Freedom from academic obligations, with funds
for months in Europe, came with an appointment
as Distinguished Research Professor during the winter of 1968. We returned to our former room in
Amalfi looking on public square and cathedral.
There Olive observed the swarming life that enriched
her fiction and poetry published in succeeding years.
I explored steep Atrani, that Lawrence passed
through in walking between Ravello and Amalfi.
Guidebooks celebrate the great bronze door of the
cathedral of San Salvatore, concealed under a locked
wooden slab like the side of a barn. Daily access
provided by a small door at the east side is close to the
stair that goes up the Valle del Dragone to Ravello.
Lawrence was an explorer of churches. Just within, I
found in dusk on the south wall a medieval marble
relief of two peacocks so closely resembling D. H.
Lawrence's emblematic phoenix that if he stepped
inside they must have stirred him with recognitions.
Eaglelike in beak and vigor, each surrounded in tail
feathers like a sunburst, they mirror each other on
either side of a small bird nested atop a palm tree.
One of them grips as with talons a human head
between sirens, the other a rabbit snared by beaks of
ravens. In splendor of spread brilliance and crested
heads uplifted, they seem to be subduing the lusts of
the intellect and the flesh, not in rejection but in
triumph transcending division, restorative of body
and spirit to unity.

In Athens I saw similar symbolic sculptures of
rabbits in the talons of birds of prey, all of them
eagles. Remnants of the rich civilization of ancient
Crete, observed in museums and crumbling ruins of

Marble sculpture of peacocks in the Cathedral of San Salvatore di Biréto, Atrani, Italy

the island, that we drove across in the time of flowering anemones, provided further insight, indispensable for studies of vital transcendence in central poems of *Country of the Minotaur*, published in 1970.

One poem, written in Amalfi and published in *Letteratura*, "Presente"—"Present"—celebrates, among many things, deliverance from the stress of attention to past and future required of us almost constantly for sheer survival. It associates in one perspective the voluble swallows, cousins of our barn swallows, dipping and rising and rocking in twittering flight over slopes of flowering orchards, the peach trees below them no less alive, though silent and motionless "in the rose of the instant," "*nella rosa dell'istante.*" Such concentration in deliverance from the rack of time is a mode of transcendence: sought by mystics, sensed by artists at work and by others who accord with works in which it is realized, and felt perhaps also—as Wordsworth believed—at moments by children.

That timeless vision was a recurrent theme in years before my retirement in 1971 and after, when I was often lecturing or involved in conferences on the arts, considering among various matters the psycholo-

gy of visual experience, in the invention of form and in its apprehension. In 1965 I published in *Aperture* a study of Edward Weston's work as consummate visual artist in photography and, in contrast, as talented literary aspirant. When *Aperture* sponsored the symposium "Photography: 1982," I was one of sixteen participants: "artists, writers, editors and other members of the creative community whose views and experience would stimulate, renew, and broaden the dialogue within and beyond the photography community." Lodged in a guest house at Esalen on cliffs above the Pacific, dining at the main building, and freed for formal and informal explorations, we enjoyed utmost opportunity, in privacy, amid the solicitous provisions of an intelligent management. The redwoods, the exemplary ocean, and the ashen middens of the slopes were admonitory. Undivided attention to the theme of concern, diversely presented, produced material for concentration in the winter issue of *Aperture*, 1983. The volume comprises photographic evidence, statements by each participant, and transcripts of discussion. I provided the "Foreword" and an examination of the psychodynamics of visual experience, illustrated by Paul Strand's photograph

"Dunes, Abiquiu, 1931," of which we had the original in view. In statements and exchanges, we learned from one another, and no doubt also from our own diversely stimulated talk. The symposium was a paradigm of fruitful procedure.

In an interval between discussions at Esalen, I picked up from a heap of rocks exhumed in a ditching project a rough-hewn stone ax tapered to an edge that may have been idle a hundred years—or more than four thousand. Hand to hand with remote shapers of artifacts, as I had been in childhood, when even my dreams, like a miser's, were glorious with rich finds, I recalled Thoreau's response to a stranger's inquiry about where one could find Indian arrowheads. His answer, recorded by Emerson, was "Everywhere," as he leaned and picked one up at their feet.

During years of nominal retirement, never quite finished with academic involvement, advising former students and others, once on the committee of a candidate awarded the Ph.D. in psychology, writing, publishing, dealing with responsibilities in season, I have continued to look close and far, less to a turbulent wake than over the climbing prow. My poem "For My Children and Their Children" begins with rascal ancestors who sailed up the river Lys nine hundred years ago and burned and became Christians. It concludes in celebration of ceaseless passage, looking

To the white mist and deep of the ocean past
And the mist before us that ravels and clears
        and moves
Away and away
As we move.

That coda may seem barren, apart from the body of the poem, that records of many whom it cites diverse and fruitful action in the objective world and in luminous subjectivity.

For My Children and Their Children

Vikings blown from the mist and the smoky
        spume of the sea
Nine centuries past,
The oak of their black boats hard with ocean
        salt,
Rounding the river reaches inland
To burn and to build:
On the Lys, Busbecq—of Flanders and France.

Six hundred years:
Knights and burghers, seigneurs, and one a
        saint,

One a musician,
Master of countersong, shaper
Of madrigal, mass, motet,
Of the North and the court of Ferrara,
One an ambassador,
Man of tongues,
Bringer out of the East of tidings and tokens,
Peace and its bloom,
Green of antiquity lifted up from the dust,
A flowering tree,
Coin and codex and flower,
Tulip to astonish and craze the west
And lilac to scent the world.

Six hundred years—and then
The long flight north to the freedom of God,
And west:
The worker in silver and gold that crossed from
        England,
Artist and founder, father of artificers,
Men of the land and shores—
Philadelphia, Annapolis, Norfolk;
The Captain fighting long to unking;
The diver from the high rigging of ships in
        Hampton Roads,
Deaf in his old age from the smash and press of
        the waters,
He whose horse pistol, ironblue, tooled and
        balanced for use,
Lay after use in war, honor and loss,
In my childhood, beautifully useless
Pointing beyond his death, beyond us all,

To the white mist and deep of the ocean past
And the mist before us that ravels and clears
        and moves
Away and away
As we move.

(From *Windrose: Poems 1929–1979.*
Copyright © 1980 by Brewster Ghiselin.
Reprinted by permission of the
University of Utah Press.)

BIBLIOGRAPHY

Poetry:

Against the Circle. New York: Dutton, 1946.

The Nets. New York: Dutton, 1955.

Country of the Minotaur (with two phonodiscs). Salt Lake City: University of Utah Press, 1970.

Light. Omaha: Abattoir Editions, University of Nebraska at Omaha, 1978.

Windrose: Poems 1929–1979. Salt Lake City: University of Utah Press, 1980.

Editor of:

The Creative Process: A Symposium. Berkeley and Los Angeles: University of California Press, 1952; London: Cambridge University Press, 1952; New York: Mentor/New American Library, 1955; paperback edition with "Foreword 1985." Berkeley, Los Angeles, and London: University of California Press, 1985.

Arthur Gregor

1923-

BASIC MOTIVATIONS

Dislocation

1

The experience of uprootedness, of cultural loss, loss of the familiar—how many innumerable times had occurred to others what was occurring to me then, in New York harbor, on that grey day in September 1939, two weeks after war had broken out in Europe?

. . . Europe! How I began to feel, to live the sound of that word as though saying it for the first time, how different its meaning for me when weeks later I trudged through fallen leaves down streets totally unlike any I had ever known, and the word of the continent lost to me rose from within like the name of someone taken for granted, an essential closeness, part of myself, unobserved until separated, removed and disappearing like a seafront's lights receding in a fog.

Arthur Gregor on his first return visit to Vienna, 1949

So opens my autobiographical book, *A Longing in the Land* (Schocken Books, 1983), subtitled *Memoir of a Quest.* This might well have read, memoir of a loss and quest, though, in a sense, the addition of "loss" is redundant since there can hardly be a quest that does not proceed from loss—the absence of something that had made for the deepest contentment and that needs to be regained or the void is ever more unendurable, an ever-deepening impediment to psychic health and growth. This need not be of a specific person or place—though in my case it was—but a general sense of loss, a loss more vague and not easily defined. For individuals of heightened artistic and spiritual temperament, that sense of loss and the dichotomy between what is needed and desired inwardly and exists, is available externally, need not originate in a physical displacement, a loss of home, a geographical and cultural uprootedness, as had been the case with me in early adolescence. For them, if that urge cannot be otherwise assuaged, that quest is also unavoidable—their journey toward the discovery and toward the possession of spiritual selfhood regardless of the cultural character of his or her world. And when I refer to this book as an autobiographical work, I mean to imply that it is not an autobiography as such, and that, though entirely based upon personal experiences, it is not just one man's story, or it can be said to be one man's story of every man's quest—for every man (or "everyman" in the sense of *Jedermann*) seeks harmony, peace: everyman is capable of deepest and far-reaching belonging; everyman knows what is

Arthur (right) with his parents, Benjamin and Regine Goldenberg, and older brother, Fred, in the Czech spa Lázně Luhačovice, 1929

meant by feeling "at-home." In this sense, autobiography can become allegory.

Before writing this memoir (I am referring to *A Longing in the Land*) I had frequently been asked in interviews, some of which were published, about influences and events that had had a marked effect upon me, experiences that had caused the direction of my work and life, etc. I always held—and continue to hold—that while the artist's life is inseparable from his work, much of it, of the life, can be discounted, those details which are of strictly personal character and of little value beyond their occurrences, and that those which were significant have been embedded— though transformed, molded to its requirements—in the work itself. In my view, the artist's life is his material but only those aspects of it are worth using which are more generally applicable and relevant to the human condition as such. I continue to maintain that what can mingle with musings and what memory finds worth retaining has been woven into the poems, and it is the poems themselves that remain as the best source and evidence of my true engagement. Still, I

know from my own pleasure in reading that curiosity about a work's history and about the author's life increases the more the work itself has seized me and made me its adherent. But the pleasure with which one has become the work's captive surely exceeds the interest with which one learns later of its genesis. Nevertheless, it is intriguing to discover—or at least to be made aware of—the secrets of the creative process by being able to see the author's life as the soil of the work.

For that one needs to go back to the beginning. It is often said, and I think that there can be little doubt about it, that childhood has lasting effects upon the artist's development, if it doesn't determine it altogether. Rilke's poems on childhood, on the range and depth of perceptions, on its sensitivity, hopes, and fears, give us a penetrating look back on the origins of a most mature—hence not ever divorced from the continued reality of the inward child—artistic personality that had, by the time those poems were written, reached the full scope of his genius. Similarly, in the most mature phase of her life—toward its end— Elizabeth Bishop tells of events in the little girl's world that were the beginnings of a bewilderment, amazement, of terrors that had led to the travels, to the painful, unanswerable questions that had formed the substance of her great art, her strikingly vivid poems. And with Stevens, so insistent on the reality of joy, of the sublime, so courageous in his acceptance and penetration of mortality, we find that when he was yet a boy in his native Pennsylvania, he was lured, entranced by nature's majesty and more delighted by than afraid of its mystery. Eliot too refers back to moments of his childhood, to images of the Massachusetts coastline, to silences in a garden, to bird sounds and other instants of momentary clarity that transcended the limits of time and became, years later, or rather decades later, exemplars of timelessness in, no doubt, the most mature of his works. The reverence he had struggled all his artistic life to become grounded in, or to be returned to, he had known deeply in his earliest years, and had never forgotten. It would appear then that the unique character, namely, the poet's unmistakable tone, announces itself early on. Somehow, mysteriously, somehow the child knows it, it has been sounded deep, deep within; and the poet's life is a struggle never to forget it, to create the work embedding it, to create the poems whereby the tone is realized, marbleized.

If in my first book, *Octavian Shooting Targets* (1954), there was in the poems a tone of nostalgia that was tinged with irony, that was only a natural expression of my life at that time. We had come to

New York from Vienna at the outbreak of the war. I was fifteen when we fled from the Nazis. My most treasured and most useful possession at the time, deprived as we had been by the German Reich's racist policies of all material ones, was a good command of the English language; by twenty-two, seven years after arriving here, my poems began to appear in the literary journals.

We are nostalgic for what we have lost and loved and are ironic about what we have in its place. Not only my home but a whole culture lay in ruins. Combined with it, with this dismay on a grand scale, was, in my case, the arrogance of youth, of spiritedness that felt itself superior to, and inviolate from, human folly and its disasters. History seemed a chronicle of the extremes of vanity, of corruption and perversity, and some of its episodes, combined with the more recent atrocities, became the subject for the arrogant disillusionment natural in youth—its brief period of quick passions, volatile attachments, untested ideals.

I felt instructed in the shaping of these early poems which made up my first volume by the great masters of modernism still then in evidence, Eliot, Stevens, Moore, Williams, their poems appearing still in what were then referred to as "The Little Magazines" (*Accent, Partisan Review, Poetry, Quarterly Review of Literature*, etc., etc.), and I awaited with eagerness the publication of their latest volumes. Their fresh, to me new approach to language and form showed me the way to bring into contemporary awareness fragments of history that served, and were representative of, my own experience, desires, and mood. Pound was the great teacher in that regard and a belated—it was by then the mid 1940s—discovery for me. But the poet of that group who meant the most to me then, and to whom I turned repeatedly for sustenance, was Wallace Stevens. Entering his poems I felt at once uplifted, at once removed from the cynicism and turmoil of the world around me and raised into, restored to where I wished to be, where I longed, with all of what I had already recognized as my inner, poetic reality, to be. But how? How get there? How find the external manifestations of an inwardness I craved to experience, to release and, consequently, be centered in? Quickly Stevens lifted me to the sublime, to an underlying, undisturbed sense of joy I seem always to have had and in those days was keenly aware of, an innate optimism despite the lessons of history and the horrors war's end revealed. There was, beneath the turmoil of the time, a recognition of a permanence unaffected by it and worthy of continued praise. But

it was shrouded in vagueness, a notion easily obscured that I wished, nonetheless, to cling to, tossed about, as I felt myself to be, by the effects of uprootedness and the horrendous news from overseas. I clung to at least the memory of a sublimity I seemed to have had in abundance in childhood and felt myself returned to by means of art—of poetry and music. To be grounded in it, returned to it in adulthood by means of experience and hence conviction: to regain the loss of not a place, which of course could never be, but of that inward glimmer, that joy, that sense of the worthiness of life—it was that which became my ardent desire and struggle, that which is the quest chronicled in the memoir written decades later.

2

It has frequently been said of my work, by reviewers and critics, that though "despite a middle-European background, his American voice is unac-

"A 1938 identification photo. By a Nazi decree Jews had to carry identification with a photograph taken at an angle to show the subject with one ear exposed."

cented" (*Poetry,* October 1968) and "as a poet of our post–World War II generation, he stands safely established within the matrix of contemporary poetry" (*Choice,* September 1975), I have followed an independent course and "have clearly stood against the mainstream with his insistence upon the continuing human validity of symbolist modes of perception." And Hayden Carruth continues, in his critical essay in *Contemporary Poets* (St. Martin's Press, 1980), that "it has not been an argued insistence. Though Gregor has been a journalist and editor . . . he has rarely resorted to theoretical statements about his own work. But in his poetry his philosophical affinities are clear: they are with the great symbolists of the European tradition." Well, I suppose that, though I continue to hold firmly to the belief that only the work, the work alone, matters and must speak for itself, I have since resorted to, if not writing strictly theoretical statements, giving certain background facts, certain situations critical to the development and character of the poems. I did this to some extent in the memoir and am doing so now here in this much briefer sketch.

If, indeed, my work has been, and continues to be, away from what is referred to as the mainstream—and if by that is meant, as I take it to mean, current trends and fashions, attitudes rooted in

"This photo was used with my first publication in Poetry, *the November 1947 issue. I was awarded the magazine's First Appearance Prize the following year."*

strictly native realities—then, certainly, this assessment is correct. The experience out of which my direction has grown—one further back even than that of my childhood, but one of a collective, ancestral nature—originated neither on this, the American soil, nor in an ingrained, deeply personal memory of the American experience in a historic sense. To be part, therefore, of that American mainstream would contradict the impulse many a poet has ascribed to poetic vision and voice, namely, the articulation of a collective spiritual condition, if not ambition, as Yeats put it. If such is restricted to national, to geographic boundaries, then I must needs be out of, away from such a mainstream. But if we take the ancestral memory to apply to a cultural ambition and heritage, if not entirely universal, at least comprising half of our planet, namely, the occidental, our western cultural tradition, then I find myself firmly placed in it, firmly part of an ongoing heritage, and in its mainstream: art and philosophy as a means for transcending the limits of separateness and stirring us into an apprehension of unity in and beyond the human realm. The expression of that may, of course, have a collective, a national character; in my case, it can only have a personal one, and by that I do not mean a private, hermetic quality but those personal aspects that are common to us all: those that have to do with desires, with dreams, with spiritual ambitions, with momentary fulfillments and, alas, failures; with mortality and the mysterious manifestations of a wholly *other* presence we respond to, are more than gladdened by, but cannot define.

I must confess that in literature, and more specifically in poetry, I am leery of distinctions that would place poets in categories. Of course, there are apparent differences: a poem by Marianne Moore can in no way be likened stylistically to a sonnet by Edna St. Vincent Millay. But when it comes to romantic versus classic, free verse versus conventional, symbolist versus imagist, symbolist versus objectivist, etc., etc., then I am cautious and often not convinced by the distinctions. (Free verse is certainly not free of the considerations behind form, and conventional verse not of the flexibility freedom provides, etc.) Whatever school, whatever stylistic tradition a poet may be said by critics and scholars to belong in, there is only one school—if by school is meant approach to language and to the practice of the art—that can apply to all who have written well enough to have become part of the lasting canon in poetry, and that is, it seems to me, that poetry is the art of summary. The means for evoking the most by saying the least, and only a precise use of language can accomplish that. (All of this is, of course, obvious and need hardly be stated but necessary here so that I may make my point.) The word must be so used, so placed, that it reverberates in all its inherent suggestiveness, all its implied meanings must be activated: that and that alone is excellent usage, that and that alone, poetic language—the summary by which so much more is suggested than is said. Certainly this was the aim of the imagists, to let the image speak for itself, to find the word whereby it will retain and convey all its emotional, all its suggestive content. By being shown as being all that it is, the thing represented becomes more than it is, transcends itself ("O reine Übersteigung," to quote Rilke's opening of his *Sonnets to Orpheus*). By placing a tree in the total context in which it is seen, it becomes all that a tree suggests, all that it symbolizes. This has to do with visual accuracy and verbal adroitness. It also has to do with memory. For in memory a thing's connotative meaning often dominates, has prominence over its denotative, over the thing's specific and most obvious attribute. If then the poet perceives the object in its totality and is fortunate enough to possess the faculty for recreating, or creating anew, its impression so that all that the object stands for is caught and conveyed, where then is symbolism, imagism, objectivism, etc.? Surely there is a difference between reporting and depicting. He who depicts can be labelled as belonging in any one of these schools, it hardly matters, and he who merely reports doesn't merit a place in any one of them, for poetry is summing up, poetry is metaphor, and not merely calling a thing by its name. All of our great poets have demonstrated just that, Dickinson and Frost and Eliot and others, and not to regard their art as our models is to demean its greatness.

But regardless of where one stands—or rather where critics place one, for it is rare that a writer of note proclaims himself adherent to a specific trend or school—memory is a critical faculty for all. Critical in both the originating and receiving of the work. The poem recreates an impression and by selection and emphasis incorporates the writer's response to it. If that impression is highly charged, has behind it history, and has for long been absorbed by others into memory; if the impression of an object—a fresco, silent and thoughtful; a street dense with trees and dim light between the leaves; a landscape and a river's glow on the horizon—if that impression, for long looked at by others, is therefore itself an expression, the articulation of some hidden aspect vibrant though as such undeclared; if, in short, the visual experience vibrates with associations, suggestions of something

hidden, does the object then not become *symbolic* of them? And is it not precisely this unstated quality that appeals to memory, where it is received, where the object incorporating it is harbored, and from where it will arise as language? Would it then be wrong to say that what some call the symbolist tradition is merely one way of being truthful to the impression, to actuality, to its impact upon memory? The soil where I must assume my sensibility originated was rich in these unstated, these implied associations; and what has become my soil continues to be so, and ever more so. For, of necessity, it has shifted inward. Interiority, the human inner realm, has been the soil of my work, rather became it in due course as will be pointed out later on here—inwardness, the human response to a spiritually impoverished environment, the thirst for the reflections in art, landscapes, faces that nonetheless affirm what even a world addicted to materialistic values cannot vanquish; the spirit for which, tradi-

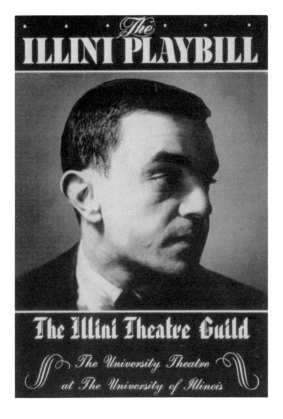

Playbill for Arthur Gregor's Fire!, *which won the Illini Theatre Guild's national competition and was produced at the University of Illinois at Urbana during its annual Festival of Contemporary Arts, 1952*

*The author in Venice, on his way back from India,
1955*

tionally, the poet has been the spokesman and, in any
period, legislator.

Let me now illustrate with some scenes from my
boyhood the effect that my early conditionings and
the soil where they occurred must have had on me
and how this must have provided a solid base for the
direction my work and my life took. It was a soil
whose suggestive aspects outweighed the actuality,
nostalgia draining it of vitality, but where nonetheless
the reality of a permanence, of a principle outlasting
the history that expressed it, glimmered around the
edges. The scenes revolve around an episode dealing
with my first experience of remorse and love for a
friend. I was not yet thirteen; it was the fall of 1936 in
Vienna.

Memory

1

What had come over me? Why had I turned on
him, taunting him, scoffing at him, telling him
to leave us alone, to "get lost"? And he did, stayed
behind, let us walk on ahead, then turned away and
took another path through the park. Why had I done
it? And why to him and not the others, Jacob and
Rudy, with whom I used to walk back home from

school? Of the three, it was Willy who had been closer
to me even then. We lived on the same street, a few
blocks away from each other, and I often used to wait
for him in front of his house, took the tram with him
going to school, spent time with him when I was free
from homework and tutors, went to the movies with
him on Sundays, for walks through the Prater on
Saturday afternoons. What had made me attack him?
To prove that I too could turn on someone who
unlike most of the boys in the class was not rowdy and
loud but gentle, considerate, polite? To prove to the
others that I was not like him because I knew by then
that in fact I was? That I too would rather daydream
along the Hauptallée so thick with trees the sunlight
was reflected on the gravel walks in flickering
patterns; that I too would rather sit pensively by the
canal, losing myself in the watery reflections of
bridges and barges, than run yelling across the soccer
field with the other boys or be one in a gang of them
pursuing and annoying some of the girls from our
class. Or had I wanted to test myself? To see that I
too could be mean to others? In young adolescence
we are likely, in a friendship, to challenge the
strength of the tie and test the other's feelings by
ridicule or a show of meanness, but, although Willy
and I had spent much time with each other, such a
deep and strong bond had as yet not been formed
between us; our friendship had at that time still been
casual and had as yet none of the intensity it acquired
a few months later, in early spring, when the sounds
and colors in the park would be other than they were
on that afternoon—the leaves were already falling
and the grounds were covered by them. What had
caused these two events, what conditions had sponsored them, the irrational outburst in the park and
the joy at the reconciliation, the closeness between us
that followed months later—a sorrow and an ardor, a
mutual responsiveness between two young friends
unclouded by memory, undiminished by years?

Was it the park, not only the large Augarten that
lay between the districts where we lived and where
the school was, but the many other parks as well, their
melancholy in autumn, the sadness of leaves falling,
of a city that lay sunk in its past as though lulled into it
and asleep in it? Was it a reaction against this
prevalent sadness, a need and desire for a contrary
reality that had made me strike out, had made me
turn on someone kind, gentle, someone who did not
deserve to be hurt and insulted? His injured feelings
which I had caused, the noncomprehension of my
unjustifiable action, the pity—for me and for himself—lay like a cry of outrage and hurt in the look he
shot at me as he turned and left. Though it did not

last, came back only, and most vehemently then, a few months later during gym when he came and stood by me, my immediate response was regret—a feeling more deeply embedded in me than I could have suspected then.

2

Not only its parks, the city itself had evoked a sorrow for what, by the looks of things at the moment, was lost, irretrievable, and missed. A musicality in the minor key, the key of sorrow, despite the popularity of songs and dances in three-quarter time. But these too—waltzes and polkas—had originated in a former age, when they were sung or danced not nostalgically in dance halls or outdoors at inns in the suburbs, but with fervor and enthusiasm at some imperially sanctioned public celebration. An unending greyness seemed to cover everything around me by the time this outburst had erupted in me and I had behaved in a reprehensible manner.

The trees were turning bare, and the leaves, collected into heaps, were burned in the parks, often in the stone basins of empty fountains. Walking along the deserted paths in the parks, through streets wrapped in slumber as the entire city seemed during those long autumn and winter months, I was impatient for the vitality that I sensed lay still ahead for me. I had not yet experienced any of the aspects of the amorous life of which there was also ample evidence around me, and which provided, in contrast to the sloth and greyness, a sense of anticipation.

There had been around me many hints of what I had to look forward to. Of an intimacy, not merely sexual—though the prospects for that had engaged us endlessly on our walks home from school or, at other times, on the prowl, three or four of us, through the meadows and bushes of the Prater, for couples lying on the ground or on benches in tight entanglements—but a fully shared togetherness, a oneness with someone else that would wipe aside the drabness of grey days. The promise of such heightened union seemed entirely realizable whenever I would see, either in or at the entrance to a park, young couples or friends, arm in arm, totally involved with one another. For an instant, the two together would merge, would turn into a brilliant vision, a sign of anticipation, the early stirrings of desire fulfilled at the sight of others, of two together, in a late afternoon's strong glare. Or, and this occurred perhaps a year or so later, it would strike like a promise when I was walking in one of the narrow cobblestoned streets in the venerable old Innere Stadt (inner

district)—near the vast grounds of the Hofburg with the tall monument of a seated empress, Maria Theresa, in the center, and with open spaces from where you could on clear days see the mountains beyond the city—there would appear, coming out of the shadows, a figure that would intrigue me. A youth, perhaps somewhat older than I, already working, wearing a long white apron and carrying coffee or tea on a tray, who just as he entered a shop on the other side, one foot already over the threshold, turned toward me as though he had known me and smiled in recognition, a familiarity that astounded me. Though this youth from the working class was, in fact, a stranger, someone with whom I could not possibly in the past have shared the intimacy the moment conveyed, such incidents spoke of something not only possible but already entirely familiar, as if foreknown and coming from nowhere but myself.

And they were not infrequent then, such moments that on the one hand thrust me away from where I was, out of time, into some promise of the future, but on the other cast me into a state of collectedness more immediate and more connected to me than the things actually around me and the very observations that occasioned it. This occurred again and again when I walked through a park, or along the river, or the canal, or anywhere that gave unto extended perspectives, unto distance and open spaces. It would, however, not come upon me when I was with the other boys from the class. I had to be alone. Solitude promoted these moments. And often, more often than not, the park, the Augarten, at one time the empress's private estate. The wide lawns and flower beds, the straight and long paths, the ornate baroque palace, had all been part of a plan to transform what had once been wild nature into carefully arranged stately grounds. How easy it was, how quickly I could soar here into the most treasured, most intimate aspects of mind and heart, closer than dreams. The very gravel underfoot, the round metal bars separating the lawns, the statues in their thoughtful poses, flowers in strict rows—these all partook of an inaudible music that listening to music would bring me back to, years later and even now.

The silences accumulated amidst the ivy climbing the long walls speak, and the children and old women always found in the park are well aware of this. They need not even listen to hear it, they come there to participate and add to it. They merge with the long, long moments that have lingered there, merge into this *other* time, this time that has shed the sense of time time has and is where they belong, where they are most simply, most easily at home. Nature transformed and time absolved by accumulation take them to where they need to be. A vision of order still contained within the arrangements of trees, flowers, and stones. The grandeur may be of a former age, of a world now gone, but the perspective is not empty.

While these were not my thoughts then, could hardly have been, such echoes from a background still in evidence were nonetheless the contents of my daydreams, whereby I stepped out of the present by means of the past; the trees and fallen leaves, the smell of leaves burning, the drowse of history in autumn reminding me not only of something lost, but of something I was beginning to desire.

3

Oddly, the parks connected me also with the period of the year I cherished the most, the summer months free from school, the months I spent in the country. Peasants and farmyards, haystacks, pitchforks, piles of manure, the squeals of pigs being fed, geese wobbling across the puddle-filled yard, a chicken flapping about trying desperately not to be caught—the precise opposite of nature's character in a formal city park. But like the views gained of the park's spaciousness when coming in from the entrance that was at a slight elevation, or of the sweep of the city when walking along the canal, or of its panorama from the surrounding hills; or even when, usually against my will, I stood in long marble halls looking up at portraits of emperors, conquerors, saints, I would have a swift awareness of a time and dimension other than the one I was accustomed to, just so expressions of nature would strike and transport me to something invisible, mysterious, and would stir the imagination whether I was in a city park, museum, or in a meadow, field, or forest in the country about two hours south of the city.

In Burgenland, the land of the castles, where unless I accompanied my mother to one of the spas, I would spend the summer months on the farm. It lay in a slight valley about a kilometer from the village and five or six from the neighboring ones where there were a good many boys around my age; the fact that I was from the city and they the sons of farmers or farmhands had not yet become a barrier between us. When they were free and did not have to help

their fathers either out in the fields or in the yards looking after the livestock, we would roam around together, went bathing in a nearby pond deep and wide enough to swim in, played ball, set traps for catching rabbits, or staged fights with groups from nearby villages. Those I joined really against my will; although they were only a game, I didn't enjoy these mock battles and didn't always understand what the boys were saying when in the excitement of a fight they broke into the most extreme of the local dialects. One day we, that is, the boys from the farm and the village close by, were to stage an attack on "the enemy," boys who were from some of the neighboring farms and villages. The attack was not to take place until the "commander" of another unit gave the signal to do so. I was assigned as courier between the outpost where that unit was stationed and our "headquarters," and it had been agreed that when the signal was given I was to gallop at full speed (this was a pretense, of course; galloping meant running at full speed) and carry the message. The outpost had been set up on a ridge overlooking the farm and the valley, and on being given the go-ahead sign, I was to run downhill to our camp about a kilometer away.

The "commander" was the son of the manager of the farm, a boy who, though two years older than I, had befriended me, and whom, as he lived on the farm, I saw more frequently than the others. It was he—his name was Hans—who had made me join the group in the first place. He was a good deal taller than I, but rather than bullying me, which taller and older boys were likely to do, he had always treated me kindly and had taken me to the treasures of the neighborhood: the convent where he had to bring milk every other day; the fountain in the center of a village said to have been inhabited by an animal that had poisoned the water and caused a pestilence ages ago; the brook lined with weeping willows—the most romantic spot in the area, where the older boys and girls had their trysts; the tombstones where at full moon in the dead of winter the dogs came to howl because of the ghosts that only they could see; and other spots noteworthy for beauty, terror, or for being the sites of folklore and legends. At harvest time, I would not see him, he was busy with the farmhands in the fields, but in spring when the cherries were turning ripe and he climbed the trees to pick them, he would always leave a basket of them on our porch. He was musical and played the harmonica very well, could manage not only the popular tunes but songs from operettas and even arias from operas. In contrast to my sandals and lederhosen he went around barefoot and in overalls. Despite the fact that he had never been there, or perhaps because of it, he had a great interest in the city and asked me about all sorts of details regarding it and our lives there. He even wanted me to tell him about the Opera and the theatres, and I gave him, as best as I could, descriptions of the splendor of the buildings and told him about the one or two operas and plays that I had attended the previous winter. On days when he was not needed on the farm he took part in the games or took me on long walks to show me the wonders and secrets of the neighborhood he knew so intimately. During the "war games" he managed always to assign me a duty under his "command," and so it was that I was with him that day when he had taken charge of the outpost and had given me the signal to run down into the camp and tell the "general" to charge. As I left him to carry out my mission, he began playing his harmonica. It was a game, after all; the beauty of the day—the clarity as if the entire landscape had been washed so that everything, trees, fields, roofs, church steeple, stood out with dreamlike sharpness—called for music, and as I was starting my descent, Papageno's tune from *The Magic Flute* which Hans was playing seemed the most appropriate melody, simple, innocent, joyous.

I had started on my downhill mission but hadn't gotten very far when some inner sensation caused me to stop. The harmony of the scenery that lay before me had captured me; it seemed as if the cows grazing below in the sun or drinking in the shade of a pond, as if the fields rising to a hill on one side and on the other falling off into a distance glowing like a sea—it felt to me as if these and the houses and trees interspersed among the fields and meadows were each part of the song, each singing of and for the same thing. It had rushed through me, this sensation, and instead of running I sat down in the grass, put my head in my hands, and joined the song, singing to myself. The buzz of insects very close to me and the shouts and cries of the boys waiting for me in the distance brought me back. The boys were now not charging at the "enemy" but at me. They came running toward me, and behind them, in quick pursuit, the boys from the village whom my group was to have surprised in a well-planned, but now failed, attack. I had ruined this plan, and in a minute they would be upon me to punish me. Suddenly, Hans, who hearing the screams had hurried down, stood beside me. I had slipped, he explained to the angry boys who were threatening me with raised fists, I had fallen, had hurt myself, I heard him say on my behalf. And in the commotion I was able to slip away unnoticed.

Gregor at his desk at Industrial Design *magazine, where he was technical editor from 1956 to 1961*

This had happened when I was twelve years old, and there were not many more summers spent at the farm after that. But that experience of the country—and there were others when sights, sudden arrangements of sky, land, and habitations, seemed to serve as though they had been conveyers of messages—has remained intact and at my disposal like an imperturbable reference.

4

In themselves externalities are inadequate indications of the condition they impart in us, of their human import. And by what other means but their effect upon us can we measure their value? An interior crammed with antique furnishings, heavy damasks, tall mirrors, paintings, artifacts from exotic civilizations does not in itself make for the beneficial repose a well-provided interior should be conducive to. Perhaps what we respond to is the intention, or lack of it, behind the arrangement. An impulse from and for centrality? A log cabin in the wilderness by a lakefront will in all likelihood instill its occupant not with the deep sense of belonging, of being part of something vast and greater than oneself, that had come over me frequently in the parks or in the countryside cultivated for centuries, but with loneli-

With Marianne Moore, New York, 1967: "From 1962 to 1970 I was a senior editor at the Macmillan Company, where among other responsibilities I looked after its poetry list, which included The Complete Poems of Marianne Moore.*"*

ness and fear, a full moon sailing through dense trees, a dog, or even a wolf, howling across the snowy distance. Only the sight of smoke rising from the cabin's chimney making its human statement would provide some comfort. Screeches do not console us, sounds of harmony do. Is it not we who are the expression of objects and arrangements? As spiritual beings, it is only an environment that contains and conveys that of which we are a part that can be adequate to our needs. Looking back upon the environments that have affected me, I can say this much with certainty: we yearn to be comforted and not assaulted by what surrounds us. The city atmosphere in which I grew into early adolescence, the nostalgia with which parents and teachers recounted the past, spoke of the better days, and listened to music, gave me, as already mentioned, not only a sharp sense of loss but also of longing, of yearning for the one return that could restore the loss. Just what this replenishing might consist of, I felt only in the vaguest terms.

School did not help me in this. School to me was another facet of the general greyness; it was drudgery, not joy. The professors too seemed to be stuck to their surroundings like flies to flypaper and when together appeared to us, the students, as part of the general ranks of grown-ups, remote, forbidding. No doubt it was because of this pervasive grimness that I so cherished those moments of solitude when something of an entirely different order, glimmers of a salutary reality, presented itself to me.

They happened sometimes in dreams. In one, when I was about twelve years old, I was walking with a friend who, in real life, was a boy younger than I whom I knew because he lived in our building. We were not friends but in that dream we were. We were strolling down the lawn that ran along the canal. Colors were prominent in the dream, of the sky, of the grass, of the flowers uncommonly large as though transposed from exotic lands. The air itself had the sky's royal blue color. Voices were coming from everywhere, although there were only the two of us walking in increasing enchantment by the water. We heard them all around us, singing a haunting song—on waking I remembered the tune as that of a Brazilian lullaby that had then been popular. In the dream, it had an inspiring choral harmony and I felt entirely enfolded by this musical reality—of voices that were coming from everywhere, from the lawns, the sky, the buildings on the opposite bank. Had I glimpsed, had I lived in the condition of happiness by now hidden in the real world, yet once possessed and now yearned for again?

Whether any of this—a clash of contradicting realities, of a world rendered almost incapable of living in the moment by long memories of lost glories and an adolescent's need and desire for the experiences that were part of growing up and lay ahead promising much precisely because of the richness of the past—whether any of this lay behind my irrational behavior in the park that autumn afternoon on my way home from school, or had in part affected it, I cannot say. Certainly it was the background within which it had occurred. A background evident to me in remnants dating back to Roman times, when the city was a camp called Vindobona, ruins pointed out to us with severity by parents and teachers on walks and tours intended to instruct us in our heritage. The silence in the Wertheimstein Park in Döbling, not far from the vineyards surrounding the *Wienerwald,* where decades before the city's noted poets, painters, and musicians had sauntered across lawns accompanying their delicate hostess, was not muted. It was heavy with memories, a denseness of the past, a fullness, not an emptiness. A stone head from Roman times had been found there, and centuries after the soldiers had camped there, the elegant inhabitants of the villa had mused on the endlessness, the irretrievability of time in sad, poetic reveries. Young Hofmannsthal had read his poems there, full of lament and longing for a nobility of spirit that belonged in the past. The once-private grounds were public by the time I sat by its ponds bordered by willows with low-hanging branches and lured the swans to come close by throwing them the stale bread I had brought for them.

I loved going there in the early spring or fall when we were back from the country. To get there I either took the tram, which often passed through narrow, cobblestoned streets, or walked. Walking, I went by Schubert's house on the way or often past the statue to him that stood in the center of a little park near the quai of the canal. Whether the lilacs, the lime and chestnut trees were in bloom or the leaves drifted along the sidewalks and gravel paths when greyness covered the city, the melancholy of time was always present. But the fact of a historic background for someone young, for me at least, though I also sensed this in others, held a strong promise for a future actualization of some of its hidden aspects.

And whether standing in front of the Ruprechts-kirche, dating back to the eleventh century; or running up the flight of steps to Sankt Maria am Gestade, where before it was erected a wooden chapel had stood, built by the fishermen when the nearby river was wide and nights were fraught with danger; or looking up at the second-floor windows of the seventeenth-century Camesima house where Mozart had composed *The Marriage of Figaro;* or above the Widow of Sarepta Fountain in the courtyard of a convent for Noble Ladies, at the fresco depicting wisdom as a goddess floating upward on vaporous rays of knowledge; or standing before the Pestsäule am Graben, a baroque white marble monument—of clouds, angels, and a kneeling emperor—erected in thanksgiving for the end of a plague: out of this time past, time congealed in supple, often luxurious forms, out of that, as though hidden behind these façades, leapt a strike of joy that easily enraptured me. Ongoingness, some hidden fact, perhaps even purpose. The new grass around stones. The shaft of light in a church's tall and dim interior. The enigma of a smile. Silence spoke: the plain towers from the Middle Ages, the later cupolas and tapering Gothic spires, the crests, equestrian statues, the crowned lions, winged putti, wrought-iron gates, a baroque summer palace behind them as though painted on a faded backdrop. Time was itself a setting, a square, housefronts on all four sides of it, the space so vast it dwarfed the buildings grouped around it. Parades commenced there, couples and friends passing across it. The setting continuing beyond the traversals, fitful, brief. The anticipation of life ahead. Promises, everywhere promises, whispers whose indistinct meanings eluded me; at any moment, walking in crowded streets, looking down a long *allée,* the assumption of the marvelous—the marvelous in all its splendor about to overwhelm and bring me into its reality of intimate being.

Promises, anticipation, but also, even by then, even in one so young, a responsiveness to disappearance, to betrayal, to someone's hurt.

5

I had started to go to the Opera when I was no more than ten. At first, by myself on Saturday afternoons, to the Volksoper; later, when we were friends again—and how that came about will follow, how despite that shameful incident we became the closest of friends a few months later—with Willy, and with his younger brother and sister, to the Staatsoper for matinees. I was too young for the defiance and arrogance of *Don Giovanni,* a performance of which we had attended one afternoon, although the majesty of the music, the contrasting emotions it conveyed, had impressed me greatly. But Madame Butterfly's dilemma, the reversal she suffers from innocence to betrayal, I seem to have grasped fully even then, at the age of ten.

Those winter afternoons afforded me glimpses into the life of adulthood which I enjoyed. I made my way alone to the Volksoper, walking there as we did not live too far away. Mingling with the Saturday crowds hurrying, people huddled in their coats, along the canal adrift with ice floes, or heading up through the streets to shops, cafés, or other destinations, being part of this flow on a day of the week charged with the anticipation at week's end, gave me the welcome feeling of participation beyond the concerns of school and home. And then the contrasts that followed, from the cold outside into the building's warm vestibule, from its domed enclosure up the broad staircase into the large auditorium where hung still the long, heavy, dark curtain. Soon it would eliminate the barrier that I had frequently felt when standing in front of a canvas or a face, a heraldic symbol in stone; the barrier between actuality and the imagination, ordinariness and artifice. With my class I had attended productions of the classics in noble surroundings suitable for Goethe, Schiller, Shakespeare; but such matinees had always been part of the planned process of learning, of the established order of education, and had all the strictness and formality of a classroom session about them. But by myself, and by my own choice, an afternoon at the Opera allowed me to enter and to explore my own realm of feelings and imagination without restrictions and, due to the music and singing, with an immediacy the verbal equivalents did not possess for me then. Perhaps the plays were more stately, but the lyrical power that swept over me in the dark in the gallery took me even beyond stated conflicts and ideals. I was beginning to learn something of the heart's reality, of its authority, for the response with which I met the human condition conveyed by the music was, in a way, beyond me. I did not envision it, force it, it simply happened. And I felt enlarged due to it, due to such response which brought me strangely and deeply close to myself. Yet oddly enough, it was not Butterfly's happiness that had moved me, it was her despair. I was, I suppose, too young to participate in

the rapture of the lovers that occurs during the first act, but when the separation sets in later on, when Butterfly sings her heartrending aria of waiting, and when she and her faithful servant, having strewn cherry blossoms all across the floor, sit down at the sliding doors and join the offstage chorus in humming a peaceful chant of arrival and praying for return as the dark vanishes and day breaks, I could not hold back my tears. Of course, I had wept before, but I am certain that, at the age of ten, this was the first time that art had stirred me to tears.

My involvement with Butterfly's tragedy and my response to it grew more intense as her condition changed from anxiety and waiting to despair, as she finds her love betrayed by insincerity and deceit and must confront her ruin as though staring down into a bottomless pit. The music of inescapable doom, followed after her suicide by her husband's repentant cry, calling out from afar, "Butterfly . . . Butterfly . . ." as she falls and dies, so affected me that I could not wait for the end and the applause. Sobbing, I ran from my seat down the stairs and out down the steps of the theatre into the cold daylight— ran sobbing as though I myself had suffered an injury and averting my face because anyone seeing me might have thought that I had been beaten, had been unjustly punished by parents or friends.

So penetrating had been this recognition—that there is no defense against hurt unjustly caused, no defense against betrayal, and that helplessness in the face of it can result in a sorrow so deep only the cessation of life itself can end it—so devastating had been these moments, which I somehow sensed had to do with an inescapable truth, that I couldn't hum any of the opera's music for days without breaking into tears all over again.

Was I the more vulnerable to such anguish because of my extreme youth? Because such revelations also foretold something of what lay ahead and would have to be suffered, and because they were in direct contrast with sudden joys that I had also known? I couldn't then, of course, have thought of such contrasts in such terms, but as I stormed out of the theatre into the wintry city I knew instinctively that they existed—like light and darkness, anticipation and dismay, joy and despair, innocence and betrayal.

6

One day, a few months after my disgraceful behavior toward Willy, I was sitting atop the gym horse during gym. We had seen each other, of course, in class or in the hallways, but not a word had passed between us. I had, by that time, put that incident in the park out of my mind, but on that day, looking down on the class divided in teams each doing a different exercise and seeing Willy walking toward where I sat, it flared up vividly, and painfully. Waiting to join my team, Willy had awaited his turn standing leaned against the horse. I had seen him walking across the gymnasium toward it and was surprised when he took his place next to me below where I sat. Surely, he hadn't noticed me there, I thought. We hadn't been talking; why would he come and stand near me? He did not look up, leaned against the horse, his head touching the leather seat, one foot resting on the knee of his other leg.

But what had I, in fact, seen in him, seeing him standing there near me, below me, in that pose? Though he was no more frail, not less sturdy than most of the other boys, there was something about him, something suggesting frailty, that seemed to have touched me—the frailty of leaves adrift in autumn air, of a face, of an actress, a singer stumbling across a stage, of summer days that turn to mist. Perhaps in a quick moment I had seen embodied in this human reality next to me the sorrows and joys that my young years had made me experience and had led me to expect. And regret; for this was someone whom I had hurt, whom I had treated unfairly, unjustly. A mixture of joy and deep sadness took hold of me. For the first time I felt my feelings

expressed in the form of someone else. For the first time I seemed to have recognized my own reality in another person. The sameness between us at that instant was the sheerest joy. But I could not express it, could not touch him on the shoulder, could not smile down or talk to him if he looked up. Which he didn't. There was not a gesture from him indicating that he had been aware of me. He was called to join his team, and he left.

For me this had been the beginning of weeks of torment. Not for a moment did the emotion that had seized me that morning leave me. I had never as yet known such intense caring for another individual, such concern for the reality of someone else. I relived again and again, and always with shame and regret, that afternoon of a few months before when I had turned on him and had driven him away. Now a totally new emotion had taken hold of me, and I had to find a way by which I could make up for what I had caused. From a casual school friend he had changed for me into a youth of the noblest attributes, into someone with whom I could share those inspired moments that had meant so much to me, during which I visualized, however vaguely, some secret greatness, the advent of something marvelous, sitting by a pond overhung with willows, walking down sun-drenched lawns amongst statues and their shadows, their dark silences. From that day on, when he had come and stood near me in the gym, I had been haunted by a new joy, but by regret as well.

At home, whenever I was alone, doing homework or between tutors, before going to bed or even at the breakfast table, I would hum the sad tune I used to hear my father sing to himself after lunch, reclined on a sofa, with his eyes closed and lost in nostalgic revery. This sadness fit my mood. How often in my wanderings had I noticed young couples wrapped around each other strolling under trees and complementing the lyrical setting. But never before had I viewed such lovers or friends with a heaviness of heart. I had hurt the one person who was now constantly on my mind. I had to have his forgiveness. I became obsessed with finding a way to heal the breach I had caused.

I thought of Rudy, a boy from the class who was on friendly terms with both of us and who had been with us on that fateful autumn afternoon. I confided in him, and he brought us together again.

What seems to me now, in long retrospect, perhaps the most memorable aspect of this entire event is the naturalness with which it had occurred and had unfolded. There was neither hesitancy to

"Since 1983 I have been spending part of the year at a house I acquired in Châtillon-sur-Loire in France's Loire Valley. Here I am with my brother, Fred (right), in the garden," 1986

*Arthur Gregor with his friend Hanna Axmann-Rezzori, a painter and novelist, at a restaurant
near his home in France, 1987*

admit to myself that I was experiencing a feeling that
although unknown until then had the quality of
something deeply familiar, nor to talk about it freely
to a classmate. That one was understood seemed
inherent in all one was exposed to. There was no fear
of being misunderstood or ridiculed because of one's
emotions. Alas, we know that inhuman acts can be
perpetrated in humane surroundings and kind deeds
rendered in violent ones, but, despite ideological and
political factionalisms and harsh prejudices—all this
occurred in 1937 only months before the annexation
to Germany—my world, my immediate world, as
such was not an enemy to me. (Not yet!) It was not
foremost an arena of competitiveness in which one
was expected to prove oneself; the very environment
and atmosphere in which I was born and grew into
early adolescence seemed to have prepared me for a
life of feelings. Even amongst the rougher boys in my
class, although they were always making a great show
for the attention of the girls, there were affectionate
and open friendships. And though when, following
Rudy's talk with him, Willy and I became inseparable
there were occasional derisive comments, these were

meant to mock us slightly, as boys are wont to do, but
not to mark us. Never, though sex was on everyone's
mind and much of the talk amongst the boys revolved
around it, was there the slightest suggestion of
inappropriateness in such close and faithful friendships. We knew of them, of where and between whom
they existed, the teachers knew of them, parents
knew of them. I made no secret whatever of my
happiness, and when Willy telephoned and Julie, our
maid, answered, she would call me saying: "Your god
is on the telephone."

The main element that underlay and sustained
this attraction was discovery. A mirror wherein the
outlines of one's being gained focus; a sharing of new
responses; a commitment to the reality of someone
else; the joy of identity; the state of affection. Nothing
more was wanted than each other's attentiveness to
one's own existence. And with that came apparently
unforgettable times of sharing, of plain happiness.
Perhaps such have never been matched. For although
it could be said that a history of the cultivation of
human sensibilities (which is, finally, culture in its
most pertinent meaning) sustained them, they were,

in themselves, extremely simple and not fraught with the complications that beset relationships in adult life. Happily we waited for each other in front of our homes, school bags strapped to our shoulders; walked through parks; took excursions to the Wienerwald or for skiing to the nearby mountains; looked down upon the city's panorama in the evening light; sat close to one another on Sunday afternoons in the dark of a movie theatre, fully absorbed in the drama unfolding on the screen before us but aware at all times that we were together, walking home afterwards often troubled by what we had experienced, by what we sensed lay ahead for us and would not be avoided.

Toward Inner Centeredness

1

I chose this episode and some scenes leading up to it because they seem to me to demonstrate a condition of belonging which I had absolutely taken for granted as long as I was part of it, but missed sorely and unexpectedly when torn from it. Until the rupture and subsequent relocation had taken place, I could conceive neither of being without it nor of the wrenching awareness of its absence. It was only once the event so much desired had actually occurred— namely, we were freed from the oppression the Nazi takeover of Austria had imposed on all Jews and were safe beyond its borders—and, following a harrowing flight recounted in the memoir, we had arrived in the United States, that my encounter with contradictory feelings, elation at America's great and uplifting freedom and torment at my uprootedness, first began. The web of connectedness such as I had known and been quite unconsciously part of, the nature of which I hoped to suggest in these boyhood memories, made in retrospect for a steady, quiet joy which only this natural and deep sense of at-homeness can yield. It promotes as well an ease of sharing and an understanding, when it happens between friends, that is natural and charged with an innocence that can perhaps not be equalled, unless we are fortunate to find again those conditionings of a common ground that adulthood may place us in. Identity, commonness, as I have discovered step by step, as it were, from the fervors of youth to the more tempered acknowledgments in later life, is simply good for the soul; there can be no full inner life without it. Perhaps it can be said that an environment, a culture has achieved its potential; or the degree to which a culture has achieved itself is dependent upon its

capacity to relate to the demands of the inner being, to uplift it to that condition of in-placeness which is, consciously or not, deeply desired by all. For it and it alone allows for the expansions of which the heart is eminently capable.

It seems to me that every culture has addressed itself to this need in one form or other. In our Western, Judeo-Christian tradition, it is held that man is God's coworker, God's helpmate. The implications this has are too far-reaching to discuss in this essay, but the principle of human participation in the reality of permanence, of an absolute condition, is clearly indicated. The Chinese speak of *Nei Zai Qui Zhi* (the characters transliterated), the sovereignty of a deep, most inward acknowledgment which alone can sanction the justness of the character of externalities, of a person, of buildings that make up a city, of the soil transformed into fields that combine with rivers and mountains into soul-soothing, soul-enriching harmonies. And the Hindus mean the same thing when they speak of an atmosphere having *rasa*, of an environment being *satvic*. And despite the inertness that had resulted from a crippling sense of nostalgia and had caused me in boyhood to regard things American—by way of the movies, and stories and rumors brought back by travelers—as symbolic of hope and revival; despite such stagnation, that sense of deep belonging, of connectedness, and hence a blending of a boy's lively imagination with the existing visual realities that had shaped and defined it, that natural feeling of at-homeness had been entirely mine in childhood and into early adolescence.

2

The newness and vitality, the attraction of the modern, the display of energy and power of an industrialized society thrilled me, intrigued and engaged me for many years after I arrived here at the age of fifteen, held me as much as the loss of the familiar, the details that had made for a cherished intimacy, unsettled me. The possibilities that lay ahead for me, the promise of artistic fulfillment in the pursuit of poetry preoccupied me, but I knew, and this became my struggle, that I could not develop, could not become effective in them, could not realize them unless I felt rooted again, could say again, this is where I belong, this is what I am part of. Headlong I threw myself into New York's artistic milieu, had the keenest interest in what was happening in all the arts, worked hard, was published widely—in *Poetry*, the *Saturday Review, Quarterly Review of Literature, Accent, Contemporary Poetry,* and many others of the literary journals prominent then—and, outwardly at least, belonged to the current literary scene. But the gnawing sense that inwardly this was not so, that I was a bit like an intruder, that unlike the others I was not on my own turf, never left me. And tormented me. I knew of course that the foothold I had once had in my environment I could never have again; I did not share with my peers in their earliest memories, the quality and nature of the world into which they were born. That could never change for me, and I knew that my rootedness now had to lie elsewhere—it could be nowhere but inward, nowhere but within myself. I knew that I would not succeed in my literary ambition unless I were securely centered in myself. That and that alone could now become the anchor, the point of reference from where the world around me must be viewed. But I also knew that this inward turn could not be accomplished by myself.

A Longing in the Land deals with this; the book's subtitle, *Memoir of a Quest,* speaks for the drive behind the events the book chronicles. A journey to India at the age of thirty-one in order to be in the presence of and study with a great Vedantic sage—and be instructed in localizing the inward center and maintaining contact with it—removed from me the loss that had so troubled me, and returned me to a rootedness not within a given place but within the interior of myself. I stayed three months in the south of India, and although I had by then published my first collection of poems, *Octavian Shooting Targets,* it was not until then, until my true identification had been revitalized—and hence, from that angle, identity with my world renewed and a vital relationship established—that my real work began. Within a few months I wrote the poems that make up my second collection, *Declensions of a Refrain,* and gradually the others followed, the most recent, *Secret Citizen,* my ninth volume, published during the early part of this year, 1989.

I concentrated in all these collections on two aspects of the art of the poem, the tight, briefer lyric and the freer, long sequences, whose range and movements allow me to explore and suggest awareness of the permanence the human being sorely craves, the indwelling spirit from where alone compassion flows. Such has been the challenge of the poets who have stood as the great models, from Shakespeare to Wallace Stevens, the "legislators of the spirit," and however inadequately, however poorly one may measure against them, they are the guides in this ultimately inward endeavor.

Having lost my footing in boyhood and having, as it were, regained it, though relocalized, in adulthood, I have over these decades come to understand the grave importance to those of acute artistic and spiritual temperament of living within surroundings that can substantiate, at least to a reasonable extent, their visions of a world helping to make of the outer and inner being a unified whole. Ignoring the inner being can have nothing but the most detrimental consequences. It seems to me the subject of the age—one worthy of pursuit and one still in need of spokesmen.

BIBLIOGRAPHY

Poetry:

Octavian Shooting Targets. New York: Dodd, Mead, 1954.

Declensions of a Refrain. New York: Poetry London-New York Books, 1957.

Basic Movements. New York: Gyre Press, 1966.

Figure in the Door. Garden City, N.Y.: Doubleday, 1968.

A Bed by the Sea. Garden City, N.Y.: Doubleday, 1970.

Selected Poems. Garden City, N.Y.: Doubleday, 1971.

The Past Now: New Poems. Garden City, N.Y.: Doubleday, 1975.

Embodiment, and Other Poems. New York: Sheep Meadow, 1982.

Secret Citizen. New York: Sheep Meadow, 1989.

Nonfiction:

A Longing in the Land: Memoir of a Quest. New York: Schocken, 1983.

Books for children:

The Little Elephant (illustrated by Ylla). New York: Harper, 1956; London: Hamish Hamilton, 1956.

1 2 3 4 5 (verses; illustrated by Robert Doisneau). Philadelphia: Lippincott, 1956.

Animal Babies (illustrated by Ylla). New York: Harper, 1959.

Plays, selected first productions:

Fire. University of Illinois Festival of Contemporary Art, Urbana, 1952.

Continued Departure. Cubiculo Theatre, New York, 1968.

The Door Is Open. Cubiculo Theatre, New York, 1970.

Lee Hoffman

1932-

"*A Christmas* Wild Bunch. *I'm the tall one with the drawn weapon.*" *Chicago, 1937*

My favorite uncle was my mother's youngest brother, Hershel, who was also the black sheep of a rather tattletale gray family. Hershel came and went, drank a lot, and occasionally served time. When I was in high school, he settled for a while in Savannah, Georgia, where my family lived. He had a buddy who had a printing press in his garage and the two of them decided to start a magazine. They called it *The Savannah All-Amusement Monthly.* My first "professional" writing was done for them.

This was during the 1940s. Radio was our home entertainment and had always been a factor in my life. At the time, my ambition was to own a radio station. I spent hours after school hanging around the local stations. My uncle proposed that I write a column of radio news. He also sent me on a reporting assignment: an interview with some acrobats who put on a performance above the main intersection from the roof of the tallest building in town.

One slim issue of the magazine came out and I got five bucks for my contributions. I also got a couple of copies, one of which I still have—for all I know, the only remaining copy in existence. My uncle Hershel was not the type to make a success of a business venture.

My mother's people had come from the Carolinas in the 1880s to homestead in Alachua County, Florida. There were family stories of the Old Plantation that was lost to them because of the Civil War, which I had envisioned as something like Twelve Oaks, until I found out "plantation" was simply a regional term for "farm." I don't know whether or not my mother's ancestors had been landed gentry or simply dirt farmers before the Civil War, but Great-Grandpa Ray was never a dashing Confederate cavalry officer, only an enlisted man in the horse artillery. He had been wounded and captured at Spotsylvania, and carried a piece of Yankee shrapnel in his neck for the rest of his life.

I never knew my great-grandfather, and I have only a dim recollection of Grandpa Ray. He was not disposed kindly toward Yankees, but he made the best of it when his daughter decided to marry one. My lone memory of him is of an old man with a billy-goat beard who teased me until I cried. At the time, Grandpa and Grammy were living in Florida, while my family was living in Chicago, and I only saw Grandpa on our annual visits south.

My father was born in Frankford, Pennsylvania, a couple of months before the sinking of the battleship *Maine.* His mother's people had come over from England early in the 1800s. His father's parents had

The author's parents, William Ellwood Hoffman and the former Vera Leola Ray, as newlyweds, Savannah, Georgia, 1918

come from Darmstadt in Germany but I haven't been able to determine when. Grandpop Hoffman relocated to Savannah, Georgia, sometime before World War I. Grandpa Ray was sent there about 1905 by the railroad he worked for. In Savannah, my parents met.

During World War I, my father was working in a shipyard. Anticipating being drafted when he turned twenty-one, he proposed to my mother and they were married in April 1918. A photo taken just after the wedding shows my mother as a slender dark-haired nineteen-year-old, smiling with a look of shy pride. My father, a boyish twenty with a stiff collar and protruding ears, appears somewhat dazed.

As the oldest girl among eight siblings, my mother spent most of her childhood as her mother's helper: cleaning, cooking, and tending the younger kids. Hers was not a prosperous family, or a happy one. Grandpa drank and Grandma nagged. They fought so fiercely there were times my mother was afraid one might kill the other. They disciplined their children with a strap.

In her teens, Mom worked in a cannery and then in a laundry. She had dropped out of school as soon as the law allowed, in part because she was embarrassed at not having decent clothes to wear. That was unfortunate. She had a good mind. She was an avid reader and had talent for writing. But in her family, a woman's business was making a home for her husband and children and she devoted herself to that. Her writing talent went into making up bedtime stories for my brother and later for me.

My only sibling, my brother, Curtis, was born in 1922. My father had made a down payment on two empty lots next door to his parents' house in Savannah and had begun building a house of his own. When a boiler exploded in the stocking mill where he worked as a maintenance man, he salvaged beams from the wreckage to support his house. In his spare time, with the help of kin and friends, he framed it and got on the roof and clapboard. It was a story-and-a-half house, and once the attic was finished, he and my mother moved in. The plumbing hadn't yet been installed. They lived with a chamber pot, a pitcher, and the use of the facilities in the house next door.

A while before my brother was born, my father had taken up a hobby, the exciting new technological marvel of radio. My mother was upset when he spent a whole week's salary on a radio receiver, but then he took it apart to learn its workings, and began building sets for sale.

After the stocking mill closed down, he worked at various jobs in various places: plumbing, laying carpet, mixing cement on bridge construction, and whatever else came along. In 1925, during the boom in Florida, my folks had gone to Lake Worth, where Mom's parents were living, and Dad spent a summer as a rough carpenter on some of the luxury hotels that were being put up.

Then in the late twenties, he moved to Chicago, where he found employment in a radio factory. Even during the worst of the Great Depression, there was work for a good radio technician. One radio factory might fail, but there was always another. Occasionally the work was only part time, but he was seldom without any job at all. And their home was never without a radio.

As I said, radio was a factor in my life from the beginning. When I was born, in 1932, one of the very popular programs was "Little Orphan Annie." The title role was played by a young actress named Shirley Bell. My mother liked the program, and the name, so she called me Shirley—a name I have never appreciated and stopped using in my teens.

As a preschooler, my favorite programs were "The Lone Ranger" and "Tom Mix" and my favorite activities were pony riding and playing *cowboy*. Going to the fairgrounds so I could ride a pony was a Sunday-afternoon ritual. The dream of my life was to have a pony of my own. According to my mother, one of the first words I learned as a baby was "horsie."

I was one of the reasons my parents decided to move out of Chicago. Dillinger had been killed at a movie house a few blocks from our home. Murders were regular news. Tramps were wandering the streets, begging and stealing. (On days when the taste of chlorine in the drinking water was particularly strong, my brother'd say they'd found another body in the reservoir.) My parents felt this was not the ideal environment for bringing up children. I was approaching school age and they did not want me walking back and forth to school in the city streets. My mother's parents were still living in Lake Worth, and my parents liked it there. They decided to go back.

My father was never a man for taking risks. He had an income from his factory job, and my brother had only two years of high school left, so they stayed on in Chicago while my mother took me to Lake Worth, rented a suitable place on the Federal Highway, and opened a rooming house for tourists.

Things didn't go well for us that season. Florida had an unusually cold winter. Central heating wasn't common in the area and the portable kerosene heaters that generally sufficed weren't up to the job.

Tourists either continued on further south, or returned north to their hearths and furnaces, to get warm.

We gave up the very big house on the main highway and moved into a smaller house on Palm Way, where we offered a few rooms for rent to seasonal tourists. For me, this move had one virtue. I met Leroy.

When we left Chicago, I'd left half my family and all my friends behind. In Florida, my mother was too busy with the rooming house to spend much time with me. I was shy to begin with, and slow making new friends, so I'd been alone a lot. I suspect Leroy was lonely, too. He was a frail boy who attended a private school and spent much of his time reading comic books. He lived across the street, and once we made connection we became inseparable buddies. Our games usually consisted of making up and acting out stories.

This winter was no better for tourists than the previous one. It got so cold the birdbath froze, and the kerosene heater went wild, smoking up the entire

"Pony-riding in the park," Chicago, 1937

house. It began to look as if we weren't fated to be magnates in the tourist business.

My parents had one more resource. They still owned the house in Savannah. My father decided our best bet was to move into it. At least we'd have a roof over our heads.

My mother didn't like the idea. She didn't like Savannah. She didn't want to live there and she shared her feelings with me. I learned to hate my new home before I ever saw it. And I was upset at the idea of leaving Leroy. Maybe it was because I was upset that my mother promised me that in Savannah I could have the pony I had always wanted.

When my parents built their house, it had been outside the city limits, in a neighborhood where one could keep livestock in the backyard. During the years they'd been gone, the area had been built up and taken into the city. I didn't get my pony. And that year, I didn't get a cowboy suit for Christmas either. I got a cow*girl* suit instead. I was big for my age, and it was the only kids' Western outfit in the Montgomery Ward catalog that came in my size.

My father got a job as radio repairman for the local Western Auto store. We had a radio in every room but the bathroom (where he felt electrical appliances were unsafe). I listened to radio drama as I did my homework. On Saturdays I went to the movie house that showed a Western, a second feature, a chapter picture, a cartoon, and a newsreel, all for a dime. I read a lot: comics, Nancy Drew mysteries, and the anthologies of horror and supernatural stories that my mother brought home from the adult section of the public library. I found a few playmates among the neighborhood kids and spent my time with them, playing cowboys or gangsters or winning World War II, but I had no really close friends until I met Audrey.

One autumn day I was out playing, when my brother hunted me up to tell me there was someone selling pony rides across Wheaton Street, a block away. He'd brought me a dime and was willing to walk me over.

Between Wheaton Street and the streetcar tracks was a vacant field of several acres, lined on the street side with oaks and pignut trees. Until World War II, an annual New Year's Eve bonfire was held in it, with wooden crates and castoffs piled as high as a small house, and a fire engine standing by to see nothing went wrong. Now an aluminum-painted box truck was parked in the field. A canvas awning extended out from the side of the truck, and a small horse was tied in its shade. There was no sign of ponies.

"In front of the house where we lived in Savannah, Georgia," Christmas 1940

A heavyset woman and a blonde girl about my age appeared from within the box of the truck. The woman told us her husband had the ponies out in the neighborhood selling rides. I wasn't to be put off. I hadn't been on a pony since we'd left Chicago. We set out to search for them.

We found them a street over from the one we lived on. There were two Welsh mares: a small chubby piebald and a slightly larger, very fat bay. Their names, I learned, were Pansy and Alice. I paid my dime to straddle Alice, the bay.

I don't recall exactly how I got to know Audrey, the blonde girl. It just naturally happened. She was as crazy about horses as I was. Nominally Pansy, the piebald pony, was hers. Audrey and I soon became the very best of friends.

At one time Audrey's parents had owned a pony farm in New York State. I don't know what had happened to it, but I would guess that, with increasing urbanization and the Great Depression, the demand for ponies had fallen off appreciably. Audrey's parents, with their two daughters, two Welsh

"Riding Alice, the Welsh pony," Savannah, 1940

ponies, and one half-horse, had joined a carnival and sold pony rides. The carnival broke up in Savannah and they'd parked on a convenient piece of land with good graze and begun looking for a way to survive.

The box of the truck had built-in bunks that folded up against the walls, two on each side. When they traveled, the bunks were up and the ponies were carried in the box, while the family squeezed into the cab of the truck. When they camped, they set up the canvas lean-to for the ponies, unfolded the bunks, and lived in the truck.

The half-horse belonged to Audrey's teenage sister, Grace, and only she or her father rode it. The Welsh ponies were the money-earners. Since the family depended on them for income, I never got to ride for free, but if I brought my dime when there were no other customers, I'd get Alice and Audrey would get on Pansy and we'd ride together, up and down in the field, until another paying customer showed up.

Audrey's father found work at the kraft paper plant, and after a while the family moved. I lost touch with Audrey then until she and her father moved into the farmhouse at the other end of our street. I learned her mother had died and her sister had married and they'd had to give up the ponies. Much later my mother told me that when they were camped in the truck Audrey's mother had known she was dying of cancer, and had asked Mom if we would please take Audrey in when she was gone. But my mother had not dared take on the responsibility.

Although Audrey and I were in the same grade, we were never in the same class at school. None of the kids I played with in the neighborhood were in my class, and it wasn't until I reached junior high that I had class friends who were also after-school friends.

I never liked school. Even before I started I'd seen enough "Our Gang" comedies to know it was something kids despised. I didn't understand the concept of education. To me, the goal was to satisfy the teachers, make grades that would keep my parents happy, and get it all over with. I had a knack for that. I could remember what the teachers said in class and feed it back on tests, without having to study. The only homework I bothered with was the paperwork that had to be turned in the next day. Instead of reading textbooks I was reading adventure stories.

I was in the sixth grade when I started writing one. It was after the fashion of the Nancy Drew mysteries. I worked on it in class. I imagine that as I bent over my desk intent on my story I looked like a conscientious student. I didn't finish that first one. But the next year I moved into a different genre. I began writing the kind of stories I saw in movies— episodic cliff-hanger Westerns and war adventures. I'd found my field. I turned out dozens of two- and three-pagers which I passed around among classmates. I wasn't thinking about writing as a possible career. I was too naive for that. I did them for my own entertainment and to entertain my companions. At the time, my ambition was to own a horse ranch.

That was not my first venture into literary composition. I don't know how old I was when I first turned the tables on my mother and, instead of having her tell me a story, I told her one. When she stopped reading me bedtime stories, I took to making up my own as I lay waiting for sleep. And I'd usually imposed plots of a sort on the games of *cowboy* or *war adventure* we kids had played.

As far as I remember, my first try at publishing was a newspaper, three columns in pencil crudely lettered on a single sheet of ruled notebook paper. It contained war news gleaned from radio broadcasts, condensed into items a sentence or two long, and an admonition to buy bonds. It appeared in an edition of one copy.

Later the boy next door and I produced a cookbook plagiarized from our mothers' recipe collections, done in an edition of two using carbon paper, on the old Underwood typewriter in my attic, and saddle-stitched on my mother's sewing machine.

We sold these for ten cents each to our respective mothers.

At times I messed around with a rubber-stamp kit of the kind with moveable type, but I don't recall anything I produced on it.

While I was in the seventh grade, a program was begun to put selected kids through four years of high school in three years. These were to be bright kids who intended going to college. I was invited to join. I had no intention of going to college, I just wanted to get done with school as quickly as possible. I jumped at the opportunity. In this accelerated class, I fell in with Bob, Albert, and Louis.

In grammar school I had seen a most marvelous device. One of the teachers had used a shallow rectangular pan of jellylike material to reproduce a drawing of a bird. When I came across a magazine article that identified such a device as a *hectograph,* I asked for one for Christmas. I got it, and the four of us decided to put out a newspaper.

This was far more ambitious than my earlier effort. It consisted of several pages of class chatter and news and included some cartoons. Albert's parents weren't home when we set out to run it off at his house. With a hecto, the ink—brilliant purple stuff—is transferred from a master to the surface of the jelly. Then you press a blank sheet of paper onto the jelly and it picks up some of the ink. Each copy comes out a little paler than the one before, until it becomes illegible. You're supposed to let the jelly sit overnight while the ink settles to the bottom, and then you can run off something new. According to the instructions, if it were absolutely necessary, once you'd finished a run you could wash the ink off the surface and do new copy.

Of course we were too impatient to wait overnight to do the second page. But something went wrong. Somehow we ended up washing the jelly down the sink, leaving a large purple stain that we couldn't scrub out. I don't know what Albert's parents said when they got home. I took my empty hecto pan and left.

This aborted our career as printers but not as publishers. Our school homeroom was oversize, with twice the usual amount of blackboard space. Arriving before the teacher one morning, we commandeered a portion of blackboard and chalked our publication up there. The teacher didn't complain, so we continued this routine until we tired of it.

It was during this period that I got onto the other side of the microphone. A new radio station opened in Savannah. It went on the air on my birthday. I went to see the facilities, and somehow got

to going back, hanging around. When my favorite deejay started a regular spot with "guest disc jockeys" I was one of the first, and I recruited my friends to make appearances. Bob turned out to have such a naturally good voice the station offered him a part-time job.

My ambition shifted from owning a horse ranch to owning a radio station. I would have liked to become a deejay, but I did not have a good voice, and in those days radio announcing was a male occupation anyway. I decided the way into my chosen field would be as a radio engineer. As high-school electives I opted for physics and extra math. In trig class I met Hank Rabey.

Hank was an amateur magician and puppeteer who aspired to become an actor. He picked up pocket money doing magic and puppet shows at parties, and I became his assistant. We spent our Saturdays together. We'd have hot dogs for lunch at my house, bike to a local hacking stable, hire a couple of horses, and ride for an hour. Then we'd bike into town, buy

"Queen Isabella and King Ferdinand, second-grade style. (I don't remember my costar's name.)" Lake Worth, Florida, about 1940

carryout sandwiches and drinks, and smuggle them into a movie house that showed a double feature, chapter picture, and cartoon. After supper at the theater we'd go back to my house to watch Sid Caesar's "Show of Shows" on TV.

My family had one of the first TVs in Savannah. There was no local station at the time. We got our snowy signal via stacked yagi antennas from Jacksonville. But that wasn't stopping Savannahians from buying sets.

During World War II, my brother had been in the Army Air Corps, stationed in England. He came home with a bride, and went to work for Dad, training as a radio repairman on the GI bill. My own aspirations toward a career in radio didn't fare so well. To my parents it was inevitable that, as a female, I would get married, keep house, and have children. They figured if I held a job between high school and marriage, it would be as a shop clerk or waitress or possibly in the kraft paper plant. When I talked about wanting to go off for technical training after I completed high school, nobody paid much attention.

I don't know whether I'd have stuck to my goal if I'd had encouragement. As it was, by the time I graduated high school I'd changed my plans.

Hank had introduced me to theater. The Savannah little-theater group was run in conjunction with Armstrong Junior College. The college offered one class in theater. The school auditorium was the playhouse and the teacher was producer-director. Students and townsfolk together made up the crews and casts. Hank was in the cast of *The Taming of the Shrew.* He invited me to the dress rehearsal. This was my first encounter with live theater since my appearance as Queen Isabella in a second-grade play about Columbus discovering America.

I was fascinated. I was too shy to consider acting on stage, but I wanted to become involved in the theater. I decided I wanted to go to Armstrong.

My mother's memory and mine diverged on this point. In her later years she said she and my father had been willing to send both of us kids to college if we'd wanted it. As I recall, in her opinion colleges were hotbeds of immorality. Besides, college was for rich kids, not for the likes of us. I remember threatening to join the army if I couldn't go to Armstrong and even going to the local Air Corps recruiter for information.

Attending Armstrong was a different matter than going off to an out-of-town campus. I'd be living at home. To my parents, the big difference between it and high school would be the cost of tuition and

books—around two hundred dollars a year. They gave in and I enrolled.

It was while I was at Armstrong that I ran into Audrey again. Sometimes she'd go along with Hank and me to ride on Saturday afternoons. Then the man across the street got a horse, a sorrel mare. He kept her with a gelding belonging to a friend of his within walking distance of my home. Audrey and I were allowed to ride all we wanted to, and we wanted to a lot. The mare was bred and dropped a he-foal which later served as a model for the colt Banner in my book *The Valdez Horses.*

My first year at Armstrong, I became thoroughly involved in the theater. I took to building scenery and operating the light board and was given a work-scholarship as assistant to the teacher. For the first time in my life I was treated as a valued, contributing member of a group in a major activity. We did one-week runs of quality plays. Many of the townspeople who participated had been in little theater for years and were polished performers. One of our students, Ross Durfee, who was there on the GI Bill, had worked as a professional actor. We did good work. I took an intense pride in our productions.

Several important things happened to me at Armstrong. I had my first encounter with semantics, a study that changed my whole view of life and reality. I was treated as other than a child by adults for the first time—by the teachers and the townspeople in the theater group. And one of the stage crew, Walt Kessel, introduced me to science fiction fandom.

In 1950 science fiction was not a widely popular form of literature. A lot of people didn't even consider it respectable, and many thought the idea of sending a man to the moon was ridiculous. Even so, there were fans scattered all over the world who were in touch with others of like mind through correspondence, fanzines, and even occasional conventions.

The typical fanzine was mimeographed or dittoed (a technologically advanced form of hectography), with a circulation of from fifty to a couple of hundred. Some of these were devoted to the discussion of science fiction and amateur attempts at writing it, but more often the contents included articles and essays on any and everything that interested the editor-publisher.

I had not known about science fiction as a category of literature, but I'd been including it in my reading, from comics about *Buck Rogers* and *John Carter on Mars* to novels such as George Orwell's *1984.* I began seeking it out on bookstands and magazine racks. And I began publishing my own fanzine.

The college had an old mimeograph in the basement. I got permission to use it. Walt Kessel had published a fanzine himself several years earlier. He taught me to use the mimeo and gave me his old mailing list and the lettering guides and styli he'd used. That summer I became avidly involved in fanzine writing and publishing.

The next term the college administrators decided the meager enrollment in the theater class didn't warrant continuation of the school-community program. They dismissed the teacher and made theater an extracurricular activity just for students, under an English teacher who switched from full-scale major productions to simple one-act plays. Without the enthusiastic leadership of our previous director and the participation of experienced townspeople, the productions became typically amateurish. After one quarter of this, I gave up my work-scholarship and quit the school theater.

The community people had formed a little theater of their own, and I stayed with them a while, but they were working in the round. I worked as assistant to the lighting technician—who didn't really need an assistant. Without scenery to build and move, I felt unnecessary and out of place, so eventually I quit that group.

Between the college courses and the fanzines I received, my world had been flooded with new ideas, viewpoints, and insights. The limited, and limiting, conceptual structures of my childhood were breaking down. I'd lost my place in the theater, and with it my enthusiasm. Audrey had moved away again and Hank had been drafted, and I had no other close friends. During my second year in Armstrong, I became more and more involved in fandom. I published my fanzine monthly, I corresponded avidly with other fans, and I attended the 1951 World Science Fiction Convention in New Orleans.

By the time I graduated Armstrong, I had no idea what I wanted to do with the rest of my life. The one thing I was certain of was that I did *not* want to be a housewife and mother such as my own mother was. But my parents continued in their faith that this was my inevitable fate.

My first job after graduation was temporary, hand-feeding a C and P Gordon printing press. Then my father and brother, in partnership, opened a radio-TV sales and service shop of their own and put me to work at the front counter. Since I was still living at home, my salary was small, but it was all

"On Kehli, during a pause in the Saint Patrick's Day parade," Savannah, 1955

mine. I was responsible only for my clothing. I realized if I saved the rest I could actually achieve my one unswerving ambition—I could get a horse of my own.

With help from my mother and friends of hers, I located some people less than a mile from our house who had pasturage with a couple of stalls in it. They were keeping a cow and a pig and were willing to let me put a horse in the pasture for five dollars a month. I got some money together and got my brother to drive me out to see the local used-horse dealer.

The dealer had only two horses in stock at the moment. One was a shabby, bony old roan that he didn't even show me. The other was a big bay gelding that he didn't think would suit me. But I was eager enough to buy just about anything with a leg on each corner and no horns. I had the price. I said I'd take him.

I think Kehli had been trained originally as a harness horse. He was a pacer, and much preferred pacing to a canter or gallop. He was a marvelously agreeable horse, good-natured and unflappable. When I dressed him up in full English tack and took him out, he stepped lively and looked classy. When I rode him bareback, with only a Johnson halter and no bit, he'd mosey along, ears flapping, looking for tidbits to eat as he ambled. He was fond of Spanish moss and would grab a hank as we passed under oak trees, nibbling it up into his mouth on the move. I recall a small child hollering for his father to look see the horse "with a moustache" as we went past.

He had one quirk though. There was scar tissue in his nigh ear, and he did not want that ear touched. He was very bridle-shy until I bought a split-ear Western bridle for him that only went over his off ear. When he learned that taking the bit didn't mean getting his bad ear pulled, he'd stand to be bridled in the pasture.

One day I was riding in a park at a distance from my house when I encountered some other riders—a man with a young boy behind him on one horse, a woman on another, and a slightly older boy sharing his pony with a monkey, all followed by a couple of dogs. I got into conversation with them. They were the Belfords, they owned a grain and feed company, and they had a large place a short distance from where we were. I rode home with them and met the rest of their "family"—a small flock of sheep, a large herd of free-roaming Siamese cats, sundry other creatures, and assorted fowl, including peacocks. The pony was especially privileged. On Sunday mornings, he got to join the family in the kitchen for a pancake breakfast.

For a couple of years, instead of going to science fiction conventions, I spent my vacations on working ranches in Colorado and Wyoming. I went on a trail ride from Laramie to Cheyenne for the Frontier Days Rodeo, rode in the grand entry, and watched the rodeo from horseback. At work I was reading more horse magazines than science fiction. I gave up publishing my fanzine, and my fannish activities dwindled.

I saw an ad in one of the horse magazines for a young woman to assist a horse dealer in Kansas who supplied mounts and taught riding at a girls' school. I answered the ad and got the job. My new employer and his wife came to Savannah in a pickup truck to convey me and my horse to Kansas.

The job did not turn out to be quite what I had envisioned. My employer and his wife and small daughter lived upstairs over a store instead of on a farm or ranch. They installed me in a spare room. She worked as a waitress, and he worked mostly at shoeing and trading horses. I don't know just what the deal with the school was. I never saw it. My boss claimed to be kin of the late Jesse James, and I believe him. It seemed the main reason he wanted a young female assistant was as a shill to offer horses at the sale barns (buyers were likely to pay more to a young woman) and to buy them for him to resell (sellers were likely to sell cheaper to a young woman).

The job didn't last long. My boss got into trouble with the law, and I took my horse home to Savannah and went back to work in the family store.

I bought a second horse, a palomino named Wrangler, but he turned out to be a spoiled barn rat, so I traded him in on Brandy, a bay gelding that could not only canter and gallop beautifully but rack as well. I saved up some more money and bought a station wagon so I could haul my own grain and hay to the horses. Occasionally I piled it full of neighborhood kids and took them to the Belfords to enjoy the animals.

I rode in the mornings before work and on weekends. At work, I did a little bookkeeping and some minor radio repairs, answered the telephone, waited on customers, and spent a lot of time just sitting waiting for something to happen. While waiting, I read a lot, mostly Westerns. After a while, sitting there at my desk with a typewriter in front of me, I began writing my own Westerns.

I still had a few connections with science fiction fandom, and was corresponding with a fan who was also into Westerns. I'd mail him my manuscripts to read, but I didn't think of trying to sell them until he suggested one should be submitted. Another fan I corresponded with was also a professional writer of suspense novels. I got him to read the manuscript. He thought well enough of it to suggest I send it to his agent. The agent returned it without so much as a note, and that ended any notion I had at the time of selling my writing. I thought maybe I'd try again when I was older and more competent. Until then I'd just write for the fun of it.

In 1955 I decided to go to the Annual World Science Fiction Convention in Cleveland. That was where I met Larry Shaw.

Larry had been in fandom for years. He'd sold a few stories and gone into editing. At the convention, he had the unbound first-off-the-press copy of a new SF magazine he was editing, *Infinity*. We saw a lot of each other during the convention and after it, we corresponded. The letters flew thick and fast. Larry came down from New York to visit me during the New Year's holidays. Not long after, he wrote and proposed.

Meanwhile, back at the ranch, I lost part of my pasture. It was taken under eminent domain for a new public school. Once the school opened, the kids delighted in having a couple of horses just the other side of a fence. The horses weren't enjoying it so much. People told me kids were crossing the fence, harassing the horses, trying to ride them. Somebody put a beebee into Kehli's neck. I realized it was no longer practical to keep the horses there.

In retrospect, I believe I was strongly influenced by the depressing situation in Savannah and wanted to get away. And perhaps unconsciously I was obeying my parents' longtime admonitions that I must eventually get married. I accepted Larry's proposal, gave my horses to the Belfords, and packed my most treasured possessions into my station wagon. Larry came down and drove me to New York. We got married at city hall and for a time I read slush for the magazines he was editing.

Larry had not ridden before, but he began going to a Staten Island stable with me, taking lessons. Soon, he bought me a horse and we moved from our tiny flat on Sullivan Street to a two-bedroom apartment near the stable. I stopped going in to the office and tried to become a proper suburban housewife. It was a job for which I was not emotionally fitted. Despite having the horse and some friends at the stable, I was lonely and depressed. I tried bringing out another fanzine, but the old fire wasn't there.

After a while we sold the horse and moved back to Manhattan, this time to a fairly large apartment in the West Village. And I got involved in the Village folk-music scene.

This was before the Kingston Trio, Bob Dylan, and Joan Baez, a time when the term *folk music* still referred to traditional and ethnic music rather than to a genre of popular music.

I'd always liked folk music. In my teens, I'd scoured the local record shop and come up with records of performers like Burl Ives, Susan Reed, and Richard Dyer-Bennet. In the Village I discovered the small recording houses that issued authentic field recordings and performances by people like Oscar Brand, Jean Ritchie, and Pete Seeger. I found out that on Sunday afternoons aspiring young performers and people who wanted to play for the fun of it gathered to pick and sing in Washington Square. I got to know some of the people and got invited to other gatherings where they played.

This was fun. I wanted to participate. But I couldn't pick or sing. What I could do was publish a fanzine. So I put together one devoted to folk music and the local scene. I called it *Caravan*. I mimeoed a hundred copies of the first issue and gave them away in Washington Square. When I put out the second issue on the same terms, Izzy Young, proprietor of the Folklore Center, told me people had been coming into the store asking for it. He wanted a batch to put on the counter as handouts to bring in customers. I went back to press and ran off another hundred copies.

"Collaborating on 'Lost in the Marigolds' with Robert E. Toomey, Jr.," New York, 1970

Increasing the press run meant increasing the cost. I couldn't keep giving it away. I put a dime price tag on it to cover the cost of materials, and Izzy agreed to pay me with records for store copies. One day in the store, Izzy introduced me to Pat Clancy, who'd recently begun Tradition Records. Pat gave me some discs for review. Other companies began sending review records. People all over this country and the U.K. were subscribing. John Brunner, whom I knew through fandom, began doing a column of British folk music news. Folk music shops and coffee-houses in other parts of the country ordered quantity lots.

Circulation increased until it just wasn't practical to keep turning it out on a mimeo and hand-collating. I got some estimates from cheap offset printers and went around talking to people like Pat Clancy at Tradition and Jac Holzman at Elektra Records. They gave me their support in the form of ads, and *Caravan* went offset with a press run of two thousand copies.

*C*aravan was a success, but my marriage wasn't. Larry and I decided on a trial separation. We gave up the big apartment in the West Village and moved into separate small apartments on the East Side. This was the first time in my life I had lived alone. It suited me. After a few months, we agreed on a divorce.

My apartment was a railroad flat in the basement of a tenement on Seventh Street just east of Second

Avenue. It consisted of four very small rooms—or three very small rooms and a very large closet. The john was in the hall and the bathtub in the kitchen. The rent was thirty-five dollars a month, which included utilities. It was always too small, but it was cozy and comfortable and convenient to shopping and bookstores. It was a great place to live.

I continued to publish *Caravan* for a while, but it had been a labor of love, never a commercial venture, and it grew to the point where it was more work than pleasure, really too much work for one person. A clever business person would have turned it into a commercial venture and acquired a staff. I wasn't a clever business person. I sold it to Billy Faier.

I had no particular ambition at the time. I got a job with *MD* magazine, processing reprint sales. After a while the boredom got to me, and I left to become a claims clerk with a foreign-car importer. Boredom got to me there, too. I took a home-study course in shorthand and got myself hired as secretary to the vice-president of Arrow Press, a large letterpress printing house that specialized in quality five-color work.

I was no better as a secretary than as a housewife, but instead of firing me, the boss moved me around, having me sit in for various office people on vacation. Finally everybody got back from vacation and I wasn't reassigned. I wasn't dismissed either. With nobody telling me what to do, I took my choice. I liked the production department, so I located an unused chair and a typewriter and table, moved them into a convenient corner, and began soliciting odd jobs from the production crew.

The head of the department was happy to have more help, and when a desk became available, he gave it to me. I attached myself to a particular account and set in to learn the job of production assistant on it. This was fun work. So, of course, it eventually fell through. The account I'd picked moved to a larger printer and my company laid off a bunch of people, me included. But before doing so, they found me a job with a typesetter in the same building.

This might have been fun, too, but the chapel chairman objected to a nonmember doing what I'd been hired to do. Again I found myself with a paycheck and regular hours, but nothing to do. And this time I couldn't help myself to work. Not being in the union I couldn't work on the floor. And I didn't want to work in the office. When the boss proposed it, I quit.

I found an offset printer looking for a Girl Friday, who promised to teach me offset production.

Good. But somehow nobody there ever got around to the teaching part, and I ended up doing general secretarial work. Foosh!

By then I had done a small amount of nonfiction writing. A gang of us—Dick and Kiki Greenhaus, Don and Jo Meisner, Aaron Rennert, Ray Sullivan, and I—had been going to sports-car races together, and had gotten interested in go-kart racing. We put together some short picture articles about them for small-car magazines in trade for a kart kit and some parts. And I'd gotten a trip to Nassau for Speed Week by borrowing a camera, conning a press pass, and doing a picture article on the first Grand Prix of Go-Karts for *Cars* magazine.

During the early sixties I got back in touch with fandom and began going to Fanoclast meetings at Ted White's house in Brooklyn. Fanoclasts was a hotbed of aspiring young writers. Ted and Terry Carr, who was then assistant editor at Ace Books, had just had a science fiction novel published, and Ted was sharing his enthusiasm. He suggested to me that we collaborate on a science-fictional western. We did several chapters and worked up a presentation, submitting them around. Nothing ever came of it, but it inspired me to try writing a Western on my own.

By the time I finished the Western novel, I'd had my fill of the boredom of being a second-rate secretary and had quit yet another job. With great trepidation, I submitted my manuscript to Ace Books. Don Wollheim was editor there then, and was well known for encouraging new writers. I was still waiting for some encouragement from him when Terry Carr phoned and asked me if I "had time" to do a funny Western. Time I had. Talent I wasn't sure about. Terry thought I did. He explained that with the new movie *Cat Ballou* making such a hit, Ace figured there'd be a market for comic Westerns and wanted to get one on the stands. He was familiar with my fan writing and had read the manuscript I'd submitted. He said if I'd work up a presentation and get it in quick, there was a good chance Ace would buy it.

I did and they did.

And Don Wollheim got back to me with an encouraging word. He said if I'd cut the first book to a suitable length, Ace would take it for half a double. When I contacted Ted White's agent to see if he'd handle my stuff, I already had one sale for him to deal with and another in the works.

I had begun a second traditional Western when Terry called me. I put it aside, did the book for the comic Western fad that failed to materialize, and then wrote another straight Western, *Bred to Kill*. My agent sold it to Ballantine Books. I decided not to look for another office job until this book-writing bonanza ran out.

My next book, *The Valdez Horses,* was the most successful of my Westerns. It sold to Doubleday, was reprinted by Ace, won the Western Writers of America Spur Award as Best Western Novel of 1967, and eventually was the source of the movie *Chino.*

Westerns came most naturally to me. Altogether I did seventeen of them. But my agent, a science fiction fan himself, kept suggesting I try my hand at SF. I had just come back from a SF convention when he called to tell me Belmont Books was planning a line of SF doubles. Since they were only asking for around thirty thousand words, he thought it would be a good place for me to start. Still enthusiastic from the convention, I gave it a try. The result was *Telepower.* Belmont took it. After that I did two full-length SF adventure novels, a short-short for *Again, Dangerous Visions,* a long short story coauthored with Robert E. Toomey, Jr., for *Orbit,* and a science-fantasy, *Change Song.*

It was while I was working on *Change Song* that I decided to leave New York. It had been a great city and I'd loved it, but it was changing and so was I. The old gang was breaking up. Greenhaus had gone to New Jersey. The Lupoffs, Silverbergs, Carrs, and a bunch of others went to California. The Whites were off to Virginia and Van Arnam to Mexico. My once-cozy neighborhood had been invaded by rats and muggers. And during my thirteen years there, I had used up all the available wall space in my tiny basement apartment for bookshelves. Even the kitchen cabinets were filling up with books. I needed more space.

I got a tip on a two-bedroom third-floor walk-up with a real bathroom that was available. The rent was appreciably more than thirty-five dollars a month but still cheap for Manhattan. I checked it out. The living room was nice, but the bedrooms were each six and a half feet wide, the bathroom was a tight fit, and the neighborhood was no better than the one I was already living in.

My parents had retired and moved to Florida in the mid-sixties. I'd visited them a few times and had taken a liking to Port Charlotte, the small west-coast community they'd settled in. I especially liked the prices. I could buy a large three-bedroom house with a swimming pool in Port Charlotte, with the mortgage payments about the same as the rent on the apartment I'd looked at. And I liked the idea of having so much sky and greenery around. I took it.

At the time, Robert E. Toomey, Jr., was living across the hall from me in New York, and suffering from bronchitis. He agreed to drive a U-Haul truck to Florida for me and I agreed to his staying in one of the spare bedrooms. So in August of 1971 my few close friends still in New York—the Meisners and Aaron Rennert—came over, we loaded my stuff and Toomey's cat into the truck, and I left the Big Apple for the Sun Coast.

When I started planning to move to Florida, I was hoping we'd be able to get the whole family together again. My brother, who'd sold out his share of the family business and gone to work for Western Auto, and his wife and three children were living in Tampa, just a couple of hours away. But as I was negotiating for the house in Port Charlotte, he got transferred to Atlanta. We never did manage to get the whole gang together at once. He died in his mid-fifties of cancer.

I discovered that having a house and yard and nearby parents in a small town makes for a completely different way of life than apartment living in the big city. I missed the secondhand bookstores, the museums, the old movies, and the exotic restaurants, but I loved the yard and pool, the greenery and the sun. I bought a bicycle and started a garden. Picking a salad fresh from the yard is an incomparable pleasure.

After Toomey left, it took me a while to connect with other writers, but eventually I found—or rather was found by—Louise Bergstrom, who wrote romances and ran a writers' workshop for the local adult-education program. I joined the group, and occasionally sat in for Louise.

I wrote several more Westerns, but the market for the kind I preferred was in decline and my agent was after me to turn my hand to other genres. With some nudging from him and some encouragement from Louise, I did a historical romance, *Savage Key,* under the pen name Georgia York. I'd always been fascinated by history, and I set my story in Florida, which gave me a good excuse to learn a lot more about my new home state. It was fun to write, and a lot of fun to research, but as I was completing it, my mother was taken seriously ill. I finished up the submission manuscript between visits to the hospital and housekeeping for my father.

During all this, I had begun to slide back into a low-level depression. I put together two more historical romances, both of which were fun to research, and both of which sold quickly, but neither of which really satisfied me. I enjoyed the history, but I didn't have a natural talent for writing romance. I decided to try a historical saga. I did extensive research and made a lot of notes but never got a first draft worked up.

A good friend from the writers' workshop, a former flyer who'd been working on a novel of the barnstorming era, died, and I spent a long time trying to complete his manuscript before I finally realized I couldn't do it. It was too much his own and too much had been in his head. I couldn't capture his vision of the completed book, or achieve a vision of my own that was compatible with what he'd done.

I started a fantasy novel, but wasn't satisfied with it either and soon junked it. The enthusiasm was gone.

I decided to take some time off and indulge a few of my other interests. I took adult-ed courses and was reading a lot, particularly in anthropology, mythology, Jungian psychology, and related fields. Rather casually, I went along with a friend to take an introduction to computers, and got hooked. We both ended up with PCs of our own. The computer became a major preoccupation.

All along, I maintained peripheral contact with fandom. I kept up sporadic correspondence with a few old friends and still got a few fanzines. I attended SunCon, the 1977 WorldCon, in Miami Beach. Nominally I was still publishing my lustrumly fanzine, *Science-Fiction Five-Yearly*, though in fact I farmed it out to "guest editor-publishers" who did all the work while I continued to collect egoboo for it.

Then in 1982 I was invited to be one of the guests of honor at Chicon III, the Annual World Science Fiction Convention in Chicago. For the convention, the New England Science Fiction Association Press published a hardcover combining the works of the three guests—short stories by A. Bertram Chandler, a collection of my fanzine writings, and a dust jacket by Kelly Freas.

The same year, I was guest of honor at the first Tropicon, which was held in conjunction with the International Conference on the Fantastic in the Arts in Ft. Lauderdale, and got to know some of the east-coast Florida fans. I began being invited to other Florida conventions.

But my primary concern had become my parents. By then they were both in their eighties and more and more they needed help around their house. Several days a week I'd help with the indoor chores.

"With my parents," Port Charlotte, Florida, 1973

In time I took over all of the yard work, grocery shopping, and general maintenance.

For years my mother had been legally blind and had suffered bouts of arthritis. Once when she had a particularly severe attack, the doctor told us all we could do was keep her comfortable and expect the worst. But before long she struggled her way out of bed, onto a walker. In time she was on her own two feet again, keeping house and fighting off all our efforts to make her take it easy.

In his youth, my father was seldom ill. When he did get sick, it was hard to get him to a doctor. He began to suffer from arthritis in the knees. He complained of pain in one foot. It got so bad that he could hardly walk, but he refused to get medical help. Then he became feverish. One night he fell and couldn't get up. He went to the emergency room then—in an ambulance.

The diagnosis was infection from undiscovered diabetes. An operation on his foot left him in a wheelchair. He was still hoping that he'd get back on his feet before long, when he was found to have cancer of the colon. Despite his age, he went through the operation well, but during his recovery he stopped breathing and almost died. He was never the same after that. His vision, his hearing, his memory, and his spirit were all failing him.

In October 1985, my mother had the first of a series of heart attacks. It was obvious they could no longer continue to live on their own. I didn't want to put them through the stress of giving up the home they'd occupied for nearly a quarter of a century, and I couldn't maintain two houses, so I held a rush sale of assorted accumulated possessions and put my own place up for sale. I moved in with my parents, sleeping on the living-room floor while we made plans to have an additional bedroom built for me. But before it was begun, my mother had her final heart attack.

For the next year and a half, taking care of my father was my full-time occupation. He never got over mourning for my mother, and continued to decline. Unable to walk, with his vision and hearing both failing, his only pleasures in life were going for rides in the car and being wheeled through stores. He had always enjoyed grocery shopping, so we'd usually go twice a week, whether we needed anything or not. At least once a week we'd go to a department store, usually just to sightsee. Other afternoons I'd take him for drives through the woods in areas that had been platted and paved but not yet developed.

"Relaxing with a friend," Boca Raton, Florida, 1988

Just before Christmas in 1987, he went into a really severe decline. In February, a few weeks after his ninetieth birthday, he died.

Abruptly I was alone again. My parents were gone, my house was gone, and most of my possessions were sold or stored. There was no going back. It was time to start a new life.

I began renewing old connections. I went to Boca Raton to visit fan friends Edie Stern and Joe Siclari. I went to the Ninth International Conference on the Fantastic in the Arts and several local science fiction conventions here in Florida and made a number of new friends. My older nephew, Gary, invited me to visit him and his wife, Nancy, in Florissant, Missouri, and attend a convention in St. Louis. Another fan friend, Felice Maxam, invited me to visit her in Oakland, California. The Annual World Science Fiction Convention in New Orleans offered me a guest membership. So I went traveling.

Back home again, with a new year just getting started as I write this, I am still hooked on the computer and have joined the local users' group. I am taking adult-ed courses again. I'm accumulating videotapes of old movies. I'm reading a lot of fanzines and looking forward to the next science fiction convention. And I've begun a new novel.

When Ted White and I discussed our goals back at the Fanoclast meetings in the early sixties, when both of us were just breaking into the business, neither of us had high literary ambitions. We wanted to write the kind of books we enjoyed reading—good, competent entertainment. This is still my goal as a writer.

The true autobiography of a novelist is in her novels, of a fan in her fanzine contributions, of a letter writer in her correspondence. My real autobiography is scattered through the ephemera of my times. What I've offered you here is a skeletal framework of my activities so far. I am too young yet to look back on my life and draw valid conclusions about who I am and why. I'm still changing day to day.

BIBLIOGRAPHY

Western novels:

Gunfight at Laramie. New York: Ace, 1966; London: Gold Lion, 1975.

The Legend of Blackjack Sam. New York: Ace, 1966.

Bred to Kill. New York: Ballantine, 1967.

The Valdez Horses. Garden City, N.Y.: Doubleday, 1967; London: Tandem, 1972.

Dead Man's Gold (bound with *The Silver Concho* by Don P. Jenison). New York: Ace, 1968.

The Yarborough Brand. New York: Avon, 1968; London: Hale, 1981.

Wild Riders. New York: New American Library, 1969; London: Hale, 1979.

Return to Broken Crossing. New York: Ace, 1969; London: Hale, 1982.

West of Cheyenne. Garden City, N.Y.: Doubleday, 1969; London: Tandem, 1973.

Loco. Garden City, N.Y.: Doubleday, 1969; London: Tandem, 1973.

Wiley's Move. New York: Dell, 1973; London: Hale, 1980.

The Truth about the Cannonball Kid. New York: Dell, 1975; London: Hale, 1980.

Trouble Valley. New York: Ballantine, 1976; London: Hale, 1982.

Nothing but a Drifter. Garden City, N.Y.: Doubleday, 1976; London: Hale, 1980.

Fox. Garden City, N.Y.: Doubleday, 1976; London: Hale, 1980.

Sheriff of Jack Hollow. New York: Dell, 1977; London: Hale, 1979.

The Land Killer. Garden City, N.Y.: Doubleday, 1978; London: Hale, 1981.

Science fiction:

Telepower (bound with *Doomsman* by Harlan Ellison). New York: Belmont, 1967.

The Caves of Karst. New York: Ballantine, 1969; London: Dobson, 1970.

Always the Black Knight. New York: Avon, 1970.

Change Song. Garden City, N.Y.: Doubleday, 1972.

In and Out of Quandry (bound with *Up to the Sky in Ships* by A. Bertram Chandler; illustrated by Kelly Freas). Edited by Charles J. Hitchcock. Cambridge, Mass.: New England Science Fiction Assn., 1982.

Historical romance novels, under pseudonym Georgia York:

Savage Key. New York: Fawcett, 1979.

Savannah Grey. New York: Fawcett, 1981.

Savage Conquest. New York: Fawcett, 1983.

Colette Inez

1931-

My mother's last letter to me reads:

Nérac, France
August 31, 1986

I am late in answering you but my health is not good. I can recover slowly with the help of God. I do not share your opinion about a religion which needs celibacy in its priesthood. It is a religion to which I have thoroughly adhered.

God does not want our happiness in this world, and Christ did not give us that example. Your father asked me to give him companionship so that he would have the strength to renounce the venal women he received regularly.

He realized it would lead to madness, as he could not renounce his early vows, and was grateful to me in the last period of his life to have been saved from suicide which he contemplated. Thanks to me he died in peace in the bosom of the Catholic church, bringing no shame to his family.

You were to be adopted by Mrs. Inez L. who was satisfactory in every way but some one told her or saw in person that you very much resembled your father, which was true, and she thought that as people knew she was a friend of your father, they would quickly guess where you came from.

She decided at the last minute not to take you, and since the American family wanted a child, it seemed a good solution.

. . . I cannot make myself explain to my cousin, Maurice, who you really are. It would bring a lot of worry to him. I have already told you the fact of your birth and those circumstances were entirely independent of my will.

I am trying to read your book of poems, *Eight Minutes from the Sun,* but I must admit I do not understand very much of it. I notice at the end of the book you invoke St. Francis. I wish it were true.

As ever,
M.

Colette Inez, 1988

The beginning, June 1931. My French mother, a scholar, medievalist, carried her pregnancy from Paris into Belgium. The same month during which I was covertly born in an unwed-mother's ward in Brussels, my father, an American priest, prepared for his ordination as a Monsignor in the Roman Catholic church. A stout and lusty man, middle-aged, respected, an Aristotle scholar and linguist, he was marked by the Vatican for high investiture.

On July 4, ten days after my birth, my mother bundled me off to the Institut de Puericulture, a Catholic children's home on the Rue Chant d'Oiseau, Birdsong Street. I was left among other abandoned infants presided over by the Sisters of Charity. My mother resumed her archival calling, perusing the medieval tracts of Pictaviensis, Saint Otto, and Saint Blaise, obscure intellects of the faith.

Years. I would wake in the half-light of dawn, file in line in my white nightshirt to a bare washroom, part my hair, rinse my mouth, splash cold water on my face and pat it dry with a large, rough towel used by others in my section.

There were no mirrors. They will make us vain, the Sisters insisted. Beauty is empty, they said. I trusted others to tell me if my clothes were in disarray. We shuffled in our *pantoufles,* brown plaid felt slippers, to the floor's communal closet. Here we secured our uniforms; one in blue wool for winter, one in brown cotton for summer, undergarments, knee socks. Two pairs of shoes, heavy and light, galoshes for snow or rain.

Herded down the stairs each morning to join others at matins, we were lambs kneeling on cold stones, praying for God's mercy, for the forgiveness of sins. Breakfast in a cavernous refectory demanded we speak only when addressed by a Sister. The concert of spoons clicking against porridge bowls, the clamor of slurping children seated on hard benches in the grey light of day still drums dimly in my ears.

I memorized the alphabet, sang songs in a round: "*Frère Jacques*," "*Il Etait un Navire,*" plainsongs and Latin chants in harmony. That incantatory rhythm was part of the cadence of my childhood, its particular music. I also learned numbers, which sometimes were menacing. Fractions on the blackboard were a parade of digits, beheaded, mutilated, wounded like the beetles we crushed as they scuttled from under our beds.

Favorite subject? Geography, with its paraphernalia of pastel-tinted maps, compasses, place names, latitudes, longitudes, ways to locate myself in the vast world beyond me.

Lunch at noon. Cabbage soup, bread, mutton. Fish on Fridays, bones in our teeth. I would file out of the refectory and join the other girls at embroidery, cross-stitching palm trees, windmills, fleur-de-lis, hemming towels, handkerchiefs, doilies, tablecloths, items sold to raise funds for our African missions.

"You will always remember this day," said the seamstress with pins in her mouth as she fitted me for my communion dress. I had been at the institute six years when a thin young priest placed the wafer, fragile as a moth, on my tongue. Defying the rules, I allowed a tooth to touch it, and envisioned a tiny Christ in my mouth: Lord Jesus wounded and bleeding, weeping with the pain I inflicted. I collapsed in a limp heap over the railing of the altar, creating a discord that spoiled the ritual. In anger and reproof,

nuns insisted I purposely misunderstood the symbolic nature of the host. To that incident I trace the beginnings of my distrust of ceremony, the beginnings of my faith in the powers of a spirited imagination.

During my sixth year, a startling announcement interrupted my needlework, "You have a visitor." I was puzzled and excited. Mother . . . father? I was never told if they were dead or alive. Hope flickered—years of such questions had been turned aside by the nuns: "Have faith in God . . . pray to the Lord for patience in all things." I had imagined they were missionaries remote from telephones or letter carriers. Perhaps they languished in an infirmary, ill with jungle rot, fevers, and agues.

"*Elle est votre tante* . . . she is your aunt," said stout Sister Paul. The somber woman who greeted me wore her brown hair wound in a bun at the back of the neck. A sliver of gold flashed from a front tooth. A crucifix on a fine gold chain hung from her neck, and her eyes in a long sallow face gleamed yellow in the whitewashed light of the reception room.

She had me kneel and pray with her. We did not embrace and she met a few venturing questions about my family in awkward silence. I pressed her no further. Sister Paul had warned me not to speak without being spoken to. She asked after my health and studies, and withdrew a stuffed animal from her handbag before leaving. "It's for the child," she said, but returned it to her purse after being told that toys might incite jealousy and resentment among the children and were not allowed. I didn't like this gloomy woman and was indifferent to her departure. While she came several times after, her visits seemed only curious diversions in the institute's monotonous rule of life. A very distant relative is how I described her to friends in my ward who thought to ask.

Two years passed. I was that much closer to the age when orphaned or abandoned children left for labors on Belgian farms, in households or factories. Girls of fourteen who flourished in school might accept the veil and join the Sisters in their pious duties. Although I was considered clever, my willful and sensuous nature seemed at odds with the career of the religious. Example: in the presence of a nun, in a fit of pity or passion for our Savior, my lips caressed Christ's body on the crucifix in a rush of kisses. A repudiating slap across my face knocked me to the floor.

One day in the spring of 1939, my hour of embroidery was again interrupted by a Sister. "Two

L'Institut de Puericulture, rue Chant d'Oiseau, Brussels, Belgium

men have come for you.'' I was introduced to stylishly dressed civilians, one with the symmetrical good looks of film stars I had seen in magazines smuggled into the wards. The shorter of the two had a trim auburn mustache and brilliant blue eyes. Mother Superior stood near. ''Colette, these gentlemen from America will be taking you away.''

I caught my breath, my heart pounded. America? Are these family friends bringing me home at last? I asked this hesitantly but could make out no clear answer from the handsome man's stumbling French. If their mission was a secret covenant with others, even with the mysterious aunt, I was not told. They were to be companions for a long voyage, nothing more.

The hours following our meeting flew by in a swirl of happenings: my first shopping trip to a department store and its magical bounty. I chose a red dress with embroidered flowers at the neck, a blue coat with brass buttons. Then tearful good-byes to my friends. ''Come back when you're a fine lady,'' a child cried out as I stepped through the iron gate, carrying a valise light with few belongings, leaving

with the Americans for the port of Antwerp and embarkation.

Although unfailingly kind, my shipmates continued to ignore my many questions about parentage. Mr. Bale confessed only to being a lawyer involved in the complex paperwork of my emigration, and lived with his wife, Sue, near New York City. I further learned Mr. Branigan, his bachelor friend, was a classical scholar returning home after a yearlong European stay. He denied knowing my visiting aunt, who I had been told was also a student of history. The men had been fellow college students whose earlier friendship now bridged Bale's New York law practice and Branigan's university post in Massachusetts.

During the last self-indulgent days on shipboard, days of freedom and abundance I thought would augur the miracle of America, I was assured that ''the family you are to meet will explain everything.'' We arrived at the port of New York in thick fog. The great lady in the bay and the *gratte-ciels*, the skyscrapers I yearned to see, vanished behind flotillas of clouds. I assumed my relatives were waiting beyond the customs door. ''Would we be met?'' Bale idly nodded and said in slurred French: *''Tout sera bien.''*

All will be well. We later moved into a reception hall; I heard thunder and the spatter of heavy rain outside. Was it an omen?

The approaching slim, blond woman called out, "Bob . . . Paul." I could see it was not Sue, whose picture in Bale's wallet I had memorized, but she appeared to know both men equally well. Her pale eyes probed my face, keenly inspected its features. I sensed she wasn't my mother, but who? Bale touched my shoulder. "Mrs. Inez Londeborg is a school friend from California." How admirable to come this distance just to meet old companions, but why, where is my mother?

"There has been a delay. *En retard.* We must wait." We spent that evening in a New York hotel and left the day after for Pennsylvania Station. Branigan boarded a Boston-bound train with a promise to write. Mrs. Londeborg glanced aside and counseled prayers to God for patience and strength. "Let's not kiss, I have a terrible cold," she dabbed her eyes and nose as Bale translated. I was to leave with him for his Rockville Centre, Long Island, home.

Sue was waiting, prettier than her snapshot, radiant in mid-pregnancy. During the weeks I remained in their cozy one-bedroom apartment, bedded on the living-room sofa, Bale was even less communicative. But raised voices sometimes reached me through the bedroom walls. I overheard breakfast talk about house hunting and the threat of a European war. There were calls to New York City and Richmond, Virginia, where Sue had family. Weekends were spent at Jones Beach or at the Shelter Pines Golf Club watching Bale stroke drives down the fairway. It was tempting to pretend I was Sue's daughter as she cradled my face in her hands, combed and parted my hair, fed me cocoa and cookies.

One day at dinner, Bale announced, "It's time to tell her." I sensed the importance of that moment as he lit a cigarette while gathering his thoughts. Were they planning to give their new baby a sister . . . to keep me? No. "Your family is here and wants to meet you." We left for his law offices the next day. I recited my rosary in tempo with the towns speeding by the train window in a soft blur, while praying for a mother as affectionate as Sue, a father with Bale's princely stature.

They were waiting. *Ma Mère,* mother. She stood by the office door in a Persian lamb cape and matching hat pierced with a jewelled sword, her hair coiffed in dark ringlets. Elegant. I flung my arms around her, but felt only tenseness; she withdrew, opened her compact, and powdered her face. Puzzled, I was more circumspect with the older man who

Colette, age seven or eight, in Belgium

could not possibly be my father, the one I fantasized. Small and graying, nattily dressed in a Prince Albert coat and black derby, he stared at me vacantly through shallow, glassy-blue eyes. A large, red-veined nose protruded from a long face. When he drew closer, his breath was sour and unpleasant. Raymond and Ruthie Bieghler, my family?

Good-byes at Pennsylvania Station, and assurances from Bale we would soon meet again, perhaps at the golf club to which the Bieghlers also belonged. With a few ungainly French phrases, Ray escorted me to our seats and retreated behind his newspaper. I was left to silently admire the doll-like woman who spoke only English. "Freeport," called the trainman as Ray helped us into our coats. Then "Merrick." "*Amérique . . . Amérique!*" I shouted loudly, intrigued with the similar sounds of each. The Bieghlers seemed annoyed, and embarrassed by the outburst.

Bayview Avenue. The stucco house resembling others on the tree-lined street was small and drab, hardly the mansion I assumed this debonair couple would own. I was told to expect a crowded household, three parents living with them under one roof. They were waiting. Nana: Ray's thin, widowed mother, erect and imperious in a straight-back chair. Maude: Ruthie's obese mother, frowning behind rimless glasses. I was also introduced to Ruthie's father, a sullen figure with a long ashen face. George Burt was immobilized by a hangover.

"*Souper*," I asked for supper, a finger pointed at my open mouth and a hand circling my belly. Family life began with a bowl of canned tomato soup and Ritz crackers secured through the universal language of gestures. A glass of ice-cold milk was the only accompaniment to that first meal in the house of my presumed family.

Spring days, 1939. Ruthie was quickly exhausted by my exuberance, and after a few gestures of mothering, shopping for my clothes, and arranging my grade-school registration, she resumed her secretarial job. "Headaches and pinched nerves" explained why I must tiptoe soundlessly past her room during early morning hours and weekends. The child must avoid all forms of speech and clatter when at breakfast with the two generations of gruff and brooding people.

Ruthie commuted daily to the Manhattan offices of the Kraft Cheese Company. She and Raymond, a fabric salesman, had met and married in Chicago, then relocated to the East with Iowa-born Nana. They said nothing about my origins until the night I drew an answer from the usually aloof Ruthie, mellowed by several highballs. I was "someone special" to comfort a childless marriage. Nana later insisted the idea of taking me was *hers* more than Ray's. Bale had shown Ruthie my picture during cocktails at the golf club: "Cuddly as a puppy," she had said, or words to that effect. A family doctor also prescribed a child to help her cope with bad nerves, depression, and drinking.

Our basement had been remodeled into a bar with a dance floor, a concession to Ray's fondness for Latin music and passion for the samba, rumba, and mambo, danced smoothly with Ruthie during full evenings of drinking. While they slept through Sunday mornings, I attended church services with Nana and later shared their afternoons at the country club—among other golf orphans in the community room behind the restaurant and bar. The Bales had since moved to Virginia.

During weeknight dinners alone with my foster grandparents, the women treated me as another irritant in a tense and quarrelsome household. Lean, dry-eyed Nana scorned fat, tearful Grandma Maude who loathed Nana's condescension and bossiness. Accord was reached only in their disdain for Grandpa Burt and his alcoholic binges and public urinations. He would greet my enthusiasm with loud groans, clapping hands over his ears.

There were moments of generosity as rare as they were baffling. Nana would invite me to her room to rummage through a box of Louis Sherry chocolates. But grateful kisses were discouraged: "Don't maul me, child, get your paws off me." And there were private pleasures, a small basement library of frayed books which challenged my beginning English while nurturing an early love for the evocation of words, their tones and melody. I can catalog them still: Zane Grey's Western potboilers, *Anthony Adverse*, the Bible, *The Collected Works of Rudyard Kipling*. I committed "Gunga Din" to memory, basking in its sounds, the muscular swagger of "you limping lump of brick dust," wrapping my tongue around pure rhymes and Burmese words, the steamy glamor of "Mandalay." Some Damon Runyon stories, books about sports, another of Ray's loves, and a threadbare hymnal completed the hoard.

And there was escape at the Episcopalian Church of the Redeemer, where I added my natural alto to militant Protestant hymns, joining hearty choral voices so unlike those who sang the hypnotic chants and plainsongs of my early childhood.

Although Nana often declared a dislike for children, she became my grudging caretaker: "You were a mistake, but they can't send you back." Small concessions and favors: freedom to sway back and forth on her personal rocking chair, leftovers from her delicious home-baked pie crust, visits with her elderly lady friends.

Ruthie was dazzlingly attractive in paisley dresses, furs, scatter pins, and glittering earrings. I learned to obey one of her few French phrases, "*Ne touchez pas*," when my hand or cheek heedlessly approached her rouged and powdered face. When I was not simply dismissed, a vague melancholy or peevishness sometimes bridged the distance; her eyes might well up with tears, or she would point to my flyaway curls and command: "Your hair, go comb your hair." Late one night, I happened on her nude body sprawled lifelessly across the bathroom floor. I cried, "Mama . . . *elle est morte!*" and woke the grandmothers. Ruth was sick, they explained without visible concern. She would be fine.

That autumn I brought my smattering of English to beginning classes at the Merrick Grade School. Within a year, Ruthie was dead, a victim at thirty-two of cirrhosis of the liver and pneumonia. Her death coincided with a visit Nana and I made to the Cleveland home of Nana's sisters. Kate and Agnes shared a decrepit house with Uncle Ed, Kate's fitfully employed piano-tuner husband. Other such visits would follow during summer lulls, intervals in an odd household that introduced me to the pleasures of poetry read aloud.

Crookbacked, deranged Aunt Agnes would aim a gnarled finger at my face and demand I identify myself. Aged and cantankerous Aunt Kate, who dusted at midnight, was barely on speaking terms with her husband, Ed. But it was he who tempered my view of adults as adversaries with a warmth and tolerance he reserved for few others. He took me to visit his piano-tuner friends, and I danced for him on the empty stage of a vaudeville theater as he rippled "Tiptoe through the Tulips" across the keys of the piano he tuned. In exchange for his gift of copious moron jokes, I washed his feet in white vinegar; he called me his treasured foot doctor and rewarded me with a velvet-lined, gold-painted ring box he had fashioned out of a walnut. Daily, to my delight, Uncle

"The Bieghlers' house, Bayview Avenue, Merrick, New York"

Ed stood to his full six-foot height in the kitchen and theatrically recited poems published in the *Cleveland Plain Dealer,* precious interludes in our alliance.

Ruthie's funeral interrupted our stay. The burial was held in mid-August heat. To Nana's evident disgust, Ray, reeking of whiskey, flung himself on the open coffin and sobbed. Nana pushed me towards the casket, prompting me to place a nosegay of wildflowers in Ruthie's hand. Afraid to pry open the stiffened fingers, I flung the flowers at the corpse's chest and fled into the crowd of mourners. I could not bring myself to cry. "You're a cool little number," said Grandmother Burt, who believed my arrival had hastened Ruthie's death.

A parting of ways. "I'm sick of supporting these goddamn leeches," Ray often said before Ruthie's parents were finally ejected from the house. "Good riddance," Nana agreed. Life on Bayview Avenue was less acrimonious during that last year of the great World's Fair. I was free to ride my blue bicycle, to read library books in the crook of a huge maple tree overlooking the backyards of Bayview and Hewlett Avenues.

Ray was a weekend occupant, visible only at noontimes behind concoctions of tomato juice, raw eggs, horseradish, and Tabasco sauce. Although sharp-tempered and moody, Nana was a remarkably undemanding custodian, mostly unconcerned with my dress, schooling, or hygiene. She declared my fascination with reading a waste of time.

Shortly after Thanksgiving, Ray announced he had met "a helluva gal" in a Flushing bar near the World's Fair. "She's lace-curtain Irish and an absolute knockout." Dee appeared in a white ski suit whose hood framed a shiny fall of dark red hair; she studied us through mascara-caked eyes and chain-smoked red-tipped filter cigarettes. Not exactly the film star I first believed, she was nonetheless an ex-chorus girl who had also modeled. Mechanically, she asked about my school and hobbies before driving off to the city in the silver Cadillac of an adoring Ray.

"Very full of herself and a barfly in the bargain." Nana, a teetotaler, condemned her son's dalliance. I was also uneasy at the prospect of a new self-absorbed and haughty foster mother who at twenty-nine could be Ray's daughter. They married in January 1941; neither Nana nor I were invited to the wedding.

During the second year of the war, Ray left New York for sales trips to southern nylon mills. Frequently on the road for months, and flush with high commissions, he would travel with Dee on evening rounds of taverns along his route. One day a postcard addressed in Ray's oversized and swirling script arrived from North Carolina. "Darling, having a swell time. Love, Daddy." Despite its phoney endearment, the gesture and message astonished and moved me. Daddy. Father.

I continued my summertime Cleveland escapes through the war years, sometimes with Nana and later alone. The house on Columbia Avenue, which today spears through the city's Hough district, was at the crossroads of great migrations up from the South. Toward the war's end, our household and a family of Orthodox Jews were the only resident whites on the block. Not much melting in that brimming pot: Prague, Cracow, and Budapest were separately anchored around the corner. I read personal letters to illiterate women, charging a nickel for each. Partly out of curiosity about other lives, I would sometimes reread them without extra charge, reaching for the pleasure of language and the dance of words that I might articulate and share.

My first attempt at a poem was an ode to a milk bottle; my second a love poem to Roone Arledge, a red-haired schoolmate and Long Island neighbor who kept photographs of film star Brenda Marshall and baseball player Mel Ott in a backyard tent on Kenny Avenue in Merrick. Although Uncle Ed had charmed me with the rhymes of John Greenleaf Whittier and Longfellow, I later chose the more subtle music of Emily Dickinson's quatrains as a model.

Since school poetry seemed bland, and we were obliged to commit individual poems to heart for classroom recitation—an undertaking I thoroughly disliked—I decided to learn about poetry on my own. So much in life was arranged alphabetically, I ventured an A-to-Z voyage through the poetry shelves of the Merrick Public Library. Auden was admirable. I tussled with Browning and Donne. A mad and eloquent John Clare was followed by Emily Dickinson, and my hair stood on end. I recall the bliss of opening *Bolts of Melody,* turning its satiny pages, my eyes dancing with the cadences of ". . . Brazil, he twirled a button . . . from tankards scooped in pearl." Even during air-raid drills and neighborhood blackouts, I read poetry by flashlight under the nighttime cover of a blanket. Books were life rafts, and like my cherished blue bicycle, were modes to flight and freedom.

My foster parents' general disregard of me went on. I had learned to forge Ray's signature on report cards, stopple holes in shoe soles with cardboard, and even pull teeth with a string and doorknob. But whatever moved Dee and Ray to dutifully attend my 1944

grade-school graduation? They wove to their auditorium seats: Dee in elbow-length white gloves, jewelled wedgies, a turban, and a tawdry red, white, and blue dress that mocked the flag. I heard wolf whistles. Ray was a five-foot-three George Sanders in white slacks, blue blazer, silk foulard, and Panama hat. Mortified and ashamed to introduce them to my teachers, I hid in a school closet and slinked out only after the graduates dispersed. Driving home in the car, Dee slapped me in the face. Ray tooled the Cadillac through stop signs bawling "Praise the Lord and Pass the Ammunition," a song he claimed he wrote. Long Island days.

The following winter, Nana fractured her hip after slipping on a patch of driveway ice; I was accused of ignoring orders to clear the snow. Corrective surgery at her age was ruled out and she was confined to her bed in a brace of heavy sandbags. I was assigned to the tasks of bathing her and scrubbing the bedpans of an irascible patient who deeply resented the loss of her treasured independence. Her infirmity would influence my life until her death.

Alcoholism had begun to demolish Ray's career. When her diversion as a volunteer driver for the U.S. Army Motor Corps was over and Ray no longer traveled, Dee grew restive and bored. In a brief fling at domesticity, she tried her hand at decorating the master bedroom in white organdy and powder-blue taffeta. The room seemed to me more suitable to a Southern belle than to an unruly and hard-drinking couple.

Until closing hours, Dee and Ray boozed nightly at Al's Bar on Merrick Avenue. Nana spoke of financial problems and rumors that Ray had embezzled funds from his former company. A new siege of abuse began.

One night in mid-sleep, I woke to a rain of body blows as Dee cursed me for failing to empty the trash pail. I was yanked from bed, pushed downstairs, and locked out of the house in my nightclothes. Even though I later slept in Nana's room, I learned to sleep lightly, prepared for eviction at any time and to seek shelter in our garage or in neighboring parked cars.

Thankfully there were books, always books, and I strongly believed in the power of language to change my reality. When discovering Thomas Wolfe's *Look Homeward, Angel,* I conscientiously copied out new words: stertorous, lambent, ptotic. I memorized these and other unfamiliar words, and invented paragraphs for them to live and work in. Curiosity about other lives led me to biography, and to the encyclopedia as a sourcebook for information about Picasso, James Joyce, Virginia Woolf, artists and writers whose names and accomplishments I would record in a notebook. I wanted to be a cultured person.

My faith in a biblical, benevolent God and the assuagements of prayer was ended. I sought consolation in the beauty of the physical world and succumbed to a form of pantheism—that a walk through the woods, the truth of it, was more divine and real than the ritualistic clutter of the church. I lived various lives: the private, concealed life in a debauched house, a life of intermittent hours guiltily spent shoplifting clothes and gifts, and a public, extroverted life among others at church fairs, county choir, tea dances, picnics, and parties. Through it all, I spun my fantasies and wrote my poems.

Never quite divulging to any the humiliations of Bayview Avenue, I reached for and won friendships. Among those I still value and keep are Joe and Syl Silverman, whose Quincy Street home was an oasis, and whose beloved daughter, Barbara, once an object of my envy, remains a good friend. Too proud to ask outright for food, on hungry mornings I guilefully lingered under the kitchen window of Nancy Kent's house until invited in for breakfast. My first published poem, which appeared in 1959 in the *New York Herald Tribune,* was dedicated to the mother of another friend, Inge Streek, whose freely given kugels and cupcakes spoke of her opulent spirit.

After convalescence, Nana was fitted with a large corrective shoe. "Witch!" children shouted as she hobbled by on crutches in baggy stockings, thrift-shop clothes, wisps of white hair escaping from a high-brimmed hat. "Snot-nosed brats," she would yell back. Conflicted, I hated her capriciousness but admired her spunk and stoicism. Even as blindness encroached with the onset of diabetes, Nana rarely complained. But she continued to berate and harangue me without much or any cause, yet I needed her ebbing protection against the Bieghlers.

A small annuity from her late husband netted her several hundred dollars, a few pennies of which were just enough for our suppers of lavishly salted boiled onions, potatoes, and carrots. Huddled over our bowls of steaming vegetables, Nana would sometimes delight in me as a confederate in league against the Bieghlers. The refrigerator had been padlocked by Dee in fierce response to my nibbling into a cup of coleslaw she set aside for a late-night snack. "This is the last time you will ever take my food," she wrote in a note.

Imagined or not, my offenses seemed to multiply. Was it the time I left a telltale footprint in the talcum powder Dee sprinkled on her bedroom rug?

"You are a liar and a thief," she howled, choking me almost to unconsciousness, releasing me only at Nana's shriek for the police. I was hurled out of the house and bicycled for miles, numb with fear and rage. After a night in a parked car, next morning I freshened up in the school lavatory and reported for class. During a study period in the library, I tried to absorb the insights of Dale Carnegie's *How to Win Friends and Influence People.*

With compassion from the Streeks, I spent the following week with Inge, sharing her clothes, food, and small room. It could not last; the modest means of a family of five would hardly support another, and a regretful Mrs. Streek suggested I solve my problems elsewhere. I left my refuge at night, walking aimlessly along a highway. Cars streamed toward me like phosphorescent sea creatures. Confused and mesmerized, I dove headlong into headlights that in the moment before blackness seemed to scream and wail. I was struck by a speeding police car on call.

The groans of women in labor punctuated the long, insomniacal hours of my first night in the charity ward of Meadowbrook Hospital. Diagnosis: concussion, fractures of the nose, spine, and collarbone, and whiplash injuries. My face was raw, its skin ripped off. I meditated on my toes, ankles, and wrists, on those limbs not in pain. I was clamped into a body cast and placed among poor and disfigured women in an amputee ward. While the Bieghlers never came during my months of recovery, Nana would cadge rides from neighbors or church members, limp to my room with a thorough scolding for my heedlessness. "You never look where you're going."

In early spring, during my senior year, I returned to the spiraling frenzy of Bayview Avenue. Night. As I crouched on a rooftop outside the window, a drunken Ray splintered his way through Nana's bedroom door with an axe. "Bitch, I'm going to kill you . . . you've ruined my goddamn life." Defiantly, she teetered up to full height on two canes. He retreated before her icy stare. Other instances of decline and delirium. I was forbidden to answer the doorbell or telephone for fear of creditors. Ray gibbered about spiders and roaches infesting the walls. "You're the bastard of a priest and a nun," he once declared, an eccentric charge that caught my attention. It seemed too fanciful for Ray's confined imagination. But I wondered.

Nineteen forty-eight. Returning home after a Junior Prom Committee meeting at W. C. Mepham High School, I opened the vestibule closet which stored my poems, letters, books, and keepsakes. Empty. I raced to my room in panic; my clothing and other belongings were gone. Dee strode through the hallway: "You want your things, you'll find them in the back lot. I want you out." Behind our house, a heap of smoking ashes was all I found. My precious writings, books, word lists, and letters from Uncle Ed and from Claude, a French pen pal, were gone. I drew some comfort from knowing I had committed numbers of my poems to memory. All that remained to me were a few items in my school locker: a change of clothing and a class notebook which is today one of the only surviving mementos of those times.

The next day was my last in the house. I waited in the living room for the clunk of Dee's wedgies on the stairs. "She's not human," I said loudly to Nana, "she's an 'it.'" I spat out the word. Dee leapt at me, punched me. I struck back. We struggled, staggered to the kitchen and fell. I hammered her head against the floor until she rolled over me with pounding fists and bulging eyes. Nana limped toward us and lashed our legs with her cane until we were exhausted. In the rumpus room below, Ray uncorked a bottle of Jim Beam.

With some money stashed at school and a few borrowed dollars, I rented a room in Mrs. Hoppen's Boarding House near the Wantagh Avenue railroad tracks. I had been hired before graduation as a Freeport telephone operator earning $28 a week. Nana, who by then was legally blind, joined me several months later. Although she never revealed how or why she left the Bieghlers, she believed Ray was simply the innocent victim of Dee's evil.

We slept head-to-feet in a double bed. I had also absorbed something of Nana's frugality and painstakingly saved $1.25 a week to buy a Modern Library classic. One year and fifty books later, a well-thumbed volume became companion to brown-bag lunches at a new and higher-paying job as a file clerk with the Textile Banking Company in New York City. Habitual tardiness was a chronic flaw inflamed by dull work. But before I was fired for lateness, coworker Alex Scotti yielded to my missionary zeal by accepting the gospel of the Modern Library. Born to Italian traditions in a tough Bronx neighborhood, ex-sailor Alex was adrift in indecision about his future. With encouragement from me and other good friends, he entered college and gradually worked up the ranks of accountancy to head the comptroller's office of Simon and Schuster and then of W. W. Norton and Company. Knowing my book love, Alex has over the decades sent me many editions in acknowledgement.

Other short-lived office jobs followed. American Cyanamid was a compromise between the stupefaction of alphabetizing file folders and the lure of its nearness to Rockefeller Center and bookstores I could visit during lunchtimes. As a government contractor, the company ran a routine security check of all employees. I was called to personnel and declared subject to deportation. The Bieghlers had never filed papers reporting my status as required by the Alien Registration Acts of 1940 and 1948. In the government's view I was a nonperson.

Recalling Nana's parsimony, I rummaged through her boxload of old Christmas cards saved for recycling, looking for something, anything, that would technically anchor me in America. It was there, a greeting card from the Bales with a Richmond, Virginia, postmark. After tracking the name in an out-of-town phone book, I boarded a Greyhound bus for an unannounced visit to Bale's law offices.

It was recognizably him. Although at first bewildered, he smiled in recognition when I identified myself, and invited me to visit several days with Sue and their children. A gracious and stylish Sue met us

With Alex Scotti, 1950

Sondra Ewing, Colette Inez, and Carmen Gonzalez in Copenhagen, Denmark, 1952

at the door of their lavish suburban home. After driving her that evening to a church bingo game, Bale and I remained in the car and conferred about my dilemma. "Your California-born father was a Roman Catholic priest who died when you were four or five. He pledged us to secrecy, and I cannot reveal his name. Do you understand?" I didn't entirely, but I nodded. "You resemble him, but your walk, your gestures are like those of your mother who still lives in France." My birth certificate stamped "illegitimate" was on file and he would soon process citizenship papers. Above the drone of voices from the nearby church basement, I thought I heard someone call out, "Bingo!"

France seemed a fortune away, and my savings were almost nil. More scrimping as I cut back on food and spent nights addressing bank envelopes for extra income. By chance I met Carmen Gonzalez, a Peruvian blue blood whose quest for her Spanish origins harmonized with my own pilgrimage; we plotted a backpacking trip to Europe. My citizenship papers were issued in the spring of 1952. Another seeker joined us on the *Île-de-France:* Sondra Ewing, bound

for Germany, her maternal grandmother's birthplace.

The face reforms itself in the doorway of a modest cottage near Oxford, England—the flash of a gold tooth. Marthe Dulong's eyes are level with mine. She is heavyset with grey-streaked, disheveled hair, full breasts curving under a threadbare sweater. Mother, the pretended aunt who visited the institute. From clues in my birth certificate and through pretext, I had traced her path from Nérac in Gascony to her only sister Jean's address in Paris, then to the university town where she glossed ancient documents for the revelation of church fathers.

"I have no money to give you." The words indented the fluent English of her flat and orderly conversation. I had blundered into a scrupulously censored life. I may write her only without reference to our bond and promised to keep the twenty-year secret. Nine months later, I returned as disenfranchised as before to Nana, who had grown frail and sickly and was now supported by checks from a prosperous niece in Chicago. Since there was no further need for my meager financial help, I moved out with my crate of books to a furnished room under the shadow of the Third Avenue El in downtown New York.

More jobs. Gal Friday for a correspondent, Leo Sauvage, at the New York office of *Le Figaro*. Clerk-typist at the Roosevelt Music Company, where I took dictation in longhand from composers of rhythm-and-blues and early rock-and-roll songs. Switchboard operator at Hunt and Winterbotham and Company, luxury English woollens.

September 1953. A heat wave. At the Meadow-brook Hospital, Nana brushed flies from her emaciated face and dismissed me with her terminal words: "Your best was never good enough." At her death, I was on my own. All three elderly Cleveland relatives had died within a year. The house on Bayview Avenue was emptied and sold. Raymond disappeared, likely into the dark night of unredeemable drunken men. A neighbor's son claimed that Dee had entered the lesbian life and hit Southshore bars with a lover.

Broke, despondent, and out of work after a dozen or more office jobs were lost to habitual lateness, absences, and poor attention, I met Bill Crosby, a Greenwich Village artist who had served in the Lincoln Brigade during the Spanish Civil War. As a member of his social circle I was marginally weaned on left-wing politics and the maelstrom of Bohemian life of the time and place. Toward the close of nearly three stormy years spent in his West Tenth Street flat, once occupied by Marlon Brando, I fitfully ventured into self-betterment: Speed-writing that promised ten extra dollars in secretarial paychecks, and psychotherapy at a New York clinic. In their own ways both nurtured enough stability to go after a night-school degree at Hunter College.

My first flirtation with the poetry classroom came with Jean Starr Untermeyer, whose course I audited at the New School. A gracious teacher, she treated her small brood of poets with an affection, tact, and flexibility that appealed to me. Although assignments were optional, I usually chose her suggested exercises, working with delight against the limits of the sonnet, the triolet, and the maddening sestina.

After an amicable split with Bill in November 1956, I settled into a fourth-floor walk-up on Twenty-third Street and was magnetically drawn to poetry readings, largely those held at the Cooper Union and the Ninety-second Street YMHA. Padraic Colum, e. e. cummings, and Léonie Adams were some among other artists who fueled my dedication to the Muse.

I sporadically exchanged formal, noncommittal letters with Marthe—bland "weather reports" that

The author with her first husband, Philip Rosen, 1961

sometimes lifted the curtain on a fact or two. She admitted to feeling only admiration and pity toward my father. Her motive for leaving me in an austere orphanage? To endow me with Catholic virtues and purity.

Much like a fruit bat's first taste of plum, publication whetted my appetite for more. I relished the image of countless *Herald Trib* readers sighing over my first published poem ("For Mama Streek"). Self-esteem was also nourished by winning Hunter College's Hotchner Poetry Award and the Richter Memorial Prize for "conspicuous ability in some field of English" during a single year. About this time I was elected to the Poetry Society of America, on whose board of directors I would later serve.

Support also came from the late Elizabeth Culbert, a librarian at *Recreation Magazine*, where I served as secretary and factotum to the editor. Elizabeth, who spoke fluent Spanish and French, had been a protégée of poet José García Villa as well as a professional chronicler and storyteller to children throughout the U.S. and Mexico. For almost twenty years, we met on and off in her London Terrace apartment to discuss translations of Lorca, Guillen, Machado, and the T'ang dynasty poets Tu Fu and Li Po. She became a rare and occasionally testy poetry-mother who respectfully read and encouraged my work.

My B.A. degree in English literature was a latchkey to the euphoria and exhaustion of teaching in some of the city's backwater schools. Never an early riser, sleep-short and stunned, I made my first journeys to a Bronx junior high school helping so-called "adjustment classes" learn parts of speech. But the adjustment was mine as I learned the custodial skills of public-school education, mediating among and soothing a hodgepodge of foreign-born, hyperactive, retarded, passive, or enraged students. "Never turn your back on a class . . . travel stairwells against the wall with an eye toward the rear," were some of the rules of engagement.

I left the often hair-raising world of junior high school for calmer precincts at year's end to teach English as a second language at New York University's American Language Institute. Foreign-born and feeling out of the mainstream, I identified with the dislocations and confusions of my adult students; their struggles at orienting to the unfamiliar had been mine as well. It was an awareness I clung to through the next decade of teaching.

I hardly gave up hopes of identifying my father despite my mother's and Bale's refusal to name him. Another avenue was Branigan, my other escort to America. I wrote to his still-active university address, and we agreed to meet at the Algonquin Bar during his next New York trip. "No," I lied over drinks at his clear concern about protecting my father's reputation, "I'm interested only in his looks and character—no names." Branigan was forthcoming with these innocent details, but inadvertently dropped a clue. "The Monsignor often dined with Jacques Maritain in Paris of the 1920s, and was friendly with John Meng." Meng was then president of Hunter College.

My letter to Meng, contrived as a heartfelt appeal from a former student, asked for the name of the "priest" described by Branigan. The ruse: the anonymous priest might lead me, an orphan, to lost parents he once had counseled. I trembled while opening Meng's reply weeks later: "Undoubtedly, the man whose name you want was Monsignor L." Meng's question, how I learned of his friendship with the Monsignor, went unanswered. My search for more facts was reserved for later.

At teaching split classes at NYU I felt a growing confidence born of status. And equally important, there was more time for writing. "The Inmost War of Jack Be Nimble," my second publication, appeared in *Noble Savage,* an early-sixties journal edited by Saul Bellow and Keith Botsford. I policed the Eighth Street Bookstore, furtively signing copies and spreading them about the magazine racks.

Years of therapy were drawing to a close. At my psychologist's parting prescription for a treat instead of a treatment, he recommended an aesthetic and affordable escape to Monhegan Island, Maine. Summer 1962. While bracketed by two lusty painters on a Monhegan House sofa, I spied a tall, attractive free-lance writer entertaining some nearby vacationers with a dazzling array of statistics about the Sane Nuclear Policy and strontium 90. Saul Stadtmauer's high forehead and boyish smile brightened an otherwise melancholy face. While drawn to him, at the time I was erratically involved with Phil Rosen, a jazz musician, postman, playwright, social worker, English teacher, and poet then traveling in Europe.

Saul and I fed hamburger meat to rock-pool anemones, slogged through moonlit marsh water, and flung wildflowers from the prow of the *Balmy Days* returning us to the mainland and home. By tradition, if the cast-off flowers floated back to shore,

Colette with Saul Stadtmauer on their wedding day,
July 26, 1964

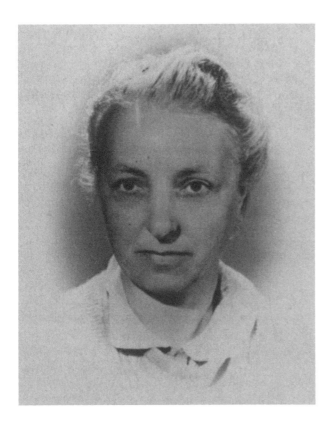

"My mother, Marthe Dulong, in her fifties"

so would we. Both happened, with a few detours between. When Phil returned from the Continent, he asked for breathing room that was filled by Saul bearing gourmet cheeses, canned anchovies, and pimentos from his father's Connecticut grocery store. Congenial talkers, agnostics, stargazers, and word and book lovers, we were also bound by our histories of childhood frustrations and psychotherapy.

Through an unconscious calculation, I became pregnant at the same age as did my mother, a conception that might even have coincided with the month or week of her own. Neither of us was ready for parenthood, and Saul was then at an emotional arm's length from marriage. Angry and remorseful after the abortion, I turned for solace to Phil, my intermittent lover who unexpectedly proposed. Despite his last-minute forebodings, we married on Saint Agnes' Eve, January 1963, during the week of Robert Frost's death. A poem that appeared in the *Nation* brought little comfort during days of desertions and shaky reunions as Phil shuttled his scant belongings between our apartments. By agreement, I was served with annulment papers at the end of the year. But the

mythic wildflowers had rooted deep on the beachfront of Monhegan.

Unexpectedly, Saul and I met again on the island. The wildflowers we once more cast overboard were as resolute as before, and one year later, we returned as honeymooners. I felt safer in marriage, more conventionally settled, and more inclined to enter the prevailing currents of contemporary poetry. I registered for a workshop conducted by Denise Levertov at the Ninety-second Street Y. Although the competitive mood in the class chilled my inspiration, I was touched by Levertov's artistry and erudition. I continue to recommend a number of her reading suggestions to my Columbia University, private, and West Side Y students: Rilke's *Letters to a Young Poet,* Ezra Pound's *ABC of Reading,* Stephen Spender's *Making of a Poem.*

Seeing "Colette Inez" in print made me feel quickened and visible, a spur to writing which I attacked with greater zest and purpose. And prizes and awards, how they gladden the heart of the striver. My first, earned in 1967 for "The Woman Who Loved Worms," judged by Peter Davison, was presented at a New England Poetry Society dinner. With a large body of work published through these decades, and with the toehold on immortality that printer's ink just might confer, I can understand the appeal of membership in what arguably may be the world's oldest profession. Could there be a finer balm for the questing ego?

That same poem titled my first collection, published by Doubleday in 1972. Saul and I were renting a cottage in Rockland County, New York, when the acceptance letter arrived. The book was a catalyst, and other letters and notices came after. A telegram announced it had won the 1972 Great Lakes Colleges Association National First Book Award, pollinating that garden of delights, poetry readings at colleges and universities. The mails delivered a *New York Times* review by Thomas Lask, who called it ". . . a book of substantial achievement." Perhaps on the strength of that review, I was invited in 1973 to conduct a poetry workshop at the New School, New York City, a post lasting ten years before I joined the Writing Program at Columbia University.

Before these appointments, I had also taught English to illiterates with Operation Second Chance, a federal antipoverty program whose intimacies introduced me to the foment of my students' family lives. Family. How might I go on to reclaim my own? It was then that Meng's letter, like an unpaid bill, finally goaded me to contact various chancery offices for information about my father. A web was spun.

"My father, the Monsignor"

School records reported my father earned his Ph.D. in Romance languages at Stanford University. An obit in the *San Francisco Monitor* placed his death in Paris, struck down by a heart attack at age forty-eight. An article in the *New Catholic Encyclopedia* filled in some of the gaps . . . "historian of medieval philosophy whose writings and participations in international historical societies stimulated basic research into the history of medieval thought."

More deception. Posing as a scholar, I wrote to my aunt Elizabeth, whose name was through stealth provided by her lawyer cousin. Would she supply details for a biography I proposed writing about the Monsignor? Her gracious replies, flushed with pride in her older brother, spoke of his illustrious career. Other letters glowingly mentioned the family's Jesuit novitiate, a nephew, and another seminarian at Saint Joseph's. Clearly, she idealized my father's saintliness and probity, his modest posthumous fame.

Revealing my origins would be a cruel shock to an aging lady and a *cause célèbre* within a family that would hardly countenance a priest's bastard. Then what is it that now prods me to open the pages of a closed book? Aunt Elizabeth is probably buried in Holy Cross Cemetery with her kin and mine. I have visited the cemetery, stood by the Monsignor's stone. And while I have not yet made any overtures to my father's people, he appears in my poems of loss and longing.

*

A postscript. The last of two meetings my husband and I shared with Marthe at the family's riverside home in Nérac came during my 1986 Guggenheim Fellowship year. Her earlier comment on news of my second marriage had been cool and vaguely critical: "Saul, I note, is not a Christian name."

After two years the house appeared shabbier, the wooden shutters a paler blue than I remembered, although the garden tended by her Jehovah's Witnesses tenants was as luxuriant as it was several springs before. I looked up at the second-story window, which framed nothing but emptiness. At the last visit, Marthe had leaned from it, beckoning us up a flight of stairs to her rooms. This time, we walked to the door, called out our names, and were greeted by a tall, elderly man with a benign face and manner who introduced himself as Maurice, her cousin from Paris.

"You are the American friends, of course." He shook our hands and led us up the stairs. When I saw no one on the top landing, I imagined he would tell me his cousin died in her sleep. A stroke or heart attack. He whispered: *"Elle est fatiguée,"* and accompanied us into a spacious room where I saw her looking immensely frail, packets of medication scattered on the side table. She pointed to a wheeled walker in the corner of the room and told us she suffered a badly bruised hip and arm during a recent fall. Her once-fluent English had begun to limp perceptibly.

Our words flew across her thin body, interrupted by the same questions she asked two years ago. "Where will your holidays take you?" "Have you seen the château of Henri de Navarre?" She looked at me indifferently, as if I were a casual visitor come to idle away part of the afternoon. We learned Maurice, who spoke no English, is a retired Latin professor summoned from Paris to attend her. An affable gentleman of the old school, he guided Saul and me on a tour of the property he would inherit. How pleased he was to show us the valuable antiques and to quote a price for each.

My mother relinquished her fragile hold on the hours. I saw her drift away. Her indisposition and age formed a shield I could not pierce; I remained an ally in her strategy of denial, an accomplice in this playlet which allowed her to pretend I was someone else. A letter sent to her the following month read in part:

New York, New York
June 19, 1986

Chere Marthe,

. . . I had hoped to speak to you about what is in my heart and has occupied and concerned me these many years, but I do not wish to alienate you, the only living relative who recognizes me, knows of my existence. And since cousin Maurice was not aware of our mother-daughter tie, it seemed inappropriate to ask for private time to talk to you.

Certainly, you know that through circumstances of my illegitimate birth, I am a stranger to my family both in France and in California. As the Monsignor's daughter, a fact I cannot even prove, his relatives would likely shut their doors to me.

Perhaps the case would not be the same from the point of view of the Dulongs. I am your rightful daughter with proper papers . . . but to come to the point, this is what I wish: for you to finally let the secret out, to announce my existence to the family.

Needless to say, times have changed since you gave me birth. With today's growing acceptance of births out of wedlock, I can only imagine compassion for your plight as a young single woman with a child in the early 1930s. Surely the family will be understanding and curious to know your daughter shares their bloodlines. You and they would have reason to be proud of my accomplishments as a poet and a teacher.

In the time left to us to make things right, I appeal to your sense of justice and look forward eagerly to your response.

With love,
Your Daughter

Her answer asked for mercy and my continued silence. Since you have waited this long, can you not wait a little longer, until after my death? she pleaded. Cousin Maurice has since written that Marthe has charged him with the duty of telling me she has taken to her bed and will no longer correspond. There was no answer to the last two letters I have written him. Has my mother told Maurice to discourage this strangely persistent American friend? Has she told

him in a deathbed confession who I am? Will Saul and I again see the snowcapped Pyrenees from Espien's churchyard cemetery in which my mother and my family are buried?

Spring 1986. When I last saw her, the withered stretch of day slumped toward mid-afternoon. My proud and willful mother appeared without knowing it to have won a reprieve from my need to break the silence. "Go with God, or whatever you believe in." Were those her thoughts following Saul and me down the steps and into the garden my grandparents planted at the century's turn? Episodes, large and small, are framed in God's will, she will say to herself, holding firmly to her faith as I to my doubts. Birth and alienation are to be endured. We are part of a blueprint, a celestial master plan; this is her credo. From a vase on her night table, Marthe handed me a rose before we left. It wilted during the long, hot drive to our distant hotel.

Without Toys at the Home

No dolls, nuns thought we would
quarrel, no spinning tops, tin
what-have-yous, wind-ups, anything
which might distract offsprings
of the solemn church. Nuns meant
well as did their priests mumbling
over games of chess.

At the Home, I gave my fingernails names
and jobs: old thumb, Pierre, the cop,
pinkie Francine, slim-hipped one-note
pianist.

In my palms I loved the roads
that led me to my realms: Lantasah, high
in the reaches of Ti, Whoa and Neigh,
crofts for my shires, stallions and nags.

The rocking horse I wanted lived in a yellow
book where a boy arranged trains
on the floor. His sister held a china doll
with lambswool yellow hair. I let my playstone
sleep in the doll's chiffonier,
in a velvet-lined drawer.

At the Home, our beds used to float like yachts
in the waves of our sleep. My sheet was a sail,
the pillow, a horse I rode calling to my second
finger, Dulce: "Stay away, nuns will find us
in my cloud."

A cloud won't stay put. More than once I've
been found out. My cheeks still smart from
being caught. Spring clouds, war clouds,
summer thunder, lulls and calms. Behind the
    gate
of the Home, the children have fallen in a
    mumble
of years, and their children have toys enough
to break, and their children enough for
    quarreling.

Setting Out from the Lowlands

Do buildings in America grow taller
than Saint Julian's?
What will eat you when you drown?
The questions swirled
as the gate unlocked,
and hungry to be noticed
in my new, red dress,
embroidered flowers at the gathered neck,
I left them in the afternoon,
a child singled out for departure
at the start of the war,
before tanks
bulldozed the Do Not Trespass signs
in the capital.

Nuns in black and white,
children in weekday brown
waved me good-bye. Birdsong Street,
Brussels, Belgium, farewell.
"Come see us when you're a fine lady,"
a child blew a kiss
that flew over paths
straight as the rule of nuns
who kept us in line for the Liturgy
of the Eucharist, midday prayer,
the daily chanting at Evensong.

Who would eat my morning gruel,
sing my praise to God at Lauds?
What kept the ship afloat?
A great fish? I expected no less
than such miracles.

In America I have made the sign
of the cross in buildings
taller than Saint Julian's
and sailed into years
beyond that child's imagining
of a fine lady come back to gloat
in the children's home
whose corridors caught echoes

from small, red mouths
that set whispers afloat,
calling "pray for us, pray for us."

Seasons of the War
For foster mother, Ruth

In the foggy spring of the far off war,
what could I have given her?
A wind-up doll instead of the child
the doctor told her might cure pinched
nerves, migraines, a fraying marriage of
fifteen years. What did she want?

I wanted her amber pomade, lip balm,
lotions, and lilac cologne, little jars of
rouge, vanishing creams, the lie of
"you are beautiful."

In the summer of the war,
on our porch with the blue glider
and white wicker chairs, what did she want?
Another start? Another drink? A body
not tricking her with blissful dreams
of mothering?

I longed to step into her paisley dress
with the fringed epaulets, to button
her yellow silk blouse, black birds on it.
I wanted them to fly out of her small breasts,
to sing to us in the morning.

In the stormy fall of the year,
I found her naked body in the hall.
"One too many," someone said. I'd seen the
    shot
glasses lined up on the bar downstairs
where she sat on a stool that spun
like a record on a phonograph.

Rumba tunes pulsed softly
when she convalesced. In her peach robe
and matching bandeau pulling back her hair,
how fragile she was and inconsolable.

I envied her cream of tomato soup,
orange pekoe tea, the red lacquered tray
with parasols stenciled in gold.
They were close to her.

"What can I do?" I wanted to run to the store
    for her.
"Go comb your hair," I was dismissed.
She'd return to exposes in True Confessions,
Silver Screen.

I stole her tortoise shell mirror,
her apple green comb
in the winter when F.D.R. declared war here.
She huddled by the radio,
sipping double scotches, straight.
"My nerves are raw," she'd sigh
and drape a hand across her eyes.
I learned to tiptoe up the stairs.

The war streaked headlines, dark bands
of birds, flying in a line.
Spring came. Summer. One day
she didn't answer to her name.

I thought I could have caught her last breath
in the tortoise shell mirror,
parted her hair with the apple green comb.

She was laid out in a beige
lace gown, lavender sash, her face,
a peaceful mask, but I stood by the casket
in a pink, puffed dress and choked back rage
as if it were a bone stuck in my throat.

Later, alone in her room, I did a rumba
with her empty clothes, held on to the sleeves,
imagined her soul lolling on the deck

of a Caribbean party boat.
And I combed and combed my hair.

Family Life

In his cups, he tore a twenty dollar bill
to make his mother, Nana, wince,
unzipped his mouth and shrieked out: "Bitch,
  you've ruined
everything, my goddamn life."
She turned her back to his whisky breath
and climbed the stairs like a martyred saint,
hummed a tune from the Hit Parade

while Dollie Dee in a purple snood was doing a
  samba
to Cugat's boom downstairs in the Whoopee
  Room;
lined up trophies from chug-a-lug beer fests,
  sozzled nights,
her maraschino cherry lips smeared in prints
at the edge of her glass, cocktail napkins,
  cigarettes.

Who was I to them? A guttersnipe, they said,
  one of the Pope's

unwanted, Brussels-born, a dingy sprout sitting
  in its dampness.
Dimwit music caving in my ears, snarls and
  battered silence,
I grew up hunched and humbled, pretended to
  forgive them—

but in dreams, Dollie fizzles, and her hubby
  chokes
a wad of money down his throat.
"I've Got a Feeling I'm Falling," his mama
  croons,
standing tall as a post I must leap past to scrap
  the lessons
I learned by rote in that skewed house.

Meeting in Nérac

My mother's face, a lantern at the window
lights a path to her door, to openings I hear
in her voice asking me to climb the stairs
to her booklined rooms.

I try to read the small print of her lips.
She turns away like a page too quickly skimmed.
The parchment of her skin whispers a story
of two scholars humbled by illicit love,
my lettered sires who signed me away.

When she crosses slowly to the room's far end
and perches on a brown wing chair, she is a
  queen
in ravelled sleeves who offers me a Baedeker
and the history of her town.
What she won't say floods the room with
  images:

she is naked, heavy breasts graze the water
as she wades into the river. In a shadowy cove,
the body swims languorously, one arm, then
  another
pulling her forward to the far shore.
There my father writes marginal notes on the
  edges
of a manuscript. He will comb her wet hair.
She will hum a song.

"How long is your holiday?" I am pulled short
from my musings by her voice. "The region is
  filled
with interesting ruins." Her English accent
  rings
in counterpoint with the sigh of palms on her
  red
tiled roof, in the south of France

where we speak after an absence of long years.
"Next year Halley's Comet returns" I say.
She recalls its glow and how she tugged at her
    father's
arm alongside the same blue-shuttered house
in which we talk of traveling
through the mother country.

Ruler of wanderers and lanterns of night, let
    her study
the comet one more time. I ask this for a woman
    of Nérac
from whom I inherit a love of quandaries: my
    doubt
of heaven, hers of the here and now. What else
    we meant
to call into question or deny stays unresolved
like an unfocused star.

The Papal Saw in a Roman Blind

I can almost hear the bells
rung by the priest who sired a child.
Nuncio, let that father rise
to sit at my right touch. One last
kiss to ease his grief in the afterlife.

I, his bastard, bid for calm
like a Papal See in a murmer of signs.
Confessor, hear my doubts of the Seven
Dolors of Mary, Elevation of the Host.
I can see the church walking

on its knees and offer my alms
to a ghost who cannot see the weight
of years, blood-soaked stones and
the orphanage drilling its wards
on the telling of beads.

My father, does he hear the lambs
bleating the hundredth psalm
of man's praise to God? Vicar of Christ,
here is a silver monstrance, here is
a chasuble of gold to pay for his release.

All our wrongs take refuge in the hospice
of time. I make this offering to lift up
my father's heart out of his remains,
mysterious as particles of light
flooding the earth from the sun.

Winter Modes

What rose from those fallen days?
Tricks of light the ancients construed
as proof of doom or bliss.
We slept beneath the whale of night
and dreamed seven blue eggs in
the Pleiades would hatch blue fire,
or damsel fish in a coral reef.

You said the saline level of primordial waters
was a quotient in our blood.
I tasted salt on your tongue.

Summer tides. The silver play of waves
whispered syllables of fish, sighs of lost
turtle years in underwater groves.
And inky clouds, the squids' defense
against insomniacal sharks.

In the jack pine, sparrows and jays
said who they were by their call.
Speedwell, lobelia grew in meadows we trailed.
We danced from happiness on the path to the
    sea
in that first summer of gazing at the Perseids,
of feeding anemones on the island rock pool.

Years later in winter, I ask if the nature
of snowflakes is known. You say temperature,
moisture, wind defines what transforms,
the single-planed, six-sided forms, not one
resembling the other since snow began.
You've gathered facts in a bouquet.

I ask you to look through the keyhole
to threadbare winters of another love.
Ragged snow, bridal lace. My fingers are almost
    blue
with cold on the January night I curse Saint
    Agnes
for blessing my first union. When did I drop
the gold band in the sea?

Was it in summer? The residue of blasted stars
dims in my recollection of hungers and desires
before we married in July on the feast of Saint
    Anne.
And in a union of circles moving towards their
    core,
I hold you fast, my love,
under the thorns of a red heaven
blooming planets and stars.

BIBLIOGRAPHY

Poetry:

The Woman Who Loved Worms and Other Poems. Garden City, N.Y.: Doubleday, 1972.

Alive and Taking Names and Other Poems. Athens: Ohio University Press, 1977.

Eight Minutes from the Sun. Upper Montclair, N.J.: Saturday Press, 1983.

Family Life. Santa Cruz, Calif.: Story Line Press, 1988.

Party Lights. Forthcoming.

Nonfiction:

Notes from an Exiled Daughter (memoir). Forthcoming.

Damon Knight

1922-

Damon Knight at the Clarion Writers' Workshop, 1988

I was born in Baker, Oregon, at midnight on September 19, 1922, the only child of Frederick Stuart Knight and Leola Damon Knight. They seem to have decided I was going to be a writer even before I was born—at any rate, my father told me he had chosen my name, Damon Francis Knight, to be a euphonious byline on the model of "Stuart Edward White." "Francis," which I dropped in adolescence, was for my grandfather Frank Knight. He was a senator in the Dakota Territory, then a South Dakota farmer; he moved to Oregon after my father was grown.

My mother's people were from Ames, Iowa; they also emigrated to Oregon, around the turn of the century. My mother's father tried his hand at store-keeping and teaching school, but was never successful

at either; his wife died when my mother was six, and he married another, a sharp-tongued woman who kept him under control. He left some very passable verses.

On both sides, my ancestors were midwestern Protestants. My father was taught that drinking, smoking, dancing, and card-playing were all sinful; he relaxed his views on all but the first when he was grown. On my mother's side most of the men were ministers; I have a crayon portrait of her grandfather, a stern-featured man with a full beard and shoulder-length hair; and one of his wife, an even sterner crone who looks thirty years older, even allowing for the evident fact that she has lost all her teeth.

My father ran away from the South Dakota farm when he was sixteen, went to the West Coast and put

Mother, Leola Damon, about 1903

himself through college by washing dishes. He met my mother when she was an elementary-school teacher in Bingen, Washington, and they were engaged; then he went off to teach for four years in a rural school in the Philippines. She broke off the engagement, but when he came back they were married anyhow.

In photographs he brought back my father is slender, but when I knew him his paunch and deep chest made him look stocky. He was thirty-eight when I was born, and my mother was thirty-five. It was her third pregnancy; the first two children were stillborn girls.

My father was a frustrated newspaperman, and taught a journalism class in the high school whose principal he became in 1928; his heroes were Irvin S. Cobb and Will Rogers. He was a shy man who felt emotion but could not express it. Although he had run away from the farm, he always loved farming and believed in hard physical labor; he was concerned about me because I didn't sweat enough. He owned a farm left him by his father and kept tenants on it, hoping that someday I might want to live there. It

had good water, pasture, etc., as he described it, but when I went there with him as a child and tramped over it with the tenant, it was nothing to my eye but a sea of partly dried mud.

In the summers, while my father took more education courses in summer school, my mother and I went to the seaside resort town of Newport, where her stepmother kept a boarding house called the Damon House. The stepmother was a wrinkled, shrewd old woman, famous for her table. (It was wasted on me—I wouldn't eat seafood.)

We spent the long afternoons on the beach. There were dunes of golden sand that broke away in chunks, nascent sandstone, and I pretended that it was gold and that I was rich. At low tide there were cratered rocks covered with anemones that closed and squirted if you touched them, and there were miles of flat sand on which to run trailing a stick or a long strand of kelp. A few miles away there was a cove, accessible only at low tide, where the sand was covered inches deep with the polished shells of periwinkles. Somewhere there must have been crabs, for I remember bringing home a bucket of them, and waking up later to find them all over the walls.

I loved this place, and looked forward to it all year with longing and disbelief. There was a little library shaped like a lighthouse; on the boardwalk I remember on one side a jewelry shop whose windows were filled with polished pieces of moss agate and jasper; on the other, a candy shop in whose window the taffy machine endlessly revolved its shining arms. The taffy was hard and brittle; you bought it in porous chunks broken off with a nickel-plated hammer, and it crunched and melted sublimely in the mouth.

I drew pictures from the time I could hold a pencil, and in my teens made some clumsy attempts at painting without any instruction. It seems curious to me now that my parents did not send me to the local artist, Percy Manser, who occasionally gave lessons, but I don't remember thinking this was odd at the time. My father was a frugal man; he owned few luxuries, bought nothing he couldn't pay cash for, saved string and lead foil, and when he died left my mother a modest nest egg, which she multiplied in the stock market.

Hood River, where my father was principal of the high school for twelve years, is a little town on the confluence of the Hood River and the Columbia. (It appears as "Dog River" in my novel *The Man in the Tree*.) The climate is mild and wet. Two snowcapped mountains are visible from Hood River—Mount Hood and Mount Rainier. The town is built on a hillside as steep as San Francisco's, and I was forever walking up and down it to and from school, until I could go as fast uphill as I could on level ground.

Although toward the end I longed to get away, looking back I can see that Hood River was not a bad place for children to grow up. The streets were ours for bicycling and skating; we even skated down Creamery Hill, reaching a velocity that would have killed us if we had run into anything, but we never did. In the spring evenings we gathered in a group of ten or twenty to play hide and seek or red-light or king of the hill. I remember the purple twilights and the scent of lilacs and the lonesome sound of "Allee-allee-out's-in-free."

Because of my slow physical development I began losing touch with my contemporaries when I was about eight, and got most of my ideas about life out of books. When I tried to apply these to the world around me, I was usually disappointed. *Boys' Life,* for example, published a series of stories about a bunch of boys who had a secret club, with mysterious hailing signs and so on. I organized one like it on my block, but when I chalked the assembly symbol on the sidewalk, the other members went on riding their tricycles. Later I tried to organize another club which would assemble model airplanes and sell them for profit, but when I tried my first kit, I put it together wrong. In shop, I could not plane a board smooth or wash the paint out of a brush. I continued to read novels, especially English novels, because England was a long way away and I could believe that life was different there.

There was one family of Jews in our town; the father ran a butcher shop and the children were fat. There was a Chinese restaurant which must have had a Chinaman in it. About half the kids in school were nisei, but they all lived out in the valley, where their parents were orchardists, except Roku Yasui's father, who kept a little store. I can't remember ever going into the store, but Roku sometimes brought strange and wonderful things from it—paper flowers that bloomed in water, tiny pieces of paper that turned into photographs of temples when you put two together and moistened them, candy covered with edible rice paper. The Japanese kids had their own dances, out in the valley, and did not attend the school dances. (I didn't either, so I don't call them "ours.") When the war came, the Japanese were rounded up and sent to concentration camps; signs went up in windows, "No Japs Served Here," and the names of nisei servicemen were removed from the register in the park.

Father, Frederick S. Knight, in the Philippines, about 1914

About the school year, what I chiefly remember is the wet galoshes, and the pain of opening their snow-choked metal clasps with cold fingers. Zippers were new, and frequently got stuck. They were used on windbreakers but not on the flies of trousers yet, and one of the favorite schoolyard tricks was "ripping" another boy—pulling all his fly buttons open with two hooked fingers. One year I remember the snow thawed and froze again—a "silver thaw"—forming a glassy crust. We children struggled up the hill, three steps forward and two back. On another day the sky was black at noon—all across the river, smoke was pouring up from the burning forest.

Our house in Hood River was one of two identical white frame cottages on adjoining lots in a neighborhood of much older houses. It had a living room and dining room, symbolically separated by a false beam, two bedrooms, bath and kitchen. When I grew too old to sleep in my mother's room, my father hired a carpenter to help him and built another room beside the back porch. There was no central heating; the kitchen was kept warm by the old wood-burning range, and the living room first by a potbellied coal stove and later by an oil-burning space heater that was not much bigger. On cold nights we took hot-water bottles to bed with us.

Our street was just outside a respectable residential area and was not far from being a slum, although that never occurred to me then. Up the hill, separated from our house by their back garden and ours, was the elegant home of Mr. Breckinridge, the school superintendent, whose daughter Ada May was my playmate up until the time she started experimenting with high heels and lipstick. Around us were old two-story houses in various stages of decay; the one next door even had a barn, weathered gray like the house. The children who lived there were barefoot and ragged and had the gray-brown faces of the poor, but they were active, alert, and good-humored. The oldest, a boy of sixteen or so, drew cartoons that were better than mine—and I was not modest about my drawing—then dropped them on the ground; I never could understand why he valued them so little. I kept everything, and counted my possessions like a miser. I knew and cherished every marble; when a boy talked me into playing "for keeps" and took four of mine, I mourned. I was inconsolable when a tree surgeon cut off the low horizontal limb of the cherry tree in the front yard, the one I had used to climb on. When my father took down the old metal toothbrush rack in the bathroom and put up a porcelain one, I made such a fuss that he put up the old one on the back porch, and let me hang my toothbrush there until I got tired of that.

As I grew older I played with younger children, sometimes joined by another outcast, a boy even older than myself. He was called Break, short for Break-a-leg, from an incident when he had fallen off his sled and bellowed that his leg was broken.

As time advanced I lost even these playmates and fell back on solitary pleasures. I attacked the Hood River library in various ways, by authors—all of Dickens, all of Dumas—then by subject—all the pirate books—and finally at random. One of my pleasant memories is of some illness when the librarian sent me out a pile of books, all by authors new to me. I read children's books and fairy tales, but I also read romantic novels and novels of manners that I only half understood. I read a novel called *V.V.'s Eyes*, which had belonged to an uncle of mine, and found that he had written in the margin encouraging comments such as "Go it, V.V.!" This was my first

experience with the defacers of books. For years I could not bring myself to make any mark in a book, even when I had it for review; now I do it, but always with a feeling of guilt, and I use a soft pencil in case anyone should want to erase what I write.

In the thirties I became intensely aware of pulp magazines. There were *Spicy Adventure* and *Spicy Mystery*, which I did not dare buy, even in the dingy little secondhand store at the bottom of a side street in town. There were air-war magazines, which I did buy. One story concerned a squadron leader who was having headaches and whose hair was falling out; it turned out that a German agent had been concealing a capsule of radium under his pillow.

Then I saw and bought an issue of something called *Amazing Stories*. It was bigger than other pulps, about 8½ × 11, and the cover, in sick pastels, showed two helmeted and white-suited men aiming rifles at a bunch of golliwogs. This was the August-September 1933 issue, and the cover story was "Meteor-Men of Plaa" by Henry J. Kostkos. That was the beginning.

The illustrations in *Amazing*, the work of a man named Leo Morey, were sketchy, gray, and ill-defined, but that somehow increased the feeling of mystery and alienness in them. In Hugo Gernsback's magazines, especially the back issues, I admired the work of Frank R. Paul in other ways, but I got from it much the same satisfaction. Paul's drawings look a little quaint now, because of the knee breeches and the statuesque poses, but he was endlessly fertile at inventing strange landscapes and filling them with the flora and fauna of alien worlds.

Not all the science fiction magazines were available in Hood River, and I could not always afford to buy them, but when we made our annual family trip to Portland it was not only Jantzen's Beach (the amusement park) that drew me, it was the second-hand stores with their stacks of *Science Wonder*s and *Amazing*s. On one visit I found a new magazine on the newsstands, one I had never even heard of before—*Astounding Stories*. Back in our hotel room I developed a fever; it turned out that I had the measles and we were all quarantined. My parents must have been chagrined, but I was blissful, lying there reading "The Son of Old Faithful" by Raymond Z. Gallun.

At home along one wall over my bed I had shelves put up, and presently these shelves were filled with science-fiction magazines. I read and reread every one, including all the parts I didn't understand. I read the editorials and the readers' letters; I read the ads. I read the stories believing that something like them must be true. I yearned to go to Barsoom, and I spread my arms to the red planet, but nothing happened. I tried to calculate if I was likely to live to see the year 2000. I haunted libraries and bookshops, and seized on any book whose title made it sound as if it might be science fiction. But I also read with fascination all the Saint novels of Leslie Charteris. The Saint was precisely everything I was not and longed to be—grown up, strong, handsome, fearless, cool in the presence of women. I yearned after Leslie Howard in *The Scarlet Pimpernel*, too, and I read my way through eight or ten of Raphael Sabatini's novels. These were particularly satisfying, because the heroine always misunderstood the hero and had to apologize later.

I kept running into incomprehensible responses in other people around me, as when I criticized the new comic strip *Flash Gordon* because the natives of Mongo spoke English, and a friend of mine said, "What else would they talk?" I came to believe that somewhere in the outside world, probably in New York, things were altogether different, and Hood River became hateful to me because I couldn't get out of it.

Everything I saw around me led me to the belief that the world was badly organized: politics, religion, and education were incomprehensibly absurd, social relationships only a little less so, and all the young people were under the thumbs of the old. Even science fiction, to which I had fled as a refuge, eventually began to seem unbearably conventional. I never became a Marxist or revolutionary, being too skeptical of dogma of any kind, but in my own fiction, over and over, I blew the established system apart as thoroughly as I could. "Not with a Bang," "To Serve Man," *Hell's Pavement, A for Anything*, and many others were expressions of this urge, and I am still at it in the series of near-future novels that begins with *CV*.

My father had an old Corona portable on which he taught me to make soldiers with ampersand bodies, capital M's for legs, virgules for guns, and quotation-mark feet. Later he traded this in on a Royal portable, and still later gave me the Royal when he got a newer machine. I taught myself touch typing from the school manual, and used this machine for the next twenty years. When I gave it away it was still working.

In high school I became the cartoonist for the school paper, the *Guide*. It was a mimeographed paper, well produced under my father's direction, and it won some state prizes. We had a big A. B. Dick mimeograph (which had to be hand-fed because of the folded sheets we used) and other modern equipment, including a mimeoscope on a floor stand, then not a standard item (in fact, I have never seen another). We had shading plates, lettering guides, and a set of ballpoint styli, with which I learned to make a graduated line that might have been drawn with a brush. I dropped out part of one year when the editor offended me by tattling on me to my father for a minor offense; except for that, my cartoons appeared weekly for three years, and by the time I graduated I was an expert in an art that turned out to be dying.

My parents were concerned about my physical weakness and tried to build me up in various ways. All one summer my father took me up to the high school every day and played a set or two of tennis with me in the hot sun—not bad going for a man of fifty-six. Later he bought me a membership in the country club, and I went out there with my bag of secondhand clubs fairly often and bashed my way around the course, topping and slicing.

I went through a phase when I wanted to go out on the country roads and drive as fast as I could. I had fantasies of meeting some girl in the yard of an undiscovered farmhouse, but I knew nothing like that was going to happen, and I took it out in speed. Once as I made a left-hand turn at an intersection I failed to notice a pickup truck approaching from the right until I looked out my window and saw it bouncing along in the ditch. The accident was clearly my fault, but the man in the truck was good-natured about it, and the insurance company paid for his broken axle.

In the late thirties, after a few years in the doldrums, the science-fiction magazines began to pick up again. *Astounding* became livelier under a new editor, John W. Campbell, Jr. *Wonder* had been converted into *Thrilling Wonder* and was bad but interesting. There was a rash of new magazines. Campbell brought out *Unknown*, which enthralled me. Among the other new magazines were two called *Super Science* and *Astonishing*, both edited by Frederik Pohl, and in one or the other was a regular listing of magazines published by fans. I sent for some, and got into correspondence with Bob Tucker, the editor of *Le Zombie*. I did some cartoons for him. I published my own fanzine, *snide*. From this, other correspondence followed, including some with Richard Wilson, Donald A. Wollheim, and Robert W. Lowndes, New York fans, members of a group that called itself the Futurian Society.

I wrote and illustrated *snide* myself, and produced a hundred copies or so on a tray hectograph I had been given for Christmas. The cover of the first issue showed a man with a briefcase running after a rocket ship which had just taken off; he was shouting, "Hey, wait!"

When *Astounding* came into full flower in the late thirties, with stories in every issue by Robert A. Heinlein and L. Sprague de Camp, and beautifully realistic brush-drawn illustrations by Hubert Rogers,

I would have given anything to be Campbell, or Heinlein, or Rogers. I sent Campbell stories, and he sent them back with letters of rejection on gray stationery, signed with his looping scrawl. I now know how much more this was than I had any right to expect, but I was frustrated because I couldn't sell the

With The Pioneer Man, *University of Oregon, 1923*

stories and had no idea how to make them better. I drew cartoons and inked them in, and *Amazing* bought one for three dollars. (A spacesuited man has found a robot in a cavern, and is about to push one of the buttons on its chest; the robot is waving a huge mallet behind its back. Caption: "Wonder what this one does.") This success elated me, and I sent *Amazing* more cartoons and proposals, but they never bought another.

I kept trying to write, spurred on by one of Campbell's periodic announcements that he would pay sixty dollars for a short story (inconceivable wealth). I could start stories but could not finish them; baffled, I gave the manuscripts to my father with a covering letter to myself and asked him to put them in his safe-deposit box. Later, without opening the box, I did succeed in finishing two or three new stories and mailed them to Robert W. ("Doc") Lowndes, who was then trying to set himself up as an agent. Lowndes sent most of them back with patronizing letters about plot and characterization; then he wrote me that Donald A. Wollheim was putting together the first issue of a new magazine and would print my story "Resilience" if I would donate it. (Wollheim had no editorial budget for the magazine, and had to fill the whole issue this way.) I of course agreed.

My last year in high school was a nightmare of boredom. When it was over, my father offered to send me to college, but that was the last thing I wanted. We agreed that I would go to Salem for a year and attend the WPA Art Center there. I lived in a boarding house at first, run by an insurance man and his fat, comely, cheerful wife. At her table I ate my first steak and found it unchewable; it was not until years later that I discovered steak did not have to be tough.

Later I moved to a rooming house run by a Bohemian lady and her twenty-year-old daughter. (She was not a carefree artist with loose morals, but a Hungarian from Bohemia.) There was also a son who was studying for the priesthood, and who surprised me by sitting around with us one evening drinking beer, smoking, and telling dirty jokes—three pleasures I was having for the first time. I was mildly smitten with the daughter, but as usual she was too old for me.

The Art Center occupied the basement of a building that I think must have been an abandoned school. There were classes in ceramics, figure drawing, design, lettering, sculpture, and other things. My sculpture teacher was a shy, almost illiterate, scrawny, unshaven little man named George Blais, who had got

himself written about in *Time* the year before by teaching sculpture to a class of blind young people. His scorn for the conventional heroic half-reliefs then being carved in front of the new capitol building, and for the gilded woodsman on its dome, was pure and noble. He cared about nothing but art, and when I last knew him was working in a sawmill to support his family while he taught himself abstract painting. Under his direction I made a few small statuettes and cast them in plaster, and did one piece in sandstone (stolen from a building site). It was one of the best times of my life.

While I was in Salem, Don Wollheim's first issue of *Stirring Science Stories* appeared, with my story in it. The printers had changed "Brittle People" to "Little People" in the first sentence, rendering the story unintelligible, but I was proud of it anyway. In one of my classes was a marvelous little old woman who told me she was also a writer, and had just finished a story called "The Hegira of Hector Hepplethwaite." I was so impressed with this title that I have remembered it ever since, although I have forgotten her name. She was kind to me, as everyone there was—took me to lunch in Portland and introduced me to borscht. We had gone there to see a statue put up by a Portland sculptor who taught at the university; it was a commissioned piece for a park on the waterfront, and what he had done was a stylized male figure, very simple, with its hands crossed on the hilt of a sword. Seen against the sky and water, it gave me my first intense esthetic experience. The Portland women's clubs hated it ferociously, and a year or two later, when some work was being done on the park, a bulldozer happened to knock it down.

The year after I graduated, the school board decided not to renew my father's contract, and he retired. He bought a mimeograph, set up shop in my old room, and wrote and published (on long newsprint pages, just like the *Guide*) a book called *The Stencil Duplicated Newspaper*. (He would have called it *The Mimeographed Newspaper*, but A. B. Dick would not give permission.) I contributed a chapter on cartooning to this work. He published an edition of five or six hundred copies and sold them himself through the mail. It was from this book, probably, that the Library of Congress got my middle name, Francis. I dropped it in my teens and never used it professionally, but librarians across the nation have patiently written it in on the title pages of all my books.

I considered "Damon Knight" unusual enough and once wrote irritably to a Blue Cross person who had asked for my policy number that I thought I was the only Damon Knight in Southern California. It turned out later that I was probably wrong in this: an actor named Damon Knight made wire-service headlines in the mid-sixties by shooting holes in a closetful of his own clothes. Keith Laumer told me about another Damon Knight, an air-force engineer in England, and I have a second cousin by that name who lives in Eugene now and confuses people who try to call me on the phone.

I began to feel that I had no vocation as an artist, or any desire to go on to school, and when the Futurians invited me to come to New York and live with them, my parents agreed to let me go. The World Science Fiction Convention that year was in Denver, and they drove me there over precipitous mountain roads. It was late at night when they dropped me in front of the hotel, but I found a few fans standing around in the convention room. Sick with embarrassment, I goose-stepped toward them and raised my hand in a Nazi salute. They asked me who I was and I told them. "Ah, Damon Knight," said Forry Ackerman kindly.

The Futurians, when I met them later, were an odd-looking group. Wollheim was the oldest and least beautiful. (Kornbluth once introduced him as "this gargoyle on my right.") He was, I learned later, almost pathologically shy, but he was the unquestioned leader of the group, and John Michel, who worshiped him, later informed me that Donald's personality was such that he could have any woman he wanted. Lowndes was ungainly and flat-footed; he had buckteeth which made him lisp and sputter, and a hectic glare like a cockatoo's. Michel was slender and looked so much more normal than the rest that he seemed handsome by contrast, although he was pockmarked and balding. He had a high voice and stammered painfully. Cyril Kornbluth, the youngest (a few months younger than I), was plump, pale, and sullen. He had narrow Tartar eyes and spoke in a rumbling monotone; he looked ten years older than he was. He liked to play the ogre; at the art auction that weekend he bid fifty cents for a Cartier illustration, got it, and tore it in half. At the costume ball, where I made the mistake of appearing, in pajamas dyed green, as a character in one of Jack Williamson's novels, Kornbluth said loudly, "I know it's John Star, but who *is* she?"

Chester Cohen, about my age, had wavy blond hair and a yellow beard grown for the occasion (he appeared at the ball as Nehemiah Scudder, a "prophet" in a story by Robert A. Heinlein). Although he was neurotic and jumpy, a nail-picker (not enough left to bite), he was able to freeze on command and hold a pose indefinitely; once Michel pretended to hypnotize him in the elevator and left him there, to the consternation of the hotel employees. They had to find out who he was and carry him up to his room, where he lay like a corpse until Michel arrived and snapped his fingers.

Heinlein, a handsome man in his thirties, was the guest of honor at the convention, and we glimpsed him and his slender brown wife Leslyn occasionally. Cohen was struck by the punch line of one of Heinlein's anecdotes ("Evidently you don't realize I'm half Jewish. Come, Leslyn!") and kept making up variations on it for years, e.g., "Evidently you don't realize I'm half pissed. Come, Leslyn (hic)!"

After the convention we divided into two groups; Kornbluth, who had been on a trip to Los Angeles with Cohen, got into one car with Wollheim, Michel, and me, leaving Chet to go home with Lowndes. "I've seen a lot of Chester Cohen," Cyril said. We were traveling by "wildcat bus"—sharing expenses with a good-natured man named Jack Inskeep, who was driving to Cleveland. On the way, Wollheim expanded on an idea of his that the surface of the earth was composed of strips of solid material about two miles across, with roads running down the middle, the rest being hollow. Kornbluth played up to this, thinking of feeble objections which Wollheim demolished one by one.

We stopped overnight at The Mark Twain Hotel in St. Louis, where we shared an antediluvian room. The bath was across the hall, but the tub had evidently not been used or usable in years; it was full of large beetles. Here, probably, we picked up the bedbugs which we battled for months afterward.

Near Columbus, our driver obligingly stopped so that Cyril could meet his girl, Mary Byers, who lived on a farm with several fierce uncles. We went to a bar, and Inskeep played the pinball machines while Cyril and Mary gazed into each other's eyes. In Cleveland he left us and Wollheim took a train, while the rest of us went on by bus. It had been a long, hot trip, and Michel was growing irritable. He was bothered by the gas fumes in the back of the bus, and wanted me to tell the driver to move us. "Tell him we're three sick boys," he said.

The Futurians at that time lived in a railroad apartment on 103d Street. It had five rooms in a row: first the kitchen/bathroom (the tub was under the drain board), then three small bedrooms for Michel and me and a guest, then the living room, which was also Lowndes's bedroom. It was bare but sunny and clean. I paid my share of the rent (I don't remember how much, but probably about seven dollars), and

Damon with a friend, Baker, Oregon, about 1924

was expected to keep my room clean and wash the dishes. Lowndes did the cooking; his specialty was Futurian Chop Suey—noodles, hamburger, and a can of cream of mushroom soup; it was better when it had rotted a day in the refrigerator. I don't now remember what Michel's contribution was. We had wall newspapers, in which Lowndes published communiqués about our campaign against the Enemy (bedbugs). We squirted the mattresses with kerosene, and eventually vanquished them. All the Futurian apartments, then and later, had names; this one was the Futurian Embassy. Kornbluth stayed over on weekends; he lived with his parents, and so did Wollheim.

None of us had any money. For amusement in the evenings, we played poker for stakes of fifteen cents each, and drank California wine at fifty cents a gallon. When the game broke up about midnight, we would walk down to Times Square to look at the advertising signs, have a cup of coffee in the Times Square Cafeteria, and walk back.

I adopted all the Futurians' attitudes. They looked down on fannish activity, and so did I. They said they were Communists; I said I was a Commu-

nist. They expressed contempt for Campbell and his stable of writers; I lost interest in *Astounding* and stopped reading it. They were nearly all native New Yorkers who would have died rather than get on a sight-seeing bus; I lived in Manhattan for ten years and never went to the Statue of Liberty, or the Cloisters, or took a boat trip around the island. We lived quite near Grant's Tomb and I passed it frequently, but never went in.

Kornbluth organized something called the Inwood Hills Literary Society, which met once a month either at his house or at ours. It was a forerunner of the Milford Conference; each writer was expected to produce a story every month for criticism. When the group met in the Embassy, everybody there but me was a member, and I had to leave the room. I thought this was a bit thick, since I lived there. When the group met at Cyril's, however, I used the time to write, and gradually my work got a little better.

Kornbluth was writing stories under various pseudonyms for all the Futurian magazines. He was nineteen. One of his unfinished stories, which I found abandoned at the Embassy, began with a flashback in the stream of consciousness of an intelligent mouse during intercourse. Another fragment of his, which I found in a drawer, was a long poem in the style of Edgar Guest that ended, "Emulate the idiot who eats his own shit—*it's delicious!*"

At home in New York Kornbluth played the ogre seldom; his humor was sardonic and sometimes cruel, but he was the least malicious of the Futurians. He played at being grown up. One fall day he came in wearing a hat, solemnly explaining that in cold weather a man needed headwear in order to balance the bulkier silhouette of his overcoat. When drunk, he was playful.

Michel was a poseur; he affected corduroy jackets and trousers, smoked a pipe, talked about his dates. He had had several operations for bone tuberculosis, and had ugly craters in his legs. He took me on an Elevated tour of New York, borrowed a dollar, and said, "Don't tell Donald." He had had three or four stories published, and managed to give the impression that he was the most professional writer of us all. When drunk he was pettish and quarrelsome.

Lowndes was the one we always found ourselves talking about when he was not there. Often when we were going somewhere together, for no evident reason he would cross the street and walk by himself. His parents had been fundamentalists who thought even the Sunday comics were sinful, and Lowndes as a small boy had had to crawl under the porch to read them. In his youth he had been in the CCC, and his arms and legs remained muscular although the rest of him was flabby. When drunk he lurched hideously, and sometimes passed out with his eyes open.

Wollheim had two parlor tricks. One was to put one arm behind his back, bring the hand up all the way around his face and lay it on his opposite cheek. The other was to put a small flashlight up his nose and turn it on; his whole nose would then light up like a pink cucumber. He dressed like an undertaker and carried a black umbrella. He did not drink at all, and his remote brown eyes were always watchful.

I myself looked like the ghost of a blond Charlie Chase. We were a gallery of grotesques, but we were all talented to one degree or another, and we counted on that to save us. We were anything but a close-knit group, and yet we stood together against the outside world. A Futurian crest, designed by Kornbluth, had a large flat-headed screw with the legend *"Omnes qui non Futurianes sunt."*

None of us knew any girls, or had any way of meeting them, except Wollheim, whose girlfriend, Elsie Balter, was part of our circle. Wollheim's courtship was slow. Elsie, who was older than Donald, was a decidedly plain but beautifully good-natured and kind woman. Wollheim gave Elsie a friendship ring after about five years, and after another year or so they were married. (Telling me about the friendship ring, Elsie said, "And then, do you know what Donald did? He *kissed* me.")

I see now that if any of the rest of us had gone to work, or to school, we would have met girls in any desired numbers, but this did not occur to us. We once got dressed up and went to a Trotskyist meeting because we had heard the Trotskyists had a lot of horny girls. There were a couple of girls, but they wanted no part of us. Another time we went down to Greenwich Village to Anton Romatka's poetry circle, because Donald said we were the real writers and would command instant respect, but it did not work out that way.

We were too poor to go to movies often, or buy books, or travel, or eat at restaurants, but we were used to that and did not mind it. Our recreation was talking. We played endless word games—People (a form of Twenty Questions), Plastered Bastard, a rhyming riddle game, and Tsohg (Ghost backwards). When on rare occasions we did have money enough to go out, it was usually to the Dragon Inn in Greenwich Village, where I ate fried rice because it was the only Chinese food I could stand.

We moved so many times that I can't remember the sequence. It was a renter's market then; if we wanted to move we just hired a truck and went, usually owing the last month's rent. On one occasion we had to pay up, though, because Lowndes wrote two letters, one to the landlord wishing him bad luck in the hereafter, and one to Elsie giving our new address, and put them in the wrong envelopes.

Lowndes and Michel and I shared another apartment after the Embassy; it was in Chelsea and was called the Futurian Fortress. At various times Lowndes and Michel, Lowndes and Jim Blish, Michel and Larry Shaw briefly shared apartments.

I liked living in the Embassy and the Fortress, but I didn't like washing dishes, and I hated cleaning up my room. After a while it was noticed that there were dust balls under my bed. Coincidentally some tension developed between Michel and me, beginning when I flicked him with a rag as he came out of the bathroom; the rag happened to be dirty, and Michel was morbidly afraid of germs as a result of his recurring illness; he exploded into rage and kicked me. I thought it best to accept the invitation of a fat, pimply fan who had turned up trying to get any one of us to go to dinner at his house. That night or shortly thereafter, the Futurians held a council and decided that I must mend my ways or get out. I chose to get out. Chet Cohen, who was living in an apartment called the Raven's Roost, formerly occupied by Richard Wilson and before that by Dave Kyle, invited me to move in and I did so. Chet was more my style; he was cleanly by nature but too lazy to work at it, and we happily let the dust gather.

The Raven's Roost was a two-room apartment in the east sixties; originally it had been Dave Kyle's place, and he still paid the rent on it sometimes in order to have a place to stay when he came into town; other times nobody paid the rent, and there had been such a shifting population that the landlord didn't know who was living there anymore. If he caught any of us going in or out, we always said no, we were just using the place for a few days, and referred him to Kyle. It was unheated (and when I think of it now, I remember the blast of cold wind that blew down the street from the East River, making us walk at an angle and squeezing tears out of our pink faces), but it had hot water and a gas stove. When we were cold we turned on the stove, and if that was not enough, the shower. Steam then filled the kitchen/bathroom, and on at least one occasion it rained.

Lowndes got tired of his unsuccessful agency and turned it over to me. I dutifully trudged around to various editorial offices with my unsalable manuscripts. In the anteroom of Campbell's office one day

I met the illustrator Hannes Bok, who showed me a check for a thousand dollars, then a huge sum: he had just sold Campbell a novel for *Unknown.* Campbell was a portly, bristled-haired blond man with a challenging stare, who told me that he wasn't sure how much longer he would edit *Astounding.* He might quit and go into science. "I'm a nuclear physicist, you know," he said, looking me straight in the eye.

Fred Pohl had persuaded Popular Publications to publish *Super Science* and *Astonishing* in 1940 and had edited both magazines for a year or two; then he had been asked to step down, but had been rehired as an assistant editor to Alden H. Norton, to whose group at Popular the magazines were added. In 1943 there was a vacancy under Norton, and Fred recommended me to fill it; he also lent me a white shirt to appear in when I applied for the job. I was hired at twenty-five dollars a week.

Norton was a large, amiable man in his forties, bald, with a blond mustache, who was responsible for half a dozen pulp magazines at Popular. He had one or two sports magazines, the two science-fiction pulps, a detective magazine, and *G-8 and His Battle Aces.*

As was customary at Popular, he read all the manuscripts, bought stories and scheduled them; the rest of the work—copyediting, proofreading, and so on—was done by his assistants. These consisted of Fred, a young woman named Olga Quadland, and me. Each of us had two or three magazines for which he was responsible every month, but *G-8,* because it was so awful, was rotated among us. The one I did concerned a plot by the Germans in World War I to make their soldiers incredibly fierce by injecting them with rhinoceros juice.

Popular Publications at that time had forty titles and was the largest pulp publisher, followed by Better Publications under various corporate names, then Street and Smith, then a straggle of little companies with eight or ten magazines apiece. A few years before I started work there, Popular had bought up the assets of the Frank A. Munsey company, including a number of pulp titles. One of these was *Argosy,* which Popular turned into a men's slick, and at the time I was there it had been losing money steadily for years. The pulps were still the principal enterprise of the company, and there was no hint that they were coming to the end of their time.

Our offices were roomy and airy, on the next-to-the-top floor of a large office building on East Forty-Second Street. Each department head ran his own magazines with very little interference, and our work relationships were relaxed and easy. The work was not onerous, even though we often took manuscripts home on weekends.

There were three large editorial departments, run by Norton, Tilden, and Harry Widmer, each employing a secretary and one or two assistant editors, plus two editors who ran a couple of magazines each with a secretary—these were love magazines in both cases, for some reason. I omit *Argosy,* which had a large staff (including its own art department) and a high turnover.

After I had been at Popular a month or so, there was a vacancy in another department headed by Mike Tilden, who had been until recently an assistant editor himself, under Rogers Terrill. (Terrill had moved up to *Argosy;* later he opened an agency.) I was transferred to Tilden's department and felt at home there immediately. Mike was a sloppy, beer-bellied man with a quiet, rumbling voice; he was one of the kindest people I ever knew. He always looked unlaundered. He had troubles at home, financial and otherwise, and was always borrowing small sums from other editors, but never from people who worked for him. Once I passed his door and looked in, to find him sitting with his feet up and his hands in his pockets. "I'm just sitting here saying *shit,*" he said.

My number came up, and I went down to the Induction Center in Grand Central Station. Lines of men dressed only in undershorts, socks, and shoes moped back and forth across a huge hall. Every expression given by the Creator to the idea "Man" was there. When some of them jumped up and down on command, their stomachs flapped. The whole tour took hours, and by the time I got toward the end of it I was numbed and apathetic. Three psychiatrists interviewed me; the first was intelligent and evidently trained, and wrote on my papers, "Schizoid. Does not think he would do well in the army, and I am inclined to think he is right." The second man wrote down, "Split Personality," and the third followed his lead. When I handed my papers to the colonel in charge, he read them and said the magic words, "Oh well, he's underweight anyway. 4-F."

New people began coming into our circle. Virginia Kidd was from Baltimore; she was fat but shapely (had an hourglass figure, like a John Held drawing). Her face was soft and pretty. She had had polio as a child and had spent years in bed, having her bad leg rubbed by her parents with cocoa butter. She had been a bar girl in Baltimore, and was a science-fiction fan; *Wonder Stories* had printed some of her letters. James Blish had been in the army and was still in uniform when I met him in a bar; he spent the whole time talking about Joyce. Larry Shaw was from a Catholic family in Rochester, which he hated. He was a funny-looking little man with upstanding hair and bottle-thick glasses; he spoke with difficulty, his face writhing.

At a party one afternoon I was introduced to Judith Zissman, a quiet, intense young woman who had just moved back to New York from Philadelphia. She was eager to know science-fiction people, and carried me off to dinner in her cluttered Greenwich Village apartment.

In the spring of that year I had grown increasingly restless at Popular. I sat with a thick manuscript on my lapboard, a Western novelette by Harry Olmsted, and found that I absolutely could not penetrate it. Olmsted always needed heavy editing, but in order to edit him you first had to find out what he meant, and I couldn't. When this had gone on for some weeks, I gave notice and quit. I wrote to my mother that I wanted to have another try at being a painter, and she agreed to finance me. She sent a lump sum, which I deposited in a savings account, and drew out a little every week. New York in the spring was very pleasant, and it was marvelous to be able to ride uptown on the top of a double-decker bus while everybody else was at work. I set up my easel in the living room and actually completed a few paintings; all but one were very bad.

Then I went job-hunting. I tried all the conventional things, read the ads in the *New York Times* on Sunday, typed up resumés, went to agencies, was sent on interviews. At one point Chester and I were reduced to typing envelopes for an addressing service. The woman in charge showed us each to a typewriter and gave us a stack of address cards and envelopes. We got a penny for each envelope we typed, and were told that if we applied ourselves we could do as many as sixty an hour. After two hours our backs were breaking and we quit.

We went down to the Merchant Marine office to apply as yeomen and took the typing test. The standard was forty words a minute; I barely made it. Chester and Larry Shaw actually shipped out later, but I never did; the Merchant Marine ID card came in handy, though, and got me into the Museum of Modern Art at half price. Chester met a girl in England, jumped ship, and lived with her about a year, long enough for their child to be born; but she insisted on naming it after a former boyfriend, and Chester came home disgruntled.

For a while Chester and I journeyed out to Queens twice a week to have our eyes treated by a marvelous old fraud named Dr. Cooley, who had a

With tomatoes, about 1934

battery of peephole machines of various sorts into which we peered. He looked like Colonel Sanders, and had been in some other line of work before he "discovered his vibrations." He told me solemnly that he had determined that nervous impulses were carried by the bloodstream, and when I pointed out that that was contrary to the general impression, he said, "Yes, I know." His other patients all seemed to improve their vision, but we didn't. The time was not wasted, because I used Dr. Cooley as the central figure in a story called "Thing of Beauty" in 1958.

I met Phil Klass, who was nonviolent but excitable; his voice would begin rather softly and then at a certain point, as if he had shifted gears, would begin to blare as he warmed to his subject. He had a set of comic Jewish gestures and grimaces which through habituation had become second nature. When I first knew him he had fallen under the spell of Scott Meredith and was writing a series of commercial sf stories which he published under the name of William Tenn. He was saving his own name for the *New Yorker* pieces he meant to write later. His brother Mort told me it was hard to get him up in the morning because he could carry on a perfectly rational conversation while sound asleep. Mathematics was the one thing he could not handle in this way, Mort said: if you asked him, "How much is two and two, Phil?" he would reply, "Well now, that's a very interesting question. The Babylonians—"

I also met Ray Cummings, a really frightful-looking man, cadaverous, gray-faced, dressed all in black with a turned-around collar. He was a survivor from the Gernsback days; he had been a secretary to Thomas Edison, and had filled the early *Wonder Stories* and *Astounding*s with long stories such as "Wandl, the Invader" and "Brigands of the Moon." Lowndes had been reprinting these, and I was given the task of illustrating a couple. I also illustrated a long novelette by F. Orlin Tremaine in which a young man blundered into a lost civilization and became its dictator. I was so indignant over this that I drew the hero in a black leather uniform with jackboots, wearing insignia that I made as close to swastikas as I dared, against a background in which little people were dying in the stench of factories and under the whips of overseers. Nobody noticed.

Still at loose ends, I had signed up for a free class in radio writing and had attended the first session, at which the instructor had told us how he felt about the expression "But first—," when I was notified that my father had had a heart attack. My mother wired money and I flew home by available aircraft, being bumped at every stop by people with higher priorities. I found my father convalescing, and stayed a week in the familiar house now grown intolerably small. To stave off boredom, I wrote part of a story called "The Third Little Green Man."

I sold the story to Malcolm Reiss of *Planet Stories,* an editor who is remembered with affection. I sold one or two other stories to the same magazine, but by then Wilbur S. Peacock was the editor. I was getting a cent a word for these stories, and I wrote so slowly and seldom that I could hardly consider myself a professional writer. I was also trying to continue as an illustrator, and got a few assignments from the editor of *Weird Tales,* a man named Buchanan, who when offered a cigarette always replied, "No, thank you—I have no minor vices."

Theodore Sturgeon came back from the Virgin Islands and took up residence in the Village with L. Jerome Stanton and Rita Dragonette. Jay was a pop-eyed, dark-haired man with a quiet, slow voice that never stopped; Rita, called Ree, was a tiny brown woman, attractive in spite of some missing molars. Sturgeon was my agent for a while; he expressed the belief that since Jay was working for Campbell,

manuscripts submitted by him would have the inside track, but it did not work out that way.

Lowndes had remained at Columbia Publications, where he edited all the magazines (including one ingenuously called *Complete Cowboy*), with the exception of the two love pulps, which were edited by a large woman named Marie Park, who later appeared in reducing-salon advertisements headlined, "I looked like a water buffalo." She was a southern lady, and went into hysterics one day when she discovered that a Negro illustrator had sat in her chair.

Wollheim, after the demise of *Stirring* and *Cosmic,* had gone to Avon, where he edited the *Avon Fantasy Reader,* and then to Ace, whose editor-in-chief he was to be for fifteen years. Michel did comic continuities for Mort Weisinger. Richard Wilson went into the army, and won a short-story contest. When he came out he got a wire-service job in Chicago, and for a while Cyril Kornbluth worked with him there.

Judy Zissman (born Juliet Grossman) was then in her twenties, a strong, rather shapely and good-looking woman with dark skin and hair. She was so full of energy that she could not abide sloth and indifference around her, and she soon stirred us up. She and her husband Danny were Trotskyists, and Judy in a political argument was a juggernaut. Danny was in the navy, serving aboard a submarine, and Judy struck up a friendship with Johnny Michel. This displeased Wollheim, and presently Judy came to tell us that Wollheim had forbidden Johnny to have anything more to do with her (because she was a Trotskyist) or Jim Blish (because he was thought to be a fascist). Our indignation was acute, and we sat up half the night composing a document in which we read Wollheim, Elsie, and Michel out of the Futurian Society. We mimeographed and mailed this out to a fanzine mailing list. Wollheim then filed suit for libel in the state supreme court, naming the seven of us who had signed the document: Judy, Blish, Lowndes, Virginia, Chet, Larry, and me. The suit was thrown out of court, with costs charged to Wollheim; but it cost us a hundred dollars apiece in legal fees.

A little later I was dragooned into appearing at Judy's divorce hearing, in which I testified that Danny and a girl not his wife had spent some time in a bedroom in my apartment. The divorce referee was an old man named, appropriately, Schmuck. He asked me, "What were you running, a whorehouse?" and muttered frequently, "There'll be no divorce in this case, no divorce." He granted it, all the same, and Judy at her request became legally Judith Merril.

I was fascinated by the permutations of Judy's name, and once when we were in a restaurant together wrote a poem about them on a napkin:

Juliet Grossman Zissman Pohl
Hated her name from the bottom of her soul:
Went to court in imminent peril;
Changed her name to Judith Merril.

Blish and I were rivals at first, and I sniped at him in a mimeographed magazine called "   ," whose missing title was supposed to satirize the meaninglessness of all titles; but his ability to absorb criticism without anger disarmed me and we became friends. (The mimeograph was Shaw's, and the magazine was produced for a Futurian amateur-press association.)

Blish and Virginia Kidd had an affair which ended in their getting married in the late forties; Jim, who had been trying unsuccessfully to make a living as a free-lance writer, went to work for the Scott Meredith Literary Agency. Presently he got me a job there too.

Scott Meredith, born Feldman, was a small, slight man who as a young writer in Brooklyn had been so poor that he had walked across the bridge to hand-deliver his manuscripts. He and Kornbluth had lived on the same block as children. He had saved his money in the air force, and after the war, in partnership with his brother, had opened the agency, which at first did such a feeble business that the partners had to sweep the place out themselves. This stage did not last long; Meredith was intelligent, an ingenious advertiser and self-promoter, and at a party one night, a little drunk on one highball, he confided in me that his personal bank account was "not one figure—not two figures—not three figures—not four figures, but *five* figures."

Sid's role in the agency was not clear. He had an office of his own and stayed in it most of the time, emerging only to distribute manuscripts and collect finished work, and to deliver an occasional homily about the resemblance of the agency to a shoe factory: "They have the raw materials, the *leather,* you know, and they take that and put it through the machines just like we do here, and make *shoes.*"

Meredith also had a list of professional clients, including P. G. Wodehouse, whom he had got simply by writing him a fan letter, but this end of the business was kept separate from the reading-fee operation, and Scott managed it himself. Later, as the agency grew, he handled only the most important

clients personally, and the rest were turned over to an employee at what was called the "pro desk."

Meredith took full-page, back-cover ads each month in *Writer's Digest;* these ads, which were lively and ingenious, encouraged amateur writers to send us their manuscripts for evaluation at five dollars for a short story and twenty-five dollars for a novel. When the manuscripts came in the morning mail, they were distributed to us, and it was our job to read them and write letters of comment, for which we got one dollar out of the five, and five dollars out of the twenty-five. (In fact, Meredith offered us a choice of two plans, a straight salary of twenty-five dollars a week with a quota of twenty-five short stories or the equivalent, or else a piecework arrangement, as above; but since in practice nobody could turn out more than five short-story letters a day, it came to the same thing.)

The first letter to a new client always began by explaining that his story was unsalable because it did not follow the Plot Skeleton. The letter went on to enumerate the parts of the Plot Skeleton, viz.: 1) a sympathetic and believable *lead character,* 2) an urgent and vital *problem,* 3) *complications* caused by the lead character's unsuccessful attempts to solve the problem, 4) the *crisis* (this element was added by Blish), 5) the *resolution,* in which the lead character solves the problem by means of his own courage and resourcefulness. In a concluding paragraph the letter pointed out which of the elements were missing (ordinarily all of them were) and invited the client to try again. Subsequent letters grew more detailed. We really tried to help the clients, and in one or two cases I think we succeeded.

We were certainly exploited, but the training we got was invaluable. A long line of Meredith employees went on to become editors. Meredith encouraged this, on the theory that such people would be inclined to buy from the agency, and in most cases he was right.

When I first saw Lester del Rey I thought he was not more than fourteen. Only as he came nearer across the office did I realize that he was a grown man, but very short and slender, almost stunted. He had a mop of wavy dust-colored hair, hooded green eyes, and a gap-toothed grin. He spoke in a deep, firm voice. In the late thirties he had attracted some attention by his stories in *Astounding,* but since then he had been in a slump, and he had come to work at Meredith's. Meredith presently made him office manager, and he took his responsibilities seriously, frowning on our paper-throwing and other games.

The fact that we were a shifting population and that all the letters were signed by Meredith (or by his

A Milford Writers' Conference, about 1958: (left to right) Judith Merril, Gordon R. Dickson, Richard McKenna, Fritz Leiber, Carol Emshwiller

brother Sid, imitating Scott's handwriting) sometimes led to anomalies. Jim got into a lengthy correspondence about modern music with one client, then quit, and the client was turned over to Lester. The client, who had been hearing from Jim about Bartók and Hindemith, now began getting letters about Ravel's "Bolero."

After a while Meredith grew prosperous enough to hire an office girl. This was Diane Diamond, a startlingly beautiful eighteen-year-old redhead with high, pointed breasts. Jim and I watched them with appreciation for more than a month before the weather got too hot and she left them at home. Virginia did not see the humor of this story.

Diane left and another girl took her place. She was just out of high school; her name was Trudy Werndl. She was a blond, plump and pretty, and seemed to be impressed with Jim and me because we were writers. We took her out for a beer after work, and I invited her to come and see me that weekend. One thing led to another, and when I asked her to come and live with me she agreed, but her girlfriends

were shocked when she told them that, and with some misgivings I married her instead.

Just at this point the Blishes had taken a house in Staten Island, and asked us to come and share it. We were married in the Little Church around the Corner (chosen by one of the girlfriends) during the worst snowstorm of the decade; we were three hours late getting in from Staten Island and the minister was put out. There had been no rehearsal, and I discovered at the last moment that I was expected to kneel on a little prie-dieu. I had never seen such a thing before and didn't know how to manage it, froze halfway down, and had to hold that ridiculous position all through the ceremony. (Trudy's mother wept.)

Trudy's mother was named Gertraud and called Traudl; she plied me with cervelat and taught me a few naughty phrases in Bayrisch. (The Bavarians are the fun-loving Southerners of Germany and their dialect is a sort of baby-talk German: where a Low German says, "*Ich auch,*" the Bavarian says, "*I a.*")

As soon as the novelty wore off it became evident that my marriage to Trudy was a mistake. We were not well suited, sexually or in any other way. Commuting to work from Staten Island, half an hour on the ferry alone, was exhausting for me, and staying home all day was boring for Trudy.

I was promoted to the pro desk, which had a huge backlog of work. After a month or so I became ill with cerebrospinal meningitis and was carted off to the Staten Island Hospital, a few blocks away, where in my delirium I read phantom manuscripts. Shortly after I came out, Trudy got appendicitis and went in. Meanwhile we and the Blishes were getting on each other's nerves a little; Trudy and I decided to try to improve our relationship by moving back into Manhattan. This was at the height of the postwar apartment shortage, and we were able to move into a Greenwich Village studio apartment (so called because it had a little skylight in the living room) only by buying the previous tenant's furniture with seven hundred dollars put up by my mother.

Now began the most miserable and boring time of my life. My relations with Trudy deteriorated. We acquired a large circle of new friends, mostly musicians who met once a week at Julian Goodenough's apartment. Julian was the son of a distinguished Japanese painter who also lived in the Village. His mother was a Christian Scientist, and Julian was not sure what he was. He lived alone, in an apartment over his silversmith shop, and in his little bedroom, under a pink light, he kept a row of high-heeled patent-leather shoes in an assortment of sizes. At his weekly jam sessions, he sometimes played the bass, sometimes thumped on the piano, grinning around his cigar. He could not drink—one highball made his face flush red. (I borrowed this peculiarity for a character called Seu in my story "The Earth Quarter." I also put Julian into a story called "To the Pure," in two personae.)

At the height of my troubles with Trudy, one afternoon when she was out with another fellow, I wrote a story called "To Serve Man." The idea had popped into my head, and I wrote the story in one sitting of about three hours.

Our marriage ended with an emotional scene; Trudy moved out shortly before Christmas. Later we got a lawyer who was nervous about the word "collusion," and there was a hearing at which Trudy swore I had deceived her about my desire for children (which neither of us wanted, and which would have been the greatest possible misfortune), and the marriage was annulled.

In the Village I met Stewart Kerby, a former sf fan who had published a limited edition of one of David H. Keller's stories. His friend Kenneth Koch sometimes hunted Stew up and brought him to my apartment to compose tunes to his poems on the piano. One of these was called *The Blind Man Blues*, and the refrain went:

> Got no money in my pocket,
> Got no eyeballs in my socket.
> But I don't mind,
> 'Cause I'm blind.

Needing money, I returned to Meredith's, where I found myself in company with James A. Bryans, a slow, gangling man with a chronic skin ailment which made him continually rub his wrists, and Don Fine, an ineffectual-looking little fellow who later became the tyrant of Dell Books, and still later the founder of two hardcover publishing houses. I trained myself to pot either of them with a wad of paper, sitting or standing.

When Ejler Jakobsson invited me to go back to Popular as his assistant, I was pleased, particularly since Jake had inherited Al Norton's department, which included the two science-fiction magazines. (Norton was now associate publisher.) This was the reason Jake had wanted me, anticipating my help in a field unfamiliar to him, but in this we were both disappointed. Jake rejected stories I recommended with enthusiasm, including two early Charles Harness stories, and filled the book with other things that I thought barely publishable. We disagreed about the merits of the pulp-style covers, and he was not amused when I traced one of them, putting football uniforms on the figures instead of spacesuits.

My companions in the office were Mary Gnaedinger and a young man named Hank Levinson, whom Jake had hired from the Columbia University placement agency. Hank and I became good friends; his main interest was the theater, and he was full of amiable lunacy.

We took our lunches together at an East Side bar where the Tom Collinses and sandwiches were cheap, and spent our afternoons dueling with toy pistols, the kind that shoot suction-tipped darts. Our aim was to plant one of these things in the middle of the other fellow's forehead, and I may be romanticizing, but I think we achieved this once or twice. Mary bore it all with unruffled equanimity. Later Hank was drafted, and sent me a large glossy $8\frac{1}{2} \times 11$ of himself in an officer's cap and sunglasses, with a corncob pipe, and the legend "I shall return." Still later he got out and married a daughter of that Dr. Rock who pioneered the Pill.

Wollheim married Elsie at last; they moved out to Queens, to an apartment with a sunken living room and a photomural. Kornbluth married Mary Byers and they went to live in Levittown. Lowndes was also married and living in Westchester. Pohl married Judy Zissman. They went househunting in Red Bank, New Jersey, and because they were wearing old clothes the house agent assumed they were rich and showed them a huge three-story house. They bought it and Fred lived there for years after they were divorced. Chet Cohen married a music teacher from Chattanooga and they had three children, one of whom they named after me.

At a party I had met Lester del Rey's wife Helen and later had learned that their marriage was breaking up. I took her out to a Chinese movie, and again one thing led to another. I turned the studio apartment over to Dick Wilson and moved in with Helen. Her parents were Lithuanian immigrants named Schliazas, shortened to Schlaz, but nobody could pronounce that either. Her father worked as a cook for Horn and Hardart for more than twenty years. He was a quiet old man who brought home neatly wrapped pieces of meat every day. Once I saw him unload from various pockets in his overcoat what must have been twenty pounds of steaks and chops. Later he developed a cancer of the stomach and was operated on at company expense. The surgeons removed his entire stomach, and he starved to death.

Lester del Rey signed his early letters to *Astounding* R. (for Ramon) Alvarez, and he had four or five other given names; the whole thing went something like Ramon Felipe Maria something something Alvarez–del Rey. He explained that his father was descended from a royalist branch of the Alvarez family, and so on. In conversation he liked to defend unlikely propositions. If he tossed out some assertion that aroused his hearer's incredulity he would immediately repeat it with more emphasis, and even if he had only thought of it a moment before, he would be prepared to defend it all afternoon, quoting sources which might or might not be imaginary: all this with a goblin grin and such evident enjoyment that it was hard to hate him. I described this aspect of Lester, among others, in "A Likely Story," in which he appeared as Ray Alvarez. In the introduction to one of his stories I once called Lester one of the most contentious men alive. His second wife, Evelyn (formerly Harry Harrison's wife), later told me that when he read this Lester shouted, "I am *not* contentious!"

I was tired of Popular again, and wished I had my own science-fiction magazine to edit. I asked Fred Pohl if he knew of any publisher who might be interested; he suggested I try Alex Hillman of Hill-

man Publications. I sent Hillman a written proposal and was called in for an interview. Hillman, who looked something like an evil Charles Coburn, hired me in ten minutes. When he asked about salary, I said I was getting seventy-five dollars at Popular (an exaggeration) but would like to do better than that; we settled on eighty-five dollars a week, the most I had ever earned in my life.

I wanted to call the magazine *Science-Fantasy*, but the firm's lawyers, after a haphazard search, advised against it because both words were in use in the titles of other magazines. We finally settled on *Worlds Beyond*, swiped from the title of a symposium edited by Lloyd Arthur Eshbach, *Of Worlds Beyond*. My handshake agreement with Hillman was so hasty that I discovered afterward I didn't even know if the magazine was to be a monthly. I was too green to ask for a contract guaranteeing a minimum number of issues, or to settle details of production and format. Hillman was leaving on a vacation, and told me to have a cover ready for him when he got back.

Fred laughed with delighted disbelief when I told him I had sold Hillman the magazine. I bought several stories for the first issue from his clients, and one or two others from Meredith. From a young writer named Richard Matheson, then almost unknown, I bought a story called "Clothes Make the Man," a deft little satire about a suit of clothes that takes over its owner's personality. This was the story I chose to illustrate on the cover. I called in an artist named Herman Bischoff whose work I admired and gave him the commission; he turned out a fine spooky painting of an empty suit of clothes waving its arms at a startled girl. When he came back, Hillman rejected the painting and would not be dissuaded, even though a vice president took my side. I discovered that I had only thought I had authority to order the painting made; what Hillman had meant was for me to get a sketch made for his approval. Bischoff was never paid. I turned to Paul Callé, who I knew had a painting that had been turned down by Popular, and we bought it for a hundred dollars.

The atmosphere at Hillman Publications was utterly unlike that at Popular. I had an office to myself for a week or two, then was put in with the staff of Hillman's fact detective magazines, headed by an irascible, pop-eyed man whose name I have forgotten. Every editor seemed alone at his little desk, even though several of us worked in the same room. There was no camaraderie and no fraternization. Meeting Hillman in the hall was an unnerving experience. Smoking a cigar, he lumbered down the hall staring straight ahead, hands clasped behind his back.

When I said good morning, he continued to stare and lumber. (I used him as the Boss of Colorado in my novel *A for Anything*.)

I had the tiniest of budgets, but since I was using about half reprint material I could afford to pay the going rate for new stories. Fred sent me an elegant satire by Phil Klass which I retitled "Null-P." I got stories from Poul Anderson, Fred Brown and Mack Reynolds, John Christopher, and others. I wrote a book-review department, which I called "The Dissecting Table"; Harry Harrison drew a heading for it which showed me bending over a helpless book with scalpel in hand.

The first issue appeared, with a dumb headline sticker contrived by one of Hillman's lieutenants (something about FLYING SAUCER MEN). It was printed on the poorest grade of newsprint I had ever seen, worse even than Lowndes's magazines. When the first sales report came in three weeks later, it was so bad that Hillman canceled the project at once. Two more issues were in preparation and appeared. The cover for the fourth had been painted. The firm did not want to pay the artist for this, either, but this time I stood by him (his sketch had been approved), and he got his money.

In the forties nearly every science-fiction magazine had a book-review department, but these were mostly of what I later called the shopping-guide type; the reviews were about an inch long and always ended, "A must for every science fiction fan." Besides the *Worlds Beyond* reviews, I had already written one long critical essay (about the works of A. E. van Vogt), which Larry Shaw had published in one of his amateur magazines, *Destiny's Child*. When Lester started two new magazines, *Space Science Fiction* and *Science Fiction Adventures*, I was able to talk him into letting me do the book department in one. He paid me, if I remember, fifteen dollars a column.

After a year or so Lowndes also offered to run any reviews I sent him, no matter what the length, and to pay his usual rates, i.e., half a cent a word. At various times I also published reviews in Harlan Ellison's huge sloppy fanzine *Dimensions* (where my column was called "Gardyloo," a call formerly used when throwing the contents of chamber pots out of windows), in Walt Willis's *Hyphen*, in *Infinity*, and finally in *The Magazine of Fantasy & Science Fiction*. When I quit, in a dispute over a review *F&SF* refused to print as written, I had been reviewing books for nine years.

Horace Gold, the editor of the new magazine *Galaxy*, bought "To Serve Man," and I wrote him

another story. He bought that, and a third story, and a fourth. I wrote them one after another sitting on the sofa bed Lester had given us, with my typewriter on a kitchen chair between my knees. When I sold Horace still another story, I realized that as a successful author I was no longer tied to New York. Helen and I stored our furniture and bought air tickets to California.

A client of Pohl's, a Los Angeles writer named Kull who wrote as Dean Evans, had offered to put us up while we looked for a place to live. He did, but we quarreled over some beans and window shades; Helen and I found ourselves outdoors without a cent. We wired my mother for money and sat up in the bus station all night.

Later we rented a cottage on the side of a mountain in La Sierra. The view across the valley was magnificent, and there was room for a little garden. I put my typewriter on a chair under the peppertree in the yard and finished "Double Meaning," the novelette I had started before we left New York. Gold rejected "Double Meaning," my first clue that all was not well in the writers' paradise. (Sam Merwin later bought it and published it in *Startling*.) I wrote another story and Gold rejected that one too.

My relationship with Helen was affectionate and companionable rather than romantic. As long as we were poor we got along beautifully and were very happy together. If we were down to a dollar and a half, we spent it on a movie, knowing that something would turn up in a day or two.

Feeling too isolated in La Sierra, we moved to Santa Monica, where we met Richard Matheson and his girlfriend. We lived in a garage apartment owned by a TV actress and her husband, an ex-policeman. It was one room, fifteen feet square, with a sagging sofa bed in it. I got a job at an aircraft plant as a file clerk. I worked in the experimental section, in a big concrete-floored room lined with vertical files. Every part came back to the file room after every operation, with its papers, and I walked back and forth over the cement floor for eight hours a day.

I worked the late shift, and I remember the buses that took us through the flooded streets of Santa Monica in the rainy season, under a gray sky. The lights in the plant were mercury vapor; they turned the skin yellow and the veins purple. The foreman in that department—we called him the leadman—had worked there for twenty years, and his wife had worked in the same factory, in another department, for eighteen years. Once he and I had to carry a big sheet of metal up the ramp into the shop. As we reached the doorway, he said, "Up your end." "Up yours," I said, but he didn't smile.

When I had been there six weeks I was invited to join the union, but declined because I didn't expect to be there long. Shortly after that, I was notified that because I had been rejected by the army on psychiatric grounds, I must have a psychiatric examination. The way the plant psychologist put it was: "Go get yourself psychoanalyzed."

I said, "But that could take ten years."

"No," he said, "the weekend's coming up, go get yourself psychoanalyzed and report back Monday."

I looked up a psychiatrist in the yellow pages and went to him for an interview. He said I wasn't a schiz. The factory fired me anyhow.

We decided we had had enough of southern California, with its eight months of sunshine and four months of rain. We went back to New York and stayed temporarily in Lester's apartment again. (He was living elsewhere.)

I went back to Popular one more time when Mike Tilden needed someone to fill in for a month or so. He said gruffly that I could keep the job if I wanted it, but I didn't. By then it was routine; I could do it without thinking, and didn't like it anymore. Within a year Popular folded all its pulps and let the editors go. Later I found Mike and Ejler Jakobsson working in the same office with Larry Shaw on a line of porn novels published by Universal Publishing and Distributing Company. Mike's wife had died and his son had committed suicide; he died himself a few years later, broke, unlaundered, and patient to the end.

Looking at a map, Helen and I saw names we liked in the Poconos and took a bus there. We found a four-room cabin in the woods and rented it from the owners, a bartender named Diebold and his wife. (I used him in *A for Anything,* too.) It was about a mile from Canadensis, itself nothing but a crossroads with a post office and a few stores. There was a good-sized lawn which I had to cut with a scythe. Behind us in the woods was a tiny shack, not much bigger than a phone booth, in which a halfwit lived. I found an old desk in a shed and dragged it into the house; it was fragrant with barnyard odors and had great gaps between the boards of its top. We acquired kittens; one of them fell into the well and another was caught in a trap set by the halfwit. In August of that year our first child was born; we named her Valerie. I began writing again, and finished a long story, "Natural State," which Gold bought.

This was my first editorial collaboration with Horace, and it left me with mixed feelings. Previously I had just written the stories and he had either bought or rejected them; this time I went to him with an idea and we talked it over. The idea was for a story to be called "Cannon Fodder," which was to take the form of an epic journey by some soldiers and their "cannon"—a living creature biologically engineered to be a weapon. Gold turned this around and produced the idea of a whole culture based on biological engineering rather than machines; he also contributed some of the most telling details, such as the knife-bushes. Beyond doubt, this was a much better story than the one I had had in mind, but I could not help feeling that I would rather have written my story. I bore this in mind when I next became an editor.

I had first met Gold in 1950, shortly after the first issue of *Galaxy* appeared. He was a bald, stocky man, restless and energetic, boastful, innovative, brilliant—all the things that *Galaxy* was. Under this there was a hard core of despair. Once when he reached for some small object on his desk it toppled and broke. "Gold touched it," he said. After the war Gold had developed an extreme case of agoraphobia, and now never left the East Side apartment where he lived with his wife and young son. There were frequent parties there, and he spent hours in telephone conversations.

Gold had an incurable habit of overediting stories; as Lester once said, he turned mediocre stories into good ones, and excellent stories into good ones. He bought Edgar Pangborn's beautiful "Angel's Egg" and showed it to several writers in manuscript, then rewrote some of its best phrases. He changed the description of the "angel" (a visitor from another planet) riding on the back of a hawk "with her speaking hands on his terrible head" to "with her telepathic hands on his predatory head." According to Ted Sturgeon, when the issue came out three pairs of heels hit the floor at that point and three people tried to phone Gold to curse him for a meddler.

Sturgeon got in the habit of marking out certain phrases in his manuscripts and writing them in again above the line in ink. Gold asked him why he did that, pointing out that it made it difficult for him to write in corrections. "That's why I do it," Sturgeon told him.

Gold was certainly one of the best idea men in the business, and contributed more to the stories published in *Galaxy* than will ever be known. Blish complained that his invariable response to an author's idea was to turn it on its head, but in fact sometimes he merely turned it sidewise, to its great benefit.

Once Horace called me up in Canadensis and proposed that I become what he called a utility writer for *Galaxy*, writing stories to order on whatever themes Horace needed at the moment, and under various pseudonyms—"maybe even under women's names." I wanted to say no but didn't dare, and agreed with such faint enthusiasm that Horace knew what I meant, and was disappointed twice—once for my refusal and once for my failure to come out with it. I know now that editors are constantly disappointed by authors' unwillingness to fight, and would often rather have a forthright "no" than a weak-kneed "yes." Horace expected some opposition when he suggested changes in a story conference, but I did not know that, thought his suggestions were orders and agreed to everything rather than give up the sale: hence Gold's bitter complaint later on that I was a rabbit in person, a tiger only when I got behind a typewriter.

I had been disappointed in my early ambition to become an *Astounding* writer; Campbell returned my submissions via Sturgeon with scrawled comments such as "Early 1930" or "So what?" which hurt my feelings without teaching me anything. I heard about the four-page letters other people got from Campbell, and I felt left out. Eventually I wrote to him asking for more guidance, and he wrote back inviting me to lunch, but I was about to leave for California and had to decline. No doubt I could have got myself invited to lunch long before, but Campbell's lecture-room manner was so unpleasant to me that I was unwilling to undergo it. Campbell talked a great deal more than he listened, and he liked to say outrageous things; I could not cope with this, and if my patience gave out, my only response was anger.

Now I saw *Galaxy* as the longed-for ideal science-fiction market, and the fact that Horace was buying nearly everything I wrote made it easy to overlook any defects in it. When Gold began rejecting my stories and I had to look for other markets, I felt betrayed. It's true that these were not the sort of stories he was used to buying from me, but I felt that ought not to matter, and that the whole point of a magazine like *Galaxy* was that it should buy, if it could, the best work of the best writers, no matter what kind it was. When I came to edit *Orbit* I tried to live up to this ideal and found that I couldn't. I bought five or six stories in a row from Gardner Dozois and Gene Wolfe and other writers, and then rejected other stories which they must have had every reason to think I would buy.

Helen and I wanted a bigger house, and found one for rent in Canadensis, but the owner's eyes narrowed when I said I was a writer. Finding nothing else nearer, we went househunting in Milford, with Judy Merril's energetic help.

The first Milford colonists had been the Blishes, who had answered an ad in the *Times* and had signed an agreement by which they would buy a house in instalments and would not get the deed until it was paid for. This kept them out of the mortgage mill—they had no money for a down payment anyhow—but it made them nervous for years, lest they lose the house and all their investment. Their house was a charming two-story cottage with a sun deck overlooking a long sweep of lawn down to the Sawkill (which later flooded them out).

Judy came next, rented a cold Victorian house on Broad Street, reassembled her family, and set out to be a mother. Both children had been living with their fathers and both came to Judy voluntarily, but in taking them she violated custody agreements, and that led to trouble later. Fred sued her in order to regain custody of their daughter Ann, and there was a messy court hearing at which nearly everybody we knew was drawn in to testify on one side or the other.

Milford is a quiet little town on the Delaware. The permanent population then was about a thousand. The streets are lined with old maples, and are beautiful in the fall. Most of the houses are white-painted frame, many of them Victorian houses, with gingerbread, gables, and slate roofs. The town has a high society composed of old residents, second and third generation; newcomers are never admitted to this, but anybody who stays one winter will thereafter be treated as human. Tourism keeps Milford alive; to the north of it there are towns like Hawley which are shockingly decayed. The town has always been known for its restaurants, among them the Fauchère, which serves an old-fashioned menu and requires its guests to be decently dressed.

Two excellent restaurants were opened in the Milford area during the time I lived there. One was operated by a chef who had had a restaurant in New Jersey for thirty years. He did all the cooking, and it was superb. The world beat a path to his door; before we knew it he was standing in the dining room all evening, greeting guests, beautifully dressed, while God knows who was in the kitchen, and the food was terrible.

The other was the Red Fox, owned by a couple named Alan and Ronnie Lieb. Judy's daughter Merril, who worked for them, reported that if she brought a plate back to the kitchen with food left on it, Alan would say, "Philistines," and if she brought one back scraped clean, he would say, "Pigs." His cooking was praised by John McPhee, in a *New Yorker* profile, in such uninhibited terms that the Liebs became celebrities, were mobbed by tourists, and had to leave town.

We found a cottage on Ann Street at thirty-five dollars a month and moved in. The house was painted white inside and out, had sagging wood floors and a bow window with window seats. The front room was unheated except for a fireplace, and in the winter we found that we had to close it off or we couldn't heat the rest of the house. The front room was where we kept the television, however, and there was no convenient place for it in the middle room. Our solution was to tack a blanket across the open doorway and watch the TV over it.

Our second child, Christopher, was born while we lived in this house. When he was two an ant bit him on the buttock, and for a while afterward he stamped on every ant he saw, remarking, "Don't like amp!"

In 1953 Arnold Hano was the editor of a new paperback company, Lion Books, and I went to see him when I heard he was farming out novels. I found him in a gloomy little office with my old stablemate

New beard, 1967

Jim Bryans, and they showed me a dog-eared list of novel ideas. One, I remember, was about a lustful gorilla pursuing white women through the jungle. I took the one I thought was least awful (about a fake kidnaping) and worked it up into a couple of chapters and outline. I had a good start, but Arnold turned it down because I had made things come out even by means of a real kidnaping that happened coincidentally with the fake one. Later Hano left to freelance, and Walter Fultz, an amiable redhead whom I had met in the Village, took over as editor.

Years before, I had asked Ryerson Johnson how he could manage to write anything as long as a novel. Well, he said, you get used to it in stages: first you write some short stories, then two or three novelettes of ten thousand words, then some longer novelettes, and then you're ready for a novel.

I had been writing longer and longer things, and I thought I was due for a novel, but I still shrank from the idea of doing all that work from scratch. Instead, I thought of a sequel to a story of mine called "The Analogues." The sequel, "Turncoat," was a little over twenty thousand words, and then I had enough to offer, with an outline of the rest, to Fultz. He gave me a contract, and I finished the book as *Hell's Pavement.* The novel was about the consequences of an invention, and it was more or less legitimate for it to be broken down into a short section (the original story) introducing the invention, then a longer one showing its early development, and a still longer section winding up the plot.

I thought I would try this again with another gadget, and this time I chose the matter duplicator, because I thought previous writers had handled it badly. George O. Smith, in "Pandora's Box," had preserved civilization by introducing coins made of an unduplicable substance. I thought this was a rabbit out of a hat, and that the thing to do was to let civilization collapse and then see what happened. (Later an Alaskan writer, Ralph Williams, took exception to my version and wrote a lovely story called "Business as Usual, During Alterations," in which he argued persuasively that civilization would not even shudder.) I wrote the first part and sold it to *F&SF* as "A for Anything," then, with that and an outline, got a contract from Fultz for the novel. My thesis was that following the collapse of industrial civilization a new slaveholding society would arise, and that the new masters would necessarily take over all the existing houses big and isolated enough for their purposes, many of which were resort hotels. I put my hero in a real place called Buck Hill, not far from Canadensis;

the description of the grounds and the exterior of the house is from observation.

I got to within about five thousand words of the end of this novel and then hit a block—I knew what was to happen next, but just couldn't write it. Fultz by this time had left Lion to be replaced by his former secretary; the firm had gone into liquidation and its assets had been acquired by a new corporation doing business as Zenith Books. In order to get rid of the novel I plunged in and wrote it as best I could. The treatment of the rebel leader in the last chapters was perfunctory, but otherwise the ending pleased me. I delivered the manuscript to Zenith and asked Fultz's successor to hold off publication for a few months so that I could sell serial rights; she refused, saying that she needed the book right away, and since I was late with it, I gulped and agreed. The book was not published until nearly twelve months later.

Zenith's emblem was a V-shaped thing, and the fact that it pointed downward made me suggest to the editor that the company ought to call itself Nadir Books; but she didn't get it. I was right, though.

In 1955 the partners in a new fan publishing house called Advent approached me with the idea of making a collection of my book reviews. They gave me a contract under which I was to get half the profits after the costs of production had been met. I put the collection together from tear sheets and carbons, although my agent would have no part of it and said I would never see a nickel. Anthony Boucher contributed an introduction, and I insisted that he get a percentage too. The collection was published in 1956. A revised and enlarged edition was published in 1967, and the book has brought in a few hundred dollars every year since.

Judy Merril and I had talked a little about holding a writers' conference in Milford, but it was the way you talk about building a boat in your basement. Then we went to the World Science Fiction Convention in Detroit in 1955, and found ourselves being taken so seriously that we began to think people might actually come to our party. When we got back to Milford, we called in Jim Blish, formed a committee, and issued manifestoes.

The convention the following year was held over the Labor Day weekend in New York. We set our date for the week after that, in hope that people would spill over from New York to Milford. It worked almost too well—we got forty people, and crammed them into the living room of a summer cottage on the Delaware. We were too innocent to realize that a "writers' conference" was usually a bunch of paid lecturers talking to an audience of paying would-be writers. We took the phrase literally—we sat our writers down in a circle and started them talking to each other. They kept talking for years, and in one sense they haven't stopped talking yet. (Sophisticated people stand on a pyramid of compromises, and can always give you elaborate reasons why an apple should not be considered an apple. When anybody tries putting the naive view of things into practice, it usually turns out that it works perfectly well. Sophisticated people then look at it and say, "Well, I swan.")

In the middle of the week Cyril Kornbluth invited four of us to a late-evening session in his hotel room—Jim Blish, A. J. Budrys, me, and Jane Roberts. Jane was a writer Cyril had discovered living near him in upstate New York, a slender, big-eyed brunette. What Cyril originally had in mind or what he expected I don't know, but what happened was that presently we were sitting in a partly darkened room having a séance which turned into a kind of encounter group. Jane, who was good at that kind of thing, went into trance and answered questions oracularly. (Later she wrote some best-selling books about a spirit named Seth who communicated with her by automatic writing.) We came out of it with a very strong feeling of brother-and-sisterhood which lasted for several years; I tried to keep it going with a round-robin letter, and managed to wound Virginia Kidd deeply by resisting her request to become part of the group. The feeling faded away very gradually, but it was real and important to us while it lasted.

In our second year, 1957, we didn't have the nearby convention to help us, and the Conference hit its low point. We had six writers, not enough to keep a conversation going spontaneously, and not enough, I guess, to reserve the cottage colony we had used before. We held the sessions in Judy's house and mine (Jim was working in New York, and could not come) and it just did not work out very well.

Harry Harrison and his second wife Joan, who was tinier than he, turned up at this second conference in a miniature automobile which Harry drove in lunatic circles, using roadway and sidewalk. Ed Emshwiller proposed making a film, and we did one called "The Thing from Back Issues," with a plot borrowed from Heinlein's *The Puppet Masters*.

In our third year, enrollment rose again; Judy found another cottage colony that would accommodate us, and we settled into the format we used from then on. The Conference lasted eight days, Saturday through Saturday. Every afternoon except the first (when people were still checking in) we had a workshop; that is, we met and discussed each other's manuscripts. Every evening except the last (because of the going-away party) we discussed a set topic—"Religion and Science Fiction" maybe, or "Getting Along with Editors." In between, whenever the Conference was not in formal session, people were talking. My God, how they talked!

Because of this incessant rattle of tongues, and the late hours and the general excitement, Milford was like a week-long party. After a few years of this, we began to notice that the end of one Milford was attaching itself in our memories to the beginning of the next; the series formed a nonstop party that went on for twenty years, or, depending on how you looked at it, for twenty-one weeks. This was very pleasant in a way, but also a little scary.

We were told by outsiders once or twice that we were running a conspiracy to subvert traditional science fiction, rig elections, worship turkeys, and so on. We might have been tempted to do all this, but as P. G. Wodehouse said when he was accused of wishing to overthrow the French government, "One has so little time."

In 1958 James L. Quinn, the publisher of *If*, asked me to become the editor of the magazine. Larry Shaw had been the editor in the early fifties, when he published the original novelette version of Blish's "A Case of Conscience"; but when Larry returned a story of Judith Merril's because he thought she could sell it elsewhere for more money, Quinn took this as disloyalty and fired him.

Quinn, who had been involved in writing and editing in a small way in the thirties, had later married money and set up a publishing company in Kingston, New York, where he lived. He was a rather small, sad-eyed man with a Walt Disney mustache who did not seem to enjoy being rich, although he drove a white Thunderbird and worked at an authentic Colonial desk. "I drink a lot of hard whiskey," he told me mournfully.

Quinn did the layouts for *If* himself and was good at it, but his tastes in fiction ran to conventional satires about automobiles and computers. He had been editing the magazine himself for several years, and its circulation had been going down. He was faced with the choice of folding it or trying another editor. I edited three issues of *If*, and gave it my best, but the circulation did not go up, and Quinn sold the magazine to *Galaxy*.

Among the stories I inherited when I began editing the magazine was one called "The Founding of Fishdollar Five" (I shortened this to "The Fishdollar Affair") by Richard McKenna. Quinn had prom-

ised McKenna he would buy this story if he would cut it in half. McKenna has told how he did this and how important it was to him in his essay "Journey with a Little Man." The story was cut to the bone, and Quinn said he had not expected to be taken literally, but he bought it. I was impressed with McKenna and invited him to the Milford Conference. I also invited a young writer named Kate Wilhelm, from whom I hadn't bought anything but whose stories had caught my eye.

I had visualized Kate Wilhelm as a middle-aged woman with iron gray hair and flat heels; instead, she turned out to be young, slender, and pretty. That year we had also invited an MIT student called Shag, who was not a professional writer and really should not have been there; he was hopelessly smitten with Katie. We sat up all night in the Blishes' living room the last night of the Conference, and in the morning A. J. and I took Kate to the train, where A. J. kissed her and she shook hands with me. When we got back to the Blishes', A. J. said to Shag, with a twinkle in his eye, "She was incredibly passionate," and Shag said, "You bastard."

In 1959, I got a copy of the French magazine *Fiction*, which had translated one of my stories. *Fiction* was founded as the French edition of *F&SF*, but almost from the beginning had been using the work of native writers, and at this time the contents were about half and half. It was then an attractive little magazine, with covers by Jean-Claude Forest, the artist who created *Barbarella*.

In the forties I had taught myself a little French with the intention of trying to puzzle out the text of sexy French magazines and books. (I had an exaggerated idea of the naughtiness of *La Vie Parisienne*, from references to that magazine in early science-fiction stories. I was disappointed in the texts I found, but kept at it anyhow and got as far as reading all the way through a novel by André Maurois, *Climats*.) This was by no means enough to qualify me as a translator, but I got my French-English dictionary and sat down at the dining-room table with the first story in the magazine, "Au Pilote Aveugle" by Charles Henneberg (really a collaboration between Henneberg and his wife Nathalie, who continued writing stories much like this one after his death). The story went smoothly into English, and happened to be very good, and I sold the translation to *F&SF*. Then it was easy to do more. The work of translation, and even more the correspondence with the authors, improved my French enormously, although I still can't understand spoken French well enough to carry on a conversation.

In 1960 Robert P. Mills, who had been the editor of *F&SF*, went into the agency business, first as an associate of Rogers Terrill, then with Ashley Famous Agency, and finally on his own. I was his first client, and the first thing he said to me was, "I think you ought to be in hardcover." He sent a collection of my stories over to Simon and Schuster, and Clayton Rawson bought it. My original title was *Stop the World*, but Clayt, who had never heard the phrase, vetoed it; then I proposed *Far Out*, and the book was published under that title.

Rawson came out to the Milford Conference next year and proposed to me that I should edit a large retrospective collection of science fiction, an idea that had occurred to him because one morning he had two proposals for sf books on his desk, one about old-time science fiction and another from a very young writer; and it struck him that there must be many people of that age who had never heard of the older sf.

I had always believed I could edit a superior anthology, but had never found out how you convinced an editor of that unless you had already done one. (I still don't know.) I attacked this assignment with enthusiasm, dragged out all my old favorite stories, and Clayt sent several of them back with sounds of pained displeasure. I looked them over again more carefully and realized with dismay that they were junk that had impressed me in my ignorance when I was twelve and thirteen. In spite of this I managed to put together a collection that pleased both Clayt and me (the excerpt from *Twenty Thousand Leagues under the Sea* was included at his suggestion), and then I found out that the second anthology was no trouble to sell. As my production of fiction diminished and my responsibilities increased I turned more and more to anthologies as a way of making a living.

In 1960 Thomas A. Dardis of Berkley Books asked if I would be interested in becoming their science-fiction consultant. He had approached Groff Conklin first; Groff had suggested me. I served in this capacity for six years, reading manuscripts and writing reports for Dardis, and also did some freelance copyediting. In 1963 I persuaded Dardis to let me edit four books a year, working directly with the authors and giving contracts on the basis of outlines. In this way I got first novels from Keith Laumer, Thomas M. Disch, and others, and brought Gordon R. Dickson and Poul Anderson into the Berkley list.

In a short time, Dardis picked up a feeling for science fiction and became a discriminating judge in his own right. He was a complicated man and not all of his personal characteristics were admirable. He liked to bully people, but I found that if I kept my voice down and replied patiently and firmly, he always backed off. In discussions by mail, also, I wore him down by persistence as much as by logic, and he usually gave in.

In 1960, with an inheritance from my mother, Helen and I bought a three-story Victorian white elephant on a hillside just outside Milford. It had a railed porch, gingerbread, stained-glass windows, dormers, a slate roof. Nobody wanted it but us. The house had been built by a doctor named Reed in the 1890s; I looked him up in the files of the local newspaper and found out he had called the house "The Anchorage." It was the sort of house I had always dreamed of living in. We bought Victorian furniture for it—it was cheap then, not yet antique—including a huge tall-backed velvet-covered thing called a fireside bench, with a seat so high that nobody but Joanna Russ could sit comfortably on it.

We moved the Conference to the Anchorage from the cottage colony where we had held it before. We housed people at two nearby hotels and held our sessions in the living room. After a while, the same thing happened that had happened repeatedly in the Futurian Society—tension developed between the two strongest personalities, in this case Judy and me. Judy has an enviable talent for extempore public speaking; she can go on indefinitely if nobody stops her, and it became increasingly difficult to stop her.

With occasional transgressions, we had established the principle that no one who was not a professional writer should sit in on our afternoon workshop sessions. (Spouses of writers were allowed to attend the evening sessions, but they were expected to be seen and not heard.) There were several challenges to this principle. One year Virginia wanted to be admitted as Jim's collaborator, although at that time she had not published any fiction of her own, and I made them both angry by refusing. Another year Judy wanted her daughter Merril to attend, and still another year her third husband, Danny Sugrue, did attend, and wanted to talk. Later Judy proposed a sweeping reorganization under which the sf requirement would be dropped and anyone who wanted to attend would be allowed to. She told us that she would resign as a sponsor of the Conference if the vote on this question went against her, and it did. I took over the whole management of the Conference, ran all the sessions, and felt hard-hearted but victorious.

In 1961 my relationship with Helen began to deteriorate, as if wealth had done us in. We owned property and had money in the bank (most of the time), but we no longer enjoyed each other's company. Later Helen explained it as cabin fever: in my presence she would think, "Ugh, he's breathing." We tried this and that, but nothing worked, and eventually I went to an upstairs bedroom. Helen moved out with the children, first to a little house near the river and then to Port Jervis. We were divorced after the degrading, grotesque, and cruel preliminaries then required by the Commonwealth of Pennsylvania.

Next year at the Conference Katie and I approached each other hesitantly; neither of us knew quite how to begin, but we finally managed. We agreed that Katie would get a divorce, bring her two boys to Milford, and live there for a year; then if all went well we would be married. She stayed with Judy for a week or two, then rented a little house on the Dingmans road. Kate's sons, Dusty and Dickie, were then thirteen and nine, and they circled me like strange dogs. Dickie, who wore paratrooper's boots, tried to kick me in the kneecap, but I caught his foot and dumped him. After that things went a little better, and eventually very well.

When I told Judy that Kate and I were going to be married, her jaw dropped. I had read about this in fiction, but it was the first time I had ever seen it.

We wanted a real wedding but not a minister, and on finding out that Pennsylvania law permits a couple to stand up before witnesses and declare themselves married, we asked Ted Thomas to perform a ceremony which we devised, basing it on a Unitarian service Ted got for us and altering it here and there.

Ted was a Conference regular, and so were my best man, Avram Davidson, and Kate's matron of honor, Carol Emshwiller. Mac McKenna gave the bride away.

In 1963 when I was working on a short novel called "The Other Foot" which is still my favorite, and was having difficulty with it, I turned for relaxation to another novel which I made up as I went along. I called it *The Tree of Time*. It was a wild van Vogtian adventure involving an amnesiac superman from the future and a search for a monster which turned out to be the hero in disguise, etc. I enjoyed writing it, especially the sequences that took place in a zero-G satellite of the future (a nasty little

The Anchorage, Milford, Pennsylvania, 1959

scientist I introduced here was modeled partly after J. R. Pierce). All my friends and well-wishers hated it, but I sold it everywhere—*F&SF,* Doubleday, book club, paperback. This made me cynical about the sf novel-writing business.

About a year later Helen went into a state of psychic retreat and could no longer care for the children. We took them. Leslie was three, and she followed Kate around all day talking. Kate lost more weight than she could afford; at the end she had no buttocks at all. There was nothing for her to do but to leave us. She took her two boys to West Palm Beach and got a room, rested and drank a lot of milkshakes.

After a while Helen was better and took our kids back. Katie and I wrote long letters and played chess over the phone. I was suspended between elation and despair. Kate went back to Louisville to stay with her mother, and when I had a little money I went there to see her. We agreed to live together in Louisville, and rented a tiny house in the county. We lived there about a year, but the close quarters were wearing us down—it was a miserably small house. We went back to Milford.

In 1964 I had the itch to edit something again. I realized that if I could do a series of original anthologies in hardcover, paperback, and book club, it would certainly pay its way. I wrote a proposal and sent it to Dardis. I called the series *Orbit,* expecting some discussion, but there wasn't any. *Orbit 1* appeared in 1966, and twenty others followed.

In the beginning I was able to look brilliant because I was buying all the great stories that other editors were too dumb to buy. Later the supply ran out and was not renewed, and the series went downhill, the way every series and every magazine does. The only known solution to this is to replace the editor, and even that doesn't always work.

Orbit was a ground-breaking series by design, and for that reason it didn't appeal to readers of conventional science fiction, and it didn't get book-club adoption as often as I had hoped; toward the end it didn't get paperback either. Harper and Row, who took it over with the fourteenth volume, carried it gallantly for another six years, but it couldn't make money in hardcover alone and they had to drop it. I don't regret any of this, and would do the same thing all over again if I had the chance.

Early in the sixties there had been several attempts to organize a science-fiction writers' association. What always happened was that the writers held meetings, passed resolutions, elected officers, and then everybody went home and forgot the whole

Newlyweds: Kate Wilhelm and Damon Knight, 1963

thing. I thought I saw there was a better way, but it required somebody with more clout than I had then, and I waited.

By 1965 I had accumulated a little more clout, meaning to say that I had published a few more stories and novels, and my patience was running short. One week I got three requests for flat-fee anthology rights, and I wrote an indignant flyer, mailed it to a hundred writers, and said, "If you would like to receive more information like this, send your three dollars." The checks rolled in. When I had seventy-eight writers signed up, I declared them the charter members of Science Fiction Writers of America, wrote a set of bylaws (adapted from those of Mystery Writers of America), and held an election.

I ran unopposed for President, feeling that it would be pointless to try to find an opponent that year. For Secretary-Treasurer I tapped Lloyd Biggle, Jr., whom I had met briefly when I lectured at a college in Ann Arbor, Michigan. This was a lucky choice. Biggle turned out to be conscientious, steady, ingenious, and tenacious as a bulldog. He organized our bookkeeping and records system, took charge of mailings, saw the need for a board of trustees and established it, and served on it himself until 1973, long after I was out from under. It was his suggestion of an annual anthology of stories by members that led immediately to the Nebula Awards, which I had seen only as a remote future possibility.

I wanted a trophy for the SFWA awards that would be beautiful and distinctive, unlike the Hugo rocket ship and all other conventional trophies. When I told Katie about this, she came forward with a design she had thought of years before, a spiral nebula embedded in plastic above a quartz crystal. Judith Ann Lawrence, Jim Blish's wife, turned this into a finished design after many changes and much agony, and took it on herself to procure the crystals, make the nebulas out of acetate and glitter, and find a manufacturer to do the embedments.

I organized the first SFWA Awards banquet *ex officio*, although I hate banquets and considered this one a necessary evil. For the occasion I bought my first tuxedo, and was reminded later of Thoreau's "Beware of all enterprises that require new clothes." On the way to New York we stopped at a red light and the truck behind us didn't. Our Dodge Dart was totaled and we both had sprained necks. Ann McCaffrey's VW bug was squeezed between two playful semis the same day, and *it* was totaled.

We got into New York somehow, and I wrestled with my studs and cummerbund. The banquet was held in the upstairs dining room of the Overseas Press Club, which turned out to be a rather depressing place. There was only one short speech, and I made that myself, explaining how to pronounce SFWA ("sefwa"). In order to avoid the necessity of other speeches, I had arranged for the first showing of Ed Emshwiller's later-award-winning film "Relativity."

After that I toyed with the thought of holding the banquet at the end of the Milford Conference, in a local restaurant where I knew we could get better food for half the price, and in surroundings far more pleasant. This alarmed Bob Silverberg so much that he threatened to get up a petition, and I gave in on condition that he and his wife take charge of the New York banquet. They found us an upstairs room at Les Champs, where the food and service were excellent at first. Later both deteriorated, and the management covered up the handsome gold wallpaper with a black and red combination that made the room look like the inside of a diseased kidney. The third year, when we sat through interminable slides of Mars ("Now, this is the Mare Crisium seen from the *east* . . ."), the room was so hot and unventilated that Katie felt

faint and had to leave. And the speeches went on and on.

I thought the organization should strike a conspicuous blow for freedom as early as possible, and opportunity came quickly with Ace Books' pirated editions of Tolkien's *Lord of the Rings*. Don Wollheim had said, first, that the Ace editions were not piracy, because that meant a violation of copyright and the books were not copyrighted in this country; second, that he didn't know how to get in touch with Tolkien anyhow. It was a pleasure to quote Webster's definition of literary piracy on the front page of the *SFWA Bulletin*, and, just below it, Tolkien's address.

Ace then made an extraordinary proposal to pay Tolkien half the royalties to which he was entitled, or, if he refused that, to pay full royalties to SFWA in order to finance a new set of awards to be called the Tolkien Awards. In a second editorial I said that the awards would be a good thing, but that a still better thing would be to pay full royalties to the author. (Tolkien indicated that this was his preference as well.) Largely due to Terry Carr's efforts, Ace decided to do this. Tolkien got about nine thousand dollars, and an agreement was eventually reached under which Ace undertook not to publish its editions anymore.

In 1967 Robin Scott Wilson, who had published several stories in *Analog* (as Robin Scott), was invited to the Milford Conference. He told us that he was ex-CIA, now an English teacher at a small Pennsylvania college. He arrived and turned out to be a muscular man who wore skivvies and had his hair cut very short. We became a little nervous when we discovered that every time we looked over our shoulders, Robin was there, listening. On the last day of the Conference, he told us what he was up to: he planned to start a summer sf writing workshop at Clarion College, in Clarion, Pennsylvania, and he had come to Milford to see how we did it and pick his instructors.

Robin's inspiration was to combine the Milford workshop method with a little lecturing for aspiring writers (Milford was for professionals). From the beginning, it worked. Among the students that first year were Vonda N. McIntyre and Ed Bryant. After two years at Clarion, Robin moved on to a succession of more glamorous jobs (he is now president of Chico State College in Chico, California). He continued to teach the first week of the workshop, but he was no longer able to direct the whole program. The workshop survived a tottery year at Tulane in New Orleans and then found a permanent home at Michigan State University in East Lansing, Michigan.

Every year, eighteen applicants are invited to come to the workshop for six weeks. They live in the dorm, eat cafeteria food, swelter in the Michigan summer. Each week they have a different instructor, except for the last two, when Kate and I teach together. As at Milford, we sit in a circle and take turns in criticizing each manuscript. It is understood that the criticism must be *a*) technical, and *b*) honest. By subjecting each other to this kind of examination, the students learn to become critical of their own work.

They don't get much sleep. They write all night, shamble into the workshop in the morning. They form intense personal relationships. Many of them stay in touch with each other, and with us. I won't say it is impossible not to love them, but I will say it is *difficult.*

One thing I have noticed is that the students seem to know more every year. There are things we no longer have to teach, exercises we no longer use. I have a feeling that knowledge diffuses somehow, maybe by pheromones drifting across the continent.

At her first Conference Katie had met a local newspaperman, Howard Rausch (who later became the *Wall Street Journal*'s Moscow correspondent). Howard, an amateur hypnotist, picked Katie out of a group one night for a demonstration. When she went back to Louisville, she got in touch with a psychologist at the university and studied with him for some time.

She gave birth to our son, Jonathan, under hypnosis in 1966; we had been lucky enough to find a local obstetrician who had practiced medical hypnosis before. The birth was less traumatic than usual for mother and child. When I first saw Jon he was looking calmly back at me.

My daughter Leslie appointed herself Jonathan's deputy mother as soon as she saw him, and they were inseparable companions all the time he was growing up.

I started growing a beard. I had tried this many times before and had always shaved it off again; this time I kept it, and now when people ask me how long I've had it I always know, because it's the same age as Jon. At first I had a little chin-beard, and they called me *o bode* (the goat) in Brazil; but when I saw Ed Emshwiller's beard I realized my error and let mine grow as full and frizzy as his.

In 1968 Katie and I spent a week in one of the beach suburbs of Saint Petersburg, Florida, and liked it so much that the next year we rented the Anchorage to Jim and Jane Sallis and Tom Disch, and moved to Madeira Beach. We were lucky enough to find a two-story frame house on the bay, one of the few two-story houses in that area, rented it, and moved in. Big as it was, the house was not quite big enough. Katie set up her office in the kitchen of a semidetached apartment that was part of the house; mine was in the bedroom, which had only folding doors for privacy.

In 1969 we sat out our first hurricane: piled up the furniture on the tables and went upstairs, where Jon slept while Kate and Dickie and I watched *Star Trek.* (Doug was in Vietnam.) The wind shook the house, but nothing fell down. At one point I went out in back to see what it was like; leaning back against the wind, I walked toward the seawall, where a flock of little birds had alighted. When I approached, they rose into the air and flew backward out over the bay.

Presently the owner put the house up for sale. We could hardly afford to bid on it, and were not sure we wanted to, because we knew it had termites. It was sold, and we got an eviction notice. We went back to Milford, to find that every piece of furniture in the house had been moved. My paintings were in closets. Jane had covered the kitchen floor with white tiles and had painted the walls red-orange. The Sallises' son, Dylan, had broken the hinges of the freezer door by swinging on it. Somebody had managed to move one of the big capstones of the stone wall beside the stair at the far end of the yard, and it was lying on the ground covered with blue plastic. The Sallises, with our friendship strained but intact, moved to a little house in the woods on the Port Jervis road, and we began moving furniture back. Disch had already left.

In 1969 the Brazilian government held a film festival in an effort to put Rio de Janeiro on the map, and José Sanz, a science-fiction buff, talked them into holding an sf seminar in conjunction with it. Sanz invited sf writers wholesale, and the writers suggested other writers. The Brazilian government flew us down on sumptuous Varig airliners, feeding us caviar and duck à l'orange on the way. Here I had my first batida, a drink made with lime juice and a Brazilian firewater called *cachaça,* beaten into a froth. Another name for the drink is *caipurinha,* which is more interesting (*batida* just means "beaten"). Caipur is a hillbilly district in the southern part of Brazil; the feminine diminutive makes the word mean something like "little hillbilly girl."

Rio is the only city I have ever seen that I think beautiful. One airliner a day lands at the airport. From the mountains around the city you look out over the blue ocean and see one ship.

strong, and the undertow so swift that if you try to swim in water three feet deep, you find yourself stranded as the water goes out.

A Brazilian writer, André Carneiro, was the chairman of the symposium, and several others hung around the lobby of our meeting place, but they had no part in the proceedings. I tried to organize a meeting of American and Brazilian writers, through Carneiro, but instead it was a meeting of American writers and one Brazilian publisher.

We went to the screening of a French film, forgetting that there wouldn't be any English subtitles, and walked past a barricade on the other side of which there were Brazilians, some of them shaking their fingers at us. We knew we were in a police state, and we saw the truckloads of soldiers being driven here and there, but had not realized until that moment that our presence might be taken as an offense. If I had it to do over, even knowing what I know now about the Brazilian government, I would do it again.

The Tocks Island Dam and Recreation Project was threatening to inundate the Delaware Valley, and the condemnation line ran down the middle of the highway in front of the Anchorage. Our friend Joan Matheson in Dingmans Ferry was deeply involved in fighting the Tocks Island Project. (The project was eventually abandoned, but not before many hundred-year-old farms had been acquired by eminent domain and their owners driven out.) It was evident to us that if we stayed, eventually we would be surrounded by hot-dog stands. Worse, we were getting air pollution from New York for the first time. We made up our minds to sell the Anchorage and move to Florida. We tried everything. We listed the house in the classified section of the *Saturday Review;* we thought of incorporating and selling shares to sf writers. The fall season passed, and we gave up. Then in the middle of winter a retired police chief from New Jersey came out with his wife, loved the house, and paid our price.

We spent three months househunting on the beaches, and got to be as familiar with them as any real-estate agent. Finally we found a twelve-year-old house for sale on the bay; the waterfront was narrow and at the end of an inlet, and the house was not as spacious as we had wanted, but it would do, and we bought it. In our little backyard there was an ear tree (something like a jacaranda), from which we hung a bird-feeder. Wild budgerigars clustered on it, along with sparrows, doves, and occasional jays and orioles. Herons perched on our dock. The bay was polluted, but not as much as it had been before the experimental sewage plant nearby was turned into a pumping

With Kate Wilhelm at the film festival in Rio de Janeiro, 1969

We were quartered in a hotel on the oceanfront, and were ferried every day to the French Cultural Center to listen to one of our number make a speech. This was idiocy, but we attended faithfully in order to show our gratitude, and refrained from making any speeches ourselves. A. E. van Vogt said that the universe to him was a tree with golden balls on its branches, and the next day all the Brazilian papers faithfully reported that van Vogt said the universe was a tree with golden balls on its branches.

Brian Aldiss was in our hotel and we saw him several times, but most of the others were in three other hotels farther down the avenue. Katie and I moved in a euphoric glow for the ten days we were there. I can't explain it, but there is an ambience of sexuality and romance on the Copacabana—it is in the air, you breathe it.

The beach at Copacabana is for the people, and you see them there sunning themselves, playing volleyball, the children flying tiny homemade kites that continually flutter down, swoop up, flutter. The sand looks and feels like brown sugar. The surf is

Jakarta, Indonesia, 1985

station, and I swam there nearly every day. Jon, who ignored the ocean when we first brought him down here, had swimming lessons at the Bath Club and now swam like a blond seal. Pinellas County had the highest growth rate in the country, and we knew pollution and crowding would force us to move on in three or four years, but for the present we were all right. Kate's son Dick and my son Chris, who had been living with their father and mother respectively, were now living with us, and Dick framed in two more rooms in what used to be the garage.

In 1973 Kate and I were invited to teach in Oregon at Clarion West, a spinoff organized by Vonda N. McIntyre, who had been one of our first students. The workshop was canceled at the last minute, and we were so disappointed that we moped around the house for a week and then said, "The hell with it, let's go anyway." We flew to Oregon, rented a VW van, and cruised up and down the western part of the state. Kate, who had never been here before, felt instantly at home.

I sneezed here and there, but not in Eugene (which later turned out to be the hay-fever capital of the universe), and we liked the downtown mall with

its fountain and playground. We decided to settle here: went back to Florida, sold the house, and packed thousands of books.

We lived in a rented house for about a year, then found another white elephant for sale on Horn Lane, just outside Eugene. It was a three-bedroom house which had been built onto in a haphazard fashion; in the garage there was a fourth bedroom, and opposite it in front, a large white metal shed which contained a swimming pool. (We heard later that the last owner, a roofer, had tried to get a variance to put up a storage shed in the backyard. When the neighbors voted against him at the hearing, he put up the shed in front, where they would have to see it every day.)

We brought Dick and Jon with us; other children drifted in one by one. Dick built two new rooms in the garage, filling in the rest of it (God does not intend us ever to have a roof over our car), and another off the pantry, so that we now have six bedrooms, just as we did in the Anchorage.

People in Eugene are relaxed and friendly. (Our former landlord, a disk jockey, told us about a friend who had moved out here from Cleveland, but moved back after six months because he couldn't stand the lack of hostility.) The climate is mild; it almost never snows in Eugene. If you must have snow, it is only about an hour away to the east, and the coast with its marvelous beaches is about the same distance in the other direction.

I had never expected or intended to move back to Oregon, and for about a year I felt I was living three thousand miles from anywhere. Then I began to realize that all roads lead to Eugene. We see more visitors here in twelve months than we did in twelve years in Florida.

In 1978 the Ambassador to Colombia, Diego Asencio, a science-fiction buff, invited Kate and me to lecture in Bogotá and Medellín. His first thought had been Isaac Asimov, but Asimov does not fly. His second thought was R. Glenn Wright, the director of the Clarion Workshop; Glenn's first thought was Katie, and she took me along.

The three of us had a *marvelous* time. I suppose our collective knowledge of Spanish was about ten words, and we called for "el chequo" in restaurants. (The food was great.) In a sort of gigantic red-carpeted conversation pit where we had our sessions with the Colombians, Glenn said, "Why don't you take some of this drug money that you all have and start some publishing companies?" There was dead silence. Glenn, a close friend who is dead now, also had a habit of expressing the idea "and so on" by "blah blah woof woof," and I always wondered how the interpreters handled that.

At this symposium we met René Rebetez, a Colombian writer who became our friend. I translated a story of his, "The New Prehistory," which was published in *F&SF* and was eventually included in *The World Treasury of Science Fiction*, edited by David Hartwell.

In 1979 Diego asked us back without Glenn. In anticipation of this we had made some effort to learn a little Spanish, and I had an epiphany on the third or fourth day, when we were taking part in a symposium at a *finca* outside Medellín: suddenly I understood everything that was being said. It was just like the fairy tales in which the hero has swallowed an amulet that enables him to understand the language of the birds.

In 1983 the U.S. Information Agency, having sent us out a couple of times without repercussions, sent us out again, this time to Southeast Asia (they gave us a choice between that and Siberia). We lectured in Indonesia, Malaysia, and Hong Kong, and saw a lot of temples, an experience that we would not trade for gold. On the island of Penang off the Malaysian coast, where they sent us for R and R, I asked a waiter what kind of birds were congregating by the dozen on the lawn. They were myna birds, and I realized then that I wasn't in Kansas.

In 1985, against all expectations, the USIA sent us to Brazil and we saw Rio again. It was still as marvelous as ever, and we also saw Brasilia, São Paulo, Petropolis, Santa Caterina, and Porto Alegre. We went home by way of Peru, and saw Machu Picchu, an indelible experience.

Well, what can I tell you? Our children are grown up, and some of them have children of their own, but we still have all their cats. We write every day, and the sun comes up in the morning.

Copyright © Damon Knight, 1989

BIBLIOGRAPHY

Fiction:

Hell's Pavement. New York: Lion Books, 1955; London: Banner, 1958; also published as *Analogue Men.* New York: Berkley, 1962; London: Sphere, 1967.

The People Maker. Rockville Centre, N.Y.: Zenith, 1959; also published as *A for Anything.* London: Four Square/New English Library, 1961; New York: Berkley, 1965.

Masters of Evolution (bound with *Fire in the Heavens* by George O. Smith). New York: Ace, 1959.

The Sun Saboteurs (bound with *The Light of Lilith* by G. McDonald Wallis). New York: Ace, 1961.

Far Out: Thirteen Science Fiction Stories. New York: Simon & Schuster, 1961; London: Gollancz, 1962.

In Deep (short stories). New York: Berkley, 1963; London: Gollancz, 1964.

Beyond the Barrier. Garden City, N.Y.: Doubleday, 1964; London: Gollancz, 1964.

Off Center (short stories). (Bound with Knight's *The Rithian Terror*) New York: Ace, 1965; also published as *Off Centre.* London: Gollancz, 1969.

Mind Switch. New York: Berkley, 1965; also published as *The Other Foot.* London: Whiting & Wheaton, 1966.

Turning On: Thirteen Stories. Garden City, N.Y.: Doubleday, 1966; also published as *Turning On: Fourteen Stories.* London: Gollancz, 1967.

Three Novels: Rule Golden, Natural State, The Dying Man. Garden City, N.Y.: Doubleday, 1967; London: Gollancz, 1967; also published as *Natural State and Other Stories.* London: Pan, 1975.

World without Children and The Earth Quarter: Two Science Fiction Novels. New York: Lancer, 1970.

Two Novels: The Earth Quarter, Double Meaning. London: Gollancz, 1974.

The Best of Damon Knight (short stories). Garden City, N.Y.: Doubleday, 1976.

Rule Golden and Other Stories. New York: Avon, 1979.

Better Than One (short stories), with Kate Wilhelm. Boston: Noreascon II, 1980.

The World and Thorinn. New York: Berkley/Putnam, 1981.

The Man in the Tree. New York: Berkley, 1984; London: Gollancz, 1985.

Late Knight Edition. Cambridge, Mass.: New England Science Fiction Association, 1985.

CV. New York: Tor, 1985.

Le Livre d'or de la science fiction. Paris: Presses Pocket, 1987.

The Observers. New York: Tor, 1988.

Nonfiction:

In Search of Wonder: Essays on Modern Science Fiction (illustrated by J. L. Patterson). Chicago: Advent, 1956.

Charles Fort: Prophet of the Unexplained (biography). Garden City, N.Y.: Doubleday, 1970; London: Gollancz, 1971.

The Futurians. New York: John Day, 1977.

Creating Short Fiction. Cincinnati, Ohio: Writer's Digest, 1981.

Editor of anthologies:

A Century of Science Fiction. New York: Simon & Schuster, 1962; London: Gollancz, 1963.

First Flight: Maiden Voyages in Space and Time. New York: Lancer, 1963; also published as *Now Begins Tomorrow.* New York: Lancer, 1969.

Tomorrow × 4. Greenwich, Conn.: Gold Medal/Fawcett, 1964; London: Coronet, 1967.

A Century of Great Short Science Fiction Novels. New York: Delacorte, 1964; London: Gollancz, 1965.

Beyond Tomorrow: Ten Science Fiction Adventures. New York: Harper, 1965; London: Gollancz, 1968.

The Dark Side. Garden City, N.Y.: Doubleday, 1965; London: Dobson, 1966.

The Shape of Things. New York: Popular Library, 1965.

Thirteen French Science-Fiction Stories. Translated by Knight. New York: Bantam, 1965; London: Corgi, 1965.

Cities of Wonder. Garden City, N.Y.: Doubleday, 1966; London: Dobson, 1968.

Nebula Award Stories, 1965. Garden City, N.Y.: Doubleday, 1966; London: Gollancz, 1967.

Worlds To Come: Nine Science Fiction Adventures. New York: Harper, 1967; London: Gollancz, 1969.

Science Fiction Inventions. New York: Lancer, 1967.

A Hundred Years of Science Fiction. New York: Simon & Schuster, 1968; London: Gollancz, 1969; also published in two volumes. London: Pan, 1972.

The Metal Smile. New York: Belmont, 1968.

Toward Infinity: Nine Science Fiction Tales. New York: Simon & Schuster, 1968; also published as *Towards Infinity: Nine Science Fiction Adventures.* London: Gollancz, 1970.

Dimension X: Five Science Fiction Novellas. New York: Simon & Schuster, 1970; London: Gollancz, 1972; also published in two volumes as *Dimension X: Two Novellas* and *Elsewhere × 3: Three Novellas.* London: Coronet, 1974.

A Pocketful of Stars. Garden City, N.Y.: Doubleday, 1971; London: Gollancz, 1972.

First Contact. New York: Pinnacle, 1971.

Perchance To Dream. Garden City, N.Y.: Doubleday, 1972; London: Gollancz, 1974.

A Science Fiction Argosy. New York: Simon & Schuster, 1972; London: Gollancz, 1973.

Tomorrow and Tomorrow: Ten Tales of the Future. New York: Simon & Schuster, 1973; London: Gollancz, 1974.

The Golden Road: Great Tales of Fantasy and the Supernatural. New York: Simon & Schuster, 1974; London: Gollancz, 1974.

Happy Endings: Fifteen Stories by the Masters of the Macabre. Indianapolis: Bobbs-Merrill, 1974.

A Shocking Thing: Seventeen Tales of the Grotesque. New York: Pocket, 1974.

The Best from Orbit, Volumes 1–10. New York: Putnam, 1975.

Science Fiction of the Thirties. Indianapolis: Bobbs-Merrill, 1975.

Westerns of the Forties: Classics from the Great Pulps. Indianapolis: Bobbs-Merrill, 1977; also published in two volumes as *Western Classics from the Great Pulps* and *Seven Westerns of the Forties.* New York: Barnes and Noble, 1978.

Turning Points: Essays on the Art of Science Fiction. New York: Harper, 1977.

First Voyages (expanded version of Knight's *First Flight*), with Martin H. Greenberg and Joseph D. Olander. New York: Avon, 1981.

The Clarion Awards. Garden City, N.Y.: Doubleday, 1984.

"Orbit" Anthology Series

Orbit 1: A Science Fiction Anthology. New York: Putnam, 1966; London: Whiting & Wheaton, 1966.

Orbit 2: The Best New Science Fiction of the Year. New York: Putnam, 1967; London: Rapp & Whiting, 1968.

Orbit 3: The Best New Science Fiction of the Year. New York: Putnam, 1968; London: Rapp & Whiting, 1969.

Orbit 4: The Best New Science Fiction of the Year. New York: Putnam, 1968; London: Rapp & Whiting, 1970; also published as *Nine New SF Stories Especially Written for Orbit 4.* New York: Berkley, 1969.

Orbit 5: The Best All New Science Fiction of the Year. New York: Putnam, 1969; London: Rapp & Whiting/Deutsch, 1970.

Orbit 6: An Anthology of New Science Fiction Stories. New York: Putnam, 1970; London: Rapp & Whiting, 1972.

Orbit 7: An Anthology of New Science Fiction Stories. New York: Putnam, 1970; London: Rapp & Whiting, 1973.

Orbit 8: An Anthology of New Science Fiction Stories. New York: Putnam, 1970; London: Rapp & Whiting, 1973.

Orbit 9: An Anthology of New Science Fiction Stories. New York: Putnam, 1971.

Orbit 10: An Anthology of New Science Fiction Stories. New York: Putnam, 1972.

Orbit 11: An Anthology of New Science Fiction Stories. New York: Putnam, 1972.

Orbit 12: An Anthology of New Science Fiction Stories. New York: Putnam, 1973.

Orbit 13: An Anthology of New Science Fiction Stories. New York: Putnam, 1974.

Orbit 14. New York: Harper, 1974.

Orbit 15. New York: Harper, 1974.

Orbit 16. New York: Harper, 1975.

Orbit 17. New York: Harper, 1975.

Orbit 18. New York: Harper, 1976.

Orbit 19. New York: Harper, 1977.

Orbit 20. New York: Harper, 1978.

Orbit 21. New York: Harper, 1980.

Translator of:

Thirteen French Science-Fiction Stories. Edited by Knight. New York: Bantam, 1965; London: Corgi, 1965.

Ashes, Ashes, by René Barjavel. Garden City, N.Y.: Doubleday, 1967.

Lyn Lifshin

1944-

LIPS, BLUES, BLUE LACE: ON THE OUTSIDE

"My first birthday party in Barre—my mother, father, and grandmother behind me"

There are only three things I clearly remember my father saying to me, all began with "Don't." Don't wear light pink lipstick, it makes your teeth look grey, he told me at twelve or thirteen when I discovered Milkmaid's creamy gloss. "Don't invite me to your wedding, I don't want to be involved, or come. Or pay," a few years later, just days before that August 25, on the phone. And then, in the post office, the last words he'd say to me, "Don't do anything you don't want to." When I was born my mother says he was thrilled at my long legs and thought I looked like Ann Miller. Those first years I've heard he played with me every night. I remember none of that. Only how he sat quietly in the gold chair listening for the Dow-Jones average, rarely smiling. And the stain where his head touched that chair when he was gone. But he did one thing never maybe imagining its impact, something that has stayed with me as long as all he never did or said.

Born in Russia, my father had many qualities typical of Vermonters: he was quiet, frugal, taciturn. Maybe it was that lack of warmth, that withdrawn, brooding, often depressed mood, a dark coldness, that endeared my father and Robert Frost to each other. I used to see Frost wandering around Middlebury in baggy green pants, carrying strawberries. He

233

bought those pants in Lazarus Department Store, my grandfather's store, and he would let only my father wait on him. At Syracuse, still afraid I couldn't write enough to take a creative-writing course, I submitted two of the only poems I'd written since high school to *Syracuse 10,* where Joyce Carol Oates published often. One was published. My father, without telling me, got a copy of that poem and showed it to Frost, who wrote on it, "Very good sayeth Robert Frost," and told my father he liked the striking images and wanted me to come and visit him, bring him more.

But, before then . . .

Like me, I think my mother married because she felt she ought to, at a time when there wasn't anything in the next couple of months she wanted to do. Then, on July 12, exactly nine months after my mother first slept with my father, I was born. They'd been married three months and she was beginning to wonder what kind of marriage this would be. They'd eloped July 1 in his brother's borrowed Chevy and went right to one sister's in Malden, Massachusetts. My father didn't introduce my mother as his wife and slept in a separate room, as he would as they slid between various sisters' houses in Malden, Winthrop, and Brookline, as unused condoms spilled from a bulging suitcase and he didn't touch her, even when they were alone. When he did, before she had time to think how to deal with the brother-in-law who blew up, sure the car was stolen, or get used to writing her name as Lipman, or had a day to think about what brides buy or the apartment, she was pregnant.

I was born in Bishop de Gosbriand Hospital in Burlington, Vermont. It must have been a beautiful day, my mother said yesterday when I asked her what the weather was, what songs were popular. "Everything about having you was wonderful," she tells me on the phone, that umbilical cord I've struggled to break from and always worry, dream, and dread, since I was five or six, about the time she won't be at the end of. "First," she says, "since it happened after the first time and I wasn't ready, I did panic and ask what I could take to stop it. But I felt great," she says, "not like when I was carrying your sister. With you, no morning sickness." The only bad dreams, she says, were those of war and a terror of Hitler. Even in the middle of the day she'd check the carriage I was in, swathed in cotton netting to keep spiders out, near the apartment I once tried, unsuccessfully, to find when I read at Norwich, near Barre. Perhaps she picked 23 Hill Street as higher, harder to get to should Hitler drift over the Atlantic to snatch me. In photographs of my first birthday party there, I'm the only girl, clutching a huge black stuffed animal, half dog, half horse.

My mother was the oldest girl, as I am. Only she'd been a disappointment, she always felt. I'm taping stories of her childhood and it always comes back to her father saying, "I wouldn't take a thousand dollars for her but you couldn't give me another for the world." With the smallest, unheated bedroom, my mother felt second-rate and for that reason always wanted daughters. She has few memories of getting attention or feeling special. Probably, tho she didn't even think of having children until she had them, this is why she went to the opposite extreme with my sister and me. She chose not to marry the man I think she cared most for, a non-Jewish law student she spent delicious college days at Simmons with. They went to lectures, on boat rides on the Charles River, laughed and danced until he did a Charlie Chaplin imitation of an old Jewish man and my mother, who never had much patience with acts or comments she considered symbolic, was horrified, knew then she'd have to forget him. She didn't become a librarian, an early choice, because friends said that was too prudish, too unexciting for her. Instead, she left to work in New York City, in bookstores, Macy's, a credit agency she said was ghastly, any place bustling and alive. On October 9, 1936, she gave a cousin a first-edition copy of Margaret Mitchell's *Gone with the Wind* for her birthday, the address of the apartment they shared with two other young women on the frontispiece, apt. 4J, 53 West Seventy-second Street. Within weeks of moving in, my mother knew the neighbors on all the floors so fast the owner and landlord offered her a job collecting rent. My mother loved to dance, jitterbugged, loved plays, saw *Tobacco Road,* a number of musicals, Cab Calloway, and discovered a lovely French restaurant, Fleur de Lis, where they served multicourse dinners for fifty cents during the week, including shrimp cocktail, seventy-five cents on Sunday. Often she had three dates a day tho she was never a beauty, "except for good legs," she says. Even at seventy she could walk in three-inch heels up Boylston. My mother loved the city, travel, adventure, new people. Even now she's more apt to talk to people on the bus than I am. In her college yearbook people wrote, "For Frieda, get your own phone, so someone else can get messages." Others said her room always had the most girls, in their pleated skirts, midi blouses, cropped hair, and Clara Bow lips, giggling. Bubbly, fun, full of joie de vivre were the words most used.

My father came from Russia, from a town near Kovno in what was Lithuania. He was probably ten.

No one is sure of his age. I always heard he was ten years older than my mother, and yet getting my birth certificate for a passport this week, he's listed as thirty-four when I was born, my mother twenty-eight. Even the day of his birth is unknown, and at one time May 10 was picked somewhat arbitrarily. His past, even his presence in the house with us, was shadowy, unreachable, a little dark. Unlike drawers of photographs of my mother and her three brothers and stories I'm still taping, of her birth in Mineville, New York, and the move to the house with crystal and ruby glass beads on Elm, to the house with the Chinese chair, still on North Pleasant, where she peeled barrel rings for hoops, hid china dolls so her younger brothers wouldn't smash them, and, when the family changed their name from Lazarovitz to Lazarus, heard her violin teacher say because of this she'd never become a famous violinist, what I remember of my father's childhood is fragmented and skimpy. Either he told me or I made up feather beds, chickens in the house, and tremendous pines, images I held on to, retold myself in an early poem where I imagine him coming to this country "riding a gull's

Lyn and her father

back." In photographs he seems to be touching my sister and me lightly, ghostly, as if not sure we were real. Or I was on the beach, fat, trying to catch a ball he'd never throw. My mother says he cherished me, read to me every night. I wish I remembered more than him sitting, a stranger, in that yellow chair, listening to stock reports. Or taking pills on the steep stairs up from Main Street. And how, just before my parents divorced, he'd made plans to have his stocks, on his death, go not to my mother or sister or me, but, like an eternal flame, or astronauts whose spaceship loses power, circle indefinitely. Coldly and untouchably. To this day, I'm drawn to inaccessible, cold men, those uncomfortable and awkward about intimacy.

My mother, all thru my childhood and teens, looked for a house, not an apartment. She wanted my father to want a house my sister and I would be proud to bring friends and dates back to. For twenty years she went out with real-estate agents, still lives in the apartment we moved into when I was six, a flat she never fixed up, certain they'd move soon. No accident that a house is important to me, that it is in the title of my first book, *Why Is the House Dissolving,* and that so many other books are about houses—*Shaker House Poems, Old House Poems, The Old House on the Croton, Leaning South, Audley End*—and many series of poems are about old houses in New York, Vermont, Nantucket, Philipsburg Manor, or that so many of my dreams involve houses.

My father was good looking, quiet, probably intelligent. Unlike my mother, he didn't go to college, and he couldn't dance. My own ex-husband said, "To dance is the same as to have sex." He probably said fuck. My father must have found my mother's joie de vivre, her energy, laughter, and daring irresistible. I wish I'd known her then. She'd suggest friends drive at midnight to Boston, New York, or Montreal for a cup of coffee or crash customs because they were, coming back, low on gas. My mother loved Cab Calloway, danced in jazz clubs in Harlem. Somewhere she'd heard that the Lipmans made good husbands and at twenty-six or twenty-seven resigned herself to giving up a life of adventure.

I don't know if I got my tendency to do things to an extreme from my parents, but my mother went from having no use for kids—she'd say, "Use it well," at a howling baby—to making my sister and me her life. In the cellar, in a box of musty carbons, interviews, news clips, letters, I found a twenty-five-page outline for an autobiographical novel for a Chicago press I never wrote. It tells of my grandmother coming in 1888 from Lithuania, near Kovno, or Odessa, the daughter of a strict rabbi and a violin player. There are details I'd forgotten about, like her not marrying a Marty Melnick, a name I half wonder if I made up. There are notes about her two sisters, her sister's death in the 1919 flu outbreak. I planned to link three generations and had penciled in in the margin, "The theme of betrayals." In the chapter about my mother I started with her feeling hated because she'd been born a girl, something she stressed again in part of an interview I did with her less than two weeks ago. In her early memories of the deaths of grandmothers, the left-out feelings when other children hung up stockings, loved Jesus, sang carols up and down North Pleasant Street, and later of being followed by a father who didn't trust her, are clues to our tangled closeness.

One afternoon when my mother was in her early teens in Middlebury, Vermont, the kind of small town *Life* magazine used to come and photograph after snowstorms, a calendar village, white clapboard houses, village green, Episcopal church, a town where everyone is Protestant, possibly Catholic, and there were few ethnic names, no pizza, no Chinese food, my mother had a feeling of being pulled into her father's store. It was as if against her will, she told her friend Peggy, a magnet, a leash, a lasso. As I write this, I'm thinking how in my poetry and prose there's a quality, often, of interruptions, sidetracks, parenthetical descriptions, roads that go where I hadn't expected, a breathless run-on, convoluted style, stories that move, no, leapfrog and vault between the past and the present, which is really the way my mother talks. Maybe it's the way our family related. That afternoon she found out her mother had been so badly hurt in a car accident the next days the papers reported her dead. Gramp's hair turned white overnight. My grandmother was rushed to the Bishop de Gosbriand Hospital, a Catholic hospital in Burlington. For years I heard how the nuns brought her candles on Friday night, said you pray in your way and we'll pray in ours. In what seemed to many a miracle, my grandmother recovered, never to stop worrying, to such an extent we gave her worry beads. She expected disaster, picked up the phone, as my mother does, with a "Is something wrong?" Everyone was so grateful to the sisters and doctors my mother decided to have her first child at that hospital, even when her doctor tried to talk her out of it. All they care about is the baby and the father, she told me later, remembering the pain they gave her nothing for and how when she groaned or complained they were more concerned about the suffering, poor father. I still want to know what songs were on the radio, if there was one

the morning she woke up and said she felt funny and they drove the thirty miles from Barre to Burlington. I'd like to know what my mother wore. Just this summer I put on a white and royal blue two-piece summer dress she had, wrote a poem about that. I have a black-velvet and fox cape she was given at eighteen by a man who still sees her as she was, in pleated skirt, giggling on bleachers in Boston.

After two weeks flat on her back, the day my mother brought me home my father was late picking her up and she didn't have any formula. "My insides," she said, "from being in bed so long, felt they were about to slide out." It must have been strange for her to have me howling, hungry. In the apartment she yelped, was in awe, and dragged her mother to see, not sure what to do with the first evidence I'd do more than howl in the diaper that would have to be hand-washed, boiled on the stove, hung from long lines that broke twice, plunging forty cotton diaper squares into mud.

The first baby, I was photographed it seems on the hour. August 11, four weeks less one day, wrapped in a blanket in tall grass, a house on the hill behind my mother and me. Six months and a day, January 13, against wallpaper with oriental trees I can't bring back to mean anything, tho in the hall of my mother's present apartment the wallpaper is something like that. In group photos, many of birthday parties, most people seem to be looking at me. The baby photos are labeled Rosalynn, my real name, a name my mother thought she'd made up, theatrical, good for an actress. Rosalynn Diane—a name I've used on and off. Even today, going for a new passport, I see it's the name I used on my expired one. Raisel Devora was my Hebrew name, I think. I've given myself that name anyway, liking it, finding it exotic. I wish I had some of the photographs still tied up and with the filmmaker for the documentary. In the early ones my mother's hair is dark and curly, her teeth, which wouldn't hold up well, a dentist told her ten years before, still very white.

Someone gave me a *Newsweek* from July of that first week with gas masks on the cover. On the first page, a Studebaker ad. Franco has just sentenced one hundred to death. Quaker Chemical announces a crystalline compound to make fabrics flameproof as Governor Long is rolling up his sleeves and someone looks back at Mussolini and Hitler. Stalin holds the balance, trouble brews. There's a photo of Goebbels patting blond braided young girls in Danzig as Winston Churchill's still smiling and Georges Braque and Kuniyoshi win awards. NBC resurrects the lost hit plays. I remember the ritual of curling close to my mother and father in their bed, a special treat on Fridays with cocoa and marshmallow fluff, listening to some radio program, and how at six I went into a mournful depression at the loss of a radio voice, Santa Claus, when my mother said, after the ritual and baths, and then listening to the radio reading of letters, he'd be gone for a year. I didn't believe I'd get thru that, much as I was sure I couldn't make it, losing the touch of others, on and off the radio now. *Newsweek* says portable radios are a find, about the size of a beach bag, light enough, finally, to carry. People drink Schlitz. My mother did, I bet, or Miller's, when she and my father went out for a big night at the Brown Derby. I see "Alan Carter," the father of a boy I'd have a crush on, "has created the 67 piece Vermont State Orchestra, Plain Folks Symphony." Esperanto looks good. Knox gelatin reduces fatigue. Books on the best-seller list have to do with those with Jewish blood being sadistically treated. No wonder my mother at times wished she'd brought us up as Christians, told us we had to be careful, being Jewish in a small town. Part of what always made me feel outside things, an onlooker, someone looking thru glass, as I did in the dark hall with stained glass and a black creaking grandfather clock, the stucco falling in my grandmother's house. Or, as a writer, I still feel.

When I was born, bicycles were big, and ocean liners. You could go for twenty-eight days for 127 dollars and up. Pepsodent sweetens breath. I wonder if I still use it for nostalgia. A lovesick man says, "I'll be holding my breath till I see you again," as the woman glad to get away shrugs, "Swell, dear." Skirts were just below the knees, a style not unlike this summer's. The dress my mother is wearing in one photograph could have come off this summer's Macy's rack. Except she would, having recently lost so much weight, after years of trying to, swim in it.

I said my first word at six months, "cig," for cigarette. And, before I was three, driving to Middlebury in a bumpy car on a back road over Lincoln Mountain, before the cigar a man smoked made me sick, said, "It looks like the trees are dancing," as we drove past. My mother wanted to write that down, an omen. If I wasn't to be an actress, I'd be a writer. Trees became a recurring image, and wood and women who, Daphnelike, run into trees. The first poem I wrote when I skipped and slid from first grade to third was about apple trees, and apples have been in the titles of at least three books, *Black Apples, Paper Apples* and *Forty Days, Apple Nights.* I live in a

house on Appletree, and branches, hearts of wood, are inside and outside me.

We lived in Barre, a granite-mining town, where what I remember is a bench in a park where you could whisper anything and it would circle, come back to you. As some poems do. My father worked in his brother's store. Wearing a clown suit, I beat up the boy next door, and my mother defended me as she has and does, said I didn't do it, couldn't, was too sweet, rosebud mouth, huge eyes, plump but not fat. Yet. Maybe there was a song that had "Are you happy?" in it as a refrain. My mother, I heard, asked me that so often that my father frowned, growled, "Don't keep asking her that. She might think she's not."

My deepest emotions are so tangled with my mother, sometimes in rage and anger—times I've felt suffocated, choked, sometimes with joy, often with the terror of losing her, something I felt as early as six, hearing stories of bad children playing with matches who start fires, burn their mother up. If I didn't write this piece now, with her thin, fragile, smaller, but still alive, it would be hard for years to, later.

She must have been fairly happy in Barre. There were a number of other young women having new babies, sharing terrors of war. It was before my mother and father started fighting as much as they would. Bridge games, mah-jongg, costume parties, suppers, birthday parties with those delicate crepe-paper baskets filled with jelly beans, gumdrops, peppermint patties, and a flower in a stem. Still in Barre, I'm naked in the grass, about one, with a boy who'd later invite me to Boston University. Close to three, I had my tonsils out, remember the bright-colored gum balls in the globe of glass, like stained glass I'd find magical later in Tiffany-style lamps and old stained-glass windows, bring back to my house to turn light less green. For years, perhaps because of the strangeness of ether, I was afraid to sleep on my back.

Ice cream after the hospital might have made up for the time there if November hadn't been fragmented by a rushed move my mother never wanted to make back to Middlebury. The town she was always ready to leave. Her brothers were in the army or at college or about to be, and tho she dreaded it, as if she knew once there she would never leave, reluctantly she and my father packed the white jigsaw horse that fit into a turquoise back and the Lindbergh doll I'd break in one of my tantrums, packed the black stuffed animal, ruby punch bowl, a wedding gift still on my mother's dining-room buffet, and the blond Heywood-Wakefield furniture, scorched with Marlboro and Camel and Herbert Tareyton burns, the locket with Rosalynn on it that I chewed, my first teeth marks on it, and my navy suspender skirt, my mother's camel-hair coat I never saw. And what, I wonder, of my father's did we bring with us?

They put sheets over the blue velvet sofa, still in the living room on Main Street covered over with the twentieth or thirtieth pair of sofa throws, three or four years before the small fluffy grey kitten peed on it and my mother splashed Clorox all over, turned the royal to bluish mud. They packed the gold chair my father left the stain of his head on, now a nubby yellow, and the chair I'd remember curling into the deepest curves of just before we'd move to the third house I'd live in, a night my father told me if you rubbed marbles long enough and hard enough they'd dissolve, loaded it in a van, a draped ghost in November snow, the leaves gone already.

The last thing my mother brought in the car could have been the red plaid carriage blanket downstairs, or the white and gold dishes last weekend she wanted to give me and I said, "Later." In the backseat, evening dresses my mother had many of before her marriage, now rarely needed, or the album of photographs of me, the windup Victrola, as much as they could fit into the black Plymouth my grandparents gave them that they couldn't afford, the pots and pans, and headed one and a half hours southeast for a stretch that wouldn't be anything like what my mother ever wanted.

Cold, raw, leafless. The weather a metaphor for the next many years, tho my mother might have told friends at the goodby parties, "It won't be as bad as I'm expecting."

In spite of a fairly successful department store, Lazarus Department Store, a Middlebury landmark until the January after JFK died, when it burned down and, as if the store was a part of him, my grandfather died a few months later, my grandparents' house, even with company coming and staying for weeks, wasn't without its own darkness. By the time I got married, I expected marriage to be gloomy. Both grandparents came from Russia, Kovno and Odessa are the cities I heard. My grandfather had worked as a peddler, met my grandmother, married her, and started a small store in Granville, New York, and Witherbee, where my mother was born, before they moved to Vermont, Middlebury, an unlikely place for someone Jewish to bring up four children. He was supposed to be very religious, but my mother and I, later, caught him eating candy on Passover. As

a young girl my mother was aware something peculiar was going on when her father brought the young Polish girl who worked for them into the bed in the den where my mother, sick, was sleeping and she heard them grunting in the sheets and something about "nice pussy." Later my grandmother heard about her husband's exploits, fainted out on the front lawn, then moved into her own room. Maybe this was when she began to write poems she never showed anybody, perhaps because her older brother, Hyman, was known as the family poet, coming up with rhymed couplets for family events. I don't remember them, but do remember how he'd say before he died he wished he could see me with my hair cut. Now my uncle sleeps in the mahogany bed, near the elephant statues my grandmother collected, where she watched hemlocks, shadows the moon made on mirrors years of nights she couldn't sleep. When my grandfather died she showed no emotion. His room, never entered all the years he lurked there, was padlocked. My mother knew nothing good could grow of moving her own family closer to what she had left, braiding her life up with her parents again, bringing along this man who they hardly knew, was hard to know.

My grandmother was in many ways independent. She ran much of the business of the store. At different times we all worked there, muggy Julys before air-conditioning, folding Ship & Shore blouses, watching the clock that seemed to go slower as it reached into the eighties. After her accident my grandmother was sick often. I'm sure my mother felt trapped by the afternoon ritual: from the time I was three, and for years after my sister was born, she packed us each afternoon and brought us when my grandmother was sick or depressed there, where my mother tried to cajole her, read to her, told stories. She tried to be silly, make my grandmother laugh before hurrying back to the Emilo house, a brown and white two-story with blue grapes in the backyard, where once I was told, playing in a tub of water, I tore off my clothes and ran naked in front of two stuffy, aging schoolteachers. Miss Hincks, fortunately retired before I got there and Mrs. McCormack, a woman I never saw smile. My father withdrew more and more. Behind his back, my grandfather complained to my mother about him. She and my father, who even that early I began to call Ben, began to fight. Most of the fights had to do with money and houses. "Merle doesn't have to live like this," something I heard my mother say about my father's brother's wife, who had a beautiful home with a lawn, is in several poems.

Most Sundays we went to my grandmother's, a pattern that continued even when I was in high school. Grown-ups slapped cards and ate my grandmother's brownies while I read or daydreamed in the front living room, dark with an exotic black shiny dragon of a Chinese chair and a green water-lily rug surrounded by dusky roses. Before the uncles came home to stay, they were mostly scratchy uniforms. For a while I was the only grandchild, my hair piled on top of my head as I clutched a white elephant. I outgrew a pink, itchy snowsuit, plump, still not quite fat. My mother smoked more. My grandmother peeled tinfoil from gum wrappers, Black Jack and Pepsin, rolled and stored them in an elephant-shaped vase. My mother must have been waiting for something to begin or get over. In a few years we moved from the house around the corner from her mother's. In Vermont last weekend I could see that house on a postcard with an aerial view of the town. Set back from the street, pointed roof, slanted ceilings, on Seminary Street near the Methodist church where Patty Bissette, whose adopted parents never let her go out without a prissy dress, tight tight curls, was buried after she became one of the Boston strangler's choices.

The more I think about it, the more horrid those early years back in Middlebury must have been for my mother. Soon she was pregnant with my sister. This time tho with all-day morning sickness, a mother she felt obligated to rush to see, and no circle of friends. She lost weight, and when it seemed the baby was coming early, was rushed to Burlington. My grandmother hurried to take care of me. I was four, had measles. I clearly remember delicious hours in a darkened room my mother brought fruit juices to with a glass straw. Suddenly she wasn't there and my grandmother was flushing false teeth down the toilet in a wad of Kleenex and nothing seemed quiet or still.

In photographs of me and what turned out to be my sister, Joy, I seem happy, proud, grown up, and big sisterly. But much of waiting for her to be born was awful. I missed my mother, desperately. Over measles, I was sent to play-school, where, too unhappy to play, to distract me or make me laugh, I was hosed with icy water. I was enraged, had to go home and change, and have resisted, since then, organized play. All I liked of the playground was a house tall enough to stand up in and a vat of water we made oil and water prints in, globs of paint swirling plum, mango, and jade on meat-wrap paper.

I remember my loneliness, staying at my grandmother's. An uncle told me if I ate the small candy pellets in glass ships on the piano, worms would crawl

into my belly. The bedroom I slept in seemed icy, even in July with wasps in the shades. Nothing, not making clay men in the driveway or the smell of Yardley's Lavendar in the orchid and green-tile bathroom, helped. When I fell off my tricycle, riding over cut-up cement, and bruised my leg and crotch and belly, I was furious. It was my new sister's fault. I wouldn't have been on that street if she hadn't been born.

Within months, we moved again. Not to our own house but the Zeno house, a stucco house I drove by last week. Sinks, motors, and mowers were in the front yard, the stucco almost guava. It was the end of the street then, near Battell Woods and a pine forest. Still as a church, carpeted with red needles. The house was surrounded by wildness. Queen Anne's lace in a clump of stones and, behind the house, rhubarb a baby-sitter once told us panthers lurked in, the night we put candles in halved walnut shells and floated them in pans of water. They made eerie

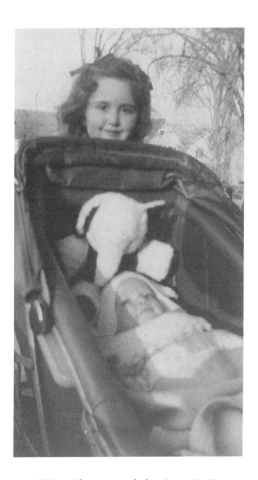

"Me with my new baby sister, Joy"

239

shadows anything could have lurked in. Upstairs the bedrooms had wide boards painted grey, with enough room between them for dead bugs to pile up, and heat grates where I could lie on my stomach listening. Eavesdropping. As I still do, spying. I learned to read early, before first grade. *Jack and Jill* magazine had stories of soldiers and dentists and a stone that would glow red and rose in a closet and transformed itself if you held it close and tight.

I painted Cheerios into rainbow beads, longed for a kitten. On the night before my sixth birthday, after my parents had tried to get one, a scraggly kitten appeared at the door, and within months she had kittens she was too young to take care of. My mother thought the kittens would die, until another pregnant cat appeared, gave birth in a coal bin, and when water rose, my father and one of the bigger cats carried many mewling, wet, scrawny bags of fur to the top stair. The boxes of cats in the kitchen near the old white and grey stove on legs is one of my warmest memories. It's cats, not dolls, I hold in most photos.

My sister was born dark with a birthmark. I was appalled, sure people would think because she had blue eyes she didn't belong in our family. She got blonde, slowly became someone to play with. One uncle was still at Fort Devon. My mother made him brownies, one of the few recipes handed down to me, and listened to the brown Zenith. Across the street in a dark house with coves and a spiral teak staircase, a house that smelled of lemon, oil, polished wood, a smell that pulled me to the house I now live in and know it probably meant the heat-vents exchanger was about to go, a Baptist minister who was always trying to convert us lived, with his two daughters, Geraldine and Priscilla, who once lured me to steal some matches from their stove and bring them out to the club we were making in chickory and wild carrot.

That last summer on Seminary my mother rented a cottage at Mallets Bay on Lake Champlain. Inside, ceilings were low and the rooms smelled of oilcloth, lineoleum, and citronella. Louis Armstrong played near a roller-skating rink across the way, where I found a girl with one blue eye and one green eye riveting. All these images haunted when I wrote about them, leaving Vermont for good. Until writing this tho, I hadn't realized how many scary memories are connected to baby-sitters. At the lake, the baby-sitter filled us with stories of atrocities in Germany and Poland, "what they did to young girls," and she painted the smoke from bodies in tunnels, said you could smell scorched hair. This may be where over a year of nightmares about fires began. And where two other obsessions got a start: wanting to be thin and

wanting to have straight, not curly, wavy hair. It was the summer before school began I started to see myself as fat and ugly, and having to wear glasses very soon didn't help. A cousin, Elaine, was skinny and pretty and snotty and always had her way. I thought the two went together. In a photograph from that summer I'm standing on the wharf looking unhappy in what seems like an old lady's two-piece bathing suit, my sister is cute and blond and skinny. A poem I often read, "Fat," deals with the loathing I had/have if I step on the scale and weigh more than I expected. I especially hated having legs I thought fat, especially thighs, and in one photo it looks like I'm trying to hide them. The first five years I took ballet, I'd only wear black tights. Until this past year I've had long hair that wasn't straight without help. I can smell the dampness of leaves near the lake, wet wooden stairs. Night smells, wild roses opening. My mother's cigarette on the next screened porch was a beacon. We washed our hair in the lake, just mothers and children, except for Saturday nights. When I combed my wet hair sleek and straight I prayed it would stay that way, horrified to find it curly in the morning.

For my mother, being at the lake meant seeing her women friends from Barre for the summer. In Middlebury, weeks before school started, we moved again, and again, not to our own house. I'm sure my mother never expected that this many years later she'd still be in those rooms.

Thirty-eight Main Street. An apartment.

We had to give the kittens and cats away. Later I'd say I got married to give my cat a home. In my own homes, I'm never catless. The first poems I sold, wrote, and made money on, were a blue book of cat poems.

The Main Street apartment, run down now and getting that way a long time, never was fixed, because my mother hoped, wanted, longed, begged, argued, demanded, but never got, a house of her own. Finally my grandfather bought the building so we wouldn't have to move again. With low or no rent, my father seemed even less interested in a house and grew increasingly distant, like too many men I've tried to know. In their louder, more frequent fights, my mother yelled that if he cared for any of us, he'd want a house. Not wanting that translated into not caring about us.

The flat jutted out over Otter Creek, rushing, falling in the spring and a trickle in summer. From the room that became my last bedroom, a whirlpool of branches, old marble mill, the Alibi, a bowling alley where I remember on a New Year's I had a date wearing a blue dress with rhinestones, hoping my hips didn't look enormous, then a bar, and Middlebury College Chapel spire slicing the last blood and purple sun. In the back of the house, the falls shut out fighting. Since then, I've run from confrontations, arguing, proving, combating. Except on paper.

Upstate Madonna has a series of poems based on the history of Middlebury, some of the haunting bits of the past I read about took place along Otter River and the river recurs in poems. And the images of water, things that flow and blur, take something important away. To this day I often put the dishwasher on before I go to sleep. The apartment still haunts when I go there, in spite of what I've brought back with me: velvet boxes of fraternity pins, rhinestone earrings I can still connect with the first Iranian man I had a crush on, who pulled me upstairs at the Middlebury Inn onto his bed. Each inch in the house is a museum. The rooms could be elegant, people usually say, but they aren't. The August we moved in my mother stayed up all night spraying, painting everything with Clorox. In dampness, hideous fuzzy bugs waddle over the grey rug that gets thinner. It was like being fat or Jewish to not have a yard: different, separate, outside what mattered.

I suppose most artists feel they didn't or don't fit in, are on the outside. That they observe carefully and redo much in a way that feels better. Another scary baby-sitter incident happened not long after we moved in. Lela, who may have stayed with us before, asked me on a night it was still light and the creek was roaring if I wanted to play doctor, pulled off my underpants, put her tongue in and all over. I didn't fight her, but when she took off her clothes and tried to push my head and mouth into what seemed a scary mess of hair I pulled away.

My mother's living room faces Main Street. I'd watch, for hours, listening, imagining. Read, draw, dream. Thru glass. At a distance. On Main Street I often ducked into store doorways if there was someone I didn't want to see, not unlike the way now I almost never answer the door unless I expect someone, keep an answering machine on.

I loved reading, and it was knowing how to, at four or five, that catapulted me quickly out of Mrs. Butterfield's first grade into second then third grade when there weren't enough chairs. What I remember of second grade is Miss Everts, skinny, ostrichlike in black silk, and that we made clay animals in a room full of lilac and lilies of the valley and that I wore a black embroidered wool jumper that was pretty but itched. Then I was in third grade with Mrs. Flag. This is where writing poems seriously started, probably

because I never learned much long division. Shoved thru those first grades, words were what I grabbed and held on to. Especially words in poems Mrs. Flag had us read, poets like Blake, Milton, Wordsworth. I loved the *Children's Hour,* the mystery and magical sensuousness, and had read *Now We Are Six* a bit earlier, judging by the pencil stabs in the margins and drawings of horses. I especially liked "I had a little beetle, Alexander was his name," "Buttercup Days," "Where is Anne? Close to her man. Brown head, gold head, in and out the buttercups," and "Binker."

Mrs. Flag had us write a lot of poems. I wrote about apples, apple blossoms, umbrellas. A packet of handwritten early poems is now in Temple University's archives. One Saturday I copied a poem of William Blake's out from *Songs of Innocence,* showed it to my mother. Since Middlebury, then, had a population of about three thousand, it's not surprising she ran into this teacher, said how thrilling, wonderful it was she'd inspired me to write this poem full of words like "rill" and "descending." So I had to write my own poem by the next Monday.

I don't know how old I was when I saw the film *Bambi* but I was horrified that a mother could just burn up. That, and stories of Germany and a terror that began on a school trip, kept me dreaming of fires and death at least two years. My father drove four of us, one of the few times I remember him being involved with anything I was doing, to Ticonderoga, a day trip my mother still has the postcard we sent her from. What the postcard doesn't say is how I was intrigued and terrified by what was thought to be the mummy of a six-year-old Indian child. Each night I imagined turning to stone, how people could lose each other. What dissolves, disappears, can't be held or touched long enough, haunts what I write.

Maybe I wanted to pare as much of myself as I could away, like a Shaker chair, so there wouldn't be more to lose, have taken from me. I wanted to be skinny but heard relatives suggest I try Chubbettes. I'm sure there really was, as in "Fat," a man in a furniture store in Rutland who said my sister was blond and pretty, and then, looking at me with disgust, asked my mother if it was hard, having this *other* child. I'm sure he sneered or growled. I curled in the brown chair and ate M & M's, read, listened to "Let's Pretend." Friday nights I'd curl up with my mother and father in their bed with hot chocolate. In the back of an autograph book I kept from the age of nine to when I was fourteen (with its recipes for Man Ketchup and puns) I drew a ballet dancer on pointe with my name under it: Rosalynn. Legs longer and thinner than I thought mine would be. I lost myself in

Lyn (bottom right) as a gypsy in a high-school talent contest

painting, took ballet, longed for tall thin legs like Sally Smith's, who was "discovered" on a ferry, became a model, was on "Today" and "Tonight," then was ditched at nineteen, as old. Louise, one of my closest friends, lived in a wonderful old brick house with window seats where we dreamed of boys, of how to get them to ask us out, walked to the river, made a clubhouse one winter in an uprooted tree. Everyone I knew went to Pilgrim Fellowship or Catholic Youth. My sister got blonder, cuter, more popular with boys, I got A's, dreamed of being an actress. Or airline hostess. I took violin lessons and baton and once, after a hurricane, walked thru broken wires to Mrs. Russo's house, tho warned not to, as obsessive about not missing those lessons as I am about ballet lately. I rode horses, painted black stallions against flame and mango sky, gypsies dancing around camp fires. I wanted to be a gypsy, to change my name to Gitana. For a while I went from Rosalynn to Lyn, was mortified when told Lyn was a boy's name. I didn't rebel much until twenty-six or twenty-eight. But I did once, with a group of other girls, leave Girl Scouts, leave Mrs. Drake, who I later wrote of as "elephantine in khaki," to form a more

adventurous club. One initiation trial was to jump into an open grave. It sounded like jumping on tin. Once in, I couldn't get out, was sure I'd be left. Still, a leitmotif.

In fifth grade, Miss Hogan, a favorite teacher, had us write how we could change ourselves. Thinner, I said, taller, no glasses, no curly hair. In sixth grade, Ginny, the prettiest girl in school, and one of the thinnest, who later would be badly hurt and scarred in a car accident, did a term paper on "Scotland, England, Whales." Blushing wildly when she realized her mistake seemed only to make her more attractive to the boys. Tho I'd skipped several grades and was younger than the other kids, I got my period too fast and wasn't happy. At twelve I was sure I didn't want children, used Kotex not with pride, like the other girls, but with resentment. I was sure I could tell by the way a woman walked if she had this nuisance. Pregnant women seemed even worse.

During grade-school years my family would go to Maine for a week or two, dolls of rubber turned brown in the backseat car window. Packing the doll clothes was more fun than going. That "looking forward" may be what Hugh Fox called the "tantalization" in my poems. I had crushes on movie stars, read about Valentino, decided dark men were for me. Men like Tony Dexter, who looked like Valentino in a movie, or Mario Lanza, kept scrapbooks on both. I loved the sadness and drama of Valentino's early death, of Pola Negri's veiled visit to his grave each year with white roses. Polio was still a fear tho hardly anybody I knew got it. I rarely felt pretty during this time. Once I remember thinking it was stupid for me to be able to get clothes from my grandfather's store (which later became my uncle's) when there were other girls they'd look better on. My mother said I was pretty but I didn't believe her.

On one trip to Maine, after eating glazed donuts on an especially hot day, my father had pains and we left suddenly, drove to Malden where his relatives still stayed. I was ten or eleven when this new, scary symbol of loss and uncertainty jammed itself into our lives. For two weeks my sister and I stayed with one of my father's sisters in a cold house we felt lonely and scared in. Especially when mystery programs on TV slithered up under the door where we were supposed to be sleeping. My sister and I felt abandoned, that things had changed. After that, my father became more depressed, quiet. He'd climb the thirty or forty steep stairs to the apartment slowly. Often, driving, he'd stop and put a white pill under his tongue. Many nights he got up with pain and sat in a chair. My mother got up with him, stayed up weeks with no sleep. One doctor, Dr. Paul White, thought he'd worried himself into a heart condition. He stopped smoking right away. My mother smoked twice as much.

Since my father couldn't play softball anymore (I'm not actually sure he ever had), my uncles, who had girlfriends, many of them, but didn't marry until late, taught me to pitch and catch and hit a ball. In photographs, the living room is still wallpapered with a design that looks like feathers. On the dusty piano, in that room, my sister and I and, somewhere in a drawer, my mother are caught in matching caramel, butterscotch, and snow pinafore dresses. My sister's long blond hair had to be curled. One uncle had a store, United Five to Dollar, with thread, buttons, and odd joke cards under the counter. One had a woman who squirted from between her knees when anyone opened the cover. There were fires in the A & P under us, as if the dreams of fire and smoke were omens, and we ran out twice in the middle of the night, in nightgowns. Summers it was often too hot to stay upstairs. We went for rides to Lake Dunmore or made tents with poles and army blankets in the front yard on North Pleasant. Or sat on my grandmother's screened-in porch. I'd wish I was still light enough to be carried back home, upstairs, sleeping. Spirea, red spirea, peonies, and yellow roses crawled toward my grandparents' house.

The summer I was eight I went to Camp Hochelaga. Two days in the top bunk with bratty Birdie Rothman, the sting of homesickness, the devastating separation from my family, my mother especially, made me so despondent that nothing, not swimming, archery, stories around a camp fire, not the smell of fresh-cut pine or apricot jam could soothe. After two days my parents were called to come for me. I wondered even then if I could ever not feel pain leaving. The pull and stranglehold of Middlebury, in spite of ambivalent feelings, makes the town a character in itself. The ache each time I left for school, or even now, started then. In "The Visit" the silences, unanswered questions, tensions, losses, separations, and deaths haunt, are that "heavy love," images that can never be unified or undone. When I came back from camp, quickly, I found *Love without Fear* in the bathroom and, reading thru it, was fascinated by the words "If a girl lets a man put his tongue in her teeth, she'll let him do anything," leaving me astonished, curious, wondering.

As early as grade school I felt even if I was fat and shy and wore glasses, was too serious, later, maybe, it would be different. In one of those red five-year diaries I wrote, "I want to be an actress," and pages later, "I want to be a ballerina." Recently I've put together a group of dance poems, and doing readings is a way of performing, of acting. Bob Peters called one book something like "Madonna as Board-walk Tease," and there is an undercurrent in many poems, a feeling of a speaker who would and could turn herself inside out to startle and stun, an actress trying on costumes: mad girl, madonna, "blond vamp," "rock star," Hugh Fox says in his book about me, Indian woman, Plymouth woman, women who are seductive, reclusive, Holocaust survivors, women married to six-hundred-pound men, women who were Houdini. It's a way of looking in, thru glass, a way to, as Fox says, "be in the world but not part of it."

People rarely see I have a temper. That rage and anger are transformed into poems. Perhaps when I saw "kike" on the blackboard I started storing barbs: my strongest poems have been triggered by rejection or rage. I wish I had, in a December 6 diary entry, written when I was about thirteen, detailed what the black mood flowered from when I wrote, "Oh God, there's only one thing I want. I want to die."

Few got divorced. In spite of a lot of fights, in photographs my parents still have their arms around each other, and there's one picture, near the Morgan Horse Farm, where my father is holding both my sister and me close; in many photographs tho, he seems to touch us cautiously, lightly, as if not sure we are real. On the way home from those nightly rides to watch the colts, watch the elms and maples leafing out, we drove thru a wooden bridge, Pulpmill Bridge, held our breath, closed our eyes, made a wish.

I wish I'd written in that sketchy diary what more of those wishes were. By seventh and eighth grade, still in the same brick elementary school with rickety fire escapes and the smell of floor wax, halved apples, they focused on boys. Pancho Gonzalez, who'd hold his hand over the lump in his crotch and jiggle it at Paula and me, grinning, taunting us to touch it. For two years Mr. Dewey taught, flirted, punished, and in subtle ways lured and manipulated. A lot of us had crushes on him. A compliment from him and we'd be floating over the wooden chairs, a snide look or sarcastic "Oh Rosalynn, a dress today? What's the special occasion?" and I'd blush. I especially hated being weighed in front of everyone, the offensive number blurted out for everyone. We still played marbles, kick the can, red rover, but what boys were thinking and wanting and saying began to mesmerize us and we'd focus on what we could do to lure those who were worth luring.

Christmas was the holiday I remember clearest. Tho we had a Christmas tree sometimes, it was usually rather small, portable enough to be shoved into a closet when my grandfather clomped up the stairs. Christmas Eve my mother and father worked in the store. Snow turned Main Street white, lights stretched from the Battell Block. We may have had Hanukkah candles but I remember the red and green lights more clearly, smell of holly. The best presents were books to curl back with under the quilts with a half-eaten maple-sugar man. One Valentine's Day I ran thru the hall, broke a thumb that had to be bandaged in a thick clumsy cast. I had a new green dress for that Valentine's party, but along with pink plastic glasses, this clunky bracelet made me feel even less lovely.

In my diary, I see notes about skating. I was never good at that. The beauty and chill of nature came to me mostly thru overnight camping hikes, lying in pine beds listening to stories, and the nearly clear blue light starting like the blue light in a painting on velvet in my grandmother's dining room.

For the first day of high school I carefully selected a black and red striped dress I hoped would hide what I wanted it to. I'd have given anything those years to have been popular, not on the dean's list, to be slutty, a cheerleader, like Joyce Menard, someone boys wanted to take across the state line, or exotic as Jo Ann, whose father came to open a funeral parlor with his daughter, who danced, who even tho she said she weighed a hundred and thirty pounds was tan, firm, flashed a white-toothed smile so many found irresistible. It wasn't until the second month of high school, October 9 or 10, that I realized I wasn't popular, sexy, grabbable or longed for, and the pain and rage of sitting with socks like absurd cotton fluffy rabbit blimps on the gym bleachers, only slightly camouflaged, slammed me. It's one of the most vivid, unpleasant images, and it carved such nightmarish anguish that, as so many poems suggest or scream, "some part of me would never stop waiting to be asked to dance." I learned that if I couldn't get attention wiggling my hips, if I had to pretend I wasn't all that studious to boys like Doug, who I never liked, but, since he was on the football team, was relieved to have ask me to dances, games, and parties closed to me before this, I could get attention drawing and painting and getting awards for that.

Three years I worked alone, like a poet, often waiting for the phone to ring, in agony, or ecstasy about some boy, on science projects that always won prizes on the local, state, and national level and gave me the chance, as with poetry readings, to be in another town, where boys didn't know I was really shy, serious, and scared. At least for a short time, in the dazzle of models, posters, newspaper reporters, I could fool them. I did an exhibit on dentistry, one on carbon, and the biggest one, complete with huge papier-mâché model of the eye using about twenty bottles of vaseline for the aqueous humor and twelve bottles of clear glue for the vitreous, a display that took up six or seven tables and quite literally was "The Eye" screaming, look at me! In my diary from then: For each of these three exhibits, three different years, the comments squeezed into those tiny allotted four lines had little to do with the science fair but were mostly the reactions of others. "Ed Foote thought I was good," one year. Another year, "Went to Morrisville and won first prize," with four exclamation points, followed by "Met Dick Frenier." And another year, "Went to Springfield Science Fair, won second. Met Bobby Jones, a doll," and finally, "Lots of congrats. Even from Mark (the intellectual macho heartthrob), at music David and Hilton said congratulations. This afternoon *Rutland Herald* took my

Lyn with her science exhibit at the science museum on the Charles River near Boston

picture for the paper. He made such a fuss over me." Only in another town, I was sure, could someone as moody, wild, hoody as Cat Callahan have found me someone he could write "To my sweet brown eyed baby" and sign it, "The Cat," on the back of the rather punk photo of him holding a Fats Domino record. When I saw the recent Sylvia Plath documentary I couldn't help but think of a similar need, a passion to win, prove, startle, lure, be alluring.

I won United Nations Poster contests, was the first Miss Middlebury High in *Tiger's Tale,* and wrote, usually with polysyllabic Latinate words from *Word Wealth,* poems, won art contests, designed dance programs for proms I was in agony I wouldn't even get asked to, did the high-school yearbook drawings. One fall I was sent to New York City to the Columbia University yearbook conference and fell in love with New York, the Rockettes, Hitchcock films, lights, crowds of people. Carmelina, the girl I went with, who I thought would later be a nun, and I were so innocent, so sheltered, that a flasher across the way captivated us, had us giggling, unbuttoning the top buttons of leather jackets. Somehow we gave him our phone number at the Plymouth Hotel so the phone rang all night in the adjoining room, where the teacher we came with grew increasingly puzzled and annoyed.

In an English class I wrote one story that showed me the power of words. I watched Mrs. Cunningham cringe and frown as she read of the speaker being petted and stroked. Then I saw her relief, at the end, discovering it was from a dog's point of view. I loved how I could hold students on the edge of their seats. At twelve or thirteen, when I saw a poem in a Middlebury College literary magazine about trading freedom for a ring of gold, I felt the same way.

I never thought of marriage and children as a goal or dream. Important as attention from boys was, I often preferred reading alone, knew clearly I didn't want to be just someone's mother. I didn't want to run down for nylons, as my mother did, rush out for those bottles of vaseline for any daughter's science projects. The ambivalence and longing and running to and away from the same thing with equal wildness that gives my best work its intensity, I'm sure began in high school. To not get a phone call from some boy, to feel someone I wanted didn't want me, was as devastating as later being thought of as someone's wife would be.

Summers after my father's heart attack were spent on Cape Cod, where the water was warmer than in Maine. I loved Hyannis Music Tent. *Brigadoon* and *Countess Maritza* were favorites, and being in summer stock a daydream. I wanted to write, too, remember trying on a rainy day in a cabin, the Henry House, to find something worth writing about, wondering if I'd ever have anything to say.

The cliché about bad love making good songs applies to poems too. The January I was fourteen or fifteen, David Lane, a rather strange, tall, aloof, dark-haired, difficult senior on the brink of a navy career called me and began the pull, the attraction, of a string of similar men, adept at the yo-yo technique: slam you in and slam you away, something I've often been too vulnerable to, the agony-ecstasy poem trigger. If I had written poems then, I'd probably have churned out orange crates full. Instead, I worked on those science projects. Waited, refused other boys. Waited for the phone too often, bought sheer blouses, not unlike some recent contortions, lace this time. Now there's a number of poems with blue lace in them. At fourteen, it took weeks to feel fingers inch toward plastic and rhinestone buttons, towards bra straps. I agonized when he didn't talk in study hall or on the Middlebury College campus, where for months, after a fire burned the high school down the night I saw *Giselle,* we had classes. When he left, not even saying goodby, I felt my life at fourteen or fifteen was over. Those feelings, even so many years later, are not at all unfamiliar. That July my parents took me to Saratoga, perhaps to distract me. Groucho Marx, after a play where he came out onstage and answered questions, motioned to me, pointed out what he called my "astonishing hair." I was too despondent to bother noting it in my diary. When I saw David in the fall he wrote on a photograph, "To my dearest from her swabby in his brother's civvies—to you Ros with all my fondest thoughts and deepest affections I love you." I wasn't prepared for him to disappear again. Wordlessly. Something to this day I hate. I think it was the impetus to lose enough weight to finally become pretty. "You'd better start eating," Ginny Lafayette wrote in the yearbook, and Linda Goulash wrote, "To the girl with the biggest waist," by then a joke.

Like my mother I looked forward to leaving Middlebury in my new body, leaving high school, letting those Junior Women's Club dances and hayrides women had to invite men to, wait for them to "decide," and then often get no for an answer, fade. Even the best of those events, even when Ron Agassipour pulled me up to his room at Middlebury Inn and peeled rhinestone spray earrings from where they were making holes in my ears. I was looking forward to leaving even Dick Wood, who died before he was twenty-eight, Fitzi, brazen and charming but difficult at the Drive Inn, tho a great subject for poems, like a beached whale in a poem just published in *Deep Down* and a prose piece forthcoming. It was goodby to Annette, who had two babies, came back to school, walked the babies up and down Frog Alley, and to Paula, whose sister lured Leo Durocher back to Middlebury years later, only to have him run off with Paula's and Carolyn's mother, their father's wife, end up with an alienation-of-affections lawsuit, and even to Martha with her iris torn—enough characters, like callers on local nighttime talk radio, to write a Spoon Riverish unending play.

At graduation, tho I had, like no one else, won local, state, and national science contests, the school opted not to give a prize for outstanding science work that year, as if there was no one worthy. I don't remember graduation night. My mother probably does, she was always there, remembers better than I do what I wore to each dance, how I'd change my clothes sometimes for two hours "to be right." I don't know if we had what's now called a disfunctional family; my father rode the Wall Street Journal. In an early poem, "Traveling," I saw him "riding the Wall Street Journal / leaving with a brown bag of loss" and wondered, "How do we learn to be whole." That he'd never told me I was pretty stung and comes back years later. To my mother, I was always a beauty. Just

yesterday, an incident I've spit out in poems, of being in that furniture store in Rutland, couldn't, she insists, have happened.

Brandeis was my first choice for college. I was drawn to the political and artistic energy, a rebellious, counterculture mood I found exciting when I went there for my first college weekend, a sophomore in high school. People in Boston smirked, "You can tell they're from Brandeis." Instead I began at Syracuse University as a drama major. Within the first week everyone I met had exotic names like Neela Dunay and it seemed years of summer stock or off-Broadway experience. I switched to English with a minor in radio and TV and art history. The closest I got to theater was teaching drama and ballet Saturday mornings with two other students, including Frank Langella.

Moving into Mt. Olympus that first September afternoon, the image of my roommate: cigarette-smoking woman in a tight orange-striped sheath, twisting to some music in her head. Mementos from that uneasy alliance surfaced the other day. In a box of photographs, handwritten notes this woman left me—one ended up triggering a poem in one workshop when I smelled fruit and remembered a box of oranges and grapefruit mailed me that winter, delivered on the floor outside my door, since Fran insisted on the whole green stucco room being dark early. Scrawled at the end of a Hemingway quote was "Lyn I'm trying to sleep so please be a little careful the door doesn't slam and the light is at a minimum." I drew her in crayon first as a black stick, a dead figure on the floor in a black room with everything bright as fruit a long distance from her.

The whirl of being social was overwhelming. I was informed, by an empty-headed handsome jerk who four years later appeared at another school and said, since he was leaving to serve Uncle Sam, I should, tho I hadn't talked to him for years, for my country, do him *the* service, he wouldn't date a woman who wasn't in a sorority and the sorority had to be one of three. During rushing, sorority sisters would touch your shoulder to see if your sweater was lamb's wool or cashmere. Or just Orlon or wool. I have those lilac, pink, blue, and white Dalton cashmeres with me. Still. Football was as important as cashmere. We learned placard cheering the first week. I had six dates—including a flasher who did it on one of the seventy-seven steps up to Mt. Olympus so quickly I thought perhaps a few teeth on his zipper just broke, until two years later at a sorority coffee he pulled me off into a corner and did the same thing again. One afternoon of that frantic, exhausting, confused orientation week I thought maybe marriage would be easier. But soon I was swept up in what must have been like the fervor Americans felt going to France or what artists felt in the twenties and thirties in Greenwich Village. I got a C– or D+ on my first college English composition, "purple" was written on it, crammed as it must have been with all those polysyllabic words. "Commingling," I remember the professor wrote, isn't a word. It was I later gloated. Maybe this was when I began to pare down my writing, as well as my hips, and be drawn to things Shaker. The next semester a professor made poetry magical, Mr. Marx. I was transfixed by Dylan Thomas. Only a few poems in an anthology, but enough to make me want to do my master's thesis on him. And García Lorca.

By my sophomore year I discovered the man who in an odd way, in his strange courses, most touched something that made feelings and urgency and experiences and excesses justifiable, made being aware of living in the moment, not in some vague future, what really mattered. Leonard Stanley Brown died over Christmas vacation. It was rumored to be suicide or severe alcoholism. He'd taught a number of three-figure courses: Lawrence, Nietzsche, and Dinesen, or Mann, Joyce, and Nabokov. He knew Pasternak and would come in late saying he'd just been talking to Nabokov. When we studied Joyce, he'd read, over and over, the Molly Bloom speech, half in our world, half in his, with "I got him to propose to me yes first I gave him the bit of seed cake out of my mouth and it was leapyear like now yes 16 years ago my God after that long kiss I near lost my breath yes he said I was a flower of the mountain yes so we are flowers all a womans body yes that was the one true thing he said in his life and the sun shines for you today yes that was why I liked him because I saw he understood or felt what a woman is and I knew I could always get round him and I gave him all the pleasure I could . . ." When I asked him for a reference he said, why don't you just leave school, travel, see people, I wanted to.

Art-history classes were a drug. I could barely wait to have the room darken, the slides go up. I longed to live in Athens or Florence. Some of the guest artists I remember were Lipshitz, Herbert Marcuse, Robert Frost, Aaron Copland. I was fascinated by talks on *On the Road* and Kerouac and the Beats. I joined a sorority, thought I ought to. A Jewish one, since I'd never quite belonged in Vermont, with one friend's father an Episcopal minister, most of my other friends Congregationalists. I envied

the dark stained-glass quiet of the church we'd play in during the week and the socials, parties. But I felt different, too, with these Jewish women. An outsider there, too. I never knew the Jewish or Yiddish phrases, so my roommate for the last years of college, Dorothy, tried to teach me a few needed phrases, like "drop dead," with her Rochester accent. I never fit into the sorority tho I was social chairman, found the counterculture more interesting than sororities or fraternities. I heard Emlyn Williams do his Dylan Thomas performance, Segovia, Pablo Casals; and I applied for Syracuse in Italy, only to have my parents come up, as they had one summer when I was accepted for a summer program in England, with too many reasons I shouldn't and couldn't. Somehow I got into an intermediate painting course. The first assignment was a collage. Not sure just what that was, I ended up with a still-wet purple oil and lavender, lilac, orchid, violet thing that my professor's dog tracked over her white wall-to-wall. Years later, at Yaddo, a painter, Susan Criele, said at Bennington she'd been told she couldn't be a poet and became a painter. I, told I'd never paint, didn't.

My second or third year, I wrote and directed an hour-long skit for a sorority dance that took place in Greenwich Village with artists, beatniks, and a poet. I played the poet and did a song to the tune of *South Pacific*'s "We Ain't Got Dames" about having "anapests and dactyls, sentiment so true, onomatopoeia but the thing that makes me blue is this sacrilegious habit, it happens all the time, I can't for the life of me stop making these damn words rhyme." The production was a hit. A sorority sister I admired, in law school, said one image, of carbon-copy lives, impressed her. University of Texas at Austin or Temple University, where many of my papers are, have those original scripts. I was drawn to radio and television classes, where we listened to Norman Corwin and wrote our own children's radio and television shows. Tho I wanted to write, I was terrified of taking a real creative-writing course. What if I couldn't write enough? What if no one liked any of it? An intermediate composition course was as close as I got. I've written little, really, about college, but the poem "Writing Class, Syracuse Winter" catches a lot of what was going on. And what wasn't.

I wanted to slam into life, not be, as a romantic-lit professor chided us for being, conformist, silent, nonpolitical. In an interview I said I'd choose Iran or Greece to live and work in. I wanted to move to Greenwich Village. Unlike others in the sorority, I couldn't stand the thought of being engaged or married and I didn't want children. I couldn't imagine not dying to travel, taste everything, see and feel what I felt a marriage and children would only stifle, suffocate. I wanted to be wilder than I was. (Someone sent me a "wild women don't get the blues" button. I think, then, I believed that.) But I ran when a man who would later publish notes he had near his bed that he drew me to said he wanted to show me, and win a Pulitzer prize for denying death and then dying, wanted me to wriggle out of my lavender clothes. He wouldn't let me go until I promised I'd come back, spend the night lying near him. I did, to get out. Still I did want to taste everything, be open, say yes. But if my period was late, even if I'd just danced close, upstairs in a fraternity house, I was sure I was knocked up. Once I even changed my name to Sherri Liane Russell and went, with a sweaty fist of wadded up dollar bills, to make sure.

Spring in Syracuse was wet branches heavy with rose flowers dripping, the lushness of sitting in the music room with rain bending lilacs in two, a new Wagner or Mozart record on as water beaded. I walked to have skirts I was thrilled were too big— they had to fit tight—made smaller to show how much of me I was paring away. I got contact lenses, let my hair grow longer, even pared part of my name away and went from Rosalynn to Lynn then Lyn. When a coffeehouse opened off Marshall Street where people sat on the floor and talked about books, films, art, and poetry as candles dripped turquoise, lemon, and violet wax down Chianti bottles, anything seemed possible.

Summers I went back to Middlebury, worked in my uncle's store or at the library at Middlebury College, where instead of pasting envelopes in the backs of books, as I was supposed to, I read them and tried to guess, as someone approached the desk, if they'd speak Italian, German, Russian, Spanish, or French. I wrote some of the first poems since high school one summer, triggered by a small argument I'd had with my sister over a woman in my sorority. One of these, "Disillusions," was the one my father showed Robert Frost, as mysterious to me an act still as everything about my father. I'd love to know what they talked about, how they started to talk, since neither was friendly. But from sometime in the fifties until Frost's death they stayed in touch. This summer I brought back a number of signed books and poems and cards he sent to my father, as well as my father's collection of newspaper articles, magazine clips about Frost, notices, especially around the time of Frost's death, when my father must have been more alone than ever, since he and my mother were separated

and on the verge of divorce. Since my mother had the car, my father would hitchhike or take the bus to memorial services in Amherst, Boston, Maine, check out schedules to towns he didn't make it to. But that summer he showed my poem to Frost we were still all in the apartment and I can remember how thrilled I felt opening the blue and white magazine. Frost's words were staggering, much more overwhelming to me than silver dollars once filling my hand from a carnival's scooping claw machine. I wish I had had more poems to show Frost, that he hadn't died before I could. I suspect those comments were part of what made several schools give me excellent graduate scholarships, made me, even tho I didn't really write much for years, feel maybe I could.

Disillusions

Sparkled smatterings,
　　Intoxicating as a sundazed shore;
Yet quickly melting, like showflaked beauty
　　In a burning palm,
Strangely elusive, as his shadow to a child
　　When a stormcloud breaks the spell
　　And his dreammate disappears

(The cover is falling off the *Syracuse Review*—I hadn't noticed that the only two prominent ads are

With roommate, Dorothy Yellen Appel (left), at Syracuse University

for Sylvania, where it says, "At Sylvania a man may choose from 67 plants and labs . . . will find tough, but challenging problems, salaries are excellent . . ." and then, on the back cover for Wamsutta Supercale, two whispering coeds in front of a college bulletin board where there's only a man's face tacked up. One woman, her legs demurely crossed, says, "If anybody asks you what I want for my trousseau . . . just be sure you mention lots of Wamsutta sheets . . . our first home may not be exactly a palace . . . but we do want everything to be just right . . . beige for complete heaven and of course, white with *his* monogram . . ." I'm not sure what I was thinking about when I wrote about what dissolves, what would melt like snow in a palm, be "elusive, as his shadow to a child / When a storm-cloud breaks the spell / And his dreammate disappears," in that first published poem, but it could have been the fantasy of living with just the dream of a trousseau and sheets that would last till I was sixty, or why, when I did get married, the rituals of choosing patterns of silver and china always made me cringe.)

Unlike leaving high school, I hated to leave Syracuse. I knew I didn't want to get married. I'd collected several fraternity pins but didn't "feel" pinned. I wish I'd collected more photographs from then. There are some bathing-suit photos à la Natalie Wood and shots of my roommate and me in front of bulletin boards in baby-doll pajamas I still have, a poster of Quebec, banners, mugs, a Belafonte record of mine in the background, a Sinatra album (hers)—I never cared much for him, once shocked a fiancé because I preferred Elvis to Frank. In other photos we are wearing slinky cocktail dresses, our hair long and sleek. I wish I could make out the photo on the bulletin board behind me, or the card. One might have been from a deaf doctor I couldn't imagine wouldn't call but didn't after I fainted in the elevator from flu I caught from him. (Writing this, I felt so close, tho we hadn't talked for years, to my college roommate, I tracked her down, five addresses from the one listed in the Syracuse directory. We have talked, plan to meet.)

I wish I'd saved more letters, especially from my family, before phone calls became easier, too frequent. Then obsessive. In one I was warned I might be kidnapped and sold to the white-slave market.

Robert Kennedy spoke at graduation and I said goodby for a month or two, until Bread Loaf, to a boy I found myself pinned to, and went to an all-night party with someone I hardly knew: proud I'd finally done something that wasn't expected, safe. I was excited that I'd missed curfew tho the night was totally innocent: no drugs, no booze, no sex. I showed up at my parents' motel at dawn giggling and then heard I was a slut as we drove past Bomoseen quietly home.

After Syracuse, that feeling of being outside things, not fitting, seemed outlined in a kohl black I'd begun liking my brown eyes exaggerated in. Tho I was pinned, the idea of marriage or engagement still seemed scary. There wasn't an urgent need for English majors with radio-TV and fine arts as a minor. Grad school seemed the only alternative that summer, so with the English major whose pin I never wore (I just found a photograph of us, the morning after I accepted the little TEP pearl bar)—an odd college weekend really. I'd agreed to sign out for the weekend, naively believing I would be sharing a room with one of his fraternity brothers' dates. Yet it must have occurred to me that there could be more expected, because I did buy a filmy lavender and a filmy white negligee—something I'd have no need for in the dorm or sorority house, where flannel and cotton were more cuddly. Suddenly I was with this boy in a motel room and I felt about twelve—insisted we spend the night walking on the highway someplace outside Syracuse. After that weekend, at least three TEP couples rushed into marriage, pregnant.

At Branbury Beach

It was a six-week course at Bread Loaf. We'd drive up every morning early. William Meredith taught a poetry course and couldn't imagine why I'd picked the subject I did: Jungian imagery in Yeats. There was a fascinating course on the American novel. Later I found all the lectures in another book not written by the man who taught it. Especially impressive was Moses Hadas, whose blue eyes were as riveting as his talks. And there was Donald Davidson, who I liked, who graciously wrote me a recommendation that I'm sure helped get me a scholarship to Vanderbilt. As a commuter at Bread Loaf, I felt outside things, there too. Felt restless, peeled off nail polish on the white clapboard chairs as writers I never got to know well played croquet and something in the air glued my eyelids together. My friend enrolled for the writers' conference in August. I went up for a number of the readings but, to my astonishment, remember none.

In the fall, I went to the University of Vermont. I felt more isolated, more outside things, very unconnected. I lived in a room in a house where the husband of a woman I was sure didn't want him coughed all night. I almost went to Boston University but at the last minute, frustrated with trying to find an apartment, didn't. "Why are you here?" a professor asked and, rather shakily I suppose, I said, "I want to write." I had little to say when he barked, "Then why don't you?"

I decided to write my master's thesis on Dylan Thomas. Frances and Gladys Colburn, a painter and poet in Burlington, knew Thomas, I was told, and I called them to talk about the poet whose reputation and mythic tours intrigued me almost as much as his poetry. Their son David edited a small college literary magazine, *Centaur,* and for that year and longer was another of those cool, elusive, hardly available men who've fascinated me more than is comfortable and have for so long triggered poems. Long icy walks and bittersweet exploding in an iced raw wind from Champlain started a few poems. It was there the first poem I published, "Jonathan," in *Kauri* got its start.

By next fall, with straight A's, course work finished for a master's degree, and the choice of several full scholarships, I chose Brandeis and moved into a pink room an Armenian woman with glass animals on fragile shelves was renting. It was the first time I ate baklava or artichokes—a Princeton med student who had taken a year off for an English degree made them for me, and that the first day in Waltham I wore hoop earrings and a corduroy orange mini still in my closet. Instead of *Beowulf,* which I had loved at UVM, it was *Piers Plowman.*

Early September I began to juggle something I couldn't: weekends I'd drive to Providence to see Bob, an English major at Brown and someone new, who, tho his family thought I was wrong for their son, I'd marry. J. V. Cunningham taught a course required of all graduate students. At any dreaded four o'clock Tuesday, your "exam" question could be sprung on you. No one could hear him, he whispered so, but no one dared sit up close because so often he lashed out, ridiculed. I audited a creative-writing class a few times. I've no photographs from then, no diary. Only the lamb's wool and cashmere sweaters I wore then, connect with a walk up Mount Auburn, or the Chinese restaurant I went to after the man I'd marry asked if we had school on Columbus Day.

As a child visiting relatives around Boston, Normbega Park, with its caterpillar ride, had been my favorite, that dark cave of a bug my sister and I were small enough to have my father still draw us close to him in. At Brandeis I wanted to go back there, try to remember. One weekend in Providence I threw tin cans thru a window, to my surprise: I'd always been too nice to. Another weekend I brought back the palm-sized black kitten, Othello, I'd get married to give a home to. It's astonishing how much doesn't stay. I've just read "Cabbages, Leaves, and Morphine," a poem loosely about those weekends I'd drive to Providence, but it doesn't tell me much about then. The man I married liked cats better than the one I didn't. When anyone asked what we had in common, I'd say cats and folk music. Seeing both men, I worked less than I needed to. I'm best at working full tilt on one thing: science contests, an anthology, writing. I hadn't finished my master's thesis on Dylan Thomas. Maybe I'd been in school too long without a break. In February, just after I registered for second semester, for reasons that aren't very clear, I left, as the man I'd marry less than a year later did, less than a year after he kissed me in his father's borrowed Chrysler, smelling of cinnamon Life Savers near midnight the same time of year I'm writing this.

I can't remember my feelings leaving Brandeis. I just let it go. I was exhausted from juggling the two relationships, remember nights I'd stay up in the pink room until three or four while my cat slept on the pillow. I'm surprised, with that scholarship, my parents didn't press me to stay.

Back in Middlebury that winter, nights seemed endless. Eric, the man I would marry, got a job and then took the bus to Vermont on weekends. His family feared and mistrusted, probably hated, me. They thought I'd seduced their son from an engineering career, so they took his Daimler, his coin collection. I was finishing my master's degree and my parents were finishing their marriage. My college roommate married, and on the way back from Rochester my family met Eric's family. My enthusiasm for Peter, Paul, and Mary made them think I was rather odd, as almost everything I did or felt or cared for would, and at two A.M., Eric appeared at the motel I was at with my parents, never wanting to be in his family's house again.

I boarded my cat at the vet's, noticed how much nicer this man was to him than the Brown boyfriend who seemed to think since I'd left school I could shrivel into a wife. After a Josh White concert I learned the guitar-playing poet I'd been so drawn to was marrying too. My parents weren't living in the same house by spring, and my sister, mother, and I moved for a few weeks in with my grandmother. By June we took a cottage on Lake Dunmore, where I could keep the cat. When we drove into town, we were told to keep the car windows up, not to stop on the street if we saw our father. Bob came up one weekend, Eric the next. Bob was edgy, didn't want me to wear a bikini, and one weekend had a rock in the car he wouldn't throw away, and at that moment I decided I couldn't marry him. With so little full of light, the idea of a wedding, something to not think of what was dying, seemed a cove, and that July, with only a month or two to plan the wedding, I stopped saying no and said OK. Those weeks were a giddy swirl. Still living at my grandmother's, my mother and I drove daily to Burlington or Rutland, checked out gowns, flowers, invitations, clothes. We were too busy to eat. Early in August I called my father to invite him, let him know, and he told me he didn't want to be involved. I got off the phone in my grandmother's dining room, where the stucco had pulled away, and went into the cluttered second living room, where ferns were already dying, sat quietly with my head in my hands and cried. I saw my father only one more time, days before the wedding in the post office, where all he said to me was, "Never do what you don't want to do."

"Get all the attention you can today," the rabbi said, "After this it will be your husband and your child." The motel we'd had reservations for gave the room away by mistake, definitely an omen. After a trip to Canada we picked up my black cat, guitar, and headed west for a fall that would be difficult. I'd never taught, never taken an education course, and was about three years younger than some of my students. Ten days after the wedding I began teaching at Wilbur Lynch High in Amsterdam, New York.

Nothing was as I'd expected: marriage, teaching, living in a new town. The college-prep students were fine; the others, called "terminal," were challenges I was in no way prepared for. There were thirty-six or more in most classes. I knew nothing about discipline. Most of the teachers were nearing retirement, were lifelong residents of Amsterdam. It was a nightmare. Later I wrote "Ramona Lake" about one black-haired student with her 70 IQ I can still see in a sea of chatter and noises and spitballs like a startled deer, dazed, about to be hit by a car, pleading for what I couldn't give her.

I couldn't wait to escape school in my dusty rose Plymouth convertible that the top, after putting it up while driving in a storm, didn't still go up and down automatically on. Past Division Street there were lilac rooms I could take my hair out of pins in and wonder how I'd gotten myself in all this. There were moments, as I described in "Hair," when I put my hair up and sprayed it by mistake with Raid "as if it was a living, flying thing." Two months into the

Lifshin on the porch of one of the old houses she likes to write about

marriage I began having devastatingly unsettling anxiety attacks. When I heard tachycardia I thought of my father's heart attack. At a teachers' meeting around then I passed out in a crowd of three hundred in downtown Schenectady. I felt corners go black, windows and lights blur. We'd rush to the emergency room. I felt I was someone else in clothes that just looked like mine. Downstairs in the apartment, a retired cop said he'd kill the cat. I don't remember his reason. In December, after a horrendous Friday, dressed in a gold wool suit I'd worn about two hours after the wedding, someone came up to me, said, that looks like a going-away outfit, and I thought, yes, it is. I never entered that high school again.

Snowdrifts were up to my waist that winter, panic slithered into depression. Other wives seemed to like cooking, talked of babies. I'd focus on years before to not feel the rooms go licorice. Everything seemed over. I couldn't even read. I'd hold *One Flew over the Cuckoo's Nest* and read the same page over and over. I never dreamed I'd be in residence, giving workshops and readings with Ken Kesey for a week in Virginia, sharing screwdrivers from his thermos, driving thru catalpa and live oak, red bud starting. Since I was no longer teaching, there was no reason to live in such a dreary, isolated town, and we moved into my husband's parents' in Albany to look for an apartment. I was so depressed I began to sleep until one in the afternoon. Running the water for a long, lulling bath, I could hear his mother whimper, whisper to her friends how weird I was. "No More Apologizing," perhaps one of the most autobiographical poems I've written, spits some of those afternoons out. I sat in the small guest room, the only room without a rug, feeling January wind thru panes, and tried to write poems, waited for my husband to come back. By April we moved to Schenectady into a flat where lilacs were about to bloom, and I got into SUNY grad school. We repainted the walls, got a couch, marble tables, and began to feel life wasn't really done. I was about nineteen.

I've no photographs of the apartment on Jackson Avenue, nothing from there except for a series of poems with the address for a title, "222 Jackson Ave." There's not one shot I can find of those first years, tho later my husband got into photography and took hundreds of shots. In the closet are negatives never even developed. In that first Schenectady place if you opened the back door and the front living room, the lilac breeze changed the afternoon. I sat at a marble coffee table eavesdropping on the couple with the organ whose family kept having heart attacks, who wanted oriental furniture, or on fights

the couple with a poodle and underground connections had much of the day, and tried a few poems. Weekends we'd listen to folk music at Cafe Lena, where I got into theater, considered just doing that, forgetting grad school. Or we went to foreign films, *Black Orpheus, The Joker.* The black cat I brought from Providence to Waltham, then to Vermont, rescued from the vet's, brought with me when I got married to give it a home, to Amsterdam and then Schenectady, ran away, and we got a grey one that had kittens and more kittens, some that had to be cut out of the bedsprings. In the summer we drove to Newport, saw Dylan and Baez, and in September I plunged back into graduate school. Again I was asked why and again, when I said I wanted to be a writer, was sneered at, asked why if I wanted to I didn't. Being an extremist, I made everything second to graduate school. Nothing else mattered. I attacked weekly papers fiercely. Spenser, eighteenth-century lit, Elizabethan theater. It was a new doctoral program.

Suny, formerly, the State Teachers' College of New York, was planning to move to a bigger campus and was hiring professors with reputations, trying to be as traditional as possible, as if to get an instant reputation. I got all A's. Tho I'd never studied Italian, with flash cards and a few random books, managed to be the only one of several to pass the Italian exam the first time. I'd written a hundred pages of what would be my doctoral dissertation on a comparison of the Psalms of Wyatt, who I really liked, and those of Sidney, who I didn't. I loved the ragged, explosive, jagged thought-in-process of Wyatt, the darkness, surprise, how his poems were colloquial, not polished and polished so smooth nothing caught and startled and snagged. It was, I thought, exciting to be the first Ph.D. candidate. I'd be the youngest, I was sure, to get a degree, just over twenty. I didn't pick up on one or two omens: even with the best academic record, when I talked about getting an instructorship I was told, "You aren't a man with a family to support," and during the first year with a teaching fellowship I got a note suggesting "I dress in a way that's more professional, wear my hair up," a note in my mailbox that became part of the second most anthologized poem, "You Understand the Requirements." No wonder hair has been a recurring image, the subject of two long poems, one a *New York Quarterly* Sadin Award.

"Energetic" was the way the head of the graduate department described me. Within weeks I was simply too involved in, too excited by, the literature I was studying to imagine I'd not be a professor. In early readings I often went over the experience of those written and oral Ph.D. exams. The poem "Orals" is pretty much a true account. Because I was the first candidate and many were new to the Ph.D. program, they actually asked me how many days, how long, the exams should be. I did go and buy special suits to wear for this, masks. And I was asked, perhaps the first question, what I thought of adultery, bedbugs, by Edward Le Comte, the newly hired respected Milton scholar. The exam clearly embarrassed the other professors: it was so sexist and shoddy, and it was because of that cut short. They decided I should have a written exam. I'd passed exams in other fields and was anxious to get this last written one over. The exam had two parts: first, fifty quotes from seventeenth-century poetry, all slightly misquoted. I was to identify the poet, make the corrections, and say why the original was better. The second half was to explicate a section from Herbert's *The Temple*. I knew seventeenth-century poetry and after the exam went out to celebrate, sure I'd passed. That night I got a call saying, "You have identified the poems correctly, and the poets," then added, "but in your explication it seems you do not have the religious background to work sympathetically in the seventeenth century. You don't have enough affiliation or sympathy for seventeenth-century English Anglicanism."

The department still had confidence in me, said there seemed to be a personality conflict, decided I should take a last exam from someone else. I was drained, wiped out. But I had to take it two weeks from that day, December 15. Unable to concentrate, tho it was a fair, actually easy exam, I slammed out of the room onto Central Avenue, without a coat, hoped, I think, I'd get hit by a car.

I wanted to get a Ph.D. so I could write and then wrote because I didn't get one. When I cleared out my desk in the English Annex, the hundred pages on Wyatt had disappeared. I should thank some of the department for pushing me, finally, to write. But for years I couldn't go near the university. The first time I did, nervously, to a party, I got a flat tire in the lot and then, somehow, managed to be in the elevator when it got stuck. Stuck with me was Dr. Le Comte. Many of the professors could recognize themselves in some prose pieces in an upcoming book from Applezaba, *Doctors*. As I left, to be nice one man said, "Well, why don't you just have a baby."

For months after that, I painted, did oils, abstracts, watercolors. A small gallery wanted to show them, and a few people asked if they could buy some of the stormy dark landscapes that disappeared in a move. That April I took a job at a local public-

television station editing their program guide and got a copy of the *International Directory of Little Magazines* that Len Fulton published, and I began writing for sample copies. It was thrilling to see magazines I'd no idea existed. I was drawn to the more startling titles: *Marijuana Quarterly, Blitz, Earth Rose, Ole, Lung Socket, Wormwood*, as well as the beautifully produced ones, like the *Outsider, Choice, Folio, El Corno Emplumado*, and the political mimeos, like *Kauri, Outcast, Work, New*. I learned magazines, like the *Caller*, might be published by funeral parlors, want only poems on death. At Channel 17 I began to type up the few poems I'd written. In June or July I left town for a weekend, came back to find there'd been trouble with typesetting, and tho I had nothing to do with this, I was fired.

The photographs on the back of my first book, *Why Is the House Dissolving*, show me with my arms wrapped around myself, sunglasses, sitting in what looks like a beach. It's the sand in back of 92 Rapple, the raised ranch we moved into when the landlord said the cats couldn't stay. It was one of ninety houses we saw go up, board by board. Having lived since six in apartments, a house suggested roots, belonging, not being on the run. The back of the house faced onto this lake of sand that stretched into woods a lover could hide in. And did. I discovered poetry on the radio and at noon on Tuesdays took the phone off the hook to listen, spellbound to whoever was reading. In an interview I was quoted saying, "I wrote like a hippy but was living like a nun." I was more isolated than ever. The few friends I'd had in grad school were in their own world. We no longer had what we had had in common. The other hundred raised ranches were families whose only interest (except for a strange Scientologist husband and wife with glazed eyes) seemed having 2.3 kids and keeping their lawns manicured and shaved like crewcuts. Tho the houses were modest, often the shrubbery was not. Weekdays from eight to five I was alone. Gas and oil were still inexpensive and I'd open the windows, let chiffon and gauzey long veil-like drapes blow from the bed as if I was trying to air the house of some dreary night spirits, and write. I wrote standing up at the kitchen counter. In one photograph you can see the postage scale near a jar of beans. The kitchen there was white, new, with brown delft tiles. Spotless, bright, as few other kitchens I've lived in since have been. A white wrought-iron glass-covered table is rotting outside the house I live in now, a ghost of itself. It was usually piled with little magazines and blue, turquoise, and lavender, lilac, and purple can-

*At the Grolier Book Shop in
Cambridge, Massachusetts*

images so prevalent, come from leaning against the glass, feeling the branches move nearer.

I was drawn to the most wild, direct poems, still felt torn, burnt by my graduate-school whirl, and devoured poems of writers like Bukowski, D. R. Wagner, Steve Richmond, and also the surrealistic dream landscapes of poets who later I realized had read Bly. I remember discovering Anne Sexton while sitting in a car in a snowstorm glued to "The Double Image." The only thing I can compare to the excitement of discovering so many unique, strange, bizarre, weird, and wonderful images and poets and poetry and magazines is the feeling I get now going to international film festivals, an obsession.

During that time, I lived in the past and in my imagination. My most erotic, shocking to some, poems (I was pleased to find, since I'd rarely done anything not well-behaved) were fantasy. "Nice," a poem I wrote when asked for something erotic, something that was to be published in some popular erotic magazine, was written at Union College on a piece of Spearmint gum wrapper while I watched a Bergman film. I hadn't been political but, hearing news and TV coverage of Vietnam, began writing poems about society and published many of them in *Outcast* and *Kauri* and *Win.* And I began to see my growing up in Vermont, my family, in a way I hadn't.

I felt again the outsider in the neighborhood I lived in, the setting for many poems in *Why Is the House Dissolving?* where "people wonder should they plant identical hedges, put the same screens on windows of their very similar heads." I was seen as strange, not a good daughter-in-law, since I couldn't goo and coo, call my father-in-law Daddy, didn't cook dinner for my in-laws often enough, have the right friends. But as bad, I wore my hair long and straight, gypsily free, tho I'd been told after twenty "a lady cuts it or wears it up." And most horrid, I hadn't had babies. I don't think I ever told my in-laws part of the reason, out of my control, why.

Much of that time, in memory, seems peaceful, sheltered, safe. The wildness and danger was in what I wrote. Somewhere else, women, including a woman I mentioned earlier I'd known in high school, were getting strangled or marching on Selma. But the poems knew a lot more than I did, even the early titles: "What We Grow Away From," "The Way Sun Falls Away from Every Window," and images of loss and leaving stud that first book, so many images of dissolving, a word that recurs, was a map to what was ahead.

Why Is the House Dissolving was published in 1968. It came from a probably too-large submission

dles in the candelabra I cherished for years. Bamboo, rubber trees, huge begonias, ivy, and fuchsia pulled green into the house, and thick plush wall-to-wall carpet turned the room, in bright light, into a beach. When I took any job, I used the pay to buy paintings, and large oils and prints and etchings covered the white walls along with psychodelic posters, dried leaves, books, and, after one summer when I think more than ever I wanted to twist and change and transform what I saw, rows of colored glass bottles.

First I wrote on yellow lined paper, folded into four pieces and put into a red bag. When the bag was filled, I typed them up, threw many of the handwritten manuscripts away. Except for poems in books, I have only some carbons of the first few years I wrote. Most were sold and are in the archives at the University of Texas at Austin. Each week I discovered a new poet; like a drug addict I'd float high on that. Or a new magazine. I planted red tulips, watched tumbleweed blow toward the house, watched blood maples turn fire. Maybe the women in poems running into and disappearing in trees, the Daphne

of poems to *Ole* magazine, just folding. Brown Miller had worked on it and picked a couple for *Lung Socket* magazine, then edited the manuscript for Open Skull Press. I'd wanted strong poems: nothing academic, prissy, safe. Now I can see there's a lot of bottled-up rage and anger I didn't see then, tho others reacted to what they felt was violence. It was odd to see the poems printed in mimeo, a few at odd angles. Unsettling maybe, like the first reaction to the birth of a child. The street language in the book is a mask, "knocked up" in the poem "She Sigh Happy," almost a costume I was trying on as I tried out surrealism in lines like "Lace grows in her eyes like fat weddings." The book was stapled together with a nice bright white and black square cover. Many of the poems less pared down, more imagistic, than a lot of what I write now. With the tone often mysterious, the subjects are often hard or tough: rape, castration, the brutalities of war and marriage.

Probably as important to me as Frost's encouraging words was a review of this book in *Works*, an issue that first had an article from Blazek, the publisher of Open Skull Press, saying he wanted "poetry that is dangerous." That would by itself have pleased me. But it was the review, by John Hopper, who said, "The most exciting poems published by any of the presses I covered were in Lyn Lifshin's *Why Is the House Dissolving?* There is an unmistakable—and yet undisguised—femininity at work here that reminds of Sylvia Plath and yet stands very much on its own gorgeous legs. There is not the mordant urgency of the *Ariel* poems, that despair so often overpowering, but encountering the woman alone generates such touching felicities I was sorry the poems ran out so soon." He closed saying, "I do not know what attempt the established houses make to scan small press poets, but here is an excellent example of a fine strong voice whose book, the reverse title page tells us is 'published in a limited edition of roughly five hundred copies.' I know nothing of Miss Lifshin's attitudes toward making it in the Big Time, but somebody with international distribution has a real obligation to give her a lot of bread and a wider audience. She well deserves it" (*Works* 11, no. 1, spring 1969). The review made me show people the book. Before I hadn't.

One wall in my garage is lined with notebooks, diaries I've kept since October of 1976, copies of letters, too many to go thru. If I'd kept a diary or journal or even copies of letters those first years of writing, I might remember what I did besides writing. I worked briefly at the New York State Mental Health Department, where "Office" and "Thaw"

grew out of talks with the secretaries about weddings and silver or just being outside those first early March days. Writing an autobiography reminds me how memory really is like a kaleidoscope, how it shifts, rearranges, lets different patterns thru. Writing this, I hear glass explode. The cat tears thru a sill of colored glass bottles, there at least ten years. Maybe it was a sparrow hot for the last red berries that lured him, and now an old and fragile white demitasse cup, a wedding or shower present from the sister I haven't talked to the last two and a half years, is splintered in pieces. One glue doesn't work and I try another, foul smelling. It's old and has to be mixed. It takes forever to dry or to piece what's broken together, find all the fragments, as with poems or something remembered.

I'm sure I'd have remembered different triggers, different faces, if I had written this ten years before or even next year. When I reread some early interviews some of what I meant dissolves. In my master's thesis on Dylan Thomas I explored how he made a religion almost out of poetry and I think I started doing something like that too. I'd drive to NYC, a two-and-a-half- or three-hour drive, to go to poetry readings in East Village lofts, just bought poetry volumes. Long before I wrote, I saw and was fascinated by Beat poetry readings in the Village, readings I'd change any plans to go to.

I'd been writing to a few poets and wasn't surprised when one arrogant, taunting, challenging note came from a poet in California who said he'd seen my photo in a clump of poems in a rather bad magazine. He said my poems needed work and I probably chewed gum but he'd like to take me down the Mississippi on a raft, hollering poems and blowing weed. It was outlandish. I answered. He began calling, I think from houses he broke into, sent outrageous letters, photographs of himself, including one of Dylan Thomas with his name inked on the side. I *had* been living like a nun. Suddenly wild letters from this man who looked like a cross between Clint Eastwood and Robert Redford, an ex-con poet with a pet water beetle, came daily along with bottles of Château Ausone from Pacific Grove. He sent luscious dreams, slivers of Puerto Vallerto nights he wanted to show me that were like ruby glass, twisting what was. But I wasn't prepared, never quite believed he'd actually come to Albany. In letters to him I'd been flamboyant, open, free, the mask I used in some poems but had never, not even in the house alone in front of a mirror, tried on. Even later flirtatious phone calls, one from a man in a rock group after he'd seen my photograph in *Rolling Stone,* would flatter rather than insult me. It was still such a new experience. I didn't know how to be coy or seductive or sexy, and being called wholesome in high school had convinced me I'd never haunt any man. It was one thing to respond to his letters. California seemed planets away. And safe. Even when he said he was coming, was on his way, I didn't think he would and was astonished that March afternoon, or maybe it was April, that he was real, tall, gorgeous. I gulped cognac to not show how terrified I was, something for a while I'd do other times I felt scared, with someone new or with someone special. And, for a while, at poetry readings.

I'd imagined this ex-con poet had been jailed for something like drugs, but it was armed robbery. He was still married to a woman who'd seen his smile, fell for him, drove seven hundred miles up the coast for two years, and with influence, got him released early. Probably it was his stories, his charm, something I've also had a weakness for, that got her. And so many women. East, in "Aaaaaalbaeney," as he pronounced it, he'd con motel owners (and then walk out), priests, and a number of famous poets. He was adept at conning everyone. I can never not think of him, passing the Arcadia Motel, where I walked, still not (tho I had my license at fifteen) driving since the year after I was married. When he ran out of his wife's money he started living in the trees in back of my raised ranch. Nights he'd scavenge backyards for lawn chairs, melons, beer, beach towels, and built himself a lean-to past where sand and tumbleweed ended. Every night at an appointed time, 9 P.M. or 10, he'd light a match under the white-tiled bathroom window and I'd flick the switch. Mornings when my husband's green Healy pulled away, this man came in full of leaves to make eggs Benedict, tell outrageous stories of making love in coffins, running drugs across the border. I'd been totally innocent, something he was astonished to find. Little besides his fantasies seemed real. But he was often on the verge of suicide. I expected to find his six-foot-two-inch corpse dangling or across the top front stair. He scrounged around, lifted bottles of beer. We'd laugh and he'd read while I sorted laundry. A Mary McCarthy story was one of his favorites and he loved Plath and Louise Gluck. Once John Dos Passos was talking at Union College—since I couldn't see the poet after 5 or 6 P.M., I wrote a huge note in the tumbleweed and sand. I gave him money for beer, but when I wasn't looking he stole Kennedy silver dollars, opened my mail, including one of my first invitations to read. Later I found library books in the weeds, Katherine Mansfield, letters he'd written to James Dickey and Ed Field.

It was a juggling act, a situation I found myself in more and more. He went back and forth to Carmel. Once, when I was on the west coast, I was sure I'd see him on the roof of a house, screaming at stars. In Albany he lived near where Legs Diamond had when it got too cold to live in the trees. Women were always after him. If he needed a typewriter he'd suck up to a warmhearted priest, pretending he wanted to go dry out. He even stuck it out a few months in Utica at a clinic where a woman gave him her car and a watch with her name on it, somehow now in my drawer. When he wasn't here, he wrote hilarious letters. I just took boxes of them out of the cellar to leave in between the screen door and the main door like a charm, or to get the musty smell out of them. I'd forgotten how clever, bawdy, touching, and sad they were. He thought we'd live somewhere in Big Sur, and in one envelope, a key fell out to a house where I was to meet him. He published several poems. I often found them stilted. But his letters were wild, endearing, funny, enraging, strange. He was the opposite of my husband, a split I've found myself torn between again and again.

Once, when my mother was visiting, since I couldn't feed this poet–con man in the trees, I cooked large vats of lasagna and put them in Maxwell House coffee tins so the cats wouldn't get them and left them under the window. Hearing a noise when he came thru the grass to get it, my mother was about to call the police. Once, knowing nothing about where anyone got drugs locally, when he said in jail they used nutmeg and mace, we poured A & P ground nutmeg powder into a glass of water. In two hours I was totally and unpleasantly stoned. I avoided all drugs after that. Once he brought a man who'd been a journalist and had been drinking a long time, looked as if he'd been living on the streets, over. I was sure they'd both pass out in the living room on the plush pile wall-to-wall carpet. It's still hard for me to resist men who tell good stories, especially if their eyes are blue, and they've a sense of life being a joke, often absurd. I'm drawn to them and really know they (or I) can't stay, that I need someone very unlike that, too. I knew I'd never leave to tramp around Big Sur or mooch off others, live in other people's attics or caves in the leaves. But I couldn't tear myself away from such an intense periscope on an alien life.

He lived on the edge, fearlessly, taunting death because he really didn't care; poems were all that mattered. I'm not sure which of his stories were lies. About two years after we met, he, and a new wife, he said, went off to Majorca, said they were getting rich writing porn and living in Graves's castle. Not long after that, I got a phone call and then a letter I just came across saying that on Good Friday he'd collided with a school bus. In keeping with the strangeness of knowing him, a woman later called me from California, said while she was trying to paint, this man's ghost came to her, pleading that she call me, tho he didn't want her, she said, to tell me how he'd been, before the suicide, half himself, so worn out with cirrhosis, sick. Her story was as weird as his, but she said she'd met him in Spain, seen an aura around him that meant he was extraordinary, and had fallen for him. She got extremely close and involved with him and his wife and went on about a woman in Graves's castle shooting up and bathing in vitamin E, a story I borrowed for "I Don't Want Diana in the Palace." That Good Friday she said there was to be a gross-out party, everyone trying to outdo the others in coming up with something bizarre. He had sheets of blood for a tablecloth, fruit. But he outdid the others by killing himself before it began, crashing his car head-on into a school bus on an embankment. The woman who called me suggested she and I and his wife collaborate on a play or film, catch our views of him. Often she called from California, or suggested we go to Paris for lunch or into his Majorca tomb. The oddest thing was that she sent me a box of poems he'd written about me I'd never seen. They're in the door now, losing the smell of what held them too.

I thought I'd write the past up to the spring of 1986, when something I can't write about yet started, am astonished, since I thought I left so much out, that I've typed only two and a half of six notebooks up and I've only come to the publishing of the first of around eighty books and chapbooks. For someone apt to write twenty-seven jealousy poems, twenty "The Thud of Not Seeing You"'s, as if to exorcise or catch what can't stay, maybe it's not strange that some sidetracks, these parenthetical, jagged detours, not just the way my mother and I often talk, but part of the rushed breathless slam of many of my poems, is also the way memory swirls and braids and discovers.

   It's February 1, 1989. I started pulling the past back last October and, tho I hadn't planned to, did go back to the diaries, some letters; it was like dragging nets, coming up with jewels and driftwood, bones, barbwire, ghosts. This turns out to be a beginning of autobiography. It stops before separations, divorce, and just before *Black Apples,* before I edited three anthologies—one of mother and daughter poems,

Tangled Vines; and *Ariadne's Thread,* women's diaries and journals; and *Unsealed Lips,* women's memoirs and autobiography—before I went to Europe, filled a green notebook, Appunti, with slices of Frascati, the tombs of Cecilia Metalla, catacombs, before I thought twenty-six was the end of an exciting life, as I had felt at thirteen, before Yaddo, Millay, MacDowell and Bread Loaf, and readings in towns with rivers I'd never heard of, Winona, Sangre de Cristo; it's before this house on Appletree with polished cherry that goes amber and guava in honey light, before Abyssinian cats, the first, when it seemed everyone was leaving, before I let my hair go curly, my hair lighten in sun to fire. It will take at least as long a piece as this to get to what happened before and during the eighty chapbooks and books, all this before my black T Bird, my night radio adventure, or the September a car slashed my forehead. It stops before I went from worrying I couldn't write enough to worrying I wrote more than I should, before the documentary film *Not Made of Glass* some years after I threw glass, as if to get it out of me, before so many poems became real after I wrote them and what was real dissolved and ghosts got more stubborn, before this ruby and cobalt velvet quilt I'm writing under, that I hope some no longer feeling it will remember got less thick. Now no one left still calls me Rosalynn. This stops before spaceships exploded on TV; it was when my mother could still open jars nobody else could and bolt up stairs, or up Boylston in three-and-a-half-inch heels. Vietnam moved from television to my arms and left scars there as red wood fades and the tulip trees I planted in a house I left are about to flower, before plum and quince here lost their leaves and those sticks of crab apple and elderberry I stuck in spread, tangle with black walnuts. I've left out the desert, Arizona, 1984, when I'd fill forty spiral diaries in one year, feel blue stain many nights, the blues gnaw like ants. Now blue lace means more than blue lace; diamonds and teeth chip. This ends before I wrote poems about houses of sawdust or blue towels, before *Rolling Stone* called me for poems, before my mother gave up cigarettes and began calling and calling. In the house I lived in when *Why Is the House Dissolving* was published, the ferns have doubled. This stops way before so many mad girls and madonnas. Later it seemed I was either running toward or away from men. I'd use "exhausted" and "drained" and "rushing" more and more in letters and diaries. This stops before I thought anyone would write a Ph.D. on me or a book of criticism or say, "The mask goes up, the mask down, the mask is hard irony, sarcasm and when it comes down the Lifshin behind it is the soft vulnerable Outsider" (Hugh Fox's *Lyn Lifshin: A Critical Study*). I couldn't have dreamed then I'd be packing boxes of poems and galleys and posters for archives at U of Texas, Austin, and Temple U, or read with writers I idolized in California, Illinois, Boston, Virginia, or imagined Reagan's visit to Bitburg or how I'd be haunted by Kent State or have Kristallnacht flood poems. Before skimming bits of this I realize I put in so little about my father's death, how on the way to his lawyer's, just before I was supposed to testify against him in court, he fell on the snow, left a stain of rose spreading, a story I told in one of the earliest, longest poems, "How It Happened," in *Mad Windows*. After I wrote *Why Is the House Dissolving* the roof really did dissolve. This was before I even imagined so much of what would matter. There were no videotapes of readings then, and when there were it would take years to have them or play them. I'd never heard of Emerald Lake, Diamond Head, Lerchi, or being stranded midwinter in a blue cabin in Maine. Later, Montreal in August for films made the summer ending more bearable, and I'd do workshops I'd never even thought of: mothers and daughters, diaries and journals, memoirs, publishing, creativity workshops. At the point this ends, I couldn't have imagined writing so many poems with war and nuclear landscapes, or that two and a half years would go by without talking to my sister. Some fantasies became reality; more would be roller coasters of spun glass in 250-mile-per-hour winds that shattered, left a hole, before I'd have any clue, like reading even three words, seemingly harmless, in a November 85 diary, "A delight, warmth, humanness," how they'd turn ghosts, sting.

Unstapling letters in these last years of diaries is a bit like walking on mine fields. Once I was told I had a layer of fat missing so I bruised when anyone touched me. Some of that dark spreading that didn't get into poems will I hope grow into stories. Because of some eye-muscle imbalance an eye doctor said it's hard for me to look at what's near, like much these past wild, funny, impossible years. I'll keep it for later like news clips, photos, a T-shirt someone gone away once wore.

I started finishing this on January 16 with salmon light falling thru cracked walnut branches on the red velvet quilt. Orange peels, Memento, my Abyssinian cat, 4:20 light thru lime and raspberry stained glass falling on leather, candles, just-stitched ribbons on new pointe shoes. "Tangled Up in Blue" on the air, roses in the lowest room, parched lily of

Teaching a poetry workshop

the valley. Downstairs, prisms, polished bronze, mortar and pestle my grandmother brought from Russia. Silver horse yanked from the crushed grill of my torn Mustang, near the "wild women don't get the blues" button I wore to a reading where no one could hear, a wreath of diaries bulge with letters, rages, horrors, jealousies, and highs, nights I'll never let go of, hips and lips, blue eyes, lace.

I didn't finish tho, ran off to a ballet class. Now, Feb 2, a day I still remember not as Ground Hog Day but as Janice Burby's birthday, when there were always red crepe-paper baskets full of hearts and we played pin the tail on the donkey; it's grey, and after a day it hit sixty-five it's sleet and ice, the blue stones glazed over. I'm looking not just backward but forward to the film, finally coming out, new books—*Rubbed Silk, Blood Road, Skin Divers, Reading Lips, Doctors*—to an interview in *New York Quarterly*, reading in England, my anthology of women's memoirs, *Unsealed Lips*, and more.

"Me, my father, and my sister, Joy"

Photograph

my father sister and
me in the trees with
our hair blowing my
sister as usual has
something in her
hands and pouts in
a way no one could
say no to dancing
in restaurants
until she pulls in
to her self at 19
like the turtles
she collects but
here she's the sweet
pouter my father's
pockets bulge with
things the gum
he'll give us in
the brown chair
later reading the
funnies I've got
a little pot and
my arms are heavy
My father touches
us both lightly
as if he's not
sure we're real

Middlebury Poem

Milky summer nights
the men stay waiting, First National Corner
where the traffic light used to be, wait

as they have all June evenings of their lives.
Lilac moss and lily of the valley
sprout in the cooling air as

Miss Damon, never late for thirty years,
hurries to unlock the library, still
hoping for a sudden man to spring fall from the

locked dark of mysterious card catalogues, to
come brightening her long dusty shelves.
And halfway to dark

boys with vacation bicycles
whistle flat stones over the bridge
longing for secret places where
rocks are blossoming girls with damp thighs,

Then nine o clock falls thick on lonely books
and all the unclaimed fingers and
as men move home thru bluemetal light,
the Congregational Church bells

ringing as always four minutes late,
the first hayload of summer rumbles thru
town and all the people shut their eyes
dreaming a wish

With the Bluest Eyes

talked fast faster
leaves crackled in the
fire blue the color
of a lake you
scrape snow off
in Michigan I could
see night fishes
darting thru
seaweed that would
tangle with all
my hair I was afraid
if I stopped talking
his tongue would be
a book in my
mouth I couldn't
put down

That December

my room mate Fran wriggled
in tight striped orange wool
and smoked extra long Winstons
but insisted on lights out by
8 pm so I'd stumble thru
biology textbooks and tampax
in drawers, spill ink thru
lace and nylons. Even in the
light, the room was pea green
stucco, identical closets
kleptomaniacs could siphon
red silk from. But that night
the temple oranges came, ruby
red grapefruit plums and
mandarin oranges in crates,
it was like Christmas in 4D
at Mt. Olympus women I never
knew came running in floppy
bathrobes from 4 wings like
cars to an accident as if
the orange and lemony tart
skins were jewels or stained
glass the moon turned to
garnets and diamonds, rubies.
Even Fran pulled out of the
cocoon of her darkness and
for once didn't scowl, but

staggered toward the candles
and flashlit glow to where
7 of us sat like gipsies
in some luscious fire
ritual—we could almost
hear tambourines our lips
close to dancing as we
pealed and licked juice
on our fingers wrists and
nose widly biting into
what after hours of dull
Geology and Beginning
French seemed even more
sweet and full of summer,
close as if linked
by love

Ramona Lake

In the back row of a
class that wouldn't listen
with her 70 IQ and
enormous pleading eyes

saucers of licorice
"I want to learn"
over the loud chain
saw buzz of boys
laughing guffawing

"I'd like to pass the
bar too." Ramona
in your pink check
dress hair so black
it was close to blue

still as a mannequin
oblivious to spit
balls, pokes in the
ribs. Ramona I
couldn't teach you

old enough now to have
a daughter as startled
paralyzed as the one
deer frozen
in car lights

baffled suddenly
in another world

You Understand the Requirements

We are
sorry to have to
regret to
tell you
sorry sorry
regret sorry that you have
failed

your hair should have been
piled up higher

you have failed to
pass failed
your sorry
regret your
final hair comprehensive
exam satisfactorily
you understand the requirements

you understand we are
sorry final
and didn't look as professional
as desirable
or sorry dignified
and have little enough
sympathy for 16th century
sorry english anglicanism

we don't know doctoral
competency what to think and
regret you will sorry not
be able to stay
or finish

final regret your disappointment
the unsuccessfully completed best
wishes for the future
it has been a
regret sorry the requirements
the university policy

please don't call us

*My Mother's Third Call on a Day of Sleet
and December Falling*

as if the whiteness was
gauze wrapped over the
mouth of someone dying
and she had to slash it
with a last word, or
Monday was a blank
sheet of paper only my
words would cling to.

My mother, who lugged
suitcases with me in the
78 blizzard when subways
broke in Brooklyn, says
the wind crossing the
street wouldn't let
her breathe. I'm stand
ing with my hair dripping,
turning the quilt a darker
blue the water boiling
downstairs, thinking how
long it's been since I've
gone to visit her or
haven't told her I had
to rush but just let the
words between us wrap
us like the navy afghan
on the velvet couch with
the stain where the grey
cat peed and just drifted
in the closeness linked
as we once were as if
we always would be

"My mother and me"

BIBLIOGRAPHY

Poetry:

Why Is the House Dissolving. Edited by Brown Miller. San Francisco: Open Skull Press, 1968.

Femina 2. Oshkosh, Wis.: Abraxas Press, 1970.

Leaves and Night Things. Edited by James Evans and John P. Miller. West Lafayette, Ind.: Baby John Press, 1970.

Two Women Poets. Oshkosh, Wis.: Abraxas Press, 1970.

Black Apples. Trumansburg, N.Y.: Crossing Press, 1971.

Lady Lyn. Milwaukee: Morgan Press, 1971.

Charas 2. Tacoma, Wash.: Charas Press, 1972.

40 Days, Apple Nights. Milwaukee: Morgan Press, 1972.

I'd Be Jeanne Moreau. Milwaukee: Morgan Press, 1972.

Love Poems. Durham, N.H.: Zahir Press, 1972.

Lyn Lifshin. Durham, N.H.: Zahir Press, 1972.

The Mercurochrome Sun Poems. Tacoma, Wash.: Charas Press, 1972.

Moving by Touch. Traverse City, Mich.: Cotyledon Press, 1972.

Poems by Suramm and Lyn Lifshin. Madison, Wis.: Union Literary Committee, 1972.

Tentacles, Leaves. Belmont, Mass.: Hellric, 1972.

All the Women Poets I Ever Liked Didn't Hate Their Fathers. St. Petersburg, Fla.: Konglomerati Press, 1973.

Audley End Poems. Long Beach, Calif.: MAG Press, 1973.

The First Week Poems. Plum Island, Mass.: Zahir Press, 1973.

Museum (illustrated by Eric Von Schmidt; calligraphy by Michael Rutherford). Albany: Conspiracy Press, 1973.

The Old House on the Croton. San Lorenzo, Calif.: Shameless Hussy Press, 1973.

Blue Fingers. Milwaukee: Shelter Press, 1974.

Blue Madonna. Milwaukee: Shelter Press, 1974.

Mountain Moving Day. Trumansburg, N.Y.: Crossing Press, 1974.

Poems (illuminated by Sylvia Schwintzer). Gulfport, Fla.: Konglomerati Press, 1974.

Selected Poems. Trumansburg, N.Y.: Crossing Press, 1974.

Several Things like Porcelain (illustrated by Manaseri). Sotto Voce 4. Beeston, England: Quickest Way Out Press, 1974.

Shaker Poems. Chatham, N.Y.: Omphalos Press, 1974.

Walking thru Audley End Mansion Late Afternoon and Drifting into Certain Faces. Long Beach, Calif.: MAG Press, 1974.

Green Bandages. Geneseo, N.Y.: Hidden Springs, 1975.

Old House Poems. Santa Barbara, Calif.: Capra Press, 1975.

Paper Apples. Stockton, Calif.: Wormwood Review Press, 1975.

Shaker House Poems. Tannersville, N.Y.: Tideline Press, 1975.

Upstate Madonna: Poems, 1970–1974. Trumansburg, N.Y.: Crossing Press, 1975.

Naked Charm. Columbus, Ohio: Fireweed Press, 1976.

North Poems. Milwaukee: Morgan Press, 1976.

Some Madonna Poems. Buffalo: White Pine Press, 1976.

Crazy Arms. Chicago: Ommation Press, 1977.

Early Plymouth Women (illustrated by Susan Hale Kemenyffy). Milwaukee: Morgan Press, 1977.

The January Poems. Cincinnati: More Waters, 1977.

Leaning South. New York: Red Dust, 1977.

Lifshin & Richmond. Oakland, Calif.: Bombay Duck, 1977.

Mad Girl Poems. Wichita, Kan.: Caprice Out of Sight, 1977.

More Waters. Cincinnati: Waters Press, 1977.

Pantagonia. Stockton, Calif.: Wormwood Review Press, 1977.

Glass. Milwaukee: Morgan Press, 1978.

Lips on That Blue Rail. San Francisco: Lion's Breath Press, 1978.

Poems, with John Elsberg. Filey, England: Fiasco, 1978.

Men and Cars. Ware, Mass.: Four Zoas Press, 1979.

More Naked Charm. Los Angeles: Illuminati, 1979.

35 Sundays (photographs by Gini Sorrentini). Chicago: Ommation Press, 1979.

Madonna. Stockton, Calif.: Wormwood Review Press, 1980.

Blue Dust, New Mexico. Fredonia, N.Y.: Basilisk Press, 1982.

Colors in Cooper Black. Milwaukee: Morgan Press, 1982.

Finger Print. Stockton, Calif.: Wormwood Review Press, 1982.

Hotel Lifshin. Eureka, Calif.: Poetry Now, 1982.

In the Dark with Just One Star. Milwaukee: Morgan Press, 1982.

Leaving the Bough. New York: New World Press, 1982.

Lobster & Oatmeal (journal and poems). Sacramento, Calif.: Pinch Penny, 1982.

Want Ads. Milwaukee: Morgan Press, 1982.

Blue Horses Nuzzle Tuesday. Burlingame, Calif.: Minotaur Press, 1983.

Madonna Who Shifts for Herself. Long Beach, Calif.: Applezaba Press, 1983.

Matinee. Chicago: Ommation Press, 1984.

Naked Charm. Los Angeles: Illuminati, 1984; revised edition. Los Angeles: Illuminati, 1989.

The Radio Psychic Is Shaving Her Legs. Detroit: Planet Detroit, 1984.

Kiss the Skin Off. Silver Spring, Md.: Cherry Valley, 1985.

Remember the Ladies. E. Lansing, Mich.: Ghost Dance Press, 1985.

Camping Madonna. Portlandville, N.Y.: MAF Press (Thirteen), 1986.

Virgin Mary and Madonna. El Paso, Tex.: Vergin Press, 1986.

Raw Opals. Los Angeles: Illuminati, 1987.

Many Madonnas. Edited by Virginia L. Long. St. John, Kan.: Kindred Spirit, 1988.

Red Hair and the Jesuit. Parkdale, Ore.: Back Pocket, 1988.

Rubbed Silk. Los Angeles: Illuminati, 1988.

Ballet Poems. Chicago: Ommation Press, 1989.

Blood Road. Los Angeles: Illuminati, 1989.

Doctors. Los Angeles: Applezaba, 1989.

Reading Lips. Milwaukee: Morgan Press, 1989.

Skin Divers, with Belinda Subraman. Leeds, England: Krax, 1989.

Under Velvet Pillows. Middletown Springs, Vt.: Four Zoas, 1989.

House of Skin. Los Angeles: Illuminati, forthcoming.

Mad Girl. Augusta, Ga.: Blue Horse, forthcoming.

Editor of:

Tangled Vines: A Collection of Mother and Daughter Poems. Boston: Beacon Press, 1978.

Ariadne's Thread: A Collection of Contemporary Women's Journals. New York: Harper, 1982.

Unsealed Lips (anthology of women's memoirs). Santa Barbara, Calif.: Capra Press, 1989.

Sound recordings:

Lyn Lifshin Reads Her Poems. Cambridge, N.Y.: Natalie Slohm Associates, 1977.

Offered by Owner (with a booklet of poems). Cambridge, N.Y.: Natalie Slohm Associates, 1978.

Films:

Not Made of Glass (documentary). Karist Films, 1989.

Sławomir Mrożek

1930-

Could my life story be interesting for someone who has never even heard of my existence? I have not shot elephants in Kenya or elsewhere, never worked for any secret service, nor been a lover of John Kennedy, there is nothing of the sort to be revealed. I have not committed a nice murder, nor do I have any particular perversion that might excite the general public, not even one personal secret of the kind which if told could compensate somehow for the lack of adventurous deeds to recount. I lived through the Second World War, the German occupation of Poland, the Stalinist and post-Stalinist eras, but I lived it as millions of people did, a common story. Also my immigration to the West, now twenty-five years old, can hardly be considered something special. Then what?

Even for myself, a storyteller, just the enumeration of facts, the crawling of my memory along the string of events that brought me to this very day, would not be interesting. I could break the string, set the facts loose and pile them up instead of following their linear boredom. But then the process would be to pick up one fact after another from the pile, like picking up one object after another from a pile stored by haphazard accumulation in some dusty loft, to have a brief look at it before dropping it back with a sigh, smile, disgust, relish, or no feeling at all.

So if I am going to try telling my life, it is only because I hope to discover some pattern in it, some shape, logic, and sense. I prefer to resist the idea that it has been nothing but a heap of junk. Only that kind of hope can incite me to begin the task. As to the general reader—I can only trust that he will follow.

I was born on the twenty-ninth of June 1930. My birth is one of those facts that I have to believe in, personally I have not the slightest memory of it. If there is some life or anything of the kind after death, then similarly, I think, I shall not remember the act of dying. Thus of two basic facts of our being—or not being—we cannot really be sure.

Many years after my presumed coming into existence I had a fit of curiosity about the exact hour of it, so I asked my father. My mother was already dead, she died when I was nineteen. He could not remember, probably because he was drunk during

Sławomir Mrożek in 1988

the event, and afterwards he was not sufficiently interested in the matter of its minute timing. He suggested that I was born towards midnight.

The uncertainty, the ambiguity, started right from the beginning and has followed me ever since. Maybe that is why I long to make things clear. The more I muddled through life, and the more confusion I created or was forced into, the more I disliked it, that is, the more I disliked myself and the more I desired clarity.

The official date of my birth, the twenty-sixth of June, is false. It was put on my first birth certificate by some sloppy clerk in the parish office and was copied over and over. It is false on all my passports, certificates of my marriages, tax payments, biographies, and whatnot in many languages of many countries. It gives me a certain satisfaction to know that it must be false even in the files of the Polish secret police, the institution whose task is to know the truth, whose dedication to the search for it equals that of Saint Augustine, Pascal, or Kant, only it is less disinterested, on another level, and has much better results.

I hope that one day I shall be less lazy or less busy than I am, enough to make a legal disposition to the effect that on my tombstone at least, if destiny should allow me to have one, the date of my birth will be set right. However I have no means of securing the authenticity of the date of my death in the same way, since I do not know it myself.

My father was one of seven children of a rather poor peasant in a village in the south of Poland where the hills roll towards the Tatra Mountains. He fled to town when he was a teenager, he wanted to get an education and thus to escape the predestinated lot of rural poverty and ignorance. He managed to get to school by his own means, I do not know exactly how because—to his credit—he never

bored his son with didactical stories of his self-made beginnings. I can only guess that it was tough for him.

Soon History (mark the capital H) intervened in his life as it later did in mine. In 1920 the Soviet Union, only three years old, invaded Poland, whose national independence was only two years old. My father volunteered, everybody did, so I do not think he had much moral choice, though neither do I think that he pondered the question excessively. He told me some stories of his soldiering, they were horror stories though he was not aware that they were. The extreme fatigue of long marches prevailed in his memory over hand-to-hand combat, the slaughter of prisoners, and other fragments of his narration which to his listener were most striking.

He succeeded in defending Poland, but not for long. The Soviets came back in 1939 to help the Germans, left for a while after the German attack on them, revisited us in 1945 when rolling the Germans back, and stayed on with the gentlemanly assistance of President Roosevelt. They are still there.

After the war my father did not go back to school, nor did he return home. I do not know how he lived, all I know is that he washed his shirt in the

Mother, Zofia Keozior (left), and her sisters, before her marriage

lavatory of a railroad station—probably his only shirt—and such accommodations as the boxcars on the sidetracks were his bedrooms. Nevertheless he was lucky. My more precise knowledge of his whereabouts and doings starts with the image of him as a young postmaster in a village ten miles distant from his native one. It was a remote, humble post, but an office, the post office, nevertheless it was. It meant a steady job and all the security bestowed by the state administration on its employees. The American reader cannot have any idea how much this meant, American society being so different from the European variety. Even the European reader now will have some difficulty understanding unless he is ninety years old.

The division of society into white and blue collars was sharp, its consequences dramatic. Leaping over the dividing line, my father achieved something that was rarely achieved by men of his origins. No more was he condemned to be a commodity on the free labor market, now he was seated behind a desk and had a necktie.

One day a tall, pretty girl entered the post office. She was to become my mother. I was born three years after they married and two years after my brother was born (he died at the age of four) and five years before my sister was born. They married in 1927, she was twenty-one then, my father was twenty-four.

She was not a native of the village where they met, though she lived there, nor was she of peasant stock. Her father was the local shopkeeper, the owner of a small enterprise producing butter and cheese, he also raised some pigs on the side, I mention that latter variant of his activities, a minor one, because it gave me the opportunity to study rats as well as pigs, rats like to live in proximity to pigs, profiting from their food and specific lifestyle. Those studies proved to be helpful in later years in understanding the character and the behaviour of some sorts of human beings.

My maternal grandfather was a cold, distant man, not very likable, who exploited his children in his business and was exploited in his turn by his second wife, my mother's stepmother, an awful, stupid bitch. She had absolute power over him, she was the only person against whom he was not fortified in the bunker of his soul. He let her invade all his territory and he loved the invasion. It seems that he was not happy, though I have no reason to pity him.

Before coming to that village and setting up his own business there, he was employed as the manager of one of many estates belonging to some aristocratic family. He died of tuberculosis after the war, the

The author's maternal grandfather

illness that had killed three of his children already, including my mother.

My memories of him contrast sharply with the memories of my paternal grandfather. The opposition pertains to everything about those two men, starting with their physical appearance. The first one was tall, handsome, and imposing, the other small, bald, and bowlegged. In his youth he moved from the village to the coal mines in Silesia, dug coal for some years, and then returned to the village to marry and to plough the soil. As it was only a small and arid patch of land, he supplemented his means of survival by serving as a handyman at the local church. I remember helping him ring the bells, quite a nice occupation, at least for a child. Standing on the ground, you pull the ropes, and the mighty, deep voice responds high above you, sounding for miles and miles around.

He was very likable. The only thing he had in common with my maternal grandfather was that he spoke sparingly, both men were of few words. But his silence radiated a calm warmth and friendliness, also a slightly mocking, inward smile. I liked to be around him even when he did not talk to me. I think that children know instinctively whom it is good to be around.

When I was three years old my father was promoted to a post in the city (Cracow). To the end of his long life he remained an exemplary civil servant, though of a lesser kind. Thus he arrived at the class of mini-petite-bourgeoisie and adapted himself to its customs and values, though—not being native to it— he was never really at ease. There was always a hint of fakery in his social behaviour as if he were making up something that he did not really possess. Just the feeling of inferiority might explain why he liked to mystify, not others, but himself. He neither lied about facts nor invented them, but rather chose not to speak of facts at all if they were unpleasant. Nevertheless he lived in a phantasy world when it came to emotions, motives, psychological causes and their materialised effects. In that world of his, all that he felt and did was very beautiful, of course. He suffered from fits of fury and depressive moods, but he could also be joyful and charming, especially after a few drinks. His self-knowledge was nil or it seemed so.

He belonged to that race of men who are liked instantly wherever they go and whatever they do, especially by women. Given what I knew about him, his charm, of which he was completely unconscious— that innocence perhaps was a part of it—was never comprehensible to me. Thanks to him, or because of him, I learnt very early about the difference between wishful thinking and reality. It was a useful lesson but learnt in a painful way.

In sociological terms what for him was the top level for me became the ground floor. The intermediate zone between the lower and the lower-middle class conditioned me till my late teens. I was born in that specific compartment but I also had family links with peasants, small shopkeepers, craftsmen, workers, teachers, clergy, and even, thanks to my paternal uncle Andrew—a notorious bar fighter and a bum in his youth—with drifters. In other words, with basic Poland. No higher culture, so-called, was yet on the horizon for me.

Till the age of nine I accepted the order I was born into, its values, modes, codes, and manners, as natural and universal. Then something happened that went far beyond what was needed to shake up my childish *Weltanschauung*. It was like using a megaton bomb to impress a fly. It was the war.

My early cosmos collapsed, disintegrated, and disappeared in some abyss of which I had never known before and which I have never forgotten

since. I know it is always there, ready to gulp down whatever we have and whoever we are. I do not mean just the war, I mean the *ontological* abyss. A nice expression, is it not? It sounds superbly scientific but no definition can truly describe it. That abysmal something is without dimensions and has no name.

Those five years meant for Eastern Europe not just actual fighting but also occupation by enemy forces, destruction, misery, mass deportations, mass and individual customized killings as the only, all-embracing every-day and every-night reality. I lived those five years in a state of a dull shock. As the war in its later stage coincided with my puberty, its impact on me is understandable.

The war ended, the old order was broken forever, but its values persisted. I was a teenager now. I was beginning to become myself, enough of an individual to see that those values, those modes and codes I was born into, were not necessarily in accordance with my own temperament, intelligence, and aspirations. Nor were they the only ones in the world.

Enter communism, or rather, enter communism victoriously carried in on the back of the Red Army. So we hate it as we hated the German invader before, I say "we" because all those people to whom I belonged did. But lo! Something curious but curiously common happens.

Communism or rather its practitioners and movers have a great wisdom. It is neither the wisdom of metaphysics nor the wisdom of intellect creating ideas nor the wisdom of intelligence creating things, nothing that the human spirit lives by. It is the practical wisdom of shaping individuals and the masses for the purpose of taking and keeping power over them. The full range, scope, and variety of the means employed to that end cannot be known otherwise than by being subject to them. Nevertheless the results are visible from the outside and can be appreciated. The operational excellence of communism in the power game, never mind how bankrupt communism proves to be in all other fields, explains the secret fascination of those politicians who would otherwise be its natural enemies, the leaders of so-called reactionary parties and states. It is the envy, awe, and respect of amateurs towards professionals, of bunglers towards masters.

Ah, that revolutionary youth of mine! Communism was forced on Poland, imposed by military might on those very people in whose name, on whose behalf, according to whose desire it claimed to be there. It was an invasion, not the revolution. But I chose to believe the lie because its timing was perfect for me. At the age of twenty I was waiting for any

Mrożek at two years of age

ideological proposition however stupid or crazy, provided it was revolutionary. All because I was ripe for my own personal revolt.

The movers and practitioners knew it, dealing with youth was by then a well-rehearsed operation. Disguised as romantic bards they sang:

"Join us, young man, what we offer you is exactly what you need, our aims and goals are the same as yours, only we know what to do and how to do it, while you do not. You will know for sure if we merge our souls. This world is rotten, but together we shall put it right."

Why not? I was nothing but a bunch of frustrations, resentments, and rebellions, many of them justified. Meanwhile my family situation disintegrated. I dropped out of school, I had not enough to eat, I questioned the meaning of life and began nurturing some vague literary aspirations. It was from such stuff that the Nazis recruited their hardcore adherents. I was lucky not to have been born in Germany, class of 1903, I would have been twenty in 1933.

If I am harsh on myself it is not because I am a masochist or because of any guilt feeling, I am a rather guilt-resistant type. It is only for the sake of lucidity. I let myself be cheated and that is all, I want to be clear about it. I thought I was joining the revolution while I joined the most rigid and oppressive establishment ever. My feeling of having been cheated is the private reason for my dislike, to put it mildly, of communism and the like ever since. This is not to say that I would otherwise have liked it—that is, if I did not have that private reason. But what is private, the existential, is always the strongest of all reasons.

Of course nobody is excused for being a fool, even at the age of twenty. Being a sucker is not a valid excuse for me. This is a matter of pride. If I am excused on that ground then it means humiliation for me. There is a tendency to excuse fools just because they are fools—alright, but then the humiliation calls for the revenge. Even a fool has the right to dislike those who took advantage of his stupidity. The fact that I was not the only one who was duped, far from it, does not mean anything to me. My accounts are always personal.

Luckily for me I did not do anything too nasty during my brief stint of totalitarian enthusiasm. My activities were limited to publishing articles in the local paper about the glories of J. Stalin and the beauties of collectivisation, communism promoted me to journalist. I say luckily, as I could easily have harmed people in some more direct manner which would have left me for life with unremitting remorse. To give an example, the extreme one, a man of my generation became a high-ranking uniformed official in the newly built apparatus of "proletarian justice." He meted out death sentences to predesignated people, and even, for reasons that I shall never know for sure (the will to go all the way? to take full responsibility?) he personally helped in executions (the good old pistol shot in the back of the skull). Certainly he would have some remorse today if he had not committed suicide only a couple of years after the period that I am talking about. What saved me from the worst was my nature, I am a man of ideas, not of action.

All that lasted for me some three or four years, the exact date of weaning is difficult to fix, the process was gradual though it went rather fast. After all I was too intelligent to live in idiocy for too long, also I was maturing, and outside developments helped me. We were already in the middle and then in the late fifties. Stalin was dead, and so more or less was the charm of his business.

So here I am closing in on thirty and the pattern of my life can already be detected. I mean that inner figure that shapes the outside of a man. The particular matrix that coordinates the lines of force into a specific design. I detect two tendencies in me: the quest for order and the drive to anarchy. Conflict is certain, something that Apollinaire, the French poet, called "the eternal strife between order and adventure" (a very free translation). Conflict is inevitable, as is the alteration of rules. When I came to this world it was order, the small, orderly world of my childhood. I took it for granted. But the war disclosed the other side to me, it was a mighty show of superhuman violence, of extra-cosmic forces set loose on a rampage. I was scared, but my fear was coupled with fascination. The war ended and so did the eruption of chaos, but I prolonged it in private with my teenager's rebellion. Finally having become tired of it I desired some structure again. The communist proposition promised both: the joys of revolution miraculously combined with the delights of order. It proved to be neither revolution nor order but a demeaning, stupefying drill. I shall never forget the overwhelming bliss when I understood that I was getting out of it, the elation of freedom and its unending vistas. Again it was time for adventure.

It came in the form of what is called in the jargon of curriculums "creative writing" but is much better and less presumptuous than that denomination. My stint in journalism, idiotic as it was, nevertheless gave me access to writing/publishing. When saying goodbye forever to ideologies, I discovered the possibilities of writing on my own, from myself, the most private enterprise that can be. The circumstances were favorable for debutants, the country was starved for anything that was fresh and true. After the deforestation so thoroughly practised by communism in its prime, every single plant sprouting here and there was welcome.

The nation was in the fast lane, so my Polish career also went fast. My first serious book, that is, the one written by me, not by my idiocy, published in 1957, was an instant success. It was a collection of short, very short, but politically and otherwise sharp stories. To this day, more than thirty years later, some quotations from these stories are remembered by people of my generation, that is, by those with whom I was young together and with whom I shared the joy and energy of suddenly, unexpectedly recuperated youth. Some of those quotations became proverbial, they were used by people who did not know and did not care who the author was—proof of how much I was in consonance with my fellow Poles at that time.

The nation's fast-moving days were slowed down, then brought to a halt, my career continued. The beginning of the sixties saw me in the capital city, Warsaw, where I had moved from my almost native Cracow (I lived in Cracow between the ages of three and twenty-nine) already a far-risen and still-rising celebrity of sorts. The status of the writer/artist was still very high in Poland at that time, you hardly could go any higher. This came from the long tradition established during the last century, when Poland was divided into three parts, forcibly incorporated into Russia, Austria, and Prussia respectively. Those empires had already started working on Poland in the eighteenth century and kept on pushing until there was no such thing as Poland, officially that is. For a very long time, writers, poets especially, were considered and consequently venerated as custodians of the national identity by the subjugated people of an obliterated country.

At thirteen

This tradition was cleverly exploited by the communists. But was there anything that they did not cleverly exploit? The writers/artists were given privileges, and the process of corruption began, it deserves a separate treatise, as does their later rebirth. The sixties were switching years. Already only a few collaborated actively, but the opponents had not stepped out into the open yet. Meanwhile the privileges lingered on for all.

I was adopted by the peculiar pet-set. Jets we did not have but pets we certainly were.

What added to my glory was a breakthrough to the Western markets almost as instant as my success at home. The Iron Curtain was still much more Iron than it is now, when the iron is replaced by shit. Given the adoration of everything Western, the phantastic dreams about the West cherished by the societies of Eastern Europe—the direct though unintended result of communist propaganda—the appearance of my books and plays on the Western side was the ultimate consecration of my local greatness. Those dreamy feelings of Easterners towards Westerners as well as their complete lack of knowledge of Western realities, though persistent, are much less now due to the experiences and disillusionment that followed. But thirty years ago they were as they were.

The adventure was finished. I passed the ominous watershed of the age of thirty, my future became predictable. Apparently satisfying and secure, the image of an established, well-off, well-adjusted member of the pet-set started haunting me. The movement of political opposition had not yet been born, Poland was still recuperating from the devastations of the Stalinist terror and the disillusionment that followed the effort for change, the first since the war, had been thwarted. People tried to scrape together whatever life had to offer and enjoy it apart from the official rigidity and boredom. *Nasza Mała Stabilizacja*—"Our teeny-weeny Stabilisation," as it was mockingly called—a caricature of consumerism, crept in. I enjoyed the privileges of my position, but, more and more, a strange sensation of unreality pervaded everything. I understood that I lived in a phantom world governed by rules the only purpose of which was to produce and maintain that phantomlike quality. Life was enclosed in a tightly sealed circuit, going round and round seemed to be the only way. I was locally famous, but my fame in the realm of phantoms—was it real? Did it prove anything about my real worth? I had money, but was it real wealth? The artificiality of the whole arrangement could no longer be overlooked or dismissed.

I married in 1959, much too early—not for my age, but because I still had an insatiable thirst for adventure, that almost mystic push beyond the known and possessed which, of course, translated itself in terms of Eros and sexuality. Wrongly or rightly, I felt that the marriage stood in my way, that it was a handicap in the long march towards the Absolute. So I took it as a sort of abject compromise if not a capitulation. Torn as I was between all my feelings for my wife and my crazy push, I could not make her happy.

In brief: I was established again, the world became orderly, but the walls were closing in around me. So it was time to blow it all up.

My first trip abroad had been to Russia, 1956. The mere act of crossing the border and seeing other places was a beneficial shock in itself, also I truly appreciate Russia, that special variant of spiritual and material existence of which Russia is the name. Just standing one early May morning in Odessa and watching the port from the top of the stairs is among the most important revelations of my life. However going to Russia could not really be going abroad because it was Soviet Russia. I know how to distinguish what is Russian from what is Soviet, but the two elements are so intermingled and the second one is so prevalent that, being a tourist from another communist state (let us beware of mistaking the state for the country when speaking of Eastern Europe, it is a mistake made by all of the Western mass media), I could not feel really abroad.

Really abroad was Vienna, Paris, and London. I went to those places, in that order, in the following years. I crossed not just the border but the mystic line separating two totally different civilisations. The people who live on the Eastern side are painfully aware of the difference, while the Westerners are not. By the way, it would be interesting to know why people who have access to all possible information are so ignorant about some basic distinctions, while people who are kept in ignorance are not.

But the ultimate opening of my mind to the vastness of our earth and the limitless chances of living upon it came when I crossed the Atlantic (it was in the last days of the ocean liners) and landed on the North American continent. It happened in 1959, thanks to an invitation from the Harvard University Summer School International Seminar, directed by Henry Kissinger, who was a professor of political science at that time. I had the opportunity to see the Statue of Liberty emerging from beyond the misty horizon, the classic sight and the first glimpse of the

U.S.A. for so many millions of newcomers before me. Those two months lived in America changed me profoundly, though I did not yet know the nature of the change, nor could I know its results.

Back to Warsaw. On the third of June 1963 I and my wife boarded a plane for Rome. Officially it was a tourist trip to Italy, but in private I intended to stay a bit longer than a couple of weeks, *tempo indeterminato*, to try living and writing someplace away from the confinement, somewhere in the open, in a world full of unknown opportunities.

Nowadays the people of Poland travel more or less freely, but in those days obtaining a passport was still one of the highest privileges. Once you obtained one you came under suspicion of having secret, criminal plans not to return. Defecting from the communist state was regarded as high treason. Also you had better watch how you behave and what you say when you are at large, because when you get back you will have to account for it. Those who felt guilty did not confess their sins even to friends.

We settled in Chiavari, a small town on the Italian Riviera. For the time being it was *villeggiatura*, just spending the summer in that wonderful site. But returning from beaches to the rented room full of plaster Madonnas and mosquitos—it was a modest house in the working-class quarter, far from the flashy coastline—I was nothing more than a desolate ring in which two mighty champions wrestled: Wild Hope against Grim Fear.

It was the fear of the future. The summer passed, the wave of happy tourists rolled back to the north, leaving the provincial town in all its naked, off-season reality and me stranded in it. The rain, cold, and wind settled in. We rented another room, this time close to the sea. No Madonnas, but huge tongues of humidity on the wall to contemplate. The house was cheaply built, it touched the slope of the hill, and the underground water penetrated its masonry. In stronger rains the room was soaked, in storms it was flooded. Watching the leprosy on the walls, I remembered my beautiful, warm apartment back in Warsaw.

Haggling with the Polish authorities took the next five years. My point was to establish a precedent: the case of a Polish writer living abroad by his own means, beyond the control of the Polish state. To the Western reader it seems as banal as free elections, freedom of speech and association, separation of the legislative and executive powers, the limits of what the police can do. He takes all that for granted and does not even give a thought to such trivia. The Irish government does not care if any Irish writer prefers to live in Paris or any other place of his choice, but in

Polish terms twenty-five years ago the case was unheard of. Our passports of course were valid for only a short time, and the Italian visas could not be extended beyond their date of expiration. The endless visits to the Polish consulate in Rome and to the Italian *prefettura* in Genoa made me feel what all foreigners of uncertain legal status feel (a considerable part of the world population by now).

Sensing my determination, the owners of my country proposed a deal. Oh, it was never put in clear terms, of course. How was it proposed, then? The Western, especially the Anglo-Saxon, and most specifically the North American mind will never understand the Byzantine communist ways and manners. Those who do not know can only believe or not that the message was clear, the one delivered to me in the wrappings of suave oral arabesque, in the privacy of the consular offices. They would grant me a valid, long-term passport if I would cooperate in convincing the West that things in Poland were not so bad after all, that intellectual life was free and all that was being said to the contrary was just a reactionary bias. I would be the living proof. In a subtle way I was offered a subtle job, a trade of long tradition. Its classic example and great genius was Ilya Ehrenburg, the followers have always been many and some of them very good at it, yesterday Yevtushenko was the best, today—I do not know.

The conditions of the deal are advantageous to both parties. Keep your apartments and relations wherever you wish, reap your privileges at home and your income in hard currency abroad, travel as much as you want, shuttle between Warsaw and Western capitals, do not shun contacts even with our declared adversaries, why should you? Even admit that not everything is bright on our side but who is perfect? More than that, suggest that you do not quite agree with us, even that you are a kind of victim, wink your eye, drop a remark here, make a hint there, what kind of remark, hint, or comment and in what situations—that we leave to your tact, intuition, and intelligence, which we trust.

Openings for that sort of mission were not lacking on the Western side. There was a great demand and warm welcome for such go-betweens. Immediately after my arrival in Italy I began receiving invitations to lectures, conferences, congresses, and whatnot of the type: "Let us get together," "Round Table," "The Bridges between East and West," "Culture above Politics." All expenses paid, handsome fees, lodging in luxury hotels in dream places like Taormina in Sicily or stylish Bavarian chalets in the Alps, round-trips by air to glamorous cities. It was tempting and I would have accepted if I could have agreed to play the game. Somehow I could not. I had eaten my portion of shit before, I was not yet ready to vomit it up, but I did not want to swallow any more. What I had on my stomach was heavy enough, fear restrained me from the radical cure but at least I could draw the line. The only deal I was prepared to accept was: "OK, stay away but keep your mouth shut. We shall leave you in peace." But they were not ripe yet for taking less rather than more, they were so used to taking all. The arrogance of their power had not yet been tamed by the general bankruptcy of the system.

However, as long as I did not return, the shepherds could not lay their hands on the stray of their livestock. Fifteen years passed before I saw Poland again.

I managed to stay on the Western market and even enlarge my share of it, so I could say good-bye to the gloom of cheap, rented rooms. Italy became my home country, not by birth of course, nor by legal status, but by the facts of life. After the apprentice-

The author's sister in her youth

ship of the early years, Western modes became first familiar, then natural to me. But otherwise I was still on a leash, a long one, but a leash nevertheless. The validity of my Polish passport was always of short duration, successive extensions were obtained only after soliciting and long, enigmatic delays and were never certain. Once they kept me waiting for half a year without any answer while my passport was dead again, but Italian tolerance saved me from either deportation or some desperate move. Both sides pretended not to know what the game was about. The pressure on me was never acknowledged, the bureaucracy has always been and remains the favorite excuse for the real workings of the system on all levels, from top to bottom. They pretended not to know why it happened, I pretended to believe them. But there was a difference: hypocrisy is their natural element, while I practised it with growing disgust.

My books were still published in Poland, plays performed, the authorities saw no political advantage in not letting them be, I was too popular, too well known by the general public, which was not even aware that I had stayed abroad, scandal was not wished for. The deal seemed to work by itself on my own terms, however reluctantly it was accepted by the other party, which was always probing to see if my determination endured. But was I happy?

Settling down again was an act of return, adventure receded. Again it was time for some revolution. Changing my country of residence was one way to go about it. In February 1968 we moved to Paris. If I wanted revolution I was well served, two months later the famous events of May 1968 broke out. I was looking only for my own private revolution and I landed in the center of the collective one. I was not young enough anymore to project my personal problems onto the outer background in order to satisfy my private needs and wants by joining any political faith or mass movement. I had already had my lesson in that heady but abusive and finally ineffective attempt to save my soul by saving the world.

That inability to delude myself made my life difficult in the next decade and still does to some extent, putting me in discord with most of the popular general certainties, beliefs, moods, and fashions. Again a sort of deal was proposed to me similar to that which was offered at the beginning of my Italian years. Only this time it was not the Polish consulate in Rome but—how shall I say it? the situation? the sociological process? history? *Zeitgeist?*—in short it was nobody in person, merely an opportunity due to impersonal circumstances. Also the requirements were less harsh, the deal being still

Father, Antoni Mrożek, in his forties

more subtle. It was not necessary to defend the communist dictatorship or even to keep silent about it. I was free and welcome to denounce it as much as I wished, provided it was followed by: your fight, dear revolutionaries of Berkeley, Quartier Latin, Kurfürstendamm—is mine. Your ideals, sister Jane Fonda, brother Cohn Bendit, cousin Bader—I love them. We are rebelling together against the same oppression. The Marxist source is pure, but the stream has been poisoned somewhere by the villains. You will overthrow your capitalists/imperialists, I shall overthrow my villains, and together we shall establish the Kingdom of love and peace on the earth.

On this occasion, long before the Kingdom, I shall establish my fortune, secure my public relations, smooth the ways of professional success. The waves were rolling high, the surfing could be excellent. I had no interest in defending the old order, not just because it was crumbling anyway and nothing will save it at the end, but simply because it has never been mine. I am a stranger to all that the global cultural revolution was against, the so-called Western bourgeois society. Also the idiocy of much of what

was going on in the world—still is, more and more idiotic every day—and what they denounced was obvious to me. I could sympathise with their sensibility and indignation but not with their analysis and programs. My instinct for pure aesthetics, probably dead in my early twenties so it could not protect me at that time, was now alive and did not let me take advantage of the opportunity, much to my regret. I know that "everything is relative" even if I do not worship relativity, our newest God. Because some things (but not everything) are relative, for someone like me who came from different parts, different times, and different experiences, the local show was ridiculous. What could I think about the martyrdom of Norman Mailer, whose complaints about the quality of the breakfast served to him during his overnight, fervently desired detention were widely publicised? Such proofs of how terrible the repression was—they were good for you, but they could not be good for me.

In 1969 my wife died of a sudden, violent cancer. She was a being of the highest quality. Her only fault was that she met me at a time when I was not ready for her. I am not going to say any more on that subject. My feelings and much of what I know are my private property and will remain so forever. I have a strong sense of privacy, a character trait which is a handicap in promoting oneself.

One year before this happened, another event of a different order changed my life in a different way. The forces of the Warsaw Pact invaded Czechoslovakia, the Polish army took part in it. I remember the beautiful summer day and my blind fury when I heard the news on the radio. I could put up, though with growing impatience, with my humiliating situation as one who knows but is afraid to tell. Now it was too much. One slave kicking another to please their common master, and me being that slave—no. The bliss of something deep inside exploding and pushing me to action no matter what—I have had several such moments in life and I think they are among the worthiest, most revitalising impulses that we can have.

The major papers of several countries published my protest. Oh, nothing special by Western standards. Just another letter to the editors, hardly more than any advertisement of anything. But have I told you already that all that you know about the realities of this world is not all? Immediately I was summoned to the Polish consulate. Our passports had expired again and our plea for an extension in due form of due forms was already circulating somewhere in the mysterious bowels of totalitarian decision making. At the door to the consular room I already understood that that was it. Without even looking at me, as if I were transparent, the official one announced to the wall behind my back that I and my wife were ordered to return to Warsaw within two weeks. Poor sucker, he thought that he still had power over me. I turned around and left forever.

Overnight my books disappeared from the bookshops in Poland, the police vans went from one bookshop to another and packed them in. My plays vanished from the theatres, not even "Out" remained of the usual "Sold Out" posted at the box office. At the same time the press was full of articles tearing the mask from my face at last. It was the face of a traitor, a Jewish henchman, perfidiously poisoning the soul of the Polish nation in the service of the Zionist conspiracy, corruptor of youth, slanderer of Polish tradition and patriotic values, licker of capitalist buttocks and sucker of imperialist stinking breasts, degenerated Judas of the Socialist Fatherland. Very handy as arguments in my application for the status of political refugee in France.

I do not deny that it was dramatic for me. Not so much because of the ban on my works in Poland, not at all because of the attacks in the press. The usual effect of communist propaganda, before it became so admirably sophisticated as it is today, was the opposite of its goals. The people respected me now, my books, those copies which survived the roundup, became articles of value, much asked for and high priced on the black market. But one does not blow up the bridge leading back to one's own country without emotional punishment. However, the joy of liberation, of doing something right at last, of repairing somewhat one's dignity, was stronger.

What about order and adventure? After the death of my wife and the final break with communist Poland, I was alone and free, completely on my own. A perfect time for adventure. I created for myself the image of a loner, entrenched myself in it, and for many years after worked on its elaboration. At the beginning I enjoyed it. I had never been totally free before, my tremendous push for freedom had always been blocked or conditioned in one way or another. Satisfying an exaggerated need required an exaggerated supply. Now I had it at last. The years that followed were stormy, especially in the area of so-called private life. My wild, almost maniacal assertion of independence soon put me in conflict with the basic laws of human relations and with another side of my own nature.

I travelled to North and Latin America—Brazil, Venezuela, Mexico. I lived in New York for half a

Mrożek's mother, shortly before her death at the age of forty-three

year, briefly I was a guest teacher at Penn State University. I drove from California to the East Coast via the southern states. I spent one year in West Berlin. Once freed from the Polish passport which had been hampering me in every way, I wandered through all of Europe in all directions. Also in the professional field the adventure was going strong. Thanks to the adventurous spirit of Mr. Müller-Freienfels, the head of the film production department of Süddeutscher Rundfunk in Germany, I was invited to write and direct a film. Writing the script—alright, I had been a scriptwriter before. But to direct, to have the entire responsibility for bringing an idea (the script) into material existence (the film)—that was another matter. Entrusting it to a complete beginner, somebody without any experience or theoretical preparation, says a lot about Mr. Müller-Freienfels's courage as well as about his trust in me. Accepting the invitation—about my carelessness, perhaps. We both gambled but we won. The 1½-hour-long film had a rating close to the record. I think it is quite a decent film, its technical insufficiencies redeemed by the quality of the script—I took the advice of one of Hollywood's founding fathers: "To make a good film, first you need a foolproof story"—and largely compensated for by that specific individual force which sometimes marks the works of outsiders. It went so well that we repeated the experience. But after the second film I had to decide what I was going to be, a writer or a film director, those two activities were incompatible for me. I decided to remain a writer.

Not without regret. Filmmaking is not just making a film or two, or more, it is a special way of perceiving things, other people and oneself. An exercise in one's relation to time and space, a particular approach to reality. I got hooked on it. Also adventure feels very good in that domain. How else could I find myself in the company of a farmer in Schwaben, drinking his wine and discussing with him the character of his horse, the one that I needed for the film? Or how could I penetrate a certain backyard in a town in Slovenia where we did some shooting for a couple of days and where two old women lived their lives otherwise inaccessible to me? Or how could I ever know the exact dimensions of a certain tree on a certain hill on a certain day in the year 1977 of our Christian Era? The endless opportunities of the most varied and unexpected sorts as well as permanent stimulation of all my capacities, the weight of the demands put on them, stretching them beyond what I believed to be their limits—all that was good. I became addicted to it, kicking the addiction was painful.

I have mentioned already that at the beginning of the seventies I established a vision of myself—nobody can live without casting himself in some character of his own invention—as an adventurous loner. I tried to live up to it. But with the passing years a contradiction arose between the very notion of adventure and its repetitious practice. There is no adventure without the feeling of something always fresh and new, of something exceptional. But how can "always" be reconciled with "exceptional"? The stage was set, my costumes appropriate, but opening night was already far behind, the public weary of the repeat performance. The adventure began to sour.

Meanwhile things changed in Poland. The nation found sources unhoped for in the period of collapse and prostration. New energies came into play. The workers' uprising in 1970 caused a change of the ruling set. The new ones (now dismissed in their turn and replaced by the newest) were confronted by the new reality and somewhat changed the ruling methods. Being new, they brought new personal attitudes and styles to the interplay between the governors and the governed.

In the early seventies I was resurrected in Poland as a Polish writer. The interdiction of my writings lasted only two or three years, this imprecision is due to the period of transition between total ban and full comeback. It was a way of bringing me back to life but not too suddenly, resurrection by installments so to say, step by step. Why so? Maybe because if I were reanimated at once it might be noticed that I had been dead? Or to observe the reaction of the partially reanimated subject? The scholastics of power *à la communiste* seem incredible to Westerners, and if credible—ludicrous. (They are wrong, there are serious consequences however silly it might look.) The high priests have their secret science of politics which is unbelievable to the profane and impenetrable to the faithful.

After fifteen years of exile, first self-imposed then enforced, I made my first visit to Poland. I was already a French citizen at that time. I experienced the shock of schizophrenia, I found that my personali-

Mrożek at twenty-eight

ty was split into two even parts: one the native, the other a stranger in my own country. It was the result of leading one life too many. Waking up in the morning, half hearing through the open window the voices of children playing a couple of blocks away, I could understand without thinking about it what they were saying. I was again in full and natural communication with the environment. Walking along a certain street in Cracow, rounding a corner I felt suddenly a strange comfort and ease in my body. I walked back and rounded the corner again. Then I recognised why: it was the same corner that I had walked by God knows how many times in my distant past, drunk or sober, young and not so young, nights, days, in sunshine or in snow, until it became the spatial completion of my body.

On the other hand I was a foreigner. Fifteen years lived out of the country had done their job. Even though I sojourned physically in Poland, mentally I was on both sides of the frontier at the same time. Not the frontier fixed by guards and customs, but a subtle line dividing experiences and minds. Staying with my people, and apparently one with them, I felt like a cheat. I understood that once you go away there is no real return. This is true for any situation of the kind.

I kept my visit strictly private and I do so each time I go to Poland now. Experience tells me that going public beyond what is necessary is against my nature. Also I do not need any publicity in Poland anymore.

During the time of Solidarity, that strong popular movement which almost changed "the socialism with a human face" (I always wonder how it could be that this curious, ambiguous linguistic freak came into everyday use without anybody raising any objections on purely semiotic grounds. It is being used by the proponents of socialism themselves as high praise, though it sounds like a jeer, too close to a werewolf or some other half-human, half-beastly monster. But it is probably due to the generalisation of bad taste)—well, during the time of that popular movement which almost changed "the socialism with a human face" into simply a human face, I kept a low profile. I sympathised with it but I did not declare my sympathy either frequently or in a roaring voice. I saw too many of those intellectuals who galloped to the rescue of the upper dog, or what seemed to be one. Those who shouted at noon, "The light is coming!" and claimed the applause for their perspicacity. Also those who sniffed the wind before it blew and turned appropriately in its direction.

Shedding the old skin, donning a new one, is a delicate business. Changing ideologies, religions, allegiances, each time putting the same faith and ardour into the new one—a conspicuous operation requiring close scrutiny if done in public. Shifting camps, sides, parties—if too noisily self-righteous, one cannot count on being trusted without questions and reservations. Nobody would deny that such flip-flops are legitimate, that is, that the evolution of a human being and the right to err are only natural. As long as the realignment is declared to the audience in terms of ideas only, the suspicion of bad faith is less. But if the shifter rushes to political action, then the profundity of his motives are questioned. Much more so if the shifter is not an insignificant footman of his former army, but a man of rank or a leader who now claims the leading post again, in the crusade of his latest choice.

After Solidarity was crushed I felt the same thing that the majority felt: a sort of despair combined with a feeling of insult and rage. I wrote a series of satirical items against the regime, rather nasty, I admit. They were published abroad and republished in Poland by the underground press. They were efficient forms of instant expression but, as literary art, without special value. Which brought me back to the perennial question: should the writer intervene in public issues, however pressing, noble, and just, at the expense of his art, or should he look after his art instead? Should he serve a political cause or master the spiritual regions? All general answers in the abstract must be simplistic because it all depends on the particular situation. If you are slapped in the face, it is unlikely that you will be held back from reacting accordingly by your profound thoughts at the moment. But a brawl is a brawl, and giving kicks for kicks does not favor intellectual profundity. There are some political causes which are not just political. Also much depends on the degree of urgency and pressure. I disliked the repression as such, but also because, forcing me to react, it brought me down, not to its own level, but certainly below my own. There are no mysteries to be explored when dealing with the obvious, and brute force is among the most obvious, and thus boring, things in this world. Denouncing it is not fertile ground for the intellect.

The dilemma presented above is especially acute in Poland, a country in a fight for its independence and the survival of its identity not just today but for the last two centuries, roughly speaking. The dilemma is a serious one, though it presents nice opportunities for self-justification. You can either say that you have genius but will sacrifice its fruits—you are serving the nation instead of writing great things which otherwise most certainly you would do—or you can collaborate with the establishment, saying that taking sides with the nation would deprive all humanity of the masterpieces that you are on the way to producing.

After the crushing of Solidarity, six years elapsed before I went to Poland again. I had to, my father was dying. I am glad that I was able to embrace that stranger closest to me before his great departure.

M y story is nearing its end. Not my whole story yet, only that part of it which can be known. The past has been more or less told and we are almost in the present. I say almost, because even the sentence written above already belongs to the past, only a few seconds old, but the past nevertheless. I turn fifty-eight this year and I am tempted to believe that I am beginning to understand how to solve the conflict between order and adventure. Please mark the prudence of this assertion. It is so measured, so full of reservation, that it is hardly an assertion at all, rather a hint and a hope, though not just wishful thinking. If I am ever sure that I have succeeded, it will be the high point of my life, the meeting of two parallel lines. A not entirely hopeless task, given the mathematical reassurance that they cross one another somewhere in infinity. How do I figure to do it, what is my trick? I think that any explanation, even if it were possible, would not be of any value to anybody. This is an existential, not intellectual thing, and being such it is ultimately personal. The individual makes it and it makes the individual, it cannot be shared. Everyone gets it or not in his own way, living his own life. There is no trick to be revealed and used by others, precisely because there has never been a trick to learn from the outside.

Another change that I can expect—already it has moved from being a mere hope into the range of expectation—is someday to get out of History (the most capital H possible). Out of it and far enough away that my life will become less conditioned by it than it has been. Probably you have noticed, my Dear Reader, how much space that monster occupies in this concise story of my life. The space given to General History and to the description of its impact on my particular life seems to be in disproportion to the length of the narration. Unfortunately it is not. I was born in such a place and in such a time that the reference to History must be as heavy as it weighed heavily on me. If it had been up to me, I would probably have chosen another place and another time, then my autobiography would not annoy you

The author's father in old age

with so many generalities. However, things are as they are, and the Reader is kindly asked to be patient and understanding. I can only assure him that I share his feelings. It is not my fault that historical generalities always appeared to me in the form of the most acute particularities. I could live without them.

Shall I ever be free from the exaggerated claims of History? Shall I ever get beyond what I have been so far, a sort of slave to it? To some extent it depends on me, because in some measure it is a matter of attitude. I have been not only enslaved by the monster but also fascinated by it. You can get high on anything, so you can on that kind of dope too.

In 1987 I married again. The basic facts of life always help in the process of detoxification. The apparently casual manner in which I talk about my second marriage does not match its importance in every respect. Marriage by itself never means much, it all depends on whom we marry. My second marriage marks a turning point in my life. I am not going to specify, of course. As I said before, I have a strong sense of discrimination between what may go to the public and what should not.

Just one bit of information, my second wife is Mexican. Thanks to her I am beginning to have insights into that dimension of humanity which is beyond my European, Christian heritage. I am beginning to understand that our European values, modes, and codes (I used those terms before in speaking about the restricted field of my early environment in childhood) are not necessarily all that being in Europe is about. Nor are they the only possible achievement, way, and approach. Thus the scope of my experience seems to be enlarging.

To reconcile order and adventure at last, to get some freedom from History, if that will ever be feasible for me—I can ask for no more.

May/June 1988

BIBLIOGRAPHY

Fiction:

Opowiadania z Trzmielowej Góry. Warsaw, 1953.

Półpancerze praktyczne. Cracow, 1953.

Maleńkie lato. Cracow: Wydawnictwo Literackie, 1956.

Polska w obrazach. Cracow: Wydawnictwo Literackie, 1957.

Słoń (short stories; illustrated by Daniel Mróz). Cracow: Wydawnictwo Literackie, 1957; translation by Konrad Syrop published as *The Elephant.* London: Macdonald, 1962; New York: Grove Press, 1963.

Wesele w Atomicach (short stories; illustrated by D. Mróz). Cracow: Wydawnictwo Literackie, 1959.

Postępowiec: Organ Sławomira Mrożka. Warsaw: Iskry, 1960.

Ucieczka na Południe (illustrated by the author). Warsaw: Iskry, 1961.

Deszcz (short stories; illustrated by D. Mróz). Cracow: Wydawnictwo Literackie, 1962.

Opowiadania (short stories). Cracow: Wydawnictwo Literackie, 1964.

The Ugupu Bird (includes *Ucieczka na południe* and selections from *Wesele w Atomicach*). Translated by K. Syrop. London: Macdonald, 1968.

Dwa listy i inne opowiadania (short stories; includes *Moniza Clavier, Ona, We młynie, we młynie mój dobry panie, Nocleg,* and *Ci, co mnie niosą*). Paris: Instytut Literacki, 1970.

Dwa listy. Cracow: Wydawnictwo Literackie, 1974.

Opowiadania (short stories). Cracow: Wydawnictwo Literackie, 1974.

Opowiadania (short stories). Cracow: Wydawnictwo Literackie, 1981.

Moniza Clavier. Cracow: Wydawnictwo Literackie, 1983.

Published Plays:

Utwory sceniczne (includes *Policja, Męczeństwo Piotra Oheya, Indyk, Na pełnym morzu, Karol, Striptease, Zabawa,* and *Kynolog w rozterce*). Cracow: Wydawnictwo Literackie, 1963.

Six Plays (includes *The Police, The Martyrdom of Peter Ohey, Out at Sea, Charlie, The Party,* and *Enchanted Night*). Translated by Nicholas Bethell. London: J. Cape, 1967; New York: Grove Press, 1967.

Selected Works. Translated by Konrad Syrop. London, 1968.

Tango. Translated by N. Bethell, adapted by Tom Stoppard. London: J. Cape, 1968; translated by Ralph Manheim and Teresa Dzieduszycka. New York: Grove Press, 1968; (in the original Polish) London: Polska Macierz Szkolna, 1983.

Vatzlav: A Play in 77 Scenes. Translated by R. Manheim. New York: Evergreen/Grove Press, 1970; London: J. Cape, 1972.

Striptease, Main Course, [and] *Testarium.* Translated by T. Dzieduszycka, Lola Gruenthal, and R. Manheim. New York, 1972.

Striptease, Repeat Performance, and The Prophets: Three Plays. Translated by L. Gruenthal and others. New York: Grove Press, 1972.

Utwory sceniczne (includes *Czarowna noc, Śmierć porucznika, Tango, Testarium, Drugie danie, Woda,* and *Dom na granicy*). Cracow: Wydawnictwo Literackie, 1973.

Utwory sceniczne nowe (includes *Rzeźnia, Emigranci,* and *Wyspa Róż*). Cracow: Wydawnictwo Literackie, 1975.

Emigrés. Translated by M. and T. Wrona and R. Holman. London, 1977; translation by Henry Beissel published as *The Emigrants.* New York and London: Samuel French, 1984.

Amor (includes the film scenario *Amor* and the plays *Krawiec, Garbus, Polowanie na lisa, Serenada, Lis filozof,* and *Lis aspirant*). Cracow: Wydawnictwo Literackie, 1979.

Striptease, Tango, Vatzlav: Three Plays. Translated by L. Gruenthal and others. New York: Evergreen/Grove Press, 1981.

Vatzlav [and] *Ambasador.* Paris: Instytut Literacki, 1982.

Pieszo. Warsaw: Czytelnik, 1983.

Alfa. Paris: Instytut Literacki, 1984.

Plays—Selected First Productions:

Policja. Dramatyczny Theater, Warsaw, 1958.

Męczeństwo Piotra Oheya. Groteska Theater, Cracow, 1959.

Indyk. Stary Theater, Cracow, 1960.

Karol. Modrzejewska Theater, Zakopane, 1961.

Na pełko nym morzu. Modrzejewska Theater, Zakopane, 1961.

Striptease. Modrzejewska Theater, Zakopane, 1961.

Czarowna noc. Groteska Theater, Cracow, 1963.

Kynolog w rozterce. Dramatyczne Theaters, Wrocław, 1963.

Śmierć poruzcnika. Dramatyczny Theater. Warsaw, 1963.

Zabawa. Dramatyczne Theaters, Wrocław, 1963.

Tango. Polski Theater, Bydgoszcz, 1965.

Poczwórka. Wybrzeże Theater, Gdańsk, 1967.

Dom na granicy. Groteska Lalki i Maski Theater, Cracow, 1968.

Vatzlav. Stratford, Ont., 1970.

Szczęśliwe wydarzenie. Współczesny Theater, Warsaw, 1975.

Emigranci. Współczesny Theater, Warsaw, 1975.

Garbus. Stary Theater, Cracow, 1975.

Rzeźnia. Dramatyczny Theater, Warsaw, 1975.

Lis filozof. Nowy Theater, Zabrze, 1977.

Polowanie na lisa. Nowy Theater, Zabrze, 1977.

Serenada. Nowy Theater, Zabrze, 1977.

Krawiec. Współczesny Theater, Szczecin, 1978.

Drugie danie. Nowy Theater, Łódź, 1979.

Other:

Przez okulary Slawomira Mrożka (cartoons). Warsaw: Iskry, 1968.

Wybór dramatów i opowiadań (plays and short stories). Cracow: Wydawnictwo Literackie, 1975.

Male listy (feuilletons). Cracow: Wydawnictwo Literackie, 1982.

Rysunki (cartoons). Warsaw: Iskry, 1982.

Donosy (humor). London: Puls, 1983.

Robert H. Rimmer

1917-

Bob and Erma Rimmer, 1984

As I write this in 1988, I've been married for forty-seven years to Erma . . . one wife for a lifetime. But in 1955, if she hadn't discovered that I was having an affair with Virginia, and if she hadn't sobbed her anger to David, the last of a breed of caring general M.D. practitioners, who told her that all men, including him, were led around by their cocks, I never would have met David's wife, Nancy—or finally discovered a woman whom I didn't have to play Pygmalion with. She was Galatea! And if I hadn't met David and Nancy (whose names I have fictionalized and who are similar to one of the couples in *Proposition 31*), I never would have discovered just how anti-Semitic my father and mother were, nor way past mid-life would I have found the focus for my first novel, *The Rebellion of Yale Marratt.*

I wrote *Yale Marratt* in my early forties, but it wasn't published until I was forty-seven. The reason why, and why I was never published in any paying form until I was forty-nine (beginning with my third novel, *The Harrad Experiment*), is the culmination of a kind of sexual odyssey which, combined with an early, loving oedipal rebellion constitutes the main adventure of my life.

Here, for the first time, I will try to show how my heroes and heroines are basically more daring extensions of my own life. I'm sure that recreating oneself in fiction is a way of life for many novelists, but most refuse to admit it.

During the late 1960s and early 1970s, the words "Harrad" and "Proposition 31" became a part of the vocabulary of the so-called "hippie generation." Most of the millions of *Harrad* readers had no idea that the author was long past thirty and hence not to be trusted. But since these novels and later ones offered alternatives to monogamous marriage and "solutions" to the increasing divorce rate, they became recommended reading in college courses on marriage and the family. Many readers were sure that *Harrad* was instrumental in the sudden merger of male and female colleges, and the creation of dormitories where young men and women lived together on the same floors, as well as laying the groundwork for the later phenomenon of young men and women living together unmarried.

But most critics were incensed. Bob Rimmer wasn't really a novelist but a preacher in disguise who was writing thesis novels. For many critics, this approach to the novel is a literary no-no. Purists believe that the novel should reflect reality and the author should let you perceive his moral purpose, if any, subtly and by innuendo. But, like Edward Bellamy, I believed, and still do, that the novel can be a vehicle to show people how they can recreate their environments and live more self-fulfilling lives.

Assuming that you may not have read many, or any, of my fourteen novels, without proselytizing, let me give you a little background. While I'm sure that my novels have interesting story lines that will keep you reading and wondering what comes next, and the characters are believable, there are no bad guys or evil persons in any of them. The basic underlying theme is that I believe there are saner approaches to premarital and postmarital interpersonal and sexual relationships which could stabilize new-style extended families. Postmaritally, in these novels I have proposed legal forms of bigamous marriage and what I have called "corporate marriage" of up to three couples, as well as creating the framework for more enduring pair-bondings (monogamy) which could incorporate intimate satellite relationships.

In essence, and I make no bones about it in *The Byrdwhistle Option,* I am celebrating life based on the four *L*'s: Loving, Learning, Laughter, and Ludamus (we and God are all playing together). These obviously incorporate the fifth *L*, George Bush's hated Liberal.

During our long courtship of each other's wives, David once told me good-humoredly, "Your problem, Bob, is that you haven't suffered enough. All great creative writers have suffered." Perhaps he was right, but I still don't agree with him. Twelve years ago, Nancy died, and within two years, David had also disappeared from this life. Erma and I were desolate, but we don't mourn them. We celebrate them and are fully aware that after living much of our married life in a kind of two-couple monogamy (for nearly twenty-five years), which I have philosophized about and fictionalized in *Proposition 31, Come Live My Life,* and *Thursday, My Love,* Erma and I really learned how to love not just each other, but many people—including my domineering father and self-glorifying mother—who crossed our lives.

Father, Francis Henry Rimmer, 1911: "The year he married Blanche."

On December 11, 1911, Francis (sometimes known as "Frank") Henry Rimmer, living in Dorchester, Massachusetts, age twenty-five, married Blanche Rosealma Rochefort, seventeen, who had been schooled in a French convent in Spencer, Massachusetts. Coming from a family who spoke only Canadian French at home, she could scarcely speak English, but she was very pretty. Obviously a virgin, she could play any kind of music on the piano and sing along with it. Later, when Blanche took a part-time job at Kresge where she would play sheet music for customers who wanted to hear a particular selection and also listen to her play, Frank remembered her as "my million-dollar baby from the five-and-ten-cents store."

Frank was running an elevator at the age of twelve and his schooling ended at the sixth grade. Before he married Blanche, he had discovered the International Correspondence School. With no parental encouragement, but great determination—Ben Franklin and characters in the Horatio Alger stories, which he insisted later that I read, were his heroes—Frank studied to pass the ICS exams for a postal clerk. The powers at ICS headquarters in Springfield were so impressed with his diligence and "gumption" that they offered him the job of branch manager at an ICS store on Winter Street. Part of his work was to corral passersby and convince them that

they too could succeed by enrolling in ICS courses. He continued to educate himself, and later when asked if he ever attended college, he pronounced ICS like "ice," and laughed, "I slid through."

But then ICS closed their Boston store. World War I and the draft were depleting the students. Frank first sold vacuum cleaners door to door, then Victor typewriters. He soon became Victor's leading Boston salesman.

Five years later, Frank was brokering printing jobs and quickly convinced his typewriter customers that he could get their stationery and business cards printed cheaper than they could. Some of the orders he gave to his father, George, who owned a printing business, but George didn't produce the finished product fast enough for him. Somehow, he managed to convince the First National Bank of Boston to loan him five thousand dollars (a princely sum in those days). Although he had never run a printing press and couldn't set type, he hired a plant manager and soon had two platen presses.

Blanche, who admitted later that she slept in the office sitting up most of the time, was his only

Mother, Blanche Rochefort Rimmer, sixteen years old

secretary. She never bothered to learn how to type. It was all she could do to answer the phone. Business was booming. After I was born, Frank met George Duffy, who had inherited five thousand dollars and convinced Frank to sell him 20 percent of the stock of what was to become Relief Printing Corporation. The name "Relief" described the raised printing which was produced by dusting resin powders over wet ink and fusing it over a gas oven. Most business cards then and now are raised printed. Little did I know as a growing fetus in Blanche's womb that twenty-nine years later Relief Printing Corporation would own me, and FH, as I began to call him ("Dad" seemed inappropriate when I was finally in business with him), would be subtly controlling my life.

I was born March 14, 1917, saving FH from the draft. By the time I was three, I was Blanche's Little Lord Fauntleroy. Very blonde with brown eyes and a Dutch boy haircut, Blanche had outfitted me with a cane and a beaver hat.

At five years old, I could read. In those days, there was no other entertainment. Radio was rudimentary. I read first fairy tales by the hundreds—all of Grimm, Hans Christian Andersen, and all of the expurgated Arabian Nights. By the time I was seven, I had discovered Tom Swift, Jerry Todd, and the Bobbsey Twins. You name them, I was hooked and read them all. Later, when I was about ten, I had also discovered Penrod, Tom Sawyer, and Huckleberry Finn, as well as the Connecticut Yankee. Saturdays were "go to the library" days, and I often came home with ten or more books. Neither FH nor Blanche read very much. Other than his ICS volumes and the dictionary, FH owned no books. His theory was that there was no need to own books. You could borrow all you could ever read from the public library.

Today, fortunately (or maybe not) having lived in the same house (with many additions) for forty-two years, I've accumulated over twenty thousand of them. A kind of ongoing rebellion against FH, perhaps, that has amusingly come full circle. Today, Erma reads very little, and Rob, Jr., and Steve, my sons, are not obsessed with my Faustian need to know everything. Beyond books and picture shows, neither Blanche, FH, nor I were aware that the person I was to become and the books I would write were already being fertilized by three other aspects of my childhood.

First, girls . . . later, women! Since I was five—for sixty-five years—I've loved them all, the long and the short and the tall. But like Henry Higgins (Bernard Shaw's Pygmalion), I would eventually begin wondering not, "Why can't women be like men?" but, "Why can't women be like me?" Before I entered the first grade, most of my friends were girls. In the summer, in pup tents in the backyard and in hot attics, it was a happy, giggly game to touch and kiss each other's forbidden parts. In my childhood, I was perfectly familiar with the hairless female pudenda. After I was seven, I never saw a girl/woman naked until I was seventeen. Like my peers, I spent many hours searching through *National Geographics* to see what women (black, of course) looked like. I probed the library for art books with a few reproductions of classical paintings where bulgy ladies out of mythology reigned supreme without clothes.

Next to girls, the driving force through all of my life has been a growing collection of hero/mentors. Beginning, of course, with Benjamin Franklin's autobiography and the "Bound to Rise" heroes of Horatio Alger. Basically, although I wasn't aware of it, all my mentors and heroes, including Tom Swift, were rebelling against individuals or a society who said they couldn't realize their dreams. Despite the nay-sayers, they triumphed and finally became famous, or, as I later told Erma, if necessary—infamous.

Along with the rebellion, they seeded two other words in my dream vocabulary: challenge and experiment. Unlike the childhood heroes of later generations, my hero/mentors had focussed rebellions—not against parents, but against entrenched power systems or outmoded ways of doing things. I have always been entranced by men and women who manage to defy the system, and yet make it work for them.

The third conditioning factor in my life was that in my youth FH never attended church, and Blanche, married to a Protestant and angry with her father's new Catholic wife, had abandoned her religion. Her family was sure that she'd go to hell and were, from then on, very circumspect with her. As a result, Sunday school was not a factor in my life. I was never indoctrinated in any church rituals and I never worried about God, Jesus, or the Devil.

In junior high school, it became obvious that I wasn't a man's man. In gym, I could never climb the swinging rope or balance on the parallel bars. None of the other kids wanted a physically uncoordinated kid on their softball or football team. On top of that, I was taking elocution lessons, arranged by FH, at the Wollaston School of the Spoken Word. Although FH probably couldn't have specified his plans for me, he did want me to be famous. He admired James Michael Curley, the mayor of Boston, who could entrance listeners with his cultured Boston accent. Later, when I was a junior in high school, FH was happy to pay for me to take a night course in public speaking with young men twice my age.

Although I was twelve years old when the stock market crashed in 1929 and grew up in the Depression of the 1930s, I was only dimly aware that the country was in dire straits. FH's printing business was so prosperous in 1924 that he traded in his Maxwell and bought a Phaeton Studebaker with disc wheels.

FH wasn't the only affluent one in the family. A few years later, I had a paper route which netted four or five dollars a week. Rarely a month went by when I wasn't paid at least five dollars by various women's clubs and church groups to recite five or six monologues that I had learned in elocution school. It was a repertoire which soon included fifty or more ten- to fifteen-minute recitations—complete with gestures and facial expressions. By 1988 standards, my purchasing power was nearly equal to a hundred dollars a week.

In addition, I had become assistant publisher of a mimeographed magazine called the *Boy's Pal.* It was conceived by Homer Jenks, whose father worked for the last of Boston's intellectual newspapers, the *Boston Transcript.* Homer typed the stencils, and with me and another boy using a borrowed mimeograph machine, we produced the twenty-page 8½-by-11 magazine, collated it, stapled it, and sold a hundred or more copies of each issue at five cents a copy. It was no mean feat, since many sneering kids called it "the jockstrap magazine"—and you could buy the fat *Saturday Evening Post* and *Liberty* magazine for a nickel, too.

We all wrote stories for the magazine, and now excelling in English, I fell in love with my English teacher, Dorothy Cole. She was only eight years older than I was. Look for me after school and I was erasing blackboards or doing any room clean-up chore for Dorothy, and waiting patiently until she was alone so I could call her by her first name and listen as she would suggest books that I should read. In class, she made novels like *Ivanhoe, Treasure Island, Great Expectations,* and Shakespeare's plays sound so exciting that I couldn't wait to read them, or act in them.

From six to sixteen, my interest in girls didn't diminish. My going-to-sleep dreams were always about lovely girls I had read about in novels. They all hugged and kissed me and adored me. In reality, I

Bob Rimmer, "Little Lord Fauntleroy at four years old"

was a shy, pimply faced adolescent who blushed when girls my own age spoke to me. I never bridged the feminine gap (pun intended) as I had in my childhood until I was seventeen. I was reduced to girlie magazines (*Playboy* hadn't appeared yet) which featured young women wearing abbreviated shorts, panties, and bathing suits and were easy to come by. I had found my dream woman, Dorothy. I was aware, even then, that she was on the spot because everyone said that I was her fair-haired boy. She took me to local Shakespeare productions, called for me at home (to Blanche and FH's surprise, in her own car), and never protested when I was always underfoot. Perhaps, in a way, I was her dream man, too. I loved her, but with no sexual demands.

At sixteen, just before my final year in high school, I was a rebel without a cause. An exceptional student in English, fair in languages like Latin and French, mediocre in science, and dismal in math (compare Yale Marratt in the novel), I fell in love with Rosslyn, a young girl who stayed with her aunt in Quincy during the summer so she could enjoy swimming at the private beach in Merrymount. Very pretty and very sophisticated at fifteen, Rosslyn's home was in Brookline, some ten miles away. Somehow, blushing, I dared to ask her to go to the movies with me. Before the summer was over, I finally had once again seen and touched a naked girl/woman and held her pretty breasts in my hands, kissed her nipples and touched the lovely triangle of hair between her legs. I was delirious, totally in love. That summer, I practically lived in her aunt's house. Blanche and FH knew where I was. Of course, neither Rosslyn's aunt nor uncle knew what we were doing.

I was so much in love that I didn't care if I went to college or not. When you made love to a girl every possible moment that you were with her, I was sure it was time to get married. It was now or never, especially since when summer was over Ross would go home to Brookline. I had a license to drive, but with only one car in the family, I couldn't compete with the army of really affluent Brookline guys who could take Rosslyn anywhere in their own cars and, God forbid, make love to her.

I was spending much of my time conniving with my Italian friends, who all seemed to have cars, to drive to Brookline to see how the rich Brookline kids lived. I learned that Rosslyn's father made eighteen thousand dollars a year (multiply 1934 dollars by ten), but I didn't discover until much later that FH made

even more money from his 80 percent owned Relief Printing Corporation.

Even though I flunked two college boards, four exams given in those days in a modern language, English, science, and math, FH was determined that I was going to college. Harvard, of course. So, still mooning over Rosslyn, a mediocre graduate of Quincy High School in 1934, I was enrolled in a postgraduate course at Thayer Academy near Braintree. I was still too much in love to be intrigued by calculus, chemistry, or Virgil. Needless to say, despite one more year of postsecondary education, I was no better college material than I had been in high school.

But neither I nor the deans of several colleges reckoned with FH, who proved with the Relief Printing Corporation, which now had annual revenues of $300,000, that he could have made money selling refrigerators to the Eskimos. Letting no grass grow under his feet, FH had already contacted Harry Rowe, dean of Bates College. I was accepted on trial a week after classes had begun. As a young man with no religion, I was in a very religious college. I had a full schedule, but no math or sciences like biology or physics.

The reason I'm detailing my early life in this fashion is if you read *Yale Marratt, The Harrad Experiment, The Premar Experiments,* or even my latest unpublished novel, *The Oublion Project,* you will understand some of the motivating factors in the novels and how, much later, I transformed portions of my realities into fiction. Pat Marratt, for example, is a fleshier, cigar-smoking version of FH. The conflict between Matt Godwin and his father in *The Immoral Reverend* has many similarities.

I was still in love with Rosslyn. Although we had finally consummated our incessant touching and made love without condoms—I had learned about *coitus interruptus*—I was dimly aware, and so was she, that, at sixteen and eighteen, we could never survive four years of separation. She, perhaps, more than me, because she had no lack of guys who wanted to date her. I was still shy with girls. Perhaps we were both "saved" by FH's first interference with my love life. I was already playing an early version of my Pygmalion games with Rosslyn. That last summer, among other books I was reading, I had discovered pre-Elizabethan playwrights, and I tried to persuade Rosslyn to read Christopher Marlowe's *Doctor Faustus.* Assuming that I didn't have to make dates with her because we were going steady, I would occasionally arrive and discover that Rosslyn had gone out with some other boy. Her grandmother, who had just arrived from St. Louis, felt sorry for me, so I read *Doctor Faustus* (whom I was already trying to emulate) to her.

During the first six months at Bates, I slowly became aware that I was much more sexually sophisticated than most of the guys I met. Very unusual for its time, Bates was a coed college. It was only twenty miles away from Bowdoin, a kind of male monastery with six hundred guys who depended on special weekends when they could bring in female companionship. Thirty years later, when I wrote *The Harrad Experiment,* I contrasted a fraternity weekend with the saner sexual environment of Harrad. But Bates College was no Harrad. Young women went to class with you, but dating rituals soon set in. By the end of your freshman year, you were "going steady" or you were one of the social outcasts who stood on the sidelines at the Saturday-night dances and prayed for some person of the opposite sex to smile at you.

Still a rebel without a cause, I detested the compulsory, presumably nonsectarian chapel assemblies which occurred every weekday morning at 8:30 A.M. Seat check on all six hundred students was taken by monitors sitting in the balcony of the very attractive church. You were allowed about twenty cuts a semester, which I used up in three weeks, spending the half-hour that I was supposed to be in chapel in a local store called the Quality Shop a few blocks away from the campus. I soon discovered a female rebel who managed to get through her 7:15 A.M. classes without breakfast, but needed chapel time to recover with a cup of coffee, English muffins, and a cigarette. An only child, her name was Margery McCray. Her friends called her Bunny.

With wide-apart blue eyes and deep brown hair, Bunny was as tall as I was. Later, she called me "Napoleon," because she was an inch taller when she wore high heels. She was a fast learner, received straight *A*'s in French and fairly good marks in other subjects. She could play popular music on the piano with great charisma and sing along with herself. I was soon very much in love with her, but couldn't resist trying to remake her in my own image.

Was Bunny the inspiration for Cynthia in *Yale Marratt*? Not quite, but almost. Before we graduated in 1939, I was to all intents and purposes married to her. By the end of our sophomore year, we were making love regularly. Defying all Bates regulations, we sneaked away on weekends to nearby hotels and rooming houses or, in the Indian summers or early Maine springs, snuggled together on a blanket alongside the Androscoggin River.

At the same time, because of some lucky roommate matching in my sophomore year, I was rooming with John Smith and Eddie Fishman, two juniors who were both on the dean's list. They were known in those days as "greasy grinds" instead of nerds. Womanless most of the time, they were amused by their romantic roommate. With their driving need to excel and learn everything, they became minor mentors in my life. Eddie Fishman was managing editor of the *Bates Student,* a weekly newspaper. Since there was no room for additional editorial help, I became advertising manager, conning merchants in Lewiston to advertise their wares. After hours, the keys to the *Bates Student* office provided a convenient rendezvous for Bunny and me. Once a week, on Sunday night, we'd put the newspaper to bed.

One night, in his senior year, lacking enough articles to fill the paper, I suggested to Eddie that we condense an article on premarital sex in the colleges that had appeared in *Cosmopolitan* magazine. A week later, when copies of the *Bates Student* trickled home to parents, it blew the top off. The premarital sex that was detailed in *Cosmopolitan* simply didn't happen at Bates. Eddie Fishman was forced to resign as managing editor.

By the end of our sophomore year, I convinced Bunny to major in English as I was doing. Before we graduated, we were, with a few exceptions, taking the same courses. Always studying together, with a small coterie of friends, we became somewhat notorious. Without being aware of it, I was playing Pygmalion to a willing Galatea, who turned her weekly allowance from home (two dollars) over to me. Conning enough money out of FH to support my "wife" was a continuous occupation, and all was not smoothness and light. Bunny loved to dance. I was spirited but clumsy and unpredictable on the dance floor. She was a skilled bridge player, but playing cards bored me. She procrastinated endlessly when it came to writing theses and term papers, so I often wrote them for her, being careful to make her style different from mine. In my sophomore year, I took a yearlong writing course, which Bunny did not take. I could imitate the style of well-known popular writers like Hemingway, Faulkner, and lesser stars like Vina, Del Mar, E. Phillips Oppenheim, Sax Rohmer, and even Thomas Wolfe, whose rebellion as much as his writing I totally admired.

Other literary rebels I was discovering on my own, and convinced Bunny to read, were Romain Rolland and his novel *Jean-Christophe,* George Bernard Shaw and, of course, his *Pygmalion* as played on film by Leslie Howard, along with Bertrand Russell's famous *Companionate Marriage.* The authors were all rebels in various ways and delighted me. I was also reading everything I could find—and it wasn't much—on the vagaries of human sexuality. Scarcely a month went by during these three years that Bunny and I didn't think our college days would come to a sudden end. She often had irregular monthly periods, and once, when she was a week overdue, we were sure that she was pregnant. We both hated condoms, and although I knew about diaphragms, in the mid 1930s it was difficult enough to find a doctor who would fit a married woman to one, let alone a single girl.

Four years at Bates, in love, not having as much daily sexual contact as I might have wished (but more than most of the nineteen- and twenty-year-olds I knew), studying anything I wished (FH was happy enough that I was in college and had, to everyone's surprise, suddenly appeared on the dean's list that he didn't interfere with my choice of courses), I had also discovered a new hero/mentor, Peter Bertocci, who had recently been hired to teach psychology and philosophy at Bates. I was so charmed by Peter's inquiring mind that, in my junior year, I decided I would take only minimum requirements for an English major and soon had, with Bunny, who protested at taking so much philosophy, a dual major in English plus psychology and philosophy. Before I graduated, Peter, who couldn't believe I was actually going to Harvard Business School, gave me a copy of the first of many books, *The Empirical Argument for God*, that he would write. He inscribed it to me, "With the sincere hope that your mind will continue to ask for reality and your actions continue to adjust to it."

Many years later Peter Bertocci's human-values approaches to teaching—he finally became full professor of philosophy at Boston University—became a key element of the Harrad program. Peter and Lucy (although the later Bob Rimmer would shock them, too) became partial models for Phillip Tenhausen and his wife. *Harrad* ends with a quotation from Peter's book, "Extolling not a Golden Age, but an Age of Creative Insecurity," which Peter believed could be common underlying philosophy for all of us.

On graduation day from Bates, although I had commuted on weekends to Hartford for two summers, FH and Blanche met Bunny's mother and stepfather for the first time. They were all well aware that Bunny and I were in love and wanted to be married quickly. Bunny had been accepted for a buyer's training position at eighteen dollars a week at Jordan Marsh in Boston. I proposed my plan to FH for the first time. In those days there were no married graduate students living on campus at Harvard Business School, and very few off campus. I told

him he could pay my tuition, but give me the cost of room and board at Harvard (equal to more than eighteen dollars a week), and together, Bunny and I could support an apartment in Harvard Square and get married. It wouldn't cost FH any more than he was already prepared to pay. In 1939, however, such ideas were outlandish, to say the least. FH refused. He had nothing against Bunny and thought she should be happy to wait two years until I finished my education. The problem was that Bunny couldn't support herself in Boston on eighteen dollars a week. With a combined income of thirty-six to forty dollars a week, there would have been no problem. The only solution was that she would have to go home to Hartford, get a job, and live with her parents until I graduated. How could I explain to FH that I now needed a regular bed companion? As well as a friend to save me from the Philistines at Harvard Business School. Before classes began in September at Harvard, Bunny wrote me a good-bye note. Her mother agreed with her. Two years was much too long to wait.

Without being married, I suddenly learned what divorce was like. Back in Quincy after four years, I had no friends, male or female. I was shipwrecked and totally shocked. A month later I met my Harvard roommate, Paul Williams, son of William Carlos Williams, who had written several novels and was being hailed as one of America's best poets, although he made a living as a much-loved doctor in Rutherford, New Jersey.

The shock of losing Bunny was compounded by the first lecture from the nationally known dean Wallace Brett Donham, who had, with the help of a multimillionaire, George Baker, practically created Harvard Business School. Donham told us that we could now forget our easygoing college days. At HBS, unless you devoted seventy hours a week to classes and study, you were sure to flunk out. He assured us that 10 percent of the 1941 class would be gone after the first midyear exams. Paul had graduated from the Wharton School at University of Pennsylvania. Unlike me, he had had four years of undergraduate business training. Within a few weeks, I was sure that I should have been studying on the Cambridge side of the Charles River, getting a masters in psychology or sociology from Harvard, which I knew several of my Bates friends were doing. I was sure that I had probably been accepted because Harvard Business was experimenting with a new philosophy and accepting a few people like me who might add a new kind of creativity to the business world and not be so one-dimensional as typical HBS graduates were.

My new roommate and I did have something in common. Paul, too, had lost the love of his life, Virginia Carnes, daughter of a wealthy physician in Massillon, Ohio. He had met Ginny and slept with her occasionally at the University of Pennsylvania, but now she had gone to Western Reserve and met another guy. Fortunately, although he had no interest in becoming a writer or poet like his father, because Paul had been raised in a literary household, we were on a much closer mental level than most of the first-year class, who were graduates of engineering schools and other business schools. But I never discovered anyone who had majored in English and philosophy. If you read *The Rebellion of Yale Marratt,* you will get a fictionalized version of my two years in business school. Bunny is transformed into Cynthia, who is Jewish (because of Nancy, later), and FH is an interfering Pat Marratt, who hates Jews. If Cynthia had been a WASP Pat Marratt might have liked or would have tolerated her, if she'd been smart enough to play his game.

Somehow, I survived the hard-driving, one-dimensional, "give it all you've got or you'll never succeed at business" philosophy of Harvard Business School. At the same time, I managed to continue my search for Galatea. After classes I spent many hours in the co-op acquiring nonbusiness books to read as an escape from the boredom of solving endless mimeographed case problems and writing my solutions which the professors quickly insisted were too literary and not the kind of concise writing that top management required. I also discovered a minor literary hero/mentor, Henry Miller, and after many discreet inquiries found a bookseller in Harvard Square who kept copies of *The Tropic of Cancer* and *The Tropic of Capricorn* (printed in Mexico) in a big, iron safe. When he carefully determined that I wasn't connected with the FBI or the Cambridge police, he told me the price. Twenty-five dollars per copy. It was exorbitant, but since I now had no woman in my life, I had plenty of money to spend reading about sex.

Because my grades were good enough, during the final year at Harvard Business School I was permitted to enroll in a special one-year course designed by Dean Donham and his confreres which would teach us how to mobilize the United States into a full wartime economy. The assumption was that those who completed their final year at HBS in this area would end up in Washington D.C. if war were declared, with army or navy commissions. With the wisdom we acquired at Harvard, we'd save England and bury Hitler. Another year would pass before the

Japanese surprised us at Pearl Harbor. But in a world at war, I was more concerned that I still hadn't found a woman with whom I could share a mental/sexual merger and the wide interest in literature, art, and music that I had acquired at Bates College.

Then, in the fall of 1940, I met Erma. Blanche had mentioned that the family dentist in Boston had a new dental hygienist, Miss Richards, who was a very nice girl. Since I was constantly looking for dates, why not ask her? Why not? I needed my teeth cleaned, and soon a very pretty blue-eyed brunette with a wholesome, clean-cut face and firm breasts was leaning close to my face as she scaled my teeth, creating an aura of sexual intimacy. When she finished, I asked her point-blank, with a clean mouth, "How about a kiss?" There was no kiss, and no date. Dating clients was against the doctor's rules. But she warned me I must be sure to come back. I needed some new fillings and missed appointments were charged. When I purposely missed the next appointment, I told the doctor it was because Miss Richards wouldn't have a date with me. He changed his mind.

Erma Richards Rimmer with Bob Rimmer, 1941

The Rimmers were good customers, and he was only too happy to relax his rules and play Cupid.

Erma was a most affectionate and loving woman. She had been recently deserted by a former high-school boyfriend who had decided to marry the daughter of a more prestigious Melrose family. Not only didn't Erma reject me when we were finally naked on her parents' sofa, but she encouraged me. Even though I was sure that her father would soon stomp downstairs and put an end to me, we were frequently making love in her parents' living room.

At twenty, a year younger than me, Erma needed to be loved as much as I did. To my amazement, she seemed very willing to be molded into my ephemeral ivory Galatea. I soon convinced her that while we were most certainly sexually in tune, if a long-lasting relationship were to develop, we must be able to communicate mentally. The business world didn't matter, but I told Erma that she must read and acquire what a quarter of a century later Edward Hirsch would define as "cultural literacy."

I was falling in love, and I was sure that I could recreate Erma, who was already smarter than I was in the practical world, and make her more literary than all the women I had known with bachelor's degrees, including Bunny. I told her all she had to do was read . . . read and take a few courses, particularly in psychology. I had it made—a woman who loved me and was eager to learn all the things she had never been exposed to. Was I playing Svengali? Not quite. Time would prove that Erma had a mind of her own.

Before I graduated, after playing Russian roulette in the baby-making area for nearly a year, Erma and I set the wedding date. August 2, 1941. FH couldn't believe what was happening. A year and a half ago, I had been in love with Bunny. Since she couldn't wait two years, he agreed it was just as well I hadn't married her, but Erma Richards? A girl who worked for Dr. Tracy and cleaned teeth? What did I have in common with her? Unknown to me, he called Erma, interrupting her at work, and asked her point-blank why she wanted to marry me. "Does Bob really love you? Did you know that he was madly in love with another girl just a year ago?" Obviously, FH was still trying to direct my life. In tears, Erma assured him that we were in love. If you read *Yale Marratt,* you'll find a similar story, but fused to FH's anti-Semitism, which I didn't discover until fifteen years later.

So Erma and I were married. She soon discovered that, along with our other wedding furniture, we had to make room for my close to one thousand books in our four-room apartment. I wasn't making

vast progress in sculpting my Galatea, but we were newlyweds who had many things to do, and we enjoyed sexmaking.

Erma continued to work as a dental hygienist for a couple of months, but then we bought a dog and were affluent enough for her to stay home. Not to read, but to cook and sew and decorate, at which she was very competent. In addition, for a few happy months, she was able to flit around Melrose in the handsome Ford convertible that FH had given me.

We had many Saturday-night parties with just-married friends and dating singles. Sexual flirting with others in their twenties, aided and abetted by plenty of booze, was a way of life. The idea of playing strip poker was often bandied about, and not being adverse to seeing how female friends of Erma's looked in their birthday suits, I devised a variation on blackjack, or twenty-one, which made it possible to play for several hours with a slow and tantalizing divestment of clothing. You'll find it described in detail in *Yale Marratt.* Within the first twelve months of marriage, although Erma and I were quite mono-gamous, I managed to hug at least half a dozen of her female friends after they had shed their last stitch of clothing and didn't know whether to run off or be embarrassed. But then, on December 7, 1941—Pearl Harbor Day—the top blew off and our happy day-dream was nearly over.

By late 1942, although I had quit Relief and taken a job at the Fore River Shipyard division of Bethlehem Steel in Quincy, hoping to be deferred because I was working in an essential industry, it was obvious that my number was up. To my shock, I quickly discovered that the months I had spent at HBS learning how, as a top army brass, to direct the war from a cushy job in Washington weren't about to be put to use.

I told Erma I still thought I might wangle a commission in the Finance Department of the army, but two weeks later I was drafted as a private. I ended up at Fort Devens, headed for the infantry with a lot of nice kids who had never met a guy who had graduated from college, let alone had a master's degree in business.

During four long winter months at enlisted man's finance school at Fort Benjamin Harrison, near Indianapolis, Indiana, the army had finally decided that I might prove of some value as a private first class in the Finance Department. I quickly discovered that no one gave a damn about my superior educa-tion. Survival in the army (with plenty of infantry training) depended on the strict obeying of orders and a lot of careful ass-kissing of officers and noncommissioned officers, especially master sergeants. Rebellion was heresy. With my ingrained disability to obey orders, or to conform to morons, I was continuously unable to get a weekend pass to leave the base. In April, a month before my enlisted man's finance training was completed, Erma, sure that I would be sent overseas, arrived in Indianapolis with our snazzy Ford convertible. Captains, lieutenants, and master sergeants, who couldn't afford such extravagances, soon discovered that it belonged to "that F.U. . . . Private Rimmer." Getting off the base to be reunited with my wife became almost impossible. But good fortune was smiling once again. I met another minor mentor in my life, Bill Resnick, who also was a private, a college graduate, and the well-off son of a family who owned a chain of clothing stores in Ohio.

To my astonishment, Bill laughingly offered to write me a pass so that I could leave the base and spend the night with Erma. He often wrote his own passes and had a pocketful of padded forms which he coolly signed with a fictitious captain's name so that he could spend weekends with his wife, Charlotte. Like Erma, she'd arrived in Indianapolis to spend a few final days with her husband.

Before I was finally shipped out of Fort Benjamin Harrison on a troop train destined for Shenango, Pennsylvania, a marshalling area for the European theatre, with the help of my barrack buddies, who showed me how to hide my cot under a building and respace the beds so as not to get caught and be AWOL at bed check, Bill, Charlotte, Erma, and I spent a happy weekend together at a resort in Brown's County, Indiana.

Deciding to save money by sharing a two-room cottage, we were soon such good friends that we were bouncing around half naked. Both Erma and Charlotte made it obvious that, although they were happily married, they wouldn't mind snuggling with a different man. But no sexual consummation. So we did, and later, fully aroused, slept with our proper spouses. The die was cast. I loved Erma, but I still enjoyed other women, and for the moment at least, without playing Pygmalion.

At Shenango, when it looked as if I would soon be serving in a finance office in bomb-blasted England, and was practically bidding a final, tearful good-bye to Erma, FH intervened. In retrospect, he "saved" me again. This time not from girls, but ultimately from D-Day, with a temporary residency at Wake Forest College, which was then located in Wake Forest, North Carolina. Here, the army was running a course for noncommissioned officers in army

finance. The change in my orders was the result of FH's phone call to his longtime friend Congressman John McCormack. They laid the groundwork, and if I survived Wake Forest, I could then apply to Officer Candidate School at Duke University for possible acceptance sometime in February of 1944. If I didn't flunk out, I would end up in June of 1944 as a second lieutenant—a full-fledged ninety-day wonder—and a finance officer. Three months later, I graduated from Wake Forest Finance School as a private first class.

I was finally accepted at Duke University, where arduous infantry training was combined with endless hours in a classroom learning advanced army finance. It made my first two years at HBS look like a pink tea. Erma didn't come to Durham until graduation day, which coincided with D-Day in Europe. During the entire four months at Duke, I was in continuous trouble, being "gigged" in for everything from insubordination to dust on coat hangers and the inability to make up my bunk so that the captain in charge could bounce a quarter on it.

Every month I appeared before the flunk-out board, which was composed of seven or more officers who hurled questions at you while you sat at rigid attention and tried to figure out how to answer them so that you weren't instantly told to pack your barracks bag, leave Duke, and once again become a private. What I was reading, and had read throughout my life, was a source of great interest to them, especially since I informed them that I'd not only read Karl Marx, the *Daily Worker,* and magazines like the *New Republic,* but I had also read Hitler's *Mein Kampf,* as well as a current novel called *Out of the Night,* which was about a Communist spy. I told them that I thought "an Officer and a Gentleman" should know what both our friends and our enemies may be thinking. They weren't amused. By a miracle, and possibly because of a notation that I was sure was on my records about my family friend in Washington, I survived.

When Erma arrived in Durham for graduation, we decided that the time had come to have a baby. Happily kissing condoms and her diaphragm good-bye, we made up for lost time. She was soon pregnant, and of all things, my first orders as a second lieutenant were to report back to Fort Benjamin Harrison, where I now had the opportunity to learn how officers (the upper class), as contrasted with noncommissioned officers and enlisted men, lived. Needless to say, in the army, all men and women are *not* created equal. From Harrison, I was assigned to the Air Transport Command at Grenier

"As a finance officer in India"

Field in Manchester, New Hampshire. After a hectic two weeks back and forth between Indianapolis and New Hampshire, Erma had a miscarriage.

For a time, it looked as if we might remain at Grenier for the war. I was in charge of a small finance office in a building filled with North Atlantic Command generals and top brass. But suddenly, I received orders to go to Florida. From there, I was to proceed to Karachi, India. I looked at a map of the world in shock. India was halfway around. I was assigned to the China Burma India theatre, where the British, backed by the Americans, were determined to fight the Japanese all the way across the Chinese mainland if necessary. Everyone in the CBI theatre was sure it would take at least another ten years to win the war this way. The theme song was "The Golden Gate by '58."

Three weeks later, pregnant once again, Erma kissed me good-bye as I boarded a train in South Station for Miami. I'll never forget the sight of her standing on the deserted track, sobbing as the train pulled out. In my pocket were a dozen pictures I had taken of her naked and three months pregnant. Would we ever see each other again? Both of us doubted it. The United States was not only bogged down in Europe fighting Hitler, but we were trying to defeat the Japanese island by island across the Pacific. World War II would never end.

Two weeks later, with stops in Algiers, Cairo, and Abadan (a city in Persia in those days), I was in Karachi, headed for Calcutta and ultimately an air force base in Shamshenagra, located in the upper

Assam Valley, an area of India now called Bangladesh. India was a unique learning experience. I soon discovered that the Indians were great readers. In the major cities there were hundreds of bookstores, and the Communists had gone to great lengths to supply all kinds of translations into Hindustani and other languages to prove that Lenin and Marx were the true prophets of the future.

I was more interested in Indian yoga, and particularly tantra—the wine, woman, and song approach to nirvana for those who couldn't pursue the ascetic Brahmin yoga disciplines. I soon had my own fully illustrated copy of the *Kama Sutra,* which in the 1940s and 1950s, along with James Joyce, Henry Miller, and D. H. Lawrence, would have put a United States bookseller in jail permanently if he dared to offer such a picturesque view of human sexuality.

Thanks to Sir John Woodroffe, also known as Arthur Avalon, whose book *Sakti and Sakta,* which was written in 1918, was also available in India, I discovered tantric sex in 1945 and the potential of extended sexual intercourse without ejaculation to achieve a blending of the yang and yin as a path to nirvana. I also learned about tantric rituals where sexual merger with a loved one wasn't necessarily monogamous. Joy of sex, tantric style, is discussed in the middle section of *Yale Marratt,* and it's one of the goals of a Harrad style of education that I wrote about many years later. Subconsciously, although I didn't realize it until later, my Galatea daydreams and tantric sexual merger were opposite sides of the same coin.

In August 1944, after finally receiving a telegram that my son Robert, Jr., was born on July 3, I was running a finance office in Chengkung, China, on a base with three thousand men and an equal number of Chinese "coolie" labor. A few weeks later, the United States dropped the atomic bomb on Hiroshima and suddenly it seemed that I might get home after all.

Then I was called back to Calcutta by Colonel Beaver, who directed all of the finance offices in the CBI, and was told it was a case of "last in, last out." There was still much to do. If I were lucky, I might be on my way home in January or February of 1946. Beaver gave me what presumably was a choice assignment but entailed endless flying to strange destinations. When the Japanese surrendered, the U.S. Army quickly moved into the occupied countries, and more than a month had gone by since most of them had been paid. My first flight was to Rangoon and then Singapore to pay newly arrived army officers and enlisted men their back pay so they could wheel and deal with the natives, whom they had liberated from the Japanese. In Singapore, for example, they had taken over the Raffles Hotel, where they were living in high style, to the consternation of the manager, who was trying to keep full records of what the American government owed him. I told him that was a problem for Lend-Lease, and my job was simply to take care of army back pay.

Later, I was back in Karachi and discovered that instead of flying back to the States in style in an Air Transport Command C-47, I was on orders to return on a troopship with several thousand enlisted men and several hundred officers whose cabins, twenty or so with triple-decker bunks, were topside. The only way to survive the three-week ocean crossing was to stay awake all night, try to sleep during the day, and thus avoid the snoring of your bed companions. Three weeks later, after steaming around India to Singapore and across the Pacific to Tacoma, Washington, I was on a four-day cross-country train ride. Like a Jules Verne character, I could say that I had been around the world, but it took more than eighty days.

I had phoned Erma in Melrose (where she had been living with her parents) from Tacoma and promised to call again from Chicago. Several days later, stepping off the train in the South Station in Boston, I was more than a little surprised to see Erma, FH, Blanche, and a contingent of Blanche's friends. It was February 1, Blanche's birthday, and I was her present. Since it was early Saturday evening when I arrived, she thought we should all go to a cocktail lounge and celebrate. Hugging me after a year, Erma whispered, "What the hell could I do? They're your parents." I could see my son Bobby, who was now eight months old, and be with her later. Erma had another surprise, which FH had confirmed. He had bought us a house, putting fifteen hundred dollars down on a six-room English bungalow and leaving only a fifty-five hundred dollar mortgage. I could pay him back the fifteen hundred dollars in the coming years. The thirty-year-old house was on a third of an acre and I remembered it. There was one major problem. It was only one house away from Blanche and FH's home. The trap was set and I fell into it, happily at first.

"Arriving home from India," 1946: (from left) FH, Blanche, Bob, Erma, and family friends

Obviously, as soon as I was discharged from the army, I would go to work at Relief Printing Corporation, which had survived the war with no bigger problems during the war years than how to find employees to produce the business-card orders that had continued unabated. Even today, the Japanese and the Americans have one thing in common. Without business cards, their economies would grind to a halt. Since I had a wife and a child to support, and I was no longer angry at FH for interfering in my love life, it seemed convenient to live close by. Joseph Kennedy style, FH was obviously trying to create a family compound. But it didn't matter, I was sure I could earn my new salary of seventy-five dollars a week and help the company grow.

But I did have an old problem. Neither in the business world nor in my social life was I meeting anyone who was as obsessed or fascinated with music, the arts, and literature as I was. Nor, spending my days as a salesman, was it easy to make contacts with anyone with equivalent interests. As a result, during the next ten years, I became a totally split personality—a kind of Dr. Jekyll and Mr. Hyde who no longer bothered to play the Pygmalion game with Erma. She was proving to be a fun companion and a wife in many other ways. As Dr. Jekyll, I was a sober citizen and a hard-driving businessman who soon proved that I could sell major accounts.

As a benign Mr. Hyde, I was an enigma to my family and friends. As an antidote to the business world, I was reading many current novels and collecting anything and everything that had been written about human sexuality as well as more abstruse books in the areas of psychiatry, psychology, religion, and economics. I was omnivorously searching for answers to questions about life and death that I couldn't even formulate. I was also buying and listening to a wealth of music that was suddenly available on LP records, discovering chamber music, ballet, concertos, and symphonies along with the world of art, all of which I had been exposed to at Bates, but had put aside during my HBS and war years.

With business friends or people that Erma met through women's clubs that she joined, I rarely revealed my Mr. Hyde inclinations. With a few drinks of bourbon, I was one of the boys, a hale fellow well met and a kindred spirit for men and women with whom I had very little in common. I told Erma that we were like two people on different trolley cars (they still existed in those days), going in different directions, but waving at each other as we passed. But in many areas, we were well mated. Erma soon proved her abilities on our thirty-year-old bungalow, personally painting, wallpapering, laying cement walks, expanding the house, and, in between time, cooking gourmet dinners and taking care of the boys. We had many goals in common, but little mental companionship.

Early summer in 1946, a few months after I was discharged from the army, Paul Williams (his friends called him "Willie"), whom I'd roomed with both years at HBS, came to Boston and phoned to see if I'd survived the war. He had—also as a naval lieutenant—and during the war had finally married Virginia ("Ginny"), whom Erma and I had met one night in Boston a few weeks before Paul and I graduated from HBS. They had two children. Paul thought we should get together and celebrate with a picnic at Crane's Beach in Ipswich, which had always been a springtime rendezvous area for HBS students. In May, a few months later, they arrived with their kids. A brown-eyed brunette with almond-shaped eyes, coolly sexy, Ginny thought nothing of sitting on a sofa with her arms around her knees, well aware that she wore no panties and her nether parts were beckoning. She was a sharp contrast to Erma. Before she settled down with Paul, she had known quite a few boys and men intimately.

Arriving in Quincy, she couldn't believe her eyes. Here was a house filled with more books than her father-in-law owned, plus hundreds of records. Willie read a bit, listened to some classical music a bit, but was an entirely different cup of tea than Bob Rimmer. I was charmed. Erma wasn't, but she liked Willie. During the weekend, I discovered that not only was Ginny an omnivorous reader, but she wrote poetry which her father-in-law, William Carlos Williams, thought was great. Ginny told me later that she loved Bill, as she called Paul's father, more than her husband, who was now a rising executive at the Abraham and Strauss department store in Brooklyn. Willie was more interested in his career in retailing (a subject he had majored in at HBS) than his wife's poetry. During the weekend, I managed to take Ginny alone on a fast auto tour of Quincy. We soon stopped for a torrential embrace during which she told me that their marriage was falling apart and she was having an affair with a buyer she had met at Lord and Taylor who was divorcing his wife.

The weekend ended with a few more discreet hugs from Ginny and an invitation from Paul to spend a weekend (without our kids) in a cottage owned by his father on the Connecticut River near West Haven. Within a few hours after Erma and I arrived, we were all drinking gin, and Ginny whispered that she really had to talk to me alone. How we were going to escape our spouses in such confined quarters was a mystery to me, but by nine o'clock, eating very little except hors d'oeuvres, Paul and Erma had drank so much that all they wanted to do was go to bed. And very definitely not with each other! Ginny's hope that they might end up in bed together never materialized. She and I went for a walk along the river. We were soon feverishly undressing each other. Despite the discomfort of bugs and sand, we nervously made love on a lonely inlet.

During the next two years (1947 and 1948), I arranged sales trips to New York City about every six weeks. Relief had many accounts and innumerable prospects whose headquarters were in New York City. For Ginny, a bus ride from Rutherford, New Jersey, and a covering excuse for arriving home late after an afternoon and evening with me was no problem. Did we feel guilty? A little, perhaps. We always ended shopping for presents to bring home to our kids. I loved Ginny, but I loved Erma too and never considered divorce. I kept wondering if we could ever match Paul and Erma, who really had a lot in common, but it never happened. In the meantime, Erma was regnant with our second child, Stephen King, who was born May 18, 1948. Long before I wrote *Yale Marratt,* it occurred to me that the solution to my Dr. Jekyll/Mr. Hyde dual life was not to create a Galatea, but simply to enjoy two very different women.

During these years, Ginny and I mailed books we were reading back and forth to each other. She wrote me five- to ten-page letters daily, care of Relief. I had never been privileged to enter any person's mind so completely. Ginny was like a dammed-up, pent-up river bursting through the dykes of an unhappy marriage. She flooded me with a million words, seeking answers for herself and for me. At one point, I had four file drawers jam-packed with every letter she ever wrote me, and I often thought if they were ever published, they would be among the most intimate revelations (Ginny was a colorful writer) ever put down on paper by a female.

Then, the bubble burst. Carelessly (or on purpose), Ginny left a long letter she had been writing to me on her desk, and Paul read it. Within a week, I received at home a certified letter. Erma opened it and it was from Paul's lawyers. "Cease and desist seeing Virginia Williams," they wrote, or be sued for alienation of affections.

I thought it was silly, but, needless to say, Erma was hysterical. Did I want a divorce? No. I loved her and Steve and Bobby. I didn't believe in divorce. We might not be riding on the same streetcar, but we had

a lot of good things going for us. I simply needed a female friend. I was mentally lonesome and I knew I would never meet a man like me in the business world. Surprisingly, after a rocky month or two, Erma stopped asking details about my extracurricular love life. She was sorry that I couldn't have my cake and eat it, but Paul obviously wasn't as lenient as she was. Six months later, I discovered why Erma had suddenly become so complacent. She had told David, the doctor she took Bobby and Steve to with various childhood ailments, about me. David had even been in our house and seen my overwhelming collection of books and told her: "My wife, Nancy, would go crazy if she saw these. She'd never leave. She reads all the time." But poor Nancy who read so much was a recluse. In her childhood, she had had a severe attack of rheumatic fever which damaged her heart. Although she had survived and even given birth to two very much wanted children, at thirty-nine (because of her heart specialist's orders) she spent much of her time resting in bed and wondering if the next time she was out of breath, or her heart started fibrillating uncontrollably, it would be the last time.

With David, Nancy was a loving but limited sex partner. David couldn't understand how I could neglect such a pretty, healthy, and competent woman as Erma, but he told her she should accept male reality. Man had invented monogamy, not for himself, but to keep his women under control. If men, married or not, ever lost interest in the joy of loving and being loved by a loving woman, the world would come to an end. Erma was dubious, but ready to let him prove it.

Now, without me (or Nancy) being aware of it, Erma and David became like young lovers champing at the bit. It wasn't easy for a wandering husband and wife, with four kids between them, to find a place to be alone. Erma didn't know Nancy, but she assured David that Bob would enjoy a woman with whom he could share all of his "damn books." The die was cast. David convinced Nancy, who rarely went to social events, that she should attend a local hospital ball and he'd introduce her to a man who had enough books to keep her reading for two lifetimes. Nancy was very pretty. Nearsighted with big, luminous brown eyes that you could drown in, she sighed when I asked her to dance. "I really shouldn't. My heart isn't very good." I told her that I wasn't a great dancer. "My heart is pounding too," I laughed. "We don't have to move fast. We could dance on a dime and just hug each other." And we did, most of the evening, to the exclusion of everyone else—including David and Erma.

Although we realized later that our spouses had been making love for several years, Nancy was under no pressure from me to have sex together. She knew about Ginny, and much later, I told her the finale.

Arriving at the front door of the Relief building one morning at eight o'clock, I was shocked to see a woman smiling at me a few yards from the entrance. It was Ginny. She had left Paul and her children, but not wholly because of me. "You knew our marriage was on the rocks from the beginning," she sighed. I reminded her, as I had many times before, that I didn't think divorce was the answer. I had lived with Willie at HBS for two years and I really liked him. I was sure that he loved Ginny, but she shook her head. "Paul was too possessive. He doesn't give a damn about my mind, but he wants my body exclusively," she said. Adamantly, she added, "If you don't want me, don't worry, I can take care of myself." I saw her occasionally and kept trying to tell her to go home, but then she met a man who was evidently free to take off with her. She sent me a postcard from Florida. Years later, I received a letter from her. She'd gone back home to Massillon, Ohio, divorced Paul, and converted to Catholicism. She was living with some Sisters of Charity and was occasionally housekeeper for a priest.

During the next twenty-five years, Erma, Bob, David, and Nancy became "the inseparables." This was no *Bob and Carol and Ted and Alice* scenario. We saw the film much later and shrugged at the silly ending. We weren't swingers. We never made love as a foursome. Our travels together eventually took us to Florida, the Caribbean, Europe, Africa, Greece, and Israel. We were often casually naked together and slept with each other's spouses, but we never made sexual comparisons to each other. During the first year, we passed through occasional moments of jealousy, but it became increasingly clear that our love for each other was "in addition to and not instead of." Sexual and mental sharing became a natural way of life between the four of us, but we were careful never to reveal our sexual exchange to anyone. We never merged households, but perhaps we would have, as I proposed in *Proposition 31,* had we all lived into our eighties. We maintained separate families in our attractive middle-class homes. We loved our biological children as well as each other's kids, who ranged from five to thirteen years of age. Many years later, as a foursome, we enjoyed the fun of being both biological as well as surrogate grandparents.

Each of us grew emotionally and mentally in the unique marriage that later I would fictionalize (to Nancy's horror) and expand into alternate lifestyles in *Proposition 31, Thursday, My Love, Come Live My Life,* and *The Love Explosion* (not my title). Seeing Erma through David's eyes, I learned to appreciate her abilities to tackle almost any project that required mechanical and physical adeptness and to do it all by herself, if necessary. Seeing Nancy through my eyes, David began to realize that her wide reading from childhood, her love of music—she introduced us all to the joys of opera—and the fact that she had me as a lover was making his wife a much more exciting woman. Seeing David through Erma's and my eyes, Nancy slowly became aware that David might not have had a Park Avenue–style medical practice, but he was one of the most caring medical practitioners around. A man who loved all of his patients, although many never paid him and tried to barter for his services. David blended his love for his family and ours with caring medicine and a never-ending sense of laughter and joy of life. Whenever you find laughter in my novels, in scenes like the meshugah ape in *The Harrad Experiment* or partying on Trotter Island in *That Girl from Boston,* David was the inspiration.

For me, it was a turning point in more ways than one. Two years after the four of us met, FH, now seventy years old, decided to become chairman of the board of Relief. When I was forty, he elected me president. At thirty-two, my brother, Richard, had finally joined the company. In twelve years, I had tripled the revenues of the company, which were now over two million dollars annually. FH had given Richard and myself each 14 percent of the outstanding stock of Relief. In the 1950s, I was well aware that FH was taking close to sixty thousand dollars a year out of the company (multiply that by four in 1980 dollars). I was earning about twenty thousand dollars, but portions of that were made up by stock dividends. Blanche was now wearing diamonds and mink and spending a month of each year traveling with FH. But Blanche didn't ingratiate herself with her daughters-in-law, whom she never really liked. In fact, she often told her friends that the reason they lived so well was that "I gave them my dividends."

FH wasn't making me too happy either. When I told him that I had two boys to send to college and tuitions and room and board were no longer in the area of one thousand and fifteen hundred dollars a year (as they were at HBS before the war), and I needed more money so I could save for the future, his answer involved a mixture of, "You're not doing too badly financially . . . if your Jewish doctor friend is making more money than you, that's your problem. I told you to use Relief as a stepping stone. Anyway, you don't have to worry, because someday you and Richard will own it all." He didn't say, "If you live long enough."

Nor did he or I realize that I was slowly moving a different kind of stepping stone than the one he envisioned into place. Thanks to Nancy and David, I not only discovered Jewish life and religion, but a sense of family—landsman—and a caring, ethnic continuity that was a far cry from the warring relationship that Blanche and FH had with their families.

In the meantime, it was no longer a case of "Some of our best friends are Jews." All of Erma's and my friends were Jews. While it was mentally impossible for me to convert to any religion—I was a humanist then without knowing the term—I not only read widely in all areas of Judaism, but I was fascinated with the kibbutz and was totally charmed by the Jewish love of life and learning combined with laughter at oneself as antidote to life's seeming insanity. Long before Leo Rostand, and with no credentials, I was compiling a Yiddish dictionary. Beginning with *The Harrad Experiment* and culminating with *The Byrdwhistle Option,* many of my heroes were Jewish. In the bibliography of *Byrdwhistle* I extolled the contribution of Yiddish to the American language, and I'm surprised today that most second-generation Jews denigrate such an onomatopoetic language.

Continuing to live a split life, which now encompassed David, Nancy, and Erma, we were soon under fire from Blanche and FH. They belonged to a popular local club which excluded Jews. FH's argument was that Jews did the same. There were no Gentiles in their golf or yacht clubs. Spending a week on the cape with Nancy and David, I was shocked to discover that there was no room at the inn when they saw David. But I was totally horrified when FH and Blanche refused to come into our house when David and Nancy (or any other Jews) were there. (Keep in mind that we lived next door!) FH ardently believed that he wasn't prejudiced because he did business with many Jews. "They have their ways and we have ours. They don't want you either." He was wrong, even Orthodox Jews were delighted with my curiosity and need to learn about their customs and rituals. After my first novels were published, I was invited to speak at every synagogue (Orthodox, Conservative, and Reformed) in Quincy. Not a year went by when we weren't guests at Passover dinners.

I was now writing. My anger at religious prejudice slowly combined into a larger than life hero, Yale Marratt. When the novel was finished, I knew it was much too long. Two years later, seventeen publishers had rejected the book. I finally decided I needed an agent and picked Scott Meredith (today a millionaire literary agent). For fifty dollars, he agreed to read the novel. He liked parts of it, but told me that I had committed the ultimate no-no. Women read all the novels, and I would never sell one extolling bigamy. As Nancy had told me, chuckling, when I finished the book, one of the women had to die, and since Cynthia was Jewish, she was the most likely one. My ego was rudely punctured. The original manuscript, which I had trimmed on a power cutter several times so that it didn't show such wear and tear, was unsalable. I was a prophet without an audience. But I wasn't about to rewrite *Yale Marratt.*

If I hadn't known David and enjoyed him almost as much as I did his wife, I probably never would have written *That Girl from Boston* as my next novel. Most of it takes place on an island in Boston Harbor called Peddocks. David's hobby was fishing for Boston flounder (the harbor wasn't as polluted then), and he was also the preferred doctor for all residents on the island, who, over many years, had built unheated, untoiled, and unelectrified houses on Peddocks. To support himself, David had wrestled his way through medical school, and I included a wrestling scene in the novel. *That Girl from Boston* pits upper-class Bostonians against the lower-class Irish.

Ultimately, *That Girl from Boston* sold a half-million copies. Before she literally lost her head in an automobile accident, Jayne Mansfield wanted to star in a movie based on the novel. But in 1960, after I finished writing it, fifteen publishers, and all of the major paperback publishers, thought it was much too sexy. They were sure it would be the target of local religious groups who were trying to control the distribution of paperbacks with lurid covers and sexy contents.

I now had written two novels. As Dr. Jekyll, I continued to increase the sales of Relief Printing and to handle the many problems of a growing business. I hired Neil Doherty, who was younger than I was. He had been a poorly paid editor of *Hunting and Fishing* magazine. Eventually, he asked if he could read one of my novels. I gave him two manuscripts. *That Girl from Boston* delighted him, but as a Catholic, *Yale Marratt* shocked him a bit, although he liked it. Later, he did an excellent editing job, introducing the bigamy trial scene at the beginning and then concluding the book with it. He wondered what would

Bob Rimmer, president, with F. H. Rimmer, chairman of the board, in the packaging department of Relief Printing Corporation, 1952

happen if we started a publishing business ourselves and published *That Girl.* If it took off, and he was sure that it would, we would then look for other titles and publish *Yale Marratt.*

All we needed was a little money. Neil knew how to edit and we knew how to get a book printed. One of the best book printers in the country, Plimpton Press, was in nearby Norwood. FH told us that he was totally disinterested in publishing and hoped I was keeping my eye on the main ball—Relief Printing, of course!

John Raffo, who ran the computer department for Relief, agreed to be our front man, at no pay, but as a stockholder of our new company, Challenge Press. A year later, he was still unsuccessfully trying to find investors when I told Plimpton Press (unknown to FH) that Relief would guarantee the cost of printing seven thousand copies of *That Girl from Boston.*

We soon discovered that it wasn't going to be easy. The world wasn't ready for Challenge's belief that "writers should not only reflect their society, but they have the moral obligation to become the van-

guards for a new and brighter world where the sexual relationship is no longer something hidden or depraved." This is part of an editorial on the back side of the dust jacket of the book. On the cover was a picture of the heroine, Willa Starch, wearing a pair of very abbreviated panties and walking out of Boston Harbor onto Peddock's Island. The *Boston Globe* refused the advertisement as "too salacious."

In the meantime, I had discovered Olympia Press in Paris in the mid-1950s and read all of the missing Henry Miller, Marquis de Sade, D. H. Lawrence and even Nabokov's *Lolita* by the simple process of ordering the books from Paris and having them sent to me with the return address of a fictitious aunt. (About every third shipment was opened by customs and I received many a letter asking to destroy the contents, which I refused but never got the books.) Challenge Press was ten years in advance of its time, including my belief that we might publish a few of the Olympia Press titles, including *The Perfumed Garden.* But Challenge Press's brazen invitation to enjoy sex with laughter made many reviewers and bookstores nervous.

Challenge Press agreed to publish two books along with *That Girl from Boston* in exchange for the services of their authors, Alex Jackinson, an agent in New York City, and Art Moger, a former publicist in Hollywood. In October of 1964, all three books, seven thousand copies of each, were printed and ready for sale. But Challenge Press had run out of money. After raising about fifteen thousand dollars, Raffo couldn't find any other investors. We had no money to advertise any of the books. In addition, Challenge owed Plimpton Press twenty-six thousand dollars, which, as president of Relief (still unknown to FH), I had guaranteed.

In the meantime, I had finished "Experiment in Marriage," which I had typed by a temporary office employee—a young woman in her teens—who told me with tears in her eyes that she loved the book, and other than Nancy, was the first one who had read it.

By this time, although Challenge Press was broke, Alex Jackinson had reached a Hollywood promoter named Herbert Margolis, who took an option on a movie to be based on *Yale Marratt.* Backed by a five thousand dollar campaign developed by Herb Margolis to sell *Yale Marratt* to some movie producer, I was traveling up and down the coast of California promoting "bigamy as a solution for the divorce rate." It was Margolis's slogan, not mine, and I didn't think much of it. I was soon appearing on national television via "The Regis Philbin Show." I carefully explained to Regis beforehand that my left hand didn't know what my right hand was doing, and there would be no discussion of what I really did for a living.

During this time, Challenge Press's full inventory of about twenty thousand books was gathering dust in the Plimpton warehouse. Margolis had received many inquiries on *Yale Marratt,* but no follow-through by any potential movie producers. Alex Jackinson hadn't been able to sell "Experiment in Marriage." Ten New York publishers rejected it, but I wasn't unhappy. Erma and I were enjoying our dual monogamy with David and Nancy, and I had decided that I had better keep selling printing because my daydream of joining the ranks of Norman Mailer, Irwin Shaw, James Jones, and others who had written war novels that had made them millions of dollars, had gone down the drain. Of course, *Yale Marratt* wasn't really a war novel, but some of it did take place during World War II and I was sure that millions of women would like it.

Then, because I was still accumulating an extensive sex library and was on many mailing lists, I suddenly received a circular from a new company called Sherbourne Press in Los Angeles. They were mail ordering many far-out books on such things as wife-swapping and strange and forbidden sex practices, all promoted with very lurid and descriptive mail-order circulars. "Experiment in Marriage" had been rejected for being too "far-out" sexually and Sherbourne seemed a likely prospect.

I showed Alex the Sherbourne mailing and suggested that he try "Experiment in Marriage" on them. Fortunately, I hadn't given the novel to Challenge Press as I had the first two. Challenge still existed with a telephone on a desk which often went unanswered in the basement of Relief. Within a month Sherbourne had offered me a one thousand dollar advance for the novel. I was elated. Finally, at the age of forty-eight, I was going to earn some money from writing.

It didn't come easy. The editor of Sherbourne, Shelly Lowenkopf, who I finally met when the book was published, hated the title. I finally agreed that *The Harrad Experiment* sounded better, but I was in shock when he insisted that my introduction, which originally was thirty pages, and established the raison d'etre of the novel, should be cut to five pages. (The complete introduction finally appeared as an addenda to the English paperback edition.) Shelly won that one, but when he asked me to rewrite the first few journals (Harrad is told through the journals of former students) and jazz them up, make them more sexy and change the location to Southern California, where he insisted the kids were really screwing around, I refused.

Sherbourne sold ten thousand copies of the book in a conservative-appearing hardcover edition by mail order. Promoter and owner Louis Linetsky wasn't interested in bookstore distribution and the book was rarely found in a bookstore. His audience was a mailing list of two hundred thousand sex-book buyers, which included the names of six thousand M.D.s who Louie assured me were steady buyers of his books since they had never learned anything about sex in medical school.

I often wonder who bought the hardcover edition of *The Harrad Experiment.* It never appeared in any bookstore or library that I could discover and I never received any letters from readers. Most of them probably couldn't believe their eyes when they saw the introduction and the annotated bibliography. They didn't buy the book to get educated! Louie insisted that ten thousand copies wasn't a bad sale for what he thought was a first novel. Actually, he finally produced a second edition and sold a total of seventeen thousand copies. Suddenly, I received a phone call from him and he told me that his agent, Mel Sokolow, had sold *Harrad* to Bantam, who loved it. Bantam was the biggest paperback publisher in the United States. The advance was small—ten thousand dollars—but I shouldn't worry. Bantam was going to sell millions of copies in paperback. How Louie could be so sure, I didn't know, but he was right. In September 1967, Bantam released *Harrad* with the slogan "The Sex Manifesto of the Free Love Generation." I had seen the cover before publication and protested that the *Harrad* idea most certainly wasn't "free love," but no one was listening to the author. Across the country and in major colleges and university areas, Bantam was trying a new technique. They used billboards with a very sexy come-on to promote the book.

Within a month, *Harrad* had sold three hundred thousand copies, and within the year, it was one of the top selling paperbacks of 1967 with a million copies in print. Over three million copies were sold over the next twelve years. I couldn't believe what was happening. Overnight, I was both famous and infamous. Letters were pouring in from all over the country and I was happily dictating answers to all of them at Relief, never revealing that I was in truth a rather old Dr. Jekyll.

I had already written another novel, *The Zolotov Affair,* about a high-school chemistry professor who had learned the secret of alchemy and how to transmute lead into gold. Zolotov tries to use his discovery to save the world by threatening to destroy the world economies which are based on gold. I assured Oscar Dystel, the president of Bantam, that it was a great around-the-world chase story and he'd love it. Sherbourne Press was in line to publish it, but Louis Linetsky hated it. Protesting that it wasn't sexy enough, he published it anyway because he was afraid of losing me. A year later, Bantam brought it out in paperback, but didn't push it. I was suddenly in the doghouse with both Sherbourne and Bantam.

In the meantime, on weekends, I was writing *Proposition 31,* the story of a two-couple marriage, justifying and exploring in another dimension our happy relationship with David and Nancy. The response to *Harrad* via thousands of letters that I was receiving proved that millions of people were searching for answers to their marital and premarital problems, and that a *Harrad*-style undergraduate education, utopian though it might seem, might lay the foundations for what I called "corporate marriages" of two to three couples. The novel takes place in California, and the title refers to propositions that are put on the California ballot if enough voters agree

in advance. In the novel, the protagonists form a group called "Future Families of America" and try via Proposition 31 to legalize group marriages for couples who are past thirty years of age.

Writing the novel in 1967, I was only vaguely aware of the developing "Human Potential" movement. But then Abraham Maslow, whom I had first discovered through Betty Friedan's book *The Feminine Mystique,* phoned me. "I decided that I have to meet you," he chuckled. "The kids are all reading *Harrad* and driving me crazy." He taught at Brandeis and lived in Auburndale, about fifteen miles from Quincy. It was the beginning of a friendship that would last until his untimely death in Menlo Park, California. Abe was one more hero/mentor in my life and I really paid tribute to him in *The Byrdwhistle Option.*

I was now living in three separate worlds. One, in the prosaic business world where 99 percent of the people I encountered had never heard of Bob Rimmer, the writer. A second private world with Erma, David, and Nancy where I could at least integrate what I was writing, and the publishing world, where I was slowly learning my way around without an agent.

My contract with Sherbourne was that I would give them first refusal rights on my next novel. Despite their offer of thirty-five thousand dollars for *Proposition 31* and Mel Sokolow's frank opinion that I'd better take it because John Updike had a new novel called *Couples,* which would upstage *Proposition 31,* I refused.

Then I had a brainstorm. My Sherbourne contract didn't cover publication in a foreign country. Through some fluke, Bantam had let New English Library (owned by New American Library) get the English publication rights to *Harrad.* I sent a manuscript copy of *Proposition 31* to Christopher Shaw, managing director of New English Library. Within two weeks, I received a phone call from Christopher in London. He was flying to New York and wanted to meet with me, along with Sidney Kramer, president of New American Library, Martin Levin, vice-president of Times Mirror, who owned NAL, and to my surprise, the famous Bernard Geis, who had published several of those million-dollar war novels.

I was really moving in the big time! The upshot of the meeting was that Geis would publish *Proposition 31* and sign me to one of his famous contracts that even Harry Truman had agreed to. Geis would pay a maximum of thirty thousand dollars a year for ten years, and that was all, regardless of what royalties were earned by a particular book. But he did guarantee that the author, or his heirs, would receive all the earned income eventually. As part of my agreement to sign with Geis, Sidney Kramer agreed to pay off Sherbourne Press—it finally cost NAL twenty thousand dollars to extricate me from the Sherbourne contract—and NAL would publish *Proposition 31* in paperback after the Bernard Geis edition ran its one-year course.

Sidney Kramer phoned me and I agreed to meet him at the Publix House in Sturbridge, Massachusetts, as a half-way point from New York City. A few days later, groaning that I was a hell of a negotiator, Sidney agreed to pay me an advance of one hundred twenty-five thousand dollars for the hardcover and paperback rights for *Proposition 31*. It shows you what you can do when you suddenly have several million readers out there.

I never should have told FH or Blanche. Although the royalties at first on *Harrad* were only six cents a copy (of which I got half), the book income itself, which I had legally turned over to be split between Bobby and Stephen to pay for their college education, among other things (and not including a movie sale) was obviously going to exceed one hundred thousand dollars. With my income from Relief, I was now earning more than FH. Although Relief was doing very well, he raised the question whether I was spending enough time with the company. The stepping-stone theory had been forgotten, and along with it was his continued dismay over our Jewish friends. We still lived in a house next door that we had expanded to ten rooms, but the underlying aggravation with Erma and me didn't make for great family get-togethers.

I was now a hot literary property. In the next five years, I wrote one novel after the other, including *The Premar Experiments* (very much a sequel to *Harrad* expanding the concept to include low-income and black students and introducing a thirteen-week work/study cycle). This was followed by *Thursday, My Love* (proposing another style of two-couple relationships that I called "synergamy" to replace monogamy). Next came *Come Live My Life*, involving a very practical approach for monogamous couples to switch spouses and enjoy a two-week vacation with another wife or husband. I was able to negotiate a one hundred thousand dollar guaranteed advance on each one of them. To keep down income taxes, NAL agreed to spread the payments and advances over the next ten years. On the surface, it would seem I was enroute to becoming a millionaire writer, but after *The Premar Experiments*, none of the novels earned their advances.

NAL was experiencing financial problems. Their vice-president and head accountant, Herbert Schnall, suddenly took over as president, and Sidney Kramer and their editor Ned Chase (father of Chevy), with whom I had had excellent relationships, were suddenly unemployed. Herb Schnall shocked me when he told me to reread the contract on *Come Live My Life*. It seemed that NAL could publish it any way they wanted to. It was their opinion that paperbacks made all the money. In 1970, hardcovers weren't selling well, and they were going to publish *Come Live My Life* as an original paperback. I knew that meant no reviews and no library sales, but I couldn't dissuade Herb. He assured me that they liked *Come Live My Life* and would go all out to sell a million copies in paperback. To prove it, although they didn't like my latest novel, *Looking Backward II* (and eventually changed the title to *Love Me Tomorrow*), they agreed to a continuing one hundred thousand dollar advance, but I had to agree to an original paperback publication of *Love Me Tomorrow*, too.

I was cornered and too busy with Relief Printing to argue or try to search for another publisher. During the early 1970s the printing business was changing rapidly. It became obvious that Relief would not only have to convert from letterpress and "hot metal" (linotype) production to offset and photo composition. The transition over a period of five years would cost at least a half-million dollars. None of the Rimmers would cut back their pay, and by this time, FH, who wasn't doing much so far as the company was concerned, had found a new interest— air freight. He spent all of his time trying to sell the idea to the major airlines.

During the early 1960s, in my Dr. Jekyll capacity, I had convinced FH that we needed to expand Relief nationwide. Within a two year period we acquired a former competitor in New York City, R. O. H. Hill, Incorporated, as well as related companies in Los Angeles and Walpole, Massachusetts. I was now responsible for four separate companies which produced business cards under different names. We were even investigated by the Federal Trade Commission on complaints that we were a monopoly and controlled the business-card business, and could thus set prices. In the meantime, I was trying to diversify the company into a mail-order catalogue business. A few years later, I would really explore the mail-order business in my novel *The Byrdwhistle Option*. At this point, to facilitate the growth of the company (with FH's approval) Relief had borrowed three hundred fifty thousand dollars from the First National Bank of Boston. The loan was made with only corporate guarantees and an interest rate of only 6 percent and no scheduled payback. A few years later, I needed more money. In 1970, Relief needed to borrow a minimum of seven hundred fifty thousand dollars to stabilize the company's transition to new methods of production, relocate into a one hundred thousand square foot building in Boston, and liquidate R. O. H. Hill and transfer its two-million-dollar sale to Boston.

But now, instead of being able to borrow, the First National Bank suddenly called in our three hundred fifty thousand dollar loan with one year to pay it off. During a conference with the bank and Relief's officials, which FH, who was now eighty, did not attend, the bank's president left the room for a moment. I noticed a bent-in-half copy of *The Harrad Experiment* in his fat file folder on Relief. Would you lend the 1988 equivalent of two million dollars to the author of such a work? The bank didn't. They agreed to increasing the loan to four hundred fifty thousand dollars, but we would have to pledge Relief's accounts receivable, and the Rimmers would personally

Erma Rimmer, 1988

have to guarantee the new loan. FH and my brother refused to pledge their assets. The only choice for me was to file for bankruptcy, but I refused to do that. Although I only owned 14 percent of the stock, to Erma's shock, I pledged our entire personal assets of about two hundred thousand dollars, which included our house. If Relief (FH's company) went under, he would be solvent, but I could move into the poorhouse so far as he was concerned. It didn't bother him, since he now assumed incorrectly that I was a millionaire from my writing. Anyway, he was planning his second around-the-world cruise with Blanche. Relief was my red wagon!

The company was still afloat, but I was sinking as a best-selling novelist. About this time NAL discovered Stephen King. The 1960s were over. Ten years later, I was being thought of as a "leftover hippie." New American Library didn't put any promotion behind *Come Live My Life* or *Love Me Tomorrow.* They simply issued the books and they had a two-month life span on the paperback distribution list, after which NAL claimed that they hadn't earned their advance. It was guaranteed, so they couldn't do much about it. But unfortunately, readers of my earlier novels never knew these later ones existed. I still had managed to sign a contract for another novel, which I called "Soufriere, The Volcano" with a new advance of one hundred twenty-five thousand dollars. I gave NAL a sixteen-page outline of the book and they agreed to publish it hardcover this time with another publisher as they had done with *Premar* and *Thursday, My Love.* But the year before I wrote Soufriere, the honeymoon was over in more ways than one.

Now, in 1975, it seemed as if a heart operation, performed at Mass General, would alleviate Nancy's problems and prolong her life—people with rheumatic heart disease rarely live beyond their early sixties. We were all afraid that she might die suddenly if her heart began to fibrillate out of control. The operation was successful with a valve implant, but in the process, Nancy got an *E. coli* infection. After a terrible month, hooked to every possible lifesaving equipment, unable to talk to us for weeks, none of us believing that she wouldn't recover, she died. Our two-couple marriage was over. We were reduced to a potential ménage à trois, which didn't work. David thought that sharing one wife was an inequitable situation. Then, two years later, though we remained good friends—a lonely man, missing the years the four of us had shared together—David died of a heart attack.

It was 1976. I was nearing my sixtieth birthday. Suddenly, Erma and I were very alone. Our son

Bobby, probably influenced by the fact that most of our friends had been doctors, and because he was well aware of the problem of the third generation taking over the family business, had obtained his M.D. degree from Downstate University of New York. He was doing his residency in cardiology at Boston University and was married. Steve, despite my warnings not to get affiliated with the family business, was working for Relief, but his wife wanted him to quit and become a teacher with her. Blanche and FH were still traveling. Erma and I, still very two-couple oriented, had found no new friends.

We continued to travel, first to Guadeloupe with David, his daughter and her family, where the volcano Soufriere had nearly exploded the year before. It was the subject of a documentary film by the famous German producer Werner Herzog and it interested me as a setting for a new novel. Two years later, because I wanted to experience a Caribbean island during Carnival, we went back to Guadeloupe with a couple a few years younger than we were. It seemed that we might establish another loving relationship. It never evolved, but it provided the background for "Soufriere, the Volcano," my original title for the novel. When NAL received the manuscript in the fall of 1978, several weeks passed. Then, after ten years of reasonably pleasant relationships with them, I received a curt letter from a new editor. "Soufriere" didn't meet their standards, and she asked for repayment of twelve thousand five hundred dollars, a tenth of the advance, which they had agreed to pay me. A year later, NAL capitulated and paid me the remainder of the advance outright, with the provision that they could publish "Soufriere" in any format that they wished, and with much reediting. The reediting was a silly scam to justify themselves. They assigned the job to a newly hired male editor, who practically rewrote the first half of the book, eliminated almost one-third of it and tried to turn it into a typical popular romance novel, which were then selling like hotcakes. It was published in 1980 as *The Love Explosion,* and although I protested, NAL insisted on retaining the annotated bibliography, which they thought was popular with my readers. It made no sense at all in the revised format. Today, I look upon it as an unpublished novel.

Suddenly, I was a man without a country. While this was happening, it became obvious, since no one in the Rimmer family besides myself would put a dime into Relief to save it, even though it was still potentially a very profitable company, Relief was still in trouble. We were now employing close to three hundred people nationwide, but I couldn't borrow the money I needed at reasonable interest rates with a ten-year payback, which we could have easily handled. Finally, there was no other choice. After long negotiations, I sold the company and the new owners assumed Relief's debt and guaranteed what amounted to a two hundred thousand dollar payment divided between Richard and myself over a period of ten years. I managed to exclude FH from the payoff. At eighty-five, I assumed that he already had more than enough money. But when he discovered what I had done, he was so incensed that he revised his will. Previously, my brother and I were coexecutors, but when he died at eighty-seven, I discovered that Richard and his son were trustees. My family was excluded. Until Blanche died, and maybe not even then, I would receive nothing from his estate.

It didn't matter. It was obvious that I would never become wealthy through inheritance. Over a period of twenty years, I had earned a million dollars writing. Combined with my income from Relief, it wasn't enough to make me a millionaire, but Erma and I had lived well and had a loving family with four grandchildren.

A year later, in 1976, although the new owners of Relief had given me a five-year contract to remain with the company as vice-president in sales, they decided that my time had come. Within a year, I wrote *The Byrdwhistle Option.* If you read it, you'll find that I took my revenge on the new owners of Relief.

I was sure that I could sell *Byrdwhistle.* Although it has a definite thesis and a very detailed annotated bibliography in which I continue the story, it is filled with sex and laughter. But then, to my shock, I suddenly discovered in 1980 that I was back on square one.

After so many years, it was obvious that I needed an agent. I contacted Scott Meredith, whom I knew had handled the foreign sales of my novels for Sherbourne Press. He really liked the novel. "I think *The Byrdwhistle Option,*" he announced to the publishing industry, "is a terrific book. It's one of the few novels that I have read which can incorporate technically complex psychological theories such as Abraham Maslow's being, cognition, and eupsychian community concepts into a thoroughly readable, hilarious plot line and make the whole entirely palatable, even to the doubtful reader. It's the perfect complement to Bob Rimmer's *The Harrad Experiment* and *Proposition 31.*"

One year later, Scott wrote me that he was sorry, but after contacting every potential publisher in the United States, he couldn't sell the novel. He refused to explain why. He wouldn't send me any of the publishers' turn downs he'd received, but I suddenly wondered whether I was being informally blacklisted by New American Library. It wasn't an impossible thing to accomplish. Practically all the major publishers and the key editors are in New York City. They all know each other and play musical chairs as they move from one company to another. Thoroughly incensed that they had to pay me one hundred twenty-five thousand dollars for a novel they didn't want to publish, NAL let all of my novels that they had published go out of print and Bantam followed suit with *Harrad.*

I probably never would have been published again, nor would I have continued to write, if I hadn't remembered another one of my hero/mentors, Paul Kurtz, head of the philosophy department at Upstate University of New York. A dynamo of a man, he had been editor of the *Humanist Magazine* and he was a nationally known writer on humanism and creator of *The Humanist Manifesto.* I knew that among his many other endeavors, Paul had started a publishing company called Prometheus Books in Buffalo, which published controversial nonfiction. Would he like to take a flyer with *Byrdwhistle*? He would, but it would have to be based on no advance and no royalty payments whatsoever until the novel sold five thousand hardcover copies or went into paperback. Paul was enthusiastic. We were both sure that after hardcover publication, it would be easily sold to a paperback publisher.

Byrdwhistle was published hardcover in 1983. The close to ten million readers of my other novels were potential buyers, but Prometheus couldn't afford much money for national advertising. Bookstore distribution was limited, and a year later, every paperback publisher in the United States turned it down. Had I really been blacklisted by NAL? It would seem so, but this was only the beginning.

By this time, Erma and I were slowly trying to put together a new life-style. After the death of both Nancy and David, we had joined the famous Unitarian Church in Quincy. I was fascinated by the emergence of Unitarian beliefs, deviating from the original Congregationalists and embracing all religions. Unitarian Universalists accepted the philosophy that all paths lead to God and their religious thinking included an amalgam of agnosticism, theism, deism, and even atheism and humanism, the latter of which needed no Creator.

Intrigued with the fact that both humanism and U/Uism needed some kind of unifying philosophy which would attract the sixty million or more Americans who never go to church, I wrote *The Immoral Reverend.* The basic thesis is that all religions (except the ancient Chinese and Hindu) have denigrated human sexuality in one way or another. My protagonist, Matt Godwin, a graduate of Harvard Divinity and Harvard Business School, proposes that sex itself should become a sacrament and the total wonder of all creation (a kind of Gaia belief), should become a key doctrine, and should be proclaimed from Beacon Street by the president of the Unitarian Universalist society.

I finished *The Immoral Reverend* while William Schultz, whom I had met, was running for president of the U/U Society. I sent him a manuscript copy of the novel, asking for an accolade, which I was sure Paul Kurtz at Prometheus could use to sell the book. Although it was a fast-moving story and is both sexy and controversial, I was sure that it would appeal to Unitarians. Published the year that Schultz was elected president, *The Immoral Reverend* has never been reviewed in any U/U publication, although it appeared in an era when there has been more than one "Immoral Reverend," and the title and sexy story alone should have been a natural for paperback publication, but it was also turned down by all paperback publishers. Was I blacklisted?

By this time, self-employed at the age of sixty-five, I decided to take a new tack. I wrote a nonfiction history of visual sex. The premise was that anything that could be written was no longer censorable (with the one exception of child pornography), but pictorial sex of the naked human body and humans copulating which had been drawn, painted, and sculpted for thousands of years, and in the last hundred had been photographed, was still verboten.

I wrote this book, and in the process reviewed about twenty porno movies, which in 1979 had become the backbone of the videocassette industry since regular filmmakers had not released any of their films. After several turndowns, Bruce Harris, editor and publisher of Crown Books, wrote me that Crown would be interested in publishing a book with just reviews of adult films since nothing like this existed on the market.

It was the first monetary offer for anything I had written since "Soufriere" (*The Love Explosion*). Because of my *Harrad* reputation, I had no trouble getting porno review tapes. In the past nearly ten years as a kind of left-hand occupation, I have reviewed more than twenty-five hundred adult films, which I call sexvids. My shrugging, sometimes laughing interest in sexvids is explained in detail in the first and second edition of *The X-Rated Videotape Guide,* which in 1988 was very much in print and being sold by mail order through Crown's wholly owned Publisher's Central Bureau. I have not only given, in about two hundred fifty words, a detailed review of the plot, the kinds of sex that appear, from normal to kinky and sadistic, but I keep suggesting that in a sane society, if children would grow up seeing human beings naturally naked and the media would show caring human lovemaking, it would make the portrayal of sick sex (and I include thousands of other sexual come-ons besides adult films) totally boring and unnecessary. A sane society would laugh sick sex out of existence.

As an antidote to reviewing sexvids, in the process of writing *The Immoral Reverend,* I discovered another heroine/mentor, Anne Hutchinson, America's first feminist. Anne challenged John Winthrop, governor of the Massachusetts Bay Colony, in 1636, and lost. She was excommunicated from Massachusetts, and, in my opinion, through the machinations of Winthrop and Thomas Dudley was eventually scalped and murdered by the Indians at the age of fifty-three. In my novel *The Resurrection of Anne Hutchinson,* Anne arrives naked on my doorstep on a cold winter night. She lives with me for two weeks while my wife (I call Erma "Emily") is on a two-week European art museum tour with women friends. The novel includes the complete trials of Hutchinson, and I only changed a few words here and there. I was sure that Anne's story as I told it was a natural for a movie, and filmmakers would be interested. If nothing else, since the actual trials of Anne Hutchinson are really fascinating and very hard to locate or read in the original, I assumed that the book would have a good library sale. Thus far, it has sold about three thousand copies and has been turned down by all paperback publishers.

But I keep writing. As Erma tells me, "What else would you do?" At seventy-one, after researching and studying the human brain for several years, I have completed a new novel, *The Oublion Project.* It involves a drug which eliminates short-term memory ("oublion" is from "*oublier,*" which means "to forget") and is used by a German and an Arab doctor to artificially inseminate women who are unaware that they are being used to create a new breed of humans (eugenically) who will, through a superior style education (described in detail), take over the world, and in the process, eliminate all production of lethal weapons. It's a fast-moving, highly controversial novel inspired by Jose Ortega y Gasset, who wrote a book in the 1930s called *The Revolt of the Masses* which suggests a coming takeover of the world by people

The author (right) with his brother, Richard, and mother, Blanche, 1976

with no historical sense who will finally destroy it. Thus far, after seeing a three-page outline and the first chapter, thirty major publishers have refused to read it.

Am I discouraged or angry? The answer is no. In truth, I have never been angry or hated anyone in my life. Nor do I blame my father or anyone else for the person I have become. If FH had not interfered with my life, I might have married someone else, and I might have been more successful. Or I might have divorced many times in my search for Galatea. My wife, my boys, and the people close to me long ago stopped reading what I write—even when it's published in book form. But rarely a week goes by that someone doesn't write me that one or more of my novels has literally changed their life for the better. Although I discontinued putting extended bibliographies in my novels, afraid they might frighten readers who simply wanted to be entertained, the bibliographies that appeared first in *Harrad* and in all the subsequent novels through *The Byrdwhistle Option* inspired thousands of people to argue with me and to think! All through my life, I have acquired and have been inspired by hero/mentors. In *Byrdwhistle,* through H. H. Youman, I even proposed that those who have shallow genealogical roots, like I have, should Adopt an Ancestor, as I have many times, and bring him or her back to life. All through my life, I have refused to make tragedies where no tragedies exist and have been fortunate to live a life filled with Love, Laughter, Learning, and Ludamus, and in the process, I have become a hero/mentor to hundreds of men and women who have gone out of their way to tell me so in writing.

There are always many aspects of a person missing in an autobiography—that's why biographers who dig up missing truths are so popular. Anyone interested in more details can find them in forty or fifty file drawers of correspondence—some of it preserved in *The Harrad Letters* and in *You and I . . . Searching for Tomorrow,* and thanks to Howard Gottlieb, who recognized them as a piece of mid-century Americana—preserved in the Mugar Library of Boston University.

As a futurist, I predict that long after the best-selling novelists of the twentieth century have become boring literary curiosities (and I include Hemingway, Fitzgerald, Faulkner, Updike, Bellow, and even more popular ones who have dominated the best-seller lists for the past fifty years), Bob Rimmer will be rediscovered. My major novels will be reprinted in the "Library of America" series and all of them will be in print. When? Before the turn of the century or just after. Why? Because the "I gotta be me" generation will finally wake up and a new twist on the 1960s "love everybody" philosophy will prevail as the United States faces the inevitable, and millions of men and women throughout the world slowly become aware, for multiple reasons, that we are not independent. We are all—too many billions of us—interdependent and many of the approaches to marriage and the family and premarital and postmarital sex that I have proposed will be the only way to survive and live self-fulfilling lives. As I noted in the dedication of *The Harrad Experiment,* my novels are for the men and women of the twenty-first century, who might find them quaint, but will consider them germinal.

Finally, to end with a chuckle. When I told Bhagwan Shree Rajneesh who is now back in Poona, India (still writing and speaking to an international following of a million or more), that I was writing my autobiography, he wrote me, "Now is not the right time. Your autobiography should end with sannyas. Why let the world renounce you. Why not you renounce it? When a man dies it is ordinary. But when a man renounces, his consciousness reaches to the heights that are possible. Sannyas is not a religion. It is simply a rejoicing in life and a rejoicing in death. My whole concept is that from the cradle to the grave life should be a dance." So, let's go dancing!

BIBLIOGRAPHY

Fiction:

That Girl from Boston. Boston: Challenge, 1962; London: Consul Books, 1965.

The Rebellion of Yale Marratt. Boston: Challenge, 1964; London: New English Library, 1966.

The Harrad Experiment. Los Angeles: Sherbourne, 1966; London: New English Library, 1968.

The Zolotov Affair. Los Angeles: Sherbourne, 1967; London: New English Library, 1969; also published as *The Gold Lovers.* New York: New American Library, 1969.

Proposition Thirty-one. New York: New American Library, 1968; London: New English Library, 1969.

Thursday, My Love. New York: New American Library, 1972; London: New English Library, 1972.

The Premar Experiments. New York: Crown, 1975; London: New English Library, 1976.

Come Live My Life. New York: New American Library, 1977.

Love Me Tomorrow. New York: New American Library, 1978.

The Love Explosion. New York: New American Library, 1980.

The Byrdwhistle Option. Buffalo, N.Y.: Prometheus Books, 1982.

The Immoral Reverend. Buffalo, N.Y.: Prometheus Books, 1985.

The Resurrection of Anne Hutchinson. Buffalo, N.Y.: Prometheus Books, 1987.

The Oublion Project. Forthcoming.

Nonfiction:

The Harrad Letters to Robert H. Rimmer. New York: New American Library, 1969; London: New English Library, 1971.

Adventures in Loving. New York: New American Library, 1973.

You and I . . . Searching for Tomorrow: The Second Book of Letters to Robert H. Rimmer, Plus Marriage 2000, a Participation. New York: New American Library, 1973.

The Love Adventurers. New York: Dell, 1979.

The X-Rated Videotape Guide. New York: Arlington House, 1984; revised and expanded edition. New York: Harmony Books, 1986.

The Adult Videotape Guide. Denver, Co.: Sundance Associates, 1989.

Raw Talent: The Autobiography of Jerry Butler, Porno Star, as Told to Bob Rimmer and Catherine Tavel. Buffalo, N.Y.: Prometheus Books, 1989.

Sound Recordings:

Discussion of Proposition Thirty-one. Big Sur Recordings, 1968.

The Harrad Experiment. Big Sur Recordings, 1968.

A Day with Rimmer at the University of Missouri. Big Sur Recordings, 1971.

A New Moral Minority. Cuyahoga Community College, 1981.

Frederick Turner

1943-

AN AUTOBIOGRAPHICAL MEDITATION

Frederick Turner on the Danube, 1988

I was born on November 19, 1943. I have very few memories of the time before I came to full self-awareness, in about 1951 when we were living in what was then Northern Rhodesia, now Zambia in south central Africa. We were driving somewhere along forest roads in my father's truck. This awakening was immediately coupled with the need to communicate to others the astonishing fact of my own inner personal being, and my experience of the world; consciousness, memory, and knowledge that I was a writer all came together and were essentially the same thing.

Inner personal being was an extraordinary phenomenon, but I did not especially love or even like the personality I had discovered; and it is still so. Indeed, now that I know how many writers have so excellently communicated this feeling—Rousseau, Donne, Thoreau, Shakespeare in the sonnets but not often, thank God, in the plays, and so on—it seems to me to be entirely unnecessary to do it again. The commitment I have taken on to write this memoir tells me to examine myself, to embark, as they say, on an inner journey; but the self that I discover is curiously tasteless, that is when it is not rather unpleasantly flavored—a slightly fecal smell, is it not?—with considerations of self-interest. Otherwise my selfhood tastes like clean lukewarm water or perhaps like one's own saliva.

So the exercise of self-exploration seems somewhat pointless. However, at rare intervals I have felt an impulse to examine myself and my memories, and sometimes the attempt to do so led to insight. Perhaps then there is some justification for such a memoir.

So; I was born in East Haddon, Northamptonshire, in England. My father, Victor Turner, was at that time a conscientious objector, and had been set to dig up unexploded German bombs. My mother, Edie, was in the land army, a British women's organization designed to replace male labor in the fields in order to free up manpower for the military. We lived in a Gipsy caravan, I am told, though I remember nothing of that period except perhaps an advertisement showing a map of Britain drawn as if it were a person driving a car; I still see Scotland as a craggy head looking westward.

I do not believe that there could be better parents than my father and mother. My father was great in his intellectual and imaginative achievements, so I could easily admire him; but he was also a deeply human person, affectionate, funny, and appalled by his own imagined faults. He always had time for me, and managed to convince me that my own calling to poetry was what he would have really wished to follow himself, and that he considered anthropology to be a lesser thing. Thus I was not overwhelmed by him, when in fact his almost superhuman intelligence, erudition, and creative imagination might have been too much for many sons.

My mother is the most loving and best human being I have known: readers can take this statement as they please, judging it by their general estimate of my reliability and objectivity. I do not always agree with her, and she has her annoying habits; but she is wise, generous, unfailingly cheerful, passionate, perceptive, morally noble, and at the same time utterly down-to-earth, without any airs or pomposity whatsoever. She is also courageous as a lion, and something of a desperado: a distinguished anthropologist in her own right, she recently as a widow in her late sixties travelled by sailing-boat with a pair of Eskimo spirit-doctors from arctic Alaska to Siberia, so that they could compare notes with their cousins across the Bering Sea. The year before that she was living in central Africa with tribal healers. She gave me so much love—which I now recognize in my feeling for my own sons—that I have never really feared anything ultimately, and know that I exist and that I am what I intend to be; and I am in turn—though not as much as she—capable of love and uncalculating generosity.

Father, Victor W. Turner, about 1982

After the war my father commenced his graduate work in anthropology at the University of London; we lived in Hastings, on the south coast, in a flat belonging to his mother, Violet. Gran-Gran, as we called her, was an ex-actress. She used to take me off conspiratorially, which rather alarmed me, and spoil me with sweets and teach me tricks of the theater; she wanted me to love her, and I liked her very much. Her mother, Ga, a formidable and splendid little Scottish lady whose white hair had been red when she was young, also lived either with us or in the same apartment building. I knew that she was a sounder personality than Violet. Some of her phrases have become part of family folklore—when a sulking child put out its lower lip she would say, "Don't stick your platform out, there's no show tonight," and when someone who was present was referred to in the third person she would ask sarcastically, "Who's 'she'?—the cat's mither?" My father's father, Arthur, whom I never knew, divorced by Violet for his philandering, had been a radio scientist and had worked with Marconi and with Baird on the development of television; he had been a fighter pilot during the Battle of Britain.

My mother's family were somewhat-decayed English gentlefolk, with generations of Anglican clerics, doctors, missionaries, judges, and younger sons of younger brothers in the escutcheon. Her mother, "Granny-in-Cambridge," had had a stroke

Mother, Edith Davis Turner, about 1982

and could not say any words except "no." She would say "No no no no no no no" with great force and affection when we went to visit her, and take me for rides in her electric wheelchair. My parents were both idealistic young Communists at the time, and there was some strain between my father, Vic, and my mother's family, who believed she had married beneath her. (My father's family felt on the other hand that Vic had been seduced by this wild young Communist rebel, and worried that she would hurt his promising career.) Some maternal great-uncle, to my mother's disgust, once praised my hands as being sturdy engineer's hands. Edie knew I was going to be an artist and felt an aspersion against my father's blood.

Since this time I suppose I have rebelled both against the English class system and against the Communist and left-wing opposition to it. Both seem to be ignobly interested in how people think of one, and to be so self-serving in their arguments and attitudes as to disqualify them from any validity. I have learned to tolerate prejudice of others against me rather cheerfully, and to expect it; it is my job to dispel that prejudice by my acts and my capacities, not theirs to change what is in effect a useful habit to them. Of course I cannot take their minds seriously until they show that flexibility and capacity for epiphanic self-criticism which marks a free human being. I am disturbed and hurt, though, not by their

feelings toward me but by their betrayal in themselves of the noble human destiny that we share.

It may seem strange and a little disgusting that I, a "successful" white Anglo-Saxon male, should complain of prejudice against me. But I am not complaining, merely trying to describe my experience. I suspect that we are so made that in the absence of strong and sustained assaults against our self-respect we simply become more sensitive to weak and transient ones, and that the Anglican gentry who made my parents feel defiant had themselves suffered pangs of class discrimination as great as those of Stendhal's Julien Sorel or of some lower-middle-class black youth in high school. I on the other hand very early took prejudice against me as a sign that I was special and marked out for a great destiny, an idea no doubt wisely inculcated in me by my parents: I have taught it to my own sons, who are part Chinese.

What prejudice could I possibly have suffered? Prejudice against strangers everywhere; prejudice by the little Ndembu kids in Africa because I was white (in some villages the smaller children, who had never seen white people before, would burst into tears of terror at seeing me, a real live ghost, and hide behind their mothers); prejudice against me when I lived in the north of England, because of my upper-class accent, inherited from my mother; prejudice against me by my schoolmates and friends in Manchester when I passed the English eleven-plus exam and they didn't (a large group of them, including my two best friends, waited one day on a street corner and beat me up); prejudice against me by the rich because I was poor; prejudice against me at Manchester Grammar School when I became a Catholic; prejudice against me when I came to America because I was English and in the academy because I was a poet and did not have a Ph.D. (my degree, the old Oxford B.Litt., is a Ph.D. in all but name, but many Americans take it to be merely a baccalaureate); prejudice against me now because I am a white male in a position that is imagined to be one of power.

But as I have said, I do not condemn prejudice in others, only in myself. It is impossible to live one's life at all without making generalizations, and all generalizations are prejudices.

Before we went to Hastings my brother Bob was born. I was nearly three at the time but remember nothing of the event at all. I always loved Bob with a tender and slightly envious passion, and we are still very close intellectually, emotionally, and imaginatively. He has become a rather distinguished physicist, working on nuclear magnetic resonance scanning (he also has an advanced degree in anthropology and some expertise in medicine and neuroanatomy; he is working toward the use of NMR scanning to reveal the physiology of cultural learning in the brain). He is a very good man, better than I am because less inclined to put great human achievements above the welfare of ordinary people. I am on a case-by-case basis very compassionate, but I don't have as much generalized social compassion as some. Bob has both. Bob's first marriage, to a very young local girl in the Manchester area, didn't work out, and as Bob was a Catholic at the time, I was grilled by an emissary of the Vatican about their marriage. Apparently I said the right things, because the marriage was annulled. Bob then began an extremely happy marriage with his present wife. They have a boy.

In Hastings my sister Irene (Rene) was born, an event of which I do very dimly remember one or two details. Rene has led a somewhat stormy life. She rebelled against our parents rather more than did Bob and I, though to their great delight she married a black premed student at Cornell University, where she did her undergraduate degree. We were all very fond of him but it turned out later that he would beat Rene up, and though Rene could, we knew, be pretty provoking, we forgave her for getting a divorce. Later we realized how arrogantly silly our attitude had been. Rene then married a very gentle and decent poet, and they have an exquisite clever little

Frederick, Robert, and Irene Turner in the Zambesi rapids, Northern Rhodesia (now Zambia), about 1953

girl. The older Rene gets the wiser, funnier, and sweeter she gets.

I do, now I come to think of it, remember some things about Hastings. There was a little girl called Christine at primary school whom I loved, and who showed herself to me under a rhododendron bush, and a bad boy called John Braybrooks whom I feared and admired. My father would take me on weekends to a park where we would feed the black swans and race twigs in the stream under the bridge, and he would by magic extract threepenny bits from my ear, wherewith we purchased a Wall's ice cream.

After Hastings we went to live in Northern Rhodesia. Actually my father went first to prepare the way for his young wife and family. While he was away I had a terrible nightmare about a dragon breaking through the ceiling to get at me and was discovered sleepwalking, given hot cocoa, and sent back to bed without waking up. I have always found hot cocoa very comforting.

More and more memories now begin to come back, but they are surely boring to anyone but myself, or if potentially interesting, so dishearteningly similar to those of other autobiographers as to be not worth the trouble of putting down in an amusing way. The remarkable thing about human beings is that the deeper one gets into their inner personalities the more alike they are. The glories of human individuation come from people's interaction with the world, what they do with their own talents and handicaps, and most important of all the recursive, self-organizing feedback system of soul-making that can spiral amazingly out of the original stereotypical brew. And funnily enough, when one considers this amazing spiral one is really getting quite away from what autobiography is all about, and from what readers want to hear; also from one's motivation for writing a memoir, which is, I assume, not to boast of one's success but to discover something in oneself that naggingly wants to be heard.

I do in fact find in this process of recall—one which is reassuringly unresearchable, for I either remember something or I don't, and if I don't it is by definition not relevant—an insight into myself, into my sexual nature as a matter of fact, which I shall not mention here because of its banality but which is interesting and new to me. What is the use of such insights? By the time one is as old as I am, it's too late, if one has made one's life and made it as voluntarily as I have mine. I do what I do, and my psychology will die with me. The only important thing now is the extent to which my actions affect other people, especially those not yet as fully formed as I; and more deeply still, how morally, esthetically, and philosophically beautiful those actions are.

In Africa, in any case, I came alive as a writer and as a self. It was a kind of paradise for a boy; we lived in a Ndembu village forty miles from the nearest white people, and while my parents conducted ethnological research I played with the Ndembu boys or with my brother or by myself in the savanna (Rene played with a strange tiny deaf girl called Dora and developed with her a total telepathic communication system). We would wake up to the straw smell of the grass huts we slept in, and the smell of woodsmoke from the sleepy cooking-fires, and the sound of human voices and birdsong. We ate smoky porridge with wonderfully various-tasting raw milk (brought in warm by truck in small churns from the Plymouth Brethren missionary farm) and brown sugar. In the cool of the morning my mother, Edie, would teach us out of a correspondence course, which she departed from at frequent intervals to explain things with meticulous and graphic metaphors. I liked drawing best, and did a magnificent rooster with a multicolored tail, and a fine ocean liner from the front, with a great curving bow, and clipper ships with far too many sails.

The ocean liner reminds me of something I missed out, which was the travelling to and from Africa. The delicious strange boredom of an ocean liner! We travelled by the Union-Castle line, whose colors were purple, black, white, and a thin line of red, very handsome. I would find a comfortable place in the sun near the stern where nobody came, and sit holding my knees watching the white wake turn violently over and over and over, hearing the odd shell-sound, the muted blowy hush and rumble and swash of voyaging, smelling the tar of ropes and the diesel odor and the salt clean smell of the sea.

On one of those voyages—four in all, because we broke our stay in Africa with a six-month return to England, when we lived in Manchester—I developed my first theories of epistemology, by noticing how close objects seemed double when I focussed on something distant. I tried pushing an eyeball about and found a second world, at a slant from the other. I also committed my second crime (my first had been biting my nursery-school teacher, Miss Smith, very sharply in the hand as she was taking me to the headmistress on a false accusation). I stole three sixpences from my mother and bought a bar of Cadbury's naval chocolate from the fascinating ship's store. We were very poor in those days—postwar graduate-student poor—and could ill afford the

theft. And they never found out until I told them, years later. The crime rode my conscience for weeks, and helped develop a pronounced sense of pathos for other people which still complicates my life if I am called on to be ruthless.

There were visions, sailing down to Africa, that were so masterful and so unearthly that they have become archetypal in my memory and have lost almost all of their actual detail—morning landfall on Ascension Island, the ship quartering across a lapping sea of rose and salmon pink and pure oil blue toward the great towering volcanic stump of the island rock. And our destination, Capetown: Table Mountain climbing over the horizon, the city opening up and opening up into a gold and blue afternoon, the mountain crags as clear as crystal, the great kloofs (ravines) in shadow, full of eucalyptus trees, the city white and pretty as a storybook republic. We lived in Capetown for six months, and I got into a fight with an Afrikaans boy at school, and had a strange Cathy-and-Heathcliff friendship with a little girl called Lynn Carneson. She was the daughter of a heroic protester against apartheid who was imprisoned later in the treason trials. (Vic nearly got arrested for the same sort of thing.) Lynn had the remarkable ability, which I had thought unique to myself, of being able to close her eyes and teleport herself to different parts of the universe.

But I had begun to tell about my days in Kajima, our village in Zambia. After lessons we would be free, and as gradually the heat of the day came up a group of small boys, led by the lean and charismatic Sakeru, would form up and go down to the Luakera river to swim. The banks of the river would sometimes be so thick with yellow and blue butterflies that you could not see the ground. The first time I left the streambed and genuinely paddled along in the current was immensely exhilarating. Also very interesting were the village girls, and their remarkable differences when they swam, a little further down the river.

Sometimes we—the village boys—would beg the head or testicles of a goat that was being slaughtered by the village elders, and take it down to the river, and build a fire and cook it, tearing off delicious charred pieces and scooping out hot brain. We fed the scraps to Mistake, one of the village dogs who followed us about. At times we would conduct wars with other groups of boys, and would make weapons which, now I think about it, make my blood run cold: bows and arrows, catapults made with strips of rubber from truck inner tubes with which we fired heavy round nodules of iron ore, and makeshift spears. But a salutary cowardice and good luck seemed to stave off serious injury. I am glad my mother did not know about this.

Sometimes we would watch and help out with the spring burning, when the village would burn off the old elephant grass for miles around, and great wedges and scuds of terrified duiker and gemsbok would leap wild-eyed through the flames. Among the burnt roots you could find, after the fire had passed, delicious red fruits—nshindwa—warmed with the flames, very sour and sweet and of a flavor that if I were to taste it again, would surely bring tears to my eyes. The African wild fruits! The mild gold moocha, my father's favorite; the tart wild plum, mfungu; the loquat and the fresh-carved guava; the heavy dented mango, blushing yellow, with its rigid cuttlefish-like kernel; the pawpaw as lukewarm as heaven. And then the flowers: whole valleys in spring, crimson with moist cannas; dells among the Zambesi rapids carpeted with leopard-skin orchids; a single exquisite white wild iris; a yellow and brown vine flower of astonishing scent that grew in the riverside jungles or "eetus"; and hundreds of species of dry-season flowers, very scrawny in the stem, with tiny frills of

scarlet or puffballs of blue that Bob, my scientist brother, carefully drew, recorded, and classified.

Sometimes we would watch or take part, if it was appropriate to our status, in the Ndembu rituals: the hunters' dance, with its imagery of blood and smoke and iron and its wonderful mimicry of the hunter's stalk and the characteristic gait of the animal prey; the women's puberty ritual, from which we were jeeringly driven away by the elder women; and the curing rituals, which involved fascinating and gut-wrenching practices, like placing cupping horns by suction all over the patient's back. The men's circumcision rituals took place secretly away from the village, but I, like all the boys, was so imbued with the knowledge and anticipation of the ordeal that I never felt myself to be a real man until, in the late 1960s, I was circumcised in Santa Barbara, California, for medical reasons.

The village boys were by custom permitted every sort of sexual experimentation, and there were beautiful copper-colored or ebon little girls who were equally interested. It was a delightful initiation, fraught with heart-stopping strangeness and metamorphosis, and I am sure it contributed to my very

"A game between black and white": Frederick Turner in Lusaka, Northern Rhodesia, about 1953

idealistic attitude toward sex and my lifelong love of women in general.

In the evening Musona, our cook, would prepare dinner: fresh or cured wild venison (there was a soup made of biltong—dried antelope meat—that was especially good), sweet potatoes, peas that we had grown ourselves, and afterward the Victorian steamed syrup puddings that Musona loved to make but would not dream of eating; and lovely sweet cape gooseberries or wild fruits.

Then, best of all, my father would read to us: Rider Haggard (*Nada the Lily, Montezuma's Daughter, She, King Solomon's Mines*), Kipling (the *Jungle Books, Kim*), Selma Lagerlöf, the Moomin books, *The Swiss Family Robinson* (which I then reread about eight or nine times, lying in the sun in my favorite spot where I could lean against our stores tent), *Rob Roy,* Charles Kingsley (*Hereward the Wake, Westward Ho!*), R. L. Stevenson (*Kidnapped, Treasure Island, The Black Arrow*), *Black Cock's Feather, Coral Island,* much of Shakespeare, Arthur Ransome, Edgar Rice Burroughs (whose Barsoom is still central to my imagination, though his Venusian adventures did it for me too), Arthur Conan Doyle (especially *The Lost World* and the other Professor Challenger stories, and the adventures of Brigadier Gerard and Sir Nigel), Hornblower, Doctor Dolittle, the Greek, Norse, and Irish myths, King Arthur, almost all of John Buchan, P. G. Wodehouse's Jeeves books, Jack London, Evelyn Waugh (very funny but a bit advanced for us), the poems of Gerard Manley Hopkins, James Thurber, H. G. Wells (almost all he wrote), and of course when they came out after our return to England, *The Lord of the Rings,* complete, twice through.

It is dangerous to fill the head of a boy with such stuff; it unfits him for the twentieth century, and I have always felt myself to be really a nineteenth-century, or possibly sixteenth-century, man stranded in the wrong time and wanting to get back. This, combined with my long exile in England—for so, after my life in Africa, it seemed to me—formed in me the peculiar desire to transform the coming twenty-first century into one of hope, exploration, aspiration, adventure, and wild poetry; perhaps this is why my favorite genre is poetic science fiction.

The books I list here are only a selection from the fifteen or so years of reading I got from Vic. He was a marvellous reader: each character had his or her own voice, accent, rhythm, and consciousness. We would implore him to go on reading, sometimes all evening, and developed a strange imploring ritual, like Egyptians worshipping their god with salaams, to get him to go on when the chapter ending left us in

unbearable suspense. After the story the whole family would have a big collective hug. It was like when the family would sing in the truck while we were driving across the continent. As I write this it seems suddenly and bewitchingly bizarre, and I am moved to the heart by the memory. It seemed quite normal to me at the time, but perhaps it was an anomaly, a little island of privileged blessedness in a bitter, terrified, and preoccupied world. I don't think I have given as much to my own children, though in an intermittent way I have tried. They did not seem to want it as much as we wanted what Vic and Edie had to give. It would be too easy to blame television.

It was the reading at night, I realize now, that kept me going once we returned to England. At first we lived in a grey working-class area north of Manchester; then we moved to a suburb south of the city which was pleasant enough but in which I felt like a wolfman in exile. I got very pudgy, passed my exams with Edie's coaching—the eleven-plus, for which my little companions exacted their class revenge—and got into Manchester Grammar School.

Manchester Grammar was a boys' day school, a private foundation supported by State money, which admitted on full scholarship large numbers of poor working-class and lower-middle-class boys as well as those who could pay. It was at that time of a Bertrand Russell progressive scientific socialist agnostic bent. Its academic reputation was excellent, but I was a very poor scholar. I was lazy, contemptibly weak-willed when it came to homework, unathletic, dreamy, and always ridiculed by my schoolmates for my "la de da" (highfalutin) language. Luckily for me I was quite large and able to defend myself when my tormentor was within range, though I was not very mobile. Also there was in my class an even more vulnerable boy who took some of the heat off me, a soft bespectacled Jewish kid called Goda, who was regularly tormented. I would sometimes protest at their treatment of him and once stood between him and harm, but was too afraid of reprisals against myself to be his reliable defender, a dereliction for which I still feel guilty. Part of the problem was that though I sympathized with Goda, I did not like him much myself: I felt he was rather self-centered and sometimes hostile.

At Manchester Grammar I developed a lifelong dislike for reductive logical positivist ways of thinking, as well as internalizing the rather rigorous logical critiques and correctives against wishful thinking which it embodied. I also acquired a deep respect and liking for Jews, of whom there were many at the school—an attraction mingled, I suspect, with a certain envy. They had a group with whom they could identify, which valued art and philosophy and science and morality, whereas I was beginning to feel that with the exception of my family there seemed to be no group to which I could comfortably belong. I disliked the shallow and philistine rich kids I knew, with their televisions and their Ford Zephyrs and their plush furniture. I hated even more the hypocrisy of the resentful and cynical socialists, who simply wanted the same cheap things for themselves, and would be prepared to loot them if they got a chance, and wanted to experience the cracking bash of bourgeois heads against the pavement; while mouthing impressive-sounding rhetoric about the proletariat. The upper classes ignored culture, or sought it as a status symbol; the lower classes loathed it because it was beautiful and noble and called unbearably for virtues and sacrifices that made them feel small.

The only subjects I was good at were art and English composition. I won a couple of art prizes and regularly published poetic essays and poems in *Ulula,* the school magazine, writings which also won prizes. I was very bad at languages, though my patient teachers managed to force enough French, German, and Latin into me to pass my "O" Levels. I started out well in mathematics, and loved geometry, but algebra was never explained to me properly to make me understand its real meaning, and so I fell behind. I refused to just follow a formula; I wanted to know why. By the time we reached trigonometry and what would now be called precalculus I was going through the motions. In the years since school I have been recurrently fascinated with mathematics, however, and from time to time I have made more progress, teaching myself out of books and getting my distinguished mathematical friends to teach me, in algebra, the theory of calculus, topology, number theory, set theory, mathematical logic, and the philosophy of mathematics. The same pattern applies to my science schooling; the moment I ceased to get clear explanations of why some formula should be applied in a given case, I lost interest; but even at that time I devoured popular-science books out of the library, and have since greatly enlarged my knowledge of biology, chemistry, physics, astronomy, and cosmology. I also designed and built model aircraft of various types, and learned how to use algebraic formulae in aerodynamic design. I always did very well in school geography, and in fact attained a better percentage in that subject than in English in the highest national examination, "Schol" Level, when I was seventeen. History was for me a mixed subject; I did well when I

had the right teacher. But I so disliked the deterministic and reductionistic left-wing account of history, while suspecting the "Whig" notion of progress toward a rational liberal State, that I never felt fully at home in historiography. Now with the courage of my adult convictions, having read Hegel, Nietzsche, and Collingwood, and having more recently realized how devastating the new theories of chaos are to any linear causal account of history, the subject has begun to interest me again.

In the sixth form, at last, I encountered a truly marvelous teacher, John Armstrong, who taught me English literature. His spirit, his complex thought, his strange metaphors, and his utterly personal and immediate response to literature are the inspiration for whatever is good in my own teaching. Armstrong was a great eccentric: in the middle of the class he would go and look out of the window for two electrifying minutes at a time. We could all imitate his loony upper-class fruity drawl. He had been a commando, I think, and walked with a limp. He tutored me at home, where I met his wife, with whom he had been in love for twenty years. From him I learned wonderful things about T. S. Eliot's *Four Quartets,* Shakespeare's *Henry the Fourth* and *Antony and Cleopatra, Paradise Lost,* and *Tess of the D'Urbervilles.*

When I was about fifteen the whole family was converted to Catholicism. My father and mother had realized, both because of Hungary and because of the spiritual poverty of Marxism, that they were no longer Communists. My mother had been active in the Ban the Bomb movement in Manchester, and I had helped decorate floats for the demonstrations. But it became clear to Edie, to her horror, how closely the Campaign for Nuclear Disarmament and the trades unions were controlled by the Communist party, and how in turn the Communist party was under the direct discipline of the Moscow Party Line.

We became very devout mystical esthetic Catholics. I went to mass every morning before school with my father, practiced various mortifications of the flesh, and had visions. These resembled my own personal visions, which usually involved an ecstatic transcendence of the world together with a joyful awareness of the whole universe in all its detail; but there was a more terrifying and numinous—and at the same time strangely sweet and gentle—tone about the religious visions. Once I saw the rose window of the old church in Stockport, in midwinter, covered with green climbing vines. Another time I sensed God on all fours in the nave of the church, like a huge beast, almost too big for the building. But visions is as visions does, it seems to me. If one is a

At Lake Geneva, in Lausanne, Switzerland, 1963

better and kinder person for them, or if they result in great insight or art, they can be given some credit. Otherwise someone who has them is experiencing nothing really more amazing than daily existence itself. Just to be alive and aware is a miracle that dwarfs all other miracles to insignificance. Likewise the astonishing logic and beauty of the universe as revealed by science—what could be more interesting than that? But perhaps the function of visions is to arouse in us just such a sense of the miracle of everyday reality.

During the years in Manchester I visited Scotland in the vacations, and developed an enduring passion for my father's homeland. One of my recurrent dreams is of a wild and dreadful coast under an apocalyptic sky, and a shining sea torn by fierce currents, bearing upon it a multitude of dazzling, dangerous, and barren islands—the whole place drenched with an almost radioactive feeling of danger, but also of unbearable joy and ecstasy. I saw that vision come true years later in Santa Barbara, when on a stormy day after the birth of my first son, Daniel, I saw the islands of Anacapa and Santa Rosa blazing upon a silver and incandescent ocean.

John Armstrong's coaching got me into Oxford University by the skin of my teeth. I was accepted at Christ Church, which had the reputation of being the college of Evelyn Waugh's Sebastian Flyte—a college of aristocrats, esthetes, degenerates, eccen-

trics, homosexuals, and mindless "bloodies" (upper-class jocks), a reputation well deserved in my subsequent experience. My tutor was J. I. M. Stewart, better known as Michael Innes, creator of Inspector Appleby, the detective.

But before I went to Oxford I spent about nine months with the family in California, where my father had been invited to spend a year in the Palo Alto Center for the Study of the Behavioral Sciences. This was 1961–1962. Being in California was like being in Africa again. I had the same feeling of freedom and of high adventure there that I had had in Africa; particularly when with a contingent of Catholic students from Stanford University I went down to Mexico on a sort of amateur Peace Corps expedition. We lived in the mountains and built for a poverty-stricken village a schoolhouse, a basketball court, and a dispensary. We had begged medical supplies for the dispensary and arranged for a medical student from Mexico University to come out from time to time and prescribe. I got Montezuma's Revenge and spent a week in bed, in a high fever, reading Kazantzakis's *Last Temptation of Christ* and the Book of Revelation, and having visions. My weight went down by thirty pounds. I suspect there was something strange in the curative potion that a kind old Mexican crone would make me drink and which the locals swore by. Later I discovered the joys of hitchhiking in America, and read *The Dharma Bums*. During the time in California I also read books two, four, and six of the *Aeneid* in the original Latin; this experience, and *Paradise Lost,* made me decide to be an epic poet. It was twenty years later that I achieved this ambition. California seemed paradise to me, and I hated to go back to England. I had fallen in love with America, and resolved to return the moment my formal education was over.

Nevertheless my undergraduate years at Oxford (1962–1965) were a deeply poetic experience, the more so because in the light of my resolve to leave England it was all oddly retrospective. I wrote my first long narrative poem, about America of course, an apocalypse concerning an atomic war and its mystical resurrected aftermath. All this time I had been writing poetry off and on, about Africa, Scotland, and America, and also more introspectively about my own reflexive consciousness.

There were some poems, not many, about the girls I clumsily and very prudishly courted; I was extremely unattractive and horrified at the idea of committing a mortal sin, so I could not have been a very interesting date. I have always loved women, of all kinds and all ages; it seems to me to be an amazing thing to be a woman, and I tend to put them on pedestals. At Oxford I met Mei Lin, who was reading French and German literature at St. Anne's College. She was a close friend of my then girlfriend, who was in the process of dropping me because she thought I was crazy: I clearly wanted sex but would not do it because of my religion. Sensible Jean realized that this was bad news.

But Mei Lin was in her own utterly different way just as strange as I. The daughter of Chinese immigrants who had run a laundry and a restaurant, she had by sheer willpower and intelligence worked her way up the English class and education system and become on the surface a quintessential Oxford student. Deeply religious in her values, she was also deeply skeptical. At the time we met she herself was moving toward Catholicism. She was and is very beautiful—and more than beautiful, supremely graceful in voice and movement—and I fell slowly in love with her. But Mei Lin did not make things easy, because she is especially skeptical about romance, and is a lifelong pessimist. I am an optimist. Eventually she married me in 1966 with the air of having nothing better to do. We have been happily and faithfully married ever since, our temperaments profoundly incompatible, our opinions quite different, and our interests at odds. She dislikes poetry readings and most poets, and never goes to any of my lectures or readings if she can possibly avoid it. She refuses to read my writings until they are published. Politically

Frederick Turner (left, in front of bus) preparing to go to Mexico, 1962

she is a bleeding heart, personally a stony conservative; I tend toward the opposite. Mei Lin is the biggest and most interesting intellectual challenge I have ever known—I swear at her behind her back for her unremitting negativeness—and I fall in love with her all over again every few months.

We have had two sons, both of them of entirely unexpected personality, both with all the independence and orneriness of their most eccentric relatives on both sides, fine boys actually who have resisted my attempts to educate them at every turn. But Daniel is turning into a serious philosopher, as well as an ice-blooded rock climber and white-water kayaker, and Benjamin too is going to be some kind of intellectual, I think, despite his obsessive interest in baseball.

I stayed on at Oxford (1965–1967) to do a dissertation on Shakespeare's philosophy of time, a project on which I had begun to work at Manchester Grammar School, had not relinquished through my undergraduate years, and in which I persisted against the advice of all the authorities including my supervisor, Helen Gardner. Dame Helen was finally won over by my evident intensity and enthusiasm, and the result won the approval of my examiners, Lord David Cecil and John Bayley. It was published later by Oxford University Press as *Shakespeare and the Nature of Time,* and still has a small but substantial reputation among Shakespeareans. Dame Helen wanted me to apply for a lectureship at Leeds University, but I took one look at the place and the faculty committee, disliked them, and sabotaged the interview. Dame Helen was furious but found me a job as an assistant professor of English at the University of California, which was where I really wanted to go. So began a five-year period in Santa Barbara, from 1967 to 1972.

In taking this position I unwittingly deprived Mei Lin of the fruits of her long effort to master the English class and education system, which might eventually have amounted to a headmistress-ship in a good English school, and plunged her once more into the marginal position of the immigrant. This is but one of the crimes of a lifetime, whose guilt cannot ever be expunged but whose structure helps to shape and organize the story of people's lives—a story which can have the greater elegance for the greater pain. It is quite remarkable to me that she did not leave me and return to England to pursue a career. She is very loyal, but perhaps also she felt it was too late by the time she realized what had happened.

During our first year of marriage we had lived in a tumbledown sixteenth-century cottage belonging to an archaeologist friend of ours who used to practice archaeology on the walls of the house, and had uncovered a seventeenth-century bread oven and

The author with his family, Mei Lin, Daniel (left), and Benjamin, 1982

some shards of pottery. It was at the edge of a village green in Marsh Baldon, outside Oxford. In Santa Barbara we lived in a cedar shack overgrown with peppertrees and acacias and aloes and eucalyptuses and loquats. We had magnificent windows that looked out over the Pacific. For the first few years I taught happily and successfully at the fairly new state university, as the English department gradually descended into a state of insane and paranoid civil war. But as time went on things darkened for us too. Daniel was born, and we felt a delirious but terrified joy. I was too young and inexperienced—and too self-centered—to be much help to Mei Lin, and now she discovered the horrors of American suburban isolation. Our marriage was tested then more severely than at any other time. It seemed to me that I had utterly failed in my life and that I had taken another person, and possibly a third, with me in the process. The upshot was that we stuck together but lost our religious faith.

Meanwhile my poetry was rapidly mutating towards its early maturity. I began to question the prevalent short free verse existentialist imagist lyric. I discovered the wonderful economy and suggestiveness of poetic narrative, and then more gradually refined my early formal experiments into a full-blooded return to meter. I met some of the California poets, and although we did not really have much in common, and I learned nothing from them, they were tolerant of me. I published three small chapbooks with Unicorn Press and its successor, Christopher's Books; then Wesleyan University Press took my first full-size collection of poems, *Between Two Lives*. Much later Christopher's Books, under the redoubtable editorship of Missy Mytinger, published another major collection, *Counter-Terra*.

I read Whitehead, Bergson, Polanyi, Koestler, Heisenberg, and a great deal of science, and began to work my way toward the metaphysics which I am still exploring today: one in which the universe is a radically creative evolutionary process, essentially divine, governed by laws of science that it evolved for itself, a process which generated us as its nervous system and growing point. The hierarchical structure of the universe and of our bodies was a living fossil of the stages of their own development. Especially important was the realization that matter was not basic but only one of the early forms taken by the autopoesis of the world, and that therefore the deterministic properties of matter did not apply either to more primitive entities such as subatomic particles or to more advanced ones such as life.

During this time I read Nabokov's *Ada,* Borges's *Ficciones,* and Thomas Mann's *Magic Mountain* and *Doctor Faustus.* These works turned me into a post-modernist, and I learned from them (in what I believe to be a deeper and more positive way) what many of my contemporaries were later to learn from Barthes, Derrida, Deleuze and Guattari, Lyotard, and Baudrillard. Out of this experience was to come my strange postmodern science-fiction novel *A Double Shadow,* which gained for me a brief reputation as an avant-garde novelist in France when it appeared in the French translation. So for me this was a fertile if unhappy period.

But somehow we could do nothing with California; though we had formed a few real friendships, most of our relationships were of the California mellow variety, without richness or depth, and we were lonely and disappointed. Meanwhile the counterculture, which had seemed so attractive from England, became more and more violent, drugged, ideological, and cynical. I had during the weeks of sometimes bloody demonstrations against the draft taken a position against the Vietnam War but also against the paranoia and vicious prejudice of those who opposed the war: it seemed to me that people of good will could support the war and offer good reason to do so, though I did not. My class, like everybody else's, was disrupted quite at random by the Black Students' Union, when in fact we were in large agreement with their grievances. I and some other members of the faculty would stand with arms linked between the violent riot police and the violent demonstrators in an attempt to prevent bloodshed. I was disgusted when people on the other side were shouted down and their motives questioned. My lifelong hatred of political ideology deepened further; paradoxically, in fact, it is political ideology which is about the only thing that arouses in me the true automatism of hatred which characterizes prejudice. I have lived in so many places and with so many different kinds of people that I don't find any human being alien by virtue of his or her race or religion or sex or background; but alas, I have to correct an ugly tendency to find political ideologues quite subhuman!

Finally I took a job as an associate professor at Kenyon College; and so began the longest period I ever stayed in one place, from 1972 to 1984. I was and still am very fond of Kenyon. A small liberal-arts college in the low hills and farmland of Ohio, it was the final resting place of the *Kenyon Review,* the Fugitives, and the literary Agrarian Movement, with which I had great sympathy when I found out what it was. We got to know Helen Forman, the delightful daughter of John Crowe Ransom, and her no-less-delightful daughter Liz: two of the wittiest people I have ever known. After a slow start Mei Lin found a true community there, and rose from drama secretary to associate director of the Kenyon Festival Theater, which she helped to found. We got to know a motley and delightful crew of actors and theater people. Mei Lin took several courses in Greek, which has since become one of the great passions of her life.

It was a time which, in memory, has the sweet richness and arcadian remoteness of Tess's summer sojourn as a dairymaid in Hardy's novel. One year in particular can stand for the others, 1976–1977. In that year I was awarded tenure, began work with my friend and colleague Ronald Sharp on the revival of the *Kenyon Review,* became a U.S. citizen, participated in the founding of a radically interdisciplinary educational program in the humanities, designed and helped to build a solar-heated house on a beautiful acre of forest, planted a garden, and wrote *The Return,* a long narrative poem, and *The Garden,* a collection of mystical poems, love poems, and metaphysical aphorisms in which I outlined a new religion. Most wonderful of all, our second son, Benjamin, was conceived; he was born early in 1978, and we baptized him ourselves on a dazzling snowy day surrounded by a lovely company of our best friends. In that same period I read the poems of Boris Pasternak, and his *Doctor Zhivago;* Saint John of the Cross, Rilke, Blake, Melville, Plato, Kant, Homer, Darwin; *Anna Karenina* and *War and Peace;* the *Upanishads* and the *Bhagavad Gita;* and discovered the wonderful blunt common sense of the English philosophers Hobbes, Locke, and Hume.

About that time, too, I was discovered by J. T. Fraser, the founder of the International Society for the Study of Time, and attended my first conference of that organization in Alpbach, in the Tyrol. Fraser's book *Of Time, Passion, and Knowledge* seemed to me to sum up all I had intuited about the nature of time, in a language and system that made it usable and scientifically fertile. Time, he said, was not a mere dimension of extension, but a nested evolutionary hierarchy of temporalities generated by the effectors and receptors of the increasingly complex organisms of nature, from subatomic particles to ourselves. My contributions to the society led to my later involvement with the Werner Reimers Stiftung research project on the biological foundations of esthetics, a German-flavored international group that met for five years in Bad Homburg, near Frankfurt. Out of these two groups has come a worldview which I believe will play a part in twenty-first-century philosophy and esthetics.

But these are the external events of that, for me, extraordinary year. As Ohio passed through its noble deciduous liturgy of seasons, I passed deeper and deeper into a calm blue and gold joy, a privateness and wholeness of being—or rather, of emptiness of being—that was warmed through with an unremitting fire of love. The beatific vision was the everyday condition of existence. During that time my poetry was largely ignored and unpublished, and I was happy that this was so. Since then I have always felt that paradise is in fact right here, just around the corner, that I have never left it, and that however terrible and desperate my work sometimes makes me feel, I have the power anytime to return to that white and gold light. I am indeed out of duty or karma bound to the great game of life, and there are many things I still have to do within it; but I shall when the time comes happily relinquish it.

I still feel that I could have prolonged that blessed time perhaps to the length of my life. But I also felt that I had had this experience for a purpose, and that I ought to communicate what I had learned to other people. And in order for that to be possible, it seemed to me, the whole culture must change in certain ways. For instance, people must learn again to hear poetry as song rather than just statement. And they must hear stories that sing, that do not just drag themselves along in prose; and the stories themselves would have to link up with our ancient human store of stories, so that we would be reunited with our own nature and with nature in general. The culture must come to see once again the deep unity of all knowledge. Value was real, but must be created and maintained. If it were continually mocked and undermined, it would disappear, leaving us with only drugs to fill the void. The arts of the person—especially poetry—must be reinfused with the great art of natural knowledge that is science; and science and technology must begin to take on the sensitivity, generativeness, and creative interconnection of the esthetic instinct that is still preserved in the classical arts. The wisdom of the great religions would have to be fully integrated with the new wisdom of the modern world, and with the perennial wisdom of tribal and peasant societies. It became my duty to help

The Turners' home in Gambier, Ohio, about 1978

bring about these changes, to discover a constructive and divinely affirmative postmodernism, a natural classicism in which the human race might, after the horrors of this century, relearn the art of hope.

Out of this resolve came the work on the *Kenyon Review* and on the Integrated Program in Humane Studies, and my first epic-length poem, *The New World*. With the *Review*, especially, I plunged into a world of administrative detail, fund-raising, speed-reading, literary politics, bookkeeping, and power which was the utter inverse of that golden year of the garden. Luckily I was not very good at any of these, and hated them, and yearned for the spiritual homeland I had given up.

But some important things came out of the work: for instance, a meeting at the Minetta Tavern in the Village in Manhattan with Frederick Feirstein and Dick Allen, which eventually resulted in the new movement in American poetry which has been variously called the New Narrative, the New Formalism, the Expansive Movement, and Natural Classicism, and is the only movement in contemporary poetry which can reasonably be called postmodern. For a while the *Kenyon Review* was one of the most interesting literary journals in the country. We helped to discover two very important poets, Dana Gioia (who was another key figure in the movement) and Amy Clampitt, among others. We broke new ground in the essay form, especially by expanding it to cover subjects beyond the merely literary and political. Our science essays were sometimes philosophically on the cutting edge. We also discovered the very important short-story writer Lynda Sexson, who was to become a close friend, the epic poet Julia Budenz, and many others I do not have space to name.

My circle of acquaintance widened enormously, and I realized that especially in America there were several really brilliant undamaged people around my age who were ready to accomplish a great change in consciousness. But this change was fraught with dangers, especially from philistine antiscience, from the residual hatreds of the political left, and from the fundamentalisms of the right which were awaiting their chance, given any apparent crack in the facade of modernism. The task I had set myself could not be abandoned midway; I would have to throw every ounce of my talent, however small it was, into the cooperative effort to keep the new movement positive, creative, inclusive, and pure of nasty old scores.

I took up karate, because I felt I needed some discipline that would calm the body and unite it with the spirit; and also because I did not know how to fight either literally or metaphorically. I could not write epic—and nothing less than epic would meet, it seemed to me, the requirements of the time—unless I knew the freedom of having transformed myself into another being, and unless I knew the full danger and commitment of personal combat. But this was combat in which one loved one's adversary, and in which the danger was really of pain rather than permanent physical injury or death (though there is enough danger of these latter, especially in tournament competition, to make one aware of the cost and the stakes of life). I have continued this discipline, and at the time of writing am preparing myself for my black-belt test under the great martial-arts master Nishiyama-sensei.

In 1983 my father died. He and the rest of the family had moved to America permanently while I was at Oxford; since my parents' conversion to Catholicism they had had two more sons, Alex and Rory (preceded by a dear little mongoloid girl, Lucy, who died at the age of five months). I had left my parents' home by the time they were growing up. Vic had positions first at Cornell, then the University of Chicago on the Committee on Social Thought, and finally at the University of Virginia. He had become the world's leading expert on ritual, and had made major contributions in anthropology, comparative religion, performance studies, and literary criticism. His death was a central event in my life; but although the grief was as fresh and agonizing as a wound, there was a kind of exaltation or even joy in it too: this great, good, human man had lived his life through in full observance of the Dionysian principles of his nature; his pen had gleaned his teeming brain. But the soft parts—the mannerisms, the comic boyish sense of the ridiculous, the clowning—are gone forever except in the hearts of those who loved him; so when they die he will die again. We—Vic's family and friends who flew in from all sides, his anthropological and performance-studies colleagues and students, including Barbara Myerhoff, Richard Schechner, John Macaloon, Roy Wagner, and many others—put on for him at the family home a full-scale Ndembu funeral for a chief, with drum music, masked dancers, and singing and drinking until late at night.

By about 1982–1983 it became clear to both Mei Lin and me that Kenyon could no longer support the work we wanted to do. The college's financial support for the *Kenyon Review* and the Kenyon Festival Theater dwindled away; Ronald Sharp and I increasingly disagreed on the direction of the *Review*; and the English department, which had become more and more disgruntled with my excursions outside its decent New Critical/Christian Humanist/Modernist ethos, began to close in on me. I resigned from the editorship, and a year later the theater folded. Mei Lin and I went to England for a year (1984–1985) to direct a Kenyon foreign-study seminar at the University of Exeter, and thought things over.

This return to England was both sweet and painful for both of us. The landscape of England was like a gentle seductive witch, with its green coombs and misty beaches; we visited old Devon churches in the still snow of midwinter, and lay in the heather of the moors in the mild summer sun. And yet the place seemed terribly small and trapped and safe; and like Odysseus on the island of Calypso, I yearned for America. Mei Lin, too, realized that her own loyalties had changed and that she was no longer an Englishwoman. Now I began my most important book, the epic poem *Genesis*, which in many ways summarized all I knew. The voice of the poem, whose speaker is trapped upon an Earth that has chosen ecological safety and theological subjection over the glory road of human partnership in the divine evolutionary enterprise, comes directly out of this year in England.

While we were in England I received an extraordinary letter from Robert Corrigan, the dean of the School of Arts and Humanities at the University of Texas at Dallas. This was an interdisciplinary, largely graduate research school with no departments. I had met Corrigan through Ihab Hassan, a good friend, and had been deeply impressed with him. Here was somebody I could work for. I flew from Crete, where we had gone for a vacation, and in the most extreme version of culture shock I have known, passed from the neolithic Minoan villages of Mount Dikte to the glass towers of Dallas. After an interview with the search committee in which I was sure I had totally ruined my chances—I have never been good at sitting before committees, which always seem to me to be collectively much less intelligent than their least intelligent member—I was offered the job. Mei Lin urged me to take it, and I did. We moved to Dallas in 1985.

The years since then have been ones in which some of the things I hoped for in the culture have begun to happen. American poetry is going through a radical change; the philosophical notions about nature, science, technology, human evolution, the arts, and the world of the spirit which I espouse are getting a hearing in essays, books, documentaries, and poems by various hands, including my own book of essays *Natural Classicism*, my pieces for *Harper's Magazine*, and the Smithsonian World TV documentaries in

Frederick Turner with Fanni Radnóti in Hungary, 1988

which I have taken part. I am presently working as a cowriter on a new TV documentary series on postmodernism. My two epic poems were published; two new collections of essays are being readied for the press; I am at work on a new collection of shorter poems. I have developed a remarkable dialogue in philosophy, literary theory, and critical theory with my friend and colleague Alex Argyros, a leading thinker in these fields; we are especially interested in chaos theory and its implications for esthetics and the history of thought. The hierarchy of the universe gives way in its higher reaches to self-generating autonomous feedback systems or heterarchies, which have increasingly the full characteristics of divine freedom.

In partnership with another colleague, the great-hearted Zsuzsanna Ozsvath, I have been translating the poems of the Hungarian poet Miklós Radnóti into English. Radnóti, who was murdered as a Jew by the Nazis in 1944, never lost faith in the rise of a new world after his death. His prophetic vision, courage, and philosophical instinct about nature and history offer, we believe, a convincing answer to those who believe the enterprise of human civilization to be so compromised with evil as to be not worth going on with. I have made many wonderful friends in Hungary, including Fanni Radnóti, the poet's widow, and have come to love Budapest.

As a teacher I have been able to use the freedom at Dallas to explore the use of performance in teaching, inspired by my father's work in ethnodrama with Richard Schechner, and my own participation in a Folger Library research group on Shakespeare in performance. I have also been developing a series of radically interdisciplinary courses, which use the evolutionary paradigm to pull together the sciences, the arts, and the humanities. My theoretical essay on education, "Design for a New Academy," played a small part in the recent American reevaluation of its educational system, though its message was less clear and thus less liable to partisan notoriety than that of such writers as E. D. Hirsch and Allan Bloom.

But as I have watched the ideas I wished to be aired find a place in the public debate, I have felt a corresponding relaxation of the sense of duty to them which inspired my voluntary self-expulsion from the garden. The time is approaching for another descent into the cold waters of spiritual transformation. I find myself becoming a stuffed shirt, a talking public man, a respected figure. This will not do. The world is an absurd, delightful, comical, and unfinished place—as well as being one of terror, death, and change—and it does not grow only from the measured statements of its cultural mouthpieces. And the self that writes these memoirs begins to look forward to its own dissolution; that self was a concatenation put together for good purposes, some of which have already been achieved, but it is not very valuable outside its usefulness to others. In any case I believe we are more important as husbands and fathers—or wives and mothers—than we are as public figures, however distinguished. I do not know what is going to happen next; but my life has been so full of undeserved gifts that it has made me almost expect wonderful things.

BIBLIOGRAPHY

Poetry:

Deep Sea Fish. Santa Barbara, Calif.: Unicorn Press, 1968.

Birth of a First Son. Goleta, Calif.: Christopher's Books, 1969.

The Water World. Santa Barbara, Calif.: Christopher's Books, 1970.

Between Two Lives. Middletown, Conn.: Wesleyan University Press, 1972.

Counter-Terra. Santa Barbara, Calif.: Christopher's Books, 1978.

The Return. Woodstock, Vt.: Countryman Press, 1979.

The Garden. Washington, D.C.: Ptyx Press, 1985.

The New World: An Epic Poem. Princeton, N.J.: Princeton University Press, 1985.

Genesis: An Epic Poem. Dallas, Tex.: Saybrook, 1988.

Fiction:

A Double Shadow. New York: Berkley, 1978.

Nonfiction:

Shakespeare and the Nature of Time: Moral and Philosophical Themes in Some Poems and Plays of William Shakespeare. Oxford, England: Clarendon Press, 1971.

Natural Classicism: Essays on Literature and Science. New York: Paragon House, 1985.

Translator of:

Three Poems from the German. Gambier, Ohio: Pothanger Press, 1974.

Editor of:

Romeo and Juliet, by William Shakespeare. London: University of London Press, 1974.

Alexander Zinoviev

1922-

(Translated from the Russian by Michael Kirkwood)

I was born on the twenty-ninth of October 1922 in a small Russian village six hundred kilometers northeast of Moscow. That village no longer exists. Like many tens of thousands of other Russian villages, it disappeared as a consequence of the collectivisation of agriculture. My mother was a peasant, my father a worker, a housepainter. It happened like that because many men from our locality traditionally went off to earn money in the towns, since it was impossible to feed a family on the pittance that could be earned by work in the country-side alone. This custom continued from inertia for some time even after the 1917 revolution. My grandfather worked from time to time in Moscow and my father settled there once and for all. He would only come back to the village for short periods to help my mother with the harvest and with the business of procreation. My mother gave birth to eleven children. Two of them died in early childhood during the famine years. Two died in adulthood. Seven are still alive. I was number six.

In Moscow, my grandfather and father were allocated a tiny room of ten square meters in a damp basement. Gradually other members of the family began to move in. The first was my eldest brother. He got married and acquired a family. In 1933 I too was sent to Moscow. Then my sister and another brother arrived. In short, it wasn't long, just a few years, before there were eight of us in our tiny little room. The collectivisation of the peasantry which got under way in the thirties increased the tendency of peasants to flee to the towns. All my brothers and sisters, like millions of other young people, left the village by one route or another. They became workers. They studied at evening school, in technical colleges and institutes. Four brothers became engineers. One became a colonel. I became a professor in a scientific field. The remainder of our family (my mother and the three youngest children) finally moved to Moscow in 1946. Our family fared no better and no worse than millions of other Russians in the years after the Revolution.

Alexander Zinoviev on a walk with his dog "Sharik," 1987

I lived and studied in Moscow from the age of eleven. The life we led does not bear thinking about. Endless hunger. Dirt. Threadbare clothing. Cold. The first time that I had a bed to myself and ate out of my own bowl three times a day was when I was arrested in 1939. I made that same comment in one of the interviews which I gave in the West after I was exiled in 1978. Hardly anyone believed me. Some interpreted my declaration as a glorification of Stalin's jails. And yet all I was trying to say was the following: what hardship I must have experienced as a free man if even jail seemed preferable! Every

The remains of the house in which Zinoviev was born

summer during the school holidays I would go to see my mother in our village and work on the kolkhoz on the same terms as the adults. Living and working conditions on the collective farms differed little from those in concentration camps.

The thirties were at one and the same time the darkest and the brightest years in the history of Russia, the darkest as regards reality and the brightest as regards people's illusions. A particularly striking phenomenon during those years was the schools—at least in the cities. Subjects which were particularly well taught at the school that I attended were mathematics and literature. I acquired a passion for both of them. And that helped to alleviate the hardship of everyday life. I became one of the best mathematicians in the school. I took part in mathematics olympics. My study of literature was indiscriminate. I began to write poetry and short stories at an early age. One of the first stories I wrote was influenced by Chekhov's "Vanka." It was a story about my first year in Moscow. As a matter of fact, unlike Chekhov's, my story was optimistic. My hero aroused a lot of concern at his school, and that was as it should be. My teacher praised my story. But

someone detected something seditious in it and I was advised not to write any more.

Like mathematics, literature was considered to be a main subject at school. In addition to the set books, our teacher made us read a great many more. Not that she had to force us. Reading was the fundamental and most easily available way of spending our leisure time. We read constantly, voraciously. We would organize competitions to see who could read the most, or give the most original answer during a lesson, or write the most original essay. It is impossible to enumerate or calculate the number of books that I have read. Many of them I read more than once, including books by Hugo, Balzac, Stendhal, Milton, Swift, Hamsun, Anatole France, Dante, Cervantes . . . There is no need to list all the names—I read all the great writers of the past and those still alive who had achieved recognition and whose works had been translated into Russian. The Soviet Union had begun during those years to publish and republish the greatest achievements of world literature. The people who were involved in that enterprise (including M. Gorky) performed a great service. They selected the best examples of literature and spared us the necessity of tracking down examples of real literature for ourselves. We studied Russian literature at school. Although these works were presented as propaganda, and although we tended to use chrestomathies, our lessons did teach us to read in earnest, to analyse literary texts, and in general to regard literature as the most sacred thing in human civilisation.

A significant proportion of our intellectual and spiritual life was taken up by prerevolutionary Russian literature. This was partly because we studied it thoroughly at school, but also partly in spite of the fact that we studied it at school. Personally, I did not relegate it to the past. For me it was a companion in my daily life. My favourite writers were Lermontov, Griboedov, Saltykov-Shchedrin, Leskov, Chekhov. I did not particularly enjoy Turgenev, Dostoevsky, or Tolstoy, although I read them. I knew many passages of *War and Peace* and "The Legend of the Grand Inquisitor" from *The Brothers Karamazov* by heart.

Of course we studied Soviet literature too— Serafimovich, A. Tolstoy, Mayakovsky, Sholokhov, Fadeev, Blok, N. Ostrovsky, Furmanov, Bagritsky, and others. We also read a lot that was not in the curriculum. I knew almost all of Blok, Esenin, and Mayakovsky by heart. Like many other people, I had, in general, a very good knowledge of Soviet literature. Not all that many books were published and we read them all. In my view, the literature of the twenties and thirties was of very high quality. Sholokhov, Fadeev, Lavrenev, Serafimovich, A. Tolstoy, Fedin, Babel, Leonov, Ehrenburg, Jasieński, Ilf, Petrov, Tynianov, Olesha, Zoshchenko, Bulgakov, Kataev, Paustovsky, Trenev, Vishnevsky, and many others were all outstanding writers. I still regard Mayakovsky as the greatest poet of our century and Sholokhov as one of the greatest prose writers. Moreover, we didn't merely read them. We had endless conversations about the qualities of these works and about the themes developed in them. Possibly this was because we read everything these writers wrote. The diligent and voracious reader as a mass phenomenon, such as appeared in Russia during the 1930s, was something previously unknown in the history of literature.

My critical attitude to reality began to develop when I was still a child. Among the people with whom I happened to come into contact, more than a few had no illusions whatsoever about a Communist paradise on earth and did not believe in Marxist fairy tales. I quite often heard biting jokes and anecdotes about our way of life as it really was

and about our leaders, including Stalin himself. And moreover I could see very well for myself what was going on round about me. The glaring contradiction between the reality of Communism and Communist ideology as it was drummed into us by various means aroused in me a very strong interest in social and ideological problems. I began consciously to turn into an anti-Stalinist. I became interested in philosophy and sociology. I wanted to understand the essence of Soviet society, seek out the reasons for the difficult conditions under which the mass of the people at the bottom of the social hierarchy had to live, ascertain the basis of the social and economic inequality which no propaganda could conceal. Accordingly, when I left school in 1939 with a "gold" certificate, I enrolled in the department of philosophy at the Institute of Philosophy, Literature, and History.

I spent only two months at the institute. The unbearably hard living conditions, the intense intellectual stress, and emotional protest at what was happening in the country had their effect. I entered a period of moral crisis. In despair I contemplated the

*Parents, Alexander and Appolinaria Zinoviev,
about 1914*

idea of individual terrorism. I even organised a terrorist group with some close friends who shared my views and my mood with the intention of murdering Stalin, who had become for us the incarnation of everything that was evil about the new society. Our conspiracy, however, did not get very far. I was provoked into making a statement at a Komsomol meeting in which I sharply criticised the collectivisation policy. At the time that was an unheard-of crime. I was expelled from the Komsomol and from the institute, moreover without the right of entry into any institute of higher education whatsoever. I was subjected against my will to examination in a psychiatric hospital. Then my friends from my school days organised a party at which they provoked me into making further pronouncements. This time I presented myself as an opponent of the cult of Stalin. I knew in advance that my friends would send a written denunciation to the "organs" and purposely provided them with abundant material. This was a rebellion born of despair. Soon afterwards I was arrested and taken to the "Lubianka," the main prison of the organs of state security.

During my interrogation I set out the conclusions to which I had come at that time concerning the problems of Soviet society. In particular, I voiced the opinion that a society based on universal prosperity, equality, and justice was in principle impossible, that Communism was no exception in this respect, that it did not remove social and economic inequality, but merely changed the form that they took compared with the past. The interrogator did not believe that these ideas were my own. He decided that I had been contaminated with these hostile views by someone else. My friends had also written to that effect in their denunciation. They had asked the "organs" to find these "enemies of the people" and to save me from their influence. To that end, the authorities decided to transfer me somewhere else, where I would live more or less at liberty but under the surveillance of young operatives from the "organs." During my transfer, there was some hitch or other and I was left on my own for a few minutes. Without thinking of the consequences I simply walked off.

I spent a whole year wandering about the country, avoiding my pursuers. A nationwide alert was put out for me. Clearly, there were not too many examples of escape from the all-powerful "organs" at that time. That year was a year of horror for me. I wandered all over Siberia and the north of the country. I worked as an unskilled labourer, woodcutter, bookkeeper, deliveryman, plate-layer—mixing with hordes of criminals and tramps and at the mercy of totally arbitrary bosses. I managed to escape from the horrors of vagrancy and persecution by joining the army in October 1940. The country was preparing for war with Germany, and people were being drafted into the army with no questions asked. I was presumed to be an underage volunteer.

I spent six years in the army. I served in the cavalry, in the tanks, and in the air force. I became a sergeant. I trained at a military flying school. I was made an officer. I saw action, first in the ground forces, later as a pilot of a ground-support aircraft. I flew on a few dozen military sorties. I was wounded. I was awarded decorations and medals. I changed a lot during my military service. I grew stronger physically. I played a lot of sport. I discovered that I had a capacity for playing the clown and telling jokes and gave it full rein. I drew cartoons and wrote satirical verses and articles for our army newspaper. After I became an officer I adopted a reckless, "hussar" lifestyle, without any thought of self-preservation or career, dissipating my capabilities and energy on all sorts of nonsense. This can be explained by the way things were during those years. I had absolutely no

Age eleven, 1933

The Zinoviev family, 1946: (front row) father, Alexander; sister Antonina; mother, Appolinaria;
(middle row) brother Vladimir; brother Mikhail; sister Paraskovia; (back row) brother Alexei;
the author, "in uniform, but without epaulets"; sister Anna; brother Vasily; and brother Nikolai

hope of surviving, never mind using my abilities in civilian life. As it turned out, however, this state of mind was temporary and not particularly deep-rooted. As soon as the war was over, my former attitude to life reasserted itself, if anything more vigorously. I decided to abandon a career in the military and to devote myself to literature. There was more than enough to write about. I developed my own mode of thought and speech. During 1945–46 I wrote quite a lot of poetry and prose. I had particular hopes for one tale that I was writing, harbouring the vague ambition, strange as it may seem, that I might even succeed in having it published. It seemed to me at that time that the situation in the country was bound to change radically for the better. As regards the forthcoming period of the "thaw," I was only wrong with respect to the date. Seven more years were to pass, during which Stalinism would make an attempt to arrest the course of history and destroy the lives of many more millions of people.

I was demobilised from the army in 1946 and returned to Moscow. My regimental comrades

returned to Russia with trunks filled with the spoils of war. I returned with a battered suitcase stuffed with manuscripts: I was going to become a writer. I showed my story to two writers—Konstantin Simonov and one other, whose name I won't mention in order not to speak ill of the dead. Simonov praised the story but advised me to destroy it if I wanted to stay alive. But at least he did not inform on me, which in itself in those times was a great and good deed. As for the other writer, he reported my "anti-Soviet pamphlet" (his characterization) to the organs of state security. Fortunately for me, he returned the manuscript. When they came to conduct a search a few days later, I had already had time to destroy all my manuscripts, having followed Simonov's good advice. My career as a writer had come to an end before it had even begun. It seemed to me then that I had finished with literature once and for all. Thirty years were to pass before I resolved to publish my first literary work, *The Yawning Heights,* in 1976—and in the West at that. I worked for a short time after my demobilisation as a civil-airline pilot, a job I obtained thanks to the recommendation of an important general who had taken a liking to me, and a substantial bribe. My outfit, however, was transferred to the north, which, for me, meant an end to flying. I entered the department of philosophy at Moscow University. At the same time I had to earn a living—as a loader, navvy, laboratory assistant, watchman, schoolteacher. I had also to engage in criminal activity—the resale of bread, fruit, and vegetables. Some of the vegetables were given to us as payment for our work, some of them we stole. In those days it was simply impossible to live on the lowest levels of society without doing that.

I graduated in 1951 "summa cum laude." I undertook postgraduate study in logic. I got married, for the second time in fact. I had married for the first time during the war. That marriage produced my son, Valery, but was dissolved soon after the war. My second wife was a fellow student at the university. After university she began work as a journalist. We had no place of our own to live and we had to rent privately, which under Soviet conditions is very expensive and entails a colossal amount of inconvenience. Our daughter Tamara was born in 1954. My wife was constantly traveling round the country or on night duty at the newspaper for which she worked. The work of looking after our daughter thus fell to me, in addition to work on my dissertation and my extra jobs. It was only in 1956 that we were given one room of six square meters for the three of us. And we thought ourselves lucky.

Throughout the postwar years right up to the death of Stalin, I devoted my life to anti-Stalinist propaganda. In 1953 I joined the Communist Party of the Soviet Union with the aim of continuing the struggle against Stalinism absolutely openly, within the framework of the Party organisation. At that time many anti-Stalinists acted in similar fashion. And indeed, during these years a mass campaign against Stalinism began in every institution in the country. It took the form of internal Party struggle which went unnoticed in the West. It laid the foundation for Khrushchev's "revolution"—the famous report he gave at the Twentieth Party Congress which signaled the beginning of the official de-Stalinisation of Soviet society. After the congress everyone suddenly became an anti-Stalinist, including former comrades-in-arms of Stalin himself. My anti-Stalinism lost its meaning. My Party membership became a pure formality.

As a student, 1951

In 1954 I completed and defended my candidate's dissertation[1] on the logical structure of Karl Marx's *Kapital.* It created quite a sensation in philosophical circles, was circulated in typescript (forerunner of the "samizdat" of the seventies), and was available officially only to a restricted readership. My work was not published until 1958, first of all in Poland, and only later in my own country. But once I had made it into print, I soon made up for lost time. In a short time I published a large number of books and dozens of articles on logic and the methodology of science. Almost all of them were translated into Western languages and the languages of eastern Europe. I obtained my doctorate, became a professor, was appointed to the editorial board of a journal of philosophy, and became head of my department.

My enforced temporary break with literature did not mean that I abandoned it altogether. Like many others, I engaged actively in the creation of oral literature. In addition, I regularly wrote jokes, satiri-

---

[1] Equivalent to the British Ph.D. qualification—TRANS.

cal verse, and articles for the wall newspapers.[2] I also did a lot of literary improvisation during my lessons in the school where I taught logic and psychology, in my lectures in different institutes and at the university, in public lectures, and even in the propaganda lectures I was obliged to give under the heading of so-called "social work."[3] During these years I produced a large number of stories of all kinds, usually literary reworkings of real events. My "specialty" was mockery of the Communist social system, representatives of the authorities, and Marxism-Leninism. Usually I satirised Marxist aphorisms or true stories connected with the teaching of Marxism. For instance, I would recast Marxist ideas about the exploitation of man by man as follows: under capitalism one man exploits another, whereas under Communism the opposite is the case. My formulation of the Marxist definition of the relations of production was this: relations of production are the relations between people in the process of their production. Numerous jokes, puns, and similar tales which I composed during my thirty-year "break" found their way into the books of mine which have been published in the West. Had the climate in the Soviet Union been even half as favourable towards literature as it was before the Revolution, it is very possible that I would have become a satirical writer long before 1976.

I will quote as an example of my satirical literary activity an excerpt from a satirical article written for the wall newspaper when I was still a student. It was entitled, "In the Light of the Eclipse."

Although the eclipse did not last for long, it was long enough for several significant events to take place in the department. An assistant lecturer in the department of scientific Communism seduced a first-year female student. A German teacher had her handbag stolen. Someone wrote a four-letter word on the dean's office door. Someone stole a hand from the medical institute next door to the department and stuffed it into the briefcase of a lecturer in the criticism of reactionary West European philosophy. In short, a lot of things happened which necessitated the calling of a general

departmental meeting. The secretary of the Party bureau delivered a weighty speech. "Soviet comrades," he said, "have conducted this routine eclipse in an organised and deeply responsible fashion. But in the light of the eclipse, some dark shadows have emerged as regards the moral education of our younger generation. Some politically and morally doubtful individuals have emerged in our healthy collective who have abused . . . ." During investigation of the case of the immoral assistant lecturer in the department of scientific Communism, the following came to light which intensified his guilt: he had not known that "such an important measure was being taken in the country." The outcome was that he was given a Party reprimand on the grounds that he had not read the newspapers. The lecturer in the criticism of reactionary bourgeois philosophy was very proud of the fact that someone had stuffed into his briefcase a hand destined for dissection practice by students at the medical institute. It was the most profound experience of his life.

In the post-Stalin years I also began a systematic scientific investigation of Soviet society. In my youth I had already established to my own satisfaction that the cause of the evils of our way of life did not lie in the personality of Stalin but in the very foundations of the Communist social order. But it was only after I graduated that I was able to study and invent methods essential for the study of such a complex phenomenon as Soviet society, moreover for study in isolation. In addition, I now had the opportunity to observe the inner workings of society practically under laboratory conditions. Most of my time, however, was taken up with research in logic and my work with undergraduate and postgraduate students. Nor did I intend to publish sociological works. As far as the Soviet Union was concerned, that was out of the question, and at that time there was no point in thinking of publishing them in the West. My work on philosophy and logic was published in the West. It brought me success. That suited me and I was in no particular hurry as regards my sociological investigations. I carried them out exclusively for myself. The fact is that at about this time I had worked out a system of rules for living my life which I encapsulated in the formula "I am a sovereign state." My logico-philosophical and sociological conceptions, including

---

[2] Every Soviet institution has its wall newspaper, i.e., a space for the exhibition of material about matters of interest to that institution written or produced by the employees themselves. They are considered to be of great ideological importance.—TRANS.

[3] Unpaid "voluntary" labour for the good of the cause—TRANS.

my theory of Communism, were to be the foundations of the whole intellectual content of my "state."

After I emigrated I expressed the above formula during one of the interviews I gave. Not surprisingly, it was interpreted as a delusion of grandeur and linked with the well-known assertion of Louis XIV: *"L'Etat—c'est moi!"* That interpretation is absolutely false. The king was at the apex of the social hierarchy, whereas I was on the lowest rung. The king had power over millions of subjects, whereas I did not have any subjects at all, and in the days when I did have them (soldiers, students, junior staff), I had found the role of boss tiresome, neglected it, and soon lost it. The king equated himself with a state consisting of many millions of citizens, whereas I declared myself to be a state consisting of one single citizen—myself. For the king, his formula expressed his position as absolute monarch. My formula, on the other hand, expressed the intention of a rank-and-file citizen of a Communist state to win and defend personal freedom and independence under conditions in which society and the collective had supremacy over the individual.

Already at the time of my interrogation in the Lubianka in 1939, I had declared that I would not permit anyone, even Stalin himself, to treat me as he liked. A quarter of a century separated that infantile assertion and my assertion to myself that I was a sovereign state. The former expressed an emotional and moral protest against the reality of Stalinism, whereas the latter was the formulation of a comprehensive, rational conception. The former had been a manifestation of despair, the latter—a programme for overcoming it.

Given my predilection for collectivism, setting out along that path was not so easy. I knew I was condemning myself to a solitary fate. Yet the thought of what the individual might be able to accomplish under conditions in which success was only achieved by groups, or within groups, intrigued me more than it frightened me. I was aware that my position was merely an individual defence against the extremes of collectivism, the weight of the masses, mafia tendencies, ideological vacuity, and moral degeneration which had taken over the world.

My decision to become a sovereign state did not pass unnoticed. It is true that my colleagues and acquaintances had no idea of the scale of my project. If they had guessed, my experiment would have come to an end at the very outset. Imagine an ant in a huge colony of similar ants that declares its intention of building its own ant's nest within the common ant's nest and sets to work accordingly. What would the others do? They would destroy the ant, of course. The same thing would have happened to me. The ant-people around me were painfully sensitive to all my attempts to become an autonomous ant-state of one person. Anyone who escapes from the control of the collective and society is perceived as a threat to the existence of the whole. That is why Communist society is so intolerant of independent loners. Indeed, this is primarily the reaction, not of the higher authorities or the punitive organs, but of people in the immediate environment of the individual who has deviated from the norm. In this respect, the authorities and the punitive organs are the last to enter the picture.

The 1960s and early 1970s were extraordinarily turbulent and full of contradictions. On the one hand, they were years of rebellion. People in all spheres of culture began to break down outdated norms of life, not bothering about official prohibitions, indeed seeking ways of overcoming them. The dissident movement sprang into being. So did "samizdat" and "tamizdat," i.e., many people began to circulate their work in manuscript form or have it published in the West. On the other hand, repressive measures against rebellious modes of thought and action began to strengthen.

My own position was also dualistic. On the one hand I had de facto recognition, albeit behind the scenes. I had a large number of students and followers. My school of logic had taken shape and had achieved international recognition. My work was published. I was quoted. I received awards. But at the same time, my activities, which never received more than halfhearted official approval, were eventually prohibited. I constantly received invitations to attend international professional gatherings, but not once was I allowed to go. I was put forward for membership in the Academy of Sciences and for a State Prize, but the authorities turned down my candidature every time. I was elected to the Finnish Academy of Sciences for my achievements in the field of logic, which was an honour, since Finnish scholarship in logic had great international prestige. But I was not even allowed to attend a symposium in Finland. The Soviet authorities were angered by the fact that I had been elected without their knowledge and compelled the Finns to elect to their academy a vice-president of the Soviet academy.

I lived and performed my activities among living Soviet people. My scientific results and my behaviour as one who considered himself to be a sovereign state inspired in them a certain reaction which was by no

Zinoviev with his wife Olga, 1968

means one of delight. I wrote articles and books that had nothing to do with Marxism, although I worked in an institution in which adherence to Marxism was considered to be obligatory. I did not bow or scrape before anyone, I did not accommodate myself to anyone or anything. I was known in the West. I had students who developed my ideas and who were successful. I was popular with the young. My colleagues, my fellow employees, and the people around me resented that. Accordingly, my success provoked increased opposition, which developed along two fronts—opposition from my "liberal" friends and colleagues, who were making a successful career in philosophy and who were connected with the apparatus of power, and from my untalented colleagues, who were just waiting for a signal from the authorities to activate a smear campaign against me and my group. At the same time, the authorities supported me to a certain extent in the spirit of the "liberal" era and in as much as their power gave them a sense of responsibility for the state of culture in the country. They also felt responsible for the consequences that an uncontrolled development of culture would have for ideology and were likewise afraid to permit

anything "heretical" that might cause them problems later on. They took steps, therefore, to give my colleagues to understand that they were not so much protecting me as hindering me. It was not very easy for me to live and work in such conditions, given the principles governing my sovereign state, which ruled out intrigue, accommodation, and toadying. In reality, it proved impossible to play the role of the scientist, occupied with pure science and indifferent to the hustle and bustle of ordinary life, for any length of time or to any great degree.

The authorities in charge of ideology constantly sought to harness me to Marxism. The following incident is typical. The Presidium of the Academy of Sciences had received my report on my research. Prominent scholars were present. My report was approved. But the vice-president whom I have already mentioned demanded that I signify my "party allegiance," i.e., that I write an article for the journal *Kommunist* in which I would declare that I was a Marxist and that my research followed a Marxist course. I refused. The approval of my research at that meeting was dropped from the agenda.

The break with my liberal friends followed soon afterwards. I was a member of the editorial board of the journal *Voprosy filosofii* (Questions of philosophy). The journal began to intensify its praise of Brezhnev. The number of references to Brezhnev in one issue of the journal exceeded the number of references to Stalin in the journal *Pod znamenem marksizma* (Under the banner of Marxism) during the darkest years of the Stalin cult. I resigned from the board in protest. My liberal friends, who now form the intellectual nerve centre of Gorbachev's leadership, responded by boycotting me and spreading slander. In addition, there was an incident at the university. I was told to dismiss two dissident lecturers from the department I was administering. I refused. After that, I completely lost the protection of the authorities and was left to the tender mercies of my colleagues. Publication of my work was forbidden. My undergraduate and postgraduate students began to encounter difficulties. My "disciples" began to betray me. My lecture courses at the university were taken away from me.

My marriage broke up in 1960 and I lived on my own for seven years. Often I had to change my place of residence. I reduced my possessions to such a minimum that when I moved I could carry them all by hand in one trip. In 1965 a young stenographer-typist came to work at our institute. Her name was Olga. We became friends. In 1967 I had the chance of a one-room flat, and we got married. Life then became very hectic. Olga began to study in the extramural department of philosophy at the university. She turned out to be good at running the house and was attractive and sociable. We began to have a constant stream of visitors. We ignored the instructions to avoid foreigners and not invite them to our flat. Rather we began to have more and more contacts with foreigners, for all sorts of reasons. The result was that we kept open house not only for people from the Eastern bloc but also for visitors from capitalist countries. This, of course, contributed to my reputation as an "internal emigrant" in the eyes of the authorities. Our daughter Polina was born in 1971.

By 1974 I was almost completely isolated. But, as they say, every cloud has a silver lining. For the first time ever I had a lot of time on my hands. I was ready once more to oppose the way things were going in the country. The generally rebellious climate no doubt also had something to do with it. I decided to settle accounts with my society once and for all. I was no longer a seventeen-year-old youth, but a mature fifty-two-year-old man with much experience of life and with an understanding of his society acquired through many years of research. I was now in a position not merely to voice a pointless protest, but to strike a blow at the Communist social order itself and at the whole way of life based upon it.

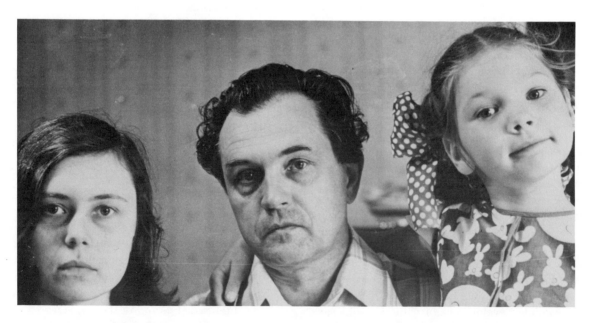

With daughters, Tamara and Polina, before the emigration, July 1978

I had a choice: either I could write down the results of my sociological reflections in the form of a scientific treatise, or write a literary work, using my experience of life and what I had learned from my activities as a practitioner of oral literature. I chose the second path, and in the summer of 1974 I began to write *Ziiaiushchie vysoty* (The yawning heights), putting all other business aside. I had thought of the title for the book as early as 1945. It was punned upon the expression *siiaiushchie vysoty* (the gleaming heights), which was often used to refer to the Communist future. By changing one letter I gave it a satirical character, which unfortunately tends to be lost in translation.

The book absorbed me totally. I thought about it constantly. There were occasions when I wrote for twenty hours at a time, breaking off for only a few minutes. It was as if a great flood of thoughts had suddenly burst through a dam and poured onto paper in an unstoppable torrent. However, such were my circumstances that surely no writer in the history of literature has produced a work of such compass in worse conditions. Certain people in my milieu had already supposed, knowing me, that I would produce something in the spirit of the rebellious atmosphere of those years. The KGB had had me in their sights for some considerable time now. The Soviet authorities had had trouble enough with dissidents and unruly members of the cultural intelligentsia. Among those in the pay of the authorities were people who knew what I was capable of. They naturally wanted to forestall my "eruption." One close friend, whom I had told about my project, was indiscreet. Thereafter KGB surveillance of me was stepped up and became regular. KGB agents followed Olga and me everywhere we went. They began to search our flat in our absence. I realised that my salvation lay in speed. I had to stay one step ahead of the authorities, who could prevent the appearance of my book. I wrote feverishly and without any corrections. Olga typed up the text. Friends of ours transmitted my work abroad, a bit at a time, mostly to France. Transfer of the manuscript was undertaken mainly by friends of Olga's, Marina Mikitianskaya Caroff, married to a Frenchman, and Christina Mestre, a French citizen who had worked in the Soviet Union, often came to visit, and sometimes traveled specially to Russia to offer us support.

The need to write the book as quickly as possible affected its form. I was not completely confident that I would be able to write a large book. My writing could be cut short at any minute. I therefore wrote each bit of the book as if it were the last. Accordingly, the book turned out as a collection of several books, each one of which was a collection of independent works. I made a virtue of necessity. I wrote in such a way that the book could be read in any order, that any one part would be a relatively finished whole. The unity of ideas and characters lent unity to the composition.

I had written a novel, but a novel of a particular type—a sociological novel. The relationship of a sociological novel to sociology as a science is similar to the relationship between a historical novel and history, or a psychological novel and psychology. But in my case, it was not as if there already existed an independent sociological theory of Communism, the results of which I needed only to incorporate in my novel. I had developed a sociological theory of my own, and I had the task of setting out its ideas in the form of a work of literature. When I began writing it, the books of Solzhenitsyn and other Soviet writers who revealed the horrors of the Stalin period were already well known. That placed me in a difficult position, since these books were sensational and had oriented the attention of readers in a particular direction. There was no point in writing a book of the "shock! horror!" type. But this had one advantage. I could concentrate wholly and exclusively on a description of a completely normal and mature Communist society, such as Soviet society had become during the Brezhnev years. The focus of my novel thus became not the excesses, but the norms of life of the mass of people at the very base of society. Thus precisely the sociological novel proved to be the most appropriate literary form.

At the end of August 1976, Western radio stations announced that my book *The Yawning Heights* had been published in Switzerland. Although I foresaw harsh forms of reprisal, I was nonetheless content. My conscience was clear. A weight which had been a burden for many long years had been lifted from my shoulders. My rebellion had taken place. I had brought my external situation into harmony with my inner state of mind. And moreover, my novel had the effect of an exploding bomb. No one had foreseen a book of this kind. Soon a large number of copies of the book appeared in Moscow and began to circulate at an extraordinary rate.

The reprisals began at once. Almost all of my friends and acquaintances dropped me like a hot potato. My colleagues demanded that I be brought to trial. I was sacked both from the Academy of Sciences and from Moscow University, deprived of all my degrees and titles, all of my awards, including my military ones. My scientific work was declared to have no scientific significance. The people who did this were the same ones who had previously recommended my work for publication, awarded it prizes, and recommended it for translation into Western languages as the best work in Soviet logic. My pupils disavowed me and began to publish my results as their own. The only one not to break off contact with me, A. Fedina, was dismissed and generally eased out of the field of logic altogether. People who had known and befriended me over decades began to discredit and vilify me in all sorts of ways. A special unit was set up in our building to carry out constant surveillance of me, Olga, and those who visited us. KGB operatives were on permanent patrol near the building. I was summoned regularly to the local militia, accused of being a parasite, and threatened with expulsion to Siberia.

The reprisals encompassed our relatives as well. My daughter Tamara was expelled from the Komsomol and sacked for having refused to break off relations with me and condemn me publicly. She has not found permanent employment to this day. My son, Valery, lived with his family in Ulyanovsk. He was an officer in the militia, an excellent worker, and had been recommended for a government award. He was warned that if he continued his contacts with me, he would lose his job and be expelled from the Party. A threat like that to a family man living in the provinces is one that cannot be lightly dismissed. And yet Valery did not heed it. When it became known that I was likely to be imprisoned or sent to the West, he came to see me in Moscow. For that, he was expelled from the Party and sacked. For many years he had to earn his living as a labourer.

My brother Vasily suffered most of all. He was a military lawyer with the rank of colonel. He was reputed to be a capable, courageous, incorruptible worker. He had been named to a post with the rank of general in the military prosecutor's office in Moscow. He had been allocated a Moscow flat. He was due to be promoted to general. When my book appeared, Vasily was ordered to condemn me publicly. He refused to do so, saying that he was proud of me. He was immediately cashiered from the army and banished from Moscow.

For two years we lived under the threat of arrest or expulsion to someplace in Siberia. In order to survive we sold books, clothes, furniture. We earned the odd ruble in the most unlikely ways. For instance, I sold a few articles along with the authorial rights to them and "edited" a philosopher's doctoral thesis for him. My wife and I both found it impossible to obtain regular work in Moscow. I was even turned down for a job in the Spiritual Academy in Zagorsk, where they wanted a lecturer in formal logic. We were offered work in the north of the country or in Siberia, but not in our field, and at a salary on which it would have been impossible to live. We got some help from readers, usually anonymously. This helped our morale rather than our pocket. The fact that people were prepared to sacrifice this money from the miserable pittances they were payed meant a great deal to us. Among those who sent us money openly were Academician P. Kapitsa and the dissidents P. Egides, T. Samsonova, and E. Kalistratova.

Our circle of acquaintances changed dramatically. The people we entertained were either dissidents or those who simply paid no attention to threats from the authorities. Our relatives visited us regularly, an event unprecedented in Soviet history. Western journalists, who played an enormous role in those years in the awakening of an oppositionist frame of mind, were also constant visitors. Many of them became our friends. The Italian journalist P. Ostellino brought out to the West my book *The Madhouse,* which I wrote after *The Yawning Heights,* and the Austrian journalist E. Hutter brought out my literary archive, for which he was later expelled from Moscow.

Western journalists kept us informed of the reaction to my books in the Western press. Their success was obvious, and that was our main source of moral support. I had not counted on such success. My book was called the first book of the twenty-first century. I was compared with Rabelais, Swift, France, Saltykov-Shchedrin, and other great writers of the past. As many newspapers and journals put it, I burst upon the literary scene completely unexpectedly, like a meteor, and immediately took my place among the greatest writers of the century. But such praise did not turn my head. I was already fifty-six years old. My life had been such that there was no room left for ambition. I was merely bitter about the fact that the Soviet authorities and their "liberal" lackeys had deprived me not only of scientific but also literary fame in my own country.

My books (a second soon appeared) reached only a limited public. People who distributed them were prosecuted, the books were confiscated if found. Thus one of the charges leveled at S. Khodorovich at the time of his arrest was that a copy of *The Yawning Heights* had been found during a search of his flat. And even a few years later (in 1983) A. Shilkov was arrested and prosecuted for distributing my books. There were many cases like that. The majority of them failed to attract the attention of the media. My books were sold on the black market for huge sums. One of my admirers copied *The Yawning Heights* by hand in a microscopic script, which resulted in a booklet about the size of a small notebook. In short, despite all the obstacles, my books were distributed round the country. The opinion of the Western press also filtered into Moscow, and there were crowds of people in our flat from early morning till late at night. A sort of opposition club took shape. This naturally aroused alarm on the part of the authorities and in the end they took the decision to expel me from the country along with Olga and Polina. We were given five days to leave. My explusion was dressed up as a voluntary trip to the Federal Republic of Germany at the invitation of the University of Munich. Literally a few days after my arrival in Munich, I was deprived of my Soviet citizenship for alleged anti-Soviet activity. As an acquaintance of mine connected with the KGB told me, they had deprived me of my citizenship even before I left the country, but had concealed the fact in order to avoid the kind of scandal associated with A. Solzhenitsyn and V. Bukovsky.

Olga and I had never considered emigration. If we had had some guarantee that we would not be sent away from Moscow or arrested, if we had found work which would have allowed us to exist on some kind of minimum level, we would never have agreed to emigrate. But no such guarantees were forthcoming. On the contrary, we were given to understand that I could expect seven years in a corrective labour camp followed by five years of internal exile. There was no work. There was no way to earn a living. We could not live on charity. It would have been, moreover, humiliating. We therefore submitted to the decision of the authorities to throw us out of the country and did not protest.

I left Russia at the age of fifty-six. Psychologically and intellectually I bore the burden of a life lived entirely in Russia. I could not escape from it. The people who hounded me out of Russia were convinced that I could bear any kind of difficulty in Russia, but that I would be broken by conditions in the West. I will not deny that I nearly was. But I survived. If I were asked what the single most significant achievement of ten years in emigration was, I would cite precisely the fact of my survival.

If we confine ourselves just to external events and actual results, the years in emigration can be considered to have been extraordinarily rich and fruitful. I have made countless journeys to different cities and countries. I have written a great many novels, essays, and articles. I have given hundreds of interviews. I have taken part in dozens of conferences. I have given countless public lectures. I have met people of different nationalities and social positions, including people like Fellini, Dürrenmatt, Ionesco, Montand, Weil, Aron, Rostropovich, Ashkenazy, Mock, Bellow, König, and many others. I have had a huge and highly flattering press. I have been awarded prizes, including the Tocqueville prize for works on sociology and the Prix Médicis for literature. I have appeared on many television programmes. I have had exhibitions of paintings and drawings. We have gone to museums and galleries, theatres and concerts, many more times than during the whole of our previous life in Russia. In short, I have led an extremely dynamic, eventful life, full of impressions, reflections, conversations, and work. However, all this has been achieved at the cost of enormous stress, together with events and experiences of a different sort which are painful to recall.

Olga and I had been trained to live in the social milieu of Soviet society. In the West we found ourselves in a different social order, in which people lived differently, had a different psychology, a different mentality. The difference between the social systems turned out to be much greater as regards the practicalities of life than we had supposed. Although in theory life in the West had little about it that was new, in actual practice everything was new, from the most trivial details to problems of vital importance. We had to learn to live all over again. This plunged us into such a morbid state that it took years to shake it off. And in fact I still haven't shaken it off completely. Perhaps I never shall.

The most difficult thing for me in the West has been the absence of a guaranteed minimum standard of living, the absence of accustomed forms of contact, the dependence on others, and the change in the correlation between the material and spiritual aspects of our life. The material side of things had never caused me any problems in Russia. Any material level of existence I took as a given, as something of secondary importance. Of primary importance for me had always been the intellectual and creative aspects. I had earned money so that I could devote myself to cognition and self-expression. The situation in emigration is markedly different. My chief concern has become providing materially for my family. My creativity has become a means of earning a living. It is not a question of our having fallen for the temptations of the West. Nothing of the sort happened. It was simply that our circumstances were such that, quite against our will, the problem of earning enough money to live on even the most modest level became priority number one. We came up against all the negative aspects of the West's high standard of living. I could have achieved a position of financial security if I had renounced literature or compromised my principles, i.e., if I had started writing and saying the things that many people in the West want to hear and which bring financial success. Many emigrants did that. For me it was unacceptable. I had no patrons. I was therefore compelled to earn a living by working harder than I could have imagined possible, even though I had always, as the saying goes, done the work of ten. And now I dare not even think of taking a rest or working on a book with the care that established writers can permit themselves.

The Soviet and first-wave Russian emigrants were not unanimous in their reaction to my books. Unofficial public opinion expressed in the privacy of people's homes was very positive. I acquired a large number of enthusiastic admirers. But the official stratum of the emigré community reacted to my books malevolently rather than benevolently. The Russian-language press tended to ignore my books

and everything to do with me. There was not one mention of my awards or the official celebrations held in my honour. Slander and false rumours were spread about me. It is hard to name a single Russian language publication in the West which has not contained something nasty about me.

The people who banished me to the West expected that my literary activity would cease with the publication of *The Yawning Heights* and *The Radiant Future*. In fact it had merely begun. And in spite of everything my books were successful. And their unofficial success was gallingly huge. I immediately detected Moscow's efforts to prevent my books appearing and circulating in the West. I still do. Threats, veiled and otherwise, direct and indirect. The spreading of slanderous rumours. The intrusion into my private life and my business relations with Western people and institutions. A whole series of my publications was sabotaged thanks to the efforts of people on the Soviet side. Two attempts have been made to poison me with bacteria and there have been two attempted kidnappings. They managed to create such an aura around me that many Western people

*The author with his wife Olga and daughter Polina on 6 August 1978—
the first minutes in the West*

on whom my activities depended became willing or unwilling helpers of the Soviet authorities.

Having entered the literary field and having been banished from my country, I found myself in a position which was highly unfavorable for a writer such as myself. Many factors enter into this situation, some of them purely literary, others relating specifically to the Russian writer in emigration.

Literature has lost its leading role in culture. It has been forced into the background by the cinema, television, science, and journalism. On the other hand, literature has attained gigantic proportions. Many hundreds of thousands of new books are published in the world every year. Literature has become a mass phenomenon not so much as regards readers, but in terms of the number of writers. It has become an industry and as such has become subject to the laws of the marketplace.

The educated reader of literature in the old sense of the word has become a rarity, swallowed up in the sea of the literarily unwashed. Literary talent has been sidelined by sensationalism and advertising in the mass media. The aesthetic criteria by which works of literary creativity are evaluated have collapsed. They have been replaced by the criteria of the market and the requirements of the press. Professional literary criticism has disappeared. The journalist has replaced the qualified literary expert. Interest in literature has declined. The ideological pressure on literature has increased inordinately. What has become important when assessing a writer is not what he brings to literature that is new, but the extent to which he responds to the tastes and requirements of whatever circles of society hold the fate of that writer and his works in their hands.

The last few decades have seen a phenomenon unprecedented in the history of Russian literature, and that is literature published illegally (samizdat) or in the West (tamizdat). It has attracted the adjective "free" insofar as it escapes surveillance by the Soviet authorities and is beyond the purview of the corresponding supervisory bodies within the literary establishment. Many of the representatives of this type of literature are well known in the West. Many representatives of "free" Russian literature were banished to the West.

All the rules that operate in the sphere of normal literary activity were broken where free Russian literature is concerned. The authorities repressed it. Soviet literary critics and the press ignore it, or if they do ever mention it, it is only to describe it as slander against the Soviet social order. The circle of readers

Alexander Zinoviev, age sixty-six, 1988

of this literature in the Soviet Union is extraordinarily small. It is practically inaccessible to the average reader who could otherwise become a severe critic of its artistic level. The readers who do have access to it are usually of a particular ideological persuasion. They have poor literary taste as a rule and a hazy notion of aesthetic criteria. There is no serious literary criticism of this free literature in the West. What there is is tendentious, superficial, and amateurish. The press pays attention to it from a political rather than an aesthetic point of view. Criticism of the literary defects in the works of certain authors has been forbidden. Artistically insignificant works are elevated to the status of literary masterpieces. Genuine literary discoveries are ignored. All the criteria by which an author's quality and importance are measured have been destroyed.

It is practically impossible for a Soviet writer who has been banished from his country to write about the West. He will always end up by writing about Soviet life. He may understand it marvellously. But that is not enough for literature. Literature needs living detail, colour, things which cannot be dreamed up, things that you will not see in the West. A Russian writer needs a reader who can appreciate the nuances of Russian literature and who can let that writer know that he derives pleasure from reading his works. Such a reader is not to be found here, or very rarely. The reader who is capable of appreciating Russian literature of a high order has remained behind in Russia. The interest in Soviet themes in the West is not as strong as it appeared from inside the Soviet Union.

In the last few years, free Russian literature has received a further stab in the back. The West has swallowed the bait of Gorbachev's "perestroika" and the "cultural renaissance" in Russia and has consigned to oblivion everything that free Russian literature did to open Western eyes to the reality of the Soviet social order and the whole Soviet way of life. Nowadays in the West, the opinions of Soviet Party officials and their literary lackeys count for more than all that the representatives of free Russian literature have spent their whole lives producing.

In spite of everything, I am destined to continue to the end of my life the work I began with *The Yawning Heights*, i.e., writing sociological novels, scholarly essays, and journal articles. I do not intend to return to Russia, I see no sense in that. During Stalin's lifetime I was an anti-Stalinist. Under Brezhnev I was the only writer in Russia to make a laughingstock out of him, which was the direct reason for my banishment. With the advent of Gorbachev, the object of my sociological analysis and satirical literary activity is Gorbachevism. I do not believe that anyone has criticised Gorbachevism as sharply or as systematically as I have. It would thus be naive of me to expect any official recognition of my creative work in Russia.

BIBLIOGRAPHY

Studies in logic:

Filosofskie problemy mnogoznachnoi logiki. Moscow: Akademiia nauk SSSR, 1960; English translation by Guido Küng and David Dinsmore Comey published as *Philosophical Problems of Many-valued Logic.* Dordrecht: Reidel, 1963; German translation by Horst Wessel published as *Über mehrwertige Logik.* Berlin and Brunswick: F. Vieweg & Sohn, 1968; Basel: Winter, 1968.

Logika vyskazyvanii i teoriia vyvoda. Moscow: Akademiia nauk SSSR, 1962.

Osnovy logicheskoi teorii nauchnykh znanii. Moscow: Nauka, 1967; English translation by T. J. Blakeley published as *Foundations of the Logical Theory of Scientific Knowledge.* Dordrecht: Reidel, 1973.

Kompleksnaia logika. Moscow: Nauka, 1970; German translation published as *Komplexe Logik.* Berlin and Brunswick: F. Vieweg & Sohn, 1970; Basel: Winter, 1970.

Logika nauki. Moscow: Mysl', 1971.

Logicheskaia fizika. Moscow: Nauka, 1972; German translation published as *Logik und die Sprache der Physik.* Berlin: Akademie-Verlag, 1975; English translation by O. A. Germogenova published as *Logical Physics,* edited by Robert S. Cohen. Dordrecht, Boston, and Lancaster: Reidel, 1983.

Logische Sprachregeln. Translated from the Russian by H. Wessel. Berlin, Munich, and Salzburg: Deutscher Verlag der Wissenschaften, 1975.

Non-standard Logic and Its Applications (lectures). Oxford: Willem A. Meeuws, 1983.

The Non-traditional Theory of Quantifiers. Dordrecht, Boston, and London: Reidel, n.d.

Fiction:

Ziiaiushchie vysoty. Lausanne: Age d'homme, 1976; French translation by Wladimir Berelowitch published as *Les Hauteurs béantes.* Lausanne: Age d'homme, 1977; English translation by Gordon Clough published as *The Yawning Heights.* London: Bodley Head, 1979; New York: Random House, 1979; German translation published as *Gähnende Höhen.* Zurich: Diogenes, 1981.

Svetloe budushchee. Lausanne: Age d'homme, 1978; French translation by W. Berelowitch published as *L'Avenir radieux.* Lausanne: Age d'homme, 1978; German translation by Franziska Funke and Eberhard Storeck published as *Lichte Zukunft.* Zurich: Diogenes, 1979; English translation by G. Clough published as *The Radiant Future.* London: Bodley Head, 1981; Franklin Center, Pa.: Franklin Library, 1981.

V preddverii raya. Lausanne: Age d'homme, 1979; French translation published as *L'Antichambre du paradis.* Lausanne: Age d'homme, 1979.

Zapiski nochnogo storozha. Lausanne: Age d'homme, 1979; French translation published as *Notes d'un veilleur de nuit.* Lausanne: Age d'homme, 1979.

Zheltyi dom. 2 vols. Lausanne: Age d'homme, 1980; French translation by Anne Coldefy-Faucard and W. Berelowitch published as *La Maison jaune.* Paris: Age d'homme, 1982; English translation by Michael Kirkwood published as *The Madhouse.* London: Gollancz, 1986.

Moi dom—moia chuzhbina. Lausanne: Age d'homme, 1982; French translation published as *Ma Maison—mon exil.* Lausanne: Age d'homme, 1988.

Gomo sovetikus. Lausanne: Age d'homme, 1982; French translation by Jacques Michaut published as *Homo sovieticus.* Paris: Julliard, 1983; Lausanne: Age d'homme, 1983; German translation published as *Homo sovieticus.* Zurich: Diogenes, 1984; English translation by Charles Janson published as *Homo Sovieticus.* London: Gollancz, 1985; Boston: Atlantic Monthly Press, 1985.

Nashei iunosti polet. Lausanne: Age d'homme, 1983; French translation by J. Michaut published as *Le Héros de notre jeunesse*. Paris: Julliard, 1984; Lausanne: Age d'homme, 1984.

Evangelie dlia Ivana [and] *L'évangile pour Ivan* (bilingual edition). Translated into French by W. Berelowitch. Lausanne: Age d'homme, 1984.

Idi na Golgofu. Lausanne: Age d'homme, 1985; French translation by A. Coldefy-Faucard published as *Va au Golgotha*. Paris: Julliard, 1986; Lausanne: Age d'homme, 1986.

Ruka Kremlia. Paris: Kontinent, 1986; German translation published as *Der Arm des Kremls*. Zurich: Diogenes, 1986.

Der Staatsfreier. Zurich: Diogenes, 1986.

La bomba all'uva passa. Milan and Trent, 1987.

Para bellum. Translated into French by J. Michaut. Paris: Julliard, 1987; Lausanne: Age d'homme, 1987.

Katastroika: Gorbatschews Potemkinsche Dörfer. Berlin: Ullstein, 1988.

Zhivi. Lausanne: Age d'homme, 1988.

Social analysis:

Bez illiuzii. Lausanne: Age d'homme, 1979; French translation published as *Sans illusions*. Lausanne: Age d'homme, 1979; German translation published as *Ohne Illusionen*. Zurich: Diogenes, 1980.

My i zapad (articles, interviews, and speeches). Lausanne: Age d'homme, 1981; French translation by W. Berelowitch published as *Nous et l'occident*. Lausanne: Age d'homme, 1981; German translation published as *Wir und der Westen*. Zurich: Diogenes, 1983.

Kommunizm kak real'nost'. Lausanne: Age d'homme, 1981; French translation by J. Michaut published as *Le Communisme comme réalité*. Paris: Julliard, 1981; Lausanne: Age d'homme, 1981; German translation by Katharina Haussler published as *Kommunismus als Realität*. Zurich: Diogenes, 1982; English translation by C. Janson published as *The Reality of Communism*. London: Gollancz, 1984; New York: Schocken, 1984.

Ni svobody, ni ravenstva, ni bratstva (articles and speeches). Lausanne: Age d'homme, 1983; French translation by Jacqueline Lahana published as *Ni liberté, ni égalité, ni fraternité*. Lausanne: Age d'homme, 1983.

Die Diktatur der Logik. Munich: Piper, 1985.

Die Macht des Unglaubens. Translated from the Russian by G. von Halle. Munich: Piper, 1986.

Le Gorbatchévisme. Lausanne: Age d'homme, 1987; published in the original Russian as *Gorbachevizm*. New York: Literary Publishing House, 1988.

Ich bin für mich selbst ein Staat (interviews), transcribed by Adelbert Reif and Ruth Renée Reif. Zurich: Diogenes, 1987.

Cumulative Index

CUMULATIVE INDEX

For every reference that appears *in more than one essay,*
the name of the essayist is given before the volume and page number(s).

INDEX